Errata

Following are corrections to *Racing Toward Tomorrow, Conference Proceedings, ACRL 9th National Conference,* April 8–11, 1999, Detroit, Michigan.

Page	Paper	Correction
v	"Recruiting More Minorities to the Library Profession: Responding to the Need for Diversity"	The page number listed is incorrect. The paper appears on page 178 in the Proceedings.
73	"Factors that Influence Online Database Use"	Table 3 was omitted and is shown below.
76	"Pay for Print: Implementing Fee for Service Programs"	The list of authors should include: *Shirley Thomas, access services manager, Virginia Commonweath University*
161	"Library Assessment Programs"	Parts of the paper were omitted. A complete text of the paper appears in this Errata.
228	"Extinguishing Slow Fires: Cooperative Preservation Efforts"	The references and endnotes were omitted. A complete text of the paper appears in this Errata.
293	"First-Year Learning Communities: Redefining the Educational Roles of Academic Librarians"	Parts of the paper were omitted. A complete text of the paper appears in this Errata.
313	"Snowbird Leadership Institute: A Survey of the Implications for Leadership in the Profession"	Appendix A was omitted and is reproduced in this Errata.

Table 3. Simultaneous Users, Magazines And Journals For Academic Libraries Database

No. of Users	Cumulative Percent Carnegie Class									
	B1	B2	M1	M2	D1	D2	R1	R2	AA	Bus.
1	95.6	94.8	89.3	85.7	95.1	91.7	83.5	80.8	91.7	85.6
2	98.2	97.7	93.0	92.8	98.9	95.5	88.3	86.0	95.6	92.0
5	99.8	99.8	97.8	99.4	100.0	99.2	95.0	94.8	99.4	99.1
15	100.0	100.0	99.6	—	—	100.0	98.8	99.9	100.0	100.0
25	—	—	99.9	—	—	—	99.4	—	100.0	—
66	—	—	—	—	—	—	100.0	—	—	—

("Factors that Influence Online Database Use" Database Use," Carol Tenopir, p. 73)

First-Year Learning Communities: Redefining the Educational Roles of Academic Librarians

Terry Taylor and Tony Stamatoplos

First-Year Classes & Learning Communities

Colleges and universities increasingly find themselves in the position of competing for enrollment, and the average student body is a mixture of traditional residential, commuter, and adult returning students. As a result, new issues have emerged concerning the assessment of learning and retention of students after their first year. Studies indicating the success of collaborative learning environments have given new weight to the concept of learning communities and the impact they have upon learning outcomes. Faith Gabelnick, et al., describe key advantages of today's learning communities:

> Learning communities [...] purposefully restructure the curriculum to link together courses or course work so that students find greater coherence in what they are learning as well as increased intellectual interaction with faculty and fellow students. Advocates contend that learning communities can address some of the structural features of the modern university that undermine effective teaching and learning. Built on what is known about effective educational practice, learning communities are also usually associated with collaborative and active approaches to learning, some form of team teaching, and interdisciplinary themes.[1]

The Coalition of Networked Information (CNI) initiated a New Learning Communities program that highlighted "increased student involvement in learning [...] and the realization that students can create knowledge and meaning out of their learning experience."[2] Learning communities foster both social and academic involvement, the integration of which appears to be central to the students' perceived success in their transition to university life. As Vincent Tinto explains: "Often, social and academic concerns compete, causing students to feel torn between two worlds so that students have to choose one over the other. Learning communities [help] students draw these two worlds together."[3]

Recognizing the significance of the first year in creating a baseline for the students' entire college experience, many institutions have revisited their general studies programs and have created opportunities for the development of new learning communities. According to Tinto: "Membership in the community of the classroom provides important linkages to membership in communities external to the classroom. For new students in particular, engagement in the community of the classroom becomes a gateway for subsequent student involvement in the academic and social communities of the college generally"[4]

Information Literacy in the Curriculum

For many years academic librarians have advocated the integration of library instruction or information literacy into the curriculum of colleges and universities. Librarians assert that students must learn information skills in the context of their courses in order for those skills to be meaningful. True integration implies that information skills are accepted as a natural and essential part of the curriculum. Attempts at integration have had varying degrees of success.

Successful integration appears to be related to a few key factors. Administrative or institutional support and commitment are vital to success, as is a clear connection to the educational mission of the institution.[5] Specific, well-defined goals are important. Hannelore Rader points out that where there has been successful integration at an institution, the institution "had a strong commitment to excellent educational outcomes for the students in the areas of critical thinking, problem-solving, and information skills."[6]

Tony Stamatoplos is assistant librarian/instruction team, Indiana University Purdue University Indianapolis, and Terry Taylor is corrdinator of library instruction, DePaul University.

Perhaps most important to success are collaborative and collegial relationships between teaching faculty and librarians.[7] Such relationships often take the form of a true partnership between faculty and librarians. D.W. Farmer goes even farther and calls for faculty, librarians, and students to step out of their traditional roles and form an "active partnership in a genuine learning community."[8] Marian Winner emphasizes that librarians "must demonstrate to faculty that they have the background and knowledge to be useful partners for faculty in curriculum planning, so that information literacy becomes an integral part of the course structure and so that skills the students develop are assessed."[9]

At the same time, and paralleling higher education curriculum reforms, many instruction librarians and programs have shifted focus to better empower students and foster independence and life-long learning.[10] This has become particularly important as more information is readily available, and our students try to meet their information needs through the use of the Internet and the World Wide Web. There probably has never been a better opportunity to demonstrate both the need to integrate information literacy into the curriculum and the significance of the librarian's role as information educator. According to Rader: "It is up to librarians to maximize their potential and to be in position to assume their role in the teaching and learning process as reforms take place."[11]

The role of teacher is not really a new one for academic librarians. We have provided instruction as part of our reference service and have taught sessions and entire courses of bibliographic instruction. Several years ago, instruction programs began to move away from library orientation and instruction in the use of specific research tools. More recently, library instruction has emphasized the teaching of process, problem-solving, and critical thinking. As this trend continues, we open up opportunities for a more direct impact on the curriculum and clearly respond to the educational goals of our institutions. As Evelyn Haynes asserts: "Librarians must be granted the authority, responsibility, and time to develop the programs that will accommodate institution-wide curriculum needs, rather than merely responding to individual requests from those faculty who already recognize the importance of information research to their teaching."[12] This sometimes means re-defining our roles or taking on new roles in the educational mission of our institution. According to Abigail Loomis we "must recognize and accept that our contribution to that educational mission involves much more than making information resources available on demand. It also involves teaching—teaching students how to find, select, evaluate, and use that information effectively and efficiently."[13]

Two First-Year Programs
New program initiatives at DePaul and IUPUI have expanded the possibilities for integrating library instruction into the university curriculum. The learning communities developed as a result of these programs present unique opportunities to integrate information and library skills into the first-year curriculum.

DePaul
As part of a larger initiative to restructure the Liberal Studies curriculum, DePaul University revised and expanded its First-Year Program. The First-Year Program has two overarching goals: 1) introducing students to the process of intellectual inquiry in a university, and 2) community building. Most students take a required sequence of English composition courses in the first year, and it is in those courses that the Library has provided a basic level of library instruction. Two new components in the First-Year Program are taught by a faculty/staff team: *Discover Chicago*, an experiential course with Chicago-related field experiences, and *Focal Point Seminar*, a small interdisciplinary seminar. The instruction team for the Discover Chicago classes also includes a student mentor. The staff professional teaches the *Common Hour* portion of the course, a seminar focusing on transition skills in four areas: student success skills (e.g., note taking and time management); university resources (e.g., student services and the library); academic and career planning; and diversity/community issues.[14]

At its inception, the Common Hour was viewed as an extension of the services offered by Student Affairs, but as the program grew, the opportunity to work with these new first-year learning communities was extended to staff professionals throughout the university. In the first year of the program, a librarian served as a consultant to the faculty planning committee. In the second year, one librarian taught a section of the Focal Point seminar. This past year, six librarians taught eight sections of the Focal Point seminar. For the first time, inclusion of a library experience, activity, or assignment was required in all sections of the Common Hour. Two librarians currently serve on the steering committee charged with designing the curriculum for next year's Common Hour component and the job descriptions for those who will teach it.

IUPUI

First-year classes have become a primary focus of library instruction activity at IUPUI. First-year seminars are now a part of the Learning Communities Program. All learning communities include a first-year experience class, and many link two or more classes. IUPUI learning communities address the general goals of learning communities, and many also serve to introduce students to their prospective majors. As an integral component of the Learning Communities Program, instruction librarians have worked primarily with the first-year experience classes.

IUPUI learning communities use an instructional team approach in the first-year component. An IUPUI instructional team is a collaborative venture that brings together a teaching faculty member, a librarian, an academic adviser, and a student mentor. The faculty member leads the team, which collaboratively develops and implements the curriculum for a particular class. Each team member plays an active role in designing and delivering the course, depending upon his or her particular expertise. Librarians are assigned to several learning communities each semester and their roles vary from team to team, always centering on the library- and information- based learning objectives.

Common Elements of DePaul and IUPUI Programs:

- A history of "traditional library instruction" placed in writing courses;
- A focus on first-year programs that introduce students to the university, build a learning community, and promote academic success;
- Administrative support, both from library administration and from the university;
- Well-defined outcomes that relate to the educational mission of the university;
- A team approach in which librarians collaborate with faculty and others, expanding our role as educators.

Benefits

The advantages of first-year learning communities such as those at DePaul and IUPUI are numerous. The impact of these programs is most evident in the following areas:

- Integration of library instruction into the curriculum from the beginning of the student's college experience;
- Development of collegial relationships with others outside the library (both faculty and staff);
- Increased visibility of librarians within the university community, which expands the perception of what are considered the "traditional" responsibilities of library professionals;
- New opportunities for librarians to participate in students' socialization into the university;
- Extension of the librarians' teaching experience in areas that can benefit from a generalist's approach.

Challenges

Innovative programs and new course models present challenges and opportunities to examine various aspects of the endeavor. One needs to ask questions, such as:

- What skills are required, and what are the existing skills, of the librarians?
- How much preparation will the librarian need, and how will the additional responsibilities balance with his/her workload?
- How are these new responsibilities relevant to the overall goals of the library?
- What impact can the librarians' participation in the new programs have on their identity and role within the university, and how does that involvement complement other public service activities?

Errata

- How might librarians pursue or maintain administrative commitment and financial support?

Conclusion

At DePaul and IUPUI, the information component, including librarians' active participation, is an integral part of students' first-year experience. Early in their academic careers, students see the value of information and connect with information professionals. This demonstrates the importance of information literacy and presents the librarian as expert in this arena. Not only are students able to see librarians as knowledgeable and skilled with information and library research but also as teachers, guides, and coaches. Most students, as well as teaching faculty, are unaccustomed to librarians fulfilling these roles. Whether working one-on-one with a student or leading a library instruction session for a group, librarians have a lot of teaching experience. First-year learning communities can demonstrate this experience to the larger university community. It is not only our opportunity; it is our professional responsibility to become involved in programs that foster these new learning environments.

Notes

1. Faith Gabelnick, Jean MacGregor, Roberta S. Matthews, and Barbara L. Smith. Learning Communities: Creating Connections among Students, Faculty, and Disciplines (San Francisco: Jossey-Bass, 1990), 5.

2. Philip Tompkins, Susan Perry, and Joan K. Lippincott, "New Learning Communities: Collaboration, Networking and Information Literacy," *Information Technology and Libraries* 17, no. 2 (June 1998): 100–106.

3. Vincent Tinto, "Classrooms as Communities: Exploring the Educational Character of Student Persistence," *The Journal of Higher Education* 68, no. 6 (Nov./Dec. 1997): 599–623.

4. Ibid, 616–17.

5. Evelyn B. Haynes, "Librarian-Faculty Partnerships in Instruction," *Advances in Librarianship* 20 (1996): 191–222; David F. Kohl, "As Time Goes by...:Revisiting Fundamentals," *Library Trends* 44, no. 2 (fall 1995): 423–29; Hannelore B. Rader, "Information Literacy and the Undergraduate Curriculum," *Library Trends* 44, no. 2 (fall 1995): 270–78; Gabriela Sonntag and Donna M. Ohr, "The Development of a Lower-Division, General Education, Course-Integrated Information Literacy Program," *College & Research Libraries* 57, no. 4 (July 1996): 331–38; Patricia S. Breivik, "Making the Most of Libraries in the Search for Academic Excellence," *Change* 19 (July/Aug. 1987): 44–52; Abigail Loomis, "Building Coalitions for Information Literacy," in *Information for a New Age. Redefining the Librarian*, ed. American Library Association Library Instruction Roundtable (Englewood, Colo.: Libraries Unlimited, 1995), 123–34.

6. Rader, "Information Literacy and the Undergraduate Curriculum," 271.

7. Haynes, "Librarian-Faculty Partnerships," 214–16; Loomis, "Building Coalitions," 426; Rader, "Information Literacy," 271; Sonntag and Ohr, " The Development of a Lower-Division, General Education, Course," 333–34; Virginia M. Tiefel, "Library User Education: Examining its Past, Projecting its Future," *Library Trends* 44, no 2 (fall 1995): 318–38.

8. D.W. Farmer, "Information Literacy: Overcoming Barriers to Implementation." in *Information Literacy: Developing Students as Independent Learners*, New Directions for Teaching and Learning Series, eds. D.W. Farmer and Terrence F. Mech (San Francisco: Jossey-Bass), 104.

9. Marian C. Winner, "Librarians as Partners in the Classroom: An Increasing Imperative." *Reference Services Review* 26, no. 1 (spring 1998): 25–29.

10. Kohl, "As Time Goes by," 426–27; Tiefel, "Library User Education," 318.

11. Rader, "Information Literacy and the Undergraduate Curriculum," 277.

12. Haynes, "Librarian-Faculty Partnerships," 217.

13. Loomis, "Building Coalitions," 127.

14. Staff professionals for the First-Year Program are recruited from various academic units, including Student Affairs, Career Services, University Ministry, and the Library.

Library Program Assessment

Thomas G. Kirk, Jr.

Assessment of academic library programs has taken on a new dimension with the concept of outcomes assessment, which has been promoted by the regional accrediting agencies. The field of library assessment has evolved from looking strictly at resource inputs (e.g., budgets, staffing levels) to an examination of organizational processes (i.e., efficiency), levels and quality of service outputs (e.g., number of circulations, reference questions) and library impact on institutional goals (e.g., student achievement, user satisfaction). Today, there is a plethora of approaches to library assessment with considerable controversy about just what outcomes assessment means, how it relates to older forms of assessment and how such assessment might be carried out. The question of what is appropriate outcomes assessment for academic library programs remains largely unanswered. This general discussion of theory and recent development in the field of assessment serve as background for a discussion of some of the practical issues associated with the utility of assessment results in improving library programs. Assessment is often viewed as an "add on" research effort or special project rather than as something integral to the operation of the library and management of its programs. This leads to a dysfunctional assessment program because it does not meet the ultimate goal of improving library services. The paper concludes with a brief description of one institution's efforts to develop an assessment program using a number of approaches to outcomes assessment. The successes, challenges and unfinished agenda of this effort are reviewed as examples of the issues surrounding outcomes assessment.

Introduction

Assessment of academic library programs has taken on a new dimension with the concept of outcomes assessment. The field of library assessment has evolved from looking strictly at resource inputs (e.g., budgets, staffing levels) to an examination of organizational processes (i.e., efficiency), levels and quality of service outputs (e.g., number of circulations, reference questions) and library impact on institutional goals (e.g., student achievement, user satisfaction). Today, there is a plethora of approaches to library assessment with considerable controversy about just what outcomes assessment means, how it relates to older forms of assessment and how such assessment might be carried out.

In addressing these issues, this paper has two purposes. One is to provide an overview of the concept of academic library assessment in the context of our current understanding of organizational effectiveness. As a special aspect of academic library assessment, the paper defines and places outcomes assessment within the larger enterprise. The paper's second purpose is to describe the assessment program of an individual college library with special attention to how the program helps to guide the organization, and the limits of outcomes assessment.

This review of our understanding of academic library assessment is based on what I believe are three essential documents. The three publications include:

1) The thorough and insightful review of the literature on academic library assessment written by Sarah Pritchard, formerly Library Director at Smith College and now director of the University of California-Santa Barbara, which appeared in *Library Trends* in 1996.[1]

2) Kim Cameron's "Measuring Organizational Effectiveness in Institutions of Higher Education," which appeared in *Administrative Science Quarterly* in December 1978. Despite its age it is still the source for much original thinking about assessment in higher education generally and could be very useful in academic library assessment specifically.[2]

3) The report of the ACRL Task Force on Academic Library Outcomes Assessment that appeared in June 1997.[3]

Thomas G. Kirk Jr. is college librarian at Earlham College.

Following my discussion of these three publications, I want to suggest a model for academic library assessment which I have called ALAM, Academic Library Assessment Model. Then I will explore how this model creates a context for academic library assessment activities. Finally, I will illustrate aspects of the model by describing Earlham's assessment program with special attention to two specific activities we have undertaken in the past couple of years.

Cameron's Organizational Effectiveness

Kim Cameron's "Measuring Organizational Effectiveness in Institutions of Higher Education," is a seminal work on assessment in higher education. It has had a major impact on the direction of assessment in higher education in the twenty years since its publication.

Cameron's work has had high visibility in the field of contingency theory as applied to organizational effectiveness and assessment of higher education. In addition to the 1978 article, Cameron has written a number of important articles on the subject that together, according to the *Social Sciences Citation Index* on DIALOG, were cited 639 times between 1978 and January 2, 1999.

Because the library and information science literature is not covered in much depth by SSCI, I cannot accurately reflect the importance of Cameron's work in the field of library assessment using the same process. However, a sample checking of the items in Sarah Pritchard's bibliography suggests that this important work is not widely cited in the library and information science literature. Therefore I feel it is appropriate to review his major ideas here.

First, it is important to recognize that Cameron's work is very consistent with the development of ideas about assessment of other types of organizations and Cameron acknowledges and takes into account the difference between institutions of higher education and other types of organizations such as for-profit businesses.

Cameron's 1978 piece is a review of literature which reports efforts to measure organizational effectiveness in higher education. We are most interested in the excellent summary and analysis of the concept of organizational effectiveness and the then new framework Cameron brings to the discussion. He identifies two sets of issues that he believes are critical to defining organizational effectiveness: types of assessment criteria and sources or originators of the criteria. Cameron's overriding point is that the criteria used to measure effectiveness is the central issue.

In describing types of criteria, Cameron enumerates four characteristic domains: (1) aspects of the organization, (2) the universality/specificity of the criteria, (3) whether the criteria are normative or descriptive, and (4) the static/dynamic dimension of the criteria. Let me explain what Cameron means by each of these types of criteria. Cameron's aspects of the organization refers to such elements as organizational goals and their achievement, the organization's resource acquisition or inputs, the internal processes of the organization, or its outputs. The universality/specificity continuum recognizes that criteria of assessment may be universal to all organizations of the same type or even multiple types or they may be highly focused on specific dimensions of an individual organization. The normative/descriptive characteristics of criteria are based on whether the criteria used have been identified as typical or common to organizations of the same type or are generated from the assessment of one particular organization. An example will make the idea clearer. Library circulation is a widely accepted measure of library activity and therefore the level of circulation is regularly included in an assessment of library activities. This is a normative characteristic. In contrast, a particular library, while studying circulation levels, might note a shift in the level of circulation when the institution changed from ten-week terms to fourteen-week semesters. This data is descriptive of the library and there is no basis for a comparison with other libraries. Cameron's fourth characteristic of criteria is whether the criteria are static or dynamic. In all assessment, there is an element of the static since the data must be collected at a particular point in time. However, data collected over time demonstrate change in the organization and therefore the criteria are dynamic.

Cameron's second set of concerns are the sources or origins of the assessment criteria. The first, and perhaps most obvious, is the constituency who sets the criteria. Constituencies include all the groups that interact with the organization either directly or indirectly. Each constituency will have a set of criteria they believe is the appropriate yardstick for measuring effectiveness. For example, students, faculty, administration and alumni are the four primary constituencies of an academic library and each of the four groups may have different ideas about the nature of an effective academic library. The second criteria source issue is the level of analysis. The organizational analysis can be at the super system level (e.g., all of higher education), the system level (e.g., the individual institution), or the subsystem level (e.g., the libraries of an academic institution). If the academic library is the level of analysis, then the super system level might be libraries of the ARL or the libraries of the private colleges of Indiana. The system is the individual library, and the subsystems would be, for example, cataloging, reference or acquisition units within a particular library. Third, Cameron points to the nature of the data collection as another source of assessment criteria. The data may come from internal records of the organization or can come from the perceptions of observers of the organization. This dichotomy, unfortunately, has often been mislabeled as objective vs. subjective measurement.

Cameron concludes his analysis by looking at a set of twenty research studies on organizational effectiveness in light of the nature and sources of the criteria. The grid he developed clearly shows that the field of organizational effectiveness suffers from the lack of comparable data. A problem that continues today—some twenty years after Cameron wrote his analysis.

In summary, Cameron provides us with the concepts of organizations as systems, and defines effectiveness contingently to depend on the types and sources of the criteria used to measure effectiveness.

Pritchard's "Determining Quality in Academic Libraries"

Sarah M. Pritchard's review article in *Library Trends*, "Determining Quality in Academic Libraries," surveys the literature on academic library assessment which reflects Cameron's analysis of types and sources of criteria. I want to highlight several key points that elaborate on Cameron's work.

In describing the historical context for determining quality, Pritchard points out how the terms quality and effectiveness, and evaluation and assessment are two pairs of equivalent terms. The first pair, quality and effectiveness, represent the performance of the organization, while the second pair, evaluation and assessment, refer to the process of determining performance. Over time, these and other terms have been used, often confusingly, to describe Cameron's two aspects, the criteria of evaluation and the process of evaluation. These two aspects should remain distinguishable regardless of the terminology used.

Pritchard goes on to point out that despite the heavy reliance on certain kinds of measures to compare academic libraries, the criteria have not been well defined and consistently applied and therefore comparisons are problematic.

In a further discussion of the challenges that academic library assessment faces, Pritchard comments that:

> Academic librarians do not have concrete ways to assess what the library contributes to the delivery of effective educational and research services by the campus itself.[4]

This issue is especially critical because the regional accrediting agencies in their recent efforts to strengthen the accountability of institutions, have formulated accrediting processes that call on each part of the institution to demonstrate how it contributes to the overall goals of the institution. Pritchard rightly points out that while we may know what we would like the contribution to be, i.e., we have goals, there are as yet no good assessment processes that concretely demonstrate the relationship between library activities and the achievement of the institutions goals.

A third key point that Pritchard makes in her critique of the state of academic library assessment is the lack of linkage between assessment and planning. Assessment is often done not to satisfy the library's need for information on which to base planning and program development, but rather to meet the demands of outside constituencies such as accrediting agencies, commissions of higher education or state legislatures.

Pritchard has identified three critical issues: the shortage of agreed upon definitions of criteria that can be used to do comparative measurements among academic libraries, the inability to demonstrate how library programs concretely influence achievement of the parent institution's goals, and the lack of linkage between assessment and planning.

ACRL Task Force on Academic Library Outcomes Assessment

These two articles by Cameron and Pritchard were important sources of ideas for the ACRL Task Force on Academic Library Outcomes Assessment which was appointed in June 1996 and issued its final report in June 1998. The Task Force was charged to:

1) Develop a philosophical framework for assessing libraries in terms of desired campus outcomes;

2) Develop prototypes for such assessment; and

3) Develop a recommendation for one or more processes for implementation of the former (#2) with a time frame for completion.

The Task Force was not asked to propose a new form for library standards, but rather to address the confusion that appeared to exist within the profession over the nature of assessment and how standards might relate to assessment.

In its work, and in the final report, the Task Force carefully distinguished between terms such as inputs, processes, outputs and outcomes. Inputs refers to the resources (financial, staffing, etc.) which the academic library uses in carrying out its work. Processes are the operations within the organization (e.g., technical services operations, staffing the reference desk) that result in outputs—circulations, reference questions, books cataloged, instruction sessions held, archival manuscripts processed. But none of these are outcomes. The Task Force defines outcomes as "the ways in which library users are changed as a result of their contact with the library's resources and programs."[5]

It seems to me that it is also important to distinguish the different kinds of outcome, a distinction the Task Force did not make. Outcomes could be as basic as changes in attitude toward libraries, and information gathering activities. Outcomes could also be a body of knowledge about libraries and the research process, and the topic being researched. Finally, outcomes could be changes in behavior. In all three cases, Cameron's characteristics and sources of criteria create a wide variety of possible outcomes assessment. If you review the library assessment literature, you see only a few examples of this variety of possibilities.

The Task Force goes on in its report to suggest ways in which such outcomes assessment might be carried out. In this suggested methodology, an outcome is selected, "indicators" of that outcome are defined, and a data collection method is developed. For example, an outcome might be "students can develop a quality bibliography on a topic they wish to study." The indicators of that outcome might be defined in terms of the criteria of quality—up-to-dateness, inclusion of a variety of types of sources, etc. The third step is the development of a methodology for collecting data such as gathering research papers in senior seminars and subjecting them to analysis based on the indicators.

Academic Library Assessment Model (ALAM)

Based on the work of the Task Force, the ground breaking research of Cameron and the helpful synthesis of the history of library assessment I have developed what I will call the Academic Library Assessment Model (ALAM) (see figure 1).

Essential Elements of the ALAM Model

This model has five essential characteristics:

1) The academic library organization is a system which has both complex internal operations and external relationships and impact. This system concept recognizes the inter-relatedness of the organization and acknowledges that assessment is therefore a complex process. Any assessment is limited by its ability to measure and evaluate portions of the system. Therefore, an overview assessment of the system will most likely be based on generalized measures.

2) The effectiveness of an academic library can be viewed very differently depending on (a)

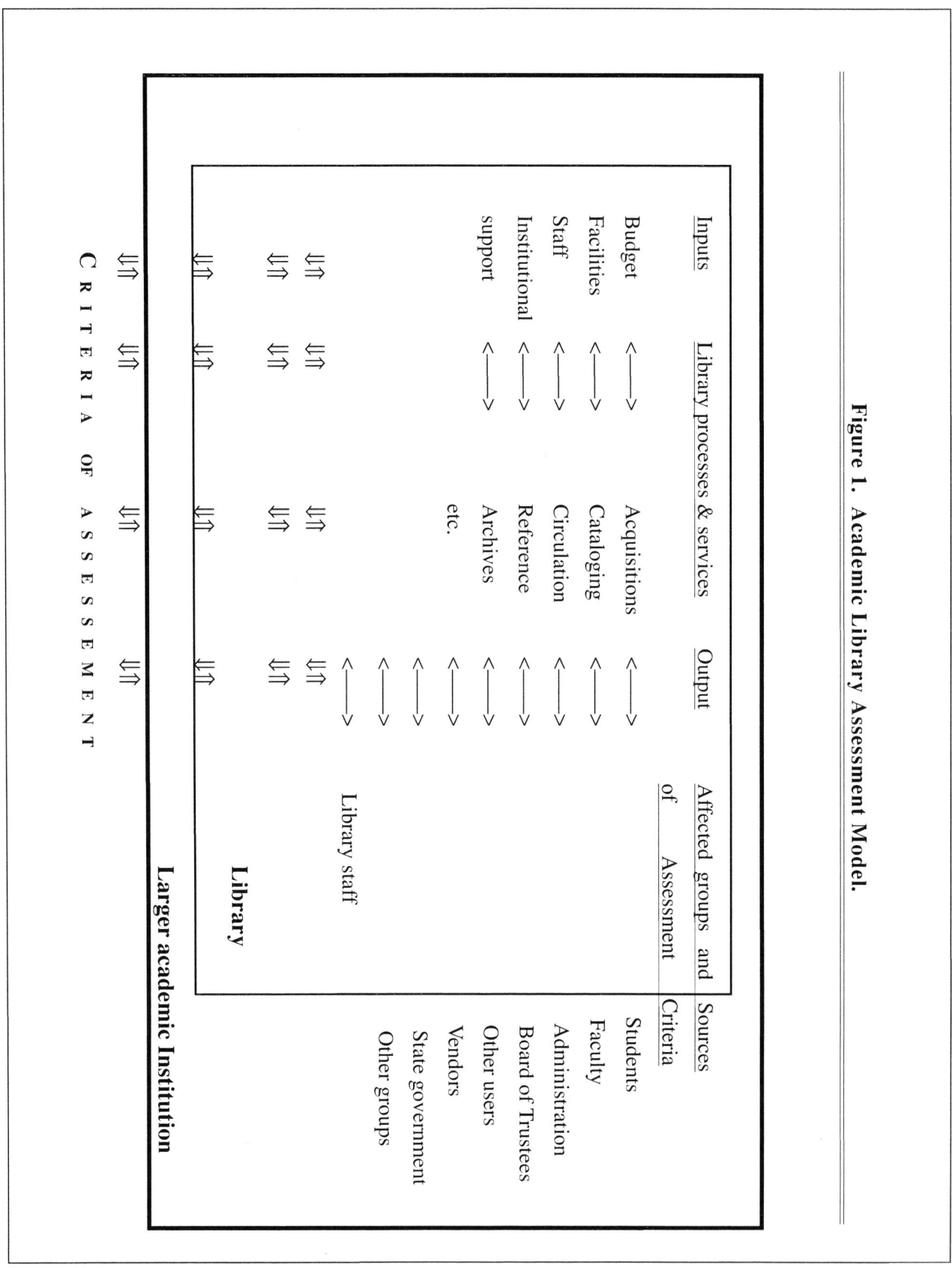

Figure 1. Academic Library Assessment Model.

who is setting the criteria of the assessment, (b) which criteria are being used to measure effectiveness, and (c) which part or parts of the organization are being assessed.

3) The library's assessment cannot be isolated from the institution's assessment program when the effect of the library, i.e., outcomes, is being examined.

4) For assessment to be more than an exercise, it must be an integrated part of library and institutional planning and management. While there may be external pressures to carry out some assessment, it behooves those who assess libraries to use their assessment for more than just political purposes.

5) Different aspects of assessment require different types of data gathering from different sources. These include, for example,

• Bench marking which is the collection of data from other institutions that is used to make comparisons.

• Collection of process indicators such as flow charts and measurement of production levels.

• Counting of library service activities such as number of books circulated.

• Attitudinal and feedback surveys of various constituent groups.

• Tests of user knowledge.

• Portfolios of both teaching materials used in bibliographic instruction and students' work based on library research.

• Techniques for measuring behavior.

• Focus groups

Assessment should not be viewed as an applied research project that has as its end goal the collection of data in order to prove or disprove a hypothesized relationship. While there are elements of research methodology in assessment, there is a tension between the demand for rigor in the protocols of research, and the needs of assessment. Often assessment attempts to look at phenomenon that are not well understood and for which there is little research basis. This means there is a very incomplete understanding of coincidental or causal relationships between library programs and criteria of assessment.

Finally, assessment needs to be placed in the context of the library's needs and therefore plans should be developed for how assessment results will be used to improve effectiveness.

Earlham's assessment

Earlham's library assessment program is not a fully planned and developed program. It is in process and in some respects groping for answers to questions. It emerged out of the same factors and pressures that all academic libraries are facing—institutional accountability, accrediting agency requirements and library staff interest in improvement. It emerged without any special expertise or extra funding.

The program has developed in an atmosphere which expects that in the library's operations and programs an effort will be made to develop ways of collecting information on the quality, effectiveness, or performance of the library's programs and activities. The nature of the assessment varies greatly depending on what is being assessed, who is doing it, and for what purpose. In each case, those aspects must be determined first.

We have consciously said that everything does not have to be measured quantitatively; qualitative assessment has a valid place. Furthermore, there is a recognition that doing assessment does have considerable costs in staff time. We therefore take a minimalist approach to assessment and design the process to make it as easy to carry out as possible.

The library staff is cautious not to over reach in our approach to *assessment* of *outcomes*. We recognize our limitations in measuring the causal relationships between what we do and how students perform, what they have learned and attitudes change,. We are focusing on bench marking inputs, measuring performance and cautiously measuring outcomes in limited ways.

Despite the recognized limits we have engaged in a variety of assessment enterprises over the past five years. The activities include:

1) Development of a set of broad goals. These goals act as guiding principles to help us choose the focus of our assessment efforts. However, whenever we conduct an assessment activity, we establish specific goals for that activity in the assessment design.

2) Administration of a library test to incoming first-year students that measures a few basic

library research and information literacy skills. The test provides us with an indication of the baseline skills of our entering students. We have not yet taken the next step, which is to use the test as a measure of the skill level of graduating students. We are working towards it.

3) Benchmarking library inputs and processes using input and output data. This data is important as we present annual budgets and make other management decisions.

4) Analysis of operations and revision of processes as a result of the analysis. Some of this has been internal, such as revision of routines associated with implementation of an integrated electronic library system. Other analysis has been external, such as the ARL national study of interlibrary loan services[6] and the surveys associated with ACRL's Clip Notes publications.[7]

5) Measuring the level of instruction activity to ascertain the status of our bibliographic instruction program. This was a study of the level and reach of the instruction program in the early 1990's based on a complete inventory of library instruction and library related assignments experienced by graduates of the class of 1993. We reported the results of this study at the last ACRL National Conference.[8]

6) Seeking feedback from focus groups to determine (a) effectiveness of individual projects or (b) directions in program development. An example of (a) is web site development where we used a focus group of student workers and paraprofessional staff to react to plans for organizing pages that provide access to web based commercial databases. An example of (b) is a survey and focus group of students we used in making decisions about the location of an after-hours study room and our instructional computer lab.

7) Conducting surveys for individual classes and user groups about bibliographic instruction activities. These are usually done with a specific question or issue in mind. For example, with the revision of the calendar, we had an opportunity to revise the introductory instruction in Humanities, a core course taken by all first year students. There had always been some question about whether an exercise we used in the instruction was useful. The survey results helped us decide to continue to use the exercise and determine ways to improve it.

8) Conducting attitude surveys of faculty and students to determine user perceptions of the quality of the libraries services, facilities and collections.

9) Conducting alumni attitude surveys to determine graduates' attitudes towards the library program and their library experiences while students at Earlham.

This list of assessment activities is probably not unique. In fact, some of the items seem pretty pedestrian and common place. However, listing all the assessment activities highlights the points Cameron made in his 1978 article. There are many dimensions to assessment. At times, one form of assessment is touted as the most important. As the ALAM model indicates, there are many perspectives on what are the important criteria for assessment. Academic libraries need to develop a *balanced* assessment program and communicate the results to a variety of library constituencies.

Attitude surveys

I would like to describe in more detail the last two activities and project our future plans. I am not going to give you a full blown research report on these two surveys. As I indicated earlier, assessment is not a research project. While it should use good methodology, the end product is not to provide a research paper. What I want to explore here is how the results were used as feedback to improve library services, and I would like to critique the approaches in terms of their usefulness for outcomes assessment.

The first example I want to discuss is a survey of alumni. The college's institutional research office regularly does a one-year-after and a five-year-after survey of our graduates. Since the library had studied the class of 1993's exposure to library research assignments and formal bibliographic instruction it seemed appropriate to survey that class after they had been away from Earlham for five years. However, to pilot the survey we started a year earlier and surveyed the class of 1992 in the summer/fall of 1997. The library items were incorporated into the larger institutional survey. The li-

Errata

Table 1. Sample alumni survey results.	
Question	Mean score* n=113 (38% response)
1. What is your current, general attitude toward Earlham College? (4 point scale)	1.45
2. Compared to other college graduates in my graduate/professional program I feel/felt well prepared (3 point scale)	1.30
3. Compared to other college graduates in my work, I feel well prepared. (3 point scale)	1.29
In retrospect how satisfied are you with the following aspects of your Earlham Library experience (4 point scales)	
4. The ability of the library's collections to meet your academic needs.	1.67
5. The ability of the library's collections to meet your general information needs.	1.52
6. The help provided by individual staff members during your use of the library	1.31
7. The *quality* of formal instruction you received about using information resources.	1.39
8. The *quantity* of formal instruction you received about using information resources.	1.57
9. The formal instruction in your major you received about using information resources.	1.70
10. The preparation the Earlham program provided for doing library research in graduate school.	1.36
11. The preparation the Earlham program provided for the information gathering you do in your work.	1.45
* Mean scores from Likert scales where 1 is highest and 3 or 4 is lowest depending on the question.	

brary portion of the survey results are presented in Table 1. This type of data provides an outcomes assessment that focuses on attitudes which the program encourages.

Certainly, the results demonstrate the respondents have a very strong positive attitude towards Earlham and the library experience. We can, therefore, I believe, make a solid claim that for a significant portion of the student body, the library experience is positive. A look at the data on academic majors of the respondents indicates this positive attitude is not limited to certain majors.

We also know that such a survey is of limited usefulness. For example, we fully expected those who feel strongly positive about the institution are most likely to reply. We might expect that those who liked the institution least might also respond to demonstrate their displeasure, but the results indicate that did not happen. We probably only have those who feel positive about the institution. Therefore, the results do not provide a very good overall indicator of the level of satisfaction. However, individual items can be compared with one another to get a sense of satisfaction with specific aspects of Earlham. For example, the library's reference service (#6) and the preparation for library research in graduate school (#10) are distinctly thought of as "very satisfying." Both of these characteristics of the library's program appear to be especially important in contributing to an overall positive alumni impression of their Earlham undergraduate experience.

As part of the survey, we asked alumni how often they used their academic or work related

Table 2. Alumni use of libraries.			
Level of use	Earlham Alumni Academic or Empl. Related Library Use	Earlham Alumni Public Library Use	National Survey Public Library Use
Not all	11%	16%	32%
1 to 5 times a year	9%	28%	29%
6 to 10 times a year	10%	13%	13%
11 to 20 times per year	11%	18%	10%
over 21 times in the last year	56%	26%	27%

library and their public library. The question design is based on a national survey conducted by the Benton Foundation for the American Library Association.[9] The results are provided in Table 2. Over all the results do not suggest a meaningful difference between Earlham alumni and the national survey population in the frequency with which they use the public library, with the exception that a much smaller percentage of Earlham graduates never use the public library. The results for use of academic or employment related libraries is substantially higher and more frequent, but there are no national figures for comparison.

How should we interpret the results of this alumni survey? On the one hand, the library experience and what they got from it while students at Earlham was highly satisfying and, in their opinion, prepared them well for graduate school and work related information research. However, the results of the library use portion of the survey suggest that the Earlham program has not made much of a difference in the level of public library use.

The problem with the library use data is that we, the profession, do not have a good research base or conceptual grounding for *relating a positive academic library experience with the level of library use by adults.*

The alumni survey typifies the problems we face in trying to measure certain types of outcome. The tools available, including the conceptual frameworks for relationships between program content and desired outcomes, are inadequate to answer the questions we ask. Therefore, if we are to move forward in building stronger outcomes assessment, we need a much better understanding of how library programs affect the life-long skills, knowledge and behaviors of our graduates. Understanding those effects and building assessment tools that will demonstrate the effects are a challenge we must address. In the meantime, we should recognize that library outcomes assessment which links specific programs to achievement of desired long-term outcomes is a problematic goal.

The second assessment activity I want to discuss in detail is a user survey of current faculty and students.

We developed a survey instrument based on the work of Joseph A. McDonald,[10] John Budd and Mike DiCarlo[11] and Kristen Smith.[12] These instruments ask respondents to rank a statement about library service, facilities or collections on a Likert Scale in terms of its *importance* to their use of the library and the library's *performance*. We were attracted to these survey instruments because they address one of Cameron's key elements of assessment criteria: the origin of the criteria. While the survey questionnaire might include items the library staff viewed as important, there is no certainty that they are important elements of library quality from the faculty or students' perspective. The survey results determine not just perceptions of the level of performance but also how divergent perceptions of performance are from the sense of the importance of the service, facility or collection to the user. While we made some modifications in the wording of the questions, we tried to keep them similar in order to have a basis for comparison with the earlier studies. A copy of the survey instrument is available in Appendix A.

We used the results (Table 3) in several ways. The median scores on performance gave us some indication of how well our patrons thought we are doing. We can say that on a scale of 5 to 1, our students believe the library is performing well. Converted to the academic coin of the realm, grades, we are, on average, doing A- to B+ work. But we were interested in more than a general sense of how well we were doing.

To dig deeper, we did a number of things with the results. First, we looked at the difference between performance and importance. In almost all cases, the performance scores were lower than the importance scores. The exceptions were statements about local and out-of-town newspapers and recreational reading material where the scores on importance were lower than the performance scores, (e.g., item 2). While we did not take any specific action, the results did indicate that in budget allocations we could reduce, or at least not increase greatly, support for those purchases. The results also confirmed an earlier decision to hold back on the purchase of additional out-of-town and international newspapers and, as an alternative, depend on the Internet for access to newspapers for recreational reading.

We also noted differences between importance and performance that were strongly negative such as "8, circulation loan period is long enough." While we had heard grumbling from the graduate seminary students, we had not received many complaints from undergraduate students about the circulation loan period. Since we had changed academic calendars from a ten-week term to a fourteen-week semester, it appeared we needed to revisit the length of loan periods. Following a review of what other similar undergraduate residential liberal arts colleges' loan periods are, a form of benchmarking, and weighing the advantages and disadvantages of longer loan periods, we changed the length for students.

There were other questions, e.g., "6. On-line library catalog is easy to use," where the results indicated, at least comparatively, that the performance could be better. We knew from experience at the reference desk that some students are having navigational problems and during this past fall that students' negative attitudes towards non-graphical interfaces has grown. These survey results provide systematic data that indicates the need to implement a graphical interface to our catalog and we hope to implement it this summer.

Finally, results from many questions do not provide clear direction for ways to improve library services. For example, "7. Adequate journals and magazines supporting your major," has a difference of means between importance and performance that is strongly negative. We asked ourselves what these results tell us. Are there specific journals (or books) that students really need that we lack? Or are there mitigating circumstances that might lead students to feel the collection is insufficient for their needs? For example, students may not be getting adequate instruction in the use of periodical indexes, or perhaps they are having difficulty knowing what we have out of the myriad of items identified thorough an index. Perhaps their expectations are unreasonable. Therefore, we have decided to follow-up with student focus groups to see if we can get beyond the superficial survey results and get a fuller sense of what is needed. It is not clear what the specific outcomes of those focus group sessions will be, but, in general, we hope to clarify the meaning of the survey

Table 3. Examples of questions and results from student survey results.

	Level of Importance*	Level of Performance*	Difference
1. Check-out procedure is handled efficiently in Lilly [Main] Library.	4.50	4.56	.05
2. Access to local newspapers	3.66	4.36	.70
3. Instruction sessions make research easier	4.20	4.17	-.03
4. Instruction adequate for understanding and using print resources	4.38	4.13	-.25
5. Instruction adequate for understanding and using on-line resources	4.38	4.16	-.22
6. On-line library catalog is easy to use	4.61	4.01	-.50
7. Adequate journals and magazines supporting your major	4.44	3.71	-.73
8. Circulation loan period is long enough	4.46	3.53	-.93

*Based on a five point scale where 5 is highest and 1 is lowest.

results on question #7 by identifying the problems that explain the responses on the survey.

In concluding discussion of this assessment methodology, I want to emphasize that the results are not simply examined with the goal of ascertaining some general sense of the quality of the library. Neither are we using the results as evidence of the need for bold actions or significant increases in resources. The responses to the results are more varied and nuanced. The results where appropriate, have been used as evidence of a need for change. But the survey results alone are never the basis for a decision. The results are being used to focus attention on the specific areas of library services, facilities and collections where our users have told us we should perform better because the enterprise is important to overall academic library service.

Conclusion

In concluding this paper, I would like to summarize the characteristics of Earlham's assessment program. Our program recognizes the four-part nature of assessment: inputs, processes, outputs and outcomes. We have been most successful in looking at inputs through benchmarking efforts and process assessment through internal analysis associated with the implementation of an integrated library system and other analysis of operations. We have also used focus groups and surveys to get students and faculty perspectives on the quality of our services. In this way, we respect the multiple origins and attitudes towards what criteria should be used and how well we perform on those criteria. We have made a significant effort to assess outputs through the earlier study of the amount and diversity of bibliographic instruction that our students receive.

We have been able to use our assessment results to make changes in the program and to identify issues that need more thorough and careful study. Our assessment program is helpful to us and not an annoying activity forced upon us.

We have been less successful in assessing outcomes. Our initial efforts were in concert with other institutional assessment activities, and our assessment has benefitted from that cooperation. One benefit is that the work of conducting the survey is undertaken by the Institutional Research Office, whose staff are better organized to handle such activities. A second benefit is the ability to use related data to compare with the library specific section of the survey. But we also know that there are limits to this approach.

In the future, we intend to work closely with faculty committees and academic programs as they conduct their assessment. A member of the library staff sits on the College's Assessment Committee, and another sits on the Curricular Policy Committee which will be doing the assessment of the General Education program. Furthermore, we are already planting seeds by talking with departments about looking at senior seminar and other major research projects as ways to assess outcomes. However, like our bibliographic instruction program itself, an effective outcomes assessment will not be created in a year or two. It will take several, if not many, years of hard work in the trenches working with individuals and groups of faculty to see that assessment of the library outcomes is viewed in the larger context of the college program and how the concept of organizational effectiveness informs the assessment program.

Obviously, these are only our current plans. Circumstances may change. However, what I hope will not change is our recognition of the several essential ingredients of the Academic Library Assessment Model (ALAM). They are:

1. Different people associated with an organization have different perspectives on the effectiveness of an organization.

2. The criteria for measuring effectiveness are highly variable.

3. Outcomes assessment is not a simple measurement of either student learning or long term changes in behavior. Outcomes assessment is an attempt to understand the relationship between what a library does in its program and how it effects, either directly or indirectly, students' lives during college and afterward.

The author acknowledges the helpful critique of this paper by Sara Penhale and Nancy Taylor of the Earlham Library staff. Correspondence with the author is possible at kirkto@earlham.edu.

Errata

Notes

1. Sarah M. Pritchard, "Determining Quality in Academic Library," *Library Trends* 44 (winter 1996), 572–94.

2. Kim Cameron, "Measuring Organizational Effectiveness in Institutions of Higher Education," *Administrative Science Quarterly* 23 (December 1978), 604–32.

3. "Task Force on Academic Library Outcomes Assessment Report," (Chicago: Association of College and Research Libraries, 1997). Available at: http://www.ala.org/acrl/outcome.html [1 December, 1998].

4. Pritchard, "Determining Quality," 575.

5. "Task Force on Academic Library Outcomes, Section II, second paragraph.

6. Mary E. Jackson, *Measuring the performance of interlibrary loan operations in North American research and college libraries*. Washington, D.C.: Association of Research Libraries, 1998.

7. *Emergency planning and management in college libraries* (CLIP notes #17.), Chicago, Ill.: Association of College and Research Libraries, 1994.

8. Sara J. Penhale, Nancy Taylor, and Thomas G. Kirk, Jr., "A Method of Measuring the Reach of a Bibliographic Instruction Program," ACRL 8th National Conference, Nashville, Tennessee, 1997. Chicago: Association of College and Research Libraries. Available: http://www.ala.org/acrl/papers.html#D29 [13 February 1999].

9. Benton Foundation, *Buildings, Books and Bytes; Libraries and Communities in the Digital Age*, Washington, D.C.: Benton Foundation, 1996, 42.

10. Joseph Andrew McDonald, *Academic Library Effectiveness: An Organizational Perspective*. Unpublished doctoral dissertation. Drexel University, 1987.

11. John Budd and Mike DiCarlo, "Measures of User Evaluation at Two Academic Libraries," *Library Research* 4 (1982): 97–84.

12. Kristen L. Smith, "Library Service Survey: Results," (Dubuque, Ia.: Lorus College, 1997). Unpublished. Used by permission of the author.

Appendix A

HOW WOULD YOU RATE EARLHAM'S LIBRARIES?

Are you a: First Year____ Sophomore____ Junior____ Senior____
ESR student____ Bethany student_____?

What is your major?_____

Which libraries do you use? Lilly_____ Wildman_____ Friends/Archives_____

To help us evaluate Earlham's libraries please rate both the <u>IMPORTANCE to you</u> of each item and the libraries' <u>PERFORMANCE</u> (<u>quality of library service</u>) in each.

Use <u>1 as the lowest rating</u> and <u>5 as the highest</u>. You may circle <u>DK, for Don't Know</u>, if you have no opinion about, or experience with, that item.

	IMPORTANCE low high	PERFORMANCE low high
1. Materials available in the Libraries		
Adequate books to support your <u>major</u>	1 2 3 4 5 DK	1 2 3 4 5 DK
General books supporting your <u>interests</u>	1 2 3 4 5 DK	1 2 3 4 5 DK
Journals and magazines supporting your <u>major</u>	1 2 3 4 5 DK	1 2 3 4 5 DK
Journals and magazines supporting your <u>interests</u>	1 2 3 4 5 DK	1 2 3 4 5 DK
Adequate out of town newspapers	1 2 3 4 5 DK	1 2 3 4 5 DK
Access to local newspapers	1 2 3 4 5 DK	1 2 3 4 5 DK
Adequate reference collection	1 2 3 4 5 DK	1 2 3 4 5 DK
Adequate map collection	1 2 3 4 5 DK	1 2 3 4 5 DK
Interlibrary loan service is <u>able to provide</u> needed materials	1 2 3 4 5 DK	1 2 3 4 5 DK
Interlibrary loan service provides materials <u>promptly</u>	1 2 3 4 5 DK	1 2 3 4 5 DK
2. Finding materials in the Libraries		
Online library catalog (PALNI) is easy to use	1 2 3 4 5 DK	1 2 3 4 5 DK
Books are shelved <u>correctly</u> in <u>Lilly Library</u>	1 2 3 4 5 DK	1 2 3 4 5 DK
Books are shelved <u>correctly</u> in <u>Wildman Science Library</u>	1 2 3 4 5 DK	1 2 3 4 5 DK
Books and journals are reshelved <u>quickly</u> in <u>Lilly</u>	1 2 3 4 5 DK	1 2 3 4 5 DK
Books and journals are reshelved <u>quickly</u> in <u>Wildman</u>	1 2 3 4 5 DK	1 2 3 4 5 DK

	IMPORTANCE low high	PERFORMANCE low high

3. Electronic resources

	IMPORTANCE	PERFORMANCE
Libraries' web page leads to useful sources for research............	1 2 3 4 5 DK	1 2 3 4 5 DK
Libraries provide adequate electronic indexes to journal articles..	1 2 3 4 5 DK	1 2 3 4 5 DK
Software used by electronic indexes is easy to learn................	1 2 3 4 5 DK	1 2 3 4 5 DK
Enough workstations for electronic indexes to journal articles available in Lilly Library...............................	1 2 3 4 5 DK	1 2 3 4 5 DK
Enough workstations for internet searching available in Lilly Library...	1 2 3 4 5 DK	1 2 3 4 5 DK
Workstations and software function properly in Lilly	1 2 3 4 5 DK	1 2 3 4 5 DK
Printers are available and functioning in Lilly Library................	1 2 3 4 5 DK	1 2 3 4 5 DK
Enough workstations for electronic indexes to journal articles available in Wildman reference area.......................	1 2 3 4 5 DK	1 2 3 4 5 DK
Enough workstations for internet searching in Wildman...........	1 2 3 4 5 DK	1 2 3 4 5 DK
Workstations and software function properly in Wildman.........	1 2 3 4 5 DK	1 2 3 4 5 DK
Printers are available and functioning in Wildman....................	1 2 3 4 5 DK	1 2 3 4 5 DK

4. Help available from library staff

	IMPORTANCE	PERFORMANCE
Lilly Library professional staff available and able to help when needed...	1 2 3 4 5 DK	1 2 3 4 5 DK
Lilly student staff responsive and courteous..............................	1 2 3 4 5 DK	1 2 3 4 5 DK
Wildman Science Library professional staff available and able to help when needed.....................................	1 2 3 4 5 DK	1 2 3 4 5 DK
Wildman student staff responsive and courteous.......................	1 2 3 4 5 DK	1 2 3 4 5 DK
Friends Collection/Archives professional staff available and able to help when needed.....................................	1 2 3 4 5 DK	1 2 3 4 5 DK
Friends Collection/Archives student staff responsive and courteous...	1 2 3 4 5 DK	1 2 3 4 5 DK

5. Instruction in library use

	IMPORTANCE	PERFORMANCE
Instruction sessions make research easier.................................	1 2 3 4 5 DK	1 2 3 4 5 DK
Instruction adequate for understanding and using print resources...	1 2 3 4 5 DK	1 2 3 4 5 DK
Instruction adequate for understanding and using on-line resources..	1 2 3 4 5 DK	1 2 3 4 5 DK
Library instruction is a worthwhile use of class time.................	1 2 3 4 5 DK	1 2 3 4 5 DK

	IMPORTANCE low high	PERFORMANCE low high
6. Circulation of materials		
Check-out procedure is handled efficiently in Lilly Library.......	1 2 3 4 5 DK	1 2 3 4 5 DK
Check-out procedure is handled efficiently in Wildman............	1 2 3 4 5 DK	1 2 3 4 5 DK
Loan period is long enough...	1 2 3 4 5 DK	1 2 3 4 5 DK
7. Library facilities		
Adequate variety of seating and work areas in Lilly Library.......	1 2 3 4 5 DK	1 2 3 4 5 DK
Adequate control of noise in Lilly Library..................................	1 2 3 4 5 DK	1 2 3 4 5 DK
Conference and group study areas are available in Lilly............	1 2 3 4 5 DK	1 2 3 4 5 DK
Temperature in Lilly Library is comfortable...............................	1 2 3 4 5 DK	1 2 3 4 5 DK
Adequate variety of seating and work areas in Wildman...........	1 2 3 4 5 DK	1 2 3 4 5 DK
Adequate control of noise in Wildman Science Library..............	1 2 3 4 5 DK	1 2 3 4 5 DK
Conference and group study areas are available in Wildman....	1 2 3 4 5 DK	1 2 3 4 5 DK
Temperature is comfortable in Wildman Science Library............	1 2 3 4 5 DK	1 2 3 4 5 DK
8. Library hours		
Libraries are open sufficient hours during the weekdays...........	1 2 3 4 5 DK	1 2 3 4 5 DK
Libraries are open sufficient hours on weekends......................	1 2 3 4 5 DK	1 2 3 4 5 DK
Libraries are open sufficient hours during breaks.....................	1 2 3 4 5 DK	1 2 3 4 5 DK

COMMENTS:

Extinguishing Slow Fires: Cooperative Preservation Efforts

Brian J. Baird and Bradley L. Schaffner

For years filmmakers in Hollywood have relied on the image of a book burning to illustrate intolerance. In the movie *Indiana Jones and the Last Crusade* Steven Spielberg utilizes this image to make clear to the audience that Nazism was an evil ideology. It is safe to say that librarians would agree with Hollywood's view of book burning as the ultimate form of censorship and intolerance. Fortunately, book burning is a rare occurrence, at least in democratic nations. However, untold numbers of books are being destroyed, not by book burnings, but through the slow fires of deterioration. These flames of destruction are not being fanned by intolerance or censorship, but by a lack of funds or indifference to the problem. One promising solution is cooperative preservation programs that can provide a viable cost-effective way to preserve important and significant publications.

There is no question that the preservation of printed materials must be given a high priority if we are to save these resources for future generations of students and scholars. Large portions of most libraries' published holdings are printed on substandard acidic paper that will become embrittled. Paper is considered brittle when it breaks after less than two double folds. Recent condition surveys at the University of Kansas Libraries indicate that six percent of library holdings have embrittled paper.[1] In addition, some holdings, such as Russian and Soviet publications, have a much higher percentage of brittle volumes with 17.43 percent currently evaluated as brittle.[2] Complicating matters is the fact that over 65 percent of the general collections and 87 percent of all Russian and Soviet holdings at the University of Kansas Libraries are printed on acidic paper that will eventually become brittle.[3] Although the percentage of brittle materials may vary by institution, most research libraries face similar challenges with significant percentages of brittle collections.[4] If these items do not receive some type of preservation treatment, they will eventually deteriorate to the point where they will be unusable. There is no debating that preservation efforts must be made to save meaningful materials—the important question is how can this be accomplished?

Preservation specialists can employ a number of treatments to save publications. These treatments range from relatively simple repairs to rebinding materials to major conservation work to reformatting materials. Generally, brittle items are preserved by the latter. Reformatting involves the transfer of the information in the original publication to digital images, microforms, or preservation quality photocopy facsimiles. Unfortunately, the process can be expensive, and a single library could not afford to save all of its holdings that need this type of preservation treatment. In an effort to be cost-effective, libraries need to work together. This paper will briefly review reformatting options and then examine past and current cooperative programs which have successfully mobilized resources to preserve publications.

It is important to use the appropriate format when preserving materials. One should not fall into the trap of using one format for all preservation projects. For example, digitizing all items in a preservation project simply because it makes use of cutting-edge technology is not the best use of preservation funds. Many publications, such as individual volumes in the social science or humanities, are best preserved on microfilm or photocopy facsimiles.[5]

There is no doubt that electronic formats are often more versatile than paper publications because full-text or key word indexing provides excellent searching capabilities. Many publications such as encyclopedias, indexes, bibliographies, and other reference works generally benefit from the enhanced access and storage capabilities of digitization. However, its limitations and drawbacks must be considered when working on preservation projects. First and foremost is the issue of cost. After an item is digitized, there are ongoing storage costs. A recent study shows that on-site stor-

---

Brian J. Baird is preservation librarian, and Bradley L. Schaffner is Russian studies librarian, University of Kansas Libraries.

age of electronic information costs a library sixteen times more than housing books and serials.[6] Moreover, there are many unanswered questions regarding the feasibility of archiving electronic information. Given the rapid development of computer technology and the lack of format and storage standards, one has to wonder if current electronic information will be accessible in five to ten years. As Marcia Watt and Lisa Biblo observed: "What use is a disc that can last 500 years, even 100 or 50 years, if there is no machine which provides access to the information on the disc?"[7]

Furthermore, when choosing a reformatting treatment, one must also consider the patron's needs and preferences. In libraries we often see users printing off page upon page of electronic text. While electronic formats provide ease of access, users often prefer to print off the text into hard copy for their use. In a recent essay, Umberto Eco observed that rather than moving us towards a "paperless" society electronic texts have actually resulted in the increased production of printed material. Rather than dealing with published books and journals, we will have to cope with "tons and tons of unbound sheets of paper."[8] Eco believes that new technologies will render only some types of publications, such as multi-volume encyclopedias, obsolete. Most printed books which are durable, portable, and economical will continue to prosper.

Of course a similar argument can be made against the use of microfilm. Most patrons find it very difficult to read microfilm and use it as a last resort in their research, often printing articles that they need from the film. In addition, microfilm does not offer either enhanced or remote access to the resource like electronic formats. What microfilm does offer, however, is a relatively inexpensive way to preserve and store materials long term. This is a low-tech preservation solution that will remain easily accessible, regardless of technological innovations.

Another reformatting alternative, and one that addresses the user's preference for a hard copy, is the use of preservation-quality photocopy facsimiles to create reproductions of the original publication. When done professionally, photo reproduction technology enhances the text and illustrations so they are sharper than the deteriorated original. The reproductions are printed on acid-free paper and bound in book format for easy access and long term storage of several hundred years. Another advantage of preservation-quality photocopy is its cost. Orders for multiple copies of an individual title lowers the overall price making this ideal for cooperative programs.

Preservation-quality photocopy facsimile is the format currently used in two successful cooperative preservation ventures, *Brittle* and *SlavCopy*, which are operated at the University of Kansas. The goal of these programs is to preserve important individual works. While *Brittle* and *Slavcopy* currently use facsimile reproductions, both programs are exploring other options, such as digitization, that may optimize preservation resources.

Brittle and *SlavCopy*

Brittle is an international cooperative effort founded and administered at the University of Kansas.[9] The purpose of *Brittle* is to facilitate the acquisition of preservation photocopies of embrittled volumes at reduced prices. The *modus operandi* for *Brittle* is an electronic listserver to which participating libraries post titles they wish to preserve. If other libraries wish to acquire preservation copies of a listed title, the price for that title is reduced. Currently there are over 60 active members of *Brittle* in the United States and Australia.

Building on the success of *Brittle*, a Slavic version of the cooperative program was established called *SlavCopy*. Brad Schaffner, the Slavic Librarian at the University of Kansas is primarily responsible for this effort and does most of the work. The focus of the list is the preservation of Slavic and other East Central European language publications. With over 20 members, *SlavCopy* is smaller than *Brittle*, but libraries actively participate resulting in the preservation of a number of important Slavic titles.

Brittle and *Slavcopy* essentially work the same way, but for ease, this paper will focus its discussion on *Brittle*. The preservation process begins when a participating library posts a title to the *Brittle* list. Full bibliographic information is given for each title along with the estimated reproduction price. Each citation also includes a list of libraries requesting a copy of the item. The *Brittle* list is distributed on the listserver weekly with updates that identify the libraries requesting a copy. Such information allows other librarians to make informed decisions regarding the need for their library to acquire a preservation copy of the work based on the number of other libraries planning to purchase the title. It is not necessary for each library to acquire a copy of every title posted, particularly if the monograph falls outside of the collection development parameters of the institution. Because *Brittle* identifies each library ordering a copy of the work other libraries know that the title will be available through interlibrary loan. Each citation appears on the list for one month so that libraries have time to examine their copy of the publication to determine if a preservation quality photocopy is needed to replace the original work.

After one month, the posting library sends the volume to the Preservation Department at the University of Kansas Libraries where it is processed as part of a *Brittle* shipment. Having all *Brittle* orders originating from the University of Kansas reduces the chance of error and helps the process run smoothly—ultimately reducing costs. In addition to the normal preparation procedures of erasing marks in the text, mending tears, and checking for missing text, the University of Kansas staff also prepare a special flag to notify the vendor which libraries have requested a copy of the title. Once prepared, the books are sent to National Bridgeport Bindery who is partnering with the University of Kansas to provide the *Brittle* photo reproduction service.

Generally, within six to eight weeks from the time a title is removed from *Brittle*, National Bridgeport Bindery will send a replacement copy and an invoice directly to each library that has requested a copy of the title. Bridgeport also returns the original volume, which was taken apart to facilitate the copy process, a replacement copy, and an invoice to the library which submitted the title for copying.

Benefits of Participating in *Brittle*
The primary benefit of participating in *Brittle* is substantial savings on the cost of preservation photo reproductions. The savings can be as much as 50 percent off the listed catalog price for photocopying services offered by some vendors. In addition to price reductions, libraries participating in *Brittle* reduce the overhead costs involved with processing materials for preservation reformatting. These reductions are achieved through the distribution of processing activities amongst the members of the cooperative and represent a significant savings of time and money to participants.

Such activities include the elimination of the need to conduct bibliographic searches to determine if a reprint is available because this search has been conducted by the posting library. In addition, participating libraries are saved the hours of tedious work needed to prepare a book for photocopying. This includes reviewing the text page by page to mend tears, erase marks, and check for missing text. This process is further complicated when pages must be ordered through interlibrary loan to replace missing text.

Often, many of the titles posted on *Brittle* are heavily used and badly damaged. One of the advantages to this cooperative effort is that the *Brittle* citations indicate that the volume is badly damaged and request that other libraries consider supply their title for photocopying. On numerous occasions *Brittle* and *SlavCopy* have orchestrated the reproduction of a single title by using copies of the work held by two or more libraries. In some cases, these titles were only one use away from disappearing forever. Had it not been for the cooperative efforts of those participating in *Brittle* and *Slavcopy* it would have been impossible to create a complete preservation copy of the item.

It is clear that libraries can benefit through cooperative preservation efforts. When multiple libraries participate in cooperative programs such as *Brittle* and *Slavcopy*, significant amounts of time and money are saved. These savings can be applied towards the preservation of additional materials that are at risk. Given the current financial environment such cooperative efforts are extremely important.

Future Directions for Cooperative Efforts
Digitization and modern communication networks have opened many new possibilities for coopera-

tive preservation efforts. *Brittle* and *Slavcopy* were made possible as a result of the creation of electronic mail which facilitates quick and easy communication with all of the participants. Thanks to digitization, it is currently possible to scan a book, store the information electronically, and print a paper copy with a high quality image; all done in less time than it takes to simply produce a preservation photocopy. Scanning and digitization allows for on-demand printing. Bridgeport Bindery is rapidly moving towards incorporating this technology into the *Brittle* and *Slavcopy* program. High resolution, high speed scanners make it possible to quickly capture, organize, and reproduce text and all types of images in a number of formats with very little degradation of text or image. A digitally captured original text can be reproduced as a near flawless book facsimile; as high resolution, high contrast microfilm; as image files on a web page; or it can be converted to a text file using OCR (optical character recognition) technology which is continually becoming more sophisticated. This technology, combined with the interactive capabilities of the Internet and World Wide Web, will allow cooperatives to maintain a catalog of digitized titles on a web site. Interested libraries, in return, may search the list at their convenience for desired titles to replace their embrittled volumes.

This on-demand capability to create copies of reformatted materials addresses a major concern that many funding agencies have had regarding the preservation of materials. In the past, government grant funds for the preservation of materials were limited to projects that used microfilm. Microfilm is a good preservation format because it has proscribed standards for the production and cataloging of three generations of film for each title including a preservation master, a print master, and a use copy to ensure the preservation of the title. It can be easily reproduced providing institutions or researchers around the world with access to the preserved material. Until recently, other formats did not offer such reproduction options, but thanks to technology there are several options available for capturing information, storing it long term, and reproducing it on demand. The success of microfilm projects have benefited national preservation efforts in demonstrating what can be accomplished with adequate leadership and funding.[10] Funding agencies need to recognize that microfilm projects have limitations which can effectively be addressed with today's technology and, therefore, preservation initiatives should not restrict themselves exclusively to microfilm.

One limitation of past microfilm cooperative efforts was the focus on preserving information at a macro level. Materials were selected for filming based on their date of publication and general subject area. Like fishing with a net, collection level preservation projects captured many less important works and items that were not in need of immediate preservation attention along with core materials that were in dire need of preservation. This approach facilitated the preservation of important subject collections. However a collections based approach to preservation of embrittled materials is no longer necessary. Using current technological advances, institutions can work cooperatively to identify embrittled materials for preservation on a title by title basis allowing academic and research libraries to take advantage of their staffs' subject expertise to select materials for reformatting based on the scholarly or cultural value of the item.

Modern communications and digitization technologies enable libraries to be much more interactive in identifying texts to preserve. Moreover, these technologies allow a library to preserve a text in the format best suited to how the text will be used— be that film, preservation photocopy, or a permanent electronic format. The challenge is now for cooperative programs such as *Brittle* and *Slavcopy* and future ventures to utilize these resources to their fullest potential. Funding agencies and other institutions which support preservation activities also need to acknowledge that there are a variety of versatile preservation formats currently available. Therefore, preservation funds should not be restricted to a single format, such as microfilm or even digitization. All formats, from microfilm to digitization to codex form all have advantages and disadvantages. Funds are best spent when we choose the appropriate preservation format based on the needs of both the embrittled title and potential users of the title.

Errata

Conclusion
Cooperative programs are not without their challenges. It is difficult to maintain the level of energy needed to develop a program and make sure it continues to thrive. To have success requires a commitment from all involved. For cooperative programs to succeed they must be managed by an organization dedicated to the goals of the program, have secure funding, and operate under accepted standards which are flexible enough to accommodate the inclusion of new technologies.

We live in a world where the cost of acquiring library materials is growing faster than library budgets. For this reason, libraries must look to cooperative ventures to reduce preservation costs. We must utilize modern technologies to save important texts from around the world in the format best suited for the text, and use cooperative programs to preserve these texts in the most cost-effective manner possible.

Endnotes
1. Brian Baird, Jana Krentz, and Bradley Schaffner, "Findings from the Condition Surveys Conducted at the University of Kansas Libraries," *College & Research Libraries* 58 (March 1997): 122.

2. Bradley L. Schaffner, and Brian Baird, "Into the Dustbin of History? The Evaluation and Preservation of Slavic Materials," *College & Research Libraries* 60 (March 1999): 4.

3. Baird, Krentz, Schaffner, "Findings from the Conditions Survey," 122; and Schaffner, and Baird, "Into the Dustbin of History?", 5.

4. Unfortunately, condition surveys at other libraries such as Yale, the University of Illinois, and Syracuse University Library have indicated that the percentage of embrittled volumes can be as high as 25 percent of the entire collection. The geographic location of the library as well as storage conditions, such as climate control, play a major factor in the deterioration of printed materials. See: Gay Walker, et al., "The Yale Survey: A Large-Scale Study of the Book Deterioration in the Yale University Library," *College & Research Libraries* 46 (March 1985): 111–32; Tina Chrzastowski, et al., "Library Collection Deterioration: A Study at the University of Illinois at Urbana-Champaign," *College & Research Libraries* 50 (September 1989): 577–84; Randall Bond, et al., "Preservation Study at the Syracuse University Library," *College & Research Libraries* 48 (March 1987): 132–47.

5. For a good discussion of this topic, see: Dan Hazen, Jeffrey Horrell, and Jan Merrill-Oldham, "Selecting Research Collections for Digitization," Washington, D.C.: Council on Library and Information Resources, 1998.

6. Charles B. Lowry and Denise A. Troll, "Carnegie Mellon University and University Microfilms International 'Vitual Library Project,'" *The Serials Librarian*, v. 28, nos. 1/2 (1996): 165.

7. Marcia Watt and Lisa Biblo, "CD-Rom Longevity: A Select Bibliography," *Conservation Administration News* (January 1995): 11–13. This issue is also discussed in: Paul Conway, *Preservation in the Digital World*, Washington, D.C.: Commission on Preservation and Access, 1996.

8. Umberto Eco, "Gutenberg Galaxy Expands," *The Nation*, v. 264 no. 1 (January 6, 1997): 35.

9. For a fuller explanation of how the *Brittle* or *SlavCopy* programs work, see Brian J. Baird, "*Brittle*: Replacing Embrittled Titles Cooperatively," *College & Research Libraries News* 58:2 (February 1997): 83-84, 95; or e-mail brited@raven.cc.ukans.edu.

10. *Abbey Newletter*, September 1991, p. 83.

Bibliography
Abbey Newletter, September 1991, p. 83.

Baird, Brian J. "*Brittle*: Replacing Embrittled Titles Cooperatively," *College & Research Libraries News* 58:2 (February 1997): 83–84, 95.

Baird, Baird, Jana Krentz, and Bradley Schaffner, "Findings from the Condition Surveys Conducted at the University of Kansas Libraries," *College & Research Libraries* 58 (March 1997): 115–26.

Bond, Randall, et al., "Preservation Study at the Syracuse University Library," *College & Research Libraries* 48 (March 1987): 132–47.

Chrzastowski, Tina, et al., "Library Collection Deterioration: A Study at the University of Illinois at Urbana-Champaign," *College & Research Libraries* 50 (September 1989): 577–84.

Conway, Paul, *Preservation in the Digital World*, Washington, D.C.: Commission on Preservation and Access, 1996.

Eco, Umberto, "Gutenberg Galaxy Expands," *The Nation*, v. 264 no. 1 (January 6, 1997): 35.

Hazen, Dan, Jeffrey Horrell, and Jan Merrill-Oldham, "Selecting Research Collections for Digitization," Washington, D.C.: Council on Library and Information Resources, 1998.

Lowry, Charles B., and Denise A. Troll, "Carnegie Mellon University and University Microfilms International 'Virtual Library Project,'" *The Serials Librarian*. v. 28, nos. 1/2 (1996): 143–69.

Schaffner, Bradley L. and Brian Baird, "Into the Dustbin of History? The Evaluation and Preservation of Slavic Materials," *College & Research Libraries* 60 (March 1999): 1–8.

Watt, Marcia, and Lisa Biblo. "CD-ROM Longevity: a Select Bibliography." *Conservation Administration News* (January 1995): 11–13.

Walker, Gay, et al., "The Yale Survey: A Large-Scale Study of the Book Deterioration in the Yale University Library," *College & Research Libraries* 46 (March 1985): 111–32.

Snowbird Leadership Institute: A Survey of the Implications for Leadership in the Profession

Teresa Y. Neely and Mark D. Winston

Appendix A

SNOWBIRD LEADERSHIP INSTITUTE SURVEY

This survey was designed to determine your perceptions of the Snowbird Leadership Institute. We are also interested in finding out if there is a relationship between your professional activities before and after the Institute and currently. Your responses are confidential and will not be connected to any individual in the reporting phase. The results of this survey will be reported at the ACRL conference in Detroit in April of 1999, and will also be submitted for publication in a refereed journal. Thank you for your participation. Mark and Teresa

1. During what year did you participate in the Snowbird Leadership Institute? _____

2. Please indicate, from the following choices, who nominated you for Snowbird.

    _____ Dean or department head, School of Library/Information Science
    _____ State Librarian
    _____ Library Director
    _____ Other (please specify) _____
    _____ I don't know

3. In what type of library did you work at the time you attended Snowbird?

    _____ Academic
    _____ Public
    _____ Special
    _____ Government
    _____ School
    _____ Other
    _____ Not working in a library at the time

3a. What was your job title at the time you attended Snowbird?
_____

4. In what state did you work at the time you attended Snowbird? _____

5. What was your undergraduate major? _____

6. What was your undergraduate minor, if applicable? _____

7. Have you earned a Master's degree in Library/Information Science (MLIS)?

Yes _____   No_____   In process _____

7a. If yes, at what institution did you complete the degree? _____

8. Other than the MLIS degree, what additional graduate degrees have you earned?

   _____   None

Degree   Discipline
_____   Master's _____
_____   Doctorate _____
_____   Other _____
                 (please specify)

9. Have you completed additional graduate courses which have not been applied to a degree?

Yes _____   No _____ go to # 10.

9a. If so, in what disciplines have you taken these graduate courses?

   Discipline   Number of credits completed
   _____   _____
   _____   _____
   _____   _____

10. For how long have you been a professional librarian? _____

11. Prior to entering librarianship, have you held (a) paraprofessional position(s) in the library science field?   Yes _____ No _____

11a. If so, how many years of such experience did you have before participating in Snowbird?
_____ Years

11b. What type(s) of position(s) did you hold?

1. _____
2. _____
3. _____
4. _____

12. Prior to entering librarianship, have you held (a) paraprofessional position(s) in another field?
Yes _____   No _____

12a. If so, what type(s) of position(s) did you hold?

1. _____
2. _____
3. _____
4. _____

Errata

13. How many years of professional library experience did you have **before participating in Snowbird**? _____ Years

14. What professional library positions had you held **prior to participating in Snowbird**? Please indicate these positions in chronological order, with the most recent past position listed first (e.g., 1-General reference librarian, 2-Social sciences librarian, etc.).

1. _____
2. _____
3. _____
4. _____

15. Please select the item which applies to your current job situation in reference to your Snowbird participation. Are you:

_____ a. In the same position at the same institution? (Go to # 19)
_____ b. In the same institution in a different position?
_____ c. Neither

16. What professional library positions have you held **since participating in Snowbird**? Please indicate these positions in chronological order, with the most recent past position listed first (e.g., 1-General reference librarian, 2-Social sciences librarian, etc.).

1. _____
2. _____
3. _____
4. _____

17. In what type of library do you work now?

_____ Academic
_____ Public
_____ Special
_____ Government
_____ School
_____ Other
_____ Not working in a library at this time

18. In what state do you currently work? _____

19. What is your current job title? _____

20. For how long have you been in your current position? _____ Years

21. In your current position, are you required to write, publish, and/or engage in research in order to obtain promotion and/or tenure or a tenure equivalent? Yes _____ No _____

22. In other positions that you have held since participating in Snowbird, have you been required to write, publish, and/or engage in research in order to obtain promotion and/or tenure or a tenure equivalent?
Yes _____ No _____

23. How many of each of the following have you published (authored or co-authored) before and since participating in Snowbird?

Before	Since	
_____	_____	Journal Articles
_____	_____	Books
_____	_____	Book chapters
_____	_____	Book reviews
_____	_____	Papers in Conference Proceedings

24. How many presentations have you made at professional conferences before and since participating in Snowbird?

Before	Since	
_____	_____	presentations at national/international library conferences
_____	_____	presentations at statewide or regional library conferences
_____	_____	presentations at other conferences
_____	_____	presentations to other (board of directors, board of visitors, city council, school boards, etc.)

25. Please indicate if you have been involved in professional associations before and since participating in Snowbird. For each item 25a–25c, select all that apply.

25a. National or international professional library associations?

Before	Since	
_____	_____	Attended conference
_____	_____	Committee member
_____	_____	Office holder

25b. Other professional associations?

Before	Since	
_____	_____	Attended conference
_____	_____	Committee member
_____	_____	Office holder

25c. What has been your level of involvement on committees at institutions where you have been employed (i.e., college/university committees, school or departmental committees, city or local committees)?

Before   Since
_____   _____ Attended conference
_____   _____ Committee member
_____   _____ Office holder

26. What other leadership activities have you participated in before and since Snowbird? Please explain.

Before _____
_____

Since _____
_____

27. To what extent did your participation in the Snowbird Leadership Institute contribute to your obtaining subsequent positions?

_____ To A Great Extent
_____ To Some Extent
_____ Not At All

27a. Please explain._____
_____
_____

28. Do you think that your career path would have been different without the Snowbird experience?

Yes _____   No _____

28a. Please explain._____
_____
_____

29. To what extent did your learnings and interaction with other Snowbird participants contribute to the quality of your experience in the program?

_____ To A Great Extent
_____ To Some Extent
_____ Not At All

29a. Please Explain _____
_____
_____

30. To what extent do you believe you received benefits and learnings from activities after the Institute for the following:

30a. Snowbird Listserv

_____ To A Great Extent
_____ To Some Extent
_____ Not At All

30b. Informal reunions at professional conferences (e.g., ALA, Midwinter, PLA, etc.)

_____ To A Great Extent
_____ To Some Extent
_____ Not At All

30c. Collegial relationships developed with other participants?

_____ To A Great Extent
_____ To Some Extent
_____ Not At All

30d. Mentoring relationships?

_____ To A Great Extent
_____ To Some Extent
_____ Not At All

30e. Please Comment here on any part of question 30. _____
_____
_____
_____

31. Have you participated in other library leadership programs in addition to Snowbird?

_____ None
_____ American Library Association Emerging Leaders Institute
_____ Association of Research Libraries Leadership and Career Development Program
_____ Other _____
          (please specify)

32. Please indicate any additional comments which are important with regard to the impact of your participation in the Snowbird Leadership Institute on your career.
_____
_____
_____

++

33. What is your gender?   Female _____   Male _____

34. What is your ethnic background?

_____ White
_____ Asian/Asian American
_____ Black/African American
_____ American Indian/Native American
_____ Hispanic/Latino
_____ Other

35. What is your age?

_____ 21 – 25
_____ 26 – 30
_____ 31 – 35
_____ 36 – 39
_____ 40 – 45
_____ 46 +

36. Are there any additional comments that you would like to make regarding the questionnaire overall?
_____
_____
_____
_____
_____

Racing Toward Tomorrow

Proceedings of the Ninth National Conference of the
Association of College and Research Libraries
April 8–11, 1999

Edited by

Hugh A. Thompson
Director of Publications
Association of College and Research Libraries

Association of College and Research Libraries
A division of the American Library Association
Chicago 1999

The paper used in this publication meets the minimum requirements of American National Standard for Information Sciences–Permanence of Paper for Printed Library Materials, ANSI Z39.48-1992. ∞

Library of Congress Cataloging-in-Publication Data
To come

ISBN 0-8389-8015-5

Copyright © 1999 by the American Library Association. All rights reserved except those which may be granted by Sections 107 and 108 of the Copyright Revision Act of 1976.

Printed in the United States of America.

03 02 01 00 99   5 4 3 2 1

Table of Contents

Introduction ix

Invited Papers

Shifting Gears: A University President's View 3
    Blenda J. Wilson

New Forms of Distance Education: Opportunities for Students, Threats to Institutions 8
    Leigh S. Estabrook

Academic Publishing: Networks and Prices 13
    Malcolm Getz

On t;he Threshold of Disconuity: The New Genres of Scholarly Communication 410
and the Role of the Research Library
    Clifford Lynch

Digital Libraries Support Distributed Education 29
    Gail McMillan

The Changing Nature of Higher Education 37
    Manuel Pachecho

Contributed Papers

Developing Alternative Resources

A Successful Partnership Library 43
    Nick Lund and Pamela M. Blome

Automated Storage and Retrieval—The Next Generation 49
    Sarah Elizabeth Kirsch

Changing Collaborations to Deliver Information in New Ways: 53
Lessons Learned in the Illinois Digital Library Initiative Project
    Timothy Cole and William Mischo

Cry Me a River: Searching for Revenue Streams in Academic Libraries 60
    Linda Dobb

April 8–11, 1999, Detroit, Michigan

EDI—Slow Walk to Fast Forward 63
    Joan Stephens and Roger Presley

Factors That Influence Online Database Use 68
    Carol Tenopir

Pay for Print: Implementing Fee for Service Programs 76
    John Jones, Michael Walker, and Mona Thiss

The UCSC NetTrail: Web-based Instruction for Online Literacy 80
    Ann Hubble and Deborah A. Murphy

Partnering for Effective Service

Bringing LOGIC to Local Government Information: A Multi-type Partnership 87
to Organize Local Government Information
    Judy K. Horn and Shirley W. Leung

Developing and Maintaining Instructional Web Sites: The Library Starter Kit 94
    Deborah A. Murphy

Directly to the Source: Will Academic Libraries Become Wholesalers of Information? 98
    Scott Anderson

Intercepting Departmental Fumbles and Running with the Ball 104
    Alexia Strout-Dapaz and Dennis Odom

Quality Undergraduate Education in a Research University—The Role of Information Literacy ... 109
    Ann C. Schaffner, Leslie Stebbins, and Sally Wyman

Partnering for the Future: Intregrating Traditional Interlibrary Lending and Commercial ... 115
Document Delivery Into a Seamless Service
    Carol A. Kochan, Daniel R. Lee, and Robert G. Murdoch

TEEAL: The Essential Electronic Agricultural Library—Getting the Literature of 120
Agriculture to the Developing Countries
    Mary Anderson Ochs

Alternative Institutions and Providers

Assessment Outside of the Box: The Need for Focused Study of Information Seekers 127
in a Changing Environment
    John Burke and Stephena Harmony

Common Ground: Creating a Unified Environmental Information System Through 134
Stakeholder Partnership
    Linda Langschied

Creating Our Roles as Reference Librarians of the Future: Choice or Fate? 140
Susan Szaz Palmer

Designing for Wow! The Optimal Information Gateway 154
Zsuzsa Koltay and Karen Calhoun

Library Program Assessment 161
Thomas G. Kirk Jr.

QUEST: A Collaborative Approach to Information Literacy 166
Susan B. Markley and Merrill D. Stein

Racing to Keep Up With an Electronic FDLP: Its Effect on Professional Relationships 171
of Academic Government Document Librarians
Ann Roselle

Recruiting More Minorities to the Library Profession: Responding to the Need for Diversity 172
Ronald Edwards

Remote Control: Creating a Technology-Centered Library in Rural Alaska 186
Anne Duffy

The Improvisational Nature of the Change Process 187
Felix T. Chu

The Roles of Academic Librarians in Fostering a Pedagogy for Information Literacy 191
Gloria Leckie and Anne Fullerton

Unified Information Access for the 21st Century: A Project of the California State University 202
Gordon W. Smith and Marvin E. Pollard Jr.

Use of the Scenario Approach for Achieving Sustainable Development in Academic Libraries 207
Steven J. Bell

"Why are You Using the Library," or the Real Goals of Library Research 214
in the Academic Curriculum
Elizabeth D. Hammond

Acquiring New Knowledge Skills

Expansion of Electronic Resources: Superhighway to Campus Visibility 223
Francie C. Davis

Extinguishing Slow Fires: Cooperative Preservation Efforts 228
Brian J. Baird and Bradley L. Schaffner

Core Journal Titles in Full Text Databases 234
Jo Ann Carr and Amy Wolfe

Getting It Right: Outcome-Oriented Redesign of a Service Program in a Team-based Management Environment — 242
Shirley W. Leung and Catherine Palmer

In Search of Services: Analyzing the Findability of Links on CIC University Libraries' Web Page — 259
Barbara I. Dewey

The Changing Nature of Work in Academic Libraries — 264
Kimberley Robles Smith and Beverly P. Lynch

Thinking Style Preferences Among Academic Librarians — 271
Linda Marie Golian

That's My Bailiwick — 280
Carol Ann Hughes and Paul Soderdahl

Emerging Roles for Librarians

Building a Campus Presence One Page at a Time: Web Strategies for the Small College Library — 289
Nancy H. Dewald

First-Year Learning Communities: Redefining the Educational Roles of Academic Librarians — 293
Tony Stamatoplos and Terry Taylor

Harvesting Hyperspace: Developing Technological Solutions to Internet Resource Discovery and Description — 297
Gregory A. McClellan and Thomas P. Turner

Reorganization: The Next Generation — 306
Rhoda Channing

Role Call—What are Library Students Training For and What Will They Be Doing? — 312
Elvira Embser and Philip Coen-Pesch

Snowbird Leadership Institute: A Survey of the Implications for Leadership in the Profession — 313
Teresa Y. Neely and Mark D. Winston

Training ITAs: A Program for Student Information Technology Assistants — 325
Angela Myatt Quick and Eugene Engeldinger

21st-Century Learners

Faculty Use of Electronic Journals at Research Institutions — 329
Deborah Lenares

How Students Use Web-based Tutorials and Library Assignments: Case Studies from Ohio State University Libraries *Nancy O'Hanlon and Fred Roecker*	335
Implementing E-reserves: Home-grown vs. Turnkey *Shane Nackerud*	342
Learning Communities, Adult Learners, and Instructional Teams at IUPUI *May Jafari*	359
Revelry, Revelation, or Research: What Are College Students Really Doing on the Internet? *Rebecca A. Wilson*	364
Strategic Positioning and the Building Project: Penn State Harrisburg's "Library of the Future" *Harold Shill*	370
Students Versus the Research Paper: What Can We Learn? *Barbara Valentine*	380
The Classroom vs. the Web: Comparing Two Ways to Teach Web-based Resources *Elizabeth Burns*	390
The Librarian as Mediator: A Significant Change in the Educational Role of Librarians *David Moody and Donna Roe*	395
Web-based OPAC's: A Leap of Faith *Norm Medeiros, James Beattie, and Carol Wu*	402
Index of Authors and Titles	419

April 8–11, 1999, Detroit, Michigan

Introduction

Detroit served as the site for the Ninth National Conference of the Association of College and Research Libraries, which took place on April 8–11, 1999. Selecting the "Motor City" as the conference location inspired the conference theme, *Racing Toward Tomorrow*. As we approach the 21st century in our rapidly changing environment, we must constantly be "shifting gears" to properly serve our users. Distinguished invited speakers and contributed papers explored various aspects of the following six conference subthemes and are represented in these proceedings:

- Environment in Flux
- Alternative Resources
- A New Kind of Learner
- Multiples Roles
- Different Players, and
- Expanding Knowledge Base

The 54 contributed papers included here were selected from more than 200 submitted abstracts, which were blind-reviewed by 27 referees. Thanks are due to all of the contributors for their fine work, to the reviewers for their careful deliberations, and to the moderators of all of the conference sessions. Thanks are also due to members of the National Conference Planning Committee and its supporting structure of subcommittees who all contributed to the success of the conference.

A special thanks to Mary Ellen Davis and Margot Sutton, from the ACRL office, who took care of myriad details, including most correspondence with presenters, moderators, and reviewers for the conference, and to Hugh Thompson, Director of ACRL Publications, who compiled and edited these proceedings.

May you find the papers within useful as we all *Race Toward Tomorrow!*

Richard AmRhein and Mary Harrison, Co-Chairs
Contributed Papers Subcommittee

Reviewers of Contributed Papers

David L. Austin
Edgar Bailey
Daren Callahan
Karen S. Croneis
Mark T. Day
Barbara DeFelice
Maggie Farrell
Jody Foote
James Gray
Philip Herold
Tom Kilpatrick
Kathryn Kjaer
Terry S. Latour
Susan Lessick

Susan Logue
Linda McCann
Nancy P. O'Brien
Lois M. Pausch
Mary Pagliero Popp
Barbara Preece
Brendan Rapple
Carrie Russell
Peggy Seiden
Cynthia Shabb
Carolyn A. Snyder
Kris Szymborski
Mark Winston

National Conference Executive Committee

Charles E. Beard
Chair

Patricia Senn Breivik
Conference-within-a-Conference

Ferne B. Hyman
Conference-within-a-conference

Barton Lessin
Conference-within-a-conference

Richard AmRhein
Contributed Papers

Mary M. Harrison
Contributed Papers

Joe K. Weed
Exhibitors Advisory

William Miller
Colleagues

Betsy Wilson
Colleagues

Betty J. Blackman
Invited Papers

Shirley W. Leung
Invited Papers

James F. Williams II
Keynote Speakers

William Gray Potter
Keynote Speakers

Marianne Hartzell
Local Arrangements

William P. Kane
Local Arrangements

Judith Lin Hunt
Panel Sessions

Carol Pfeiffer
Panel Sessions

June L. DeWeese
Poster Sessions

Glenda S. Neely
Poster Sessions

Sherrie Bergman
Preconferences

Joan G. Rapp
Preconferences

Kate Nevins
Roundtables

Ralph E. Russell
Roundtables

Liz Bishoff
Scenarios

Sue Stroyan
Scenarios

Randy Dykhuis
Technology

Eileen M. Palmer
Technology

Joseph J. Mika
Volunteers

Margaret Auer
Volunteers

Mary Ellen Davis
Conference Manager

Althea Jenkins
Executive Director

April 8–11, 1999, Detroit, Michigan

ACRL Board of Directors 1998–99

Executive Committee

Maureen Sullivan
ACRL President

Larry Hardesty
ACRL President-Elect

W. Lee Hisle
ACRL Past-President

Cathy Henderson
ACRL Budget & Finance Chair

Helen Spalding
ACRL Councilor

Althea H. Jenkins
ACRL Executive Director
(ex officio)

Directors-At-Large

William E. Brown, Jr.

Paul E. Dumont

Barbara Baxter Jenkins

Linda Muroi

Dana C. Rooks

Carol M. Pfeiffer

Mary Lee Sweat

Invited Papers

Shifting Gears: A University President's View

Blenda J. Wilson

Nostalgic Preface

As a child, *my* library was a commanding Gothic building that I passed each day on my way to and from school. Its cavernous interior and leaded windows were matched with heavy wood tables and chairs and gray haired lady librarians guarding the treasures in the beautiful oak stacks.

One of the librarians became my friend and introduced me not only to the wealth of children's books that were housed there, but led me to the window seats that surrounded the main reading room. So, I developed a habit of stopping at the Library after school, finding a comfortable window seat and reading book after book that my friendly librarian had recommended.

The building today is an Arts Center, still commanding, still cavernous, and while I consider that a very worthwhile use, I'm sorry that small children no longer enjoy the quiet world of imagination and possibility that it inspired in me.

Many years later, I was working at Harvard University and had the occasion to visit Widener Library. Many of you are familiar with its grand steps and imposing facade. Many students who passed by Widener were convinced that the mere act of walking up the steps made one smarter and potentially wise. There, too, with the guidance of a wise and generous librarian, I learned to access the stacks. I can still remember the slightly musty smell of the basement stacks where the really old books were stored. I spent many hours with my note cards, copying references from the card catalogue, reading at the reading tables, sharing in the sense of history and intellect that the Library represented.

Like most of my contemporaries, libraries have been personal and private places and librarians have been personal and knowledgeable helpers.

A Digital advertisement, a few years back, read, "Once in every millennium, an invention comes along that speeds the pace of the whole human race." I begin, therefore, by noting that the impact of technology is not only what it can *do,* but what it can *un-do.* I will return to this point later on in the paper.

University Environment in Constant Change

As with my memories of libraries, yesterday's image of university students and campus life are more nostalgia than reality. Yesterday's traditional student is today's exception. The majority of college

---

Blenda J. Wilson is president, California State University, Northridge.

and university students today are female, rather than male; almost half are over the age of 25; a greater percentage are minority students and foreign-born; many of our urban public institutions, like mine, enroll a majority of minority students. Almost as many students are enrolled part-time or intermittently as full-time and continuously. And more of all students live at home instead of in college dormitories.

Within the next decade these trends will likely become more pronounced. More of the students will be enrolled to update their skills or learn about changes in the economy; they will not be seeking degrees at all. Proportionately, the number of undergraduates in degree-granting, residential colleges will decrease, mirroring the number of 18 to 22 year olds in the population.

At the same time that the student body has changed so remarkably, the public demand for accountability has increased. Global competition has transformed the economic landscape and challenged our national strengths. Budget and trade deficits have made Americans more conscious of our need to assure that American workers are educated to levels that maximize their productivity and our economic well-being. The new economy requires workers who can handle an exploding stream of information. So it should not be surprising that the decline in the competence of graduates is of profound concern to the public. While increasing numbers of Americans receive associate and baccalaureate degrees each year, a significant percentage of these graduates possess little more knowledge, competence or skill than a high school graduate of previous generations.

I believe that the most profound challenge to higher education is not only to educate larger numbers of students to a 21st century standard of competency, but to educate them in environments that will enable them to share a sense of common purpose within a diverse national and global community.

Our institutions and libraries must respond to the changing nature of the student body and the knowledge demands of global industries if we are to fulfill our historic mission of educating each successive generation.

Changing Role of Libraries and Librarians
Changing role of the librarian

Christine Borgman, chairwoman of the Department of Library and Information Science at UCLA sees the role of librarians as the same—but different—as its always been in her assertion that, "The online world is chaotic." All of us who have tried to retrieve specific information on the World Wide Web know exactly what she means.

Librarians have served society in the past by preserving its cultural heritage, and its valued ideas. They will continue to be essential to identifying, selecting, and cataloguing valuable information. Establishing standards for telecommunications, file formats, security and communication will be critical to the digital environment. Librarians should play a leadership role by advising faculty, publishers and communications companies on the most effective ways to achieve interoperability among digital materials.

On the university campus, librarians will become closer partners with faculty members by helping them understand, organize and present information in these new media. As the abundance and speed of information increases, librarians will also perform more direct teaching roles, teaching information competence and library skills to students who need to navigate the Internet and the Web.

With the development of distance learning programs, it will be particularly important for librarians to be involved so that distance learners will be encouraged to develop the habit of lifelong use of library resources and have the skills to access those resources from off-campus sites.

I can easily envision a time in the not-too-distant future where courses will not be created by individual faculty members but by a team made up of the faculty member, librarian, technology specialist and media specialist, all contributing to the content, pedagogy and organization of a course.

Use of Technology

A generation ago, computers were so large they required entire rooms and punch cards were the standard tools for accessing computer data. Today microprocessors, miniaturization and fiber optics put far more powerful tools into the hands of five year olds than the world's finest scientists had years ago. Information from across the globe is available instantaneously to anyone with a computer. Scientists from different countries collaborate on research and friends from around the world keep in touch through the Internet. Information overload is becoming a common malady.

Libraries were, of course, early users of technology for categorizing and retrieving information and they will continue to be heavy users of technology. As information proliferates, libraries must continue to provide rational ways of organizing it and linking different sources of information to structured systems.

"To a man whose only tool is a hammer, everything looks like a nail." There is a dangerous tendency to assume that the World Wide Web is a vast storehouse of information, making libraries either unnecessary or obsolete. We must also, therefore, count on librarians to remind us that the Web contains only a small fraction of the information that is available in an average-size research library and to help institutions understand the necessary balance between print resources and technological forms of information delivery.

Most importantly, librarians must continue to remind us that *the uses of technology*, not the technology itself, are what's important. Information technology can increase access in cost effective ways by extending the resources of our campus to students wherever they may be. It can improve the quality of education by making the student a more active learner and by offering greater flexibility in time, space and the curriculum. But it is not a substitute for teachers and librarians whose roles as teachers, guides and mentors are equally important to the learning process.

Collections

One of the most difficult challenges for libraries in the future will be maintaining adequate collections in support of the curriculum. That is because at the same time the costs of print resources are escalating, institutions are having difficulty financing the high start-up costs and operating costs of technological delivery.

Collections are, and will remain, the intellectual foundations of the curriculum. It is important that faculty and librarians work together and develop collaborations across institutions so that collections do not deteriorate because of these financial pressures. Associations of libraries throughout a state or region are working together to share collections, through inter-library loans and electronic delivery systems. The result of well-planned regional collaborations can be enhanced collections and expanded services for all partners.

Changes in service/strategic planning

As technology becomes a ubiquitous tool in American life, college and university students will become more demanding consumers, attuned to accessing information at any time and in any place. Public expectations of libraries will also increase; tolerance for service delays will decrease.

Libraries should develop strategic plans that are informed by both faculty and students as a means of determining which service requirements are most important to their users. While mail delivery of reserve collections, journal articles and loaned books may have seemed fast and efficient a few years ago, today's consumers will be able to demand full-text information by downloading or email to their personal desktops. Libraries are rapidly incorporating full-text databases offered through external vendors among their services.

Unfortunately, technological services do not reduce the need for staff or reduce staff costs. Processing requests may require contacting requestors to obtain additional information, developing alternative user authentication methods, gathering information on the user's level of expertise, etc. Increased distance services will be accompanied by an increased demand for "help desk" support, including technological assistance and research guidance.

Libraries need also to manage consumer expectations by providing clear information about the turn-around time for various services, and planning ways to meet them. It would be better to promise less and meet the commitment than to promise more and fail to do so.

Information Competence or Literacy

We used to believe that literacy was a sufficient enabling skill for individuals to obtain and use the information they needed. As the Information Highway has expended exponentially, however, educators have come to realize that the abilities needed to use the staggering amounts of information made available through technology are more complex than simple literacy. As stated in the *American Library Association Presidential Committee on Information Literacy: Final Report*. ". . . the landscape upon which we used to stand has been transformed, and we are being forced to establish a new foundation called information literacy."

That new foundation should include the ability to recognize when information is needed and how to identify, locate, evaluate and use information effectively for their particular purposes; it should encompass judgments about the quality of information; and it should emphasize making ethical judgments about information and media.

Librarians should play an important role as advocates of information literacy as a core competency for undergraduate and graduate programs. They need to collaborate with faculty and help provide tools for faculty to incorporate information literacy within the curriculum. The library itself should be established as a center for student learning about information competence.

What Makes a Good Library From a President's Point of View

As sound, video and data converge in the digital environment, higher education has the opportunity to offer an astounding array of new tools to both faculty and students. Proficiency in using technology is, for all practical purposes, a basic skill. Because of its early use, and comfort, with technology, the Library is often the "first wave" of innovative and practical uses of technology on a university campus. A good library will provide leadership to the institution in adapting to the potential of these tools:

Places students and faculty at the center of its attention. The most powerful and important uses of technology are to improve the teaching/learning process. The library should be a place in which both students and faculty receive support, guidance, service, training and encouragement to utilize what is available to increase their effectiveness. The Library should be a partner with faculty in designing and creating new courses. It should be a service-oriented resource for students—both on-campus and off—in teaching them how to access the plethora of information that is available to them.

Provides excellent service. Access to information resources is essential to the academic enterprise. Students and faculty, rightly, rely upon the Library to have available what they need for their work. Whether through purchasing, interlibrary loans or digital collaborations, libraries must seek to provide "on time" service and "real time" assistance.

Supports and integrates itself into the curriculum. Whether through courses in information competence or through team effort in developing new courses, the Library should be proactive in conveying the potential of new technologies for enhancing collections, assessing student achievement and enriching the curriculum.

Actively promotes good relations with the community. Individuals and organizations in the community are not likely to have the resources or expertise that exists within the university library. Outreach activities, shared resources, training for community people and generous visitation policies will enable the library to empower the general community to realize the full potential of the information age.

Participates in institutional fund-raising. The financing of new technologies, services and support is one of the most difficult challenges to colleges and universities. On the one hand, competition with new service providers is driving continuous expansion in the use of these new tools. On the other, most financing formulas for higher education have not taken into account the costs of the technological infrastructure, resource personnel or refresh.

I would suggest that the university library and its personnel should commit to developing new sources of revenue, including private fundraising, to reduce the need to have institutional funds from ongoing instructional activities diverted to technological capacity.

Because the Library serves as the intellectual heart of the university, it has the broadest natural constituency for fundraising and can solicit private support from alumni, faculty, staff and community members and organizations that it has served.

The Director of the Library has the additional responsibility to be a leader within the institution. She or he should understand the big picture and assure that the staff works toward the University's goals and strategic priorities. By participating in the policy dialogue about educational priorities, the Library Director can be an advocate for information competence and use of technology to enhance instructional effectiveness.

Finally, to return to the preface of this paper, I would urge that, in embracing the new possibilities that are made possible by modern technology, libraries should not lose sight of the ways in which architecture, face-to-face interaction and quiet study areas continue to inspire, motivate and serve the needs of students. The contemporary library should be an environment that extols the human intellect. Those who visit should learn about data banks and online instruction in a physical setting that also ennobles the human spirit. Whether through art collections, comfortable reading places—including window seats—or simply the enthusiastic personal service ethic displayed by staff, the Library should remain a haven for reflection, inspiration and admiration.

We should be admonished to take care that in advancing knowledge through new tools and capabilities, we do not "un-do" the Library's unique place—with cathedrals—as an abiding symbol of human accomplishment and potential.

New Forms of Distance Education: Opportunities for Students, Threats to Institutions

Leigh S. Estabrook

Abstract

In 1996, the Graduate School of Library and Information Science at the University of Illinois began offering its master's degree over the Internet, with only brief periods of on-campus learning, in a program called LEEP3. This paper outlines the way in which LEEP3 is designed to allow students from Alaska to the Virgin Islands to obtain high quality LIS education. Students can obtain the full Master of Science accredited degree in a site independent *format* of instruction. Faculty employ both synchronous and asynchronous learning in classes that increasingly a blend on-campus and distance students. The program includes cooperative learning, outside lecturers, career counseling and extensive use of new information technologies to give students an experience as rich as that received by students on campus.

This paper describes the design of LEEP3 with a focus on instruction. It then turns to the broader implications for programs such as LEEP3 for colleges and universities. While distance education opens up new opportunities for students, it also promises to change significantly the ways in which colleges and universities operate. Most familiar to librarians is the demand for materials in electronic form. Other changes that may affect libraries even more dramatically include (1) new configurations of faculty both on and off-campus and (2) significant challenges to the ways in which the "Carnegie unit" of instruction (i.e., credit hours) is defined. Who are the faculty for which the library develops collections? Who are the students? What is a course? Can the library "collect" instructional materials developed for distance delivery? What is the domain of supporting materials for teaching for which the library should be responsible?

A concluding section suggests areas of greatest need in the near term for libraries responsible for providing support to distance education.

Leigh S. Estabrook is dean and professor, Graduate School of Library and Information Science, University of Illinois at Urbana-Champaign.

New Forms of Distance Education: Opportunities for Students, Threats to Institutions

In 1996, the Graduate School of Library and Information Science at the University of Illinois began offering its master's degree over the Internet, with only brief periods of on-campus learning, in a program called LEEP3. This paper outlines the way in which LEEP3 is designed to allow students who cannot commute to Champaign-Urbana to obtain high quality LIS education. It then turns to examine the real and potential impact of such design on higher education and its libraries. Students can obtain the full Master of Science accredited degree in a site independent *format* of instruction. Faculty employ both synchronous and asynchronous learning in classes that increasingly a blend on-campus and distance students. The program includes cooperative and group learning, outside lecturers, career counseling and extensive use of new information technologies to give students an experience as rich as that received by students on campus. We are cognizant of the need to support varieties of learning styles as we assure access to both human and instructional resources for learning. Above all, our faculty have been committed to avoiding a correspondence course model. We work hard to keep frustration over technology to a minimum.

When we designed LEEP3, the GSLIS faculty was committed to providing instruction and student experiences comparable to those received by students who enroll on-campus. This means that all regular GSLIS faculty are involved in teaching. Extensive and creative access to library resources is provided through online reserves and mail service for inter library loan. We have set up a "proxy" server that allow students from outside information service providers to be recognized as coming from the UIUC domain—a necessary component to their getting access to the University library's electronic collections.

During the brief periods of time students are on campus, we schedule a variety of activities—both social and instructional—that increase the sense of community not only among the students but also between students and faculty. We have begun an electronic job fair that includes live recorded interviews with professionals in the field. We are careful in selecting adjuncts—and are fortunate to have a talented pool from which we can draw because we are not limited by geography. Faculty from Pennsylvania, North Carolina and Wisconsin have taught. They, too, come to campus only once during the semester.

Faculty, while preparing and teaching a course, work closely with our technology support staff. The manager of instructional resources goes to a faculty member and asks "what is it you wish to accomplish pedagogically?" The answer to that question drives the types of technology used in a particular class. As we complete our third year of this program, all regular faculty have been involved and only a few students have found it necessary to stop taking courses in the program because of demands from work or family.

We enroll people from Thailand to the Virgin Islands: from Alaska to Columbia. Many of those who enroll are initially much less technologically literate than we had expected. But many are in jobs for which the master's degree will be a significant advantage and the students are driven to learn and take advantage of an opportunity they did not have before. Among their comments to us are the following:

> I've . . . learned that a large component of the ability to learn, to use technology, and to . . . do scholarly work benefits from the ability to work with peers. What we're facing with LEEP3 is the need to generate peer support infrastructure without face-to-face communication.

> at age 41 I'm finally learning how to swim . . . After LEEP3, I'm much braver about a lot of things.

LEEP students not only do the full workload of a class delivered in "regular" format, but must also spend extra time with technology. Communication takes time, learning how to use the technology takes time, and troubleshooting technological problems takes time. I am very grateful for the opportunity to get my degree in this manner, (one student said) but it's taking me longer than I thought it might because it's so timeconsuming for one who works a fortyhour week. Every time someone who asks about my course work says, "So it's like a correspondence course?" I want to smack `em! The thing that's different about LEEP3 is the constant, immediate communication and the synchronous instruction/discussions we are able to conduct. Not all of us are given release time and/or pay by our employers, making it even more difficult to juggle work and LEEP3. And I hope it will be clear to future employers that a degree earned in this manner is every bit as good as one earned in a traditional setting, and in some ways, more valuable.

Another commented as she was about to graduate:

> Sitting here preparing to work on my final paper, I can't help remembering that it was two years ago today that approximately thirty students gathered in Champaign to begin this bold new adventure. I remember my apprehension as I drove to Champaign, sure that I would be the only student over thirty in LEEP3, wondering what I had gotten myself into. Did I still remember how to write papers? Could I do graduate work and still hold down my jobs? What about my family? How would this affect them? Did I know enough about computers and the Internet? But the excitement and enthusiasm for this opportunity to do graduate work in library science was greater than the apprehension.

LEEP3 has truly been a marvelous, exhilarating experience. I have met and learned from a wonderful group of students and teachers. At times overwhelming, but always challenging, the GSLIS classes have taught me far more than I could have imagined. I have gained insights and confidence, knowledge and skills, and friends for a lifetime. The virtual community of LEEP3 continues to develop and thrive.

For us, at the Graduate School of Library and Information Science at the University of Illinois, the advantages of LEEP3 center on the opportunity to extend LIS education to those for which it has been unavailable (we have had someone from Alaska in each of the three years of LEEP3). Faculty have been able to explore new forms of pedagogy and to work collaboratively in new ways. We have been able to hire adjuncts of particular talent.

Most colleges and universities are considering new forms of distance education, although it is important to note that models of instruction vary. (None currently mimics the "old form" practiced by such people as Alice Lohrer in who in the 1950s took a plane from Champaign to various places in Illinois to deliver instruction.) Some institutions involved in distance education focus on the "learning unit", others focus on "skills" and still others focus on teaching courses as a whole. Some see distance education as source of new students and new revenue. There is a range of distance education models from videotapes sent to remote locations with workbooks, to whole, highly interactive degree programs like LEEP3. Many university administrators and state legislators assume distance education will save money. (It probably won't if it is done well.) Some see it as a way to use certain technologies in which a state may have invested.

As distance education moves from the control of a division of "continuing education" and becomes more firmly embedded in university structures, colleges and universities will face a number of complex questions driven by new configurations of faculty both on and off-campus and significant challenges to the ways in which the "Carnegie unit" of instruction (i.e., credit hours) is defined.

I mentioned earlier that we hire a number of instructors for LEEP3 who do not live in Champaign-Urbana. I was even called by our department of Human Resources to verify that certain individuals really were U of I employees. What responsibility does the library have for providing collection development support for these faculty? How does the library work with the adjunct faculty member's "home" library? How does the library handle the murky questions of intellectual property rights for digitized materials made part of a distance education course?

Similar questions arise when providing service to off-campus students. Many do not pay regular campus fees. Are they to be given the same library privileges as on-campus students? Does a library provide electronic reserves or mail ILL requests to individuals unable to come to the library to read or borrow materials? Does the library provide a "proxy" server so remote students can have access to electronic materials that usually can be used only from the college or university domain name? In a program such as ours, who is in residence? Many of our LEEP3 format classes are taken by on-campus students and many of our on campus students are actually at the School for limited time.

And what, we may ask, is a course? What is the meaning of the classic "Carnegie unit" that standardized measure of credit hours, when teaching is modularized. The faculty at GSLIS are undertaking a full review of the master's curriculum that has led us to confront the questions of what areas of instruction to combine and how much depth to provide. This is an issue well beyond distance education, but I believe that the modular approach to various distance education offerings in other universities, particularly in the areas of math and the sciences, has led us to question in new ways some of our basic assumptions about what topics go together. And once these questions are opened we have added problems in defining faculty load.

We see also an increased potential for outsourcing college and university services. So far, at Illinois, the campus has outsourced only the food services—not a problem for LEEP3 students. But Phoenix University, I understand, is outsourcing student support services. Not an unreasonable approach, particularly if a university can find staff who are trained to work with the issues that confront students working at a distance from campus. Certainly library services are an obvious target for outsourcing in some kinds of institutions. But then we may begin to ask, "where is the university"?

What happens to our universities depends a great deal on the economic patterns that evolve. I see a number of alternatives. First a Darwinian model in which different programs in effect adapt to their environments, driving out those unable to adapt the technologies or recruit students or convert faculty to new ways of instruction. Similar to this might be the "distance education class struggle" in which those with power, prestige, resources for technology and business connections are able to dominate the distance education markets. A third possible model could be called the "loaves and fishes" approach. For the foreseeable future there are many more students to be educated than opportunities for education. There are also many more areas that might be taught and a global demand for new educational ventures. One might argue then that there is ample "food" for hungry distance education providers.

Two other models we might posit include the "McDonalds" model, in which distance education becomes franchised. In some ways this is the pattern followed by some universities that send video tapes or live video instruction to remote sites where local staff are employed to facilitate discussion of learners. And finally, I would offer the model of "Colonialism" where we find not only economic control, but also cultural domination of the forms and shape of distance education offerings.

I offer these examples as much to trigger discussion as anything else. They certainly are not exhaustive categories, nor even mutually exclusive. But I think they give us a way to begin thinking more broadly about the impact of distance education on library services in colleges and universities. Many of us, and I include myself, have focused on issues of how to get materials to our students who live in remote locations. Some of us are beginning to address issues related to providing electronic reserve. Few of us, and again I include myself, are working out the possibilities that higher education itself may be radically transformed by distance education.

Let me suggest just three of those transformations—ones with which we struggle daily at the University of Illinois. First is the idea of learning communities and how best to create them in a distance mode. It is not only a question of how to build community for LEEP3 students, but also what models of teaching and learning are most effective when students have only short periods of time working face-to-face. When do they need the physical documents in their learning about library and information science? When will document surrogates work? Are there some things that simply cannot be taught in anything other than a face-to-face mode? For example, uses of certain kinds of higher end technology.

Second is the challenge of how to manage new interdependencies in instruction. Much of our face-to-face instruction occurs with a single instructor behind a closed door. Someone may deliver AV equipment or help order text books, but others are rarely involved in a significant way. In distance education, faculty do not work alone. They are dependent on several of our technology staff who not only help initially in the pedagogical design of a course and in getting materials mounted on the web; but work throughout in setting up and monitoring synchronous sessions, trouble shooting when students or faculty have technical difficulties and providing numerous other support services *intrinsic* to teaching.

Third is the greater "publicness" of teaching and learning. We do password protect much of the work of our students and faculty so that it cannot be seen by people outside the GSLIS community. But within that community, all of us know much more about each others work. Students' postings on webboards are read and commented upon not only by others in the class, but sometimes by students in other classes. The archived synchronous sessions, particularly when they involve outside guest speakers may be listened to by others long after a course has been completed.

For college and university librarians, who are important parts of these increasingly interdependent learning communities, the issues then go well beyond what to scan, what to mail and how to password protect. We look to you to help us understand when and why document surrogates won't work. We ask you to become part of our interdependent team trying to make the pedagogy of distance education work. We also ask you to consider whether to preserve and make accessible new forms of information that are being created as part of the teaching and learning of distance education.

Academic Publishing: Networks and Prices

Malcolm Getz

The rapid growth of the Internet creates opportunities for academic by providing new ways of communicating within academia and beyond. Our concern here is to identify the nature of the challenges. Why should we invest in using the network for scholarly purposes? Will prices play new roles? How are publishers responding to the opportunity? How are academic journals changing? Will scholarly information beyond journals come to the network? Developments are occurring rapidly and libraries and scholars are challenged to make good decisions.

Electronic networks are changing intellectual work. If we are what we write, networks are having a fundamental effect because networks are changing what we write. Networks make it desirable for us to change how we present ourselves to the world by inviting us to write for electronic distribution. We can reach more audiences more effectively by network and so networks are of growing importance to most kinds of intellectual work.

The electronic networks tied together as the Internet and its cousins provide effective ways to reach colleagues. Increasingly, work in progress is shared by network because the network is faster, less expensive, and so can reach more people. In some disciplines, formal network working-paper services are well developed. In other disciplines, working paper services are less well developed but show promise. Network newsgroups are important in many fields. A substantial number of formal, edited journals are distributed by network, and the number is growing.

Networks are an effective way to reach students. More than half of the references in my students' essays are to web sources. I routinely give assignments that assume use of the net. With e-mail, I can send brief messages to my classes between meetings. By posting notes and problems on the course web-site, I can make very targeted information available to my classes 24 hours a day. An increasing number of faculty are creating websites for their courses.

I have written an etext for the first course in statistics that is all electronic. It is highly interactive with diagrams that update instantly as students change values. It makes extensive use of color graphics. It uses simulation to give deeper insight into the nature of statistics with less need for formal mathematics. The style of communication al-

---

Malcolm Getz is associate professor, Department of Economics and Business Administration, Vanderbilt University

lows students to learn more faster.

Networks are also an effective way of reaching beyond the academy. At Vanderbilt, more than 75 percent of our students report that they exchange e-mail with their parents. An increasing number of journalists, politicians, and government agencies use e-mail and the Web as an important part of their daily activity. The Federal Emergency Management Agency (FEMA) reports a million hits a week on its home page.

Network communication is only modestly successful as a direct analog of print. Taking print documents and posting them electronically is only a first step. Network communication excels when it takes advantage of the inherent features of digital documents. Color, graphics, interactivity, linkage to other documents, and embedded algorithms are much easier in digital documents and can be readily shared by network. When Christopher Sholes invented the typewriter, he didn't design a machine to copy the hand motions of a scribe or typesetter.[2] Instead, he sought a machine that would work more quickly than the hand, produce more legible copy, and get more words per page. Network communication is not just a way of distributing printed text, it is a new form of communication. Not everyone will adapt to the new mode, but quite a number of people find an advantage communicating with the new tools.

The growing importance of network communication poses challenges for libraries and publishers.

Quality of the Library

In the nineteenth century, one measured the information available to a community by the books in its library. Many collections were of a size that could be comprehended by an individual. In the early 20th century, the invention of the card catalog supported much larger collections, collections vastly larger than could be comprehended by any one person. The card catalog took on a life of its own. Items not well represented in the catalog had dramatically lower use as if they were invisible. In the 1980s, electronic catalogs replaced the cards. Items not well represented in the electronic catalog had dramatically lower use as if they were invisible. Very large libraries that had planned not to convert all their card catalogs to the electronic form changed their minds and, with a few exceptions, have converted the preponderance of their card catalogs to the digital format.

In the 1990s, the emergence of the network allows us to see more information electronically on our desktops. Our first call is to material delivered by network. It is at least imaginable that materials not delivered by network will become as if invisible. Web access is the most convenient way of finding information and, for some purposes, fully sufficient. As network communication moves to the dominant position, most of us will want to be seen there. Many libraries have then come to the goal of delivering information by network.

For the library, the network has the great potential of allowing services remote from the campus to play an important role. The campus then need not maintain a machine room, hardware, and technical support staff to sustain the back office functions necessary to mount the data. The campus can contract out these services when the contract has significant cost savings.

Relying on remote network services opens the possibility of structuring payment systems in different ways. Experiments are underway to parse out how readers and institutions will respond to different possibilities. One important possibility is to invite individual readers to pay for services as they use them. Perhaps this approach will lower costs and improve service. To see this possibility, consider first how interlibrary loan might be transformed if the spending decisions were in the hands of readers. This sets the stage for thinking about how to put spending decisions in the hands of readers. Once we see how a payment system might work, we turn to thinking about the consequences, the advantages and disadvantages such a system might yield.

A colleague uses the *New York Times* network service to find articles to use in support of a class he is teaching. He is invited to pay $2.50 to get the electronic text of an article after finding it through an electronic search and reading the first few lines. He weighs the cost of a trip to the library with the necessary scrolling through microfilm and cost of printing it, and calls the $2.50 a bargain. The New York Times, Inc. is a for-profit company with considerable market power, so the marginal cost of supplying an article must be well below $2.50. The cost of delivering articles electronically by the network has been falling and is likely to continue to fall. This commercial network venture provides at least one benchmark for comparing library services.

Moving to Prices

If network delivery of information is to reach its full potential, we need to find a better way to manage it. Electronic systems have inherent advantages in keeping track of transactions. We should be able to use these advantages in managing network information services.

Putting prices in the hands of readers will invite them to vote with their dollars for the services they value most.

Consider interlibrary loan (ILL). The 1996 Association of Research Libraries study of interlibrary loan costs put the cost of both ends of an ILL transaction at near $28 of direct cost.[3] This figure was little changed from the cost shown in an earlier study. More than a third of the ILL transactions are photocopies of journal articles. Typically, commercial fulfillment services will supply photocopies of most of the requested articles for about $15. Yet, libraries persist in directing their readers to their ILL shops. The libraries fear both losing control and passing direct charges along to users. Each visit by a reader to the ILL shop imposes costs on the library. Because the ILL shop is in place, the library treats the staff costs as a sunk cost. Libraries use various stratagems to limit demand for the ILL service. They may offer no service to undergraduates, seek fulfillments with historic partners rather than the least cost provider, and so may create longer than necessary delays. Forms, delays, denials, and occasionally charges (all of which require staff costs) are the norm.

Consider the alternative. Suppose that readers have personal debit accounts with the library. They may search the network for a fulfillment service, shop for the least cost provider, and place an order and have the charge debited electronically from their account. The fulfillment service will supply the document directly to the reader, either electronically, by fax, or express. Interlibrary loan ought to move as smoothly and inexpensively as Amazon.com sells books. If a service with more delay offers a lower cost, the reader may sensibly choose that. If speed is valuable, the reader may sensibly elect to spend more for faster delivery. The reader may have choices of image quality. A lower quality image at a lower price may sometimes suffice, sometimes a high quality image at a higher price may be essential. Because the reader is committing funds from an account with a variety of uses, he or she has an incentive to choose appropriately. The campus library need incur no staff costs for a majority of such transactions. The campus library need only create a system of electronic accounts with authentication services to allow remote providers to reliably receive payments. Electronic funds transfers is a plausible payment mechanism.[4]

Creating Personal Information Accounts

Suppose that our mind set shifted to putting subsidized personal accounts in the hands of readers. Allow readers to see the marginal cost of their requests for service and make choices. A library might announce a $30 charge for the ILL versus a $15 charge for the document supply. The reader is free to make requests for ILL or document supply up to a budgeted limit. When the subsidized limit is reached, the reader will need to deposit more in order to get more services.

In some settings, such as law and business schools, faculty have research accounts that support travel, assistants, photocopying, personal subscriptions, and software and computer purchases. Because these expenses are paid with before-tax dollars, receiving support for such costs of doing business is better than providing higher pay and expecting faculty to pay for such services personally.

In the sciences where externally funded research is the dominant culture, the university faces the issue about what items will be institutionally provided (and so built into indirect cost recovery) versus what items will be charged as a direct cost of research. Either way, the culture is for faculty to use dollars to vote for the services that best meet their needs.

In other disciplines like the humanities, institutional support for direct faculty expenses has a more limited scope. The institution's concern is that faculty needs are more episodic, with infrequent but costly travel, and that faculty differ widely in their personal expenses. Some successful faculty may have no interest in a computer, study a few books intensely, and travel rarely. At the same time, faculty with little or no research program might spend significant amounts on computers, travel, and other services. It is easy to see that one size won't fit all.

To move to personal information accounts for faculty, universities are likely to invite individual departments and programs to make their own choices. That is to suggest that deans and provosts will see advantages in treating each discipline appropriately. Just as teaching loads, travel policies, and clerical support differ from discipline to discipline, so too will faculty accounts that may be used for incremental costs in information services differ.

For students, subsidized information accounts are likely also to be shaped in a decentralized manner. The institution might establish a floor for all undergraduates that would provide a minimal level of service. Students in honors programs, seminars, and other courses with papers, might get additional subsidized funds automatically.

The funds might have a matching component. In order to encourage use of information resources but to discourage waste, the university might expect personal funds to match institutional funds at some point. Let's suppose that an undergraduate gets a base fund per term, all institutional funds, tuition-financed. In addition, the university might offer to match personal funds for additional expenditures up to a limit. The institution might routinely add institutional funds for each information intensive course. The magnitude of the subsidized funds will depend on the prices of specific services and the institutions culture. Institutions will differ.

In short, universities already have some experience with personal spending accounts. Many should find it useful to extend these to allow personal decisions about spending on specific information services. In particular, it may be useful to treat some network information services as an extension of the photocopying service.

When the university is subscribing to a remote service rather than cumulating a stock of library materials, the cost and incentive structure shifts. The library is no longer a fixed, largely sunk cost where marginal cost pricing (essentially zero or rationing with modest delays) is reasonable. Rather the university will have few fixed costs for remotely served databases but ample variable costs. Given the cost structure, a system of prices in the hands of readers may be sensible.

Why Prices?

Prices have at least four substantial benefits. First, they empower readers. Second, they create a demand for services that is likely to be elastic to price. Price elastic demands encourage low prices. Third, they encourage innovation. Fourth, they allow more effective responses to potential congestion.

When network services are mounted remotely from a campus, the campus is incurring direct costs on a continuing basis for the information services it receives. The conventional notion of building a library by making annual investments that overtime accumulate a significant campus resource no longer applies. The campus then is in a position of paying for the services it consumes on a current basis. Some information vendors may offer front-loaded fee structures, but there is a significant continuing cost for use. It is likely to be difficult for an institution to make sensible decisions on the margin about what services to sustain. Deploying personal accounts and turning to prices is likely to improve institutional decisions. The university is more likely to focus its information expenditures on services that promote its core missions by using prices.

Empowering Readers

Turning to prices gives readers the power to decide what services will best meet their personal needs. They will become conscious of costs and aware of service alternatives. When a slow cumbersome service is inexpensive, a reader might choose it. When a deadline is at hand, a more expensive but faster service may be the best choice. When the library makes these choices in the absence of personal prices, it will make the wrong choice part of the time. Some libraries will staff heavily and provide a deluxe service nearly all of the time, even when such a response is unnecessary. Other libraries will staff at lower levels and will not be able to offer the deluxe service. Indeed, when readers face a zero price, they are likely to make demands for service even when the value is low. Libraries ration the demand with rules and delays. Putting the dollars in the hands of users gives them the power to avoid rules and delays and to select the service that meets their needs.

Elastic Demand

Libraries face high prices for journals and some other materials in part because they present demands that are inelastic to price. That is, the library must hold the best journals. One cannot have a chemistry department without the core chemistry journals. Seeing that library demand is inelastic to price, profit-maximizing publishers impose high mark-ups over their marginal costs. Indeed, a number of journals are published just for the library market place with inelastic demands and so, high prices.

If access is by article with the spending decisions made by individuals, the demand is likely to be more price elastic. Individuals make choices about what to read. Although many will view some of what they read as essential, most will also face choices about secondary things. Let's say that half of a typical bibliography has some discretion. Indeed, individuals may be particularly price sensitive if prices are low enough to invite revisiting. If prices are in the range of photocopying, then users are likely to treat per-use prices in a way that is psychologically like photocopying. A user has a variety of ways of using a service. One might store electronic copies locally after payment for items of high personal value. Don't store but occasionally revisit-for-a-fee items of secondary interest. Typical users will exhibit considerable elasticity of use with respect to price.

The net reaches beyond the campus. In each discipline, there is a community of interested persons beyond the campus who may make occasional use of academic materials. In medieval studies, there are a number of independent scholars. In the social sciences, there are lawyers, legislators, and officials with interest in specific issues.

In the sciences, engineers, the medical community, and people in industry are interested in a variety of topics. The community of readers beyond the academy are likely to show reading behavior that is elastic to price.

The ability to segment the market by faculty versus others may be limited. One might suppose that the faculty tend to have less price elastic demands than students, and that persons beyond the academy may have more price elastic demands than those within the academy. A publisher might prefer to segment the market so as to employ a different price in each segment.[5] The faculty (library) will then face the highest price, the students an intermediate price, and off-campus the lowest price. Segmentation of published journals between libraries and personal subscriptions reflects this phenomenon. With network delivery, such segmentation may be more difficult. Because the network is ubiquitous, the publisher of electronic information to be delivered by the network must make the service generally available on a low priced pay-per-look basis so as to reach the elastic part of the market. That may bring downward pressure on the price of a subscription to a campus. If segmentation is difficult, the publisher may have to set one price for all, reflecting the average elasticity of all its readers.

Encourage Innovation

When users can shop for services, innovation may be faster. A publisher of network-based information with a new product may be able to find readers on a number of campuses and generate revenues without having to persuade a library of the value of the service.

Innovations in libraries and computing in higher education take about 10 years for full adoption, that is, from the time a first campus adopts until all have adopted.[6] The library and computing innovations are adopted more quickly than most other innovations in higher education, so one might think that moving decisions to individuals would slow innovations. However, the other observed innovations each involve institutional decisions. Personal decisions may be much simpler. An innovation may reach a threshold scale more quickly and so may encourage more publishers to innovate.

Respond to Congestion
A fourth reason to contemplate prices is to address congestion. Like highways, networks are inherently congestible. As traffic builds, the pace of flow slows. With slower flow, less traffic gets through. Ultimately, traffic may become stop-and-go with a very slow flow. More traffic would get through if the rate of flow were kept higher. To sustain the flow, some move to price according to use may be necessary. In particular, different rates for use might apply during peak periods of use than in off-peak periods. On highways, electronic toll collecting systems are emerging that can collect tolls without slowing the cars. Discounts are given for off-peak users.

Congestion is a common occurrence on the Internet because prices are not related to use and do not vary by time of day.[7] The technical community's response is to request more resources to build a faster Internet. It seems natural to expect that, without peak period pricing, traffic flows will expand with network capacity, making congestion a continuing phenomenon. Internet II will be congested instantly by continuous video and other bandwidth devouring claims for service unless pricing regimes are built into the protocol. It is ironic that electronic toll systems are successfully addressing congestion on highways while time-of-day toll collecting seems difficult on the electronic network.

In sum, the thoughtful use of prices can enhance the performance of networks as tools for communication. We may expect information services to continue to be subsidized, ready access to appropriate information products is an important part of the academic process. Many information products will be licensed for campus-wide use without usage-based charges to readers. However, if access is more effective and involves lower cost when prices are attached then when they are not, then the case for prices and subsidies for some range of information products seems compelling.

Publishers
The electronic medium is changing publishing profoundly as well. Far into the 19th century, letter writing was a common means of communication among active scholars. Letters had little circulation and so had limited effect. Formal printed publication had high set-up costs and relatively low marginal costs. As a result, a decision to print a publication required some confidence that a sufficient quantity would be sold to cover the up-front fixed cost. Publication in journals has become increasingly important in the last century because journals could be sold by subscription prior to publication. The reputation of the editor and publisher sustained interest. Advance subscription sale allows the publisher to better forecast sales and to avoid holding inventory. Journals also speed the publication process. Thus serials sold by subscription in advance of publication have become the dominant means of intellectual communication.

The cost structure of printed publication has evolved. With electronic typesetting and printing processes, shorter print runs have become economical. Indeed, print-on-demand is gaining market. Publishers are able to store electronic files for their out-of-stock publications and print single copies on request with reasonable economy. With this innovation, printed publications are likely to remain "in print" (that is, available for printing on demand) for a longer period of time.

Publishers provide substantially more than economical distribution of the author's text. They engage editors who often play an important intellectual role. Editors are active agents. They may solicit material from authors. They may solicit comments from others, propose significant alterations in presentation, and may even discover and help correct significant errors. Finally, editors may work directly on the author's copy and make revisions to improve readability and suitability for a given audience. We might think of the editor as the reader's agent in seeking ideas from authors and packaging them as readers would like to have them. We may also think of the editor as the author's agent in identifying how to reach readers. The editor's intermediation has gained importance as the quantity of material available for review has increased. No one can read it all; we depend on editors to shape what we write and, most importantly, what we read.

Just how the publication process works is changing with network communication.

Personal Publishing

Personal publishing is much easier on the net. One can create an electronic document and post it on a website. Given that one is working on a personal computer and is using either a campus network service or a commercial Internet service provider, the cost of posting an electronic document is quite modest. Indeed, once the set-up is in place, the cost of posting an essay in Hyper Text Mark-up Language is about like the cost of reformatting from one style manual to another. With Adobe's Acrobat, one can create a web-available document as easily as one can print it.

Once posted, a document is instantly accessible to the world. Compared to writing a letter or even photocopying and distributing a typescript, web posting has substantial advantages. Webposting is faster, less expensive, and preserves the inherent advantages of the electronic document, particularly color and linkages. When something gives better service at lower price, we can expect to see more of it. Web-posting is growing as a means of personal communication. Faculty can communicate with students, research can be shared with colleagues, and work can be made available to all who might be moved to look for it.

Formal Publishing

Personal publishing is likely to reach only those who have a strong prior reason to seek out a given author's site. For most of us, time is too precious to spend probing personal sites. We want editors to have worked their magic before we commit our time. Thus, the formal publisher will have an enduring role in the electronic arena.

The journal was a convenient size package for periodical print publication. It's length may reflect both what an editor could comprehend and what readers could manage. With network distribution, however, the packaging may change.

The network can make available a whole database of materials and point a reader to just those components that may be of greatest interest. Indeed, the reader may establish a personal profile of interests with an indication of intensity and character of interest by subject. For new materials of highest interest, the reader may receive a copy of the full document. For material of second priority, the reader may receive an e-mail with a brief announcement. A full document may be just a few pages of summary with links to a lengthier discussion, data sets, deeper bibliography, and commentaries.

Editors then may work to build additions to the formal database. Because of scale economies in managing databases, the database may have several editors, each producing journals for specific audiences. The database may well begin with submissions. Editors may notify reviewers to evaluate specified postings to the database. The database may contain the working papers, submissions, and commentaries. Access to these may be limited to the editors. The database will track revision cycles. Once an editor gives an imprimatur to a specific document, it may be released to the general readership with abstracts sent to the profiled list of readers. The document might also be put in the print queue for the next print issue.

One might imagine a database of working papers as has developed in physics. The electronic working paper service might be enhanced by creating more ways for an author to flag the level, scope, and subject matter of an essay. For example, one flag might indicate an original empirical investigation, another might indicate original theoretical content, and another might note an interval of historical perspective, and so on, with flags appropriate to the discipline.

Access to the working paper file might be available at one subscription rate and access to fully edited essays might come at another rate. In some disciplines, the working papers might be treated as relatively private with access limited to personal subscriptions. In other disciplines, the working papers might be readily accessible to all who care to plow through a larger number of essays or where simple electronic searching may be an effective finding tool. Whether access to a working paper database is complementary to a database of published essays and so increases sale of the package is an open question.

The database might invite commentary. An author might agree to be available in real-time for network chat at a given time. Asynchronous discussion might be supported for an interval of time. An editor might moderate the discussion, posting only comments that meet some threshold of relevance. The electronic database may take on some of the quality of a professional meeting. An editor could then make a decision about what if any of the commentary to archive.

The challenge to the editor is, as always, to attract strong authors and sustain reader interest. Working with a database as the input tool may improve interaction with authors. Producing electronic documents as the end product will give speedier access to new material and give play to the other advantages of electronic documents. However, the editor will draw a line between what is carefully reviewed and various levels of ancillary postings and commentary that may have little oversight.

Hal Varian discusses a new process for electronic publishing.[8] Authors submit summaries of their work that is ranked on a numerical scale by a board of editors. Readers are notified of interesting works and are invited to rate the full length essay as well as add commentary. This regime has the potential of substantially lowering the cost of reviewing but under estimates the active role editors play in attracting and shaping manuscripts. Odlyzko (and Varian as well) suggest that the cost of producing journals can fall by a factor of ten by having author's do the typesetting and page layout and by having editors use electronic means to gather reviews.[9] That is to say, with some loss in presentation quality, the journal designed for the electronic world can create substantial cost savings.

Minimum cost, however, isn't an overriding goal. Quality matters and readers are drawn to quality in editing and presentation. In the electronic arena, quality also arises with design, with linkage from abstract to summary to longer essay to underlying data, algorithm, images, and other raw material, and with ties to a wide database of related materials. There is no doubt that publishers can produce electronic journals of substantially lower cost. However, it is certainly possible that readers will prefer and be willing to pay for higher quality.

The University of Chicago Press has converted nine journals to electronic format. They have achieved economies in the production processing by accepting electronic submissions and using the electronic submissions all the way through typesetting.[10] They produce paper and electronic versions of journals from the same input stream. Electronic methods have lowered their costs. Nevertheless, it is also possible that publishers will gain increased market power and so that journal prices will increase even as production costs fall.

Publishers are moving toward offering large databases, the accumulation of many journal titles. The master database has coherence that transcends individual journal titles and the unit becomes the article. For example, one can do a full word search of the content of all the journals in JSTOR. This feature of the electronic archive gives it a substantial edge over print. Moreover, the advantage of text searching may be larger, the larger the database. Thus, both for scale advantages in storing information and for scale advantages in searching, the larger the database of coherent material, the better. We may expect that the publishers who produce only a few journal titles or a larger number of titles but in unrelated fields will be at a disadvantage. The economies of scope in academic publishing are much larger in the electronic network arena.

Pricing the Database

Let's suppose that with the shift to electronic publication, the larger scale database becomes the norm. How will access to it be priced? There are three general ways to price the service. The publisher might license access to a campus. A university might pay a flat annual rate that would allow unlimited use by members of its community via the campus network. Second, the publisher might license use to individuals. Individuals might pay an annual subscription and have unlimited use of the database for a year. Third, the database publisher might charge per use, defined perhaps as delivery of the full article as the *New York Times* does. These three strategies are complementary and may allow a publisher to sell to several groups simultaneously, much as magazines are sold at newsstands as well as by mail subscription.

Some print journals are sold almost exclusively to libraries. Selling a campus site license for electronic access would undercut personal subscriptions and so the price for a campus might be comparable to the library print subscription. For journals with significant personal subscriptions, a campus license might be a replacement. Sale as a campus license reduces costs modestly, and in some cases there might be some reduction in price because of lower costs. By selling a database, the publisher may sell a bundle for considerably less than the total for which it would sell the individual parts. Let's say that a campus would buy two-thirds of the database on an individual title basis. If the publisher then offered the whole database at two-thirds of the total cost it would get just as much revenue. If selling access to subsets of the database requires incurring additional costs, sale of the whole at a discount may serve both buyer and seller better.

Personal subscriptions, call them memberships, may be the mode of license for independent scholars and scholars on campuses that choose not to subscribe to a given database. The publisher might seek to offer special services to individuals that would enhance the value of a personal subscription. For example, access to working papers might be limited to personal subscribers who participate in self-selected subsections. E-mail announcements of new documents that fit a member's profile may only be available to personal members. Personal subscriptions or membership may tie to other services as well, for example, discounts on submission fees.

Pay-per-use may allow access to persons from other disciplines or who are beyond the academy whose interest is episodic. (I am not distinguishing here between pay-per-use and pay-per-look although a variety of different regimes are plausible.) Think of the network as a quasi-photocopier, delivering electronic images to one's personal workstation on demand. Of course, to print one must provide the printer. If the demand for pay-per-use is highly price elastic, then the profit maximizing price will be low. The price elasticity is likely to vary by discipline.

The three pricing strategies interrelate. Where there is a highly elastic demand for pay-per-use, the profit maximizing strategy may be to offer low prices for pay-per-look. Such a strategy will put downward pressure on rates for campus and personal subscriptions because some campuses and individuals could opt for the pay-per-look approach. Where the pay-per-look market is thin, campus and personal licenses may be higher.

The for-profit publishers have come to charge substantially more for journals than do the non-profits. They do so because of the low price elasticity of demand for library oriented journals. As publishers consolidate and capture the economies of scope of databases of multiple journals in a given discipline, the demand for campus licenses for the database may become even less price elastic than the demand for library subscriptions. With lower price elasticity, price may be much higher. Consolidation of whole literatures as a single database owned by a for-profit publisher would seem to offer considerable potential for profit and alarm for universities and their libraries.

Some disciplines are served by non-profit publishers with substantial suites of journal titles that may succeed in moving to the database arena. Some disciplines seem likely to have their literature move to for-profit databases. What the consequences will be for the intellectual vitality of the differently situated disciplines will be interesting to observe.

Distance Learning, Asynchronous Learning, Remote Institutions

Another feature of the network is that is it is ubiquitous. Generally, its services are available 24 hours a day almost anywhere. One can imagine founding a new university and thinking about what information resources should be installed. Even now, a first consideration will be installing a powerful network that is accessible to all the students and faculty. One will think carefully about what electronic tools to install in classrooms. When one turns to the library, one will naturally ask about the costs and benefits of electronic services the library might deliver by campus network. Commitment to building print collections of historic materials may be limited to specific subdisciplines.

By this logic, those campuses in remote places or with short histories and so limited library resources are likely to find electronic network services a more economical buy for many purposes than retrospective print collecting. Network services diminish the disadvantages of remoteness and youth.

Of course, one might then ask why build a campus at all? Why not simply rely on network delivery of instructional and information services to homes and businesses? It is certainly the case that many businesses invest in significant amounts of training for their employees. There exists a market for distance learning and we should expect it to grow. The network has advantages over conventional distance learning in its interactivity and its ability to deliver services asynchronously.

Instructors aren't going to become obsolete. Personal interaction among students and between student and instructor will remain an important part of what many people want in an education.

Over the last two decades, the gap in earnings between those with college and those with no college has grown remarkably. The rate of return to post secondary education has soared. President Clinton has called for universal access to the first two years of college. Today, about 60 percent of high school graduates enter post secondary education. Deciding how this proportion should grow is a substantial challenge. Delivery of educational services to the fourth quintile (that between 60 and 80 percent of high school graduates) will be an even bigger challenge than was expansion to the third quintile. As a first approximation, the three quintiles now entering college are likely to be those with highest secondary school achievement. The fourth quintile will typically have lower achievement on entry. Designing post secondary education services for this group in a way that is cost effective in improved lifetime earnings will take careful thought. Perhaps, network delivery of educational and informational services will play new roles as higher education expands.

Journals

In November 1998, the number of peer-reviewed electronic journals from conventional academic publishers is approaching 2,000. The quality of the offerings is high, the covering of titles is strongest in the sciences. The pricing and technical strategies vary. In addition, there are perhaps 4,000 other electronic academic publications created specifically for Internet distribution. The intellectual importance of the latter are more difficult to assess.[11]

Table 1

Publishers distributing e-journals directly:	# of Titles
Elsevier Science Direct	1,100
Springer Link	300
American Chemical Society	33
Institute of Physics	33
University of Chicago Press	9

This is a partial list meant merely to establish an order of magnitude

Integrators supporting electronic distribution of e-journals (This list is selected so that titles are not duplicated above.)	
Highwire (several publishers)	90
OCLC (29 publishers, none of the above)	1,200
Academic Press	175
JSTOR	68
JHUP Muse	40
Kluwer	120
Blackwell	150
MIT Press	9
Taylor & Francis	50
Total	**2,765**

Counts are approximate, the numbers change as more journals are added.

PUBLISHER LINKS
http://www.sciencedirect.com/science/page/static/splash_about.html
http://link.springer.de/home.htm
http://pubs.acs.org/about.html
http://www.iop.org
http://highwire.stanford.edu
http://www.oclc.org/oclc/menu.eco.htm
Journal@Ovid supports more than 100 journals from 50 publishers. These largely duplicate OCLC's offerings.
http://www.ovid.com/wcgi/button3.map?406,18

Note: Carl Uncover offers Desktop Image Delivery of a TIFF image to a web browser with about a one-hour delay to 2,500 journals. I am unable to judge the overlap with the above.

Some publishers are offering electronic journals directly on the network. Elsevier is the largest and its roster includes more than 1,100 journal titles. Its Science Direct service lists about 1,000 titles in electronic format. (Elsevier is also participating in the University of Michigan's PEAK experiment with 1,100 titles that offers Elsevier's package on various terms with a view to learning how libraries respond to various pricing regimes.[12]) Springer offers a package of about 300 titles, most of its titles are available in both print and electronically, but they are offering a few titles that are exclusively available electronically. Some professional society publishers are offering their titles electronically, for example, the American Chemical Society offers its 33 titles.

Other publishers are working with intermediaries who package journals from a variety of sources into a common electronic environment. The publisher then can economize on the costs of electronic services, billing mechanisms, and marketing. OCLC offers about 1,200 titles from 29 publishers through its First Search electronic publishing venture, including the suite of titles form Academic Press, JSTOR (backfiles only), the Johns Hopkins University Press's Project Muse, Blackwell, Carfax, and Kluwer. The Highwire Press, a service of Stanford's Library, offers a suite that will grow to 90 titles as the titles of Oxford University Press join the fold. Several of the serials subscription agents are offering ejournal aggregation services, including EBSCO, Swets, and Blackwell.

OCLC charges libraries for access to the electronic journal service while libraries must subscribe to each journal individually from publishers. Vanderbilt quoted a charge of about $66 per journal title for access for ten simultaneous users over and above the cost of the subscriptions.[13] These rates were high enough to discourage many libraries. In late 1998, OCLC introduced a new price regime to offer access in the $16 to $26 per title range for titles to which a library holds a print subscription. OCLC's lower rate seems to apply just to titles from publishers who offer electronic access via OCLC at no extra charge. OCLC's approach inevitably treats electronic access as an add-on cost. Although it offers a common interface to many titles and easy searching, OCLC does not offer publishers economies in the production process. In addition, links to OCLC's full-test ejournals from abstract and index databases are tied to OCLC's First Search service and not from other vendors of abstracts and indices. In contrast, the Highwire Press appears to have a tighter integration with publisher operations and is able to offer electronic access without the print at a substantial, 40 percent discount to the print subscription.

Elsevier, Springer, JSTOR, and Academic Press, among others, have moved to offer all their titles as a package. They have built sets of titles in given disciplines so that the set of titles amounts to a total database that is more than the sum of its parts. By bundling the set of titles together, they can offer bundled prices that are more attractive to libraries and more profitable for the publisher than only offering a price for each title. The professional society with a substantial suite of titles in its discipline has the ability to create the dominant database for the discipline.

Libraries are buying the packages offered by specific publishers. One can visit the websites of most academic libraries and scan their offerings of electronic journals. One can quickly identify whether the library has bought each major suite of titles. Libraries are electing to buy packages for three reasons. First, the publishers offer some discount for the whole over the sum of the individual prices. Second, it is costly for a library to make a decision and render payment title by title. The libraries are, then, making decisions about bundle A or bundle B more readily than about individual titles. Third, libraries are likely to take a holistic view of a discipline and prefer to offer a complete database rather than subsets. As that database comes to define a literature, a library will prefer to make all-or-nothing decisions to support a literature.

Indeed, there are mushroom colonies of library consortia formed essentially to seek discounts on volume purchases of bundles. In the longer run, consortia who have deeper pockets and so can offer vendors financial guarantees of payments and libraries financial guarantees of the performance of the electronic services, are likely to survive. We might note in passing here that the performance of electronic services delivered by the World Wide

Web is quite variable and often poor. Network congestion is only one reason. When libraries insist on performance standards, weak consortia are likely to disintegrate. For example, when a European publisher provides access to its journals at its home site, delays in access from North America run to several minutes. By maintaining one or more mirror sites in North America, performance would be much higher. If libraries specified contracts with performance standards with financial penalties for poor performance, their consortia would have to monitor performance, stand ready to pay when performance is poor, and pass along claims for performance to publishers. Publishers might then more readily create strategically located mirrors so as to lower response times in major markets. Consortia without the substance to engage in performance monitoring of the services they are brokering and to manage penalties for underperformance are likely to be replaced by more substantial entities.

Publishers with few titles or with titles that are spotted across many disciplines will have difficulty achieving the critical mass necessary for a database of titles in any discipline. As a result, any package they offer will be less compelling. OCLC's strategy occupies a middle ground. Its title count is large but libraries must subscribe to each title directly from its publisher. OCLC then isn't able to offer a bundled price that spans beyond the offering of an individual publisher. There may be limits on its ability to integrate the offerings from disparate sources. OCLC is attracting many publishers to its electronic publishing umbrella by sustaining the publishers pricing autonomy while creating the look and feel of a common database and providing archival access.

The electronic publishing arena in academia opens an economy of scope that gives a significant advantage to large, coherent databases. The journal title, although an essential vehicle for building editorial reputation, is becoming less important as the object of purchase for libraries. Ready electronic access to current electronic journals massed in databases with a group of critical size in a discipline and licensed for campus-wide use gives a substantial edge to journal titles that are part of the database.

The database provider/publisher is positioned to add value by integrating the articles in the database electronically and to enhance their quality by taking advantage of the electronic format. The database presentation should allow searching the whole database or important subsets. The search might be for individual words in the full text. Integrating abstracting and indexing into the database will allow the discipline of a controlled vocabulary to improve subject access. The articles might be labeled for intended audience, empirical content, original theory, and in other ways appropriate to specific disciplines as mentioned above. The articles might be linked electronically to supplementary material, numerical data, algorithmic software, and more extended discussions and commentary.

Journal Prices

A thorough review of electronic journal pricing is beyond the scope of this essay. We can look at some readily available examples of journal pricing. Table 2 reports the average prices of ten journals offered by the American Society for Microbiology through the Highwire Press. Highwire is the electronic publishing imprimatur of the Stanford University Library. Journal prices are set by the Society. The average for an institutional subscription (that is a campus license to a library) to a journal is $333 for a print journal while the average electronic subscription is $200, that is, 40 percent less. A campus that wishes both the print and the electronic versions may acquire both for just 30 percent more than the print price alone.

Table 2
Average Prices of Ten Journals by the American Society for Microbiology published electronically by the High Wire Press http://www.asmusa.org/

	Print	Electronic	Both
Personal	$64	$38	$83
Institutional	$333	$200	$433
Personal/Institutional	19%	19%	19%
As % of print	100%	60%	130%

Table 3

Johns Hopkins University Press
Project MUSE Prices assuming 40 subscriptions in the package
http://muse.jhu.edu/orderingplan_a.html

Library	Campus	Building	Campus/Title	Bldg./Title
FTE>2,000	$3,300	$1,650	$83	$41
FTE<2,000	$2,475	$1,221	$62	$31
Community/2-Year	$1,650	$825	$41	$21
Public/Special	$1,650	$825	$41	$21
Corporate	$3,300		$83	
High School		$396		$10
Department		$1,650		$41

The Microbiology price pattern makes clear that electronic publication offers substantial cost savings in comparison to print. The cost savings may arise in part from the economies of scale achieved by Highwire Press in managing a common technical system for many journals. The campus license costs about five times the price of an individual subscription, regardless of format. We might suppose that the price elasticity of demand for the personal subscription is substantially above that of the library.

The Johns Hopkins University Press prices its package of 40 plus journals as Project MUSE. Table 3 reports the library rates for the package. The Press discriminates by type of library. Large academic libraries (campuses with more than 2,000 FTEs students) pay $3,300 for a campus license, $1,650 for a license for up to 25 computers in a single building. Four-year campuses with under 2,000 enrollment pay $2,475. Two-year campuses pay $1,650 as do public and special libraries. Corporations pay $3,300, high schools pay $396. Discounts to these rates are offered under certain conditions to consortia of libraries. A library that buys the MUSE package is offered a 60 percent discount on print subscriptions to journals. Individuals may subscribe to the electronic journals for $20 per title, that would be about $800 for the whole package (although it would be an unusual individual whose need spanned all the disciplines represented in the package).

Assuming that the Press will only offer the package when it at least covers incremental costs, the price to high schools then puts an upper bound on the cost of delivering the suite of MUSE titles of about $10 per title. Presumably, the demand by high schools is more price elastic than the other library markets and so a lower price is appropriate to maximize net revenue. High schools might be expected to exhibit lower rates of use, so if the price is based on a forecast of intensity of use for each class of library, the high school rate might be lower for this reason as well.

Dividing the package price by 40 gives an approximation to the charge per journal title. This per title rate allows comparison with the Microbiology titles in table 2. If we take the institutional title rate at $40 and the personal title rate at $20, we can see that the MUSE has a lower per title institutional rate compared to Microbiology. This difference might arise for several reasons. First, the MUSE title suite includes many humanities titles and few scientific titles. The demand for humanities titles is more price elastic and may have lower production costs than scientific titles. Second, MUSE is offered as a bundle and so the Press expects to gain more revenue from the bundle than it could by pricing each title individually. The bundle price strategy is most effective when the demand for the individual titles is heterogeneous, different libraries place different values on the individual titles. It is conceivable that a library that would buy none of the titles when priced individually at $100 each yet would find the bundle attractive.

This brief visit to journal prices is sufficient to establish that electronic access is frequently priced below print access. Also, many publishers are offering current issues of their journals by license for campus-wide use by network. The publishers continue to offer personal subscriptions even as they offer campus licenses. Bundles of journals are frequently priced as a package at a rate well below the sum of the individual prices of the titles. Libraries are drawn to make a single buy for a package by the discount, by the lower transaction costs, and by the value of the whole database. The market for electronic journals is now well established, a significant feature of the academic landscape. The market will continue to evolve with new pricing and packaging as publishers gain experience and as more publishers are drawn to present their journals electronically. The next milestone looks like it may be the availability of 5,000 core, peer-reviewed academic journal titles electronically for campus license and individual subscription. This count grew from about 1,000 in mid-1997 to 2,000 in late 1998. The 5,000 peer-reviewed title milestone might be about five years away in 2003.

The pay-per-look market appears to be underdeveloped. Although the New York Times is doing business this way and articles from more than 17,000 journals are available through Uncover (in a few hours by fax for $12.95), still no discipline has its core abstracting and indexing service database tied to an all electronic delivery mechanism. [Uncover has also begun to deliver articles in TIFF format to a web browser within about an hour from 2,5000 journal titles.) Depending on price elasticities and the evolution of low-cost electronic payment mechanisms, the pay-per-look market may evolve toward the availability of individual articles for prices under $5, delivered to the desktop on demand by network.

Archives

Journals are the most important part of academic information flow and the largest share of library acquisition budgets. Electronic publication, however, is also of growing importance in other arenas. Academics use manuscripts, photographs, numerical data, government documents, newspapers, maps and a variety of other material as raw material for study and as ways of documenting historic, cultural, literary, and scientific phenomena. Conventionally, libraries acquire these material in print or microfilm, they may acquire original material or facsimile. Electronic facsimile are becoming a significant alternative.

For example, the World Wide Web is a convenient way to make medieval manuscripts available to a wider audience. Less than two percent of the Western European medieval manuscripts are held as originals in U.S. libraries and those holdings are concentrated in about a dozen libraries. Printed and microform facsimile of substantial collections are held in a few libraries, with a few dozen libraries holding moderate collections of facsimile. The libraries at Columbia and Berkeley with support from the Mellon Foundation are mounting 10,000 full color images of medieval manuscripts on the Web as the *Digital Scriptorium*. The images are captured at 600 dots per inch in 24 bit color and are well cataloged. The libraries plan to offer access world-wide on a subscription basis so that any campus, or indeed, any individual will have convenient access to a substantial collection of medieval material in digital facsimile. The revenue stream generated by the Digital Scriptorium will fund growth of the database and attract more libraries to the venture. Indeed, the Digital Scriptorium should establish a technical and economic framework for all the archives of the world to share important medieval manuscripts.

An important point here is that the digital archive is established once for the world, is universally accessible, and generates revenue so that it is self-sustaining. Scholars and their libraries can buy into a much more substantial body of archival materials with better cataloging and presentation, than they could afford to do with conventional tools.

Colonial Williamsburg, also with support from the Mellon Foundation, plans to present a significant part of its archive in digital facsimile on the World Wide Web to generate a revenue stream so that the service can be self-sustaining. A centerpiece will be the complete run of the *Virginia Gazette* from 1736 to 1780, with a full-text word-searchable index and presentation of the facsimile of the pages. Williamsburg's archive will include other documents from the colonial era, photographs of museum objects, maps and plans, and research reports from the Williamsburg research staff.

A digital archive can present its content in digital facsimile to the whole world. The digital documents can be designed to take advantage of the digital medium with searching, zooming, and linking. The quality of the archives will be shaped by the amount of revenues they can generate. Those with larger audiences, who do a better job of selection and presentation, and who package and price their offerings in ways that scholars and libraries find compelling will grow. We should expect the same price regimes as we see with journals with prices scaled to the size of the institution and various bundled offerings.

Digital archives should provide access in digital facsimile to museum and art objects, to photographs and newspapers, to government and corporate documents, genealogy, to sound and video, indeed to most of what archives offer as raw materials for scholarship. Digital facsimile seem substantially superior to microfilm in ease of use, ready access, and searchability. Of course, digital archives are likely to march to somewhat different drummers than conventional archives. The value of a revenue stream will draw managers to seek out more popular items for presentation to a variety of audiences.

Cooperation

The wonderful world of the World Wide Web came into being with a cooperative ethic that finds an affinity in libraries. Libraries are for sharing, too. The sharing made possible by the World Wide Web and by libraries relies on a number of motives. At one level, we each are willing to contribute to the greater good; we have sound philanthropic motives. At another level, we see advantage in promoting our institutions by presenting what we have. At yet another level, we can use collective resources to subsidize shared goods to foster a sense of community as tuition or tax finance supports many libraries.

However, sharing has its limits. When people have little face-to-face contact, the opportunity to build communities is limited. When many people share the philanthropic service, the source of the philanthropy matters less and so we each have a weaker sense of purpose in contributing. Given the world wide scope and breadth of interests found among users of the World Wide Web, the heterogeneity of interests means that philanthropic motives are weakened. The ability to express our interests by voting with our dollars for services we like is much more likely to sustain the services we want most.

The World Wide Web will provide more information resources for use by scholars and will allow scholars to reach wider audiences when prices become more important and revenue streams allow service providers to match services to reader tastes. Putting prices in the hands of individual readers may indeed lower costs and yield more finely tuned services. Although there are risks of increased monopoly power and excess profits by for-profit vendors who control whole databases of a literature, these risks may be offset with vigorous innovations by not-for-profits. In the end, the quality of scholarly communication will improve and reach more audiences digitally than was possible with print and microfilm.

NOTES

1. I appreciate the helpful comments of my colleagues Paul Gehrman, John Haar, and Flo Wilson. The views expressed, however, are my own.

2. Sholes, Christopher Latham" *Britannica Online.* <http://www.eb.com:180/cgi-bin/g?DocF=micro/544/48.html> [Accessed 04 March 1998]. Sholes' first patent was in 1868.

3. Mary E. Jackson, "Measuring the Performance of Interlibrary Loan and Document Delivery Services." Association of Research Libraries, http://arl.cni.org/newsltr/195/illdds.html

4. See Brian Tracy, "The Color of Money" *Wall Street Journal* November 16, 1998 R28 for a discussion of the state of electronic funds on the Internet.

5. Market segmentation is a core idea in microeconomics. See, for example, Watson and Getz, *Price Theory and Its Uses*, (Boston: Houghton Mifflin, 1981)., pp. 353-4.

6. "Adoption of Innovations in Higher Education," (with John J. Siegfried and Kathryn A. Anderson) *The Quarterly Review of Economics and Finance*, 37 #3 (Fall, 1997) pp. 605-31.

7. Jeffry K. MacKie and Hal R. Varian, "Economic FAQs About the Internet," pp. 27062 in Lee W. McKnight and Joseph P. Bailey, *Internet Economics*, MIT Press, (Cambridge, MA, 1997).

8. Hal R. Varian, "The Future of Electronic Journals," *The Journal of Electronic Publishing*, September, 1998 Volume 4, Issue 1, ISSN 1080-2711 http://www.press.umich.edu/jep/04-01/varian.html

9. Andrew Odlyzko, "The Economics of Electronic Journals," The Journal of Electronic Publishing, September, 1998 Volume 4, Issue 1, ISSN 1080-2711 http://www.press.umich.edu/jep/04-01/odlyzko.html

10. Evan Owens, "SGML and the Astrophysical Journal: A Case Study in Scholarly and Scientific Publishing," http://www.journals.uchicago.edu/sgml96.html (c. 1997)

11. Private communication from Dru Mogge at the Association of Research Libraries, November 17, 1998 puts. The latest published figures are at http://www.arl.org:591/foreword.html The Association of Research Libraries publishes a list of e-journals. The July 1997 report listed 2,459 ejournals/zines, of these, 1,049 were peer-reviewed. The growth rate of titles becoming available electronically appears to be quite rapid.

12. The PEAK project quotes a per-article rate to libraries for use up to a ceiling quantity of articles per year. The library pays in advance and must pay a higher per-article fee when use exceeds the prepaid ceiling. Different participating libraries are offered different rates schemes to allow the experimenters to observe how libraries respond to the differences. One library estimated its per article rates under one of the PEAK regimes at $4.60 per article and estimated that the per article cost of its set of Elsevier journals in print at $8 to $9. Because libraries can do little to influence the rate of use of individual articles once they are made available to a campus, it isn't clear how the per-use charge to libraries will influence their readers' demands for journals. The core issue may be the extent to which libraries might change the mix of journal titles to which they subscribe or change their view of the value of a whole database of journal titles.

13. Private communication from John Haar, collection officer at the Jean and Alexander Heard Library at Vanderbilt University, November 17, 1998. The rate quoted was $32,370 for 490 journals for 10 simultaneous users.

Digital Libraries Support Distributed Education

Gail McMillan

Abstract

Many digital library discussions focus on computer processing and neglect the range of services that libraries traditionally provide. The digital library is not equivalent to a digitized collection with information management tools. It is also a series of activities that brings together collections, services, and people in support of the full life cycle of creation, dissemination, use, and preservation of information. A digital library should be a seamless extension of the library that provides faculty and students with access to information in any format that has been evaluated, organized, archived, and preserved. Access to evolving digital information is provided through global as well as personalized systems and through the services of information professionals. Digital libraries and traditional libraries should not be separate, but should coalesce to accomplish more than either can do independently to serve the user community on the highest order.

Introduction

My thesis is that many digital library (DL) discussions focus on computer processing and the limited notion that a library is just a collection of documents. Frequently these discussions are held among computer scientists and do not include librarians. As a result they neglect to consider that libraries provide a range of services and resources to anticipate as well as meet the needs of their user communities.

Through this presentation, I want to have a catharsis (in the Aristotelian sense) and I'm going to have it in public in front of what I hope is a sympathetic crowd. I will briefly express my dissatisfaction about the shortsighted approaches of computer scientists who conduct research and write about digital libraries, failing to take into consideration the range of library resources and services and the multi-faceted roles of information professionals and librarians. Secondly, I will share a definition of "digital library" created with my colleague at Virginia Tech, Nan Seamans. Third, I will share some design scenarios prepared by a variety of Virginia Tech faculty that describe their visions of the library. And, lastly,

---

Gail McMillan is director of the Scholarly Communication Project at Virginia Polytechnic Institute and State Universty Libraries.

I will make recommendations for actions we should take.

Catharsis

Through working with computer science faculty at Virginia Tech over several years, I developed the opinion that their research and development of digital libraries was so narrowly restricted as not to be about libraries at all. They usurped the word and ignored the broad range of services and resources associated with libraries. Unfortunately, reading about DLs has not dispelled what I learned through my VT experiences. For example, the October 1998 "Report of [the] First Summit on International Cooperation on Digital Libraries" defines it as "a collection of digital objects ... along with methods of access and retrieval, and for selection, organization, and maintenance of the collection." Michael Lesk's 1997 book, *Practical Digital Libraries: Books, Bytes, and Bucks,* says "Digital libraries are organized collections of digital information. They combine the structuring and gathering of information, which libraries and archives have always done, with the digital representation that computers have made possible, [ixx] and: DLs "address traditional problems of finding information, of delivering it to users, and of preserving it for the future." [p.2]

While their goals are lofty—to improve access to information—they concentrate solely on computer processing of information and ignore those aspects of libraries that can not be preprogrammed or digitized. Therefore, what they attempt to create is not a library at all; certainly not the Athenaeum-like place where writers and scholars meet. They use it more in the old fashioned sense of a circulating collection with simultaneous multi–user access. The computer scientists who discuss and conduct research and write about DLs are on a noble mission, but because they often isolate themselves from librarians and libraries, the broad range of services and the human environmental factors of the building structure, eludes them.

Librarians and information professionals do not try to meet the needs of library users and other information seekers with just one format, even one that is becoming as pervasive as digital. Similarly, few libraries limit their collections to just works available in paper, but also include magnetic tapes with audio and video recordings as well as bits and bytes, and vinyl, and microforms. We know that our library users inquiring about information want it in whatever format they can get easily and quickly.

When a diverse group of teaching, research, and library faculty came together because of our interest in applying for grant funds to support DL research, it quickly became evident that we lacked a common understanding of "library." This can, of course, be attributed in part to the jargons of our separate professions. English and Engineering faculty thought first of the building that houses *their* collections. Computer Science faculty focused on programming access to digital resources while they ignored librarians' collection development and collection management roles. Evaluating and developing library resources meet the needs of the breadth of a research university, including specific degree programs and the research needs of the faculty.

Another point of confusion was trying to incorporate asynchronous teaching and learning into our plans. The classroom, like the library, needs to be thought of as having a component that is independent of time and place. However, they would not eliminate the instructor from the course, but they would consider eliminating the librarian from the library. In both cases the one that resides wholly on a computer or a network of computers is not a complete replacement of the other, but is more effective as one component.

Because of these kinds of discussions, we initially had a difficult time agreeing on how the grant would be allocated. Therefore, using our own words and borrowing from others (including Stephen Griffin, Program Manager of the Digital Libraries Initiative at the National Science Foundation, and Digital Library Initiative Phase I participants), Nan Seamans and I developed and circulated among the grant writing group this definition of a digital library.

Digital library definition for vt dli2
(http://scholar.lib.vt.edu/DLI2/defineDL.html)
The "digital library" is not merely equivalent to a digitized collection with information management

tools. It is also a series of activities that brings together collections, services, and people in support of the full life cycle of creation, dissemination, use, and preservation of data, information, and knowledge. The challenges and opportunities that motivate an advanced DL research initiative should be associated with this broad view of the DL environment.

A DL should be a seamless extension of the library that provides scholars with access to information in any format that has been evaluated, organized, archived, and preserved. Access to this evolving collection of digital information is provided through personalized systems as well as through the services of information professionals. The DL adds value and saves time while extending the hours of access. It reduces the need for proximity to information resources, but still emphasizes the quality of those resources. It is a library that can be individually customized and, ultimately, will be easy to use.

Libraries are more than their information resources, their collections, the buildings that house them, the systems that they run on, or the services they provide. Libraries have information professionals that make judgments and interpret user needs; they provide services and resources to people (students, faculty, and others, and organizations). Some traditional library services can be replicated in the DL, partially or wholly, but some cannot be replicated. Online instruction is important, but sometimes meeting face–to–face, or having a (telephone) conversation, between student and instructor (including the information professional and librarian) is the most effective method. Information seekers should not be denied any library resource or service because it is not available online. The DL and the library should be complimentary, intertwining systems that exist to serve the user community on the highest order.

With a DL evolving within an academic library interested in research and development along pedagogical lines, we have a unique opportunity to incorporate participatory design to address user issues and collection-centered issues, as well as systems issues. While it didn't generate as much discussion as we would have liked, we used the opportunity to educate our colleagues and we received important input. For example, professor of political science, Tim Luke, wrote:

> …we seem to want "the library digitized," recognizing, as Gail's description does, that we are talking about rebuilding an entire environment, culture, space, and discourse for knowledge accumulation/evaluation/organization/preservation around digital means of access and use…we want to generate a system, like [OCLC] or the Internet, rather than a product, like an OPAC or Windows, so that it might be easily, cheaply, and widely used…This perhaps flies in the face of university's economic development mission, but this orientation seems more worthwhile and important than just throwing forth a new stream of computing commodities. …The library is a very old social institution, so we need to have an attitude of permanence when working in this area … In addition, we also need to… preserve physical things that contain/express information.

Luke goes on to suggest that the DL should have these characteristics:
- an open, adaptable notion of document;
- a flexible, expansive system of cataloging tags;
- a backward link and forward link to creators and users;
- an incomplete, emergent method of evaluative records/profiles/notes;
- a uniform, expansive, but accurate system of searching;
- a simple, shared means of dissemination;
- an adaptive, rebuildable, and error-resistant means of storage;

twluke@vt.edu
Sat, 13 Jun 1998 15:34:39 (EDT)
http://video.dlib.vt.edu:90/~fox/DLI2/ScenLuke.txt

Another faculty member, Gary Downey, professor of engineering and director of the Center for Science and Technology Studies, wrote in response to our definition: "so the focus of an ethnography project studying both the project itself and prospective participants would be on the identities of the relevant positions or groups." He commented that adding collection-centered issues in the midst of the user-issues and systems-issues is a major intervention in technology-oriented thinking that will help our DL research project. He agreed with our broad notion of a DL and its being a seamless extension rather than a wholesale replacement of the library.

Downey, however, criticized our phrase "digital library environment" because he prefers

> ...thinking about computer technologies as collections of activities—in this case, the digital library as a collection of library activities that live alongside and in the midst of other library activities. Even more particularly, I think of computer technologies as collections of activities of communication—which raises questions about who is communicating to whom about what, and what kinds of social interactions are taking place through such communications, how these modify pre-existing relationships among people, and so on.

> Gary Downey <downeyg@vt.edu>
> Tue, 19 May 1998 17:06:10 (EDT)
> Subject: Re: definition of a digital library

Stimulating discussion about resources and services that would be useful to DL users ensued. One of the ways we decided to clarify our various views of DLs was by creating scenarios to demonstrate how the DL should support distributed teaching and learning. Those who developed scenarios were from the departments of English and Computer Science. Faculty from the library also developed scenarios, one from a reference librarian and one that outlined the cycle of library activities from an instructor planning a course and determining what resources would be necessary, including library acquisitions and reference services for those resources. What follows are summaries of a few of them. The full text of the scenarios is at http://scholar.lib.vt.edu/DLI2/.

Highlights from scenarios
Reference scenario

The "reference scenario" by Jane Schillie (Virginia Tech Arts and Sciences College Librarian for the Social Sciences) demonstrates that undergraduate students are seduced by the convenience of searching the web. They are impressed by the quantity of information retrieved and they think, "all information is equal." Schillie's scenario demonstrates the advantages of the personal reference interview as intellectual access versus electronic access.

She wrote that librarians teach information discrimination through personalized research assistance, guidance, and instruction. Librarians are trained information professionals, perhaps a better label for the digital librarian cum-traditional librarian. They ask probing questions because experience has taught them that most people who ask information professionals for assistance do not initially ask the question that they really want answered. The librarian listens carefully and analyzes and interprets the responses to discover what information is needed. Then she guides them to the appropriate resources. In this particular scenario, a trained information professional discovers that a student requesting assistance in finding information about the women's movement is actually interested in finding primary source material to help her analyze Gloria Steinem's influence on the women's movement.

Teaching scenario

Dan Mosser, VT professor of English, presented a scenario for his course on the History of the English Language (HEL). His students will read, watch excerpts, play interactive games, perform workbook exercises, record their speech, and subject their speech and collected research samples to spectrographic analysis. Initially Mosser was very frustrated about the amount of time and trouble it would take to digitize and get copyright permission for all the material he wanted his students to use. Because he was so focused on a new distributed learning environment, he did not consider methods of distribution beyond the web. He lost sight of the library and only considered using the DL. He is a sophisticated library user, but because he is on campus, he had not kept up with new document delivery services, for example.

From his office he looked for specific videos in the library's online catalog, but he did not find the title he wanted. He completed the appropriate web form, requesting that the Center for Alternative Media purchase it. Preferring a digital video, it was four weeks before he received e-mail notification that it had arrived. He also received copyright permission to use it for this specific class, with access limited to users with vt.edu accounts. With a fresh sense of overcoming the technology, he added a link from his online syllabus directly to this library resource using the EReserve (electronic reserve) system.

Mosser's class will meet traditionally and with a virtual class in England. He requested and received the publisher's permission for the class in England to have access to the digital video for one week. During this week Mosser will record the "discussion" and mark points in the discussion as it takes place; later he will annotate it with explanatory text and links to video excerpts. This he archives with his other HEL class materials. Quite some time later, he will make a conference presentation that includes this segment and he will submit it to the VTDL (Virginia Tech Digital Library). This digital work will be annotated as a personal publication (i.e., lacking peer review) and given subject descriptors.

Research scenario

Robert France, Research Associate in Computer Science, created a scenario about a faculty research project. In his scenario, the fictitious Dr. Charity Miller is beginning new research on the history of photography. She uses a VRML (virtual reality markup language) browser on her desktop computer to interact with VTDL from her private space, a virtual carrel that has all the resources of a traditional carrel and more. She begins with a web search, exporting her findings into her carrel.

Next she searches the library catalog that includes not only local library holdings but many other libraries and databases such as OCLC's WorldCat. When her hits have been listed, they include brief descriptions and whether or not it is available in paper locally or digitally anywhere. These she drags into her "personal digital library." Things are accessible by all of the standard library access points, including as a shelf-list in call number order, and by any personal notes that she has added to them. The hits are color coded, designating their quality rating (which can be based on the source of the work or library bibliographers' evaluations made during collection development, etc.). Some of the works are not available digitally and some the library does not have. Dr. Miller uses an online form to borrow works through interlibrary loan, but she does not have to key in much information because there is metadata within the citations.

Stopping her far-ranging search, she now focuses on the VT library using the same catalog search and the same query but restricting the scope of the search to the local collection. Miller picks a point in the stacks where several relevant books have been "shelved," and using one book as a clue, clicks herself to the virtual stacks. Here she sees every book that the library owns in this range, even ones that are currently circulating or are physically in storage. She chooses to see them color-coded by quality, relevance to her search, or other criteria and can arrange them in any classification scheme or any other piece of metadata. Spine labels are clear and easy to read! From her research she accumulated an annotated bibliography of works in the library. Instead of walking to the library, she emailed them to Document Delivery, a library service that will deliver them to her office.

While this is in the works, Dr. Miller accesses the American Memory Project where she finds examples illustrating technological change in photography. She exports some into her workspace, uses an HTML editor to pass it to the VTDL image indexer. The indexer signifies when it finds matches in the local collection of images. A collection visualization device creates a topographical map. The documents that are near each other in the map have similar content and mountains represent many images with the same content. She can see clusters of near matches or similar images. She is ready to begin her historical investigations.

Scholarly Communications Project
(http://scholar.lib.vt.edu/)
Along with our fictional scenarios, the grant writ-

ing group was exposed to a unit of library that has been designing and implementing enhancements to traditional library resources and services since 1989, the Scholarly Communications Project. It is an early (and sustainable) model of how DLs enhance traditional library resources and services, in many cases paralleling the physical library. Libraries can have an active role in DL development, adapting to evolving needs and expectations of the user communities. Librarians educate today's casual web browsers who will become tomorrow's serious researchers, from undergraduates cruising the web to sophisticated graduates submitting electronic theses and dissertations, to powerful members of the academy publishing electronically. The Scholarly Communications Project collaborates with university researchers so that information seekers continue to have the opportunity to select resources in the environment that best meets their needs and desires (i.e., 3Qs: quality, quantity, and quickly).

Post-scenario developments

Digital library researchers have not, for the most part, acknowledged the hybrid format environment. These scenarios and library practices, however, reveal that even the very farsighted researchers agree with this reality. The format question should be resolved logically according to how the information is available and how it is to be used.

Developing these scenarios, some individually and some through group input and critique, helped our grant writing group better appreciate the range of goals a DL grant should support. Though we did not come to consensus about the definition of a DL, Nan Seamans and I contributed to broadening the scope of the research to be undertaken to the library's advantage. One goal is to improve teaching and assignments through the incorporation of library materials. The information resources that are important to a class should be format independent, whether the class is taught in a campus classroom or at a distance via a network to a distributed and asynchronous "class." To accommodate both classroom teaching and distance education (for neither will completely replace the other in the immediate future), students need access to information resources and not all are, can, or will be digital.

Because a resource is not digital does not mean that it cannot be used in distributed, asynchronous education. Digitizing an article may be one practical solution; another solution, however, may be linking to an existing article database. In some situations, sending a library book to a student's home may be the best way to get the information to the student, and making that possible through online requests should be a component of the DL, as it is the library. Offering services such as document delivery through online request forms, as well as information in multiple formats, was not initially a component of the computer scientists' DL and they did not encourage the other teaching and research faculty to incorporate this broader level of resources and services into their scenarios.

In conclusion

The DL should not be limited to a collection of documents controlled solely by automated information management tools. It should also be a series of activities that brings together the collections, services, and people in support of the full life cycle of information—creation, dissemination, use, and preservation.

The DL must also function as a social institution if it is to be a library. This aspect of the evolution of the DL can be detected in recent reports of evolving genres of digital documents that are coming out of social, though distributed, interactions. For example, there is a dispersed group of unacquainted people writing poetry together by contributing alternating lines to limericks. There is also the notion of published conversation being used by some newspaper publications to engender reader input and reaction. The impact informal communication through electronic mail has had on research in many areas is also familiar.

For now, the DL is a collection of information resources and limited library activities that live alongside and in the mist of other library activities. Cheryl LaQuardia put it well in a recent issue of *Library Journal* when she reported that "We confuse the methodology for the product, consider the means as the ends, and mistake the medium (the web) for the message. Technology will eventually recede into the background to be a silent and unobtrusive servant."

The best DL will be a seamless extension of the library that, among other things, provides its user community with access to information in any format that has been evaluated, organized, and preserved. Ideally, access to constantly evolving digital information will be provided through global as well as personalized systems with the availability of services by information professionals, librarians. DLs and libraries should not be separate, but should coalesce to accomplish more than either can do independently to serve the user community on the highest order.

Libraries and librarians are committed to their collections and to their users, and that commitment extends to the digital collection and the online user. Computer scientists have an unfortunate tendency to limit DLs to repositories of information. There is, of course, much more to libraries. People using libraries seek information, certainly, but this is just the tip of the iceberg. They also go to libraries seeking knowledge and wisdom and art and entertainment, and more, but they also seek *help*. Effective use of libraries involves library professionals helping researchers turn their rambling tales of what they are looking for, into the essential elements of well framed questions. The next step is to help them identify a well-defined body of information and avoid the misguided hunt for information. At this point, patrons are ready to continue on their own and to derive more benefits from interaction with the (digital) library.

Information professionals, librarians, know users and know domains of information. We are not indifferent to the collections we service or the users we assist. A machine is; a computer program or script is also. DLs fail to address libraries as social institutions. We need more librarians like Gary Marchionini working with computer scientists doing research on DLs who will help them understand that "To be called a library, an entity must be...guided by a service mission that is manifested in policies of acquisition (collection development), organization, and access. Libraries offer both content and services guided by such policies and exist in a social-political context that influences policies and operations."

How do we begin to overcome the current limitations of DL? We must take action, be proactive, take a leadership role, not just manage the information resources and services we know so well. Here are some suggestions:

- Do not wait to be asked to participate with faculty in preparing grant applications. For example, work with the computer science faculty and researchers to help them understand how their grant applications will present a stronger argument for funding if information professionals contribute to the "library" in "digital library" research.
- Do not wait to be asked to participate with faculty in preparing classes and instruction. For example, don't let faculty inadvertently limit expectations based on what is available electronically. Do not let them waste time scanning articles when the article database the library subscribes to has the them available online. Encourage faculty to centralize course materials through systems such as electronic reserve.
- Aggressively inform students about how to get and evaluate the information they need. Promote library services such as Document Delivery and resources such as online journals and article databases, as well as library resources available through the OPAC. Help them understand that the information they need is available in lots of different formats and many, not just digital, are within easy reach. Help them learn to evaluate Internet resources.
- Work with systems designers to improve functionality and make information easy to find. It is not enough to complain about what your OPAC does not do that it "should do." We must talk (constructively) with system vendors and offer to help put our knowledge into applications. Complex systems like OPACs do not engender unassisted, unmediated public use and independent information seeking behaviors are increasing tremendously. Similarly, DL designers devote the majority of their resources to managing content. We must help them to also focus on user services, one our areas of expertise.
- Learn from DL research. Do not assume that its limited perspective means that its findings are invalid. Do not assume that through our noble goals for educating library users, we can make people approach information and technology, as we know that they should. We must develop (digi-

tal) libraries where information is easy to find and easy to interpret (including evaluating the source).

- Take a risk: meet and respond to the changing information environment and commit to improvement. Explore, discover and create new services, and let go of some control of the known. Expect a learning curve (yours and your faculties' and students'), but realize that it is a temporary unease due to lack of confidence and the trepidation at the unknown. Seek new funding or allocations; form new alliances—facilitate activities and share leadership. Try something new, quietly, then learn from the mistakes, make improvements, and advertise successes.

There are new and evolving roles for us. I moved from a behind-the-scenes serials cataloger to become a liaison to our teaching and research faculty—working on grants, teaching classes of faculty and graduate students, working with programmers to transform building-centric services to enhanced library web services. We have new roles to fill. While the format of our resources may change, while access to information may change, while styles of service may change, the vision of high quality, service-oriented, information centers still fits the library's mission. We will serve our user communities best if we incorporate this into the DL also.

I challenge you to think differently, to think creatively, to identify the actions that librarians and information professionals should take, and then take them.

Please send comments about this paper to Gail McMillan, gailmac@vt.edu.

References

(All web resources were verified on Jan. 28, 1999.)

Akscyn, Robert M., Ian H. Witten. "Report of First Summit on International Cooperation on Digital Libraries." http://www.ks.com/idla-wp-oct98/

Deiss, Kathryn. "Steal a Base or Say Safe? Taking Risks to Grow," *ARL* 201 (Dec. 1998): 12–13. http://www.arl.org/newsltr/201/olms-risk.html

DLI phase 1 participants meeting [report], March 1997. http://www.si.umich.edu/SantaFe/Introduction.html

Duguid, Paul. "Information and Libraries," Red Rock Eater News Service: Nov. 17, 1998 (reposted to DIGLIB. http://listserv.nlc-bnc.ca/cgi-bin/ifla-lwgate.pl/DIGLIB/archives/diglib.log9811/Author/article-39.html

Griffin, Stephen M. "Taking the Initiative for Digital Libraries," *The Electronic Library*, vol. 16, no. 1, Feb. 1998: 24–27.

Hawkins, Brian, and Patricia Battin. *Mirage of Continuity: Reconfiguring Academic Information Resources for the 21st Century*. Washington, D.C.: CLIR and AAU, 1998.

LaQuardia, Cheryl. "Online Links: Users' Needs, Librarians Roles," *Library Journal,* Nov. 15, 1998: S10–S11.

Lesk, Michael. *Practical Digital Libraries: Books, Bytes, and Bucks*. San Francisco: Morgan Kaufmann, 1997.

Marchionini, Gary. "Research and Development in Digital Libraries" (article for *Encyclopedia of Library and Information Science* to appear 1998). http://ils.unc.edu/~march/digital_library_R_and_D.html

McMillan, Gail, et al. *VT DLI2=DL4U.* http://scholar.lib.vt.edu/DLI2/

Tennant, Roy. "Digital Potential and Pitfalls," *Library Journal,* Nov. 15, 1998: 21-22.

McMillan, Gail. Librarian, associate professor, director of the Scholarly Communications Project, and head of the Special Collections Department, University Libraries, Virginia Tech. http://scholar.lib.vt.edu/staff/gailmac/Gailshp.html

Seamans, Nan. Librarian, assistant professor, co-director, New Media Center, and head of the Center for Alternative Media, University Libraries, Virginia Tech. http://www.nmc.vt.edu/staff/nan/

The Changing Nature of Higher Education

Manuel Pacheco

Hello, my name is Manuel T. Pacheco, and I am the president of a medieval institution. I mean no insult to the University of Missouri, where I work. Nor to the hundreds of colleges and universities around the nation that are also medieval institutions. The fact is, in ways both visible and hidden, higher education still bears a strong resemblance to the institutions created by our monkish ancestors.

We see it, obviously, in the titles, the ceremonial robes, and the architecture around our campuses. And all those things serve as good reminders of days when knowledge was closely held, protected by a few, and imparted to a few more. The walls of the college truly once were a barrier; phrases such as "the gates of knowledge" really used to mean something. This was not an entirely negative connotation, at least in the sense that it helped define the university as a community, but it ceased to be a viable world view a long time ago.

Yet somehow, aspects of this cloistered life survived not only Gutenberg but also Mr. Rogers; not only moveable type but also television. Despite the 20th-century growth of satellite campuses, satellite courses, and extension and outreach services, we remain too inaccessible to many of our citizens. And this is at a time when access to virtually any kind of information seems to be readily available in the rest of the marketplace. The more the information age advances, the more we struggle to keep up.

To be certain, we are trying to do better, and succeeding in many ways. Today, a student sitting at home in Columbia, Missouri, can browse through library holdings in Columbus, Ohio. Not only books and journals but archival collections are increasingly becoming available to everyone with Internet access. No parts of the university community can remain cloistered in the medieval sinecure, no matter how hard some of them still try.

And while there is much to be praised in that development, cause for concern exists as well. A fair example comes from our colleagues in journalism. Some say that the Internet can make anybody—even, say, Matt Drudge—a journalist, because it creates instantaneous, inexpensive access to a worldwide marketplace of ideas. Others remark that a modem, or for that matter, a printing press, doesn't make someone a journalist, and that skills, experience, and an ethical orientation are more important.

Manuel Pacheco is president, University of Missouri System.

What makes a person a librarian? Certainly, not the Internet. It is simply the last in a long line of technical innovations that have made life at college libraries both easier and more challenging. Placing a list of holdings online no more makes a library than did converting old card files to digital databases. Librarians are, I think, the last to confuse their tools with their task. Books and computers are their tools; their task is to make knowledge available to everyone.

Knowledge is not the same thing as information, any more than Matt Drudge is the same journalist as Walter Cronkite. And therein lies the challenge I mentioned. If a new, digital age is simply about the dissemination of information, then we don't need to ask much of our librarians. Technicians would do nicely in that case. The search for knowledge would be, as they say in the computer industry, "plug and play." This attitude can be found among intelligent, well-meaning people who believe if we can just find the money for the equipment, if we can just stretch enough cable across the planet, we can tear down the medieval walls once and for all.

But as anyone who has ever set up a home computer can tell you, the world definitely is not in a "plug and play" mode. And the problems with hardware and software pale in comparison with the big questions about how we learn, how we want to learn, how we live, and how we want to live.

In our time, information has become a global commodity, as our society shifts from a manufacturing-based to information-based economy. Not all commodities are the same, of course. In the financial world, brokerage houses may deal with everything from junk bonds to Microsoft stock. On the Internet, consumers might choose to visit the Big Ten libraries, or head for a web site dedicated to denying that the Holocaust occurred. Everyone has an equal right to disseminate information, but all information is not created equal. This has led to some difficult problems that everyone here is already familiar with—such as whether public libraries should, for instance, block access to Internet pornography—but I believe more difficult and significant questions lie ahead. I will pose two of them to you today.

First, we must decide how we want to learn in an age of digital information. I am not a critic of distance learning. I believe that courses can be greatly enhanced through the use of web pages. And it is clear that the ability to access libraries and archives across the world is one of the greatest advancements in the history of scholarship. But as many critics of the information age have noted, the advent of personal computers, servers, and networks has raised some disturbing questions about access to education. The enormous outlays required to build and maintain information technology systems concern all of us who are required to sign off on such budgets. Imagine how much worse it is, as parents and employers become increasingly enamored of computer skills, for those who have no such resources. I suspect that some of you in this room don't have to imagine that situation.

It might be more intriguing to turn this problem on its head. It might seem counterintuitive, but the future problems relating to access and technology might be exactly the opposite of what we expect. Instead of poorer students and schools finding themselves left behind in the computer revolution, we might see, in twenty or thirty years, a different type of two-tier system: The wealthier among us would be able to serve our students with real, human teachers, librarians, and other staff, who have their expensive salaries and health benefits. The less-fortunate would enjoy the benefits of a "virtual" education from a "distance."

This might sound improbable, even blasphemous, given the cachet information technology has in our society. But television once had the same kind of excitement surrounding it, too. And imagine if, twenty-five years ago, you had told someone that they would deposit and withdraw money with the aid of a computer instead of a living bank teller. What might have seemed like a futuristic luxury is a source of irritation, once it is realized, for a lot of people. The cost of computing power always goes down, and the cost of staff and faculty and physical plant always goes up. Do you have any doubt which students would really prefer, given the choice between interaction with real, knowledgeable people and the digital byproducts of real, knowledgeable people? Or will we confuse tools with tasks?

The second question is closely related to the first: How do we want to live in an information age? Again, I want to praise all the wonders of our computing systems, our satellite uplinks, and our Internet servers. They are wonderful accessories, and I can't imagine doing without them. But as more talk emerges of a "virtual campus" with "virtual libraries," one does not have to be a Luddite to ask why we would settle for living vicariously through our equipment.

Some tell us that we should look to industry for guidance on this question — that the marketplace has shown higher education the way with its use of telecommunications equipment. I agree that industry often can teach us a thing or two, although I believe just as often it is the other way around. But when we do look for answers from industry, we sometimes learn things we already suspected. For example, Sprint Corporation, the communications giant whose Kansas City-area headquarters is scattered among nearly sixty buildings, is now creating a new headquarters on a 200-acre site at a cost of $700 million. The new complex will have offices, meeting rooms, businesses, and athletic fields. They even call it a campus. When a vice president of the company was asked what motivated the consolidation, he remarked on how great it would be to meet and talk face to face with his colleagues for a change.

Businesses will do what they deem right for themselves. Colleges and universities have to do the same. How do we want to live and learn? We will answer this question differently depending on the situation at hand. We will make mistakes along the way; we already have made some we don't know about yet. No one is really poised to deal with this question in a comprehensive manner, but everyone is trying.

Still, no one group in higher education has better experience or a more informed viewpoint than our librarians. They have long known that they could not equate excellence with the number of volumes on their shelves, but that the essential measure is the ability to readily identify and acquire information that the user needs, wherever it is located. They know the power that new tools have given researchers and students, but they also know that no computer can replace the human skills required to use those tools wisely.

We have politicians to regulate the Internet, or at least argue about it. We have attorneys to debate intellectual property rights. We have college presidents to worry about the expense. We can count on students and faculty to tell us what we're doing wrong and what we could change to make life better for them.

But few social institutions are better equipped than libraries to confront the changes brought on by the rapid evolution of information technology. As a matter of fact, librarians were dealing with this challenge before many of us used the term "information technology." As you continue to deal with it, I urge you—and everyone else in higher education—to keep these factors in mind:

- Again: Our society is moving from manufacturing to information as its economic basis. The skills needed for sustained employment prove not only to be new but also to change constantly. We must not only understand the need to retrain today's workers, but to adjust to the fact that today's students will be life-long learners. What is vitally important today will be obsolete tomorrow.

- The people we serve live in an internationalized marketplace in which national and regional boundaries are coming to mean less and less. We are used to issues of free trade in goods and services, but we have only begun to confront the difficulties of free trade regarding the knowledge business.

- Individuals must make their way in a world of increasingly diverse communities in which massive historical forces have created unparalleled mixtures of race, religion, language, and cultural inheritance. We do not live in what some historians have termed an "age of consensus." We must be ready to adapt to the educational needs of a truly multicultural clientele. We will face barriers of language and custom, but we will be hindered most of all to the extent that we are unwilling to understand and embrace differences.

Any library system that does not recognize the reality of these truths is doomed to failure. Any library system that does not recognize the inherent implications will be ineffective at best and irrelevant at worst. You may stack your computers a mile high, but they will not help you deal with the real consequences of change in our society.

What will help you are the skills that librarians have always brought to their work. In any age, you have shared the responsibility for helping the volumes on your shelves speak to the inner heart of each student. Each of you, in your individual work, resonates through the institutions and the societies you serve.

In an information age—one in which an endless array of words and thoughts are available at the touch of a finger, with seemingly no help from anyone else—we need the guidance of our librarians more than ever. That is not the conventional wisdom, but it should be. When knowledge was jealously held and hesitantly shared, only a few stewards were required. Now, with the explosion of information technology, we require more good stewardship than ever. For as we tear down the old barriers to knowledge, we must ensure that we are not simply putting up fancy new ones.

Contributed Papers

Developing Alternative Resources

A Successful Partnership Library

Nick Lund and Patricia M. Blome

Introduction

Library partnerships, over the years, have been put together in many forms and for many reasons. Probably the most common partnerships have been between K-12 schools and public libraries. The most common reason has been saving money.

The Academic Library is a joint-use library serving the partnership between Northern Arizona University in Yuma and Arizona Western College. The name was changed in 1997 from AWC Library to reflect this growing and prospering partnership between the university and community college.

Northern Arizona University in Yuma has grown from a distance learning site, started in 1988 to serve the needs of geographically distributed students, to what we have today. The shared campus of NAU in Yuma and AWC serves close to 7000 students. Many of these are non-degree seeking students or those pursuing a two-year associate's degree. Approximately ten per cent of Arizona Western College students wish to continue on for their baccalaureate degree while others in the community wish to continue their education beyond that level. However these students do not wish to leave Yuma to continue their education, because of family obligations, career goals, or many other reasons. Unfortunately, the nearest university campus in the state is 180 miles away in Phoenix, Arizona. For this reason, Northern Arizona University, located in Flagstaff, Arizona, set up distance learning centers throughout the state and Yuma is the most developed. We offer more than 30 baccalaureate degrees and 9 graduate degrees including a doctorate in Educational Leadership.

To support these programs, Northern Arizona University provides a budget to purchase library materials to support their programs and one full time professional librarian and one full time paraprofessional librarian. This budget is under the direction of the NAU in Yuma librarian. The librarian works with the Arizona Western College Librarians to provide library services.

Nick Lund is executive director and Pamela M. Blome is a librarian at Northern Arizona University in Yuma.

Literature Review

A review of the literature shows that there are many kinds of partnerships in many kinds of libraries. In "Shared Academic Library Facilities: The Unknown Form of Library Cooperation," Anthony J. Dedrick from Denver, Colorado's Auraria Library tells us that this is not a new phenomenon; he found several programs that have been in operation for over twenty years. He found that most were two-library partnerships between a community college and a university, with community college/public library partnerships also common. He found that management of these libraries varied a great deal. Many had one library director, but some had employees paid by both institutions. Some had separate directors for the separate institutions. Funding was also diverse. For some it was decided yearly. Others had a percentage from each institution's budget. About 50 per cent of the libraries studied said that their budget increased as a result of the joint program, others reported that their budgets stayed the same. Some had concerns that budgets would be decreased because the joint program was more efficient and as a consequence, their institutions would use this success as a pretext to reduce library funding. The majority did say, "some type of separate budget accounting is maintained for each school." (Dedrick, 441) In general Dedrick reported that there were many advantages of the partnerships including: a larger acquisitions budget, better utilization of staff, reduced physical plant costs, eliminated cost of a new facility, access to a larger collection, ability to purchase more reference materials and products, expanded hours of service. Of course Dedrick reported some negative comments, primarily administrative difficulties, such as tracking multiple budgets, developing programs and services to meet the needs of separate institutions with different missions and student populations, and separate payroll systems and personnel policies. He said that there were two clear patterns to emerge from his study: "(1) the typical shared academic library facility program does provide significant cost savings and service enhancements, and (2) there are inherently additional administrative burdens with these types of arrangements." (Dedrick, 441)

Geraldine Evans, in an ERIC document published in 1994, described the partnership between the Rochester Community College and Winona State University in Minnesota. She described a "2 plus 2" program similar to our partnership with Arizona Western College and Northern Arizona University in Yuma. Her article emphasized the history of the partnership and the financial benefit to the institutions. (Evans, 4)

In an article entitled, "Partnerships: Doors to the Future for Community Colleges," Norman R. Nielsen discussed multiple kinds of partnerships which could benefit community colleges. In a study by Kirkwood Community College (Iowa) they felt that "strong partnerships with both public and private agencies would meet the growing challenges for higher education in the nineties."(Nielsen, 3) Nielsen described several very successful partnerships between community colleges and private companies.

In "Joint-use libraries: more bang for your bucks," Sally Kinsey and Sharon Honig-Bear describe the partnership in Reno, Nevada between Washoe County Library and the Washoe County School District. They describe the benefits of their joint-use facilities and emphasize that "Agency boards and administrators look good when they cooperate and maximize resources. Students, teachers and the public gain enhanced services." (Kinsey, 37) Another point that they made was to be successful, "the top administrator and boards of these agencies must fully endorse the joint-use idea." They also point out that "smart government agencies understand that networking and resource sharing make them look good."

In "Joint-Use Library Services at Distant Campuses: Building Cooperation Between a Community College and a University," Yvonne L. Ralston and Adele Oldenburg discuss many aspects of these partnerships. They discuss how Florida was a pioneer in this area in 1972 with their *The Master Plan for Florida Post-Secondary Education* which created branch campuses and pioneered the development of 2 + 2 programs. They stress that the needs of community college and university students are different and that Interlibrary Loan between the smaller campuses and the universities would be very important. Universities would be primarily the loaners and the community colleges would be primary borrowers; but universities should accept this sacrifice as necessary. (Ralston, 144) They recommend that the sites build their collection to support their curriculum, and the university would supply access to other materials at other sites. This very thorough article also gave a checklist of what the primary issues would be and that they should be in writing. This list included mission and goals, lending policies, resolutions of conflict, advisory committee, acquisitions, etc.

Another article that looked at shared libraries in Florida was Susan Anderson's "Shared Libraries: Focus on Florida." She looked at the various kinds of partnerships that are possible and gave recommendations based on the varied experiences in Florida. In the case of Edison Community College and the University of South Florida, both institutions purchase materials, but they are intershelved with each institution identifying its own materials. Fiscal responsibility is based on the head counts for the two institutions. They also use a courier service between sites.

In looking at the literature on partnerships, I would say that in our partnership here at Northern Arizona University in Yuma and Arizona Western College's Academic Library, we implement the best of their recommendations, in a combination that has been very successful for us.

What is working for us now

The Librarian-Generalist for Northern Arizona University in Yuma is considered to be part of staff of Northern Arizona University's Cline Library staff. She works with this staff to provide library services to NAU's students in Yuma. This librarian also reports to the Associate Director, Dr. Thomas Tacke and the Executive Director, Dr. Nick Lund of Northern Arizona University in Yuma. Dr. Lund reports directly to the President of Northern Arizona University, Dr. Clara Lovett. In some respects, the administration, faculty and staff of NAU in Yuma are considered another college of Northern Arizona University, in the same way that the College of Business is a college of Northern Arizona University. The partnership between Northern Arizona University in Yuma and Arizona Western College is very important to these individuals and all involved feel that this partnership is tied very much into the continuing success of these institutions and the success of our mutual students.

The Arizona Western College Library staff reports to the Associate Dean of Instructional Technology. This individual is responsible for Arizona Western College's library services, interactive television services, computer services and their learning assistance center. Because the Associate Dean of Learning Resources has other responsibilities in addition to the library, the actual running of the library is in the charge of the three AWC librarians and the NAU librarian. The Arizona Western College staff consists of three professional librarians, two full-time paraprofessionals, and six to eight half-time paraprofessional employees.

We have evolved a team or consensus approach to running the library. We have informally divided up the primary responsibilities according to our strengths and interests. For example, this author supervises bibliographic/technical services. One AWC librarian is in charge of computer support, the second is in charge of circulation services and the third supervises reference. However, the librarians do all of these jobs, in addition to planning, bibliographic instruction, book selection, serials, etc. It is just good to have one single, final authority for cataloging or reference policy or other questions that can come up regularly in any busy library. Generally, we discuss the gray areas when a clarification is necessary, and then make sure, if there is a change in policy or procedure, that all affected are made aware of the change. The library also employs student workers from both NAU and AWC.

Book selection is also done by all of our librarians and we have divided up the subject areas again based on our strengths and interests. We ask for input from the faculty of both institutions. When recommendations are made, we will specify if the item is more appropriate for the NAU in Yuma curriculum or AWC, and then it will be ordered out of the appropriate budget. While the library keeps track of which institution pays for which books, they are all stamped Academic Library, not NAU-Yuma or AWC. Often we will consult with each other on these choices, especially if we see a review for an item that is from another's subject area. If an Arizona Western Librarian sees something, which they feel is more appropriate for supporting the Northern Arizona University in Yuma classes, they usually want my input in the decision. Our open communication and dialog helps to make this process go smoothly.

One of the key factors in our success is that all of our acquisitions, budgets, ordering, and bookkeeping for the library is handled by one person. This person is our Northern Arizona University paraprofessional. All our materials orders go through her. This eliminates the possibility of duplicate orders and facilitates working together with two separate budgets. She works very closely with all the librarians and the AWC Associate Dean of Instructional Technology.

Another key factor in our success can simply be stated as attitude. When a patron comes into the library, we serve them. The library cards are issued by the library, which means that they do not say on them if them if the student is an NAU or an AWC student (the computer knows, of course). Although NAU students make up only about ten per cent of the population on campus, they are much more likely to use the library than their AWC counterparts. This is primarily due to their differing education goals. The NAU students are upperclassmen or graduate students and therefore have more compelling reasons for using the library. NAU students make the majority of our interlibrary loan requests, but our ILL librarian is an employee of Arizona Western College. To better serve all university students in Arizona, there is a courier service between the three universities. Northern Arizona University in Yuma was included in this courier service, which gives overnight delivery of books and materials from one campus to another. We use document delivery software to transmit periodical articles between the universities also. These services greatly increase the resources available to students and supplement our 50,000-volume library!

All of the librarians give library tours and bibliographic instruction. Which librarian gives the session is determined by their schedules more than by the employer or whether the session is for an AWC class or an NAU class. The librarians often work together in creating bibliographies and other handouts to give to the students. In the case of very large classes, two librarians may work together or split the group into two for their instruction.

Northern Arizona University is committed to providing a university education to Arizona residents wherever they reside in the state. To this end they have well-developed statewide Services. This is particularly true of their Library State Wide Services. The well-developed statewide sites have Internet access to the databases to which NAU subscribes to in much the same way as the on-campus students do. All Northern Arizona University students can access these databases through their home computers, also, using their e-mail account information. Because three of the computers in our library, with Internet access, belong to NAU and are considered part of the Cline Library on the Northern Arizona University campus in Flagstaff, they have direct access to these databases without the need to log in. This access is analogous to a community college student, high school student, or any other local patron going into the Cline Library in Flagstaff and using their reference computers.

The majority of the Arizona Western College students who use the library are in pursuit of their bachelor's degree and most will matriculate to Northern Arizona University, either in Yuma or Flagstaff upon completion of their lower division classes. In that sense, they are our freshmen and sophomores. Many students are co-enrolled in both institutions. Also, some of the Arizona Western College faculty will teach NAU classes as adjunct faculty and therefore have loyalty to both institutions. The Arizona Western College and Northern Arizona University in Yuma advisors and financial aid people work together to make the transition from one institution to the other as seamless and painless as possible.

Northern Arizona University in Yuma has distance sites within the region that they work very closely with. Because Arizona Western College offers classes in San Luis, Somerton, and Parker, Arizona, as well as a couple of other sites, Northern Arizona University in Yuma also teaches classes at those sites, some in person, some through interactive television, and others through the Internet.

A Successful Partnership Library

These students can receive library services directly from the Cline Library in Flagstaff or from the Academic Library in Yuma. Arizona Western College is working very hard to improve services to their distance students and our librarians have visited the sites and are working with the faculty and staff at the sites to improve their library services. The NAU librarian is on this committee and is working to improve library services for all of our students, AWC and NAU. One avenue we are pursuing is creating partnerships for these remote sites with their local public libraries.

The Academic Library has other partners in addition to the partnership between Northern Arizona University in Yuma and Arizona Western College. This library has shared its library catalog with the Yuma County Library District for many years. This was motivated mainly for the cost savings of a shared system. These two partners are now on their second system, the original was a "home grown" system, which had outlived its usefulness and was replaced in 1998 by a SIRSI Unicorn System. Sharing the systems has been very cost-effective for both parties involved. We also work together when we have problems to solve them. It is convenient for both our students and their patrons to be able to easily check each other's holdings when we don't own the book or item which the student or patron may need. At times, we may choose not to order a particular book because the County Library owns it and we don't anticipate that the demand would justify that more than one copy is needed for the area.

The Future

Northern Arizona University in Yuma has seen that this partnership with Arizona Western College has been a good one for all involved. The main campus of Northern Arizona University has looked to Yuma as the model, when they design and improve their other distance sites. NAU in Yuma is always looking for other ways to partner that will also be of mutual beneficial to the college, university, and the community. One proposal put forth would be to create a community joint use library. There is already a K–20+ consortium in place between the University, Community College, and the Yuma Public Schools. This consortium is already taking care of busing and vehicle maintenance for the institutions. The campus which NAU in Yuma and AWC occupy would have room for a large joint use library to be used by the public schools as well as the university and college. Northern Arizona University in Yuma and Arizona Western College currently share their campus with two elementary schools and a middle school. Two of these schools were just completed in the last year and this reflects the rapid growth in this part of Yuma County.

Last year Northern Arizona University in Yuma, Arizona Western College and the Public Schools received a grant from U.S. West to provide Internet instruction and access for K–12 students, teachers, businesses, and the community, which was held in Northern Arizona University in Yuma and Arizona Western College's Academic Complex Building, with state-of-the-art computer labs and classrooms. Faculty and staff members from both the university and community college volunteered to assist with this training. The partnership would like to offer more of this type of training to the community in the future, with or without a grant.

Conclusions

The Academic Library serving Northern Arizona University in Yuma and Arizona Western College is a successful partnership library. This success is due to a commitment by the administration, faculty, and staff of Northern Arizona University, Northern Arizona University in Yuma, and Arizona Western College. In the library, the librarians and staff feel that we have no choice, we must serve all of our patrons fairly, whether they are students, faculty, staff or community members. This is an attitude that says that there is always room for improvement, and we work everyday to improve our services to all of our patrons.

Bibliography

Anderson, Susan. 1990. "Shared Libraries: Focus on Florida." *Community & Junior College Libraries* 7:1, 3–16.

Clark, Linda M. & Tullar, Phil. 1995. *Three Governmental Entities Collaborate to Build a Satellite Community College Campus in Northern Ari-*

zona: Working Together to Create a 'One Stop Learning Center'. ERIC Document Reproduction Service No. ED 395 618.

Dedrick, Anthony J. 1997, September. "Shared academic library facilities: the unknown form of library cooperation," *College and research libraries* 55, 437–43.

Evans, Geraldine A. 1994. *The University Center at Rochester: Rochester, Minnesota*. ERIC Document Reproduction Service No. ED 382 059.

Kinsey, Sally and Sharon Honig-Bear. 1994 November. "Joint-Use Libraries: More Bang for Your Bucks," *Wilson Library Bulletin*, 69:3. 37–39, 132.

Maxwell, James D. 1992. *A Summary of the Online Public Access Catalog Merger between the Library of the Franklin University and the Columbus Ohio Metropolitan Library and an Analysis of the Intralibrary Loan Relationship*. Unpublished master's thesis, Kent State University, Ohio.

McNamara, Jay R. and Delmus E. Williams. 1992. "High School Students and Libraries in Public Universities," *Academic Libraries in Urban and Metropolitan Areas*. New York: Greenwood Pr. 55–65.

Nielsen, Norman R. 1994, May. "Partnerships: Doors to the future for Community Colleges," *Leadership Abstracts* 7:5, 3–4.

Ralston, Yvonne L. and Adele Oldenburg. 1992. "Joint-Use Library Services at Distant Campuses: Building Cooperation between a Community College and a University." In *Academic Libraries in Urban and Metropolitan Areas: A Management Handbook*. New York: Greenwood Pr. 142–56.

Automated Storage and Retrieval—The Next Generation: How Northridge's Success is Spurring a Revolution in Library Storage and Circulation

Sarah Elizabeth Kirsch

Abstract

The first automated storage and retrieval system combined with an online catalog was heralded as a "pilot project" when it was introduced in 1990 at California State University at Northridge (CSUN). Librarians across the country were watching to see whether the system would succeed or fail. The automated storage and retrieval system's integration of industrial technology and an online catalog appeared to be an excellent solution to many libraries' storage problems. Since the CSUN installation, there has been little discussion in the library literature either about the exciting possibilities of automated storage and retrieval systems or the possible drawbacks of such systems. Despite the possible drawbacks, many libraries are installing automated storage and retrieval systems to meet their storage needs.

The presentation of this paper will begin with a short survey to demonstrate the audience's knowledge of automated storage and retrieval. The discussion of the audience's answers will lead into the beginning of the paper.

The paper will examine the current state of automated storage and retrieval. Beginning with the promising system installation at California State University at Northridge, the paper will consider both the expected advantages and actual advantages of the CSUN system. (One unexpected advantage is the system's resistance to earthquakes).

The paper will also discuss the forthcoming system installations at Simon Fraser University, Eastern Michigan University, and University of Nevada, Las Vegas. This discussion will explore the effect the CSUN system has had upon auto-

Sarah Elizabeth Kirsch is assistant social studies librarian at Southern Illinois University at Carbondale.

mated storage and retrieval systems' popularity. The paper will conclude by anticipating the future of automated storage and retrieval systems in academic libraries.

The lack of library space at California State University at Northridge (CSUN) could no longer be ignored. By 1990 the University's Oviatt Library would have a space deficit of 72,985 square feet. It is a well-known fact that "Large research libraries do not, by and large, ever dispose of any of their materials and the result is that their collections increase each year." The library administration knew they had to expand the library, but communication with the university chancellor's office led them to expect that there would not be money to provide for a facility to house the library's growing collection in open stack shelving.

They had a limited number of options remaining. Because the need for space was immediate, digitizing their collection was not an option. Compact shelving, remote storage, and regional depositories were all carefully considered, but the most attractive option they discussed was installing an automated storage and retrieval system in the proposed addition to the library.

Automated storage and retrieval technology had been used in the industrial world since the 1950s. The technology's original function was to do away with "the walking that accounted for 70% of manual retrieval time." An automated storage and retrieval system consists of aisles between rows of frames containing bins or pallets. Up and down the aisles, between the rows of frames, the robotic crane mechanism journeys at the whim of its operator. In accordance with its operator's instructions, the robot selects a bin or pallet and transports it to the appropriate station. When the bin or pallet is no longer needed, it is returned to storage by the robot. Automated storage and retrieval technology may be adapted for library use by bar-coding each book and bin. The computer links each book to a bin. When a book leaves the system, the link is deleted. Upon the book's return to the system, the linking process is repeated. The edge of a book may be coded with a part of the id number so that the staff member who receives the bin will have an easier job of finding one book among the hundred in the bin.

CSUN's library administrators were not the first to consider the possibilities of such a system for use in a library. Four automated storage and retrieval systems had been installed in American libraries in the 1970s. This first generation of library installations had met with disaster. Problems with suppliers, unanticipated maintenance costs, crude equipment, primitive computer control, and ignorance of user requirements had the combined effect of making these library installations a nightmare to the staff and a laughing stock to American libraries.

In contrast to the failure in America, the contemporaneous installation at Erasmus University, Rotterdam, the Netherlands survived. Their initial system installation did not work properly either. Much money and time was invested to make the Erasmus installation work. The changes made over the years included adding microprocessor computer controls, adding an error detection system and funding periodic maintenance, as well as developing an interface between the automated storage and retrieval system and their public catalog.

The Erasmus success story left little doubt that an automated storage and retrieval system could be operated effectively in a library. The question was whether improvements in technology since the late 1960s and lessons learned from both the success and failure of automated storage and retrieval systems in libraries made it desirable to try another American installation in the 1990s. CSUN thought that the experiment was worth trying. According to their research, an automated storage and retrieval system was the most economical choice available to them. They could store books in 1/12 of the space of open stack shelving at 1/4 of the cost.

Not only would such a facility be less expensive, but also the environment could be regulated for the comfort of books rather than humans. Usually the darkness, humidity settings, and temperatures ideal for book preservation must be adjusted in a library for the comfort of its users. Because the library users and staff would not be inside the enclosed automated storage and retrieval system, the atmosphere could be set and maintained at ideal preservation levels. Books printed on acid paper that are stored in an automated storage and retrieval system will last 40 years longer than if they were on open shelves. Not having to install lighting, wall coverings, floor coverings, and false ceilings in the storage area also saves on expense.

Another benefit of such a system is that tracking the actual location of an item would be much simpler. Far fewer would be the moments of frustration for both library users and library staff as the staff attempt to explain to the users that a book may not be "available" even though it is listed as such on the computerized online catalog.

Perhaps an advantage more apparent to the user would be the shortness of retrieval time, which was estimated to be around 5 minutes. The ability to request items electronically and pick them up within minutes eliminates the user's frustration at searching the aisles and floors of an unfamiliar library.

The real usage of an item could be more accurately estimated, because the items checked out of the automated storage facility would be checked out twice, once for use in the building and again if the user desired to take them out of the library. Over time, this would enable the staff to adjust what was stored in the facility to conform to real usage. Any items in storage receiving a lot of use could be relocated to the open shelves. An added bonus of this record keeping would be greater security. There would be far fewer instances of mutilation and fewer missing items.

If CSUN's experiment worked, libraries would no longer have to store their rarely used items in buildings on the remote edges of campuses. Library users would no longer have to wait hours or days to receive items from storage. Therefore not only the CSUN community was intrigued by the idea of this experiment, but the entire academic library community.

The disadvantages of such a system were also considered. One obvious disadvantage of an automated storage and retrieval system is that it is enclosed. The library user may only stand outside and watch through windows as the robotic mechanism follows its instructions. Here there is no serendipitous browsing of shelves. The books are in bins, and may be stored randomly. For materials in the storage facility, the users have to rely on the computerized online catalog. Another disadvantage is the possibility of equipment failure. Such failure would effectively cut the size of the library's collection in half, causing distress to its users.

CSUN did not ignore these potential problem areas. They hired a full-time technician for the system to minimize mechanical problems. Because of the lack of browsing, they took great care in selecting items for storage. CSUN decided to store periodicals published before 1990 and books that were not used very often. It has turned out that of the library's annual book loans, only 15% are books in the automated storage and retrieval system.

CSUN has been delighted with the success of their automated storage and retrieval system, which began operating in June of 1991. In a 1994 earthquake no books in the storage facility were damaged, although nearly all of the books on the open shelves ended up on the floor. They had a few software problems in the beginning, which have since been solved. Overall, they report "very little downtime and no long-term maintenance headaches."

Now, fifteen years after CSUN's facility was first conceived, other libraries are installing automated storage and retrieval facilities. Eastern Michigan University has installed such a system in its new Bruce T. Halle Library. The Dean of Learning Resources and Technologies wanted the expensive floor space to be used for people rather than books. Having an automated storage and retrieval system allows for more study spaces and computer workstations. The 30-foot high system is in a vault which houses 6500 storage bins each capable of holding 100 to 140 books. At full capacity it will hold 800,000 books, though it is less than half full now. The automated storage and retrieval system cost $1.6 million and an additional $100,000 for software totaling $1.7 million. It has saved 50,000 square feet of floor space.

Although the Dean is proud and excited about this technology, he acknowledges that "just like any computerized technology, when its down, it's down." To avoid system problems, EMU bought a 20-year supply of major spare parts and employs the equivalent of 1 1/2 full-time workers to care for its automated storage and retrieval system.

An upcoming installation will begin operation with the January 2000 opening of the new Lied Library at the University of Nevada-Las Vegas. Inspired by the success at Northridge, the Dean of the Library sold the idea to the legislators. They chose to economize by building a 300,000 square foot library with a $2.2 million automated storage and retrieval system instead of constructing a 425,00 square foot library.

This system's specifications indicate that it will closely resemble CSUN's system. To begin with, the 40-foot high system will have three aisles, with three additional aisles to be added at a later date. Its height will measure three stories and it will take up about 1,300 square feet of floor space This application differs from CSUN's in that a sizable portion of UNLV's collection designated for storage are depository government documents.

Yet another library poised to follow CSUN's example is Canada's Simon Fraser University (SFU). SFU's library administration chose automated storage and retrieval only after careful consideration of all of their storage options and consultation with many university committees. The proposed robotic storage system had duly been added to the university's capital plan. A report of the Library External Review Committee in May of 1998 indicated that the university community was not convinced of the value of such a system. They opposed their loss of access and ability to browse. They suggested that SFU may be guilty of trendiness. The Library External Review Committee proposed further studies and reports. It is to be hoped that as more automated storage and retrieval system installations are successful, the need for this kind of justification will diminish.

Users are concerned that they will lose the open stacks that have been around since the 1940s, which were revolutionary for their day. They see in the enclosed nature of an automated storage and retrieval system the steel prisons of multitier structural stack shelving (closed stacks) that were used in the hundred years before their beloved open stacks gave users the freedom to browse.

Therefore, users must be convinced that the choice is not between an automated storage and retrieval system or open shelves, but rather between an automated storage and retrieval system or remote storage, an automated storage and retrieval system or boxes of books stacked up to the ceiling with nowhere to put them.

Having found neither closed stack shelving nor open stack shelving to be entirely satisfactory, CSUN and its followers have found that by using automated storage and retrieval technology they can economically combine the two shelving models to their best advantage. CSUN has developed a new paradigm for the academic research library.

Changing Collaborations to Deliver Information in New Ways: Lessons Learned in the Illinois Digital Library Initiative Project

Timothy Cole and William Mischo

Introduction

Since the inception of the scientific journal in 1665, libraries and sci-tech publishers have enjoyed a synergistic and symbiotic relationship centered around the production and dissemination of the paper-based journal. In this traditional relationship, publishers have been responsible for acquiring content, packaging it, and distributing it. The role of the library has been to purchase the published product, organize it, make it accessible and then archive it for posterity. In FY '97 the ARL libraries purchased (across all disciplines) over $411 million in paper-format journals. The advent and growth of electronic journals, however, has begun to change this traditional relationship, and we can anticipate that the relationship will continue to evolve in the future.

The overall objectives—the acquisition, organization, dissemination, and preservation of information—haven't altered or become less important, but changes in journal format and delivery mechanisms are altering the ways in which libraries and publishers accomplish these objectives. As the information industry moves from paper-based to electronic journals and as publishers become involved in mounting their own complex information systems, the roles of publishers and libraries are changing. As users modify the way in which they access and process information, the responsibilities of those providing information services also change. This paper discusses our experiences with these evolving roles and responsibilities in the context of University of Illinois at Urbana-Champaign (UIUC) Digital Library Initiative (DLI) grant project. In this project we have explored issues connected with the local processing, loading, and indexing of electronic journals by libraries and mechanisms for extending the functionality of electronic journals.

The UIUC DLI Testbed

In the fall of 1994 UIUC was awarded a DLI grant

Timothy Cole is systems librarian for digital projects and associate professor of library administration, and William Mischo is director of Grainger Engineering Library, University of Illinois at Urbana-Champaign.

to explore and develop new ways of delivering the full content of scholarly journals to users. In partnership with five leading publishers of scientific and technical journals and in consultation with a half-a-dozen other publishers in the field, the UIUC Library has built an online testbed presently containing approximately 60,000 full-content articles from 63 scholarly journals published since January 1995. The initial 4-year grant was funded jointly by the National Science Foundation, the Advanced Research Projects Agency, and the National Aeronautics and Space Administration. A follow-on 3-year grant funded by the Corporation for National Research Initiatives (CNRI) and the participating publishing partners began in the fall of 1998 at the expiration of the original grant. The goals of the ongoing UIUC DLI testbed project are:

- to create and make accessible to end-users a large-scale, multi-publisher, distributed repository of SGML/XML-formatted full-content journal literature in selected fields of science and engineering;
- to investigate issues relating to the local processing, indexing, normalization (including through use of metadata), retrieval, and rendering of journal literature in digital format;
- to study end user searching behavior and needs when using such materials online;
- to develop scalable models for effective dissemination and retrieval of information in an electronic full-content publishing environment;
- to evaluate methods for integrating full-content publishing resources with existing library information systems and services.

Key to the success of the project has been the identification and development of new relationships between the Library and journal publishers and between the Library and others, both on campus and off, involved in providing information services. The UIUC DLI project was created as a collaboration between the UIUC Library, the (then) National Center for Supercomputing Applications (NCSA), the UIUC Computer Science Department, and the UIUC Graduate School of Library and Information Science. Outside collaborators have included a core group of sci-tech publishers, researchers in the Computer Science Department at the University of Arizona, and a number of commercial computer software and hardware vendors.

Testbed Technologies

When work on the UIUC DLI project began, NCSA's Mosaic 2.0 beta was the browser of choice, the HTML 2.0 standard was still under development, Netscape had yet to release its first web browser, and Microsoft Windows 3.1 was the most common PC operating system. The initial task of the testbed project team was to identify technologies that were both of sufficient maturity to be usable at once and of sufficient potential to evolve over the life of the project.

First it was necessary to settle on a testbed document format standard. The ideal format would support full-text indexing; high-granularity, field-specific search and retrieval; and robust, platform-independent rendering. While no existing format matched all criteria and it was immediately obvious that HTML 2.0 fell far short of desired structure and rendering functionality, three other document format standards showed promise.

1. Standard Generalized Markup Language (SGML), a non-proprietary, international standard, was the best of the formats available in terms of exposing the intellectual structure of documents. The Text Encoding Initiative (TEI) was built around SGML and pilot, full-content journal publishing projects using SGML were then underway at OCLC. Rendering engines for SGML were weak, however.

2. TeX and LaTeX, were well established in the mathematical sciences academic community and supported extremely robust rendering of mathematics, but available authoring and viewing tools were limited and were largely UNIX-based. Exposure of document structure in TeX as used in real-world applications was limited.

3. PDF, an Adobe-proprietary format, provided the best emulation of the printed page. Adobe Acrobat reader was free and available for multiple platforms. However, PDF lacked (as of 1994) important hyperlink functionality and vital (for our project) cross-collection indexing features. It also was then, and remains today, a primarily appearance-oriented format.

In the end, SGML was chosen because it was non-proprietary and inherently best both for indexing and for search and retrieval. This was a decision made in consultation with perspective publishing partners. Though all had experience with the 3 formats under consideration, most favored SGML or SGML with embedded TeX for mathematical equations. The assumption was made that SGML rendering would catch up. To compensate for immediate SGML rendering limitations several of the publishers provided PDF versions of articles in conjunction with SGML versions.

Choosing an index/search engine was the next task. OpenText was chosen because it could exploit the strengths of SGML. (The OpenText search engine grew out of work done at the University of Waterloo to create and index the SGML version of the Oxford English Dictionary.) OpenText also had attractive features for indexing document metadata in conjunction with document full-text, for normalizing documents created with different publisher Document Type Definitions (DTDs), and for maintaining multiple, distributed repositories. Additionally, OpenText's architecture allowed us to integrate 3rd party tools, implement locally developed scripts and code, bypass OpenText modules we didn't need, and rapidly change processing procedures in response to dynamic research needs.

Originally the UIUC DLI project had expected to influence generic web client development by influencing development of the NCSA Mosaic web browser. This proved a naïve expectation. We quickly realized that search and delivery of testbed materials needed to be done in a browser-neutral manner. A focus of the testbed project has been the development of server-side scripts and CGI executables. For our servers, we've used both NT and UNIX operating system platforms as appropriate to task. Off-the-shelf webservers are used (initially Apache and the European Microsoft Windows NT Academic Center webservers, more recently Netscape Enterprise and Microsoft Internet Information Server webservers). Webserver functionality is extended using both conventional CGI and more advanced techniques such as Microsoft's Active Server Platform (ASP). HTTPS protocols (HTTP with Secure Socket Layers) are used for user authentication and authorization as required. HTTP protocols are used for all other interactions with clients.

Accomplishments to Date

By design the testbed is heterogeneous. Materials have been provided by five publishers: the American Institute of Physics (AIP); the American Physical Society (APS); the American Society of Civil Engineers; the Computer Society of the Institute of Electrical and Electronics Engineers (IEEE-CS); and the Institution of Electrical Engineers (IEE). These materials are created by various software systems and transmitted to us by various means (e.g., FTP, CD, and magnetic tape). Though all articles are provided in SGML, each publisher uses a different DTD (implying different tagging semantics). Materials are stored on multiple servers, and the indexes reside on different servers than those on which the articles reside. Our most significant accomplishment to date has been the demonstration of the viability of this distributed, heterogeneous repository model.

A variety of techniques have been used to accomplish this end result. Figure 1 shows the processing flow for the testbed. Materials are received from publishers and distributed to repository document servers. Pre-processing scripts are run which embed links to associated figures, check character entities, and extract and create a metadata file for each document (using RDF syntax and Dublin Core semantics supplemented with project-specific elements). Metadata is heavily used in the testbed both to normalize searching and to maintain link information between objects in the testbed and related objects external to the testbed. The project-specific metadata semantics go well beyond the minimal metadata tagging semantics of the Dublin Core and similar schema designed for general use on the Web.

OpenText indices are then built. Metadata is indexed along with full-text of the articles. Indices can be searched separately or in parallel. Tag aliasing is applied to support normalized searching. CGI and ASP scripts are used to enhance search functionality, insert hyperlink information, perform transformations between SGML, XML, and HTML, and facilitate linking between testbed objects and related information both within and external to the testbed.

Document repositories, metadata repositories, and the actual indices can be maintained on sepa-

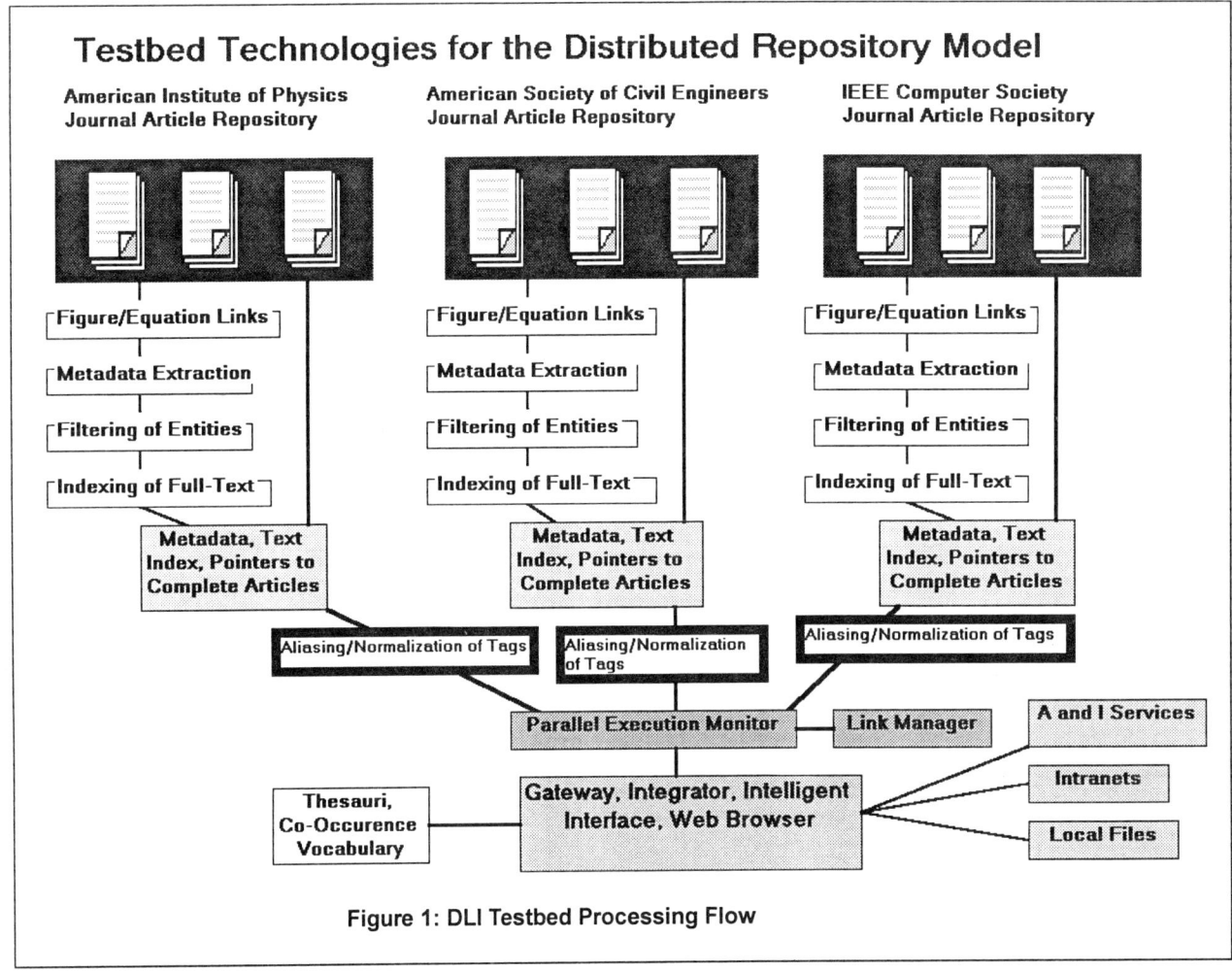

Figure 1: DLI Testbed Processing Flow

rate servers and can be searched separately or simultaneously. Figure 2 provides another view of the testbed architecture. Web browsers communicate (via HTTP & HTTPS) with CGI and ASP gateways that search the testbed indices. These indices were built from document and metadata repositories that may be collocated or distributed. Indices contain pointers both to testbed documents and to information resources in other systems. The gateways can filter links sent back to the client based on client characteristics and established authorization.

The system has been available to end users campus-wide at UIUC since October 1997, and at Notre Dame University for the past 6 months. 10,106 **end-user** search sessions have been conducted to date.

Lessons Learned

1. The potential of SGML (and now XML) has been borne out by experience. The full-text indices are extremely rich, supporting a measure of search precision unavailable in previous full-text search systems. Figure 3 shows the search fields available to end-users in the current interface. SGML has greatly facilitated extraction of metadata and insertion of hyperlinks to related resources within and external to the testbed.

2. Rendering of complex mathematical markup continues to be problematic. Until recently we relied solely on the Panorama SGML viewer originally marketed by SoftQuad. In spite of promises to improve the rendering engine, development has lagged (Panorama was recently sold to Interleaf) and there still isn't a version of Panorama for the

Macintosh. Rapid development of XML, advances in the latest version of HTML, and development of Cascading Style Sheets are improving prospects for better rendering. Nonetheless, our experience with Panorama demonstrates the degree to which libraries and information providers are dependent on the commercial sector for essential technology.

3. A detailed transaction log analysis of 4,158 end-user search sessions has been conducted.

Several interesting results have been gleaned from the transaction logs. These include: there is very little use being made of either 'Help' or 'Quicktips' functions; browsing of tables of contents is being performed in 39% of the search sessions; full-text searching is the predominant search mode, but in 24% of the sessions users chose a specific field; full-text is displayed in more sessions (69%) than extended citations (19%); in 25% of the sessions, users do multi-concept searching; and an average of 4 full-text documents are viewed per session.

4. Overall development of the testbed has taken longer than anticipated. With some notable exceptions (e.g., the lack of a robust SGML viewer), the technology needed has been available by the time needed. The development of processing procedures, the normalization of DTDs, and the development and implementation of metadata semantics have taken longer than anticipated. Technology infrastructure changes happen much more quickly than process changes that involve changing how libraries and information providers do their jobs.

5. Implementation of a digital information resource requires tighter integration of the parties involved. Small changes by a publisher in tagging semantics can require corresponding changes in indexing scripts, metadata extraction procedures, and further downstream, style sheet design. Conversely changes in browser software or rendering client can necessitate changes in tagging and indexing. Because each of these tasks may be performed by a different agency, close, efficient working relationships are essential.

6. In the electronic journal environment, roles and responsibilities are more fluid. While documents may reside on a publisher's server, metadata may reside elsewhere (e.g., on an abstracting and indexing service's hardware). Different agencies may create different metadata for the same objects (e.g., using different controlled vocabularies). Libraries may implement their own gateways and portals, or may contract for such services with consortia or other 3rd parties. A single article may be found through different gateways, using different

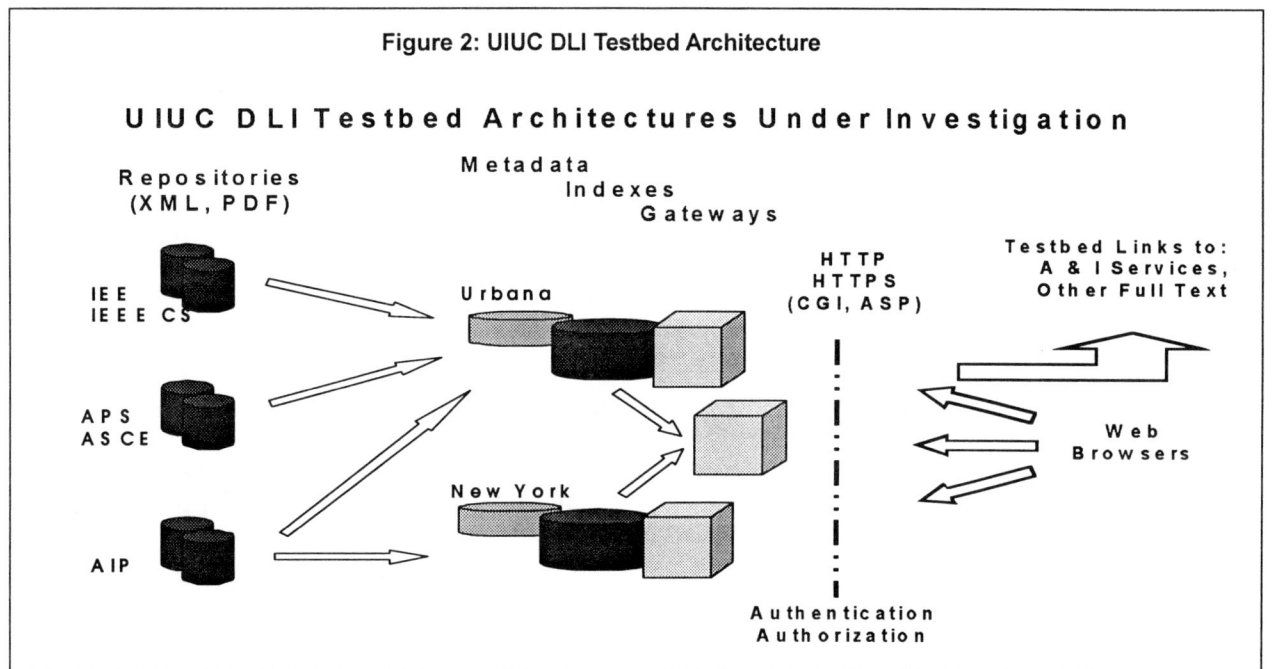

Figure 2: UIUC DLI Testbed Architecture

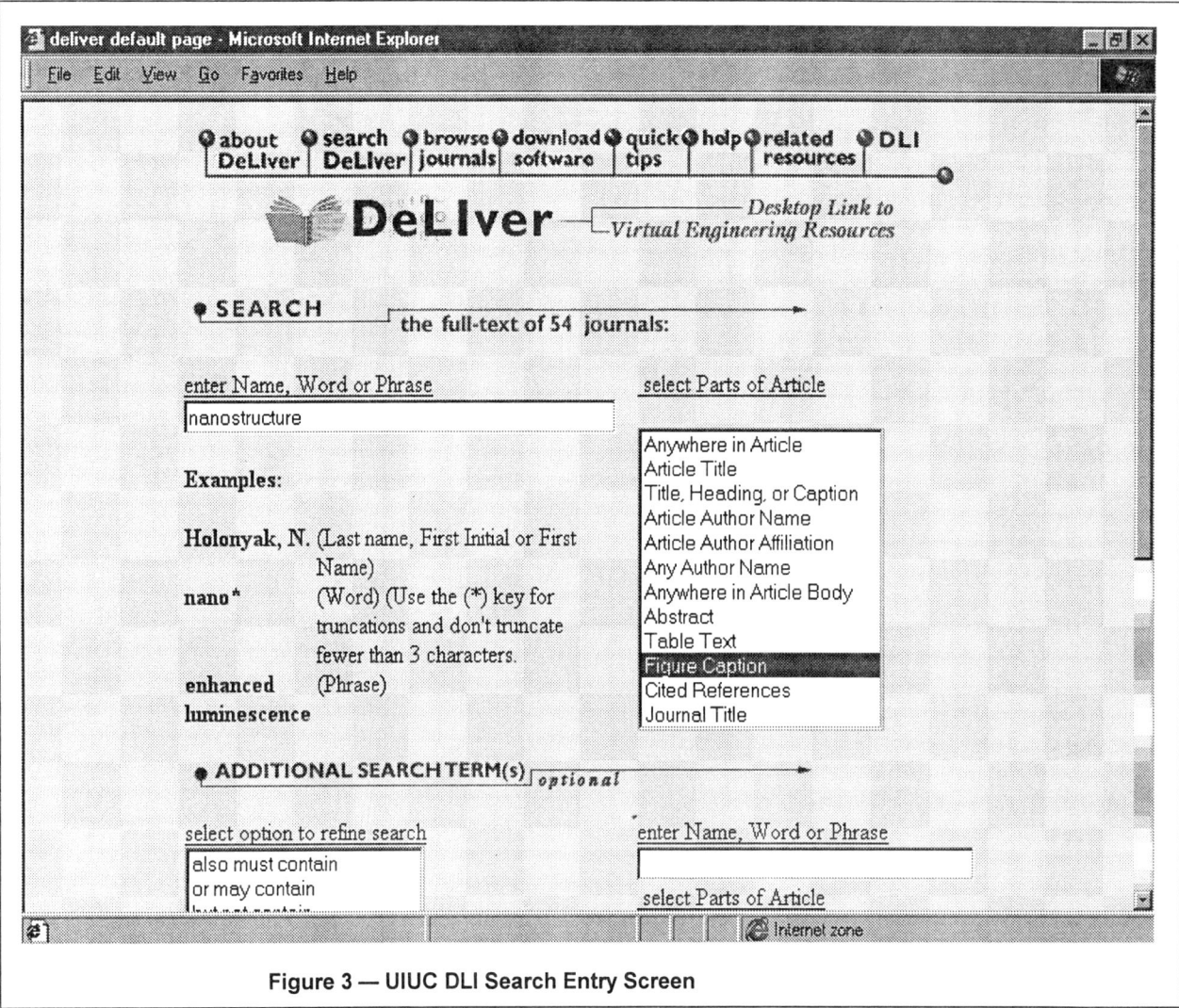

Figure 3 — UIUC DLI Search Entry Screen

index and metadata providers, even if full content of the article itself still comes from a single publisher's server. Archival responsibilities may be distributed between libraries, consortia, and publishers.

7. In the rapidly evolving electronic journals environment, academic libraries will need to re-examine their collection development policies in terms of ownership vs. access, become more actively involved in institutional and consortial licensing agreements, and become more actively involved in campus networking, server, and workstation policies and technologies.

Future Foci

In the remaining years of this project additional issues and technologies will be investigated.

1. The entire testbed was recently converted to XML. Testbed articles are now retrievable in XML and HTML as well as in PDF and SGML. This has already improved rendering options and overall quality. The potential of the Math ML standard to support even better rendering of testbed content will be investigated.

2. Further testing of distributed architecture models will be done to test scalability and performance of the options.

3. The use of Document Object Identifiers (DOIs) and other emerging standards to enhance and facilitate link management will be investigated.

4. Dynamic search mechanisms (e.g., word

wheels to facilitate data entry, vocabulary switching to enhance search recall) will be integrated into our search interface.

5. Simultaneous search features (e.g., allowing simultaneous searching of non-testbed information resources) will be further tested.

6. As part of the CNRI Digital Library Testbed suite,[3] the UIUC DLI testbed repositories and indices will be opened up to additional researchers investigating ways in which digital libraries of the future may evolve.

Notes

1. Association for Research Libraries. 1997. *Descriptive Statistics for Academic Institutions* [online]. Available: http://fisher.lib.virginia.edu/newarl/dstat.html [February 28, 1999].

2. The original UIUC DLI grant project included considerable work in addition to the DLI testbed described in this paper. For overviews of the complete grant project, see: Schatz, B., H. Chen, W. Mischo, T. Cole, J. Hardin, and A. Bishop. 1996. "Federating Diverse Collections of Scientific Literature." *Computer* 29 (5), 28–36. Schatz, B. et al. 1999. "Federated Search of Scientific Literature. *Computer,"* 32 (2), 51–59.

3. Corporation for National Research Initiatives 1999. *D-Lib Test Suite* [online]. Available: http://www.dlib.org/test-suite/overview.html [February 28, 1999].

4. Sperberg-McQueen, C. M. 1994. "The Text Encoding Initiative: Electronic Text Markup for Research." In B. Sutton (ed.), *Literary Texts in an Electronic Age: Scholarly Implications and Library Services, Papers Presented at the 1994 Clinic on Library Applications of Data Processing, April 10-12, 1994.* 35–56. Urbana, Ill.: Graduate School of Library and Information Science, University of Illinois at Urbana-Champaign.

5. Both the CORE project, in which OCLC was a partner, and the OCLC Electronic Journals Online project were making use of SGML as of 1994. For further information about these projects as they existed in 1994, see: Weibel, S. 1994. "The CORE Project: Technical Shakedown Phase and Preliminary User Studies." *OCLC Systems and Services,* 10 (2 and 3), 99–102. Dykhuis, R. 1994. "The Promise of Electronic Publishing: OCLC's Program." *Computers in Libraries,* 14 (10), 20–22.

6. Cole, T. and M. Kazmer. 1995. "SGML as a Component of the Digital Library." *Library Hi Tech,* 13 (4), 75–90.

7. Terry, D. 1991. "Sidebar 4: Open Text Corporation." In J. Price-Wilkin, "Text Files in Libraries: Present Foundations and Future Directions." *Library Hi Tech,* 9 (3), 7–44.

8. W3C: World Wide Web Consortium. 1999. *Resource Description Framework (RDF) Model and Syntax Specification: W3C Recommendation 22 February 1999* [online]. Available: http://www.w3.org/TR/1999/REC-rdf-syntax-19990222/ [February 28, 1999].

9. The Dublin Core Metadata Initiative. 1998. *The Dublin Core: A Simple Content Description Model for Electronic Resources* [online]. Available: http://purl.oclc.org/dc/ [February 28, 1999].

10. W3C: World Wide Web Consortium. 1998. *Mathematical Markup Language (Math ML) 1.0 Specification: W3C Recommendation 07-April-1998* [online]. Available: http://www.w3.org/TR/1998/REC-MathML-19980407/ [February 28, 1999].

11. Technology Update: Digital Object Identifiers. 1998. *Online & CD-ROM Review,* 22 (2), 115–18. See also: International DOI Foundation. 1998. *The Digital Object Identifier System* [online]. Available: http://www.doi.org/ [February 28, 1999].

Cry Me a River: Searching for Revenue Streams in Academic Libraries

Linda Dobb

Introduction

The hunt is on! The hunt for additional funds. The quest for a new entrepreneurial identity. The search for innovations that will attract attention, users, and of, course, resources.

Almost anything goes in this new environment. Cafes, video rentals, teleconferences, gift shops, auctions, contests. And, oddly enough, most of these will not—in and of themselves—generate much money for the libraries that sponsor them. But there is value in trying new services, creating new products, and raising the library's profile. This brief paper will discuss some of the revenue-generating activities that are currently being tried in libraries and attempt to point out the real value in exercising entrepreneurial zeal in the midst of academic enterprise.

Why Now?

The search for additional revenue to support library services is not new. The traditional sources of support—state or institutional subsidy, fines, and photocopy fees—have often been supplemented by book sales, small service charges, and special events. Additionally, most libraries have engaged in some form of fundraising and grant writing for a long time. Indeed, almost every academic library has received a gift or started an endowment at some point in its existence.

But today the need to raise additional funds beyond subsidy and fines seems more acute. Nothing can keep up with the rate of inflation in certain areas of the library budget; new forms of information demand not just product but equipment and furnishings; and, little money ever seems to exist for training, travel or other small incentives, which are needed to keep staff up-to-date and motivated.

Additionally, the environment in which libraries exist has changed. There is keen competition for every resource on campus. No unit is presumed to be an inherent good, deserving of support without demonstrating its academic worth. University and college libraries even compete with non-campus resources—local libraries, internet service providers and mega-bookstores—as pur-

---

Linda Dobb is dean, Libraries and Learning Resources, Bowling Green State University.

veyors of information. And, too, the climate on most campuses today encourages competition, salesmanship, and enhanced performance. We are rewarded by positive attention when we display an active regard for the bottom line.

In this more highly charged atmosphere of increased user demand, choice, and rivalry for attention, it is no wonder that libraries are looking for new ways to generate more income. And, like so much else in library work these days, the most successful formula for doing so may, in the end, be a blend of both the innovative and the traditional.

Older Models of Entrepreneurial Behavior
At one time a library which maintained its own copy machines or a copy service was considered "in business" and enterprising. In the late 1980's and early 1990's fee-based services were all the rage; and some highly touted business services existed at the University of Arizona, among other sites. Today most academic libraries maintain, depending on size and specialty, some fee-based reference and document supply services; although few can support a separate unit based solely on the income of these activities.

Other enterprises, such as book sales and vending machines were and are common in college libraries. Few generate sizeable returns. Larger enterprises that resulted from the provision of cataloging services or the creation of online library systems often ended up divorcing themselves from the libraries and universities where they were developed.

Libraries seldom saw themselves as "in business" or competing with other entities. For the most part, the new services they attempted to provide as revenue generators were an outgrowth of services they offered their traditional clientele. The questions asked when creating these services might be: a) is this a needed activity?; b) can we charge for this activity and at what rate; c) who, in-house, will perform this activity; d) what will be the real cost of providing the service; and, most importantly, e) do we get to keep the profits?

New Models of Entrepreneurial Behavior
Some of the "newer" services offered by libraries in the late 1990's are still outgrowths of traditional offerings, albeit with a technological twist or a more modern approach. Charging and collecting for printing from computers as well as from photocopy machines has become quite common. Provision of coffee from expresso machines rather than vending machines is in vogue. Libraries and archives which once offered microfilming or preservation services might now also offer digitizing of materials at a fee to other libraries.

Some truly innovative enterprises have also been born. the teleconferences produced by the College of DuPage generate revenue and perform an excellent service to the profession as well as to DuPage's own library technology program. Colorado State's webZAP is a fee-based product which may make web-based and server-based Interlibrary Loan requests more widely available to libraries who do not have the expertise to develop their own such services. And other exciting ventures are on the horizon which involve training, citation services, search engines and web creation.

Under the new models of entrepreneurial behavior, some of the same questions cited above might be asked but others are added: a) if we do not wish to perform this service, can we contract it out; b) how will we publicize this service to maximum effect; c) do we really care if this service makes money or is the service the basis for further partnerships, something we perform for the public good, or an experiment we use to develop new skills within our own staff; and, importantly, d) if we don't do it, will someone else step in and fill the vacuum?

Why Search for New Revenue Streams At?
The unfortunate facts of academic library finance dictate that even under the best of circumstances, revenue generated by entrepreneurial behaviors will never make up a significant portion of a library's budget. Some special libraries can charge back for all of their activities and subscriptions and survive. But the ethos of academic libraries makes them resolutely non-profit, and dependent on institutional and/or state subsidies to exist. Figures quoted by the American Library Association in 1991 show that most academic libraries generated more

than 1% but less than 10% of their total operating budgets from non-subsidy sources.

Even more daunting were figures quoted by the Association of Research Libraries which showed that in 1992 the average university library received only 8.2% of its funds from supplementary sources. And, that of those supplementary funds only 1.2% were from revenue generating activities. Most extra-subsidy funding was from gifts and endowments, fines, and grants.

So why be an entrepreneur if you are not destined to make lots of money? It is because revenue generation in academic libraries should probably not be regarded as a river or a stream but as a branch of the tree. Good ideas that may yield some cash can be more important if they yield positive attention. Business donors and alumni may be attracted to a university library that shows business spirit in experimenting with new services and trying new things. An attractive offering, such as serving expresso, may bring in new users who will think positively of the library at a later time; or think positively of the university as a community resource right now.

Additionally, some entrepreneurial activities have the ability to help libraries get grants or form new partnerships. A library may be able to demonstrate that a new process it undertook with the intent of simply marketing the service to other individuals and/or other libraries, could actually be adopted as a prototype in other institutions. For example, the Kent State School of Library and Information Science undertook to establish a new site for its library science program at Bowling Green State University with the intent of just generating additional student fees. The State of Ohio saw this new site, with its telecommunications capabilities, as a prototype for library science education throughout the state and awarded Kent $280,000 to make its single experiment a statewide reality.

Being a successful entrepreneur in an academic library is really just part of being a successful fundraiser for the enterprise. In both endeavors you need to know your population, know what will attract interest and support, and know how your activities are sharpening the image of your organization. It is doubtful that you will hook the big fish when looking for new revenue streams in an academic library; but you may be successful in creating a strong branch of the tree from which beautiful fruits can grow.

References

Coffman, Stephen. "Fee-based services and the future of libraries." *Journal of Library Administration*, v. 20, no. 3/4 (1995): 167–86.

Lomax, Joanne, et al. *A Guide to additional sources of funding and revenue for libraries and archives*. Letchworth, Hertfordshire: British Library Research and Innovation Centre, 1997.

Lynch, Mary Jo. *Alternative sources of revenue in academic libraries*.Chicago, Ill.: American Library Association, 1991.

MacLeod, Leon. "Lattes 'n libraries." *Bottom Line*, v. 11, no. 3 (1998): 97–100 (see also the author's web site at http: www.multnomah.lib.orr.us/lib/entre)

Melville, Annette. *Resource strategies in the 90's: trends in ARL university libraries*. Washington, D.C.: Association of Research Libraries, 1994.

Ratliff, Priscilla and Thomas J. Weeks, "Three years experience with fee-based services in a corporate library." *Special Libraries*, v. 86, no. 1 (winter 1995), 21–27.

Steckel, Richard. "Doing good in challenging times: how nonprofits can profit." *Wilson Library Bulletin*, v. 67, no. 4 (December 1992): 43–45.

EDI—Slow Walk to Fast Forward

Joan Stephens and Roger Presley

Introduction and History of EDI

Electronic data interchange (EDI), or the transfer of structured data, by agreed message standards, from one computer application to another by electronic means, has been used in the corporate sector for many years. Large retail companies such as department stores, use EDI to order materials and process invoices. Other industries, such as transportation, banking, and health care, have seen their production rates rise, their services expand, and their staff re-energized by implementing EDI.

EDI was first used in the book industry between book stores and publishers. EDI is now moving into library operations and shows great promise in many areas, including: improving efficiency and accuracy in daily operations; freeing staff from routine tasks in favor of developing high demand, value-added services; as well as realizing appreciable budgetary savings from incentives for participating in electronic commerce.

Friedemann Weigel, Managing Partner and Information Systems Director of Harrassowitz, a German bookdealer, said that EDI is based on two basic assumptions: 1) that communication is the central starting point for organizational and economic improvements in companies and organizations, and 2) that EDI will account for 50 percent to 80 percent of all communication activities between libraries and agents in the next three to five years.[1]

There are several reasons that EDI is not yet commonplace within the library marketplace. Even though standards groups such as SISAC and BISAC are writing and publishing EDI standards, the vendors of library systems in the United States have been slow to implement these standards. This tardiness is at least partially the responsibility of librarians. Joan Griffith wrote that librarians have not done a good job of explaining to library administrators and integrated library system (ILS) vendors that EDI is really a public service issue. "If EDI were sufficiently well understood, it would be obvious that its implementation in technical services has significant repercussions for public services. It is the backbone for improved receipt of

---

Joan Stephens is head, Acquisitions/Serials and Roger Presley is associate university librarian for Resource Management, Georgia State University.

material as well as for shipment and cancellation information. Money and time saved in technical services may be reassigned to public service activities or for the introduction of new services in technical services."[2]

Bruce Compton agrees that EDI implementation suffers from the fact that high-profile development that benefits mainly public services is of greater importance to the marketplace than improving efficiency in technical services. He writes that, "Backroom functionality usually takes a backseat to glitzy new products such as WWW, Z30.50, imaging, and multimedia services . . ."[3] Compton says that we must clearly state in our requests for proposals (RFP's), our EDI expectations from an ILS vendor. He said that such statements are often vague and phrased in terms of functional requirements rather than being specific from a technical standpoint. The real key to the successful development of EDI lies in the formation of development partnerships between all players, the ILS vendor, the library, the book/subscription agent, the vendor of the EDI mapping software, and the communications provider. If EDI is important to libraries, librarians should buy only those systems that support EDI.

Librarians must begin to play an active role in standards organizations such as BISAC and SISAC. As for our material agents, they must get the message that either they implement EDI or risk being left out of the marketplace. Librarians should carefully consider the implications of not introducing EDI.

However, not every business transaction must be run under EDI. Friedemann Weigel writes that, "Very few cost-benefit analyses about EDI have been published. One reason for this lack of information might be the *ceteris paribus* clause, which states that, during a test, only one parameter can be changed, and the rest of the parameters must stay unchanged."[4] It is difficult to assess the costs versus the benefits. EDI in acquisitions can only be properly evaluated when data have been exchanged electronically with several partners for at least a year in routine operations.

EDI at Georgia State University and Hypotheses
The Acquisitions Department of Georgia State University (GSU) has used the PALS integrated library system since early 1990. One of the unique features of the PALS system is its EDI capabilities. PALS, developed by the Minnesota State University System (MnSCU), has been on the leading edge in the implementation of the X12 standard for exchanging business data electronically since the early 1990's. At that time, Fritz Schwartz of the Faxon Company, used the PALS system to test Faxon's initial EDI activities. In the spring of 1994, when GSU was gathering information about EDI translation packages, Schwartz said that GSU was very lucky to have the PALS system because of its EDI track record.

In the fall of 1994, GSU rebased its PALS software to a version which, for the first time, supported EDI. We immediately decided to implement this feature. Working with our ILS vendor and our subscription agents, we systematically worked through the process of implementation of EDI at GSU. In May 1996 we processed our invoice for 1996 renewals with Readmore. The invoice included 2,200 domestic titles and resulted in errors or about 10% of the titles. It took several hours to correct these errors, but this was far less time than it would have taken to post the invoice manually. About a year later we transmitted our first monographic orders to YBP.

We had several hypotheses in mind when we began this adventure. They were:

1) Because Mankato State had been doing EDI for years using the PALS system, it would be relatively easy to a) set-up the process and get going quickly, and, b) be relatively trouble free in the processing of routine invoices.

2) EDI saves staff time and reduces monotony in the routine process of entering data for a million character renewal invoice;

3) EDI cuts down on errors created by repetitious data entry;

4) EDI speeds up the ordering process;

5) EDI cuts down on the paper flow of acquisitions and serials processes;

6) EDI will permit staff to be reassigned and provide services in new areas within existing budgets; and,

7) EDI will give the library increased visibility and recognition within the institution as a whole.

EDI —Slow Walk to Fast Forward

Review of Hypotheses

Utilizing our working experience with EDI processing with multiple vendors and different processes, we can now examine our hypotheses.

1. The first hypothesis stated: Because Mankato State had been doing EDI for years using the PALS system, it would be relatively quick and easy to set-up the process, and, be relatively trouble free in the processing of routine invoices.

Unfortunately, this hypothesis was not proven to be true. Because of local system and organizational differences we could not simply duplicate Mankato's efforts and expect them to run as a mirror image in our system. The first problem was that we were using the PALS system in different ways from Mankato. We also had a different configuration of staff running the process than Mankato. Mankato had a centralized unit that did all EDI processing for all libraries within the state system. At Georgia State University the work was dispersed among the University's Computer Center, the Library's Automation Coordinator, and staff of the Acquisitions Department. In addition to this, we also discovered that one of our vendors was able to transmit supplemental invoices electronically, but these invoices had to be coded differently than renewal invoices. Mankato had never processed an EDI supplemental invoice and so there was no documentation to help us. Finally, the vendors we were using to process EDI invoices were different from those that Mankato had used. So the vendors also had to solve problems without the help of Mankato.

2. The second hypothesis stated: "EDI saves staff time and monotony in the routine process of entering data for a million character renewal invoice."

This hypothesis was supported, but only partially. It is true that the monotony of manually keying a million character serial renewal invoice was eradicated in the minutes it took for the X12 process to update the file into the serials system, although the monotony of reviewing the invoices or renewal lists remains. However, the first year and a half of processing invoices took large amounts of human intervention by higher level staff, such as the Serials Librarian and the Automation Coordinator. Work that was previously done by a Library Assistant II invoice clerk is now done by her supervisor. This problem has been in part due to the fact that we were processing additional charge invoices not previously done in our ILS system, and had encountered a negative service charge with one of our vendors because of large credits accrued from the early prepayment of invoices. Those problems have been solved in part and current invoices are not as labor intensive. However, as recently as the 1999 renewal invoice with one of our smaller vendors, we have had difficulty loading the invoice. Since we are migrating to a new system, we have not pursued a solution to the problem. Our second EDI process, sending firm purchase orders in the X12 standard, has gone relatively smoothly. This process is still labor intensive if there is an error in one of the files. If this is the case, then the entire transmitted file needs to be reviewed to find the item with errors and resend it.

3. The third hypothesis read: "EDI cuts down on errors created by repetitious data entry."

Although we are not certain exactly how much error there was of the manual data entry process, we have yet to find any errors in the processed EDI renewal invoice postings. Consequently, it seems safe to say that this hypothesis is proven correct.

4. The fourth hypothesis is: "EDI speeds up the ordering process."

This hypothesis has definitely proven to be true. Until last July, when we expanded our approval plan, we processed approximately 100 to 150 firm purchase orders for monographic materials each day. Prior to X12 processing of our purchase orders, this was primarily a manual and paper driven system. PALS produced paper purchase orders in an over-night batch process, which were mailed to the vendor. Once the vendor received the paper purchase orders, they re-keyed the purchase order information into their ordering system. With EDI, our ILS creates an X12 purchase file nightly. That file is ftp'ed from our mainframe to our mailbox, where it is downloaded into a local PC in the Acquisitions Department, run through the EDI templates, and then ftp'ed to the vendor. This whole process takes about five minutes of staff time, and about two hours of local PC time. Once the vendor receives the file, it is uploaded into their system without re-keying data.

5. Hypothesis number 5 reads: "EDI cuts down on the paper flow of acquisitions and serials processes."

To date EDI has not cut down on the paper flow in acquisitions and serials processes. So, this hypothesis has not proven to be true. There are several reasons why there is no reduction in the paper flow from the EDI process. One of them has to do with the limitations of our ILS system. Unfortunately, even though we may send purchase orders electronically, the PALS ILS system's printing of those same purchase orders cannot be suppressed without suppressing the printing of all PO's, whether they are electronic or not. This is a bug in the ILS system. On the serial side, because of the problems we have encountered to date with the processing of serials invoices, we have asked our vendors to send us both electronic and paper. Part of this is to ensure that the electronic files can be trusted to include what we expect on the major renewals. In addition a paper copy is required by our University's Business Office, although this may change as we implement a new online financial system. Eventually, we do feel that there will be a reduction in paper from this process.

6. Hypothesis six stated: "EDI will permit staff to be reassigned and provide services in new areas within existing budgets."

As with hypothesis five, this hypothesis has not yet become a reality either when you look at the big picture. It is true that the clerical staff who entered the invoice data manually into our ILS system no longer have that task to do. However, because we are still monitoring the EDI process, the paper copies of the invoice are being checked against the updated EDI files. A preferred alternative is that we review a renewal list prior to receiving the electronic invoice. This allows us to notify the vendor of changes or errors that can be corrected before the invoice is sent to us. This, we anticipate, will not be needed once we have gone through at least one renewal cycle with Voyager. By then the process should have the most significant problems worked out and we will feel confident in relying solely on the electronic file. Once this is accomplished, then we can look at reassigning this staff time to new responsibilities. One area of staff time that was greatly impacted by the EDI process, and which we had not anticipated, was the increased amount of high level staff time and intervention needed to monitor and work with the process. Because of the numerous technical problems with the process, the senior support staff in both the acquisitions and serials units, as well as the librarians in each of these areas, devoted immense amounts of time making sure the process was successful. In addition to these staff, our library's automation coordinator and the university's system person on the mainframe side, were also significantly involved. As the processes become more routine, we anticipate that the professional level of staff involvement will decrease. However, we do not see an significant decline in the increased senior support staff utilization. The process, even when running smoothly, requires a high level of technical monitoring.

7. Our last hypothesis stated: "EDI will give the library increased visibility and recognition within the institution as a whole."

This hypothesis has certainly proven to be true, not only in increased institutional visibility, but also increased attention at the state, regional and national levels. On the institutional level, our EDI endeavors have been lauded as examples of how the library continues to be on the leading edge of technology. The process is viewed also as an example of how the library utilizes its staff effectively to increase efficiency. Because of our EDI processing, we have also been asked by the university's accounting services to work with them in setting up the electronic transfer of our payment information for library materials directly to their disbursement systems. At present, we are the only unit on campus that has any experience or capability of succeeding in this type of exchange. External to the library, we have been cited as an institution that has successfully accomplished EDI processing using the X12 format. There have been press releases from our vendors about our joint successes. In addition to this, our librarians have been invited to present papers, give poster sessions and publish articles on our experience with this process. This, of course, has raised consciousness of our institution in the profession.

Currently at Georgia State, we are using EDI transactions in two areas: receiving serials invoices from three major vendors and sending monographic orders to our primary book vendor. With just these two areas, we are realizing benefits already. Over 90 percent of our subscription payments are being updated automatically through EDI. This operation alone, saves several weeks of staff time that was previously devoted to routine maintenance such as posting invoices. On a daily basis, one hour is being saved in checking and mailing monographic orders. The time saved in these two areas can be redirected into other more creative tasks. This provides us with two benefits: staff who are not burned out by repetitious tasks and time to work on other important tasks.

Currently Georgia State is migrating from PALS to Endeavor's Voyager system along with all University System of Georgia libraries in the state. Voyager has EDIFACT EDI processes programmed into the ILS software. This should lead to more seamless EDI processes and reduced annual maintenance costs on our current X12 translation software. As we begin our migration we are communicating with our subscription agents and Endeavor to make sure we include all data elements needed for successful EDI use.

Once our migration is complete, we plan to implement our current EDI processes. After that we will add additional EDI processes as they are available. These processes will include: sending serial and book claims; receiving claims and order acknowledgments and the posting of their responses into our ILS records; and paying invoices electronically through the University's Business Office.

We anticipate with continued EDI development and use in libraries, EDI will continue to revolutionize acquisitions and serials work over the next few years.

Notes

1. Weigel, Friedemann. 1996. "EDI in the library market: how close are we?" *Library Administration & Management*, 19 (summer): 141.

2. Griffith, Joan C. 1996. "Why not EDI? One librarian's perspective." *Library Administration & Management*, 10 (summer): 148.

3. Compton, Bruce. 1996. "The ILS vendor and EDI: a perspective." *Library Administration & Management*, 10 (summer): 164.

4. Weigel, Friedemann, 145.

Factors That Influence Online Database Use

Carol Tenopir

Introduction

What makes a student or faculty member select a particular online database to search? We would like to think they go through a systematic process of determining which of the databases offered by their library is best for their needs each time they search or that their knowledge of reliable sources on a topic always leads them to search the best possible resource.

Realistically, however, the choice of database is more likely made by a complex mix of factors, centering around such things as convenience, recommendations by librarians, placement of a database icon on a library welcome screen, or availability for remote access. The library and library staff influence this process by their control over many of these factors.

This paper reports on a two-phase study of academic libraries to identify patterns of database use and what subtle factors might influence this use. Online data from 96 academic libraries reveal how often and when selected databases are used. Usage data do not show what each library is doing to encourage (or discourage) use of these databases, however, so usage data were supplemented with a survey. The survey questionnaire asked each library about their specific environment for online access and gathered information about what factors influence online use.

Review of the Literature

The information reported here is part of a larger study that examines patterns and factors of use for both academic and public libraries. (Tenopir, Green.) All sizes of academic and public libraries have similar usage patterns, although the amount of use varies considerably. The American Library Association's Office for Research and Statistics participates in studies regularly to gauge amounts of library use. In 1997, in cooperation with the Association of College and Research Libraries, ALA published a survey that showed how all types of academic libraries have embraced electronic services (ALA).

Early usage studies for automated resources often were done to help libraries determine how many terminals were required when they first

---

Carol Tenopir is professor, School of Information Sciences, University of Tennesee.

Table 1. Carnegie Categories For Academic Institutions (Source: www.carnegiefoundation.org)			
Category	Carnegie Class	Number in Sample	Surveys Received
B1	Baccalaureate (Liberal Arts) Colleges I	7	3
B2	Baccalaureate Colleges II	9	5
M1	Master's (Comprehensive) I Universities and Colleges	32	21
M2	Master's (Comprehensive) II Universities and Colleges	3	1
D1	Doctoral Universities I	3	2
D2	Doctoral Universities II	6	5
R1	Research Universities I	15	6
R2	Research Universities II	6	5
AA	Associate of Arts Colleges	12	7
Bus	Schools of Business and Management	3	3
Total		96	58

an online database receives. Throughout the 1990s, I measured reference librarians' attitudes toward electronic reference products and changes in university reference services (Tenopir, Ennis). Reference rooms in libraries grew busier throughout the decade. Many more workstations were added in libraries at the same time remote access was made available. Users prefer electronic reference products, both from within the library and through dial-up access, while library instruction classes now most often focus on electronic resources.

brought up an online catalog (just as much earlier studies tried to predict an appropriate number of chairs to provide in academic libraries.) A 1983 report incorporated queuing models to recommend appropriate numbers of terminals (Tolle, et al.). Turnstile counts were used to optimize reference department staffing or pickup schedules for shelving. Turnstile counts show that peak usage periods in academic libraries correspond to the academic calendar and daily class schedules (Murfin, McGrath.)

Turnstile counts are not enough to see why a particular database is used. Librarians' attitudes might be expected to influence the amount of use

Methodology: Phase 1—Usage Data

Measuring online usage is more complex than turnstile counts, sampling workstation queues, or even measuring access to a single library's online catalog. To get both remote and in-house online activity for selected commercial databases from many libraries, a major database producer and aggregator provided me with usage data for all of its online databases. This database aggregator provides online access to many bib-

Table 2. Simultaneous Users, All Databases, Academic Libraries by Carnegie Class									
No. of Users	**Cumulative Percent** Carnegie Class								
	B1	**B2**	**M1**	**M2**	**D1**	**D2**	**R1**	**R2**	**AA**	**Bus.**
1	97.8	96.8	94.5	91.5	96.4	95.2	91.8	89.9	96.1	90.5
2	99.2	98.7	96.9	96.1	99.0	97.8	95.0	93.3	98.2	94.9
5	99.9	99.9	99.1	99.7	99.8	99.7	98.3	97.8	99.8	99.3
10	100.0	100.0	99.7	100.0	100.0	100.0	99.4	99.7	100.0	100.0
15	100.0	100.0	99.8	—	100.0	100.0	99.6	99.9	100.0	100.0
25	—	—	99.9	—	—	—	99.8	100.0	—	—
66	—	—	—	—	—	—	100.0	—	—	—

liographic, full text, and directory databases, 38 of which were used by one or more academic libraries in this study.

This database aggregator provides over 100 database titles, many of which contain overlapping information that is aimed at different audiences. For example, the same journals and magazines may be available in an indexing only version, a full text version, or a combination version. Versions indexing thousands of titles may be sold to university libraries; small colleges may prefer versions with fewer, selected titles. Rarely does the same library purchase overlapping titles, although a library may purchase separate current and backfile versions or choose a combined version. Some databases are subject specific (business journals, for example); others are aimed at a general interest academic audience. For the purposes of analysis, the 38 databases used by the libraries were examined in three different groupings: 1) all 38 databases together; 2) eight databases that together cover general magazines and journals for academic libraries (including full text, indexing only, backfiles, and current files); 3) the single most heavily used database among these academic libraries (a current general magazine and journal title.)

From a customer list of over 1200 libraries, a random sample of 100 academic libraries in the U.S. and Canada was taken. From these, usable online usage data was available for 96 libraries. The 96 libraries cover every Carnegie Class of parent academic institution, with the largest number from MI: Master's Universities and Colleges I (32 libraries). Table 1 shows how Carnegie Class was distributed in the study sample.

Online usage for every library is captured automatically by the database provider in five-minute intervals 24 hours a day. Even with a random sample of only 96 libraries, a year's worth of data would thus yield over 10 million data points for every database. For this study, usage data were sampled once per hour (on each half-hour), from the hours of 8 a.m. to midnight, for a period of 6 months (July to December.)[1] Still, over 281,000 data points per database are included in this sample of academic libraries.

Usage data reveal how many simultaneous users are logged on to any one database at any of the sampled times. Time stamps on the data allow us to draw patterns that show average numbers of users by time of day, day of the week, and day of the month for each class of library and each database or database group.

Methodology: Phase 2—Questionnaires

Usage data reveal typical patterns of use within classes of academic libraries, but do not identify why or how the specific environment might influence online use. To begin to answer the questions of how and why, information beyond usage data is needed. Information about unique environmental factors that may influence online use in individual libraries was sought by sending a questionnaire to each of the academic libraries for which we had usage data. Fifty-eight libraries responded, for a return rate of 60%.

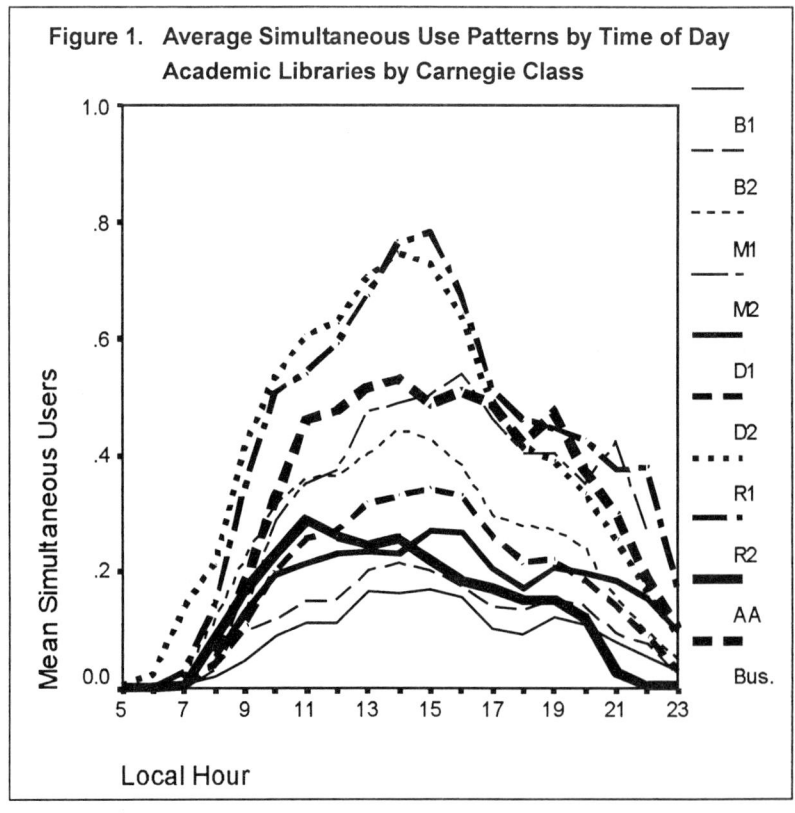

Figure 1. Average Simultaneous Use Patterns by Time of Day Academic Libraries by Carnegie Class

Factors that Influence Online Database Use

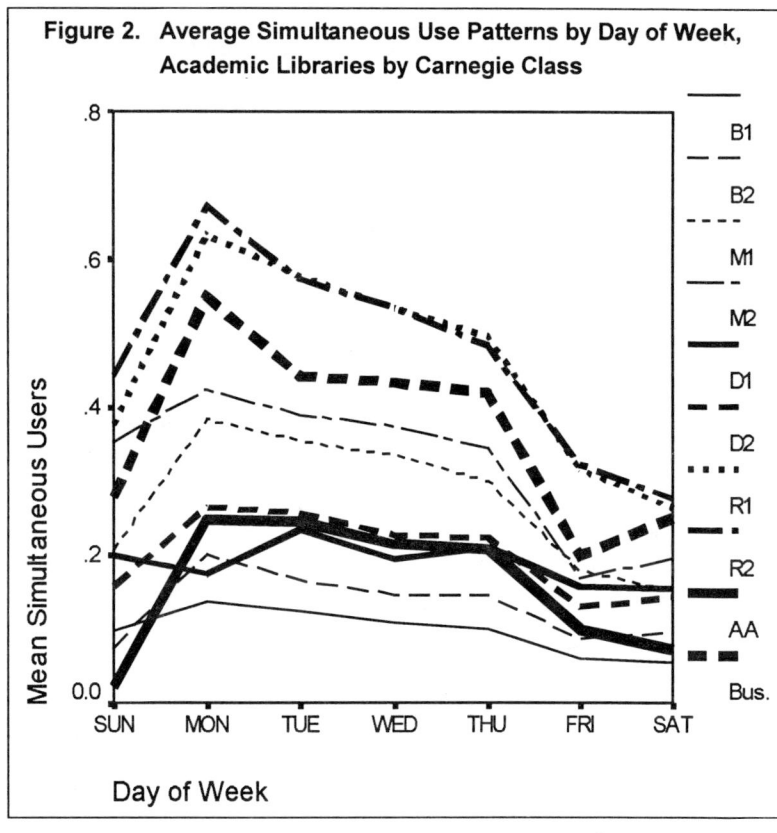

Figure 2. Average Simultaneous Use Patterns by Day of Week, Academic Libraries by Carnegie Class

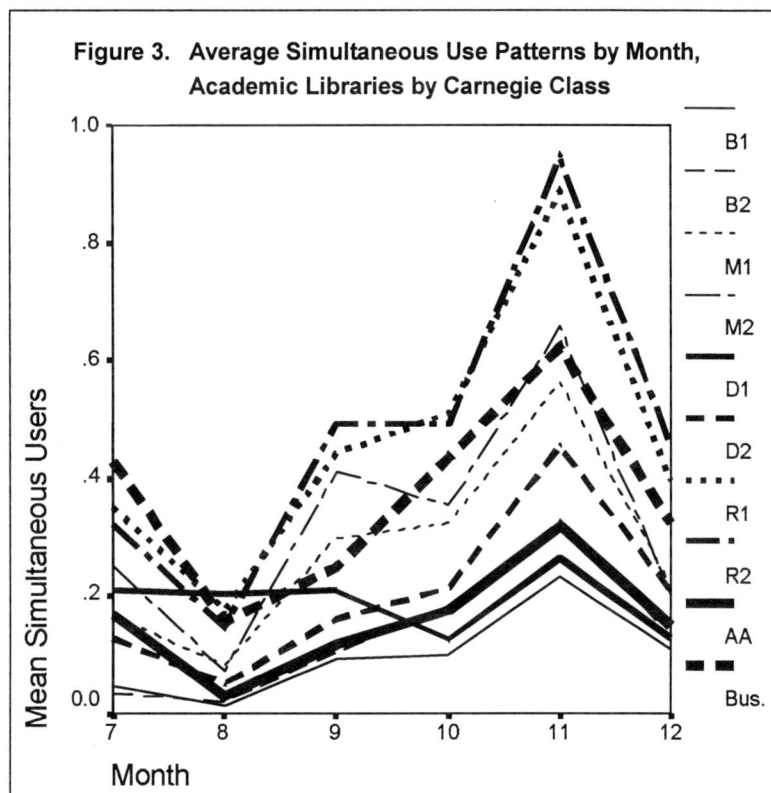

Figure 3. Average Simultaneous Use Patterns by Month, Academic Libraries by Carnegie Class

Their distribution by Carnegie Class is shown in table 1.

Analyzed alone, the survey questions reveal much about the different environments in academic libraries and the role librarians play in influencing online use. A final step will be to analyze the survey answers in conjunction with the usage pattern data.

Analysis of Usage Patterns

The number of simultaneous users for all 38 databases in all 96 libraries ranges from zero users (the mode and median) to 66 users (the mean is .28 and the standard deviation is 1.36). Periods of high use follow clearly defined patterns. Figures 1, 2 and 3 show the patterns of use aggregated for all databases, but separated by class of library. Although the range and exact number of users varies by class of library, the patterns of use, including peaks and valleys, are quite similar. Not surprisingly, the busiest time for online research in or from academic libraries is between 10 a.m. and 5 p.m., Mondays and Tuesdays, in November. (It is likely that April and May would also be high use months.)

Patterns of use for eight general databases together show similar patterns of use (figures 4, 5, and 6.) (The mode and median are still zero, but the mean is .56 and standard deviation is 2.15.) The patterns of use for the one most heavily used general database are very similar, so are not presented here. Amounts of use are higher and vary more, however, with a mean of .84 simultaneous users and a standard deviation of 2.77 (the mode and median are still zero.)

Averages do not show the true impact of multiple users on workstations, online ports, and staff. Patterns do a better job, by helping to identify times of heavy demand. Another way to show impact is to measure how often multiple users are logged on. Tables 2 and 3 show how many simultaneous users are logged on at any one time on any single database, aggregated first for all databases and secondly for the eight general interest databases. Unlike usage of a library's catalog, simultaneous usage of any one reference databases is relatively uncommon. Providing access to only one user for a general research database, for example, would be satisfactory 80.8% of the time in research libraries (R2) and over 95% of the time in the smaller baccalaureate colleges (B1). If five simultaneous users could be accommodated for a database, users would be accommodated 99.8% of the time in B1 libraries and 94.8% of the time in R2 institutions (table 3).

The single most used database in these libraries was also analyzed alone to mitigate any effects on the data from seldom-used files such as backfiles. Table 4 shows the simultaneous use figures for the general magazine/journal database used the most in these libraries. Clearly databases that are expected to be used by a wide variety of students and faculty and have general current interest appeal will attract more simultaneous users.

Analysis of Questionnaires

The 58 libraries that responded to our questionnaire offer a variety of electronic media for end user searching. Over 90% offer CD-ROM, commercial online, and World Wide Web access. Many provide access to several commercial online services. Seventy-two percent provide both in-house and remote access (table 5).

Approximately 95% of the libraries that responded to my survey offer access on ten or more workstations to the databases provided by the company for which I have usage data, but only 7% have workstations dedicated to these

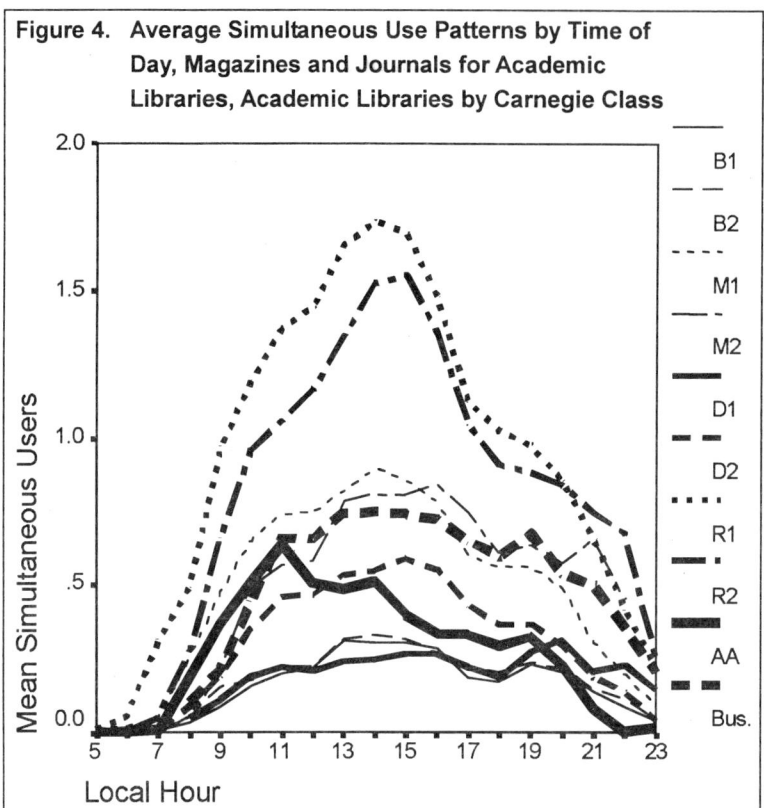

Figure 4. Average Simultaneous Use Patterns by Time of Day, Magazines and Journals for Academic Libraries, Academic Libraries by Carnegie Class

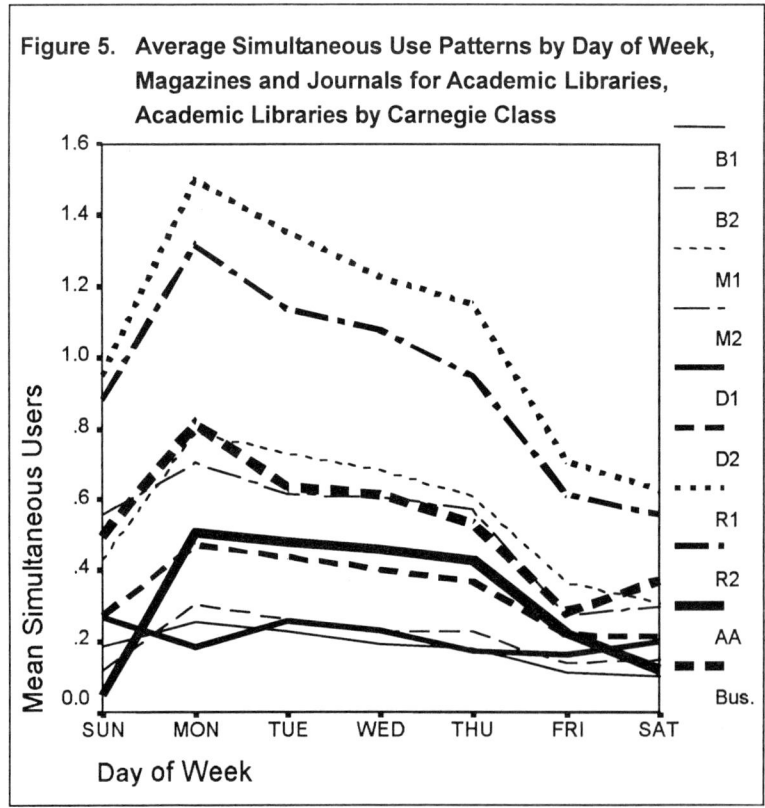

Figure 5. Average Simultaneous Use Patterns by Day of Week, Magazines and Journals for Academic Libraries, Academic Libraries by Carnegie Class

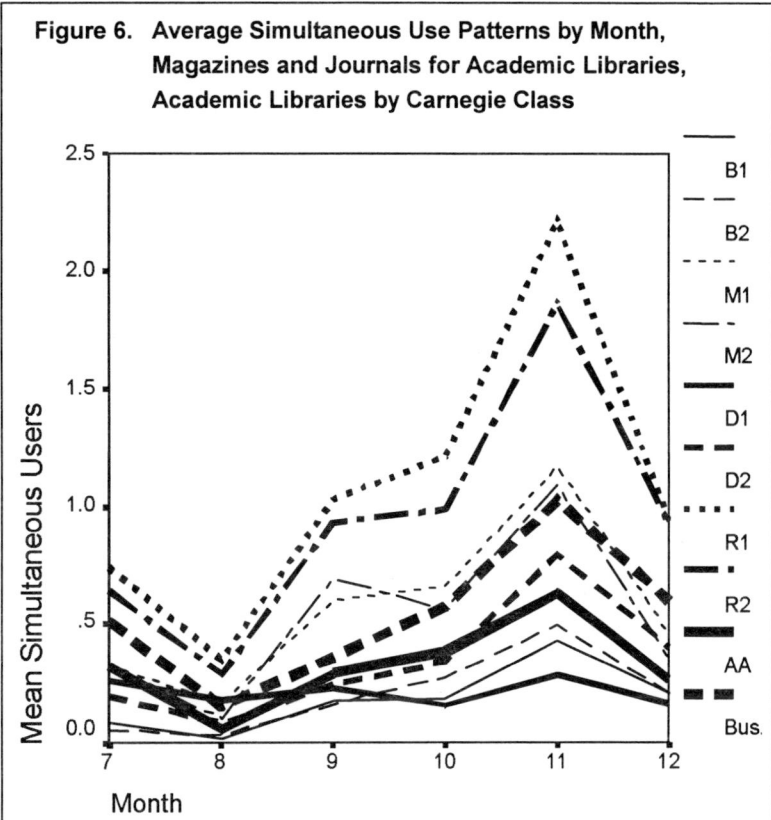

Figure 6. Average Simultaneous Use Patterns by Month, Magazines and Journals for Academic Libraries, Academic Libraries by Carnegie Class

databases. Multipurpose workstations that allow access to the library's online catalog and other online databases are the rule.

Librarians believe that the databases analyzed in this study are some of the most popular among library users. The largest number of libraries (44.8%) reported these are the most popular databases. An additional 20.7% believe these databases rank second in popularity. Some libraries actively promote one or more of these databases or, at least, make those databases easier to find. Of the libraries that responded to the survey, 62% note these specific databases on the library system's main menu, 21% post signs that promote them, 57% provide handouts that describe them, and over 79% offer training that specifically mentions this company's databases. Once a user logs in or sits down at a workstation, it requires just 1-3 steps to reach the databases in 83% of the libraries (table 6.)

Close ties with academic classes should also influence how much a database is used. Over 72% of the libraries said all of the databases from this company have subject matter related to academic classes. Although many librarians don't know for sure if the databases are mentioned in academic classes, 64% report that they are mentioned specifically and 55% said there are specific class assignments that require use of the databases.

Conclusions

It will come as no surprise to academic reference librarians that peak online usage follows clearly defined patterns. The greatest number of users is online early in the week, midday, in the month when term papers are due. A majority of academic users are accessing databases at the time they typically use the library. For all types of academic libraries there are clear valleys and peaks for online use, following the rhythm of academic life.

Even for general interest magazine databases that are available both in-house and through remote access, at many times no one is online. Peak

No. of Users	Cumulative Percent Carnegie Class									
	B1	B2	M1	M2	D1	D2	R1	R2	AA	Bus.
1	95.7	92.1	84.2	85.7	91.3	86.9	78.9	68.9	86.7	85.3
2	98.5	96.4	89.4	92.8	98.2	92.4	84.0	76.3	92.6	92.2
5	100.0	99.5	96.4	99.4	100.0	98.4	91.9	90.6	99.1	99.1
15	—	100.0	99.2	—	—	100.0	97.7	99.7	99.9	100.0
25	—	—	99.7	—	—	—	98.9	—	100.0	—
66	—	—	—	—	—	—	100.0	—	—	—

Table 4. Simultaneous Users, Most Used Database (General Magazine/Journal)

Table 5. Electronic Media for End Users

Media Types Used By Respondents	Percent Carnegie Class									
	B1	B2	M1	M2	D1	D2	R1	R2	AA	Bus.
CD-ROM	100.0	80.0	100.0	100.0	100.0	100.0	100.0	100.0	85.7	100.0
Locally loaded	33.3	0.0	33.3	0.0	0.0	40.0	83.3	40.0	57.1	33.3
Loaded on another library's computer	66.7	80.0	33.3	0.0	50.0	40.0	33.3	40.0	28.6	33.3
Commercial online from a vendor	100.0	100.0	95.2	100.0	100.0	100.0	100.0	100.0	71.4	100.0
Commercial online from an OPAC company	33.3	20.0	23.8	100.0	0.0	20.0	50.0	0.0	14.3	33.3
World Wide Web	66.7	100.0	100.0	100.0	100.0	80.0	100.0	80.0	100.0	33.3

Table 6. Ways Libraries Promote The Specific Databases Analyzed Here

Methods of Promotion Used	Percent Carnegie Class									
	B1	B2	M1	M2	D1	D2	R1	R2	AA	Bus.
Remote access	33.3	80.0	85.0	100.0	100.0	100.0	83.3	60.0	28.6	66.7
Workstations dedicated to these databases	0.0	20.0	4.8	0.0	0.0	0.0	0.0	20.0	14.3	33.3
Databases noted on library system main menu	66.7	100.0	61.9	—	50.0	60.0	50.0	40.0	85.7	33.3
Signs	33.3	20.0	33.3	0.0	0.0	0.0	0.0	20.0	28.6	0.0
Handouts	0.0	60.0	66.7	100.0	50.0	40.0	50.0	40.0	71.4	66.7
Databases mentioned specifically in training	100.0	60.0	85.7	100.0	100.0	80.0	66.7	80.0	57.1	100.0
Databases specifically mentioned in academic classes	66.7	80.0	71.4	0.0	100.0	60.0	33.3	20.0	71.4	100.0
Specific class assignments require use of these databases	66.7	40.0	61.9	0.0	50.0	20.0	66.7	40.0	57.1	100.0

usage can be quite high in some libraries, but average usage for any one database or group of similar databases is low.

A combination of subtle factors may influence use. Librarians influence use in a variety of subtle and obvious ways, including mentioning specific products in a user instruction class, advocating use of a specific database in specific class assignments, referring to a database on a library's welcome screen, or otherwise reminding users about a specific database and making it easy to get to it. The next step will be to seek statistical correlation between deviations in amounts or patterns of use and environmental factors in the libraries.

Acknowledgments

The author would like to thank Danielle M. Green for her able assistance with bringing this project to a conclusion. George Banks and Leslie Preston were involved in the project at its early stages, including the overwhelming task of figuring out how to deal with tens of millions of online data points and how to present the data in a meaningful way. Shawn Collins, technology coordinator at the School of Information Sciences, University of Tennessee, has offered expert support throughout.

Note

1. We have converted the hourly data into the local time zone for each library, but, since the database company's computer was set to eastern time, data from libraries in western time zones begin and end earlier (7 a.m.–11 p.m. central time; 6 a.m.–10 p.m. mountain time; 5 a.m.–9 p.m. pacific time; 4 a.m.–8 p.m. Alaska time; and 3 a.m.–7 p.m. Hawaii time).

References

American Library Association, *Electronic Services in Academic Libraries,* Chicago: ALA, 1997. [Executive summary available at www.ala.org/alaorg/ors/elecsvcs.html].

McGrath, W. E., "Periodicity in Academic Library Circulation: A Spectral Analysis," *Journal of the American Society for Information Science* 47 (February 1996): 136–45.

Murfin, Marjorie E., "National Reference Measurement: What Can it Tell Us About Staffing," *College and Research Libraries* 44 (September 1983): 321–33.

Tenopir, Carol and Ennis, Lisa, "The Digital Reference World of Academic Librarians," *Online* 19 (July/August 1998): 22–28.

Tenopir, Carol and Green, Danielle M., "Simultaneous Usage of Online Databases in Academic and Public Libraries," *Proceedings of the National Online Meeting, New York, May 1999.*

Tolle, John E., et al., "Determining the Required Number of Online Catalog Terminals," *Information Technology & Libraries* 2 (September 1983): 261–65.

Pay for Print: Implementing Fee for Service Programs

John Jones, Michael Walker, and Mona Thiss

Introduction

Along with the increasing use of computers in libraries has come an equal increase in the consumption of paper. This has been especially true at Virginia Commonwealth University (VCU) over the past several years. The use of the Web is gaining in popularity and so is the proliferation of full-text electronic databases to the Library's collections. User demand for printing electronic information has rapidly increased, along with the costs and use of paper, toner cartridges, and printer maintenance and repairs. It has become easier to click on the print button than to put pencil to paper, which cost a great deal to support and encourages thoughtless consumption of resources. In this paper, we will address VCU's strategy for gaining control over the high cost and waste associated with these rising printing demands.

History/Background Information

The James Branch Cabell Library (JBC) and the Tompkins-McCaw Library (TML) are located on the campuses of Virginia Commonwealth University (VCU). James Branch Cabell Library is located on the Academic Campus in the historic Fan District and Tompkins-McCaw Library is located on the Medical College of Virginia Campus (MCV) two miles east near downtown Richmond. The Libraries support learning, teaching, research, health care and public service at VCU through the wealth of information resources they provide.

TML 's end-user population consists mainly of graduate and professional students but also includes VCU faculty, staff, and undergraduates. JBC's end-user population is made up of mostly undergraduate students, although a large number of graduate, faculty and staff are served. Both libraries support a large number of community borrowers who include high school students, patrons from consortium institutions, other institutional program agreements, and registered community borrowers. As a state institution, the libraries are public facilities and the surrounding community

---

John Jones is manager, Electronic Resources, Michael Walker is reference services team leader, and Mona Thiss is manager, Information Services, Virginia Commonwealth University.

has access to public computers, printers, copiers, and most collections.

Prior to July 1996, TML had 12 mainframe dumb terminals operating as the core access to databases and health science information. Each terminal had a dot-matrix printer. A 15 computer workstation teaching facility (LIMERC) provided access to local area network resources as well as some windows based software including Internet access. Two networked dot-matrix printers were shared between the 15 workstations. The LIMERC was available for student use when no classes were being taught. In July 1996, TML replaced the 12 mainframe dumb terminals with 16 networked Internet capable computers and upgraded the computers in the LIMERC. No additional dot-matrix printers were added in the new networked environment nor were any shared with the new extra computers in the public areas. Those computers had no printing available.

The core of the computers used to access databases in JBC were located on the first floor near the Reference Services Desk. There was a total of 25 computers, 16 of which had dot-matrix printers attached. Every two computers shared a printer leaving nine computers without printers. Like TML, patrons were permitted to use the 16 additional computers located in the Library Instruction Classroom Lab (LICL) but no printing was available. A few additional computers and mainframe dumb terminals, without attached printers, were located throughout the building on the second, third and fourth floors.

Printing was problematic on both campuses and patrons and staff became increasingly frustrated with the process. The capabilities of the new computers were challenging the abilities of the dot matrix printers. Windows applications were graphically intense and web pages with graphics and formatted fonts nearly brought the printers to a stand still. Library users further contributed to the problem by spending hours at a computer printing citations and web pages that often ended up in the recycling bins. The libraries were going through reams of paper and dozens of printer cartridges on a weekly basis. Staff were put in the awkward position of asking patrons to limit printing and were constantly clearing paper jams and providing troubleshooting support. Additionally, the noise created by the dot matrix printers made the area unattractive for patrons who needed a quiet place to study.

Request For Proposal (RFP)

It became clear that the libraries needed to take immediate steps to address these printing problems. Laser printers were an alternative that would provide the robust printing needed in an academic environment, but they were beyond the limits of the libraries' small overhead budgets. After investigating a number of alternatives, a decision was made that the cost of printing would have to be passed on to the end user.

In the fall of 1996, a committee was formed to write a Pay for Print RFP with the goal to:

> establish a contract with a firm that is able to support the University in implementing a cost recovery system for computer printers that is fully integrated with existing systems, meets the diverse printing needs of its clientele on both campuses, and can be administered efficiently.

Five objectives were listed in support of this goal:
- recover at least partial printing costs;
- improve management of public printers services;
- significantly reduce wasted printing;
- increase network efficiency;
- utilize card access technology.

The RFP detailed a two-tiered service level to be provided by the vendor. Tier one was described as a complete turnkey system that required the vendor to supply all software, equipment, supplies and staffing. Tier two enabled those computing facilities with substantial investments in printing technology to maintain control of that service and equipment but provided a method for cost recovery. Since the libraries could not afford to invest in laser technology, we selected IKON Office Solutions' complete turnkey system which met our goals and objectives, was compatible with our existing vending card system, and minimized use of staff time.

Implementation

A Pay for Print taskforce was formed and services were scheduled to be implemented at both libraries during the summer session when fewer students were on campus. This would allow two months before the start of the fall semester to plan for the transition from a free printing service to a fee-based service. Planned activities included staff training, development and distribution of public relations materials, web page creation, and meetings with the various units on campus. These units included the Student Government Association (SGA) and faculty and deans from the individual schools. However, negotiations with the vendor to finalize the contract delayed the implementation date. This delay left us with only two weeks before the beginning of the semester to complete our planned activities.

In August 1997, we installed one Pay for Print workstation at TML and four at JBC. Signs outlining instructions, locations, and costs were developed and posted at each computer workstation and at the printer locations. Web pages addressing questions and pointing out the advantages of pay for print were developed and staff was given training.

The service was free to users during the first two weeks of the semester. Initially charges were $.12 for single sided black and white copy, $.55 for single sided color, and $.15 for black and white two sided. The single sided black and white copy was later reduced to $.09 per page.

User Impact

Whenever you implement a fee-based service you must anticipate some initial negative reactions. However, we underestimated the impact that pay for print would have on our users. We were not fully prepared for the initial outpouring of concern and dissatisfaction over the decision to implement a fee-based printing service. The delay in implementation of pay for print took away the time we needed to sufficiently train staff and market the benefits of the new service. Some students were outraged and expressed their anger and frustration through the student newspaper as well as to staff and administration directly. They felt that the decision was made without their input and the fee of $.12 a copy was financially prohibitive. University and Library officials met with students to discuss their issues with regard to the service.

In order to respond to the concerns of the library community, we looked at a number of alternatives, including:

- Open Forums sponsored by the Academic Campus Student Government Association (AC-SGA);
- A listserv was created to provide an outlet for users to ask questions and vent their frustrations and receive a response from administration;
- Articles to provide information on the service;
- A pay for print program survey, "Tell us what you think" to garner their input.

In an effort to address student concerns firsthand, the vice provost for the Office for Information Technology attended SGA forums. The feedback he received generally indicated that, while many students understood why the libraries were implementing the new service, they were not pleased with their lack of input into the decision making process, the cost per page, the minimal publicity, and timing of the service fee. As a direct response to the concerns expressed in these forums, the decision was made to reduce the price of printing from $.12 to $.09 a page.

While users on the Medical Campus expressed some disapproval over the new fee, the majority of the feedback had come from students on the Academic Campus. To help determine the attitudes of our students on the Medical Campus, we conducted a survey seeking feedback to determine user satisfaction at TML. The survey consisted of 21 questions and was completed by 81 patrons.

Over a year after the service was implemented, the same user survey conducted at TML was conducted at JBC. The survey was completed by 124 users and collected by staff at the major public services desks. The responses to the JBC survey were similar to the responses at TML. Although respondents at both libraries indicated that they were printing less (51% at JBC and 75% at TML) the noticeable differences (24%) between the two libraries may be attributed to users now being accustomed to pay for print services. No community borrowers responded to the survey, but staff noticed a significant reduction in printing by these users. Respondents from both libraries were more selective in what they printed (54% at JBC and 62% at TML). Over half of the respondents at JBC (52%) indicated no change in their use of pencil and paper. A year earlier, the TML respondents (62%) indicated that they were using pencil and paper more. The differences between the libraries may be an indication that users are accepting and adjusting to the fee more than when first implemented.

The majority of the respondents at both campuses agreed that the print jobs were of good quality (75% at JBC and 94% at TML). Most respondents reported that the cost was too high (71% at JBC and 65% at TML). About one third of the respondents reported that the services should be free (33% at JBC and 27% at TML) while the majority reported that $.05 (58% at JBC and 57% at TML) per page was reasonable. The most respondents were willing to pay was $.10 per page (51% at JBC and 34% at TML).

The majority (81% at JBC and 68% at TML) of the respondents would like to print on both sides of a sheet. The majority (74%) of the respondents at JBC would like to be able to print in color while less that one half (46%) would like to print in color at TML.

The majority (67% at JBC and 75% at TML) of respondents have not downloaded to a floppy diskette. The respondents who had downloaded to a diskette did so seldomly. Sixty-four percent of the JBC respondents were aware that they could e-mail search results. Less that half (44%) of the TML respondents were aware of this. The increased awareness at JBC may be the result of continued patron education about the service and its associated fee.

The respondents (66% at JBC and 77% at TML) agreed that the quality of the print copy is better than the dot matrix printer and agreed (75% at JBC and 72% at TML) that the pay for print system was easy to use.

Conclusions/Recommendations

Communication is key to the success of implementing any major change in service and especially a change from free to fee. Clearly communicate the whys and goals of the new service, and develop a marketing campaign which focuses on its benefits. Promote the service to the primary users through press releases, brochures, articles in the campus paper, displays, and web pages. Attend Student Government Association (SGA) meetings and solicit support from colleagues campus wide. Include a member of the SGA on the Implementation Task Force to help distribute the information. Help the users get used to the change well in advance of implementation.

Educate and train staff to deal with users who are not familiar with or oppose the fee-base service. Ensure that staff clearly understand the goals of the organization and the whys of implementing a fee-based service so that they can communicate this effectively to users. Sufficiently train staff to use the system before patron questions arise.

The pay for print system itself has been easy to use and we have experienced few system errors or equipment failures. Before implementing the new service, make sure that an adequate maintenance agreement with the vendor is in place. Request that the vendor provide courtesy cards, a procedure for refunds, and a customer service representative on a routine basis. Communicate troubleshooting problems and solutions to all staff who are responsible for providing any patron assistance. It will be easier for users to accept the new fee base service if it works properly. Keep the fee in line with other similar services such as photocopying and if possible, provide the service at no charge until all bugs have been worked out of the system.

Summary

The first two months after implementing pay for print proved challenging for the library users and staff. Users were very vocal about their unhappiness over the fee and staff had to deal with frustrated patrons while maintaining quality customer service. However, the benefits of changing to a fee-based printing system have far outweighed the initial negative reactions from our users. We have seen a dramatic decrease in the amount of wasted paper and in the costs of our printing supplies. Now, a year and a half later, we are faced with few complaints over the fee and pay for print is a comfortable part of the libraries' routine.

The UCSC NetTrail: Web-based Instruction for Online Literacy

Ann Hubble and Deborah A. Murphy

Background

The Library seeks to provide not just information, but the resources and assistance needed to help students become life long learners and knowledge seekers. Being able to find, evaluate and effectively use information sources from an increasing variety of formats is key to this process. However, many students arrive without essential basic online or research skills and face the lack of any centralized campus wide resource to aid them.

Instructional Need

There is little disagreement among faculty and librarians that students need to acquire basic skills to begin the research process. ItÕs the method of delivery that has proved to be a major sticking point. The logistics of a de-centralized campus allows for great diversity in a studentÕs first year experience, but it also fragments the instruction process. The majority of first year students participate in a Core Course, an ideal opportunity to make contact with thousands of students struggling to come up to speed in a research oriented environment. The challenge was how to integrate a library component given:

- no centralized organization either across campus or at the individual College Level;
- core courses occur at about the same time at all colleges, presenting the logistical challenge of working with several thousand students at once;
- current models of instruction (large group lectures, individual seminars, workbooks, exercises, etc.) were not working given limitations of library staff with classes so content packed that instructors were unwilling to give up large group lecture time;
- students were facing other courses that made assumptions about their abilities to use online tools, perform research, or use the Internet that did not match their actual skill and knowledge levels.

The UCSC NetTrail

The library was not alone in identifying a need in this area. A systemwide conference on undergradu-

---

Ann Hubble is electronic information resources librarian, and Deborah A. Murphy is instruction coordinator and reference librarian, University of California, Santa Cruz.

ate education brought together a self selected UCSC coalition of librarians, computer center staff and faculty to develop UCSCÕs first campuswide online literacy course and work began in the summer of 1997 on "The UCSC NetTrail" (http://nettrail.ucsc.edu). The NetTrail was developed to set a basic level of computer literacy on campus which would allow faculty to presume that students are able to make use of online resources without doing explicit instruction in their classes. It is just the first step along the information literacy journey. Through a set of four self-paced modules, students are provided an introduction to browsing the World-Wide Web, using E-mail at UCSC, connecting with on-line Library Resources, using Newsgroups, and understanding Netiquette. This course is aimed at users new to the online environment or those with differing starting points in terms of initial computer skills and interests. It is aimed at providing a solid grounding in basic skills as well as an introduction to more specialized applications used locally at UCSC.

Each module is designed with a similar format - self-paced learning materials that introduce and "teach" the topic, and one or more exercises that allow the students to test their knowledge. The NetTrail exercises interact with electronic scripts to provide immediate feedback to the students, as well as record exercise completion information for instructors to track which students have successfully completed specific modules. The exercises require a live connection to the resource presented. In order to complete the exercise, students need to be able to connect, then complete a task and successfully answer questions about the resource. Each module takes about 20 to 30 minutes to complete. They may be taken alone, all at once, or separately in any order.

The diverse team approach to developing this resource worked surprisingly well. The timing of this project could not have been better from a campus perspective. For example, the library was in the midst of beginning work on a similar resource at almost the same time as this project came together. Team members were for the most part self selected. The group was formed by those who worked closely with undergraduates and online resources, had been interested in instructional issues and were willing to develop supporting resources. The diverse opinions and perspectives this brought to our discussions were ultimately key to our success.

Usage

The NetTrail is available on demand as a web site. To ensure that students have help if needed, we advise students and instructors to explore the NetTrail from one of the many campus Instructional Computing Labs where assistance is available from trained support staff. Instructors have the option of having students take the NetTrail on their own, either in a lab or on their own personal computer, or of arranging for group sessions in an Instructional Computing Lab. Instructors register their courses using a short online form and are then able to query the NetTrail logs for student usage. Reports include summary course reports; detailed course reports, individual student reports and overall summary reports.

The NetTrail has been used as of winter 1998 by over 1,000 students from Core, Writing, Humanities, and Computer Literacy/ Engineering courses. Instructors can assign the tutorials without giving up class time and have been able to send students to labs where help was available. In addition to course integrated instruction, other uses for this tutorial include: on demand reference for students needing an introduction to a set of skills while in pursuit of another topic (e.g. students doing Library research who need an introduction to using the WWW), faculty and staff who may need additional Internet instruction, distance learning for students off-site, and integration into a future UCSC General Education requirement around information literacy.

Evaluation

An initial pilot phase of the NetTrail project included conducting usability tests with a small sample of students and staff. Information received via our evaluation logs and continued usability testing with more students, staff and several faculty members provided additional feedback used to fine tune the modules. Feedback has been consistently positive on content, navigation, look and feel of the NetTrail. The library module has consistently been given the best review, with even experienced users noting its usefulness. In tracking usage statistics, we discovered that students often went through additional modules even when they were only required to do one. Highest used modules are the Library Resources and Web Browsing. As of July 1998, there have been over 2,200 hits on the site with the Library section receiving the highest number of hits.

The faculty and instructors who assigned the tutorials to their students found that the additional online background aided their students in a number of ways. For writing classes, it meant that their library research sessions could move more quickly beyond introducing skills and the concept of the WWW. Instructors could assign the tutorials without giving up class time and were able to send students to labs where help was available. Several instructors took the tutorials themselves and gave their feedback on usability as well.

Continuing Development
No project of this nature is every finished or static. Many initial decisions around development involved areas which had to be deferred to a later date due to time and funding constraints. A smaller Continuing Development group has continued work on refining and updating modules as needed. In 1998, we competed for campus wide Instructional Technology funds and, based in part on the successful initial introduction of The NetTrail, were awarded a $31,750 grant that has allowed us to revisit defered items and take development further. During the summer of 1998 some of this money was used to hire an editor to give a consistent voice to all of the NetTrail modules, as they had originally been written by five separate authors.

As a project that is never really finished, it faces some unique challenges. One of these challenges is keeping the interest of a cross campus group together and focused on making sure the NetTrail site is current. Already, some members of the original development group have dropped out, as their own roles or priorities have changed within their own careers. As anyone who has put together a web site before knows, it needs continual maintenance. As an example, the web graphics within one portion of the University of California systemwide library catalog we use to teach library research skills have already changed twice since creating the NetTrail. Each time the graphics change, we must recreate all of the corresponding screen captures and substitute them for the proper ones. We hope to use part of the grant money to assist in hiring part time help to make changes such as these.

Although the NetTrail has received high praise from those who have used it, publicity is time consuming and we would like to increase campuswide usage even further. One strategy we adopted was to present the NetTrail to faculty groups working to change student general education requirements. Currently there is a proposal by an educational policy committee to revise the general education requirement on our campus to include the ability to use a reseach library and at least the basics of modern infomation technology. Members on the committe are aware of the NetTrail and are advocates of using it to address the library research requirement.

Initial Development Team (1997/98):
Library:
Deborah Murphy, Instruction Coordinator/Reference Librarian, McHenry Library (damurphy@cats.ucsc.edu)
Ann Hubble, Electronic Information Resources Librarian, Science Library (ahubble@cats.ucsc.edu)
Faculty:
William A. Ladusaw, Professor of Linguistics/Provost, Cowell College
Charles McDowell, Professor of Computer Science
Computing Center:
Fred Siff, Director of Communication and Technology Services
Janine Roeth, Communication and Technology Services
Other staff:
Kathy Jefferds, Humanities Division
Karalee Richter, Porter College

Continuing Development Team (1998/99):
Library:
Deborah Murphy, Instruction Coordinator/Reference Librarian, McHenry Library, (damurphy@cats.ucsc.edu)

Ann Hubble, Electronic Information Resources Librarian, Science Library (ahubble@cats.ucsc.edu)

Faculty:
William A. Ladusaw, Professor of Linguistics/Provost, Cowell College

Computing Center:
Janine Roeth, Communication and Technology Services

Contributed Papers

Partnering for Effective Service

Bringing LOGIC to Local Government Information: A Multi-type Partnership to Organize Electronic Local Government Information

Judy K. Horn and Shirley W. Leung

Abstract

Would you like to develop closer partnerships and working relations with public libraries or other jurisdictions in your area? Have you ever wished that there were more efficient methods of collecting, organizing, providing access to and archiving local government information from the cities in your jurisdiction? This paper presents a description of a multi-type partnership of libraries, local jurisdictions, and community organizations working together to develop a method for enhancing the community's access to full-text electronic local government information.

Background

The University of California, Irvine is located in central Orange County, surrounded by high technology firms and in the midst of what is becoming known as the new Gold Coast. Orange County is the third most populous county in California with a well-educated and culturally and ethnically diverse and economically multi-faceted population. High school graduates constitute more than 82% of the population and more than 26% are college graduates. Approximately 61% of the households have an income of over $35,000. The Orange

---

Judy K. Horn is head, Government Information Department, University of California, Irvine, and Shirley W. Leung is university librarian, Hong Kong Baptist University.

County economy is a vigorous one which ranks 33rd in the world. The UCI Libraries is the largest research library in the county. The Orange County Library system consists of 27 branches. Seven cities within the county also have city libraries. The public libraries are mostly small and have focused mainly on providing recreational reading. There are several other academic libraries in the county.

The December, 1994 bankruptcy of Orange County had a major effect on the public libraries and resulted in the reduction of hours and staff. Community use of the UCI Libraries proliferated, especially on weekends when UCI was frequently the only library in the county that was open. A survey done by the UCI Libraries in 1995/96 indicated that approximately 70 percent of the weekend users in the Libraries were from the community. Weekday usage by the community averaged about 40 percent. Community users have always constituted a large part of the use statistics of the UCI Library, given the make-up of the county and the lack of other large research libraries. However, the increase in the number of community users that the UCI Libraries experienced during the 1995/96 period was approximately 10 to 15 percent above the previous statistics. Government Information materials in the UCI Libraries which has traditionally seen heavy use by the community experienced a corresponding increase in its statistics.

Recognizing the need for demand management and desiring to develop a stronger partnership between the UCI Libraries and other libraries in Orange County, Shirley Leung and Judy Horn organized a meeting and invited representatives of the Orange County Public Library, Newport Beach Public Library, Santa Ana Public Library, and the Orange County Law Library to attend. As a Federal depository library, UCI has always maintained a strong outreach program in working with the public libraries in the area. With more and more government information appearing on the Internet/WWW, we were seeking ways that UCI could facilitate the use of these electronic resources in the public libraries.

The discussion at this initial meeting focused on how the Internet could be utilized to answer government information questions received by the public libraries. The conversation quickly moved from Federal information on the Internet to the need for better access to information published by Orange County and its cities. The need for better access to local information was identified as the most critical need with which UCI could help facilitate a resolution. The public libraries as well as UCI get numerous requests for reports from Orange County cities that are collected by various libraries in Orange County. There is no mechanism to determine which library has which report. Libraries tend to send users to the UCI Libraries since they have the most comprehensive collection. Thus, as a result of this conversation, the concept of the Local Online Government Information Center was born.

Attaining a grant for LOGIC
The LOGIC group decided to seek a LSTA grant and a proposal was quickly written with UCI Libraries as the lead agency. The original plan had two main objectives. The first was to develop a prototype of a Local Online Government Information Center with access to full-text Orange County city government information by using the WWW as the vehicle of presentation and access. The second was to explore the feasibility of, and options for expanding and continuing this effort on an ongoing basis to create on electronic archive of full-text local government information to be housed at UCI. In reading our planning grant proposal, the LSTA readers and consultants raised two important issues. They pointed out that the proposal failed to demonstrate the need for this project since numerous libraries had already established links to various local, state, and federal government web sites. They also expressed the view that we should not scan local documents into electronic format since the production of government documents, regardless of format, is a local government responsibility.

We addressed the first concern by developing a table showing that the websites of the Orange County city governments vary considerably in coverage, content and scope. A few of the 31 cities in Orange County have put important documents in full-text on their websites. The majority have only included very general information such as a list of city government agencies and their office hours and other basic information about the city. This led us to realize that we needed to make a better case in explaining the importance of making available and collecting the kind of local government information of a more enduring interest to city planners, analysts, researchers, and the community. We called this type of information "research level" local government information and it was defined to include such documents as annual budgets, general plans, zoning codes and ordinances, building codes, demographic reports, and environmental impact reports.

We felt that the second concern raised by the grant proposal readers stemmed from a more traditional perspective with information owned by clearly demarcated sectors. Their attitude showed a lack of understanding of issues related to electronic information and archiving. It was clear from our survey of the city websites that none of the cities had yet begun to archive full-text information on their website. This concern also reminded us that we must make a stronger and clearer case of what we wanted to accomplish and the role that we wished to undertake.

In the successful LOGIC grant proposal, we focused on the development of a conceptual framework and action plan based on user input during the first year of the project. The grant included funding for a consultant whose responsibilities included gathering input from constituent groups through public forums to determine the type of information deemed most important to have full-text coverage, developing a conceptual framework for LOGIC, and producing an action plan for an implementation effort in the next fiscal year with emphasis on ways city government and libraries can work collaboratively on this project. The grant proposal was written by Shirley Leung and Judy Horn with considerable input from the participating libraries.

A Steering Committee to provide overall vision and leadership for the project was established. The Steering Committee included the original representatives from the Orange County Public Library, Orange County Law Library, Newport Beach Public Library, Santa Ana Public Library and UCI with the addition of a representative of the California League of Cities, Orange County Division and the Webmaster for the County of Orange. Day-to-day supervision of the project was provided by the UCI Libraries.

In addition to the representative from the League of California Cities, Orange County Division and the Webmaster for the County of Orange, the Steering Committee decided that it would be advantageous to have a city manager or city council member serve on the group. On the recommendation of the Orange County Librarian, the city manager of one of the cities in central Orange County was invited to serve on the LOGIC Steering Committee. The city manager was enthusiastic about the project and agreed to serve. However, after the grant had been received and we were arranging our first meeting, he decided that he would be unable to participate because of other responsibilities. He appointed the city's personnel analyst to represent him but that person never attended the meetings or participated. Whether the presence of a representative from a city would have influenced the course of events of this project is, of course, unknown.

Getting LOGIC off the ground

The first item of business for the Steering Committee after receiving the grant for the LOGIC project in October 1997 was to hire a consultant to carry out the work of the project. UCI placed an advertisement in *Western Cities* and on an Internet job site. Four qualified applications were received and the Steering Committee met to interview them. The selection of the successful candidate, RRB Policy Research and Planning, was based on his considerable experience in working with various local jurisdictions. The consultant had formed a project team consisting of the himself and two colleagues. One team member was a fellow consultant who formerly worked for the Orange County Environmental Management Agency, and the second was a web page designer. The time between the receipt of the grant and the hiring of the consultant was 4 months, about 2 months longer than anticipated.

Before the consultant began work, a contract listing scope of the services and tasks to be performed by the consultants was prepared. The various tasks included researching the state of the art of local government information on the Internet/WWW including which cities have full-text information on their sites; developing an online survey form for businesses, community users, libraries and other interested individuals; publicizing the survey as well as the project; meeting with each Orange County city either individually or in groups to gain support for the LOGIC project; ascertaining the perceived benefits of the project, and its potential barriers; holding public forms to provide opportunities for open discussion and input from various users of government information; developing a conceptual LOGIC framework and action plan based on input received from the participants; and creating a LOGIC prototype. In addition, the consultant met with the Board of Directors of the Orange County Council of Governments (OCCOG) and with the OCCOG Technical Advisory Committee to make presentations about the project and to enhance awareness of LOGIC among the city council members, mayors, city managers and city staffs. The League of California Cities, Orange County Division assisted in facilitating the appearance of the consultant before these groups.

During the course of the grant, which concluded in September 1998, the LOGIC Steering Committee and the consultant met regularly to discuss the various phases of the work the consultant had completed and to discuss progress of the project. Two issues frequently discussed were the funding for the next phase and the long-term maintenance of LOGIC. The original plan was to submit a proposal for a second LSTA grant for the 1998/99 cycle but the proposal deadline occurred prior to the hiring of the consultant and the Steering Committee did not feel that they had enough information to prepare a new proposal. Funding for the next steps of this project was of major to concern to all members.

The Steering Committee discussed the possibility of securing corporate funding but did not move beyond the discussion stage until the spring of 1998 when Shirley Leung had the opportunity during a dinner occasion to sit next to the Chairman of the Board of a Fortune 500 information management system company headquartered in Orange County. She mentioned the LOGIC project to him and he expressed strong interest in the project. Shortly after, a company staff member contacted Shirley to suggest a demonstration of their system. Several meetings between the staff member, the consultants and the LOGIC Steering Committee followed this demonstration. The Chairman of the Board was so interested in the project that he brought staff who specialized in assisting customers in implementing new systems from the Seattle office to attend a meeting with the consultant and the LOGIC Steering Committee. The company has since undergone restructuring and has suffered a financial downturn, slowing down their involvement in the project. The University Librarian continues to keep in communication with the Chairman who has reiterated his interest in the project.

What we learned from Phase I of the LOGIC Project

The final report from the consultant contains several interesting facts. Among them are:

• Orange County cities and jurisdictions are interested in seeing LOGIC developed. The jurisdictions participating in this project perceived several potential benefits. They see it as a research tool which could result in savings of staff time and resources by providing electronic access to a centralized research document database that they could search for information to determine what other jurisdictions are doing in regards to a specific issue. They recognize it as a way to respond to public requests for such information without having to produce and maintain a supply of documents for the public. They find it desirable to facilitate enhanced public access to information since research level documents would be available to the public 24 hours a day. Lastly, they see the benefits of saving server space on the city servers for large documents.

• The LOGIC proposal for archiving local government full-text, research quality documents would not duplicate any existing or planned efforts of local jurisdictions/agencies in Orange County.

• The use of the Internet/WWW by local jurisdictions to serve constituents is relatively new. The direction the cities seem to be moving is toward more descriptive and current information about the services offered by their agencies rather than the provision of full-text archival quality documents which would be a "value-added" offering to existing online information on city websites.

- Many cities, even those which have city websites, are not adequately staffed to maintain their own sites, much less participate in the development and maintenance of a centralized LOGIC site. Given this, UCI will need to determine if electronically archiving documents is a service that it wishes to provide to the public as a data collection, information and resource entity
- One of the primary added values of a LOGIC site will be the ability to provide comparative research across several local government documents. This is best achieved with a centralized server and data archives
- Search and downloading capabilities and document protection are critical components to the initial development of the system; ultimate operation and maintenance costs will rise considerably as search functions are expanded, but expanded search functions will probably be most desired by system users

The consultant team recommended that in the next phase the focus should be on those documents that the cities do not currently provide or store on their local sites and documents which cities have indicated an interest in using for comparative research. These initially include:
- General plans
  - Annual budgets
  - Zoning codes and ordinances
  - Building codes
  - Demographic reports
  - Fee schedules
  - Environmental Impact reports
  - "Special" studies conducted by/for local jurisdictions

These documents are not subject to frequent revisions as some are released annually, others are released on a one-time basis or are officially updated infrequently. The consultant team did not recommend the inclusion of information subject to frequent revision since it would be detrimental to the success of the project in the early stages.

The consultant team stressed the need for the LOGIC site to have links to city web pages since the current city information and LOGIC archival information are complementary to one another. Additionally, the consultant team suggested that in the future the cities should have a direct link to the UCI site, providing the cities with the opportunity to update information on both their local site and the centralized archive concurrently. There will be a need for a data management system to allow cities to identify who has authority to alter a document and to track various versions of documents.

What we learned from the Partnership

The partnership effort for the LOGIC grant was also a learning experience for us. Some of the things that we discovered include:

- Local public libraries are interested in partnering with the University library, particularly if the topic is one of sustaining interest to the involved libraries and the community.
- While it is important for all libraries to work together, it is also necessary for one of the libraries to take the lead in submitting the grant proposal and to track the financial information.
- There also needs to be a day-to-day coordinator for the project who is a member of the steering committee, acts as liaison between the consultant and the Steering Committee, establishes meeting times and agendas, and assures that the required reports are submitted on time.
- Regular meetings of those involved in the project are important not only for progress reports but to maintain momentum and interest in the project.
- If possible, tasks should be allocated to the various members of the group as a means of maintaining interest and promoting active involvement in the project.
- Partners take a more active role when they have a strong interest in the project or when the project is tied to their daily responsibilities.
- The larger and more diverse the partnership group, the greater is the need for communication and coordination.
- Partnership activities always take longer than anticipated and they require more work and attention than planned.

- The possibility for partnerships is unlimited. Opportunities arise when least expected and being alert for these possibilities enhances the potential for finding partners for your project.
- Projects of interest or benefit to the local community have the highest potential of attracting corporate partners as well as community interest and partners.

Next steps for LOGIC

After reviewing the report of the consultant and considering the various recommendations, the Steering Committee has submitted a proposal for a second LSTA grant that will be a pilot project with two to four Orange County cities. The proposed grant will fund a web page designer to work with these cities on resolving the technological issues involved in loading full-text files on a server hosted at UCI. As recommended by the consultants, the proposal includes the development of a subject/keyword index to provide access to the files. We also propose to establish links to the LOGIC prototype on the Orange County public libraries and city home pages to widely test the prototype and indexing. As a result of this proposed pilot project, we will be able to collect data that will assist in acquiring, maintaining, and updating the site as well as cost analysis data and information that will assist in expanding the project to include additional Orange County cities. Because of the outreach and publicity work of the consultant in the first phase, the cities in Orange County are familiar with the LOGIC project. Several of them, including the City Manager of one of the largest cities in the county, have already indicated a desire to participate in this pilot project.

We have determined that we need more specific information about technological issues, indexing and file issues, and the amount of time and costs involved before we can proceed with full implementation of this project. It would be an impossible task to work with all 31 Orange County cities at one time. By concentrating our efforts in working with a couple of cities who have some full-text information and some who have not yet added full text information to their website, we hope to acquire the data that we need to fully implement LOGIC. Once we have this information, we will be ready to talk once again with the Chairman of the Board of the Orange County based information technology company. He continues to indicate that he is interested in the project. We will also look for partnership opportunities with other companies in the business of information management systems.

Conclusion

LOGIC began as a multi-type library effort to manage demands on the university Libraries by community users and to develop a strong working relationship with public and special libraries in the area for future partnership collaborations. Unbeknownst to the Steering Committee members when they came up with this idea, the concept of LOGIC is one that many different jurisdictions within the county have long had on their "wish" list. However, no one in these various jurisdictions quite knew how to go about organizing full-text local government information into a single source and bringing such a project to fruition. The LOGIC proposal was greeted enthusiastically by the community and that led to the inclusion of representatives from the League of California Cities, Orange County Division and the County of Orange to the Steering Committee.

The work of the consultant team revealed that the cities in Orange County are not as technologically advanced as it had first been assumed. Few of the cities have the resources to place full-text information on their city websites. Most cities have not yet considered the need to electronically archive their documents or how this can be done most effectively. A widespread desire exists within the county to have full-text city documents such as general plans, municipal codes, environmental impact statements, annual budgets, and demographic reports available electronically with indexing to provide comparative searches across several jurisdictions. The idea for LOGIC is a solid one but this first phase revealed the difficulties incumbent in working at one time with 31 cities with differing technological capabilities. Hence, in this second grant proposal, we plan to work with a small number of cities (from 2 to 4) to work through the issues of loading full-text documents from these cities on a server and to index these documents so that the user can search for the same or similar data issued by more than one city. The information that we gain from this new pilot project will provide us with detailed data that will assist us in expanding the project to additional cities and in renewing discussions with our possible corporate partner.

We still have a long way to go to fully implement LOGIC. If we obtain the necessary funding the project that will benefit the entire county. This is a project that numerous groups within the county would like to see succeed, though each for a different reason. It is also a project that is a perfect fit for the expertise that librarians can bring to organizing information in an electronic environment. The cities welcome the participation of the libraries in this because they recognize that none of them individually, or even collectively, have the experience or expertise to organize and develop such a body of information. It has been very rewarding to work with the cities, other libraries, county organizations, and our potential corporate partner on this project and we look forward to extending that collaboration as we continue to develop LOGIC.

Developing and Maintaining Instructional Web Sites: The Library Starter Kit

Deborah A. Murphy

The library may not see a student until an actual research project or paper is due, at which point the student often has a very narrow focus and limited interest in learning about the process of research. Point of need assistance, while intrinsically wonderful, can be problematic given a limited number of librarians and Reference Desk hours. Librarians are faced with the equivalent of someone who has never been behind the wheel of a car needing to drive from Chicago to New York. The non-driver may only want to know where to put the key and which is the pedal that makes it go. It can be difficult to explain why one might need to know how to read a map, what are the rules of the road, or where the gas goes.

Development
There has been a natural progression in the methods and formats librarians have used to reach new library users. These range from one-on-one assistance, to group tours, specialized orientation sessions, and individual class instruction, as well as self-serve resources such as self-guided tours, handouts, maps, information notes and so on. The World Wide Web (WWW) presented another potential way to reach students. Increased campus access to the Internet from numerous computer labs and high speed connections in dorm rooms, and off-campus dial-in modem access meant a resource that was available 24 hours a day from wherever a student could connect to the Internet. The Internet also allowed access for librarians when at the Reference Desk, teaching a library research course, or providing assistance to distance learners.

In early 1996, I developed an Instructional Improvement Grant to create the first Library Virtual Tour on the WWW. The grant provided funding for a limited number of student developer hours to work with me on both designing a tour as well as enhancing with my web development skills. The first version of this tour was made available in August of 1996 and provided a graphic and textual overview of both the physical layout and resources available in the McHenry Library.

The process left me with a rudimentary knowledge of HTML and image editing, and essential knowledge to maintain the tour but not yet enough to develop additional sites without additional skills and experience. The completion of the virtual tour led to an invitation from a Computer Science pro-

Deborah A. Murphy is instruction coordinator and reference librarian, University of California, Santa Cruz

fessor to submit a class project for her multi media publishing course. I enrolled in the class and learned along with the students as both project client and team developer of a new project "The Library Starter Kit." The Kit would consist of not only the virtual tour, but a guide to starting the research process, a collection of web-based subject guides to research and a directory of current on-line library workshops.

By being both a student in the course as well as project client, I had the opportunity to work on all portions of the new Starter Kit as well as provide detailed content and immediate feedback on design and organization. The first version of this site became available in 1997 (Murphy, 1997) The next phase of development occurred in the subsequent advanced multi media publishing course. By this time new technologies had come along that allowed for greater interactivity with a web site, we redesigned the entire virtual tour, creating a new navigational metaphor that utilized frames, Java scripting and MacroMedia Director software. The metaphor we chose, an elevator, provided a more consistent and "real life" framework as students moved around the tour. Links were available to both the non-frames tour as well as the text version so that users had a choice of environments.

In spring of 1997, I joined a campuswide group of faculty and Information Technologies staff to develop UCSC's first on-line literacy course available on the WWW. Through a set of four self-paced modules, students are provided an introduction to browsing the Web, using E-mail at UCSC, connecting with on-line Library Resources, using Newsgroups, and understanding Netiquette. This course, the newest addition to the Starter Kit, is aimed at users new to the on-line environment or those with differing starting points in terms of initial computer skills and interests. It provides a solid grounding in basic skills as well as an introduction to more specialized applications used locally at UCSC.

Maintenance
Web site development is only half the picture. The care, maintenance and continued growth of a web site can be a major commitment. Initially, this meant unifying the diverse sites onto a centralized server, ensuring that all sites met ADA accessibility requirements developed by the University, and negotiating appropriate locations on the existing Library web site.

Additional workload issues became evident after the initial development of the Starter Kit. The size of many of these sites meant that keeping pages current became a major workload issue. High on the maintenance list were the subject guides, which require new additions, as well as revisions to content and format of existing guides. How best to handle these workload issues has yet to be addressed, but I still retain primary responsibility for all sites. As more instructional sites were developed, it became clear that not all of these would become part of the Starter Kit. A new Library Instruction page was created that incorporated all instruction based sites into one annotated list with links to each.

Other maintenance issues that came to light over time. Given that eight different students had contributed in some way to the developments of the various sites, a significant amount of editing and programming had to be done to ensure some consistency in style and layout of both the final product and the HTML coding. Although all sites require updating and revisions, some are more demanding than others. Time has become one of the scarcest resources available. Funding for one time projects is easier to obtain than long term staffing. So authoring a web site often means being responsible for its care and well being.

Implementation
The Library Starter Kit can be used in a number of instructional environments:

• A resource available on demand to users browsing the library home page - The individual components of the Starter Kit are available in several places on the Library web site. Links back to the Starter Kit home page give users an overview of additional resources. A prominent position on the McHenry Library home page and campus wide email announcements have also helped users locate the Starter Kit.

• A link for instructors to add to their own WWW pages—UCSC faculty who create WWW based resources for their classes can place a link to the Library Starter Kit directly on their class pages.

• A lecture tool for library instruction—All of our library instruction sessions, whether conducted in the library or elsewhere on campus, include an on-line component. The Starter Kit has links to many of the key introductory resources that are presented during these sessions. This simplifies preparation for library instructors and gives students a single starting point to remember when they search on their own. The Virtual Tour in particular allows us to vividly bring the library into the classroom, presenting maps and images of materials as we lecture.

• Online Literacy instruction—In addition to course-integrated instruction, the NetTrail provides on demand instruction for students needing an introduction to a set of skills while in pursuit of another topic (e.g. students doing Library research, but who need an introduction to using the WWW), Faculty and staff who may need additional Internet instruction, assistance for off-campus students, and integration into a UCSC Information Literacy program.

Evaluation

As most web site developers know, evaluating usability is important for any site that you expect others to search and use. There are a variety of methods (e.g., surveys, questionnaires, focus groups), of which we chose field testing using student volunteers. It was an enlightening and sometimes humbling experience watching how they used the interface, how they used resources or navigational features, if they used or needed help features, and their general reaction to the site. This mix of qualitative and quantitative feedback was a key part of the design process. The UCSC NetTrail demonstrates of the impact of usability testing. Initially comprised of four tutorials with differing approaches to their content, feedback from user observations led to revisions that produced a more unified voice, layout, and navigation scheme. As one might guess, it was much easier to rework a web site early in the authoring process than after investing in extensive development. Usability testing performed on earlier sites instructed development of later ones, and new design and authoring features on these more recent sites have informed changes and revisions to earlier resources.

Another way to evaluate use is to track statistics on web site usage. While bigger does not necessarily mean better, tracking the hits to a page can be a one way to detect poor linkage, confusing layout, invisibility, or lack of interest. There are also utilities that allow you to see who has placed links to your pages, another way to gauge user audience and interest. Our web server can generate weekly and cumulative statistical usage reports. This has been a very useful means of tracking patterns and increases or decreases in usage. The numbers below reflect the cumulative number of times the top home page for each site has been visited:

Site	Dates	Visits
The Library Starter Kit	8/1/97–2/14/99	9,858
McHenry Virtual Tour	8/1/97–2/14/99	4,069
Constructing Your Research Paper	8/1/97–2/14/99	57,017
Subject Guides	8/1/97–2/14/99	17,175
UCSC NetTrail	11/22/97–2/13/99	4,039

Areas with lower than expected usage prompted a re-examination of the pages themselves for usability, as well site visibility and accessibility. It was also interesting to note which sites are being used by nonUCSC researchers. We were surprised to see how heavily the "Constructing Your Research Paper" site was used and discovered that it is a featured site in several on-line web directories, specifically those aimed at students new to the research process.

Conclusion

There is a difficult balancing act to maintain between the hours spent in developing and updating web pages vs. the return in terms of instructional value. Evaluation may take many forms, from usage statistics to individual feedback. Additionally, continued web development requires continuing acquisition and practice of development skills, keeping up with software and hardware changes, and adequate time to maintain existing sites. Educating one's colleagues about web site authoring issues may become almost as important as developing one's own skills—the more others know of what is involved in developing and maintaining web sites, the greater chance of creating an environment which supports publishing in this new format.

Librarians face many of the same issues other academics do in publishing and developing resources in new media and formats. Peer evaluation can be a key part of advancement and promotion, and work outside the more traditional areas of publication and research can be difficult to evaluate. Those publishing in nontraditional multi media may find that acknowledgment of the value of their work may not come primarily from the resource per se, but from the articles or papers published in more traditional formats that discuss the resource (Guernsey, 1997).

The Library Starter Kit remains very much a work in progress. It will require a continuing commitment to maintain and expand existing components, add new WWW search and multimedia features, and develop additional resources. Given the changing nature of technology, it can be safely assumed that most of these resources will need to migrate to new formats in the not so distant future. In spite of these issues, it has been an exhilarating experiment in exploring innovative approaches to instruction and has expanded the range of the Library's instructional programs.

Web sites:

The Library Starter Kit
http://bob.ucsc.edu/library/ref/instruction/skit

McHenry Library Virtual Tour
http://bob.ucsc.edu/library/tour

The UCSC NetTrail
http://nettrail.ucsc.edu

Constructing Your Research Paper
http://bob.ucsc.edu/library/ref/instruction/research/libres.htm

Subject Guides
http://bob.ucsc.edu/library/ref/instruction/refguides/noframes_index.html

Online workshops
http://bob.ucsc.edu/library/ref/workshops

McHenry Library Instruction
http://bob.ucsc.edu/library/ref/instruction

References

Guernsey, Lisa. Scholars who work with technology fear they suffer in tenure reviews. *Chronicle of Higher Education* v.43, n.39 (June 6, 1997): A21 (2 pages).

Murphy, D.A. "The Library Starter Kit: using new technologies for training and instruction." In: *Proceedings. ACM SIGUCCS 1997 User Services Conference XXV. Are You Ready?* 25th SIGUCCS '97 Conference, University and College Computing Services 25th User Services Conference, Monterey, Calif., USA, 9–12 Nov. 1997. New York, N.Y.,: ACM, 1997. 239–46. (http://bob.ucsc.edu/library/ref/instruction/siguccs)

Directly to the Source: Will Academic Libraries Become Wholesalers of Information?

Scott Anderson

Introduction

As libraries begin addressing growing numbers of remote (although not necessarily off campus) users, technology has and will continue to play a primary role in how information is conveyed to this new class of library users.

While remote access to library catalogs has been around for years, the growing number of traditionally print indexing and reference tools available anytime, anywhere, represents an interesting paradox in the extension of library resources and services. The monopoly position of the library as the institutional information provider could appear to some users as being broken by increasingly seamless computing and communications technology. If it is viewed as such, what happens to the position of the library in the information hierarchy of our users?

While today's talk isn't intended to be highly scientific or densely packed with reams of survey data, it is intended to get you thinking about what may happen after all of the resources and services that libraries have historically provided become available "out there."

Utilizing the competitive intelligence process, I'll attempt to extrapolate some possible "answers" to this presentation's primary question "Will academic libraries appear to become wholesalers of information?"

The Competitive Intelligence Process

What? Competitive Intelligence process? Why? The 'CI' process is a simple four step process (that could be continuous) that anyone can use to help them think about and formulate possible courses of action (hopefully) in anticipation of developments that are going to warrant *some* type of response. The four-step process as outlined by Larry Kahaner, in his recent book *Competitive Intelligence*[1], is as follows.

Step 1: Planning and Direction.

What do you need to know? This could be viewed as the first step and the recurring last step as your plans and directions will probably change the more you know about what you're investigating. What do you need to know or understand is often stated as a question to help facilitate the process.

Scott Anderson is information technologies librarian, Millersville University.

Step 2: Collection
Gathering information. As practicing information professionals you shouldn't be surprised that just about everything needed is already available someplace. Personal observation is also a valid resource and shouldn't be forgotten when gathering information for use in the analysis phase.

Step 3: Analysis
Utilizing the information gathered in the previous phase of the process, begin the process of weighting the information for importance and creditability, timeliness, etc. Determining patterns or establishing a chain of events would be useful, as that can be used when developing various scenarios that may prove possible. Developing realistic future scenarios and how your institution may be able to prepare or respond is part of this phase of the process.

Step 4: Dissemination
At this point, the various scenarios and possible responses have been "documented" and are ready to be set to the person or persons that make policy or determine the general direction of the organization. As with any information, the best format is the one most suited to the intended audience.

Competitive Intelligence in the Library Setting
The CI process within a library setting isn't concentrated so much on the "what are competitors doing" as "what events involving us are taking place" and how do we want to address them. While institutions may compete for students, and libraries are certainly part of that recruitment effort, libraries themselves hardly actively compete with each other with any destructive intent.

While it's likely that someone or a group people in the library attempt to keep up with the latest and greatest that vendors have to offer or with larger political and policy issues, it's important to make everyone at least aware of what to expect. Additionally, whenever there are a number of choices or when possible trends start to emerge that are all plausible, it's time to start outlining some responses.

Taking two issues that my own institution should be addressing within the next year or two, I will attempt to utilize the CI process in part to formulate a response to a possible or probable scenario. What follows in the next section are some thoughts on what effects the library's "brand" presence could have among library users based on the two examples.

Integrated Access to "Not Indexed" Periodical Collections
Seamless electronic passage between 3rd party indexing and the article or document itself may represent if not the last technical hurdle, at least a large step, to easing the connection between accessing the literature and the relatively mechanical step of obtaining the literature itself. The following is an example of using the CI process in a library setting regarding the "integration" of periodical indexing and periodical literature driven by vendor products and/or technology.

Step 1: What's the question(s)?
Anybody could pose the question(s); what's more difficult is getting someone, or a group of someones, to finish the process.

How, when or should the library pursue integrating electronic collections of periodicals into indexing resources? At what cost and from what points will the articles actually be available to users?

Step 2: Information collection.
As part of the Pennsylvania State System of Higher Education, Millersville University is part of a consortium that purchases about two dozen databases from SilverPlatter, of which Millersville subscribes to eighteen. Given that Millersville subscribes to eighteen databases (mostly indexing) and generally is able to add about one new title every year, there is certainly already "critical mass" on the indexing side to make integrating full text from strictly full text aggregators via "SilverLinker" feasible.

Without getting into reams of data, list comparisons, etc., we'll make the assumption that there is a sufficiently high match between the periodicals indexed in various databases to which Millersville subscribes, and full text in other products to which Millersville subscribes. Additionally, we'll consider the cost of the adding on the

SilverPlatter product SilverLinker to be within the grasp of the Library Department.

Step 3: Analysis
As stated above, analysis is the most difficult part of the process as building scenarios can get complicated quickly, and it is often necessary to make some educated "guesses." For this issue, I'll try to keep the scenarios simple and sufficient to illustrate the idea of analysis.

Scenario #1. Linking will function seamlessly within a specified IP range, but not from off campus, even though a user will have access to the indexing portion of the product off campus via validation services. This is caused by lack of off campus access to electronic periodical collections.

Scenario #2. Linking will function for any validated (enter of barcode) user, regardless of physical location on or off campus. (For Millersville this scenario would require that additional issues be addressed as the library presently deploys IP passthrough whenever possible to aid ease of access and on campus library instruction).

Scenario #3. Linking will function on campus via IP passthrough, and off campus via existing validation for indexing, but additional validation will be required prior to gaining access to the actual article. Passwords for validation would have to be issued for each periodical database that a user might encounter.

None of the above scenarios is intended to be the definitive word on how the technology may or may not work, but they are intended as some possible examples of scenarios.

Step 4: Dissemination
At Millersville, whoever has assembled the report would pass this along to the Collection Development and Management committee for review. Should that committee find it useful and something to pursue, it would be forwarded to the entire Library Department for discussion.

One could make an argument for the process to end with a decidedly neutral recommendation, or it could favor some method of deployment. The Library Department at Millersville traditionally likes to have some sort of "recommendation" for or against after something has come from committee, so the dissemination and discussion process will have to take into consideration how your organization reaches decisions (or doesn't) on issues.

Delivery of Physical Materials
Despite the talk surrounding grand schemes of the paperless office and the promise of electronic publication, it is very likely that one has too look no further than one's own office to find that this is not true. Information stored on some sort of physical medium (usually known as paper) continues to clutter our offices and arrive in the mail at what seems an ever-increasing rate.

Delivery of physical materials that cannot be accessed electronically, or that a user elects to review in a physical format could represent an area of extension of library services in response to student needs when they are not physically present at the library. These materials could consist of simple articles, various governmental documents, or items from the general collections (we'll exclude restricted access collections).

In an effort to meet the needs of remote users (primarily those off campus) and provide equitable access to information resources, libraries will eventually have to develop a mechanism and surrounding policy about how to deliver these materials to students. Millersville is developing distance education courses and programs, and yet the library has no means of delivering physical information to prospective students. Millersville is not alone. To truly support a distance education program, there is little doubt that some delivery mechanism accommodation has to be made, but remote library users may find delivery services just as convenient and useful.

Step 1: What's the Question(s)?
Should the library consider sending physical items to remote library users? For what cost? For everyone who is registered and wants to pay, or just people not on campus?

Step 2: Information Collection
If this phase were being performed right now, there would be considerable secondary resources to consult, and various institutions doing something similar to this already. The phone and e-mail would

likely be very useful resources for this phase as talking about various success and/or failures at institutions that have a service similar to this could yield very useful results.

Step 3: Analysis
Analysis of this question would likely yield several existing models with varying degrees of service and cost associated with each. Scenarios for this would probably concentrate on who qualifies for the service, where something would be delivered, speed of delivery, the costs associated with speed of delivery, and return mechanisms for items that are to be returned. It would be appropriate in this phase to explore some financial "break-even" points as well.

Step 4: Dissemination
Dissemination and discussion of any report for this type of service (unknown, usage based, and having monetary transactions) will likely go to library faculty, staff, and administration as this involves multiple areas and some sort of billing/funds collection operation.

The Library and Extension of Services
Simple observation reveals that most incoming students are largely unprepared to effectively utilize the increasingly technologically oriented tools of an academic library or library system[2]. However, with some instruction (one tries for systematic instruction) and experience, many students obtain sufficient skills to understand the general concepts of the library catalog, periodical index and, it has increasingly been my experience, where students can get access.

If convenience of use for the average remote library user is at the top or near the top of desired attributes from a library[3], what does that do for any particular academic library trying to meet the needs of its users? It's paradoxical that the easier a library is to use, resources are to access, services are delivered, the easier it becomes to forget about it as a specific entity and think of it in a more generic sense.

Using myself as an example, I'm not overly concerned about my bank, I'm concerned about where and when I can do my banking. Making arrangements to get to Detroit, I wasn't concerned about any particular airline, but rather point of departure and departure/arrival times. Notwithstanding that I work at a library, my second trip through graduate school didn't see me using too much of the physical library since I could do most of my research from the comfort of my office, 50 miles away. I don't consider myself lazy; I just prefer to take full advantage of options that save me time and movement, even if there is a direct cost. What I consistently see in daily library thinking and discussion among my colleagues is a failure to understand that there is a cost associated with place. If a library enhances the ability to deliver services, what happens in the long run as users no longer think of the library as an entity because it's been "replaced" with resources purchased by the library, but delivered to the end user by vendors?

I hold office hours in computing labs on the Millersville campus specifically for business and economics students. I also provide increasing numbers of "library instruction" sessions for business students, often outside the library, but still making full use of the resources they will need for their assignments. What I see happening I think is very interesting. Students are acting and talking of information needs and specific products, not of the library. Hence, I have adopted a few strategies that help students understand that there is a "library" that supports all of these technologically accessible products and services that are available.

What follows are some of the activities that I am undertaking to keep library services (but not necessarily the library) in the forefront of student and faculty research activities.

Getting "Out There" with the Students
Similar to many other academic libraries, Millersville has a liaison program. I am the liaison librarian to the Business, Economics, and Computer Science departments at Millersville. If the information is "out there" and services are "out there" I should be out there as well. Beginning in the spring of 1998, I started holding office hours in general purpose computing labs and had what I thought was modest impact. I'd average about one student ev-

ery office session. I was unable to hold office hours in computing labs in the fall 1999 semester, but have reinstated the service after numerous requests from other faculty to help students with their research projects. In interactions with students, they aren't inundated with "this is a library resource" so much as a tangential comment that the library purchases the product for use with this and other assignments as part of the learning process.

Network with New Faculty
New faculty orientation at Millersville is a great opportunity to meet with new faculty in my areas and talk about what resources and services are available and how I can be of assistance in the learning process. While this takes time to develop since I'm casting a fairly small net, in only three or four years it has become a major tool for getting "library instruction" inserted into the curriculum at the most appropriate time for all parties concerned. You can often learn a lot more about the intent of various assignments, and what's happening in departments by asking your fellow faculty at any meeting involving food. Never underestimate the "schmooze factor."

Just a Little Advertising
Walk into many libraries and you'll likely see a list of workshops, who to contact, where to sign up, etc. Using a simply one page flyer sent directly to faculty in my areas, I have several hundred flyers distributed directly to students in their classes addressing essentially the same concept. If students have a research question in one of my subject areas, they are encouraged to attend either my office hours, or make an appointment with me for private consultation. To my surprise, I've even seen some of these informational flyers posted on faculty office doors and in areas where students congregate to use computers or work on group research projects they have been assigned.

Associate with Products & Resources
Increasingly I attach my name and e-mail address to resources being made available via the library in my subject areas. Starting with web enabled bibliographies for classes that list me as the person to contact with any questions, to simply being listed as the "expert" for a particular resource, there is a *name* and a *means of contact* for students when they have questions.

Managing Expectations
Despite every intention of meeting user needs, there will be instances when either myself or services provided by the library will not be able to fulfill a need, in either the immediate or distant future. Managing expectations about what can realistically be expected is another way I attempt to continue fostering interaction. Users will view services as being adequate more often (and consequently view myself and library services with less dissatisfaction) with a better understanding of what is available[4].

Conclusion
While I expect to continue seeing, and actively encouraging, the deployment of new technologies to enhance access to scholarly information, I am also drawing the conclusion that the library as an institution will be the conduit for information. No longer will the library be the sole aggregator, repository, and only legitimate information purveyor in the academic setting. I tend to agree with Andrew Odlyzko's comments that publishers (or their vendors) could be assuming more of the aggregation and storage functions in the digital arena very similar to what the library has historically performed in the print arena[5].

While it is unlikely that academic libraries will be relegated to strictly wholesale storage locations of information anytime soon, we need to recognize that publishers of information now have the means to bypass the library and its functions should they elect to do so.

Notes
1. Larry Kahaner, *Competitive Intelligence: How to Gather, Analyze, and Use Information to Move Your Business to the Top* (New York: Touchstone, 1997), 43–47.
2. Cheryl A. McCarthy, "Expectations and Effectiveness Using CD-ROMs: What Do Patrons Want and How Satisfied Are They?" *College and Research Libraries* 58 (March 1997): 128–42.

3. Rosemarie Cooper, et al., "Remote Library Users—Needs and Expectations," *Library Trends* 47 (summer 1998): 42–64.

4. Christopher Millson-Martula, "Customer Expectations: Concepts and Reality for Academic Library Services," *College and Research Libraries* 56 (January 1995): 33–47.

5. Andrew Odlyzko, "Competition and Cooperation: Libraries and publishers in the transition to electronic scholarly journals," January 19, 1999, white paper, http://www.research.att.com/~amo/doc/eworld.html

Intercepting Departmental Fumbles and Running with the Ball

Alexia Strout-Dapaz and Dennis Odom

Academic libraries may find themselves drawn into inter-departmental partnerships with diverse campus units whose goals often run counter to the libraries' mission statement. Inter-departmental cooperation—while perceived as an ideal scenario—can be the source of disruption when fueled by conflicting research agendas or customer service goals. The challenge is to ensure that the partnership will be mutually advantageous to all concerned. This becomes increasingly complex when shrinking budgets and space considerations are the prime motivators for establishing a partnership. The library should not become an academic black hole for products or projects that have become inconvenient for other departments to handle. The objective of this paper is to outline steps to turn a potentially disadvantageous alliance into a win-win solution.

Recently, two departmental fumbles were intercepted by staff members of the Mary Couts Burnett Library at Texas Christian University (TCU). The first involved the selection, by the School of Business, of the electronic product Compustat. The second concerned the creation of a new non-library computer lab by the Intensive English Program. Via these examples, we intend to illustrate effective ways of handling politically charged situations which, at the outset, do not appear to be in the library's best interest. Following the "fumbles" and "interceptions" overview, is a solutions framework that may be adapted by any library to successfully negotiate potential academic minefields.

Compustat

Compustat is a [family of] CD-ROM product(s) produced by Standard and Poor's, a division of The McGraw-Hill Companies. Compustat is non-bibliographic in nature; it is used to generate statistical reports using raw financial data. As a data series product, its format is more appropriate as an instructional aid and/or laboratory application than as a library reference product. Furthermore, practitioners in the field of Finance—not students doing financial research—are Compustat's intended search audience. The product is also math intensive in its application and requires a math

---

Alexia Strout-Dapaz is business/reference librarian, and Dennis Odom is acquisitions librarian, Texas Christian University.

co-processor chip to perform the statistical calculations.

Although the library recommended against its purchase in 1993, the School of Business made a financial commitment to the product. After realizing that the product was going to take much more support in the Business computer lab than was previously anticipated, the School essentially unloaded the product onto the library since, in their words: the library "handles CD-ROMs." In effect, the School of Business determined that the product was appropriate for the library with no regard to its content, only its format. This last action was undertaken with no library staff consultation. The lack of library input resulted in improper planning and improper product implementation that took many years to resolve. Although they did not want to be involved in the maintenance, training, and upkeep of the CD-ROM, the School of Business continued to finance the product from their budget.

Departmental Fumbles
Product did not fit the selection criteria/policy document, employed by the Collection Development Department, used in purchasing electronic data products.

Professors, and library staff, were unaware that the purchased subscription was an **academic**, not a corporate subscription; resulting in mass confusion when professors demanded to know why certain data was not available for their calculations.

Once the School of Business realized it did not have the resources to appropriately accommodate the product, the library was put in a position to assume the ongoing upkeep, maintenance, product check-in and routing. To further complicate matters, the library lacked the proper electronic equipment required to effectively run Compustat since, in 1993, the Reference area PCs lacked math co-processors.

A specific point of service was not established. Guidelines for the routing of archival discs were either unclear or ignored, resulting in staff confusion and delays. Miscommunication between campus units, (Information Services/School of Business/Library), downgraded user support and increased end-user frustration.

Of the three departments involved (Information Services/School of Business/Library), not one wanted to endorse a "product champion" or "product troubleshooter." The lack of a product expert resulted in poor training procedures. All reference staff were now required (theoretically) to have extensive knowledge in the fields of finance, statistics, and the Compustat product with absolutely no training from Standard and Poor's.

Library staff became "couriers" or intermediaries between the Business faculty and Information Services. Faculty wanted certain disks loaded and available at the drop of a hat and any available Reference staff was expected to expediently deliver the product for quick loading onto the network CD-ROM tower.

Faculty had unrealistic expectations for the type of services Library staff could, and should, provide to users. For example, professors would encourage their undergraduate students to consult the product with no training, instruction or usage guidelines, assuming librarians could properly direct students in the product's use.

Library Interceptions
The list of challenges facing the Library staff provided an opportunity to strengthen the Library's position on the campus, while ensuring that Compustat found the most effective "home" for its user base. The first priority was establishing a clear communication link among the three campus entities previously mentioned. Since communication had broken down from the very beginning— with the library's initial rejection of Compustat as a Library database—a committee of concerned departmental representatives was established to spotlight problems. The library took the initiative by inviting both Business and Information Services to a procedural brainstorming meeting. The problems faced by library staff in effectively implementing Compustat were outlined. The suggestion was to continue meeting to devise a policy manual, for non-bibliographic electronic products, whereby all concerned departments would have input into the procedural document.

An effective communication process finally began after five years of miscommunication between the School of Business, the Library and Information Services. This amount of time should not have elapsed before the problem was identified and tackled by staff members. One of the reasons for this alarming time lapse in cementing a policy stemmed from the atmosphere of intimidation the library and Information Services perceived to be coming from the School of Business. Only when this fear was overcome and the key library staff committed themselves to an empowering role did the situation begin to improve. After many years of a frustrating situation, the library finally realized that the only way to pursue a solution was to be proactive, by taking a leadership role in forcing the other departments to face up to their fumbles and miscalculations.

The Compustat documentation that developed in the inter-departmental meetings became a detailed guideline, not only for Compustat implementation, but for future non-bibliographic electronic products as well. This policy and procedures document—after many drafts—became the guiding instrument which clearly delineated the commitments and responsibilities to which each department must adhere. In this complicated scenario, the Library was instrumental as the guiding force in strengthening cooperation between departments with antagonistic agendas.

Intensive English Lab

After many attempts, the Intensive English Program at Texas Christian University received a grant dedicated to the construction of a language learning lab on campus. The lab would house state-of-the-art computer equipment geared to facilitating instruction to non-English speakers. Campus Administration decided the best location for the Lab would be the library.

Departmental Fumbles

- The library space selected for the Intensive English Lab housed the graduate study carrels.
- The library was already very limited on space, having established an off-site storage facility the previous year.
- The loss of precious library space caused an immediate negative reaction from the staff, heightened by the fact that the location was to house another university department's program.
- The Intensive English Program had done very little planning beyond writing the grant. Implementation and the impact on the library and its staff had not been considered in detail.
- The library's instruction program, under-equipped and desperate for space, had suggested the graduate carrels as a location for future growth.
- Lab maintenance guidelines had not been established, causing concern over who would be responsible for the technology: Information Services or the Library.
- Many library staff members were concerned about how much staff time would be required in implementing a lab in which their role, or its benefits, were not clearly defined.

Library Interceptions

Once it became evident the Intensive English Lab would be housed in the library, staff attitudes, not surprisingly, were uniformly negative. Disbelief and anger with the campus administration's commandeering of library space was the norm. How could they take the building space, when they must know how much we needed and deserved it? Polite protest to the contrary, this is where University Administration felt the Intensive English Lab should go. When the charge came to the library's Instruction Committee to help in implementing the project, this negative attitude was the first hurdle.

Was gaining a lab with state-of-the-art equipment geared toward instruction really a negative? True, it was paid for and would be run by another campus department, but they were very grateful for the space. Also, beyond the classes scheduled by the Intensive English Program, the lab had many vacant time slots available. Why not work out an agreement where the library gained access to the lab for instruction purposes during these windows of availability? As soon as the Instruction committee began perceiving the forced intrusion of the lab as an opportunity, rather than as a threat, negative attitudes began changing. Since a new library instruction facility, with hands-on capabilities, was not in the library's foreseeable future, this was a golden opportunity to quickly gain access to a fully stocked instruction facility: an opportunity not to be missed.

As communication between the Intensive English Program and the library began, it became increasingly clear that much of the necessary planning required to bring the lab into existence had not been initiated. Intensive English had primarily focused on obtaining the grant, not on what would be done once the money was available. This became the logical place for the library staff to step in, offering assistance and guidance. If the new lab was to benefit the library, staff members needed a voice in the all important implementation phase. Librarians must be diplomatic, calm, and clear headed in this process. They needed to confront the often troublesome and time-consuming task of bringing a project into viable existence. The library was willing to compromise by supplying staff, time, and expertise in return for access.

The focus, as stated throughout this paper, is how to turn a potentially bad situation into a positive one. How to pick up another department's fumble and run with it to a successful outcome. This may sound like an "us-against-them" scenario, but, unlike football, the goal is a win-win outcome. By agreeing to play ball with the Intensive English program, versus passively sitting on the sidelines, the library gained an enhanced campus image. The library avoided becoming a victim of campus politics, by remaining proactive in a potentially disadvantageous situation.

The library, often considered a passive player in campus politics, can become a valuable intermediary in the negotiating process. Frequently, the library's nebulous status in the university can work to its advantage when conflicts develop. The ability to step back, then find the core of the problem, and spearhead the solution is a enviable position to have. Using the following steps as guidelines, successful inter-departmental resolutions can be negotiated and implemented.

Solutions Framework

When conflicting campus agendas collide, we offer these basic steps in developing a potential win-win solution for your library:

1. Communication
2. Negotiation
3. Planning
4. Documentation
5. Implementation
6. Maintenance

These six basic steps form a solutions framework that will enable you to accomplish positive results. The initial negative attitude of librarians can be a major stumbling block; possibly stemming from fear of risk-taking as well as a sense of powerlessness. We may not be in control of all outside forces impacting the library, but we can become empowered risk takers when we decide to become players, not spectators, in the problem-solving arena. Creative solutions can be explored when we walk onto the playing field. Sitting on the sidelines will only result in watching the other players further their agendas without valuable library input.

Naturally, the first step is communication. Zero in on the specifics of the issues and begin a dialog with the other campus unit(s) involved. In the discussion phase, become the mediator or the facilitator. Whenever possible, take the initiative to direct the proceedings. In taking this first step you will open the doors, illuminating the issues at hand. In many situations, the willingness to start the ball in motion may help strengthen your bargaining position.

With the relevant goals and agendas identified, you can move on to negotiation. What steps need to be taken and who will be responsible for seeing them through? And, how will the project be implemented to the satisfaction of all involved? For a tense and potentially political situation to begin moving to a resolution, compromise must happen. Once again, do not be afraid to take the first step. By being willing to negotiate initially, you will gain in the long run. The library has demonstrated a willingness to lead combined with a desire to negotiate.

When compromises have been committed to, a natural bridge to the planning phase has been constructed. Planning will move the project toward a smoother implementation. When developing a plan of action, you begin crystallizing the project's goals and objectives. A well-devised plan provides a solid implementation framework; a framework that will become the basis for creating accurate documentation. A properly devised plan irons out any remaining issues left unresolved in the negotiation phase. The communication that began the entire process is now beginning to gel into solutions.

It is imperative to properly document the entire project life to reduce, if not eliminate, future disparities. Via a written agreement, record all the processes involved in the development and upkeep of the project. Additionally, identify and gain commitment from designated "project champions." A "project champion" is the responsible party overseeing all aspects of the project's implementation, documentation, and maintenance. The champion will insure that policies and procedures are followed. He, or she, functions as an inter-departmental arbitrator when future questions arise and require resolution. The need for a "project champion," combined with good documentation, was recently reinforced when a business professor at TCU attempted to sidestep the policy document inspired by Compustat. The written procedures outlining database selection underscored the library's position, ensuring that the previous pitfalls encountered with Compustat were not repeated.

Now that the documentation and people are in place, it is time to proceed with project implementation. If the communication and planning phases have been effective, implementation will fall into place. The framework for solving new pitfalls has been established. Smooth implementation, and successful maintenance, are the rewards of a productive partnership.

This process need not be a power struggle between two departments. It should be a willing partnership with a common goal. The building blocks of a successful partnership are accomplished via the planning stage dialogue, where guidelines and policies are mutually agreed upon by all parties. Concerns and problems are brought to the table, ensuring solutions that will be beneficial to all sides. Involvement in the planning process helps ease negative feelings at the project's end. By working together in a spirit of good will, positive results are realized. A proactive mindset is always preferable to a reactive one.

While the two examples described in the paper are unique to the Mary Couts Burnett Library, the solutions framework can be universally applied. Each potentially volatile campus partnership will require a unique set of solutions. The goal is to think globally while exploring out-of-the-box solutions, ignoring artificial boundaries inhibiting successful progress. By utilizing the basic concepts detailed in our solutions framework, campus partnerships can flourish. Intercepting departmental fumbles will enhance customer service, strengthen campus cooperation, and reduce end-user frustration. A secondary benefit is a subtle reinforcement of the library's importance in the overall campus environment. Take the ball, run with it, and win.

Quality Undergraduate Education in a Research University—The Role of Information Literacy

Ann C. Schaffner, Leslie Stebbins, and Sally Wyman

New concerns about undergraduate education, particularly in research universities, present new opportunities for us as librarians—opportunities to strengthen our information literacy programs, to enhance our role in undergraduate education, and to improve the quality of that education.

Of course, concern about undergraduate education has been with us in one form or another for decades, from early reform efforts by John Dewey, and Alfred North Whitehead to the experimental colleges of the 1960's and the "culture wars" of the 1980s.[1] In the last 5 years, however, the level of concern has intensified and the flood of reports, position papers and recommendations has crested at an alarmingly high level. Reports with catchy and compelling titles continue to roll off the presses with increasing regularity: "Shaping the Future: New expectations for Undergraduate Education in Science, Mathematics, Engineering and Technology," "Beyond Bio 101: The Transformation of Undergraduate Biology Education, Physics at the Crossroads," to mention just a few.[2] The reports, in turn, have generated a lively discussion in the literature of just about every discipline—including mathematics, German, geology, and many others.

Most important for us as librarians is not the quantity, but the focus of this new round of criticism and debate – a focus on issues central to our own missions—research skills, active learning and critical thinking.

The Boyer Commission Report, "Reinventing Undergraduate Education: A Blueprint for America's Research Universities,"[3] brings together many of these concerns in a well-developed critique of undergraduate education at U.S. research universities. Released in April of 1998, the report's conclusions, while aimed at research universities, applies to most U.S. institutions of higher education, whether classed as research institutions or not. In the months since its release, the report has been a catalyst for discussion, defensive action, and reform at a number of institutions—Rochester, SUNY Binghamton, University of Michigan and the University of Southern California, to mention just a few. Many of our campuses are actively engaged in creative efforts to improve undergraduate education.

Ann C. Schaffner is associate director, public services, Leslie Stebbins is reference librarian/instruction coordinator, and Sally Wyman is librarian for research services, Brandeis University.

The Boyer Report asserts that undergraduate education in research universities does not take full advantage of the unique opportunities available in these institutions. Links are often not made between undergraduate education and faculty research; opportunities to enrich and strengthen undergraduate education through exposure to the research process are missed. Undergraduates are too often the passive recipients of a segmented curriculum presented by untrained graduate students. Uninspired, unmotivated, pushed through their education as unwilling participants, students often emerge from this process without an understanding of how knowledge is produced, ignorant of the relationships between different fields, and incapable of expressing themselves clearly.

We can all see some of these results in the students we work with at research universities. What are the solutions proposed by the report? There are ten major recommendations, and they will sound familiar to those of you who are instructional librarians:

1. Make research-based learning the standard
2. Construct an inquiry-based freshman year
3. Build on the freshman foundation
4. Remove barriers to interdisciplinary education
5. Link communication skills and course work
6. Use information technology creatively
7. Culminate with a capstone experience
8. Educate graduate students as apprentice teachers
9. Change the faculty reward system
10. Create a sense of community

Sound inspiring? What can we do as librarians? What role does the Boyer Commission outline for us? None! The report advocates involving undergraduates in research, exposing them to primary source materials, and educating them about the production of knowledge. Yet libraries are given only a passing mention (as a part of the resources students may expect at a research university) and no mention is made of the role of librarians or information literacy programs.

At the same time, library instruction programs at many of our institutions have begun to work on precisely these issues. We are all contributing to changing undergraduate education in exactly the ways envisioned by the report.

At Brandeis, where we have the advantage of being a small research university, library instruction programs reach every first year student and many students in advanced courses. Through these programs we encourage research, teach evaluative skills, encourage the use of primary materials, provide one-on-one guidance, introduce many of our students to the concept of a "discipline", encourage and support multi-disciplinary approaches and introduce active learning techniques to many students.

The Brandeis library instruction program takes place through two formal programs: the Freshman Library Instruction Program (or FLIP), for all first-year and transfer students, and the Library Intensive Program for upper-level and graduate students.

The FLIP program began in 1994, as a component of the writing lab portion of the University Seminars in our newly-revised curriculum. The University Seminar program pairs small groups of first-year students (rarely more than 18) with established faculty members from all different disciplines in the University. The course topics are designed to catch the attention of the students, while at the same time, give faculty members the opportunity to experiment with particularly interdisciplinary topics. The adventurous spirit of these courses is best illustrated by two of the recent course titles: "Everyday Activity", taught by a Computer Science faculty member, and using such activities as playing a CD and carrying on a conversation to explore models of skill acquisition and problem-solving and the role of culture in everyday activity; and "Don't Get Mad, Get Even: The Ethic and Aesthetic of Revenge", taught by a faculty member from the Theater Arts program. Accompanying this discussion portion of the course is the writing lab taught by a writing lab instructor. It is within this context and in anticipation of writing their first research paper for the writing lab, that the students visit the library for their FLIP experience.

FLIP's are 50-minute hands-on active learning sessions, utilizing a specially designed interactive web page. Prior to the session, students are instructed to complete and electronically submit a web-based worksheet on topic analysis and construction of a basic search strategy. The session begins with a brief introduction by the librarian. Students are then paired up to complete an in-class web exercise requiring that they use their previously-devised search strategy to search the Brandeis online catalog. Next, they choose from a selection of journal indexes to find articles on their topic, and, finally, they venture out onto the Web to look for more information. The last ten minutes of the session are devoted to a group discussion of the differences encountered in the different types of databases. This portion of the session provides a chance to emphasize the need for critical evaluation of the references the student retrieves, and to discuss the cues useful in distinguishing between popular and scholarly literature. While the librarian is there to conduct the session, his/her role is secondary to the self-instruction and collaborative learning taking place in the working pairs at the workstations. The librarian does, however, make an effort to orchestrate the closing discussion to make sure that certain key points are made in a "guide at the side" model.

The goals of the FLIP were, from the beginning, modest. They were, first and foremost, to get students into the library and to make contact with an approachable and knowledgeable librarian, who could serve as a resource when needed later on. Additionally, the program was designed to introduce students to the concept of a discipline, to the research process, to the types of resources available, to the differences between popular and scholarly literature, and to plant the seeds of the idea of critical evaluation. One other goal is that there be little preparation time involved, so that librarians have time to devote to the lengthier preparations required by the Library Intensive Program. We are conducting a preliminary evaluation of the FLIP program this semester, with a full-scale one planned for the fall.

The Library Intensive Program is a formal program providing course-integrated information literacy instruction for upper-level undergraduates and graduate students. From the beginning it was viewed as, centrally, a partnership between librarians and interested faculty members to design instruction highly tailored to the needs of the students in a particular course. To that end, certain expectations are made of the faculty members who join the program. Each faculty member must make a commitment to the program well in advance of the start of the semester of instruction; that commitment must include the faculty member's agreement to begin working closely with the librarian well in advance of the in-class sessions, to design instruction and a closely linked assignment jointly. Finally, the faculty member must agree to provide the necessary amount of class time to accommodate the library instruction—from 1 to 3 in-class sessions.

The cornerstone of the program is the Faculty-Librarian Workshop, held near the end of each semester. Faculty members from the past semester are invited, along with those faculty members who have been identified as participants for the upcoming semester. Any faculty members who might be potential participants are also invited, along with various University administrators. We find that the workshop is one of the most important aspects of the program, exposing faculty members to the possibilities for instruction and assignment design, engaging them in broader discussions, and allowing them to make connections with librarians and with faculty members in other disciplines. The glue for all of this is the library and library instruction.

The instruction taking place in the Library Intensive sessions, while very loosely guided by a model curriculum, is highly individualized in its approach. The choice of tools taught, the emphasis of the instruction, and the nature of the assignment, help convey to the students that information is transmitted in a particular way in the particular discipline. At the same time, features common to library research across disciplines are also taught.

Increasingly, just as the University curriculum is reflecting greater emphasis on inter-disciplinary instruction, so is the Library Intensive Program required to address those needs. To meet this demand, library intensive courses are frequently team-taught now, with each librarian contributing his/her expertise to the enlarged partnership with the faculty member. It has been interesting to note, in these instances, that it is sometimes the librarian who is providing the bridge to the less-familiar discipline for the faculty member. Such was the case this past fall, when a chemistry professor taught his first forensic science course. One library instruction session focused on the wide diversity of scientific literature and tools. The second library session, taught by the legal studies librarian, introduced the students—and, not incidentally, the faculty member—to some of the intricacies of researching court cases. Both elements of the library instruction were integral to the success of the students in completing their research paper assignment.

The Library Intensive Program is considered a great success. We know this from the comments of students and faculty members, who almost unfailingly remark on how much they have learned. We know this also from the growing demand for Library Intensive instruction, and from the rising attendance levels and active participation of faculty members at the Workshops. One of the reasons the Program seems to work so well is that the faculty members who participate do so out of choice—and it is their commitment to the importance of this instruction that motivates the students.

Of the major points in the Boyer Report: "Ten Ways to Change Undergraduate Education," the following are incorporated in library instruction at Brandeis:

1. Make research-based learning the standard
For library instruction to be meaningful, there must be a need. The Library Intensive Program has played a part in encouraging faculty at Brandeis to require a research paper or other type of research effort — this phenomenon has been most noticeable in the sciences, where movement away from complete reliance on textbooks has been most difficult, but is taking place slowly. The greatest benefit occurs when the instruction is timed in the semester to the period when the students are beginning their research efforts, and will be most open to instruction.

2. Construct an inquiry-based Freshman Year
The Brandeis USEM program, with its real-life questions and writing and research requirements, has provided a good venue for the training of first-year students in research and critical evaluation skills in the FLIP sessions.

3. Build on the Freshman Foundation
Library Intensive instruction assumes that students have already been introduced to basic research and introductory critical evaluation skills through their Freshman Library Instruction sessions. Library Intensive sessions can, thus, begin on a slightly higher level, and proceed commensurately.

4. Remove barriers to interdisciplinary education
Oftentimes, we have found that it is the librarians who encourage faculty members to think in more interdisciplinary ways, as they begin their planning for Library Intensive sessions. The team-teaching of Library Intensive sessions by librarians specializing in different disciplines incorporates the idea of the librarian as the bridge to a new discipline. Even in Library Intensive courses which are not team-taught, the fact that most librarians are generalists fosters a more an inter-disciplinary approach to classroom instruction of all kinds.

5. Link communication skills and course work

6. Use information technology creatively
The use of the interactive web page for FLIP provides instruction that feels comfortable to this generation of students. In Library Intensive courses, custom web pages and PowerPoint slide presentations are often used in creating hand-outs and as teaching tools in live demonstrations.

7. Culminate with a capstone experience
While Brandeis does not have a campus-wide "capstone experience", the Library Intensive instruction, in a particularly in-depth format, plays an important role in several senior honors programs, including those in American Studies and Chemistry.

8. Educate graduate students as apprentice teachers

9. Change faculty reward systems

10. Create a sense of community
The Library Intensive Workshop held each semes-

ter provides a forum for discussion of information literacy issues. Many of the faculty members who attend are "regulars". This is one of the few times during the academic year that issues of concern to both faculty members and librarians can be freely discussed. Recent discussions have covered such topics as use of the web for research, copyright, and critical evaluation.

The Freshman Library Instruction and Library Intensive Programs at Brandeis are not atypical of library instruction programs in other universities and colleges across the country. Many of these programs already address some of the issues and imperatives detailed in the Boyer Report. Clearly, library instruction is but one component of the much larger picture of higher education, but, just as at other institutions, the two Brandeis programs described here are working together to make a difference in that larger picture.

What are the lessons here for librarians? We think there are several:

1. Participate in the debate about undergraduate education.

Find out what is being discussed or planned in your institutions. National discussions about curriculum are being mirrored on individual campuses in major reviews and revisions of the undergraduate curriculum. Work with faculty and academic administrators to generate interest and discussion on these issues if the debate is not already taking place on your campus.

2. Publicize the role that library instruction has played or can play in improving the undergraduate educational experience.

Make sure that academic planners know the role that an aggressive library instruction program can play in encouraging faculty to expose their students to the research process. As already mentioned, we have evidence at Brandeis that our library instruction program has changed the way that some science courses are taught—inspiring faculty members to incorporate library research (as opposed to lab research) into courses that previously relied entirely on texts, reserve readings and lab work. Administrators may not be aware of this. Make sure that the role we play in introducing research skills and critical thinking skills is also understood and appreciated.

3. Publicize the unique skills and talents that librarians can bring to the undergraduate educational reform effort.

In addition to the core skills in research and critical thinking, many librarians have broader skills and knowledge to contribute. Often we are among the few people on campus who have a broad view of the disciplines and of how knowledge is produced, transferred and preserved in different disciplines. This perspective may prove valuable on a campus which is beginning to embrace multidisciplinary or interdisciplinary studies.

Librarians are also often among the most knowledgeable people on campus about the educational use of technology or active learning techniques. We can be valuable resource people for efforts to incorporate technology and active learning into the curriculum.

4. Seize the opportunity presented by the interest in curricular reform to strengthen your library instruction programs.

Now is the time to make the case for that new instructional position or a new classroom. Now is the time to increase participation in our programs. By tying requests into the broader goals of educational reform, we have a better chance at success.

Finally, there is the lure of outside funding. Corporations, foundations, and government agencies are all supporting undergraduate educational reform. Library instruction programs can be linked to broader educational funding proposals. At Brandeis we have done just this with a proposal to incorporate multidisciplinary learning and critical thinking into the undergraduate curriculum. If funded, our proposal will bring added resources to our library instruction program, allow us to incorporate more critical thinking into our program, and integrate it more thoroughly into the curriculum.

Librarians and library instruction play an important role in a quality undergraduate experience. It will take some work to make sure that role is understood and appreciated on campus.

Once it is, we can all realize real benefits for our programs, our profession, and the undergraduates we serve.

Notes

1. For a good review of the history of curriculum development and change in the U.S., see *Handbook of the Undergraduate Curriculum*, Jerry G. Gaff, and James L. Ratcliff, eds., San Francisco, Jossey-Bass, 1997.

2. For a good collection of recent reports see *Case Studies in Science*, http://wwwublib.buffalo.edu/libraries/projects/cases/sites.htm.

3. http://notes.cc.sunysb.edu/Pres/boyer.nsf

Partnering for the Future: Integrating Traditional Interlibrary Lending and Commercial Document Delivery into a Seamless Service

Carol A. Kochan, Daniel R. Lee, and Robert G. Murdoch

Abstract

Utah Academic Libraries developed a partnership with EBSCO to develop an innovative program to improve resource sharing. This paper discusses the original project initiation, the revised project after EBSCO was no longer a participant, and evaluates the success of the service from the Consortium's and the users' viewpoints.

It is hard to imagine an academic, public, or school library, today, whose stacks and associated collections would not be open to its general clientele for the purpose of providing personal access and selection of desired materials. Today's librarians are rapidly expanding the notion of open access to patrons for collections beyond the walls of their own library buildings. Library patrons, with the assistance of sophisticated library systems and digitized information, now have the opportunity to have "open stack access" to Virtual Libraries worldwide. We regularly read in library and information literature of new programs being established to empower patrons—allowing them to play a more direct and active role in selecting and accessing needed materials. Many of these new programs revolve around permitting patrons to order materials directly from commercial document delivery suppliers and having materials delivered to their home or office.

Recognizing both the need and the opportunity to embrace themes such as virtual libraries, digitized information, consortia strength, and patron empowerment, the Utah Academic Library Consortium (UALC)[1] began working in 1996 to develop new operational models, planning and

Carol A. Kochan is coordinator of interlibrary services, Utah State University, Daniel R. Lee is head of circulation services, University of Utah, and Robert G. Murdoch is deputy of library services, Utah State University.

accountability strategies, and a series of funding initiatives. These planning activities were based on the Consortium's long and successful tradition of cooperation with its aim focused on improving academic library collections and services on a statewide basis as we move into the twenty-first century.

One of the very most immediate needs was for a program to enhance patron access and rapid receipt of journal resources as a supplement to traditional interlibrary borrowing and lending services. With this in mind, the UALC Resource Sharing Committee accepted the assignment and challenge to develop such a program. In 1997 the Committee responded to their challenge by designing an innovative resource sharing service to provide articles to the Utah higher education community. The new service, named Utah Article Delivery (UTAD), was developed in partnership with EBSCO Information Services and was prepared to begin beta testing in February 1998. The development of this new service was based on the following objectives and parameters:

Objectives
- Increase awareness and access to relevant journals in an efficient and timely fashion.
- Satisfy the increasing expectation for information through solutions found in telecommunications technologies, electronic publishing, and World Wide Web access.
- Meet the challenge of providing article delivery in a time frame based on "patron expectation."
- Reduce article delivery time from the traditional average of six days to 24 hours.
- When possible, supply requested articles from UALC collections
- Promote the notion of a single Utah academic library collection as opposed to individual institutional collections.
- Provide opportunities for the end user to initiate and directly receive desired information.
- Establish a strong partnership with a commercial document delivery supplier who shares the same values of UALC, and whose access to scholarly journals is broad based and will supplement the UALC journal collections.
- Serve as a collection development tool and resource by identifying journals that should be part of a statewide collection and titles that would be more appropriately accessed outside UALC owned collections.

Parameters
- Funds for the program development were limited and based on a one-time funding commitment.
- In-state journals needed to be promoted and used as a "first source" whenever possible.
- The service must be easy to use and must allow for students, faculty, and staff affiliated with UALC institutions to equally participate.
- Simply adding additional staff to traditional ILL departments/units was not an acceptable solution.
- Acceptable article delivery time frames must be viewed in terms of hours rather than days.
- Service must reduce end-user document delivery from the current status of days to hours.
- Program must be developed and implemented without the aid of a current or complete union list of serials for Utah.
- The service must foster a statewide collection development program focused on diversity in holdings and decreasing duplication.
- An evaluation component must be associated with the program.
- Minimize the impact on existing ILL staff.[2]

EBSCO/Utah Partnership
In early 1998, EBSCO Document Services created a master list for journal titles held in Utah. While this list was not a complete representation of UALC journal titles, it did identify the majority of the Consortium's active holdings, since it was based on titles currently ordered through EBSCO Subscription Services. Additionally, considerable work with EBSCO took place to establish procedures for how the article delivery service would actually work. In brief, registered students at UALC institutions, as well as faculty and staff, could request journal articles via a World Wide Web form. Requests were sent via e-mail to EBSCO Document Services where staff members check the request against their list of UALC journal subscriptions. If

the requested information was held in a member library, EBSCO then forwarded the order to the appropriate library to satisfy the request. Requests for articles from journal titles not currently available at UALC were filled by EBSCO Document Services. In all cases the desired article(s) were delivered by fax to the end user's designated fax address. The only limitation to this service was that UALC set a maximum cost of $35.00 per article. The results of the testing with pilot sites were promising—UTAD was now ready to go live!

A Setback in Service—A Contingency Plan
Only days before the formal announcement of Utah Article Delivery going into day-to-day operation in September 1998, EBSCO Information Services notified UALC with the disappointing news that they were planning to discontinue EBSCO Document Services. After a moment of discouragement, frustration, and doubt about the future of UTAD, a contingency plan was quickly developed. The void left by EBSCO Document Services was satisfied by adding three new components to UTAD. First, as an ARL library, the Marriott Library at the University of Utah would serve as the primary supplier for documents. Second, UALC hired a temporary full-time employee, located at the Marriott Library, to manage the clearinghouse functions of verifying holdings and directing requests which EBSCO had performed. Third, following an informal bid process Infotrieve Systems was selected as the vender of choice to supply document delivery services for articles not owned by member libraries.

On December 1, 1998, UTAD was officially introduced to the entire Utah higher education community. Initial service was limited to article requests from journals available at member institutions. Beginning January 2, 1999, the service was expanded to include ordering from Infotrieve Systems. UTAD requests trickled in slowly the first month; however, usage of the service seemed to explode in January.

Initial Observations
While the initial project seemed simple, it soon became apparent the overall task of actually implementing a document delivery program founded on the established objectives and working within the limitations of our project parameters proved to be a more complicated process than originally envisioned. Fortunately, while we were extremely disappointed EBSCO Document Services was not able to continue as a business partner and key foundation piece to Utah Article Delivery, the time, experience, and lessons learned during the testing period proved to be a tremendous benefit. The association with EBSCO Document Service coupled with information gathered during the beta phase provided useful information, allowing the Resource Sharing Committee to:

• Solve problems associated with identifying and delivering articles from state owned serial holdings before forwarding article requests to a commercial supplier.

• Establish effective communication channels and protocols with appropriate Consortium staff members, the commercial document delivery supplier, and with UALC clientele.

• Program staffing requirements and operational procedures.

• Resolve issues relating to copyright permissions, royalty payments, and billing/payment procedures.

• Establish reporting and evaluation methodology.

• Develop institutional promotional materials and strategies.

• Bolster institutional commitment to the overall project.

By the time the Committee had made changes necessary to accommodate the loss of EBSCO and launched UTAD as a statewide service, renewed commitment and enthusiasm to the goals of the project had been restored.

During the inaugural month of December 1998, client activity was relatively low. However by January 2, 1999, we were encouraged by the number of patrons who had learned of the service and were now placing self initiated orders and directly receiving journal articles without the aid of Interlibrary Loan personnel. Table 1 identifies the institutions of the Utah Academic Library Consortium and lists the activity of each college and university, along with their associated percentage of total requests placed during the first six weeks of the new year.

Table 1. Patron Requests per Institution Jan. 1, 1999—Feb. 12, 1999		
Institution	No. of Requests	% of Total
Brigham Young University	397	24
College of Eastern Utah	0	0
Dixie College	5	1
Salt Lake Community College	10	1
Snow College	56	3.4
Southern Utah University	64	4
University of Utah	369	21
Utah State University	371	22
Utah Valley State College	112	6
Weber State University	72	4
Westminster College	184	11
Total Requests	1,640	100

Table 2, documents the UALC libraries and commercial vendor providing requested articles, the number of journal articles supplied, along with corresponding percentages of the total.

Obviously, at this early stage of the program, there is too little data and experience to make solid conclusions or judgements about the success of the service or need to make operational adjustments. There are, however, a number of interesting observations, considerations, and questions generated by this first glimpse of data:

- The nine percent unfilled rate represents requests for materials available at the patron's home institution, inappropriate requests (i.e., book loans, etc.), incorrect citations, and copyright fees that exceed $35.00 cap for ordering.
- The number of patron initiated requests placed at several of the smaller colleges is significantly higher than historical Interlibrary Loan borrowing. If this pattern continues, it will be interesting to determine the factors contributing to this trend.
- The three research universities generated majority of the use, which parallels traditional Interlibrary Loan trends.
- What impact and role will commercial document delivery suppliers, such as Infotrieve Systems, have on institutional and state collection development policies, decisions, and practices?
- What liabilities and opportunities will UTAD present UALC libraries in terms of reallocating personnel resources?
- How discriminating will patrons be in their selection and appetite for journal articles in a self initiated document delivery environment?
- At the present time, no usage fee is assessed to the patron. Can or should UALC support this policy?

Are We Meeting Our Objectives?

UTAD is built on a number of desired objectives and goals. Perhaps most fundamental of these objectives is the intent to enhance patron access and delivery of required information resources by offering both rapid fulfillment of requests and providing quality copies. With this in mind, relevant client survey and assessment tools will be administered. The ultimate measure of the success and worth of the service is determined by the end user. While knowing our experience with UTAD is too brief to make formal assessments, we were curious to receive some initial feedback. A simple survey was sent to 30 UTAD clients seeking input on the speed of the service, quality of the articles,

Table 2. Articles supplied for UTAD Requests: Jan 1, 1999—Feb 12, 1999		
Supplier	No. supplied	% of requests supplied
Infotrieve Systems	528	32
University of Utah, Marriott Library	435	26
University of Utah, Eccles Health Sciences Library	248	15
Brigham Young Univ. Lee Library	76	4
Weber State University	68	4
Utah State University	60	4
Southern Utah University	30	2
University of Utah, Quinney Law Library	29	2
Westminster College	10	<1
College of Eastern Utah	7	<1
Dixie College	1	<1
Unfilled or Canceled	148	9
Totals	1,640	100 %

Table 3. Survey Respondents Rating of UTAD Services					
Speed of Service	**Faster than expected**	**Fast**	**Adequate**	**Too Late**	**Too late couldn't use**
Number of Responses	6	4	3	1	1*
Quality of text and Graphics	**Very high**	**Good**	**Adequate**	**Poor**	**Couldn't read**
Number of Responses	3	4	4	1	1*

*Note: Did not receive requested article(s).

and service expectations. Fifteen individuals responded, with 87% indicating UTAD had satisfied their information needs. Table 3 reports the survey rankings on the timeliness and quality of articles delivered.

The majority of the respondents reported turnaround time and quality of the delivered article as being adequate or better. While this small and unscientific survey appears to be positive, it is clear there is room for improvement. Knowing the importance of patron satisfaction, UALC will be responsive to patron input.

The Future

We are encouraged with the initial implementation of UTAD and are optimistic about its future. We recognize there is more work to do on our part in meeting the Consortium's objectives.

Undoubtably there will be a number of operational adjustments that need to take place as the service evolves.

Work is continuing on the development of a comprehensive electronic UALC Union List of Serials. This resource will significantly benefit both patrons and library staff by providing complete and accurate journal information, plus serve as a major aid in reducing labor costs and delivery times. We are hopeful that we will find a document delivery supplier who is willing to assume the clearinghouse responsibilities, which where originally intended to be supplied by EBSCO Document Services.

The print quality of articles delivered by fax is a continuing concern. Future document delivery enhancements include providing journal articles by either scanning requested materials into a digital format housed at a secure web site for patron pickup, or delivering articles via e-mail. If these delivery opportunities are realized, UTAD will take a big step forward.

Building on a history of cooperation, we are succeeding in developing a creative, beneficial, and popular service. It is anticipated UTAD will become an important tool for developing stronger and more responsive cooperative statewide collection development programing, along with the additional benefits associated with consortium purchasing opportunities and leverage. We are confident Utah Article Delivery will prove to be a valued foundation piece in UALC's efforts to improve library and information services through cooperation, shared goals, and values.

Notes

1. Membership in the Utah Academic Library Consortium is composed of Brigham Young University (Howard L. Hunter Law Library and Harold B. Lee Library), College of Eastern Utah, Dixie College, Salt Lake Community College, Snow College, Southern Utah University, University of Utah (Spencer S. Eccles Health Sciences Library, J. Willard Marriott Library, and the S. J. Quinney Law Library), Utah State Library Division, Utah State University, Utah Valley State College, Weber State University, and Westminster College.

2. Kochan, C. A. and D. R. Lee, "Utah Article Delivery: A New Model for Consortial Resource Sharing." *Computers in Libraries* 18 (4), (1998): 24–28.

TEEAL: The Essential Electronic Agricultural Library—Getting the Literature of Agriculture to the Developing Countries

Mary Anderson Ochs

What Is TEEAL?

In one sense, TEEAL (The Essential Electronic Agricultural Library) is a self-contained library of the core journals in the field of agriculture. It is available at cost ONLY to research institutions in the developing countries. It is a system being produced at Mann Library at Cornell University with the cooperation of many scientific publishers, database producers and the Rockefeller Foundation.

In the larger sense, however, TEEAL is the solution to a problem. In the last decade, there has been a huge investment in research and education in the developing countries. The goal has been to make the research and education programs in these countries self-sustaining. In spite of the monumental strides made in improving these programs, little has been accomplished in bringing these countries access to the world's scholarly publishing. Without access to the scientific literature, researchers in the developing countries cannot know that solutions to the problems they are struggling with have already been found by others. Many students from the developing countries come to the United States and Europe to complete their graduate work. Upon returning to their own countries, they no longer have access to the literature that they have relied upon for their work.

Providing access to the literature is a key to the success of research programs in the developing countries, but providing access to literature in all fields was too great an undertaking. So which fields were the most critical? The research area most fundamental to the improvement of conditions in many of the developing countries is food production and nutrition. Thus, the choice was made to focus on this literature (Olsen, 1994). By gathering the opinions of over 600 scholars in the field of agriculture, with 250 scientists focusing on the developing countries, the most important literature was identified.

The work to identify the core literature of agriculture began at Mann Library in 1988, and beginning in 1991 a multi-volume series, *The Literature of the Agricultural Sciences* (Olsen, 1991–1996),

---

Mary Anderson Ochs is deputy director, TEEAL Project, Cornell University.

Getting the Literature of Agriculture to the Developing Countries

was published by Cornell University Press. This extensive bibliography defines the literature most critical to researchers in all areas of agriculture. The ultimate goal in identifying the most important current literature was to make its full-text available to researchers in the developing world, where research libraries are few and far between.

After visiting universities and agricultural research stations around the world, officials at the Rockefeller Foundation agreed that one of greatest barriers to the improvement of agricultural research in the developing countries was the absence of literature and libraries to support the research. There was a tremendous need to make this core literature available, but it had to be in a form that the libraries in the developing countries could afford, support technically, and maintain under less than ideal environmental conditions. TEEAL, a CD-ROM system, was the answer.

In today's presentation, you will hear a bit more about the selection of material for inclusion in TEEAL, the creation of the system, marketing the system and thoughts on measuring the impact of the introduction of TEEAL in the developing countries. I must say at times I feel a bit like the producer of a low-budget movie. TEEAL may not be quite as flashy as other information retrieval systems, but I believe it will have a powerful impact by bringing agricultural information to those who have never had it before.

Who Are the Players?

TEEAL is the result of a successful multi-player partnership. Jan Olsen, the former director of Mann Library, and Wallace Olsen, a research associate at Mann Library, are the originators of the idea. Six years ago, and again three years ago, they performed a marketing study to determine whether there was a need for TEEAL. Responses in both cases were positive, and a decision was made to proceed with the project.

Even though the need was determined, the system could not be built without the cooperation of the major publishers of the agricultural journals and some significant start-up money. The publishers were approached with the idea, and most of them, including the major scientific publishers, such as Elsevier, Academic, Kluwer, and Springer, agreed to provide free copies of the journals selected for inclusion in the system. With a list of 80 journals approved for inclusion in the system, production could begin. The Rockefeller Foundation agreed to provide the funding.

Last April Mann Library signed a contract with a scanning vendor to perform the digitizing of the journals, and they sub-contracted with an information handling company to build the information retrieval system. At this point, I will demonstrate the system so that my description of its creation will be more meaningful.

The system is designed to support the three main uses scholars make of the literature: current awareness in their field; subject searching to support research proposals, student papers, and ongoing projects; and "known item" searching, such as finding a specific article by a specific author. I will demonstrate each of these functions.

Why CD-ROM?

Perhaps the first question some of you may be asking is, "why did they use CD-ROM technology?" While online access is now ubiquitous in this country, wide-spread access to the Internet in the developing countries is still many years off. Even where institutions do have access to online information resources, connections can be very poor and costs astronomical. With CD-ROM, once the system is purchased, it stands alone. At some point we will be looking at DVD technology, but costs for DVD were still too high when we made the decision to use CD-ROM.

Creating the Database

The core literature of agriculture spans a wider range than what one might expect. The journals selected for TEEAL include journals in crops, animal science, veterinary science, soils, environmental management, human nutrition and diet, food science, genetics, and other subjects. No one of the agricultural databases indexed all 130 journals included in TEEAL 1993–1996.

We started the production of the index with a set of records from CAB International, one of the major agricultural databases. We made an assessment of how complete their coverage was of each of the journals included in the system. If they covered less than 90% of the articles in a volume, we supplemented the indexing with records from another database.

In the initial TEEAL set (1993–96) there are 47,808 CABI records, 21,748 Medline records, 6,248 BIOSIS records, 2351 EconLit records, 396 Agricola records, 275 Agris records, and 602 records created at Mann Library. All of these database producers provided records to include in the system either free or at a reduced cost.

In order to combine these records into one database, we had to carefully reformat the non-CABI records to match the standard CABI record structure. For each database, we analyzed the record structure to determine how, for example, the BIOSIS fields would be transferred into the CABI fields. Each field had to be transferred into an existing field in the CABI-based record template or a new field had to be created. All data elements had to be reformatted. For example, authors with names spelled out had to be cut to include just initials, and language codes had to be converted to the full name of the language.

One particularly interesting challenge was translating BIOSIS and Medline codes into CABI codes. We created translation tables and converted codes by machine, and then did a manual check of the results. One slight error in the translation table created some rather amusing subject coding, with animal behavior articles receiving human codes. There may still be some of these lurking in the system, so we hope our users have a sense of humor.

Inconsistencies in the databases also created problems. In writing the programs to convert the data, our student programmers based their programming on the expected appearance of the data. Any time the data did not conform to this standard, the program needed to be adjusted to accommodate this. Seemingly simple problems took much programming time to find and troubleshoot.

Because the index for the system was created using records from many different databases, and all records for each journal from the 1993–1996 date range were added to the database, we had to write a duplicate checking program. This program had to match all the records against each other and delete the duplicate records. The CABI records were considered the primary records, so if there was a CABI record, it was retained. Records from the other databases supplemented the CABI records. The duplicate checking program matched the records on issn, year, volume, issue number, pages and the first 10 characters of the article title.

The index in the final product, as in the demo, will appear to be one large index, as seamless as possible, considering the multiple sources of the data. Our records were sent to the information handling vendor responsible for the construction of the TEEAL information retrieval system. There they were massaged yet again, and inserted into the Folio software that runs the TEEAL system.

The Folio software is not a traditional DIALOG or BRS-style bibliographic database. It was designed to be a full-text search and retrieval system, so it really looks at our index as a huge full-text document. It is possible to scroll through the entire database record by record without performing any kind of search. The search system simply creates pointers to the hits in this huge text file. The Folio software was selected because traditional bibliographic database software could not accommodate the browsing functions of the system. Using Folio was a relatively inexpensive way to build a system with as many of the desired features as possible. A custom designed interface would have been superior, but would have cost a great deal more and taken much longer to create. We began the actual production of TEEAL only about a year ago, so it has come a long way very quickly.

Scanning

Any of you who have undertaken a large-scale scanning project know the pitfalls of such a project. The sheer volume of the TEEAL material, over 700,000 pages, presents a challenge, but the complexity of the material, with its complicated pagination and multiple numbering schemes, adds to that complexity. Linking each article to its corresponding index record has not been an easy task.

Behind the system, lives a set of index files, one for each journal issue, that provides a link between the name of each image file and its corresponding page number. It is the "lifeline" that runs between the Folio database software and the

Figure 1:	Index file matching page numbers with file names.

```
Cover 1,13562001.tif
Cover 2,13562002.tif
       i,13562003.tif
      ii,13562004.tif
     iii,13562005.tif
      iv,13562006.tif
       v,13562007.tif
      vi,13562008.tif
       1,13562009.tif
       2,13562010.tif
       3,13562011.tif
```

separate image viewer. Figure 1 shows a small portion of an index file.

The majority of the images are bitonal scans. They are TIFF files, scanned at 300 dpi. Many of the scientific illustrations required grayscale scanning. The grayscale and color images are JPEG files, scanned at 200 dpi. These resolutions are much lower than typical preservation scanning, which is often done at 600 dpi. However, with the volume of material to be included in a CD-ROM system, it was important not to create files that were too large. The images at these resolutions are of good quality, although certainly not perfect. We are expecting the 1993–1996 set to fill approximately 150 compact disks.

Marketing

Unlike most other academic library projects, the undertaking of TEEAL required a business and marketing plan. We had to decide how much to charge for the system and how many sets we needed to sell in order to cover our costs at that price. The start-up money was provided by the Rockefeller Foundation, with the intent that the system would ultimately pay for itself in its second year. The price for the initial 1993–1996 set is $10,000. The cost of the actual subscriptions to these journals for four years would be $365,000. It is a bargain by US standards, but for institutions in the developing countries, $10,000 is a great deal of money.

Many of the countries eligible to buy TEEAL are in Africa. In Africa, the marketing of the product presents particular challenges. Marketing efforts must be directed at decision-makers, not users, who do not have control over how money is spent. Many of the institutions eligible to buy TEEAL will need to find development aid to use to buy the system. In African countries, $10,000 may be the entire budget for the library at some institutions.

The distances involved and the difficulties experienced in communication with the African countries have presented additional challenges. As a result, we have put in place a marketing coordinator working out of Zimbabwe. More and more, administrators are becoming convinced that putting money into an information product is worthwhile. It will be the role of our African marketing coordinator to work with administrators to convince them that TEEAL is a good investment for their institutions.

Conclusion

Throughout this project, librarians have taken on many non-traditional roles. The TEEAL system is the brain child of librarians who were committed to the goal of bringing the literature of agriculture to the developing countries. They found the money to build the system, they persuaded publishers to join them in their efforts, they hired staff that could build a system, and they marketed the product to its intended audience. What remains to be seen is the impact the system has in the developing countries. Before it is in place, we hope to be able to take a benchmark reading of how scholars in some of the institutions buying TEEAL currently get access to the research literature. Over the course of several years, we will try to measure the impact of providing quick and easy access to the literature through TEEAL. We are certainly counting on making a difference in the research and teaching in these institutions.

Bibliography

Olsen, Wallace C. "The Current Core Literature of the Agricultural Sciences." *Journal of Agricultural & Food Information* 2.3 (1994): 99–109.

Olsen, Wallace C. *The Literature of the Agricultural Sciences.* 7 vols. Ithaca: Cornell University Pr., 1991–1996. 7 vols.

Contributed Papers

Alternative Institutions and Providers

Assessment Outside of the Box: The Need for a Focused Study of Information Seekers in a Changing Environment

John Burke and Stephena Harmony

Introduction and Background

As academic librarians, we are certainly familiar with the ongoing mandates from a variety of federal, state, and accrediting agencies to evaluate educational programs and services within our institutions. We periodically complete detailed statistical questionnaires on our collections, budgets, staffing, and public services to demonstrate how we support our students and faculty in the learning and teaching process. While statistics do provide helpful information on such issues as the use of the collections and the number of reference inquiries, this data does not give the complete picture, nor does it provide explanations of why any changes might have occurred. To find out what our users need and why, a proactive model of library assessment is required in which users are not only counted for their transactions with the library, but are also consulted for their perspective on the library's success in providing them with information. The assessment model, as described in this paper, looks to user satisfaction and expressions of users' needs to complement the statistical data libraries traditionally collect.

Before describing the assessment model developed by the Raymond Walters College Library, it is necessary to provide some background information on the College and why we designed this particular model. Raymond Walters College (RWC) is a two-year suburban regional campus of the University of Cincinnati with an enrollment of over 4,000 full and part time students. The College offers over 50 programs of study in business, computer support, office administration, the allied health sciences, and liberal arts. Approximately 60% of the students are enrolled in career degree programs and 40% are planning to transfer into baccalaureate programs.

In March 1999 the College underwent an accreditation site visit by the North Central Associa-

---

John Burke is systems/public services librarian, and Stephena Harmony is library director, University of Cincinnati

tion (NCA). One of the requirements for the NCA accreditation was to develop an assessment process that focused upon student outcomes to evaluate teaching effectiveness and student academic performance. Approximately five years before this site visit was to take place, the College created an organizational structure to develop an assessment process and gather the required data. Three committees were established: Academic Assessment Committee to evaluate the degree and transfer programs; Non-Academic Assessment Committee to examine support services such as Student Services and the Library; and NCA Issues Committee to coordinate all of the assessment activities and to address institutional and administrative areas such as policies, governance and finances. The Library/Media department had representatives serving on all three of these committees.

The Academic Assessment Committee created the College-wide model that included the following components:

- Academic or service outcome statements based upon the College and/or departmental mission statement and goals;
- Multiple measures (e.g. surveys, test scores) to quantify each outcome statement;
- Results of the measures;
- Changes made in the academic program or service area based upon the results of the measures.

The RWC Library Assessment Model

The RWC Library/Media department is unique within the College because it is an academic unit with a dual function. It supports the educational mission of the College through its services and collections, and it offers associate degrees and professional certificates in Electronic Media Technology and Library Media Technology. While the academic assessment of the degree programs would be handled by the program directors, the Library and the Media Services Center staff would be responsible for developing a plan to assess services and collections. During the summer of 1997, Library/Media Services faculty and staff met and identified the department's four primary service areas:

- Instruction and reference: developing and providing classroom instruction sessions and workshops on the effective use of information resources and media technology; providing reference assistance on research, course assignments, and media resources for classroom use;
- Facilities: providing appropriate study space, hardware to access information resources (e.g. computer workstations, photocopiers), and media production facilities;
- Management of resources: selecting and purchasing materials for the Library/Media collections; cataloging and organizing information resources for access by students and faculty; providing interlibrary loan services; maintaining equipment;
- Production and dissemination: designing and developing instructional media programs; developing web sites and guides for students and faculty to access information resources; providing support services for distance education courses.

For each service area, the Library/Media staff developed goals, outcome statements based upon these goals, and multiple measures for every outcome statement. Because the number of outcome statements to be assessed for all of the service areas was too many to handle at one time, the Library/Media department established a three-year cycle. The outcomes for instruction and reference services would be measured every year because they are the highest departmental priority. The outcomes for the other three service areas would be measured alternate years. Table A illustrates the assessment cycle and associated outcomes for the Library.

The RWC Library/Media faculty and staff have spent a considerable amount of time in developing this assessment model and in analyzing the results. When we began our discussions, we struggled to articulate outcome statements that focused upon our users. It was also a challenge to identify a number of *different* methods of measuring these outcomes. For most of the outcomes, user surveys were appropriate, but we had to find additional ways of measuring each outcome statement. It was difficult in deciding upon what the level of achievement for each measure should be. For example, when measuring reference services, we had to decide what would be an acceptable

Table As: Raymond Walters College Assessment Cycle and Outcome Statements		
Year	Service Area	Outcome Statements
1997–1998	Instruction & Reference	Students will be offered effective reference services.. Students will be taught how to locate, evaluate, and effectively use information.
	Facilities	Students will have an inviting, well-equipped, and secure environment for the purposes of study, research, and use of information technology and other resources.
1998–1999	Instruction & Reference	Same as 1997–1998
	Management of Resources	Students will have access to a collection of informational material, both in-house and available through resource-sharing, that will support their studies.
1999–2000	Instruction & Reference	Same as 1997–1998
	Production & Dissemination	Outcomes to be developed.

percentage of students who would respond that they had benefited from using reference services. We needed to identify a realistic percentage, but also a percentage that would indicate that we were reaching enough students. Although the assessment model described in this paper focuses upon Library services, some of these services, specifically reference and bibliographic instruction, are more closely aligned with academic assessment than with non-academic assessment of support services. However, reference and bibliographic instruction do not fit into the traditional classroom/student performance mold either. We had to be creative in designing meaningful outcome statements and measures for these quasi-academic service areas. Although the planning and implementation of this assessment model has consumed a significant amount of time, the results have benefited our students and have generated a meaningful examination of how and why we provide the services that we do.

Based upon our experiences in using the student outcomes assessment model described above, we would like to share several suggestions in creating an assessment process that measures library services in both a meaningful and practical way. A number of the measures and results from the RWC Library assessment model are provided as illustrations for each of these suggestions.

Five Suggestions for Assessment Success
1. Focus on users and what they use.
We mentioned above the importance of considering users' perceptions along with quantitative data. When deciding upon your outcomes and measures for assessment, try to answer this question: what services or collections are most often used in the library? You may need to rely on both quantitative data and your staff's perceptions to decide on these areas, but your next step is to measure the effectiveness and usefulness of these areas to the individuals who use them. While you can know from your record keeping that circulation has increased or decreased, only by questioning your users will you be able to analyze why this has occurred.

Since our entire assessment process was established with this concept in mind, most of our measures are focused on users' reactions to heavily-used services and resources (see a complete list of the measures we have used in Table B). In both years that we have been following our plan we have utilized surveys as measures. Through these surveys we are able to gain feedback on services and resources that we either perceived were used heavily or that we could measure the usage of quantitatively. A library user survey sought to gather background information on respondents and a sense of whether and how they used the Library. We also asked questions on the survey that served as service area-specific measures (i.e., were students aware of and satisfied with reference services, were the Library's physical accoutrements and its staff acceptable for users' needs?). In addition to these questions, we called for general suggestions on improving the Library.

The feedback gained from the survey was very interesting and helpful to our service planning. We learned that 11% of our respondents had never used the Library, that 35% had never asked for reference assistance, and that only 58% believed we had enough workstations available in the Library. There were also a good number of written suggestions for improving the Library, many of which were related to collection development in specified areas. While these are just a few of the results, they demonstrate the types of information that a survey can gain from users which are impossible to assess quantitatively. The 1999 version of this survey, which asks some new service area-specific questions in addition to the general ones from 1998, is currently underway. It should produce a larger sample due to a new means of distribution. We have asked the help of faculty mem-

---

Table B: A Measures Used By the RWC Library, Organized by Area of Assessment

Instruction
- A tally of students attending library instruction sessions during the academic year.
- A survey of student satisfaction with, and understanding of, the instruction session they attended.
- A survey of faculty members who requested instruction for their classes to gauge changes in student research skills.
- A survey of student satisfaction with the library resources section of the Computer Awareness class.
- Primary trait analysis of student exams from Computer Awareness to assess student understanding of key library resources concepts.

Reference
- A survey of library users which assessed users' knowledge and use of reference services.
- A survey of reference service quality, following a reference transaction.
- An analysis of class assignments which utilize library reference sources.

Facilities
- A survey of library users which assessed users' opinion of : (1) the Library as an environment for study and research, (2) the Library staff's approachability and helpfulness, and (3) the availability of workstations for accessing library resources.
- A measurement of available student study space, based on the ACRL Standards for Two-Year College Learning Resource Centers.

Management of Resources
- An analysis of the RWC Library's holdings of recommended materials in nursing, veterinary technology, and dental hygiene.
- A survey of library users which assessed users' opinions and awareness of the ability to request materials from libraries within OhioLINK.

bers to distribute the survey in their classes so that we can reach more students, particularly those who may have never entered the Library. To date, the survey has been offered to students in the Library and in the nearby hallway.

Your outcomes and measures may also include services or collections which are known to be rarely used, or for others which you have no current perception or measurement of usage. An attempt to measure their use could be used to promote them. Surveys can both create awareness and assess it.

2. Make an assessment plan that does not overwhelm the library or its users.

The twin temptations of assessment are to do too little or to do too much. While the first temptation is addressed under Suggestion One, this suggestion addresses the latter. There are countless measures available for assessment purposes, and the idea of assessing several different aspects of the library at once can be very attractive. Library staff may find, however, that administering too large a number of measures is extremely difficult to do while fulfilling their regular duties. Likewise, library users may grow weary of filling out interminable surveys or experiencing service delays caused by certain measures. Selecting a reasonable and comfortable amount of assessment for any one time is essential.

The assessment model used at RWCL, as described above, addresses this potential difficulty. By only assessing half of our service areas annually we are able to control the impact of assessment on both our library and our student body. We decide upon a certain number of Instruction & Reference-related measures to use each year. Then we devise measures for the other service area that will not compete with those for Instruction & Reference but which will still provide good information about that area. A workable method for lowering the demand on staff and users is to space assessment measures out over the year's academic quarters or semesters. We have also been able to have a single measure serve a dual purpose. For instance, in our first year we conducted a survey of library users that included questions related to both Instruction & Reference and Facilities. We are repeating this survey in the second year of our cycle, this time combining Instruction & Reference and Management of Resources. This has helped our administration of assessment and increased the willingness of students to give their input by requiring only one survey to cover a variety of separate measures.

3. Pick measures that will provide meaningful samples and useful information.

Make sure your measures actually measure something. Will your measure reach enough individuals to provide an accurate sample of your user population? If you do reach a meaningful sample, will the information you ask of your respondents actually help you with assessment?

Our measures, particularly the surveys, owe their success to two reasons. First, we have kept our surveys short (ranging from three questions to twelve questions) and fairly easy to understand in order to ensure the cooperation of our intended respondents. Neither the length of the survey nor difficult to understand questions should try the patience of respondents. This last point can be a difficult one to achieve with certain library activities (such as aspects of instruction), which demand terminology that sometimes defies layman's terms. Second, we have tried to offer some measures in a controlled environment which help ensure participation. For instance, our library instruction surveys are offered to students right before the end of the instruction session, when they are still a "captive" audience. Students rarely refuse to complete the survey.

On the other hand, our survey of reference quality was an abject failure. Here the problem was probably not the survey itself, but how it fit (or intruded) into the process it was meant to measure. The survey involved handing out a form to students who had asked a reference question once they either had an answer or when the reference interview ended. Though we can certainly not fault the model for our instrument, our survey was loosely based on the forms used by the Wisconsin-Ohio Reference Evaluation Program.[1] Reference staff members either found it awkward at times to hand out the survey, particularly when they were away from the reference desk, or simply forgot to do so during busy periods. Library users were not unwilling to complete the survey, but some did not have time to fill it out once they had located their needed materials. Other reference users who were, unbeknown to staff, offered a second or third survey refused to fill it out again. After reaping only forty-three surveys out of a total of 360 reference interactions, we decided to call a halt to this measure. The service was heavily used and the information would have been useful, but our method could not reach a meaningful sample of our users.

Whether you are using surveys or not, be sure to take the time to carefully design your measure and its distribution to ensure user participation. There are many sources in the assessment literature that can guide you in the use of focus groups or any other measure you have in mind.

4. Experiment with new measures.

You certainly want to have some measures that you use consistently so that you can compare data from one year to the next. However, this should not restrain you from finding new ways to measure your assessment outcomes. Experiments can come about at various times and for various reasons. An experiment may be a measure that is just new to you (never before tried by your library) or an entirely new instrument. When you begin your assessment plan, you may wish to try something new (not just another survey, for instance). Once you have been working under a plan for some time, you may find that your original measures do not assess all of the important aspects of a given collection or service. You may even need to scrap an "old faithful" measure that is no longer fitting to your library. At any time, new services may be added which require a different approach. Whatever the reason, be open to trying new measures as long as they do not violate Suggestions Two or Three.

Even in the short duration of our assessment plan we have attempted experiments at several different points in the process. Our planning process allows for staff to critique current measures or suggest new ones so that changes or additions can be made quickly. Three experimental items that we have tried are the survey of reference quality (described above in Suggestion Three), an analysis of library-related class assignments, and the primary-trait analysis of student exams following a required library session.

Like the reference quality survey, our plan to analyze class assignments to see if they were supported by our reference collection was introduced as an experiment in the initial year of our assessment plan. It was unlike anything we had ever tried or read about before, and could have become a staple measure of our plan. Sadly, and again like the reference quality survey, this measure failed. Our call for assignments netted a small number to work with, and a significant number of them did not use library resources (despite the fact that our call made note of this requirement). In the end, it was possible to only minimally evaluate the reference collection in just a few subject areas. We will not be repeating this measure in the future, but we cannot rule out the possibility that we will, through experimentation, eventually arrive at a measure that accomplishes our objective.

Our latest experiment is still ongoing. As part of our Instruction & Reference measures for 1998–99, we are attempting to use Primary Trait Assessment (PTA) to analyze student exams from RWC's Computer Awareness course. Primary Trait Assessment is a method for assessing student learning which focuses on the required elements for a given assignment. Instructors can use their grading criteria to construct a scale with which they can analyze students' assignments.[2] Computer Awareness (CA) is a one-credit course which teaches incoming students the fundamentals of word processing, e-mail, browsing the Internet, and library resources. We conduct a two hour session for CA students and then contribute five multiple choice questions to their final exam.

We have already been surveying students on their satisfaction with the session and surveying faculty members on the potential effect of Computer Awareness. Now we hope to use a primary trait scale based on the key concepts we test for in the exam. Since each of the five questions concerns one of the five concepts taught in the session, our scale is determined by the number of questions a student answers correctly, thus demonstrating understanding of the underlying concepts. Preliminary results show that 55% of students are missing one or fewer questions, placing them at what we have designated as either Level One or Level Two on our scale. For students missing two or more questions (Level Three on our scale), we hope to see if there are trends in the questions they are missing and whether we can improve the session to better stress the most crucial concepts.

5. Make assessment a regular part of your operation.

In order for assessment to be truly effective it has to be continuous. Do not just wait to assess immediately prior to an accreditation visit. Do not assess on only an ad-hoc basis (although this can be a fine additional method of assessment if you discover something that should be assessed immediately). We believe that our model of assessment is in keeping with Suggestion Two (do not overwhelm) and Suggestion Five (do not forget). Our hope is that our measures will cause us to make changes. By assessing regularly, meaningfully, and with a certain number of consistent measures, we will create a feedback loop in which these changes can then be assessed. We can only decide whether the changes have been successful by going back to the same (or quite similar) measures the next year and then comparing the results. If a change works, then we will keep it in place and keep measuring that service or resource. If it does not, then we will have data in place that may suggest a new change.

Another reason for regular assessment goes beyond the changes that you initiate. Academic libraries by their very nature are constantly in flux, with new services and resources appearing and being created to meet needs and demands that may be beyond the ken of your assessment model. Campus environments change regularly, most obviously though the departure and influx of students. You cannot base today's changes on survey results from five years ago. Annual and semi-annual assessment will provide the recent data you need for decision-making.

The Future of Assessment at the RWC Library

We expect to continue following our three-year cycle and to repeat our most successful measures. When the three-year cycle begins to repeat in 2000-2001, we plan to modify the outcome statements for our four service areas to reflect any changes in the Library's goals. We will also review all of our measures at that time to decide which ones should continue to be used.

We will continue to experiment with measures, one of which (the Primary Trait Assessment of Computer Awareness) was discussed above in Suggestion Four. A measure we would like to implement is some kind of information needs assessment to better understand the types of resources and services our entire college community expects from the Library. An instrument has yet to be created for this measure and we will be combing the assessment literature for ideas. We also hope to experiment with focus groups to measure those service areas where they would be appropriate.

Assessment is not exactly a science and is hardly an art. It is, however, an honest attempt to make sense of the daily activities which make up library work. With a good plan and enough determination any library is capable of better evaluating its services and collections and improving its offerings to its user population. It is not merely an additional activity for us to undertake; it is our professional responsibility.

Notes

1. See Stalker, John C., and Marjorie E. Murfin. "Quality Reference Service: A Prelimary Case Study," *The Journal of Academic Librarianship* 22 (Nov. 1996): 423–9. The Wisconsin-Ohio Reference Evaluation Program is very well described in this article, and its list of references has a number of other pertinent sources.

2. See the Web page http://www.rwc.uc.edu/phillips/Assessment/AcadAssess.html for more information on Primary Trait Assessment (PTA). Under the "General Education Assessment" section of the page there are links to PTA activities at Raymond Walters College and to an introductory essay on the topic by Barbara Walvoord and Virginia Anderson.

Common Cause: Creating a Unified Environmental Information System through Stakeholder Partnership

Linda Langschied

Introduction:
This paper begins with a basic premise: universal access to and sharing of scientifically-sound research helps to promote rational decision-making about environmental and related societal concerns (e.g. transportation, land use and development, public health). The preservation of any state's natural heritage depends largely on the ability of government policy makers to plan and to allocate resources for both preservation and remediation. It is of particular concern that usable and timely data be made available to local government officials who bear the major responsibility for environment-related planning within their communities, as well as to the citizens, researchers, and environmental organizations who work to influence policy.

Currently, however, the state-of-the-art in distributing such information to diverse users leaves much to be desired, and the uneven availability and usability of environmental data compromise informed decision-making. Multiple investigators, representing multiple disciplines are involved in data collection and analysis, usually for a specific purpose and with little thought of possible secondary uses of their research. The resulting studies constitute a large and growing body of environmental "grey literature"—both print and digital—that resides at best across distributed networks; at worst, in the offices of individuals, unknown to other potential researchers. This paper will illustrate by example the benefits and pitfalls of working with non-library partners towards the common goal of making New Jersey's environmental research record available to researcher and citizens.

Background Notes on New Jersey's Environment
In 1996, when the New Jersey Department of Environmental Protection announced a campaign to promote Ecotourism in the state, the citizens of New Jersey responded with some, perhaps considerable, skepticism. The polite ones did, any-

---

Linda Langschied is information services librarian, Rutgers University.

way. The notion of environmental excursions in tourism to the state of New Jersey somehow provokes comedy—even burlesque. (Remember filmmaker Michael Moore's scurrilous reference to the imaginary New Jersey theme park—Chemical Land—in his movie, "Roger and Me?") And in truth, New Jersey's environmental condition, by many measures, does present a troubling picture. After all, we hold the dubious distinction for:

- the greatest population density;
- the greatest automobile density;
- the most miles of paved road;
- the greatest number of federal Superfund sites—116;
- troubling, if yet unproven, occurrences of "clusters" of disease, and speculation about environmental causation.

Certainly continuous development and a long history of industrial and agricultural pollution compromise New Jersey's environmental health. But the environmental situation in New Jersey is an extremely complex one. Despite the tremendous pressures of past and present environmental practices, the state is replete with areas of tremendous natural beauty: pristine beaches and sand dunes, lush green countryside, historic towns, rolling hills, scenic river valleys and mountain overlooks, lush wetlands, and dense pine forests. New Jersey's environmental challenge is a dual one: to preserve and protect its natural heritage, and to address remediation of its tainted lands, air, and water.

Federal/State Partnership

How New Jersey and other states will address their environmental challenges is in many ways shaped by federal objective. A major Environmental Protection Agency (EPA) initiative is having a tremendous influence on how states conduct their environmental planning activities. The National Environmental Performance Partnership System (NEPPS) is a framework for joint priority-setting and decision-making between the EPA and states. NEPPS represents a new approach to environmental management, with a focus on measuring progress towards better environmental protection through the use of goals and indicators of environmental improvements.

The use of "environmental indicators" as a way of focusing program priorities on desired outcomes, and as a useful way of communicating results to the public, is a critical component of NEPPS. Environmental indicators are viewed as the best, if long-term, way to measure meaningful progress in improving human health and the environment. Scientists might, for example, monitor a stream's sensitive macro-invertebrates over time to determine whether point-source pollutants are entering the ecosystem, rather than trying to detect transitory occurrences of discharge. NEPPS is an innovative management system is designed to foster identification of state environmental priorities and to allow states the flexibility to better direct federal resources to address their distinct priorities. New Jersey, for example, would obviously have environmental concerns differing from those of Alaska; the set of indicators each would measure would be determined by the individual state, in understanding with the EPA. Examples of state "Performance Partnership Agreements" are available from the EPA's Office of State and Local Relations/NEPPS Signed Documents and State Agreements site at: http://www.epa.gov/regional/pps/docs.htm.

A key provision in NEPPS—and one that impacts directly on information services issues—is based on enhancing accountability to the public. NEPPS commits both the EPA and state environmental officials to share information on environmental priorities, status, and trends broadly and effectively with the public. No specific approach to achieving that objective is prescribed, however. The general concept is to involve the public more actively in understanding environmental issues and choices.[1]

A Widening Circle of Partners...

The New Jersey Ecological Research Partnership was formed about the same time as the NEPPS initiative, with a specific purpose: to promote the use of environmental information in decision making. The Partnership represented members of state and local government agencies, citizens groups, and local corporations; however, the initial effort was primarily led by scientists in the NJ-DEP and researchers in the biological, geological, environmental sciences at Rutgers University. The federal mandate to enhance public access to environmental data coincided with the Partnership's goals, since the development of environmental indicators depends upon data availability. New Jersey's signed agreement with the EPA clearly includes, in its mission, provisions for making information available:

> ...as critical environmental issues have evolved over time, and knowledge of the limitations of existing strategies to address these increasingly complex issues has matured, the need for reinventing many environmental protection practices is now frequently acknowledged. The goal of this next generation of environmental protection is to focus efforts on achievement of improved environmental results while allowing flexibility in how results are achieved. Key elements of this new philosophy are long term direction setting, and development and reporting of specific, scientifically sound measures of progress toward meeting these goals. Additionally, reinvention relies on increased sharing of information and decision-making with all stakeholders, creates opportunities for compliance assistance with environmental requirements, and attempts to lessen the burden of complying with these requirements. Through reinvention practices, environmental agencies can improve the ways in which they protect the environment and the public, while setting clear priorities and making the best use of limited resources.[2]

Ultimately, the Partnership, led by a scientist at the NJ-DEP's Division of Science, Research and Technology, backed a proposal to create a web-based data directory, which could be used by any researcher to identify environmental data and experts. The project's accordance with the goals of the NEPPS program no doubt contributed to the Partnership's ultimate ability to secure funding for the project

...Encompasses the Library

The NJ Ecological Research partners—most of them researchers themselves—were keenly aware of the difficulty in determining the existence and location of extant data on the environment. What was needed in the partnership was the inclusion of those with the skills to discover elusive information, organize it, make it available to the public, provide outreach services and, most importantly, have the technological know-how to bring about the information management system envisioned by the Partnership.

In a tremendous show of keen, collective insight (for a group of academics), the idea of *librarian* took hold and grew. The librarians of Rutgers, the State University of New Jersey, seemed the likely candidates to approach. The Rutgers librarians' familiarity with scientific research collections and connections to the state's leading environmental research faculty clearly recommended them to the project.

Moreover, the Library had recently opened its new Scholarly Communication Center (SCC). This SCC is a state-of-the-art technological information facility, equipped with computer and distance education labs, teleconferencing and satellite transmission capabilities, and Humanities and Social Science Data Centers. We are confident that the year spent in meetings and negotiations about the project in this environment, represented by librarians who had planned and implemented the Center, sealed the deal!

The New Jersey Department of Environmental Protection awarded a $50,000 seed grant to investigators from the Rutgers University Libraries and Rutgers Ecopolicy Center to create a web-based resource to facilitate discovery and access to scientific reports and data related to New Jersey's environment. The resulting product, the prototype New Jersey Environmental Research Record, is part traditional catalog, part digital library, part data server for GIS, and part community outreach tool. Some of the basic elements of the Record are:

- World Wide Web used to create/modify records, search/browse contents, retrieve/download data;
- Computing platform: NT 4.0 with Internet Information Server, FrontPage, Cold Fusion, and MS Access;

- FGDC metadata standard to describe digital/non-digital objects; all entries are geo-referenced for discovery through a map-based graphical interface;
- Contents ultimately to be built through self-submission by data holders.

Development is ongoing, but because of shifting priorities of our funding partner, the NJ-DEP, the project has undergone significant upheavals in scope and direction. Partnership relations can shift as new developments arise, and new players enter the picture.

All Partners are Equal, but Some are More So

What do librarians bring to the table in a partnership? Certainly not hard resources—we are much more likely to be on the receiving end of a money-granting situation. Instead, we contribute our "in-kind service"—the commitment of our time and expertise to the project. In-kind service is valuable and, in grantsmanship, a most justifiable and quantifiable contribution. Nonetheless, the fact is that the partner putting up the hard resources is going to have tremendous influence over the direction of the project.

At last year's ACRL conference, Kate Nevins, the Executive Director of SOLINET, delivered an excellent and insightful paper entitled "Partnerships and Competition," in which she asserted: "… it cannot be assumed that our partners don't compete with libraries, or that others partners on the project don't compete with each other."[3] Insofar as our partnership evolved, truer words were never spoken. The direction of our project has been radically altered—twice—as our partners engaged either directly or through "third party" partners in parallel projects. In each case, the library partners were expected to conform to the new goals of the funding partner.

In the first major shake-up, the "ever-widening circle of partners" benefit took a direction that was simultaneously exciting and disquieting. The partnership circle kicked-off by the EPA's NEPPS initiative came full circle, back to the EPA. The EPA's own adherence to the NEPPS initiative spawned the development of a number of information management systems within the agency. Among them was the Environmental Information Management System (EIMS), intended to provide uniform data access to the multiple EPA offices. When the EIMS concept became known to the NJ-DEP, it was viewed as a possible option for New Jersey. Our immediate contacts within NJ-DEP quickly recognized the significant overlap of projects, and redirected our activities to actively partnering directly with the EIMS staff, with the goal of merging our prototype with EIMS. Our work was radically altered as we joined with database developers in Washington, D.C. to act as consultants to their (and potentially our own) database and user interface design. Development of our own database project—with the exception of content development—froze in place.

But our commitment never lessened. While working in good faith to cooperate with EIMS, we continued to openly discuss with involved NJ-DEP managers the problems of merging New Jersey data into the federal agency system as we saw it: the lack of local control, the over-complexity of the database, the rigidity of EPA's security system, and the loss of New Jersey's specific imprimatur on the whole project. Ultimately, the partnership between NJ-DEP and EIMS faltered, and we rather elatedly returned to our originally slated activities of prototyping the New Jersey Environmental Record. Until then we had concentrated the project on handling documents and like objects; now we hired a new staff member who had years experience in GIS, and began the next stage of prototyping for GIS and other data resources.

The next upheaval was swift to arrive, and came from a source closer to home: the NJ-DEP itself. In the time that had transpired since the beginning of our grant award from DEP's Division of Science, Research and Technology, the DEP's Geographic Information System's (GIS) Division had secured a large sum in state funding to consolidate GIS data from all the state's agencies. The proposed GIS "clearinghouse," Endex - The Environmental Data Exchange, has as its stated mission the very same one that we based our entire project on: to fashion an approach to support environmental management and decision making. Specifically, Endex would:

- Establish an "electronic trading post";
- Use the Internet and GIS for cooperative problem solving;

- Demonstrate advantages of open information access and data sharing;
- Create an information sharing service;
- Work smarter by organizing environmental monitoring data.

Once again, a project so like the one that we were funded to create was in the making, and given the resources and DEP talent behind it, would certainly prevail. Everyone involved realized that the continuation of our project as initially envisioned threatened a wasteful duplication of effort, not to mention creating a state of confusion for the state's environmental researchers.

As of this writing, negotiations are underway to determine how our projects can be realigned to work with, and benefit from, the Endex initiative. The tentative plan is for all state GIS collections and services to reside within the DEP. The Library proposes that it will take on the creation of a digital library for documents, including maps.

The exclusion of GIS from our immediate purview is disappointing, for we have significant expertise in management of data in our organization. However, we agree that areas of responsibility must be clearly delineated—in effect, competition reduced—if the relationship is to prevail. Ultimately, our commitment to the aims of this project outweigh our sense of "ownership," and we continue in our commitment to work towards what is still, after all, our common cause—creating universal access to environmental information for the benefit of the state's citizens and researchers.

Summing it All Up

What do libraries gain from these partnerships? Successful partnership ventures generally cite common benefits: increased breadth of expertise, enhanced resources-sharing capabilities, and making connections to potential new contibutors. Subtler benefits are derived, as well, and among those that librarians might expect to achieve are as follows:

Working in non-library partnerships aligns academic libraries with national campus trends toward university engagement with community and government. Librarians need to develop collaboration beyond those of their immediate colleagues in order to meet the increasing campus objective to make their services available to the state's citizens. Ernest Boyer, former President of the Carnegie Foundation for the Advancement of Teaching, noted:

> Increasingly, I'm convinced that ultimately, the scholarship of engagement also means creating a special climate in which the academic and civic cultures communicate more continuously and more creatively with each other, helping to enlarge what anthropologist Clifford Geertz describes as the universe of human discourse and enriching the quality of life for us all.[4]

By working in partnership with other stakeholders, the university library can achieve goals unreachable on its own. Partnerships allow us to share both costs and benefits; this is a winning strategy for the University, and for the citizens whose tax dollars help to support it.

Partnerships furnish opportunities for development of original services. Because partnerships enhance resource-sharing, they can occasion the development of creative pilot projects that would not find support in the mainstay budget. It is important, for example, for librarians to stretch their knowledge and capabilities in the digital library environment. Too often, however, budgetary and time limitations constrain our capabilities to undertake experimental projects.

Partnerships furnish opportunities for individual growth...

The benefit that partnership support brings to projects like ours goes beyond mere technological support to improve library services. Partnership relationships can serve to significantly improve the knowledge of the individual by expanding the circle of expertise in which we move, and by affording us time and resources for creativity and invention.

... which will in turn promote institutional growth.

I predict that as faculty librarians will increasingly seek to garner the support necessary to create digital library projects, and that they will do so though the development of partnerships with academic departments, government agencies, and citizens. Through this expansion and redefinition of work and scholarly activity, a secondary benefit is bound to emerge. The reinvention of individual librarians' view of their work may ultimately produce a fundamental shift in our organizational behavior and beliefs about what librarianship is and can be.

References

1. United States Environmental Protection Agency. Office of State and Local Relations Performance Partnership System. "Background on the National Environmental Performance Partnership System." (1998). Online. Available: http://www.epa.gov/regional/pps/faq.htm.

2. New Jersey Department of Environmental Protection. Division of Science, Research and Technology. "Executive Summary: Environmental Directions for New Jersey Performance Partnership Agreement." (1997–1998) Online. Available: http://www.state.nj.us/dep/dsr/exesum97.pdf

3. Nevins, Kate. "Partnerships and Competition," ACRL National Conference. (1997). Online. Available: http://www.ala.org/acrl/invited/nevins.html

4. Boyer, Ernest. "The Scholarship of Engagement," *Journal of Public Service and Outreach*, 2, no. 3 (fall 1997): 20.

Creating Our Roles as Reference Librarians of the Future: Choice or Fate?

Susan Szasz Palmer

During our lifetimes, new technologies have changed the roles of many individuals: supermarket clerks now scan groceries for speedier checkout service, doctors employ MIR or CAT scans to help diagnose patients, telephone operators at financial services assist callers with paying bills or transferring funds. Most of these changes, I believe, are generally considered by all (providers and consumers or clients alike) to be beneficial and are regarded as signs of progress. Can we say the same thing about all the new technologies in the library? Has the increase in new technologies added to the stress of playing multiple roles, or lessened it? Has our fundamental role as reference librarians really changed, or rather only the tools and methods we employ to carry out our mission? Should user expectations, or perhaps what is really our perception of user expectations, define our role, or should we be more proactive in directing our own mission, our own futures as professionals?

In my time with you this morning, during one of the opening sessions of this conference titled "Racing Toward Tomorrow," I plan to explore the issue of our roles as reference librarians of the future—and suggest that our professional futures, no less than our personal lives, might best be served by another image than that of a race. I will at times refer to some of the literature that has addressed these issues, and will also discuss how we approach them in the Reference Services Division of Olin•Kroch•Uris (OKU) Libraries at Cornell University.[1]

It may be useful for you to know that I came to Cornell 20 years ago as a Reference and Instruction Librarian at what was then called the Uris Undergraduate Library. About three years later, I moved a building away to become a Reference Librarian at the John M. Olin Graduate Research Library (you may note here that "instruction" geared towards graduate students and faculty was not in favor yet in the early 1980s, at least not in the

---

Susan Szasz Palmer is reference collections coordinator, Cornell University.

Cornell Library). Olin Library is the largest library at Cornell, and is sometimes referred to as the main library, a distinction it held with more prominence when we had the only so-called "union" card catalog on campus. For those of you who became librarians only since the advent of online catalogs, this meant that Olin was the only library, of 17 on campus, whose card catalog contained records not only for its own holdings, but for all of the other 16 libraries as well.

Approximately five years ago, the reference departments in Olin and Uris were administratively merged to form one division. While we maintain two reference desks (a third if we include the Map Division which is also now part of Reference); we have combined our staffs (9 Reference Librarians, 1 Map Librarian, 6 Reference Assistants, 2 office support staff, and the Head of the Division); and we continue to offer cross-training for both the librarians and the paraprofessionals (we call them Reference Assistants). All of today's professional staff except for the Head of the Division were here before the merger; in fact, I believe the most "junior" librarian has been in the Division nearly ten years. Needless to say, turnover among the Reference Assistants has been much higher, although we have a few loyal veterans.

As for the scope of our services, Olin and Uris are essentially Social Sciences and Humanities collections, and while Uris is no longer formally referred to as the Undergraduate Library, it continues to house a college-level stack collection, the largest reserve collection on campus, and most recently, two electronic labs (one of which we use for classroom instruction). The Division also serves as the *de facto* government documents department, providing reference service for United Sates, United Nations, and European Union documents, for each of which we are official depositories. And speaking personally of multiple roles, I serve as bibliographer for the Olin and Uris reference collections as well as for the Uris stacks; I am the resident documents "expert" in the Division; I teach both lower and upper division course-related instruction sessions as well as Internet classes; and last, but sometimes not least, I schedule the librarians' hours of service at the Olin and Uris reference desks.

We at Cornell may serve as an example of one institution's approach to the issues facing our profession, but I do not want to suggest we have created the perfect model for any or all of you to adapt to your own institutional settings. I would also be remiss if I led you to believe my colleagues and I always agree among ourselves on these issues. Most important, I want to stress overall that as we address the issues facing our roles as reference librarians of the future we do something that may seem totally at odds with our tendency to pride ourselves on answering questions. None of us, myself included, has the answers to the questions I am raising today. However, as the great German poet Rainer Maria Rilke said:

> Do not now seek the answers, that cannot be given you because you would not be able to live them. And the point is to live everything. *Live* the questions now. Perhaps you will then gradually, without noticing it, live along some distant day into the answer.[2]

I believe we would all agree that the core mission of reference librarians in academic libraries today is to provide service to students and faculty as integral members of the learning process; that our overall primary function is to support the curriculum of the students and the research of the faculty. I would further suggest that everyone in academia—both we the providers, as well as students and faculty, the clients—take reference service for granted. Don't get me wrong. I don't mean this in a pejorative sense. I mean only that we accept it as a core service, indeed a core commodity. We do not need to justify our existence. Yet it is worth reflecting that reference service has neither a very lengthy, nor a very universal, history.

The very concept of reference service—librarians eagerly and willingly available to answer patrons' queries—is a very American idea. And even in this country, the prevailing notion in the mid-1800s was that "helping readers represented a distraction from the librarian's important duties... ."[3] One of the earliest descriptions of the role of a reference librarian is described in an 1876 article by Samuel Green, aptly titled, "Personal Relations

Between Librarians and Readers."[4] A decade and a half later William Child, then a reference librarian at Columbia University, offered the following definition of reference work, still useful today:

> By reference work is meant simply the assistance given by a librarian to readers in acquainting them with the intricacies of the catalogue, in answering questions, and, in short, doing anything and everything in his power to facilitate access to the resources of the library....[5]

University libraries were slower to accept the importance of reference service than public libraries. According to one historian of librarianship, "...with the exception of Cornell and Columbia, the private universities were still without reference librarians specifically so titled in 1896."[6] Not until the early 1900s—not yet a hundred years ago—did reference service take hold as an integral function in academic libraries. To those who are thinking a hundred years is substantial, "...the history of reference is much shorter than that of the two other primary functions of the library, collection development (which dates back thousands of years) and collection organization (which dates back at least 400 years)."[7]

It seems that throughout this brief history, debate has continued to ensue as to the scope of reference and the responsibilities of reference librarians. For the most part, this self examination has, and continues to be, a good thing for the profession. But as we approach the next hundred years, I would suggest not that we stifle the debate, but that we not get caught up in it either. That we not spend so much time on self reflection that we lose sight of our core mission—serving others.

With this in mind, let us examine the place of the reference desk in the provision of reference service. The desk is now an entity at once as seemingly essential to what we do as the courtroom is to a trial lawyer, and yet its importance is regularly being called into question. One of the first apparently successful efforts to eliminate the general reference desk is described by Virginia Massey-Burzio, who did this in the early 1990s at Brandeis University.[8] Brandeis has gone to a model where most questions are filtered by paraprofessionals, with professional librarians acting as consultants. In his controversial article, "Shaking the Conceptual Foundations of Reference," Jerry Campbell argues more radically that we not only remove the reference desk, but that we remove most of the human interface altogether. In his view, the notion of reference *desk* service "... is a building-centered, old style, 'make them come to us' model [which] cannot survive in the information age."[9] He suggests that "we should set ourselves the goal of answering no less than 75 percent of the questions that currently come to our reference desks using computers and yes, without human intervention."[10]

Yet it seems this revolutionary idea of eliminating the desk only skirts the issue of what *service* reference librarians can and should provide. Does it really matter whether we do it at a formally designated, and at least to some also a familiar, spot in the library? If the issue is helping patrons find the information they need and assisting with their research, if we aren't at a desk, where should we be? Tucked away in our offices, harder to find than at present, in effect coming to resemble European libraries where patrons have to ferret out human help.

Two things are troublesome about the view, strongly held by some, that we do away with the desk. The first may sound trite, but to paraphrase the notion about baseball spectators from the movie "Field of Dreams"—if you build it, they will come—isn't it all too likely that when it comes to reference desk patrons, "if we take it down, they will go away"? And if they go away, where will they go? To the Internet? Or ironically, to Barnes & Noble, as described by Renee Feinberg in a 1998 issue of *Library Journal*. She surveyed patrons in a Manhattan Barnes & Noble, many of whom were area college students, for an explanation of why they weren't using their college libraries. No, it's not simply that B&N serves coffee (which some libraries actually do now as well). It is because, as one interviewee expressed, "'The library has information, but B&N has books' [suggesting] that patrons may have been turned off by libraries that emphasize electronic information."[11]

The decline in desk statistics at many college and university libraries might be playing into the notion that we are needed less. But we need to be careful about confusing quantity with quality. I suspect that most people go inside banks less frequently than a decade ago, thanks to ATM machines. But I would argue that when you need a banking service that the ATM cannot provide, you want to go inside the bank and easily find a knowledgeable employee available to help you. Simply put, the increasing presence and ease of technology in our lives does not eliminate the need for human assistance, it heightens it—if not in the frequency with which we seek out that human assistance then in the intensity for it when needed. If we keep this distinction in mind, we will be able to more clearly see technology as a tool, as something we choose how to employ, rather than as a force driving what services we should provide.

To me, there is another curiosity about the eliminate-the-desk theory of the future of reference. It is puzzling how this theory relates to a generally agreed upon presumption of user behavior in libraries—that many, if not most, patrons are hesitant to approach the desk for help. This may result from a kind of basic human nature that people don't like to ask for help because they don't want to admit their lack of knowledge (and I'm not just referring to the stereotypical view of men not being able to ask for driving directions). Think here of the number of times, even during only one short shift on the desk, that someone comes up to you and says, "I'm sorry, but I have a really stupid question." Or, "I'm sorry to bother you." What makes us think that patrons who feel this way when they enter the library—either the unsophisticated undergraduate with a term paper to write or the professor with a complex reference she cannot decipher—will feel better when we are even harder to find? What will make them seek us out when we are farther away?

I would suggest that the undergraduate will conclude the library is not a place that offers help and the professor will conclude that we have made things too complicated for them to understand. Or perhaps more important, we will have lost the opportunity to intercept that hesitant undergraduate and take his intimidation of his assignment to do a term paper and turn it into curiosity and excitement about a new topic to explore. Similarly for the professor, we will have lost the opportunity not only to show her that we have skills that can help untangle that thorny citation, but also to talk to her about her research needs in general. In both cases, by distancing ourselves from the patrons we send the message that the user is not our primary focus anymore. At an institutional level, we also weaken our connections to the teaching and research missions of the university as a whole. Rather than working towards greater involvement with the educational mission of our institutions, we marginalize ourselves. Rather than emphasizing the value of human interaction in this era of technology, we make it easier for our patrons to find a computer than a librarian.

I would argue that rather than eliminating desk service we need to enhance it. As one librarian has noted, "we first need ... to cure ourselves of the suicidal notion that has taken hold of the library profession's soul in the last decade, that providing service within our walls is our primary weakness when in fact it is precisely our primary strength."[12] One way to build on this primary strength is to offer to meet with patrons by appointment as an extension of the routine service provided at the desk. This allows for patrons, again either the beginning undergraduate or the senior faculty member, to meet individually with a librarian and discuss in private his or her needs. Maintaining desk service alongside this consultation service supports the majority of users who don't need in depth assistance, and will be put off by any extra effort required to get help. In addition, routine traffic at the desk allows, perhaps only for now, a familiar and easy mechanism both for us to advertise this additional level of service, and a place from which patrons can be efficiently referred—either by a librarian who would like to spend more uninterrupted time with the patron than can often be done at the desk, or by a paraprofessional who might help the patron get started because she is the only person on duty at the time and then refer the patron to a librarian for a follow up appointment.

Although we have been taking referrals at the desk informally for as long as I can remember, in the last year we have formalized this into an additional service. We have a flyer advertising our "consultation" service that we keep in handout racks near the desk; we list it as a service on our Division web-site; and we also keep all the librarians' business cards at the desk which we regularly hand out. By this I don't simply mean that we hand out our own cards, but that we (and the paraprofessionals) also hand out each others' cards as we think appropriate based on the patron's needs and our individual areas of expertise. We also keep on hand the business cards for our colleagues in Collection Development, and hand those out as well, either when the patron's needs are in a subject area outside those covered in the Division, or more often when the patron has a specific question about obtaining material for the library's stack collection.

As I have alluded, one motivation for removing the reference desk may be what I would call a "defensive strike." If our statistics are going down, and our administrators judge our performance by our statistics, it's not good if we are less busy. Worse yet, the very idea of us "sitting there" is perceived as not a good use of our time. The difficulty lies again in whom we are ultimately serving. Administrators may want to see the desk busy, with lines of people waiting; but patrons want prompt service without waiting in a long line to get it. Administrators see the same phenomenon as overstaffed; patrons see it as well staffed.

I have said here that the library's administration is judging our performance, if not our essential value, by our numbers because I think that is how most of us tend to view this issue. But perhaps we have created this problem ourselves by fostering a quantitative method of evaluating reference service, and consistently failing to develop qualitative methods to evaluate what we do. It is not simply that we should reject the notion of "more is better." But only if we attempt to measure what we do qualitatively can we learn the true strengths and weaknesses of the services we provide. To put it differently, measuring the number of questions we answer may help us better manage our staffing patterns, our hours of service, but it won't tell us what kinds of questions are being asked, by whom, and how well our staff are answering these questions. As one writer noted nearly a decade ago:

Reference service is too complex and too important to be judged simply on the basis of how many reference questions any group of people answers. At some point, we have to deal with the quality of that service. If we don't know what quality we have, we have no way to determine if we're improving or getting worse, what kind of training for the reference desk works, and whether or not individual reference librarians are doing a good job.[13]

Perhaps less extreme than removing the desk is the proposal that we should at least be getting up from it more and seeking patrons out in the reference area. Generally called "roving" or "rovering" it has been compared to the concept of "Management by Wandering Around."[14] To the degree that we do this in order to be proactive, I would agree that it is indeed helpful, although I would again suggest that like private consultations, it functions best as an extension of traditional desk service. Roving might help us connect with some users who are hesitant to come to the desk, but others might also find it intrusive. To the degree that we hope to teach patrons over time to be as independent researchers as possible, roving may send an opposite, "in your face" sort of message.

I would suggest that the concept of roving is not all that new: we were very much encouraged to do this when I worked at the Undergraduate Library, on the assumption that the value of capturing the more helpless user outweighed the potential of our being intrusive. But I'm also reminded in this context of a story a colleague once told about one roving experience, back in the card catalog only days: He went up to a student who appeared to be confused and inquired if he needed any help. The patron turned to my librarian colleague and said, "Yeah, you can put these drawers away for me," and walked away. In today's library, will our implied offers of help in the research process be met with requests to unjam a printer or format a disk for downloading? We have tried to adapt to this new era by adding another level of staffing to assist in the roving: Students, whom we call "database assistants" move about the area where the bulk of our computer terminals are clustered, looking precisely for this kind of non-research problem. They not only help with the mechanics of the computers, but they are also trained in the basics of searching the major databases we support. So if a patron is having trouble distinguishing an abstract from an image in *Periodical Abstracts*, or can't figure out how to email the full text of an article from it, the database assistant can help. But if the patron then says, "I'm really not finding very much on my topic, can you help me?," the database assistant refers the patron to the librarian on the desk.

If roving is not as new as some suggest, it may be that it does require a fresh examination for a different reason: When we are at the desk now, we *sit* there much more than we used to, because we tend to spend more time helping patrons find electronic resources, which we can do without ever getting up. When we had to leave the desk to consult the print collection with patrons, we routinely got up and moved around the room thereby encountering other patrons attempting to use those collections. To the degree that we have ourselves become too glued to the computer, either when helping a patron or during quiet moments in between patrons, we do have a problem. But the problem may be more fundamental: Has the computer at our reference desks, our electronic gateway to the world, in fact made us less approachable and narrowed our methods of answering questions? If so, getting up and walking around may or may not be the only appropriate remedy.

Getting rid of the desk, keeping it, sitting or moving around, all still beg the questions: What are we doing and what should we be doing in the future? In the last year alone, two conferences have been held where the future of reference or the future of librarianship generally has taken center stage: Last spring, a conference was convened at Harvard around the theme "Finding Common Ground," the title alone conveying the message that we are not always moving forward together on these issues. In July of 1998, the Library of Congress held a two-day "institute" on "Reference Service in a Digital Age." The major issues addressed at the institute were as follows:

I. Skills and personality attributes—how do we personally prepare/react to technology changes?

II. Definition of core service—how do we define those we serve?

III. Philosophy of service to the digital researcher versus the traditional in-person or telephone researcher—how do we provide service to those we serve.

IV. And finally: What, if anything, can reference librarians **stop** doing as we enter the digital age?[15]

And in 1996, an entire issue of *The Reference Librarian* was devoted to the theme "The Roles of Reference Librarians: Today and Tomorrow."[16]

One underlying theme raised at these conferences and in the literature centers around the so-called skills reference librarians of the future will need. I say so-called, because we seem to be falling into a way of speaking about what we do that belittles it. It is also the language of technology. Master these skills and, voila, you are a reference librarian, or as one article describes it a "master reference librarian."[17] We speak of training today (or retraining or cross-training) as though what we do can be found in a user manual—absorb the contents and go. Even the way we approach new electronic resources being added to our reference collections has seemingly changed the way we, ourselves, describe what we need to know. We spend more time learning the intricacies of each new database than we ever did about even the most sophisticated print tool, and as a consequence, I believe we are spending less time continuously honing the *process* of doing reference. We emphasize now, more than we ever did with print resources, actually knowing *how* to use a resource, rather than *when* to use it. This is, of course, a futile exercise with electronic sources, especially those on the Internet, which is a seemingly infinite universe. For example, "From some 130 Web sites in mid-1993, the Web grew to over 646,000 sites by January 1997, with an estimated net gain of 1200 sites being added each day!"[18] But how many of us work (or ever did) in libraries where one could really "master" the print reference collection, never mind the print collections of our libraries' stacks? "Mastery" is the wrong goal.

I am not suggesting that content is not important. But just as we have confused mastery of sources with the process of doing reference, so too do we confuse the value of format with the value of content. And so we focus more on the so-called retraining of "older" reference librarians in how to use particular sources, in how to adapt to the new formats technology has brought us, rather than on training (perhaps we should call it teaching) "younger" reference librarians the content of our collections, the process of attempting to answer questions about which one knows very little. Perhaps the problem does lie in our language of "training": one can train someone to use the *MLA Bibliography*, but that is not the same as knowing something about 19th century literature. I still believe part of the challenge and thrill of reference work is being able to approach questions about which one knows very little, maybe even nothing at all. This is why we sometimes call ourselves generalists. But we mustn't confuse the impossibility of our knowing everything about all subjects with the notion that all content knowledge is irrelevant. Or worse, that technology has made the value of this content knowledge less necessary for us as reference librarians. As the late John Swan noted a decade ago,

> ... librarians, and not only academic librarians, have an essentially external relationship to knowledge. Our role is to provide access to information, not to master that information ourselves. ... [But] the simple fact is that the more a librarian knows about a particular topic, the better access she or he is able to provide to information about it.[19]

We have all heard the phrase "techno-stress," and while it refers to a wide range of aspects in the digital library, it is commonly invoked by reference librarians regarding the proliferation of different electronic resources, with many different interfaces.[20] To my best recollection, I have never heard a colleague of mine say he or she was suffering from "print-stress" or "microform-stress"—despite the fact that our reference collection alone has over 20,000 volumes and the library has over 6 million pieces of microform, most of which are not analyzed in the catalog. Our "stress" comes from the notion that we need to "know" (master) each new electronic resource inside out, before we can help our patrons use it, rather than learning how to approach a new, unfamiliar source, sometimes for the first time with a patron. We expect our users to admit their lack of knowledge and approach us with their questions; we need to be equally vulnerable with our patrons, and admit that we don't always know everything—particular when it's the "mechanics" of knowing, not the substance or content. We need to re-emphasize for ourselves the process of reference, something on which we used to pride ourselves.

At the same time, we need to encourage librarians not simply to learn new skills (which is really a euphemism for becoming more computer literate), but to learn more content, to attempt to have some specialization, some knowledge base. New technologies are indeed exciting tools that can enhance what we do. But without that knowledge base, we risk being "content with showing people which keys to push when."[21] I'm not suggesting that using electronic resources is exactly the same as using print resources. But teaching someone how to construct a search statement is one thing; trying to remember whether the truncation symbol is an asterisk or a plus sign is not useful. It's information, not knowledge, and we should be leery of "...the current obsession with delivery systems that many equate with information, research, and knowledge itself."[22]

Why do I think electronic access to information isn't a substitute for content knowledge? Why do I think learning the reference process is not about mastering a body of electronic sources? Let me give you an example from my experience providing reference service for government documents within a general reference department. These functions have been combined in our division at least since Olin opened in the early 1960s, an unusual consolidation of services at that time. When I began working in Olin, a core level of knowledge in these materials was expected, even among the paraprofessionals. What was "core"? I can't tell you precisely, but I can tell you that everyone was expected to be able to tell the difference between a Congressional Report and a Public Law, and be able to retrieve these documents from the current paper collection we housed. Most everyone could also track the status of a current federal bill, thanks to the one print resource that provided this information, *Congressional Index*. And while, as I mentioned, I have been the resident "expert" on documents, I frankly didn't get many referrals, or only very thorny ones. Today, we not only have access to what everyone with a computer has—*Thomas*—we also subscribe to *Congressional Universe* and *Lexis-Nexis Academic Universe*.

Have these tools made it easier for patrons to be self sufficient? More important here, have they made my colleagues more knowledgeable about the legislative process? It might surprise you to hear that while these tools have helped *me* immensely—I can certainly answer the same kinds of questions much more quickly than I used to—they have not raised the level of core competency in these materials among my colleagues. I get more referrals now than I used to, for many less complicated documents questions. I believe there are two possible explanations for this: The first, that my colleagues believe the hype that because it's now available electronically, patrons don't need our assistance as much; the second, that my colleagues no longer take the time to refresh their knowledge of the *content* of these materials, regardless of their format.

It may also surprise you to hear that while it is easier for me to answer this type of question today, it is not easier for me to teach legislative research to patrons, as I do both in course-related instruction sessions and in specialized workshops. Why? The explanations may be similar to those about my colleagues. Patrons often presume that it's all much easier than it used to be, and are frustrated when it isn't as simple as pushing the right buttons. And for those who start with very little knowledge of the legislative process, explaining the relationship of one piece (say a Bill) to another (say a Public Law) is more difficult where both documents appear as nothing but text on a computer screen. Explaining the context, the hierarchy, the relationship of these distinct items is still necessary for truly helping the patron do his or her research. It is no less important in the electronic era, but it is seemingly more elusive.

So why are many of my colleagues no longer spending their time building their knowledge base in government documents, or for that matter in subject areas in the Social Sciences and Humanities? I would suggest that despite the glitz of electronic access not only to government documents but to other categories of materials, the provision of traditional reference service (and I hesitate to even use that phrase) in all subject areas, is seen as something we need to move away from. Instead of focusing on what I believe are our unique skills and services—those areas of expertise that we alone can provide in academic libraries—we have been seduced by the new electronic technologies into completely changing our vision. We hear more and more talk about distance learning, and it often sounds as though we are more concerned about making sure those distance learners have reference service than we are about those on our own campuses. Many of us spend more time creating web pages than we ever did typing or word processing. And now, at least in OKU Reference, we actually teach classes on HTML, Endnote, and are contemplating offering classes on Word—all of which could be offered by other units on campus (and sometimes are), outside the library.

All this seems to have led us a long way from our mission of helping patrons find the information they need, to simply processing results. It almost makes me want to agree with Terry Ann Mood, who suggests that reference librarians actually *do* the research for patrons, even students, rather than simply guiding them towards the right sources, always in an effort to teach the patron to be self-sufficient: "No more library instruction in the guise of reference help, no more explaining, no more wandering the library in tandem with a user."[23] While I confess this idea at first made me cringe, compared to the way we seem to be going, Mood's suggestion at least keeps us centered in our core mission of providing research assistance, and requires us to maintain that knowledge base I think is essential. Perhaps more important, it may serve our patrons better because, as she puts it: "The result: users who can spend their time reading, absorbing, and applying the information provided... ."[24]

Could it be, sadly, that librarians of the future (if not of the present) have lost their interest in the mysteries and wonders of the research process, be it "traditional" or "digital"? Two short quotes from two articles in the same 1997 issue of *Collection Management* are revealing in this connection. The first reads: "For the researcher, the curse of the Web is that it's spontaneous, uncontrolled and unorganized, one can slog from irrelevant link to irrelevant link finding nothing useful and wasting vast amounts of time."[25] The second reads: "Of course, librarians have been assisting users in finding information and answers to questions all along, but slogging through countless print sources, following leads, has little of the flash and dash of sitting at a computer terminal and bringing things up on a screen for the users to see."[26] The problem with both these attitudes, one towards print the other towards electronic, is that it reduces the research process to the very negative concept of "slogging." I would suggest that you take these words to heart—whichever format you more closely identify with—and ask whether you have lost our interest in what reference librarians claim to be all about.

Think for a moment about how you respond when a student asks, "do you have a database that does X?" Do you say "yes, here it is" or "no, I'm sorry, we don't." Or do you inquire into the student's true question of substance, the subject of her pursuit? Why do we take, without question, interlibrary loan requests from database searches for undergraduates—when we no doubt have sufficient resources in our libraries to serve their needs? Perhaps you scrutinize these requests more than we do at Cornell, but I confess it sometimes puzzles me why we do not, when we have one of the largest libraries in the country. Is it because we don't want to pry? Or have we really given in to the notion that it's easier to just take that request, attach that electronic printout, and send it off, than it is to pursue the underlying question? If the latter is true, we have given up our evaluative function in guiding students to the best sources available to them in the most efficient manner. For are we actually saving the student any time in this interaction? She will have to wait two weeks for the requested material to arrive, when more time on *our* part pursuing the deeper question—even just listening more closely to the question—might get the student something useful that very afternoon.

I believe, as one participant at the Finding Common Ground conference stated, that we need to re-find reference, not redefine it, to think more about "why" we do what we do rather than "how" we do it.[27] We need to re-commit to focusing on content, not on format, to process rather than mastery. We do need to be more proactive, but ". . . proactive does not necessarily mean standing up and talking instead of sitting down and listening."[28] We need to reject the clever but meaningless suggestions to change our names to "librinfotist"[29] or "access engineer."[30] We should "enhance the meaning of *librarian* and have it take on new meaning [rather] than abandon the term."[31]

I'm not suggesting that we tear down the Information Superhighway with its ever growing valuable stops, but rather that we stay our course on the Research Road and steer carefully into the future. I'm not suggesting we choose between print and digital. But just as the old conflict between reference and instruction once consumed the profession and the two now seem reconciled into one mission, so too this new alleged conflict between print and electronic must be reconciled. They must be blended and balanced as we move forward. For if one or the other alone "wins," we may all lose sight of our mission along the way.

Twenty years after becoming a librarian, I remain as excited and challenged by reference service as ever. Not by the new technologies, some of which surely enhance what I do and some of which I resist. But rather because I remain committed to my fundamental role of providing service to students and faculty, to being a part of what I believe we each sought when we chose to work in an academic library, "... to offer the opportunity for discovery, even at the cost of convenience; for depth, even in exchange for simplicity; for richness of perspective, even if it means the loss of precious seconds."[32] We need to use every format and means possible to achieve this end, this goal. We need to take off our answering hats, and keep asking ourselves the questions asked of us.

Bibliography
Baker, Betsy, Natalie Pelster, and William McHugh.

"Refinding Reference: Carrying the Reference Mission into the Libraries of the 21st Century." *Finding Common Ground: Creating the Library of the Future without Diminishing the Library of the Past*. Eds. Cheryl LaGuardia and Barbara A. Mitchell. New York: Neal Schuman, 1998: 99–110.

Berger, Christopher. "Reference Service: A Thing of the Past?" *The Reference Librarian* 54 (1996):115–23.

Berger, Kenneth, W. B. Ilene Nelson, and Johannah Sherrer. "Encountering the Twenty-First Century: Libraries, Reference Departments, Reference Librarians." *North Carolina Libraries* 50 (Special Edition 1992):15–19.

Berring, Robert C. "Future Librarians." *Future Libraries*. Eds. R. Howard Bloch and Carla Hesse. Berkeley: University of California Pr., 1993:94–115.

Berry, John N. III. "Risking Relevant Reference Work." *Library Journal* (May 15, 1998):6+. Online. Available: Proquest/Periodical Abstracts. 25 January 1999.

Bristow, Ann. "Traditions: Research and Reference Services." *Finding Common Ground: Creating the Library of the Future without Diminishing the Library of the Past*. Eds. Cheryl LaGuardia and Barbara A. Mitchell. New York: Neal Schuman, 1998:116–20.

Bryan, Jane G. "Where is the Reference Desk Now?" *Finding Common Ground: Creating the Library of the Future without Diminishing the Library of the Past*. Eds. Cheryl LaGuardia and Barbara A. Mitchell. New York: Neal Schuman, 1998: 124–26.

Burkhardt, Robert R. "A Role Transformed?: Technology's Challenge for Job Responsibilities of the Reference Librarian." *Advances in Library Administration and Organization* 14 (1996):125–90.

Campbell, Jerry D. "Choosing to Have a Future." *American Libraries* 24 (1993):560–66.

———. "Shaking the Conceptual Foundations of Reference." *Reference Services Review* 20 (1992):29–35.

Constantine, Paul J. "Reference Service in a Larger Research Library: Finding Common Ground in a Time of Change." *Finding Common Ground: Creating the Library of the Future without Diminishing the Library of the Past*. Eds. Cheryl LaGuardia and Barbara A. Mitchell. New York: Neal Schuman, 1998:121–23.

Dawson, Alma and Kathleen de la Pena McCook. "Trends Affecting the Roles of Reference Librarians." *The Reference Librarian* 54 (1996): 53–73.

DeVinney, Genna. "Rushing Toward the Emerald City?" *The Journal of Academic Librarianship* 20 (1994):91–92.

DeVries, JoAnn and Patricia M. Rodkewich. "Master Reference Librarians for a New Age: A Study of Characteristics and Traits." *The Reference Librarian* 59 (1997):203–14.

Dougherty, Richard M. "Editorial: On Becoming All We Can Be: A Last Word." *The Journal of Academic Librarianship*. 19 (1994):355.

Ensor, Pat. "How Do I Keep Up On Everything in the New Electronic Information World." *Technicalities* 16 (1996):7–8.

Evans, Anita K. "Electronic Reference Services: Mediation for the 1990s." *The Reference Librarian* 37 (1992):75–90.

Farber, Evan Ira. "Plus ca Change. . ." *Library Trends* 44 (1995): 430–38.

Faries, Cynthia. "Reference Librarians in the Information Age: Learning from the Past to Control the Future." *The Reference Librarian* 43 (1994): 9–28.

Fark, Ronald, Anne Cerstvik Nolan, and Tovah Reis. "Technology and the Network: Redesigning an Academic Library Reference Department." *Finding Common Ground: Creating the Library of the Future without Diminishing the Library of the Past*. Eds. Cheryl LaGuardia and Barbara A. Mitchell. New York: Neal Schuman, 1998: 47–57.

Feinberg, Renee. "B&N: The New College Library?" *Library Journal* (February 1, 1998): 49–51.

Ferguson, Chris. "Reshaping Academic Library Reference Service: A Review of Issues, Trends, and Possibilities." *Advances in Librarianship* 18 (1994): 73–109.

Ferguson, Chris and Charles A. Bunge. "The Shape of Services to Come: Values-Based Reference Service for the Largely Digital Library." *College and Research Libraries* 58 (1997):252–65.

Franks, Jeffrey A. "Forming a Reference Philosophy: The Role of Shared Values." *The Reference Librarian* 59 (1997):15–23.

Goding, David P. "Chapter One: The More Things Change, the More They Stay the Same: The Future of the Library and the Library Profession." *Collection Management* 22 (1997): 9–28.

Grealey, Deborah S. "Leveraging the Wave: The Role of Today's Academic Reference Librarian." *The Reference Librarian* 59 (1997): 93–102.

Green, Samuel Swett. "Personal Relations Between Librarians and Readers." *Library Journal* (October 1876): 74–81.

Hale, Martha L. "Getting Ready for Tomorrow—Or Today." *Reference Services Review* 19 (1991): 77–80.

Hansel, Patsy J. "Quantity is *Not* Necessarily Quality: A Challenge to Librarians to Develop Meaningful Standards of Performance for Library Reference Services." *North Carolina Libraries* 48 (1990): 184–87.

Heckart, Ronald J. "Machine Help and Human Help in the Emerging Digital Library." *College & Research Libraries* 59 (1998): 250–59.

Hinojosa, Susana. "Re-thinking Reference—A True Change?" *The Reference Librarian* 54 (1996): 95–102.

Hisle, W. Lee. "Roles for a Digital Age." *Creating the Future: Essays on Librarianship in an Age of Great Change.* Ed. Sally Gardner Reed. Jefferson, N.C.: McFarland & Company, 1996: 29–41.

Hopkins, Richard L. "Countering Information Overload: The Role of the Librarian." *The Reference Librarian* 49/50 (1995): 305–33.

Jackson-Brown, Grace. "The Academic Librarian's New Role as Information Provider." *The Reference Librarian* 39 (1993): 77–83.

Kathman, Michael D. "Response to Swan and Evans: 'Problems and Opportunities." *The Reference Librarian* 37 (1992): 87–90.

Kelly, Julia and Kathryn Robbins. "Changing Roles for Reference Librarians." *Journal of Library Administration* 22 (1996): 111–21.

Kemp, Barbara E. "Chapter Two: May You Live in Interesting Times: The Impact of Revolutions and Shifting Paradigms on Public Services Staff." *Collection Management* 22 (1997): 29–41.

Koyama, Janice T. "http://digiref.scenarios.issues." *Reference & User Services Quarterly* 38 (1998): 51–53.

Kresh, Diane and Linda Arret. "Do Birds Fly?: Some Thoughts after the Library of Congress Institute on 'Reference Service in a Digital Age.'" *Reference & User Services Quarterly* 38 (1998): 17–21.

Kupersmith, John. "Technostress and the Reference Librarian." *Reference Services Review* 20 (1992): 7–14+.

LaGuardia, Cheryl. "Online Links: Users' Needs, Librarians' Roles." *Library Journal* (November 15, 1998): S10–S11. Online. Available: Proquest/Periodical Abstracts. 25 January 1999.

Lester, Linda and Karen Kates Marshall. "Traditional Library Services and the Research Process: Are Social Sciences and Humanities Faculty Getting What They Need?" *Finding Common Ground: Creating the Library of the Future without Diminishing the Library of the Past.* Eds. Cheryl LaGuardia and Barbara A. Mitchell. New York: Neal Schuman, 1998: 211–18.

Lewis, David W. "Making Academic Reference Services Work." *College & Research Libraries* 55 (1994): 445–56.

———. "Traditional Reference is Dead, Now Let's Move on to Important Questions." *The Journal of Academic Librarianship* 21 (1995): 10–12.

Lipow, Anne Grodzins. "Reference Service in a Digital Age: Introduction." *Reference & User Services Quarterly* 38 (1998): 47–48.

———. "Thinking Out Loud: Who Will Give Reference Service in the Digital Environment?" *Reference & User Services Quarterly* 37 (1997): 125–29.

Lorenzen, Michael. "Management by Wandering Around: Reference Rovering and Quality Reference Service." *The Reference Librarian* 59 (1997): 51–57.

Mann, Thomas. "Reference Service, Human Nature, Copyright, and Offsite Service—in a 'Digital Age'?" *Reference & User Services Quarterly* 38 (1998): 55–61.

Mardikian, Jackie and Martin A. Kesselman. "Beyond the Desk: Enhanced Reference Staffing for the Electronic Library." *Reference Services Review* 23 (1995): 21–28+.

Martell, Charles. "Editorial: Sometime Soon: A New Renaissance." *The Journal of Academic Librarianship* 20 (1994): 129–30.

Massey-Burzio, Virginia. "Education and Experience: Or, the MLS is Not Enough." *Reference Services Review* 19 (1991): 72–74.

———. "Reference Encounters of a Different Kind: A Symposium." *The Journal of Academic Librarianship* 18 (1992): 276–86.

McConnell, J. Christopher. "Technology and Teaching in Academia." *The Reference Librarian* 39 (1993): 31–40.

Mood, Terry Ann. "Of Sundials and Digital Watches: A Further Step Toward the New Paradigm of Reference." *Reference Services Review* 22 (1994): 27–32+.

Moore, Audrey D. "Reference Librarianship: 'It Was the Best of Times, It Was ....'" *The Reference Librarian* 54 (1996): 3–10.

Nardi, Bonnie A. "Information Ecologies: Highlights of the Keynote Address." *Reference & User Services Quarterly* 38 (1998): 49–50.

Papandrea, Virginia A. "Managing Reference Services in the Electronic Age: A Competing Values Approach to Effectiveness." *The Reference Librarian* 60 (1998): 111–26.

Rettig, James. "Future Reference—'Sired By a Hurricane, Dam'd By an Earthquake.'" *The Reference Librarian* 54 (1996): 75–94.

Ritch, Alan. "Back to the Future: From Desk Set to Desklessness?" *Reference Services Review* 19 (1991): 74–76.

Rothstein, Samuel. "The Development of Reference Services through Academic Traditions, Public Library Practice, and Special Librarianship." *The Reference Librarian* 25/26 (1989/90): 161–72. [originally published 1961].

———. "The Development of the Concept of Reference Service in American Libraries, 1850–1900." *The Reference Librarian* 25/26 (1989/90): 7–31. [originally published 1953].

Sarkodie-Mensah, Kwasi. "The Human Side of Reference in an Era of Technology." *The Reference Librarian* 59 (1997): 131–38.

Sherer, Johannah. "Thriving in Changing Times: Competencies for Today's Reference Librarians." *The Reference Librarian* 54 (1996): 11–20.

Shreeves, Edward. "Embracing the Inevitable." *The Journal of Academic Librarianship* 20 (1994): 136–37.

Sloan, Bernie. "Electronic Reference Services: Some Suggested Guidelines." *Reference & User Services Quarterly* 38 (1998): 77–81.

Snow, Marina. "Forward with People." *The Journal of Academic Librarianship* 20 (1994): 142–43.

Solomon, Alan. "The Scholarly Bibliographic Record." *Finding Common Ground: Creating the Library of the Future without Diminishing the Library of the Past*. Eds. Cheryl LaGuardia and Barbara A. Mitchell. New York: Neal Schuman, 1998: 127–30.

Stanley, Deborah and Natasha Lyandres. "The Electronic Revolution and the Evolving Role of the Academic Reference Librarian." *North Carolina Libraries* 56 (1998): 100–04.

Strong, Gary E. "Toward a Virtual Future." *The Reference Librarian* 54 (1996): 153–61.

Summey, Terri Pedersen. "Techno Reference: Impact of Electronic Reference Resources on Traditional Reference Services." *The Reference Librarian* 59 (1997): 103–11.

Swan, John C. "Books and Screens, Readers and Reference: Bridging the Video Gap." *The Reference Librarian* 37 (1992): 65–74.

———. "The Electronic Straightjacket." *Creating the Future: Essays on Librarianship in an Age of Great Change*. Ed. Sally Gardner Reed. Jefferson, N.C.: McFarland & Company, 1996: 42–50.

———. "Rehumanizing Information: An Alternative Future." *Library Journal* (September 1, 1990): 178–82.

Tenopir, Carol and Lisa Ennis. "The Digital Reference World of Academic Libraries." *Online* 22 (1998): 22–28.

———. "The Impact of Digital Reference on Librarians and Library Users." *Online* 22 (1998): 84–88.

Tyckoson, David. "What We Do: Reaffirming the Founding Principles of Reference Services." *The Reference Librarian* 59 (1997): 3–11.

Whitlach, Jo Bell. "Enhancing the Quality of Reference Services for the 21st Century." *Reference & User Services Quarterly* 38 (1998): 15–16.

Wisner, William H. "Back Toward People: A Symposium." *The Journal of Academic Librarianship* 20 (1994): 131–33.

Notes

1. The Head of the Division, Paul J. Constantine, offers another view of the activities of the Reference Services Division in his, "Reference Service in a Large Research Library: Finding Common Ground in a Time of Change." *Finding Common Ground: Creating the Library of the Future without Diminishing the Library of the Past.* Eds. Cheryl LaGuardia and Barbara A. Mitchell. New York: Neal Schuman, 1998:121–23.

2. Rilke, Rainer Maria. "Letter No. 4." *Letters to a Young Poet.* Translated by M. D. Herter Norton. New York: W. W. Norton, 1934. 34.

3. Rothstein, Samuel. "The Development of the Concept of Reference Service in American Libraries, 1850–1900." *The Reference Librarian* 25/26 (1989/90): 9.

4. Green, Samuel Swett. "Personal Relations Between Librarians and Readers." *Library Journal.* (October 1876): 74–81.

5. Rothstein, op cit, 8.

6. Rothstein, Samuel. "The Development of Reference Services through Academic Traditions, Public Library Practice, and Special Librarianship." *The Reference Librarian* 25/26 (1989/90): 85.

7. Tyckoson, David. "What We Do: Reaffirming the Founding Principles of Reference Services." *The Reference Librarian* 59 (1997): 4. One of, if not the, first "textbooks" of reference did not appear until 1930: Wyer, James I. *Reference Work: A Textbook for Students of Library Work and Librarians.* Chicago: American Library Association, 1930.

8. Massey-Burzio, Virginia. "Reference Encounters of a Different Kind: A Symposium." *The Journal of Academic Librarianship.* 18 (1992): 276–86.

9. Campbell, Jerry D. "Shaking the Conceptual Foundations of Reference." *Reference Services Review* 20 (1992): 32.

10. Ibid., 31.

11. Feinberg, Renee. "B&N: The New College Library?" *Library Journal* (February 1, 1998): 50.

12. Mann, Thomas. "Reference Service, Human Nature, Copyright, and Offsite Service—in a 'Digital Age'?" *Reference & User Services Quarterly* 38 (1998): 59.

13. Hansel, Patsy J. "Quantity is *Not* Necessarily Quality: A Challenge to Librarians to Develop Meaningful Standards of Performance for Library Reference Services." *North Carolina Libraries* 48 (1990): 184. For a related discussion of the importance of a philosophy of service see also: Franks, Jeffrey A. "Forming a Reference Philosophy: The Role of Shared Values." *The Reference Librarian* 59 (1997): 15–23.

14. Lorenzen, Michael. "Management by Wandering Around: Reference Rovering and Quality Reference Service." *The Reference Librarian* 59 (1997): 51–57.

15. Taken from a handout distributed at the Institute. I did not attend, but obtained a copy from a colleague who did. For additional information on the Institute, see generally *Reference & User Services Quarterly* 38 (1998). Articles of particular relevance are included individually in the bibliography.

16. See issue no. 54 generally; articles of particular relevance are included individually in the bibliography.

17. DeVries, JoAnn and Patricia M. Rodkewich. "Master Reference Librarians for a New Age: A Study of Characteristics and Traits." *The Reference Librarian* 59 (1997): 203–14.

18. Goding, David P. "Chapter One: The More Things Change, the More They Stay the Same: The Future of the Library and the Library Profession." *Collection Management.* 22 (1997): 12.

19. Swan, John C. "Rehumanizing Information: An Alternative Future." *Library Journal* (September 1, 1990): 179–80.

20. See, for example, Kupersmith, John J. "Technostress and the Reference Librarian." *Reference Services Review* 20 (1992): 7–14+.

21. Swan, op. cit., 181.

22. LaGuardia, Cheryl. "Online Links: Users' Needs, Librarians' Roles." Library Journal. (November 15, 1998): S10–S11. Online. Available: Proquest/Periodical Abstracts. 25 January 1999.

23. Mood, Terry Ann. "Of Sundials and Digital Watches: A Further Step Toward the New Paradigm of Reference." *Reference Services Review* 22 (1994): 28.

24. Ibid.

25. Goding, op cit., 19.

26. Kemp, Barbara E. "Chapter Two: May You Live in Interesting Times: The Impact of Revolutions and Shifting Paradigms on Public Services Staff." *Collection Management* 22 (1997): 36.

27. Baker, Betsy, Natalie Pelster, and William McHugh. "Refinding Reference: Carrying the Reference Mission into the Libraries of the 21st Century." *Finding Common Ground: Creating the Library of the Future without Diminishing the Library of the Past*. Eds. Cheryl LaGuardia and Barbara A. Mitchell. New York: Neal Schuman, 1998: 99–110.

28. Ibid., 106.

29. Foster, Constance L. "On My Mind: Ask Your Librinfotist?!" *The Journal Of Academic Librarianship* 16 (1991): 362–63.

30. Campbell, op. cit.

31. Lewis, David W. "Making Academic Reference Services Work." *College & Research Libraries* 55 (1994): 447.

32. Swan, op. cit., 182.

Designing for WOW!: The Optimal Information Gateway

Zsuzsa Koltay and Karen Calhoun

Abstract

Increasing reliance on electronic systems for access to resources and services is a fact of life in today's libraries. Users have grown to expect reliable, powerful and intuitive systems that "do it all." The Web has raised library users' expectations for simplicity of use. At the same time the emphasis on customer service in academia has produced an atmosphere in which it is essential to adapt quickly to the changing needs of faculty and students. In this fast-paced, technology and customer-driven environment, the library as a slow-moving, stable institution is a thing of the past. To continue to succeed, academic libraries must transform themselves into high-performance organizations committed to delighting their users. This can only be accomplished if we have an accurate understanding of what the users need and want. This paper presents the results of a focus group study that was conducted to find out just that.

Introduction

The title for this paper comes from business visionary Tom Peters' *The Pursuit of WOW!: Every Person's Guide to Topsy-Turvy Times*.[1] Peters wrote the book—a collection of sometimes-brash stories, interviews and observations—to help individuals and organizations stay on top of the chaos of the nineties. Peters urges us not to be timid in fending off staleness, and he claims that "stepping out" (individually) and "standing out" (organizationally) from the crowd is and will be crucial for surviving and thriving in a world of uncertainty and upheaval.

Zsuzsa Koltay is public services librarian, and Karen Calhoun is head, Original Cataloging, Cornell University.

Designing for WOW!: The Optimal Information Gateway

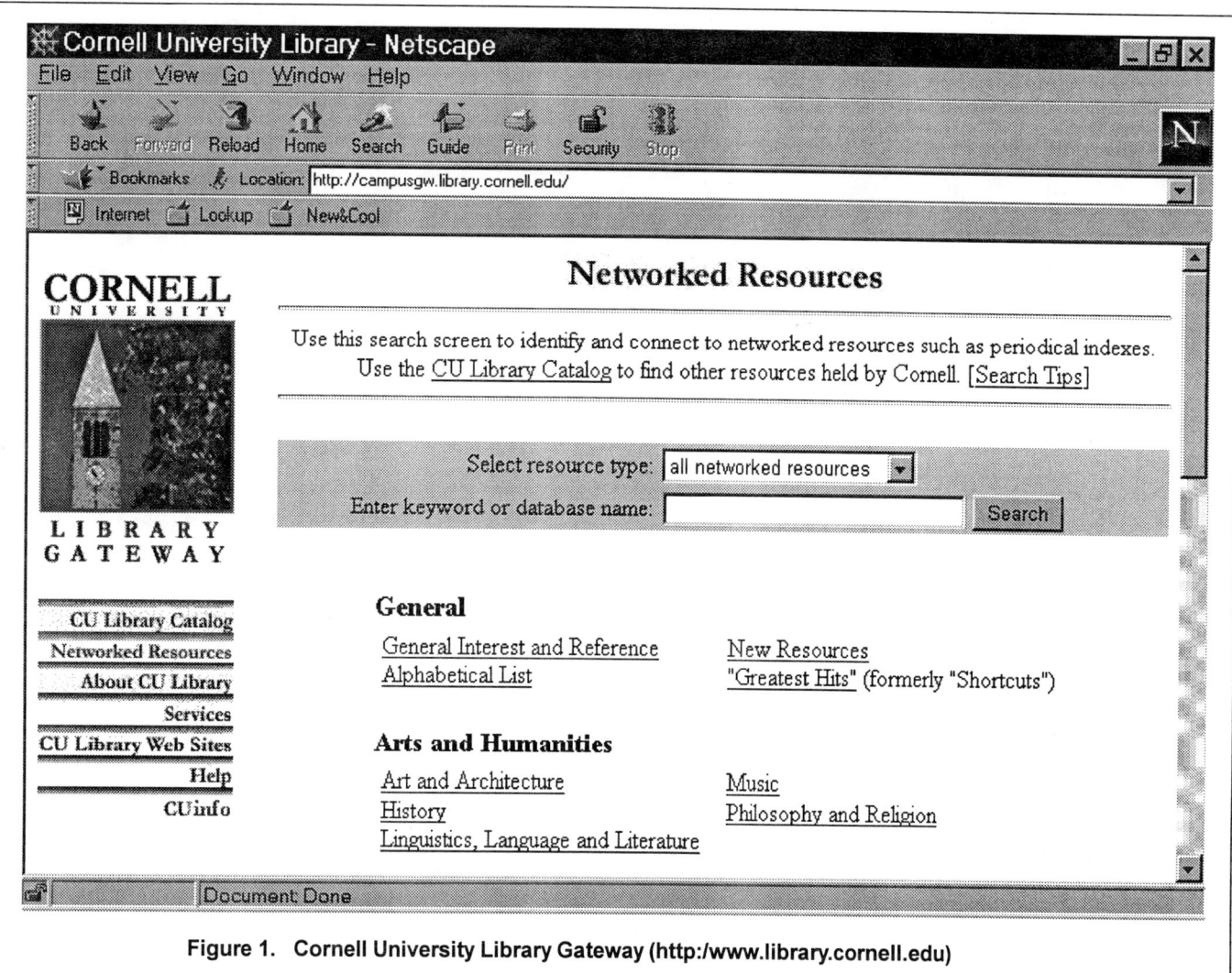

Figure 1. Cornell University Library Gateway (http:/www.library.cornell.edu)

For academic libraries, pursuing WOW! increasingly means producing easy-to-use yet powerful systems for information discovery and delivery. Such systems cannot be developed based on what we *think* users want. They can only be developed by people and organizations that can gauge and respond creatively and rapidly to shifting user needs.

To gauge user needs and reactions to the systems we develop, librarians need reliable tools and research methods. This paper reports the results of one attempt to uncover user needs and expectations for an information system, the Cornell University Library Gateway, using the focus group methodology.

What's the Gateway and Why Study It?

The Gateway is Cornell University's library on the Web (Figure 1). It is the common entryway to the networked resources, services and information that Cornell University Library (CUL) provides for its users. The system's introduction on January 5, 1998 brought to an end years of confusion for CUL users. Before the launch of the Gateway different unit libraries provided different ways to connect to different subsets of these offerings.

The Gateway uses a searchable (MySQL) database to provide access and connections to over 1200 networked resources. The resources are all cataloged in CUL's OPAC and the MARC cataloging records get transferred into and augmented in the separate Gateway database. The system can be browsed by subject caption or searched by keyword (including resource title, LC subject headings and short descriptions) to help users identify the networked resources that will be helpful for them.

The Gateway was built in just seventeen weeks. Because of the tight implementation schedule, no user studies were conducted to guide the system design process. User studies had been conducted by Mann Library[2] about the Gateway's predecessor, the Mann Library Gateway, but extrapolating the results from the disciplines that Mann serves to all disciplines across campus seemed problematic.[3] So the Gateway was essentially based on the librarians' understanding of user needs and behaviors. We wanted to conduct a study that would give us a user-centered report card for the Gateway as well as a roadmap for future development.

Other Gateways
The literature has little to offer that is directly applicable to the present study. Therefore, to place our research into the context of what is happening at other institutions, we evaluated the library Web sites of the nine largest U.S. ARL university libraries and three additional peer libraries (Penn, Dartmouth and Brown). As a follow up, we queried the libraries about user studies they have conducted or plan to conduct of Web-based access to their collections.

Our evaluation of library Web sites suggests that the sample libraries, just like CUL, have striven to:
- Use their Web presence to pull together the catalog, networked resources, services, and library information into a single interface;
- Make networked resources highly visible;
- Raise awareness (i.e., "market" the library) and educate; publicize "what's new" and digital library projects;
- Provide access to both telnet and Web versions of the catalog;
- Integrate e-resources into the catalog (in varying degrees);
- Allow e-resources to be browsed and searched separately from the catalog;
- Provide separate lists of e-journals (searchable if possible);
- Point to individual library Web sites;
- Provide online forms, help and instruction
- Encourage online communication with librarians (most);
- Link to consortia resources (some);
- Provide subject guides to online resources (a few);
- Provide standard interface to databases (some).

Most sites treat "databases and reference tools" differently than they treat "Internet resources" despite the artificiality of this distinction. Most sites maintain an elaborate system of static Web pages to present their electronic resources separate from the library catalog. Only a few libraries use a searchable database of electronic resources, as CUL does. It has proved difficult to gather information about user studies that may have been conducted or planned at these twelve institutions. To date we have received only four responses, all negative.

Methodology
We had four objectives in mind when designing and carrying out the study:
- Assessing how the Library Gateway is being used;
- Ascertaining Gateway users' satisfaction levels, likes and dislikes;
- Determining enhancements for the current Gateway;
- Identifying future, long term improvements.

To achieve our objectives, we decided to use focus groups to gather the information we needed. We, the authors, played instrumental roles in the development of the Gateway. Familiar with the Gateway's features and limitations, we knew what needed to be examined from a library user's point of view, but we lacked the expertise to conduct a methodologically sound, impartial user study. To assist us in planning, designing, and carrying out the study, we engaged the owner of Marketing Backup, a research consulting firm specializing in library-related projects and user studies.

Focus groups are a purposive sampling method—that is, participants are deliberately selected based on a set of criteria. They are not randomly or blindly chosen, as is often the case with other user research methodologies, such as transaction log analyses, intercept interviews, questionnaires or phone surveys. A tool for collecting in-depth, thoughtful feedback, focus groups represent a qualitative rather than a quantitative methodology. Focus group interviewing is well suited to the study of needs, perceptions, satisfaction, and user expectations, as it overcomes the limitations of pre-determined, closed-ended questions. While the results are not statistically representative (that is, they may or may not reflect the attitudes of all users), they provide useful information for planning and evaluation.

The focus group method involves choosing groups of eight to twelve participants. Selection is based on similarity of background (e.g., undergraduates who are Gateway users), but possible dissimilarity of attitudes (e.g., use different CUL libraries; come from different disciplines).[4] Our study targeted current users' perceptions of the Library Gateway. We did not study non-users of the Gateway, because their inclusion would have required a different research design. Once the focus group convenes, a trained facilitator, who remains neutral throughout the session, provides a framework (called an "interview guide") for the discussion and serves as the catalyst to solicit feedback from all and to encourage candor.

For our study, we had the consultant lead six focus groups for us—two each of faculty/graduate students, two each of undergraduate students, and two each of library staff members. We worked closely with the consultant on the design of the interview guide; canvassed for, screened and selected the participants; and made the local arrangements for the focus group sessions. Each session had a note taker and was audio- and videotaped.

We are glad we had the opportunity to engage an outside consultant to run the focus groups. Her training, expertise and impartiality were important in getting good results and having these results trusted. She also saved us a lot of time that we would have had to spend on preparing to run the groups and doing the initial analysis of the data. However, we did find that we had grossly underestimated the amount of time and effort that we had to invest into the project ourselves. The local arrangements took a long time and a lot of attention to detail, especially the recruitment of focus group participants. We also found that having some knowledge of CUL and its library system was essential in interpreting the results. Consequently the consultant's report was only a first cut at the data analysis. To complete the final report to the library, we needed to go back to the session notes to rework and supplement her analysis. For example, it took some further analysis to be able to separate the "report card" and "roadmap" functions of the project.

Summary of Selected Findings
Awareness
Too many of our focus group participants "just stumbled across" the Gateway and learned to use it by trial and error. The primary use is access to networked resources; use of other Gateway features is less frequent, and awareness of them is low. Many felt a need for instruction but the level of awareness of the different kinds of library instruction available was disappointing. We need to be proactive about building awareness and educating users about our information services and systems. Another word for this set of activities is "marketing." Whatever we call it, users want us to get their attention, connect with them, keep them informed, and reach out to them.

Hierarchy of use, hierarchy of needs
Undergraduates use the Gateway when they do papers; their use is intermittent, and usually their need is for quick information. Most come to a campus library to use the system. In contrast, faculty and graduate students use the Gateway more frequently and steadily, and they prefer access from their offices. Some go to the library so they have the help of a librarian. Their information needs are highly focused, and they typically use a handful of databases associated with their specialties, but they also want to be kept up to the minute on what's new in their areas. This set of findings suggests that we should be designing for various levels of information system use and need.

The trouble with Help
Focus group participants admitted they not only rarely use Help, they laughed about how no one

ever uses help pages and manuals. At the same time they reported initial confusion about what the Gateway is and how it works, and they suggested developing context sensitive Help, search tips, online tutorials, and online interactive user support. Most of all, though, they stated a preference for human (including e-mail) over system help. This set of findings suggest that we need to maintain personal connections (either physical or virtual) to users of our systems. This appears to be as critical to excellent service as the technology and design of the system.

Full text and more full text
With respect to the networked resources available on the Gateway, focus group participants said they want more resources, more full text, and more electronic journals. Asked what they liked *most* about the Gateway, faculty and graduate student participants chose full text.

Finding the (right) resource
Many participants found the process of selecting an online resource from the thousand plus available through the Gateway confusing and unpleasant. Comments from our focus groups suggest that systems should permit both searching and browsing of networked resources (e.g., by subject). Asked what they liked *least* about the Gateway, participants picked confusing searching, having to know multiple query languages, databases with more than one interface to choose from, and lack of immediate access to library holdings information from citation databases.

An embarrassment of riches
Even though they appreciate the variety and increasing number of resources available to them, and they want more, our focus group participants made it clear that the Gateway is already somewhat overwhelming to them. This finding suggests that we must keep working to find a design that can make a full (even cluttered) information space easy and intuitive to use.

Conclusions
The following issues emerged as overarching themes throughout the six focus group sessions.

Complexity of the information scene
The most often heard complaints were the sense of confusion that the novice user faces when using the Gateway, the complexity of the system, and the fact that keyword searching is "useless." These complaints are related to each other and they all stem from the complexity of the information scene that the Gateway presents. Changing cataloging practices and redesigning the interface could provide a slightly better or slightly worse result, but they won't fundamentally address the core of the problem.

In the print academic library most users expected and accepted complexity as a fact of life. Indexes, catalogs, reference books, encyclopedias, dictionaries, journals, monographs, magazines, manuscripts, etc. were somewhat daunting for the average user but since they had to come to the library anyway, they could ask for help at the reference desk and they had no expectation of simplicity. The librarian helped them acquire the basic research skills they had to have to translate their information needs into the language of the library, the first and most important step towards getting the answer.

Today the information scene is even more complex. By adding enough full text and bibliographic databases, numeric, visual and geospatial data to the mix to create a digital library, we have not eliminated the need to translate between the users' information need and the available resources. The only thing that has changed is the users' expectation that all this should be easy and their perception that they are alone in this process with no easy help available. In the era of remote access, the World Wide Web, and search boxes, needing library research skills is a hard concept to sell.

Any system that requires searching a metadata catalog of such diverse items as the full text of the Oath of Hippocrates, Science Citation Index, LEXIS/NEXIS, the CRL Catalog, and the Americans and Food Quiz will cause some confusion for the novice user who is interested in something as specific as the link between anorexia in adolescent women and gender stereotypes in mass media. When they encounter the search box on the Gateway Networked Resources page, oftentimes they type in their specific keywords not understanding the granularity of the catalog, not knowing that their best bet might be a general or multidisciplinary index that they can only get to if they type something as broad as social sciences. Tweaking keywords in the records and changing the interface will not address the underlying problem that we have no intelligent agent to find the best databases for the user and no way to search multiple databases and present the different level results in a meaningful way. At this point we need the user to have the necessary skills to navigate by themselves, or ask for our help. This problem will no doubt be a major challenge for any future Gateway as well.

Overall satisfaction with the Gateway and the library

Overall, everyone in the focus groups seemed to be happy with library collections, services, staff, and online resources. Even when they were critical about something, users kept reminding themselves how lucky they were to be served by such a great library. The criticism and suggestions we heard came from users who are generally satisfied or very satisfied with the Gateway and their library. This comes in contrast with the widely shared perception in the library staff groups that users are very confused, that they need lots of help and that they don't always get the help they need.

Personalized and subject-specific services

Because of the complexity and size of the system, users welcome any shortcuts we offer. "Greatest Hits" is a short list of the most widely used databases on campus with connection links just one click away from the top page. Users like "Greatest Hits" and are eager for a way to create their own "Greatest Hits." They would also like to be notified of new resources that are of interest to them. In other words they would like to be able to bypass the Gateway but without missing out on new developments. This is mostly of interest to faculty and graduate students whose research interests are already quite focused and constant. They are also interested in getting suggestions for the best resources for a specific subject or discipline now that the Gateway subject captions bring up too many resources to comfortably scan.

Recommendations and Lessons

The study produced a long list of recommended actions. The following is a short, somewhat generalized summary of these specific items.

Continue to do the good that we're doing, such as providing more resources, especially full text and e-journals; allowing for both searching and browsing the collection; providing both Web and telnet access to databases; and making networked resources highly visible as a separate category.

Improve what's not perfect, such as keyword searching; the display of search results; the degree of integration with the OPAC (especially holdings information); and expand the ways of "slicing and dicing" the collection such as allowing an easy way to search for e-journals.

Explore new ways of doing things, such as simplifying the task of navigating a complex information scene; providing personalized and current awareness services; adding features like "what's new," "hot topics," and subject guides; adding services like multimedia tutorials, document delivery and chat reference; involving users in systems design; and providing a common search engine and simultaneous searching of databases.

Aside from producing a list of recommended actions, our study also reinforced some general design lessons. First and foremost it served as a great reminder to always involve users in the design process, and the earlier the better. Yes, it takes time, yes, it slows down the pace, but the results will be better. Besides improving the final product it also sends a strong message to the users that the library clearly sees serving them well as its first priority.

One thing users will tell you time and time again is to always provide multiple ways of accomplishing the same task. In our case, for example, it became clear that providing the "institutional" entryway to the resources via browsing and searching is not enough. Users have a real need for a more personal way to approach the information scene, a way that is built on their specific interests and use patterns. Redundant? Yes, but it is worth it for the added comfort and convenience for the users.

Naturally, all system producers strive to build a product that is so user friendly that it practically "drives itself." Unfortunately, the result always falls somewhat short of this goal. Consequently, users often need help, but their reluctance to use manuals and help pages is legendary. The solution seems to be twofold. Making help indistinguishable from the system via good design, intelligent responses and error messages eliminates the need to click on that uninviting "Help" button. Also, building in some "real human" help such as chat or e-mail accommodates most users' desire to just ask someone.

Academic Libraries As System Producers

To operate in today's uncertain and competitive world, librarians are increasingly called to question their assumptions about what libraries are, what they do, who they serve, and what those users need. We are not sure what academic libraries are coming to be, but it is clear that they are in transition. Our highly standardized catalogs that provide access to collections housed in buildings are being transformed into scholarly information networks with a growing number of novel capabilities, and today's library gateways are only the beginning.

We believe the university library is becoming a producer of systems for gathering widely distributed resources and expertise into a unified whole. Such systems will support the creation, storage and transmission of scholarly information in at least two ways. One way is through attentiveness to library users (both in the immediate sense of eye contact and the more abstract sense of heeding what they say and do, then acting on it). Another is through information system design, production, support and enhancement.

So where does WOW! come from? It comes from the deployment of technology—the building of systems—to lead library users through the maze of available resources and to facilitate scholarly communication. At the same time, the system alone is not enough, and the power of personal connections should not be underestimated. Our research suggests that for an academic library information system today, connecting with users and system design are two sides of the same coin, contributing equally to a user's perception of the system.

Acknowledgments

The authors thank the Cornell University Library administration for their support in the form of a grant to fund the Gateway user study. We also gratefully acknowledge the significant assistance of Diane Cellentani and Marketing Backup.

Notes

1. Peters, Tom. *The Pursuit of WOW!: Every Person's Guide to Topsy-Turvy Times*. New York: Vintage Books, 1994.

2. Albert R. Mann Library is one of Cornell's 19 unit libraries. It serves the College of Agriculture and Life Sciences, the College of Human Ecology, the Division of Biological Sciences and the Division of Nutritional Sciences.

3. Several studies of the Mann Library Gateway have been published. The most recent is Payette, Sandra D. and Oya Y. Rieger, "Supporting scholarly inquiry: incorporating users in the design of the digital library." *Journal of Academic Librarianship* (March 1998): 121–29.

4. The information presented in this section is based on several useful sources: Rao, Vithala R. "Identifying unmet needs." In *Analysis for Strategic Marketing* (Cornell University Press, date), 83–86; Paley, Norton. "Getting in focus." *Sales & marketing management* (March 1995): 92–95; and Connaway, Lyunn Silipigni, Debra Wilcox Johnson and Susan E. Searing. "Online catalogs from the users' perspective: the use of focus group interviews." *College & Research Libraries* (September 1997): 403–20.

Library Program Assessment

Thomas G. Kirk Jr.

Assessment of academic library programs has taken on a new dimension with the concept of outcomes assessment, which has been promoted by the regional accrediting agencies. The field of library assessment has evolved from looking strictly at resource inputs (e.g., budgets, staffing levels) to an examination of organizational processes (i.e., efficiency), levels and quality of service outputs (e.g., number of circulations, reference questions) and library impact on institutional goals (e.g., student achievement, user satisfaction). Today, there is a plethora of approaches to library assessment with considerable controversy about just what outcomes assessment means, how it relates to older forms of assessment and how such assessment might be carried out. The question of what is appropriate outcomes assessment for academic library programs remains largely unanswered. This general discussion of theory and recent development in the field of assessment serve as background for a discussion of some of the practical issues associated with the utility of assessment results in improving library programs. Assessment is often viewed as an "add on" research effort or special project rather than as something integral to the operation of the library and management of its programs. This leads to a dysfunctional assessment program because it does not meet the ultimate goal of improving library services. The paper concludes with a brief description of one institution's efforts to develop an assessment program using a number of approaches to outcomes assessment. The successes, challenges and unfinished agenda of this effort are reviewed as examples of the issues surrounding outcomes assessment.

Introduction

Assessment of academic library programs has taken on a new dimension with the concept of outcomes assessment. The field of library assessment has evolved from looking strictly at resource inputs (e.g., budgets, staffing levels) to an examination

---

Thomas G. Kirk Jr. is college librarian, Earlham College.

of organizational processes (i.e., efficiency), levels and quality of service outputs (e.g., number of circulations, reference questions) and library impact on institutional goals (e.g., student achievement, user satisfaction). Today, there is a plethora of approaches to library assessment with considerable controversy about just what outcomes assessment means, how it relates to older forms of assessment and how such assessment might be carried out.

In addressing these issues, this paper has two purposes. One is to provide an overview of the concept of academic library assessment in the context of our current understanding of organizational effectiveness. As a special aspect of academic library assessment, the paper defines and places outcomes assessment within the larger enterprise. The paper's second purpose is to describe the assessment program of an individual college library with special attention to how the program helps to guide the organization, and the limits of outcomes assessment.

This review of our understanding of academic library assessment is based on what I believe are three essential documents. The three publications include:

1) The thorough and insightful review of the literature on academic library assessment written by Sarah Pritchard, formerly Library Director at Smith College and now director of the University of California-Santa Barbara, which appeared in *Library Trends* in 1996.

2) Kim Cameron's "Measuring Organizational Effectiveness in Institutions of Higher Education," which appeared in *Administrative Science Quarterly* in December 1978. Despite its age it is still the source for much original thinking about assessment in higher education generally and could be very useful in academic library assessment specifically.

3) The report of the ACRL Task Force on Academic Library Outcomes Assessment that appeared in June 1997.

Following my discussion of these three publications, I want to suggest a model for academic library assessment which I have called ALAM, Academic Library Assessment Model. Then I will explore how this model creates a context for academic library assessment activities. Finally, I will illustrate aspects of the model by describing Earlham's assessment program with special attention to two specific activities we have undertaken in the past couple of years.

Cameron's Organizational Effectiveness

Kim Cameron's "Measuring Organizational Effectiveness in Institutions of Higher Education," is a seminal work on assessment in higher education. It has had a major impact on the direction of assessment in higher education in the twenty years since its publication.

Cameron's work has had high visibility in the field of contingency theory as applied to organizational effectiveness and assessment of higher education. In addition to the 1978 article, Cameron has written a number of important articles on the subject that together, according to the *Social Sciences Citation Index* on DIALOG, were cited 639 times between 1978 and January 2, 1999.

Because the library and information science literature is not covered in much depth by SSCI, I cannot accurately reflect the importance of Cameron's work in the field of library assessment using the same process. However, a sample checking of the items in Sarah Pritchard's bibliography suggests that this important work is not widely cited in the library and information science literature. Therefore I feel it is appropriate to review his major ideas here.

First, it is important to recognize that Cameron's work is very consistent with the development of ideas about assessment of other types of organizations and Cameron acknowledges and takes into account the difference between institutions of higher education and other types of organizations such as for-profit businesses.

Cameron's 1978 piece is a review of literature which reports efforts to measure organizational effectiveness in higher education. We are most interested in the excellent summary and analysis of the concept of organizational effectiveness and the then new framework Cameron brings to the discussion. He identifies two sets of issues that he believes are critical to defining organizational effectiveness: types of assessment criteria and sources or originators of the criteria. Cameron's overriding point is that the criteria used to measure effectiveness is the central issue.

In describing types of criteria, Cameron enumerates four characteristic domains: (1) aspects of the organization, (2) the universality/specificity of the criteria, (3) whether the criteria are normative or descriptive, and (4) the static/dynamic dimension of the criteria. Let me explain what Cameron means by each of these types of criteria. Cameron's aspects of the organization refers to such elements as organizational goals and their achievement, the organization's resource acquisition or inputs, the internal processes of the organization, or its outputs. The universality/specificity continuum recognizes that criteria of assessment may be universal to all organizations of the same type or even multiple types or they may be highly focused on specific dimensions of an individual organization. The normative/descriptive characteristics of criteria are based on whether the criteria used have been identified as typical or common to organizations of the same type or are generated from the assessment of one particular organization. An example will make the idea clearer. Library circulation is a widely accepted measure of library activity and therefore the level of circulation is regularly included in an assessment of library activities. This is a normative characteristic. In contrast, a particular library, while studying circulation levels, might note a shift in the level of circulation when the institution changed from ten-week terms to fourteen-week semesters. This data is descriptive of the library and there is no basis for a comparison with other libraries. Cameron's fourth characteristic of criteria is whether the criteria are static or dynamic. In all assessment, there is an element of the static since the data must be collected at a particular point in time. However, data collected over time demonstrate change in the organization and therefore the criteria are dynamic.

Cameron's second set of concerns are the sources or origins of the assessment criteria. The first, and perhaps most obvious, is the constituency who sets the criteria. Constituencies include all the groups that interact with the organization either directly or indirectly. Each constituency will have a set of criteria they believe is the appropriate yardstick for measuring effectiveness. For example, students, faculty, administration and alumni are the four primary constituencies of an academic library and each of the four groups may have different ideas about the nature of an effective academic library. The second criteria source issue is the level of analysis. The organizational analysis can be at the super system level (e.g., all of higher education), the system level (e.g., the individual institution), or the subsystem level (e.g., the libraries of an academic institution). If the academic library is the level of analysis, then the super system level might be libraries of the ARL or the libraries of the private colleges of Indiana. The system is the individual library, and the subsystems would be, for example, cataloging, reference or acquisition units within a particular library. Third, Cameron points to the nature of the data collection as another source of assessment criteria. The data may come from internal records of the organization or can come from the perceptions of observers of the organization. This dichotomy, unfortunately, has often been mislabeled as objective vs. subjective measurement.

Cameron concludes his analysis by looking at a set of twenty research studies on organizational effectiveness in light of the nature and sources of the criteria. The grid he developed clearly shows that the field of organizational effectiveness suffers from the lack of comparable data. A problem that continues today—some twenty years after Cameron wrote his analysis.

In summary, Cameron provides us with the concepts of organizations as systems, and defines effectiveness contingently to depend on the types and sources of the criteria used to measure effectiveness.

Pritchard's "Determining Quality in Academic Libraries"

Sarah M. Pritchard's review article in *Library Trends*, "Determining Quality in Academic Libraries," surveys the literature on academic library assessment which reflects Cameron's analysis of types and sources of criteria. I want to highlight several key points that elaborate on Cameron's work.

In describing the historical context for determining quality, Pritchard points out how the terms quality and effectiveness, and evaluation and assessment are two pairs of equivalent terms. The first pair, quality and effectiveness, represent the performance of the organization, while the second pair, evaluation and assessment, refer to the process of determining performance. Over time, these and other terms have been used, often confusingly, to describe Cameron's two aspects, the criteria of evaluation and the process of evaluation. These two aspects should remain distinguishable regardless of the terminology used.

Pritchard goes on to point out that despite the heavy reliance on certain kinds of measures to compare academic libraries, the criteria have not been well defined and consistently applied and therefore comparisons are problematic.

In a further discussion of the challenges that academic library assessment faces, Pritchard comments that:

> Academic librarians do not have concrete ways to assess what the library contributes to the delivery of effective educational and research services by the campus itself.

This issue is especially critical because the regional accrediting agencies in their recent efforts to strengthen the accountability of institutions, have formulated accrediting processes that call on each part of the institution to demonstrate how it contributes to the overall goals of the institution. Pritchard rightly points out that while we may know what we would like the contribution to be, i.e., we have goals, there are as yet no good assessment processes that concretely demonstrate the relationship between library activities and the achievement of the institutions goals.

A third key point that Pritchard makes in her critique of the state of academic library assessment is the lack of linkage between assessment and planning. Assessment is often done not to satisfy the library's need for information on which to base planning and program development, but rather to meet the demands of outside constituencies such as accrediting agencies, commissions of higher education or state legislatures.

Pritchard has identified three critical issues: the shortage of agreed upon definitions of criteria that can be used to do comparative measurements among academic libraries, the inability to demonstrate how library programs concretely influence achievement of the parent institution's goals, and the lack of linkage between assessment and planning.

ACRL Task Force on Academic Library Outcomes Assessment

These two articles by Cameron and Pritchard were important sources of ideas for the ACRL Task Force on Academic Library Outcomes Assessment which was appointed in June 1996 and issued its final report in June 1998. The Task Force was charged to:

1) Develop a philosophical framework for assessing libraries in terms of desired campus outcomes;

2) Develop prototypes for such assessment; and

3) Develop a recommendation for one or more processes for implementation of the former (#2) with a time frame for completion.

The Task Force was not asked to propose a new form for library standards, but rather to address the confusion that appeared to exist within the profession over the nature of assessment and how standards might relate to assessment.

In its work, and in the final report, the Task Force carefully distinguished between terms such as inputs, processes, outputs and outcomes. Inputs refers to the resources (financial, staffing, etc.) which the academic library uses in carrying out its work. Processes are the operations within the organization (e.g., technical services operations, staffing the reference desk) that result in outputs—circulations, reference questions, books cataloged, instruction sessions held, archival manuscripts processed. But none of these are outcomes. The Task Force defines outcomes as "the ways in which library users are changed as a result of their contact with the library's resources and programs."

It seems to me that it is also important to distinguish the different kinds of outcome, a distinction the Task Force did not make. Outcomes could be as basic as changes in attitude toward libraries, and information gathering activities. Outcomes could also be a body of knowledge about libraries and the research process, and the topic being researched. Finally, outcomes could be changes in behavior. In all three cases, Cameron's characteristics and sources of criteria create a wide variety of possible outcomes assessment. If you review the library assessment literature, you see only a few examples of this variety of possibilities.

The Task Force goes on in its report to suggest ways in which such outcomes assessment might be carried out. In this suggested methodology, an outcome is selected, "indicators" of that outcome are defined, and a data collection method is developed. For example, an outcome might be "students can develop a quality bibliography on a topic they wish to study." The indicators of that outcome might be defined in terms of the criteria of quality—up-to-dateness, inclusion of a variety of types of sources, etc. The third step is the development of a methodology for collecting data such as gathering research papers in senior seminars and subjecting them to analysis based on the indicators.

Academic Library Assessment Model (ALAM)

Based on the work of the Task Force, the ground breaking research of Cameron and the helpful synthesis of the history of library assessment I have developed what I will call the Academic Library Assessment Model (ALAM) (see figure 1).

The author acknowledges the helpful critique of this paper by Sara Penhale and Nancy Taylor of the Earlham Library staff. Correspondence with the author is possible at kirkto@earlham.edu.

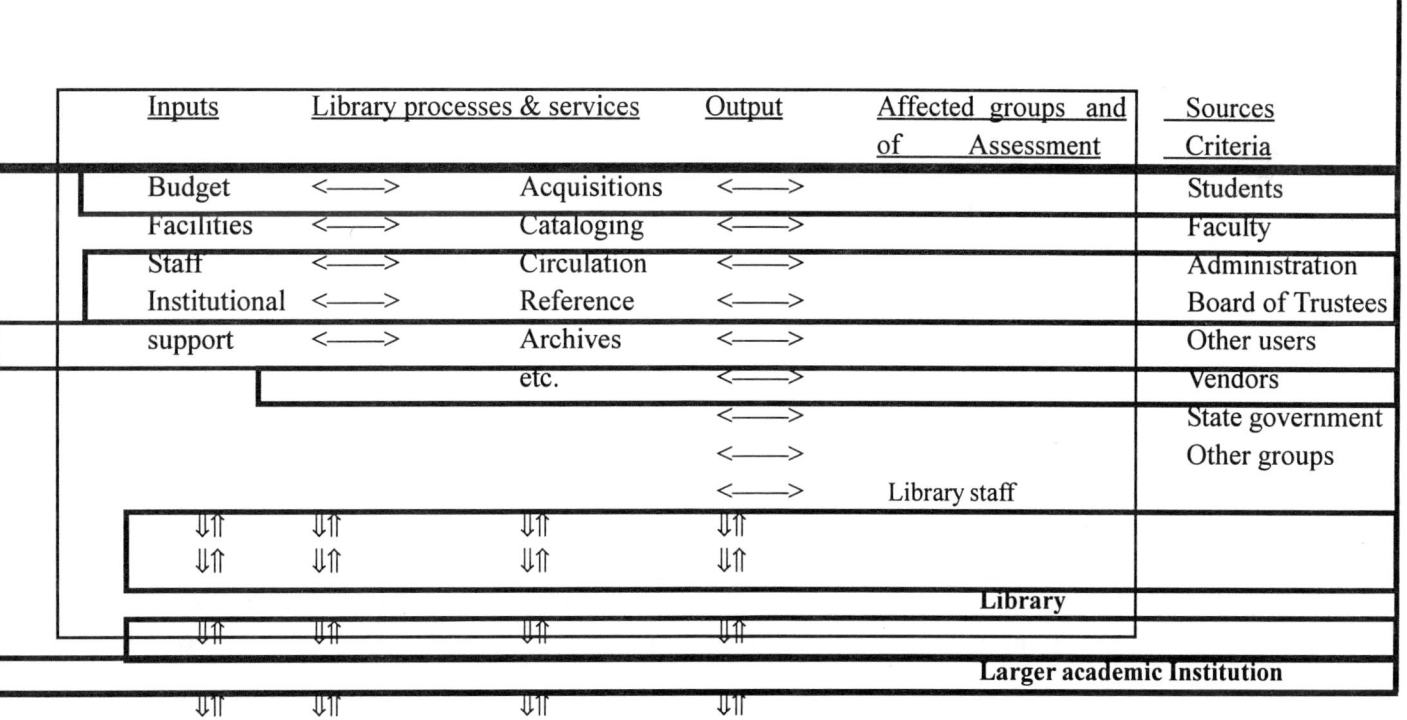

Figure 1. Academic Library Assessment Model (ALAM)

QUEST: A Collaborative Approach to Information Literacy

Susan B. Markley and Merrill D. Stein

Abstract

QUEST, a joint venture of Villanova University's Falvey Memorial Library and the Core Humanities Seminar (CHS) faculty, began as a one semester self-paced online tutorial to introduce freshmen to the basic concepts of information literacy. Since Core Humanities is required for all incoming freshmen and is a cornerstone of the Core Curriculum at Villanova, it was felt that a foundation for information literacy initiatives should start here. Through these entities on campus, an Information Literacy Committee was formed and tutorial exercises were customized to course syllabi for 1,600 freshmen in over 100 sections. Librarians introduced the tutorials in a classroom setting and then corrected them as they were received via e-mail. Feedback was provided to the professors and students. Second semester included hands-on library instruction sessions on Boolean logic and critical resource evaluation techniques. This further encouraged the collaborative process with faculty at the same time it increased awareness of the librarian's role in the education process. Middle States guidelines for a broader institution-wide information literacy component were also addressed. Reference and non-reference librarians, CHS faculty, CHS staff, Media Graphics, and Systems personnel were integral parts of the project's success.

Susan B. Markley is head, Periodical Department, and Merrill D. Stein is head, Access Services, Villanova University.

QUEST: A Collaborative Approach to Information Literacy

Introduction

It has become apparent to most educators and academic librarians that instruction in library and information literacy is essential if students are to learn to be mature and self-directed learners. To achieve this end at Villanova University, an Information Literacy Committee was formed by the Library Director, Dr. James Mullins, and charged with developing an information literacy program. The program's goal was to bring to the students a sense of order and organization when dealing with the overwhelming explosion of print and electronic information.

The Committee volunteers consisted of three Reference librarians, the Head of Public Services, the Head of Access Services, the Head of Periodicals, and the serials cataloguer.[1] Our objective was to reduce library anxiety by introducing basic information literacy skills during the first semester via a self-paced tutorial on the Web and then, second semester, build on these skills by teaching more sophisticated search techniques of specialized resources using a hands-on approach in the library. Included in this second semester presentation would be how to critically evaluate resources for accuracy, validity, bias and relevancy. The Committee anticipated that such a program would also satisfy the Middle States guideline to evaluate "the extent to which bibliographical instruction supports a broader institution-wide emphasis on information literacy."[2]

The Committee considered integrating its proposals into the Core Humanities Seminar Program (CHS for short) on campus. This Core Curriculum Program, required for all incoming freshmen, is an interdisciplinary approach that encourages reflective examination of the primary texts and sources in Ancient, Medieval and Renaissance thought through to the Present. A year before, the Chair of the Core Program, Dr. John Doody, had agreed to integrate a relatively simple PowerPoint orientation to the library into their curriculum. Though this effort met with limited success, both the Chair and many of his staff supported attempting a tutorial-based information literacy effort. To ensure the success of this massive undertaking, garnering broad faculty support would be essential. Ultimately, several faculty agreed to serve on the Committee as liaisons for the Core Humanities Department and became deeply involved in all aspects of the planning and implementation process.

Efforts to Develop the Tutorial

For the Committee, the first priority was developing a project time line to implement the tutorial. Several underlying principles were generally agreed to late in 1997. Freshmen library orientation tours would no longer be offered before the semester began and CHS and the library would commit to orientating students to the library and library research skills through a joint initiative. The Information Literacy Program would not formally teach mechanical computer skills, such as using the mouse. Those tasks would be left to the computing services department on campus.

The elements composing the tutorial would address a list of library information seeking competencies developed over the years in the Reference Department, supplemented by input from CHS Committee faculty and from concepts presented in The Brief Holt Handbook [3] (recommended for all freshmen). How to prioritize and coherently present these elements were issues wrestled with over the next several months by the Committee.

Initially, fourteen tutorials were reviewed by the Committee. Review criteria included content, hardware/software requirements, graphics presentation, logical organization, and interactivity. Tutorials were suggested through personal experience, the Library Instruction Round Table Tutorials General Guides to Research[4], Villanova's list of peer institutions, and other literature sources citing criteria for web-based tutorials.[5]

Committee members then prepared a list of comparable institutions to contact about their information literacy programs. Form questions were developed to help evaluate how these programs were incorporated within the overall campus and freshman orientation experience.

Ultimately, it was agreed to seek permission from the University of Dayton's Roesch Library to adapt their elegantly direct and concise tutorial for this exciting initiative christened QUEST. It was determined that after the first semester tutorial, freshman should know some of the physical layout of the library (such as the Reference and Main Stacks sections), how to access the library homepage, how to use the local catalog (VUCat), and how to do basic citation searching in online databases and web sites.

The tutorial was evolving into an online lesson that could be completed from dorm rooms or elsewhere on campus. CHS faculty were then encouraged to submit topics to the Committee related to their syllabi which would form a core list of subjects from which students could choose in completing the tutorial exercises. However, as faculty had requested, one section required the students to physically come into the library and search a specialized print encyclopedia for several short answers.

The tutorial instructed the students to use one topic from the faculty-supplied list, such as Jane Austin, Islam, or St. Augustine, in completing all facets of the tutorial in the library's catalog, the specialized encyclopedias, such as The Encyclopedia of Philosophy, selected databases, such as Humanities Index and Expanded Academic Index, and pre-determined web sites. Optional links were embedded to explain to students such research issues as scholarly vs. popular materials, LC classification, the correct citation of sources, and Interlibrary Loan. Tutorials would be submitted to the librarians for correction via e-mail. Professors had an option of grading the tutorial, giving credit for it, or providing additional follow-up assignments. QUEST was launched after the above plans received the necessary faculty approval.

Introducing QUEST to Participants

At various stages in the program, public relations efforts were employed to inform the campus of this joint venture. The January 1998 Library newsletter, distributed campus-wide, carried positive comments by selected faculty describing their successes with library instruction. By April 1998, a prototype version of QUEST was being tested in one of the CHS classes. At this time, the library also invited all Core Humanities faculty to an Open House for a demonstration of the tutorial and to elicit feedback, thus furthering the collaborative process.

Later in the spring, it was determined that the librarians, rather than the CHS faculty, would introduce the freshmen to QUEST by way of a five-to-ten minute classroom presentation. This was a daunting endeavor to schedule, as there were over 100 classes and a total of 1600 freshman to reach. The presentation would include the various elements of the tutorial, how to access it from either the Library or Core Humanities homepage, and a description of the goals of the QUEST project.

At this juncture, most of the librarians were familiar with the idea of QUEST but unaware of its potential impact on their work routine. Some librarians were apprehensive about the prospect of visiting classrooms in the fall and briefly introducing QUEST to the students. They were also concerned about the perceived time necessary to correct the tutorials and provide feedback to the professors. In an attempt to ease these concerns, it was decided to contact the Chair of the Communication Department, Dr. Teresa Nance, and her colleague, Dr. Heidi Rose, to address the librarians on the fundamentals of classroom presentation and communication. Their workshop included various exercises and video feedback sessions and was well-received by most of the staff.

Early in the Fall semester, each librarian was supplied with the name and class schedule of two to three Core Humanities professors with whom they would work all semester to introduce freshmen to QUEST. Preferences were given to matching library liaisons with their academic departments since Core professors often taught in other departments, such as History or Philosophy. The librarian was responsible for contacting each professor and arranging a preliminary office visit to further explain QUEST and what was intended to be accomplished. A date was then determined for the librarian to visit the classroom and briefly introduce the students to the online tutorial.

The Chair of CHS encouraged faculty to integrate the tutorial into their lesson plans. The class presentations were staggered over a three-month period so the librarians would not receive all completed tutorials at the same time and so student use of the specialized encyclopedias could be spread over the course of the semester. E-mail connections were established so when students entered the name of their professor, the completed tutorials were sent directly to the corresponding librarian's e-mail address for correction. Corrected tutorials were then returned to the professors for distribution to their students. In selected classes, a pre-test and post-test was administered by the librarian to measure whether anything was learned by completing the tutorial. QUEST was now well underway, and by having the librarians establish these contacts with the faculty, relationships developed, collaborative efforts increased, and the librarian's role in the learning process of the students and faculty expanded.

Public relations efforts continued as displays of QUEST-related material were prepared for the library lobby. Articles were placed in the student newspaper, *The Villanovan*, and in the faculty/staff newspaper, *Blueprints*. Informal brown bag lunches and planning meetings with Committee members and faculty continued to be held during the fall 1998 semester to maintain a high level of communication, especially as preparations for the second semester part of the program, QUEST STRATEGIES, was being developed. In the fall of 1998, evaluation forms from the Chair of Core Humanities were also distributed to the faculty to obtain additional feedback.

Efforts to Develop Second Semester QUEST Strategies

By August 1998, work had begun on the initial development of the information literacy program for the second semester, christened QUEST STRATEGIES. Emphasis was placed on teaching the more sophisticated Boolean search techniques used in retrieving material from VUCat and selected databases and on discussing criteria for evaluating the appropriateness of those resources.

A fifty-minute PowerPoint presentation was developed to coincide with the University's *Worlds in Collision* theme and with Villanova's Irish connections. "England and Ireland in Conflict: An Interdisciplinary Investigation of the Rebellion of 1798" was selected as an example of this broad theme. To create an Irish mood, slides and music of Ireland were incorporated into the presentation.

Students were then taught to extract concepts from a narrower, more focused topic, form a Boolean search statement and execute it in one of three different databases (Historical Abstracts, MLA Bibliography, and the library's online catalog). Students were also given two pre-selected web sites to evaluate based on a set of detailed criteria.

Committee and Staff Efforts Second Semester

As the technical preparations for QUEST STRATEGIES progressed, it was apparent that some of the non-reference librarians had reservations about leading sessions. They were being asked to teach freshmen classes material unfamiliar to them and to use multimedia equipment with which they were not comfortable. To try to alleviate these concerns, the Committee decided to pair a Reference librarian with a non-Reference librarian for each session. It was also decided to invite Carol Weiss, Ph.D. from the Villanova Institute for Teaching and Learning (VITAL), to address the librarians about teaching college students. Dr. Weiss detailed the levels of intellectual development in college students and gave insight on how best to approach them in a teaching situation. In a second visit, she critiqued the QUEST STRATEGIES presentation and answered additional questions. Her visit was another example of the collaborative efforts underscoring the program.

To further reduce any remaining librarian anxiety, the Committee prepared a script that closely followed the PowerPoint presentation. Librarians could follow or adapt the script as they chose. The presentation was loaded on the library server so staff could practice it in private.

Effforts to Launch QUEST Strategies

At the start of the 1999 spring semester, the Chair of Core Humanities sent memos to his faculty reiterating what QUEST STRATEGIES hoped to achieve and requesting them to schedule their classes for the advanced research instruction in the library.

Sessions were then adjusted around the other instruction classes normally held during the spring semester. The Committee planned the QUEST STRATEGIES sessions to run from January through April in hopes of encouraging professors to integrate skills taught at the presentations into their class curriculum.

At the same time, to further publicize QUEST STRATEGIES, a significant library display was mounted from the Irish material in the Library's

Special Collections. During this time, faculty were also encouraged to provide the librarian with any research assignments for that semester so they could be integrated into the QUEST STRATEGIES presentation.

Conclusion

This type of collaborative effort may not be new, but it is also not the norm in most academic institutions. It is hoped that under the proper circumstances and direction, this can become more prevalent on campuses. Although drawbacks exist, many more benefits accrued. For the faculty, this partnership with the library provided another dimension to their teaching of information literacy and was an opportunity to upgrade their own skills.

For the librarians, this was another opportunity to promote team-building within the library and encouraged collaboration with the faculty. It provided a way to familiarize themselves with various disciplines, departments, and programs. On a more personal level, it increased self-confidence and fostered a new sense of accomplishment.

For the students, the pro-active approach of QUEST and QUEST STRATEGIES re-enforced the concepts of self-sufficiency while laying the foundations for building information literacy skills. These skills will be further enhanced as the Information Literacy Programs expand to incorporate higher-level research in upper-level classes.

For the University, this project attempted to address the Middle States Information Literacy guidelines and added another component to the University's Learning Communities theme. It also increased awareness of the importance of collaboration between the various teaching elements on campus.

As for the QUEST tutorial itself, an analysis of pre- and post-test data, collected from six different class sections, containing one hundred students, produced extraordinary results. As the figures in-

Test Conducted	Test Results	Significant at
T Test	.0004	>.05
Analysis of Variance	.0178	>.05
Chi-Square	65.179	<3.84

dicate, the improvement rate from the pre-test to the post-test, after taking the tutorial, was dramatic, clearly demonstrating the value of the tutorial process.

As for QUEST STRATEGIES, the quality of future individual class assignments will be an indicator of how successfully the presentations conveyed searching and evaluating techniques.

Notes

1. The Information Literacy Committee is composed of the following librarians: Judith Olsen, Chair; David Burke; Michael Foight; Louise Green; Susan Markley; Barbara Quintiliano, and Merrill Stein. The following faculty represented Core Humanities: Professors John Doody, Chair of CHS; Earl Bader; Peter Glomset; Marylu Hill; Gaile Pohlhaus and Lauren Shohet.

2. Commission on Higher Education, Middle States Association of Colleges and Schools. *Guidelines for Librarian Evaluators.* Philadelphia: 1997

3. Kirszner, Laurie G., *The Brief Holt Handbook.* Fort Worth: Harcourt Brace College Publishers, 1998.

4. Library Instruction Round Table. *Library Instruction Tutorials; General Guides to Research.* LIRT. 29 December 1998. <http://diogenes.baylor.edu/Library/LIRT/lirtgen.html>.

5. "Special Issue: The Best of Library-Related Web Sites." *Library Hi Tech* 15 (1997). 3–4.

6. We are indebted to Dr. Joseph Pigeon, Department of Mathematical Sciences, Villanova University for his work on the statistical analysis of the QUEST tutorial.

Racing to Keep Up With An Electronic FDLP: Its Effect on Professional Relationships of Academic Government Documents Librarians

Ann Roselle

Internet-related technologies, such as e-mail and e-conferencing, along with the enormous amount of information over the World Wide Web (WWW), have had dramatic impacts on the field of academic librarianship.[1] These electronic vehicles for communicating and disseminating information have been particularly influential on academic government documents librarians as a result of the U.S. government's commitment to disseminating information electronically. The Federal Depository Library Program (FDLP) is now moving from paper and microforms distribution to electronic access, including the Internet.[2] Efforts to revise Title 44 of the *U.S. Code*, which stipulates the roles of the FDLP and the responsibilities of the Government Printing Office (GPO), are underway to reflect, among other things, electronic dissemination of government information.[3] Documents librarians have increasingly had to adjust their work activities to utilize Internet-related technologies.[4]

This paper discusses the extent to which Internet-related technologies and the WWW, which have affected academic government documents librarians' roles and responsibilities, have impacted the professional relationships of these librarians. The professional relationships in this study include those with library administration units, instruction units, systems/automation units, reference units, academic departments, government documents librarians at other institutions, and government representatives. Concentrating on modifications among professional relationships is important because they may affect the resources that academic government documents librarians have to do their job successfully; the patterns of collaboration and cooperation; the status of academic government documents librarians within and outside of the library;

Ann Roselle is assistant librarian, Eastern Washington University.

and career options and career mobility. The study of professional relationships among academic government documents librarians thus has importance for the study of professions more generally.

Research Methodology and Profile of the Sample

In July 1997, a mail survey was sent to 226 academic government documents librarians working at U.S. depository libraries, representing a simple random sample of one-third of all academic government documents librarians listed in the *Federal Depository Library Directory*.[5] One hundred eighty-seven responded for an 82.7% return rate. Table 1 shows considerable variation in a number of key sample characteristics.

Beginning in December 1998, follow-up telephone interviews were conducted with respondents who indicated their willingness to be interviewed on their returned survey. At the point of writing this paper, sixteen 45-minute telephone interviews had been completed. Select results from the survey and preliminary findings from the interviews will be presented in this paper.

Work Activities and Professional Relationships

Several survey questions were developed that asked about the respondents' work-related activities with the WWW and other Internet-related technologies. The activities included participating in the development of the library's Web site; providing hypertext links for the Web site; using e-mail to contact GPO, other federal agencies, political figures, and web masters; participating in GovDoc-L, an active electronic discussion group; searching the Internet to locate relevant government sites; using the WWW to locate information for users; using Internet resources for collection maintenance; serving on Internet-related library or campus committees; providing instruction on government information available over the Internet; and training librarians on accessing such government information. Based on a principal components factor analysis, these activities were grouped into four factors: the "E-Mail Activities" factor, the "WWW and Listserv Activities" factor, the "Committee and Web Site Activities" factor, and the "Instructional Activities" factor.

Along with Internet-related work activities, the researcher surveyed respondents on the nature of

Table 1. Characteristics of Respondents and Their Place of Employment

	%	Range	Mean	Median
Gender	72.7% female			
	27.3% male			
Age		23 yrs.–67 yrs.	46.2 yrs.	47 yrs.
Employed as docs librarian		6 months–31 yrs.	10.3 yrs.	8.0 yrs.
Hired on tenure track	50.8% yes			
	49.2% no			
Type of institution	62% public			
	38% private			
Student enrollment		675–60,276 students	9,874	6,321
Highest degree conferred	19.8% bachelors			
	44.4% Masters			
	35.8% Doctorate			
Library holdings in vols.		57,000–64,000,000	1,427,964	427,812
Depository selection rate		2%–99%	38.72%	30.0%
# of professional librarians		1–145 librarians	19	11
# of support staff		1 ½–500 staff	38	17
Separate unit from computer center	89.3% yes			
	10.7% no			
Length of Internet connectivity		3 months–17 yrs.	4.2 yrs	4 yrs.

Table 2. Descriptive Statistics for Variables Related to Professional Relationships				
		Frequency of Contact (%)		
	% Indicating Working Closer with Unit or Individuals	Frequently	Sometimes	Seldom to Never
1. Library Administration	16.4	56.9	33.1	9.9
2. Systems/Automation Unit	47.8	56.6	28.0	15.4
3. Instruction Unit	23.0	62.5	25.5	12.0
4. Reference Unit	27.3	85.5	11.8	2.7
5. Academic Departments	28.6	33.3	56.5	10.2
6. Documents Librarians at Other Institutions	70.1	N.A.	N.A.	N.A.
7. Government Representatives:	41.6			
Political Figures		1.1	20.8	78.1
GPO		7.6	57.3	35.1
Other Federal Agencies		4.8	42.9	52.2
		% Responding "Yes"		% Responding "No"
8. Made Contact with New Person(s) while Performing Tasks Related to the Internet		28.8		71.2

their professional relationships. Table 2 provides descriptive statistics on respondents' perceptions of modifications in their professional relationships, their frequency of contacting individuals, and their development of new professional relationships.

The researcher through multivariate analysis tested whether academic government documents librarians who are more involved with activities involving the use of the WWW and other Internet-related technologies are more likely to be forming professional relationships with new individuals, both on and off campus, and are more likely to observe modifications in their pre-existing professional relationships. Table 3 shows the results from running a regression analysis with the professional relationships variables as the dependent variables and with work activity factors as the independent variables. R^2s range from .035 to .195, five of which are significant at the .01 level. Internet-related work activities explained the most variation in the development of closer ties with government representatives (19.5%), and the extent to which respondents felt they were working more closely with academic departments (10.1%) and with their systems/automation units (10.0%). Detailed analysis of these results will not be presented in this paper due to space limitation but will be available in a forthcoming publication.[6]

Table 3. Variation in Dependent Variables Explained by Work Activities Factors		
Dependent Variable	R^2	Significance
Extent of Working More Closely with Library Administration	.034	.215
Extent of Working More Closely with Systems/Automation Unit	.100	.002
Extent of Working More Closely with Instruction Unit	.044	.112
Extent of Working More Closely with Reference Unit	.035	.200
Extent of Working More Closely with Academic Departments	.101	.001
Developing Closer Ties with Documents Librarians at Other Institutions	.089	.003
Developing Closer Ties with Government Representatives	.195	.000
Making Contact with New Person(s)	.089	.003

Statistical tests were also conducted to determine to what extent changes in professional relationships were dependent on respondents' background characteristics, opinions about the Internet, and institutional characteristics of their places of employment.[7] Results show that the tendency to form closer relationships is only minimally correlated with characteristics of the respondents and their institutions. Only "years served as a documents librarian" was significant, when controlling for the work factors, with "making new contacts" at .048 and with "developing closer ties with other documents librarians" at .000. This suggests that respondents who have been working for a longer period of time as documents librarians were less likely to be developing closer ties with other documents librarians as a result of Internet-related technologies, and less likely to be making contact with new persons while performing tasks related to the Internet. This may be because more experienced documents librarians already have a well-established network of professionals with whom they can consult.

Discussion
Relationship with Government Documents Librarians

A majority of respondents (131, 70.1%) believed that they were developing closer ties with documents librarians at other institutions because of the Internet. As shown in Table 2, in performing tasks related to the Internet, 53 (28.8%) respondents indicated coming into contact with a new person(s) who helped with these tasks. A documents librarian was identified as the new contact by 25% of the respondents making new contacts. There was a significant correlation at the .01 level of .239 between the development of closer ties with documents librarians at other institutions and the establishment of completely new relationships due to the Internet.

One interviewee describes her experience making a new contact with a documents librarian as follows:

> Respondent: I sort of got a real serious case of hero worship of [the librarian]. Primarily when I first decided, okay, you have to come up with an approach to creating a documents home page, I looked at a lot of depository home pages, whatever I could find that was up. And when I looked at [the librarian's pages], it was like, this is to me *the* thing to aspire to.
>
> Interviewer: Had you ever met [the librarian]? Did you know her before seeing her web pages?
>
> Respondent: I had met her once. [The two states] sometimes get together for state documents/GODORT meetings, but it had been a long time ago. I knew, of course, who she was. I really had not had real contact with her. I didn't feel like, gee, I've talked to this woman a lot. At the time that I was really looking at her home page, trying to work on my page, going back and visiting her pages a lot, I was sort of drafted into doing a program for the [state] documents group. And I contacted her and asked her if she would come and do a program for our [state] GODORT. And she agreed to do that. I don't think it would have occurred to me to ask her to come. And so, we spent a couple of days with her. We had all sorts of chats before the program and after.

In addition, the use of GovDoc-L may be influencing relationships with other documents librarians. There was a significant positive correlation at the .01 level of .236 between those respondents who indicated meeting a documents librarian through GovDoc-L and those developing closer ties with documents librarians. In addition, there was a significant correlation at the .05 level of .167 between the number of hours per week respondents used GovDoc-L and the development of closer ties with other documents librarians.

As another interviewee explains:

> I have either had people see something, like a posting on GovDoc-L, and contact me directly or vice versa. I've contacted someone and it has caused us to develop

a relationship where one or the other of us felt, because we did establish this contact—this repertoire—, [they could] use the other person as a resource for something else later on.

Relationship with Systems/Automation Unit

A total of 87 (47.8%) respondents felt that, because of the Internet, they were developing closer ties with their systems/automation unit. This was not unexpected because this is *the* library unit that is generally most engaged in Internet-related work. 139 (74.3%) respondents indicated that they could go to the systems/automation librarian for help with the WWW and other Internet related-technologies. In fact, when respondents were asked to identify the individual whom they went to most frequently for Internet help, the systems/automation librarian was listed by 69 (38.5%) respondents. Among the 126 respondents who worked on the development of their library's Web site, 53 (43.8%) indicated that they worked with the system/automation librarian during the process.

Relationships with Government Representatives

A total of 77 (41.6%) respondents believed that they were developing closer ties than they otherwise would with government representatives as a result of Internet-related technologies. This is an interesting finding considering that, in general, respondents less frequently contact GPO, other federal agencies, and political figures compared to contacting library units or other documents librarians (Table 2).

As one interviewee explains:

> The askLPS[8] really does make you feel closer [to GPO]. People I haven't even seen, when I send messages to them (well, I know [the GPO staff person]) . . . people who we've sent questions to about something that has happened, and when they respond, it's like we have a personal relationship with them. It really does bring you closer, or at least I feel that way, to the folks at GPO. It is not like some unknown person, they are not foreign to us anymore.

Another interviewee describes the changing relationship with GPO as follows:

> It used to be that communicating with GPO was like pulling teeth. I mean we used to have to send in these silly inquiry forms, and they fell into a black hole most of the time. The relationships between depositories and GPO was never, now this was years ago, was never really very good. The communication flow was very bad. You never knew who to talk to. If you did get a hold of somebody, frankly they would or they wouldn't help depending on their mood. I don't know if is entirely due to the fact that we now have GovDoc-L and we can communication via e-mail and we have askLPS and all these things. But that certainly has revolutionized, and I really mean that word, communication between depositories and GPO. It's just incredible the difference it has made.

When respondents were queried about persons they met through GovDoc-L with whom they communicate on a regular basis, 41 (21.1%) respondents indicated they met a GPO representative and 8 (4.3%) indicated that they met a representative from another government agency. There were significant positive correlations at the .01 level of .313 between those respondents who indicated meeting a GPO representative through GovDoc-L and those developing closer ties with government representatives.

Another interviewee describes traffic on GovDoc-L and its impact on federal agencies:

> Respondent: One thing that does stand out [about GovDoc-L] is the discussion that went on last year about STAT-USA, and the way they were changing their structure. STAT-USA and the Commerce Bureau were much more responsive to what documents librarians wanted because we were so vocal on GovDoc-L. The criticisms were out there, and there were enough people saying the same thing that I do think it changed the way they set up their interface. I think

it was very useful to them to hear how people are searching. The agencies know how they use the material, but they don't know how users use it. Since we are talking to users all the time, we know how people are searching.

Interviewer: What do you think the documents community would have done to try to communicate that STAT-USA was difficult to use? In your opinion, would we have done anything?

Respondent: I think something would have been done if a committee had time, at our twice a year ALA committee meetings - - if a committee had time to take a look at it and set-up a task force and make suggestions. Something might have been done much slower.

Other Relationships
In performing tasks related to the Internet, 53 (28.8%) respondents came into contact with a new person(s) who helped with these tasks. As previously discussed, the survey identified a quarter of these new contacts as documents librarians. The other types of positions identified include: systems/automation librarian, librarian in same state, librarian in different state, campus computing/college webmaster, paraprofessional, student/teaching assistant, vendor, faculty member, other campus webmaster, information specialist, writer, person from listserv, reference librarian, GPO representative, documents librarian outside the U.S, and associate director of budget & technology at another university.

One interviewee gives an example of the formation of a new contact:

Interviewer: Were there any of your colleagues, that you normally, wouldn't have talked to, but during this process of [creating Web pages] you got to know them a little bit better?

Respondent: Yes. I would say I did. For example, there was a humanities librarian who's really good at learning the Web, and generally I wouldn't have had that much contact with a humanities librarian. I did have a lot more contact because of this shared learning experience.

Interviewer: Do you still keep in contact?

Respondent: Yes. We've developed a closeness because of that.

Conclusion
Survey results and preliminary interview findings indicate that there is a perception that modifications are occurring among professional relationships of academic government documents librarians. For the most part, this is occurring for some academic government documents librarians regardless of who they are and where they work. This suggests that an electronic FDLP, which requires the utilization of an array of Internet-related technologies, may be affecting the academic government documents librarian profession by altering internal and external relationships.

These findings raise several important issues. For example, how well will academic government documents librarians manage these new relationships? On campuses, academic government documents librarians may find themselves within altered work environments where they are now required to interact and communicate with units or individuals in new capacities. Will academic government documents librarians have the appropriate technical knowledge and skills to collaborate with these units or individuals? Likewise, will they be able to communicate the goals and objectives of an electronic FDLP to persons with whom they might not have had to interact previously? It is not clear to what the extent new knowledge and information is being shared or produced, and the extent to which barriers to effective communication between different professions and occupations are being overcome. However, increased communication may be achieving these goals to some extent.

In terms of alterations among off-campus professional relationships, there are potential benefits of an expanded network. This study discovered the development of closer ties with government representatives. Will this, in turn, affect academic government documents librarians' ability to influence the FDLP? Developing a broader range of relationships may directly affect the opportunities that documents librarians have in integrating government information within a wider arena and providing enhanced access to library resources, more generally.

This study also suggests that changes in work as a result of Internet-related technologies are necessitating changes in the specialized body of knowledge required by academic government documents librarians. Moreover, it suggests that academic government documents librarians may be attempting to develop this new knowledge through new patterns of collaboration and cooperation with individuals on and off campus. Since the work of other professional academic librarians is also being impacted by Internet-related technologies, it is plausible that these changes are occurring at least to some extent for them as well.

Notes and References

1. Charles R. McClure, William E. Moen, and Joe Ryan, "Academic Libraries and the Impact of Internet/NREN: Key Issues and Findings," *Proceedings of the 56th American Society for Information Science Annual Meeting*, 30 (1993): 32–38; Diane K. Kovacs, Kara L. Robinson, & Jeanne Dixon, "Scholarly E-Conferences on the Academic Networks: How Library and Information Science Professionals Use Them," *Journal of the American Society for Information Science* 46 (May 1995): 244–53.

2. See Peter Hernon & John A. Shuler, "The Depository Library Program: Another Component of the Access Puzzle Shifting to Electronic Formats," in *Federal Information Policies in the 1990s: Views and Perspectives* edited by Peter Hernon, Charles R. McClure, and Harold C. Relyea (Norwood, N.J.: Ablex, 1996), 259–78; Ad Hoc Committee on the Internet, "Government Information in the Electronic Environment: A GODORT Whitepaper," *Documents to the People* 24 (March 1996): 21–39; "Symposium on Federal Depository Libraries: Challenges and Opportunities for the 21st Century," *Government Information Quarterly* 15 (1998): 11–121; Duncan M. Aldrich, "Depository Libraries, the Internet, and the 21st Century?" *Journal of Government Information* 23 (July/August 1996): 389.

3. See the *Federal Information Access Act of 1997*.

4. McClure, Moen, and Ryan, "Academic Libraries and the Impact of Internet/NREN," 32–38; Daniel C. Barkely, "Public Service Guidelines in an Electronic Environment," *Government Information Quarterly* 15 (January 1998): 73–85.

5. *Federal Depository Library Directory* (Washington, D.C.: Government Printing Office, Superintendent of Documents, Library Programs Service, 1996).

6. See "Internet-Related Work Activities and Academic Government Documents Librarians' Professional Relationships," forthcoming publication in *Government Information Quarterly*.; Magali Sarfatti Larson, *The Rise of Professionalization: A Sociological Analysis* (London: University of California Pr., 1977); Andrew Delano Abbott, *The System of the Professions* (London: University of California Press, 1988); Leonard S. Cottrell Jr. and Eleanor B. Sheldon, "Relationship Expectations," in *Professionalization*, edited by Howard M. Vollmer and Donald L. Mills (Englewood Cliffs, N.J.: Prentice-Hall, Inc., 1966), 232–37.

7. Ibid.

Recruiting More Minorities to the Library Profession: Responding to the Need for Diversity

Ronald G. Edwards

Abstract

The issue of recruiting a diverse population to the library profession has been a concern for many years. The library literature is replete with articles and reports documenting this issue. Task forces, committees, and focus groups have been formed to discuss this situation and provide recommendations. The bottom line still remains the same. Comparatively little progress has occurred regarding the recruitment of minorities into the library profession. This paper will examine some of the barriers that exist concerning more effective minority recruitment and offer some suggestions for improving this overall situation.

Introduction

For an issue that has generated so much discussion over the years, the library profession cannot speak well of accomplishing its goals and objectives regarding minority recruitment. Although there appears to be enough activity and involvement in some areas of the library profession, and ample discussion of the relevant issues surrounding the topic, the library profession continues to lack success in diversifying its ranks. Minor gains are being made, but they are not keeping pace with the ever increasing minority population in the United States.

Recent statistics compiled by the Association for Library and Information Science Education (ALISE) reveal disturbing figures regarding minority recruitment efforts and corresponding graduation rates. White students enrolled in ALA-accredited master's degree programs from 51 schools that reported ethnic data constitute 83 percent of the students. Black students accounted for 4.8 percent, Hispanics 3 percent, and Asian or

---

Ronald G. Edwards is head, Curriculum Resource Cnter, Bowling Green State University.

Pacific Islanders 2.7 percent. In comparing census population figures with student enrollment in ALA-accredited master's degree programs, Hispanics comprise the most underrepresented.[1]

Although some library schools have been conscientious about minority recruitment efforts, most institutions still lag behind. In fact, statistics comparing the number of ethnic minorities in ALA-accredited programs reveal marked disparities in student enrollment. Two institutions account for over 61 percent of all ALA-accredited master's degrees and certificates awarded to American Indian or Alaskan Natives in 1996/97. Just eleven library schools account for over 68 percent of the ALA-accredited master's degrees and certificates awarded to Asian or Pacific Islanders. Ten library schools account for over 56 percent of all master's degrees and certificates awarded to Blacks, while just ten library schools account for over 72 percent of the ALA-accredited master's degrees and certificates awarded to Hispanics.

The globalization of the economy has radically altered the way business has been conducted and undoubtedly has affected the field of librarianship in the process, especially regarding the provision of information services. Ironically, though, a relatively insignificant amount of change has occurred concerning the recruitment of minorities into the library profession. A more varied work force has developed during the past ten to fifteen years in the United States, but the library profession, and specifically accredited library schools have not responded to these changes by recruiting librarians who reflect this diversity. The negligible increases experienced by some ethnic populations in some library school enrollment figures is not consistent with the overall minority population explosion in the country. Blacks, American Indians, and Hispanics have been noticeably ignored and are still certainly underrepresented.

The issue of recruiting a diverse population to the library profession has been a popular and fashionable concern for many decades. It has been a concern, but unfortunately not a mandate or a high enough priority. The library literature indicates this dilemma has existed for decades. The American Library Association (ALA) and its various sections have been involved with the creation of a multitude of committees, task forces, initiatives, caucuses, and focus groups to explore diversity in the library profession. In addition, ALA has attempted to find solutions to the overall problem. Too often, these groups of professional and dedicated librarians and key administrators have failed to live up to their expectations. In many cases, goals and objectives have been developed and written down, but not fulfilled. Issues have been discussed, subcommittees formed, recommendations made, and procedures drawn up, but a lack of continuity and long-range commitment on the part of many of these participants exists regarding minority recruitment.

Barriers to Recruitment
Library Schools and International Students

So why does this shortage of minority librarians still continue to be the norm? Part of this responsibility rests with the accredited library schools in the United States and their ineffective methods and efforts to attract a diverse minority population to their respective library programs. For many years, and until recently, many accredited library schools sought to remedy the lack of minorities by recruiting a variety of international students to their graduate degree programs. Indirectly, these international students filled the gap left open by the lack of American Indian or Alaskan Natives, Asian or Pacific Islanders, Blacks, and Hispanics. Classified as people of color, most international students satisfied the cosmetic need of many accredited library schools to fill their ranks with students from diverse backgrounds. The prestige associated with attracting international students and the funding acquired were additional benefits. Likewise, some library faculty were able to arrange various reciprocal agreements with countries who had sent their students to graduate library school in the United States.

The major difference with international students, though, is that library schools were not resolving the more important need of recruiting minorities to the profession. Foreign students often came from totally different cultural or socioeconomic backgrounds in comparison to American minority students. Many international students came to the United States with the desired prerequisite lacking in American students, enough financial aid up front. This factor, coupled with the financial problems and possible school closings faced by many library schools, made the selection of international students an easy decision on the part of accredited library school administrators.

Complacency and the Status Quo
This same lack of initiative regarding minority recruitment is manifested in the way library school administrators recruit their main constituents. Library school administrators are fully aware that a majority of their prospective student population enrolls automatically into their programs, year after year, without very little recruitment effort or intervention. The abundance of white females has been consistent for many decades. Although an integral part of the overall student enrollment picture, this steady influx of students has resulted in library school administrators becoming somewhat complacent, taking for granted that this majority group of individuals will always be there, filling the student enrollment ranks. On the flip side, this blase attitude has indirectly prevented more vigorous attempts to recruit minorities. Why bother with a system that has worked for decades, especially if no one holds you accountable. This attitude has too often been the norm with complacency overcoming more ambitious efforts. Apparently, library school administrators have yet to learn that diversity may be the panacea and not the problem.

Racism
Although many people in the library profession will deny that racism exists, especially as we approach the new millennium, it is certainly prevalent at many institutions. Major initiatives to recruit and retain minorities in the library profession are hampered by this very real problem. Many libraries and library schools try to ignore this issue at their respective institutions, but racism is alive. According to St. Lifer and Nelson, the prevalence of racism in the library profession is as common as in other professions.[2] The irony of this situation is that the library profession has sought to hold itself to a different standard, a standard which takes into consideration an individual's intellectual freedom and human rights in general.[3] Although ALA promotes the ideals behind the Code of Ethics and Bill of Rights, it falls short in actually implementing these ideals. The American Library Association has fought for years with the conflict between promoting pluralism and maintaining the status quo.[4]

Competition
Another reason for the meager attempts to recruit a diverse work force is centered on the idea of competition. A significant number of leaders in the field of librarianship firmly believe, or so they say, that little progress is being made in the recruitment of minorities because minorities basically don't want to be librarians. As a continuation of this same attitude, other individuals state that fields such as law, medicine, and business offer too much competition for attracting the best and brightest to the library profession. I maintain that this perspective is extremely inaccurate and just an excuse for not pursuing minority applicants more earnestly. Whether they are the best or brightest, or just average people like many librarians, is not really the issue. To say that competition from such fields as law, medicine, engineering, or business is responsible for the scarcity of minority library students or professional librarians is quite ludicrous. It ignores a number of basic facts. First, it doesn't take into consideration that many librarians are not the same type of individuals who end up pursuing law, business, or engineering degrees. Most librarians who pursue master's degrees still come from the undergraduate areas of English, history, education or other social sciences. More than likely, those individuals who chose librarianship would not have selected law, business, or engineering in the first place, or even been eligible to pursue graduate degrees in these disciplines. Many of the students who pursued these other disciplines have a fairly good idea, well in advance, that they will focus on law, business, engineering, or business. This is not true of many library school graduate students who end up choosing librarianship comparatively late in their careers. In fact, many library school students choose the library profession as a second career, an option not as readily available or possible in other professions because of time constraints, tuition, and prerequisite courses required for admission.

Thus, to claim that minorities are not being recruited to the library profession because of competition from other fields, or that the best and brightest are not being recruited for the same reason, is a fallacy. This display of apathy also presupposes that library school recruiters should go out and seek only those individuals who are the best. Many individuals can become excellent librarians, not just the brightest. Although I know quite a few bright librarians, I also know many others who may not be the brightest, but are certainly competent librarians.

Lack of Marketing

The lack of conscientious and systematic efforts to market existing library school programs is yet another obstacle in recruiting minorities into the library profession. Other than increasing the already disproportionate blend of students in library school, and adding more tuition dollars to the library science programs, very little attention is devoted to increasing minority student enrollment. Although library school administrators believe the creation of bigger programs ensures a continuing supply of qualified people into the profession, the bottom line is really increasing critical mass and university support for their respective library programs.[5]

Instead of attracting more minorities to their library programs, library school administrators seek to expand their existing programs by offering courses at various satellite locations throughout the state or country. Many of these locations, though, are not located in urban areas accessible to minorities. As a result, most individuals who end up enrolling in these courses and subsequent degree programs represent the preexisting gender/ethnic mix which already dominates the library profession. Blacks, Hispanics, Asian or Pacific Islanders, and American Indian or Alaskan Natives are virtually ignored. An inordinate amount of time is expended developing new courses for these satellite campuses, time which could have been spent on recruiting more minorities to the profession.

In addition, adjunct instructors are often hired to teach these courses. Many of these adjunct instructors are qualified, but they do not possess a high degree of commitment to the overall library science program. Because of this fact, these adjunct faculty devote little time or effort mentoring their students or guiding them through the ups and downs of a graduate degree program. Recruitment does not become a general part of their vocabulary.

Second Master's

And then there is the second master's degree, or as it is often referred to, a subject master's. Others refer to this phenomenon as credential inflation.[6] Librarians who peruse the literature have seen a second advanced degree referred to in The *Chronicle of Higher Education*, *College & Research Libraries News*, *American Libraries*, and *Library Journal* job postings. Listed under desired or preferred qualifications it stands as a symbol of the library profession and a means of identification. Although second master's degrees apply primarily to academic library positions, public libraries use it as a form of credentialling, also. Library school programs give this requirement credibility by promoting its existence and availability through dual master's degree programs. Prospective employers give it importance by making it part of the position vacancy announcement. Is it really essential for practicing librarianship, though? Or is it important enough to be added to the basic requirements for employment? In most cases, no! At best, it gives some individuals more familiarity with a discipline they might encounter as a subject specialist in various academic or public libraries. Given the time, effort, and cost factor associated with its acquisition, its advantages are practically limited.

To begin with, acquiring a second master's requires significantly more tuition dollars in order to take the additional courses needed for degree completion. Since financial aid is such a key factor in determining a minority student's decision in either attending or not enrolling in graduate school, these extra monies become a very real obstacle. Likewise, more credits mean additional time consumed completing the degree program. This translates into finding future employment later than anticipated.

Even though there may be some statistics that support the acquisition of a second degree as the road to success in librarianship, I think the jury is still out regarding its utility. Search committees may place value on achieving this plateau when interviewing candidates for particular positions, but most positions are filled by individuals who meet other selection criteria first. Most librarians who get promoted are not advanced because of a second master's degree. Librarians get promoted for more subjective reasons such as conformity, seniority, or always being a team player. Instead of placing more barriers or roadblocks in the way of attracting minorities to the profession, library administrators and library school personnel would do well by eliminating second master's degrees as requirements for success in the library profession. The time, money, and effort necessary is not worth the end result of steering minorities away from librarianship. If the profession is truly going to move ahead and prosper, it must vigorously address these issues.[7]

Recruitment Essentials
Mentoring

The process of mentoring is one of the key ingredients in attracting and retaining minorities to the library profession. Mentors serve as key advisors and role models for prospective librarians. 8 Mentoring has been shown to be the most critical factor in inflencing minority librarians to initially pursue their library careers.[9] The roles of the mentor are replete and invaluable, especially for minority librarians and students. Mentors provide access to the inner workings of the library which allows minority librarians, and librarians in general, an easy way of communication. Mentors provide a less formal way of initiating an individual into the complexities of management and the overall communication network within the library or library school. A good, effective mentor will act as an advocate, running interference as the new librarian learns the system and hierarchy of the library or institution. The mentoring relationship may give a new librarian the confidence and motivation required for continued self-growth and personal risk.[10]

This process is extremely vital at the higher education level regarding the recruitment and retention of minority library school faculty. Although the mentoring process is important for prospective library school students in high school, in preprofessional library positions, and in community college settings, it is a key factor in recruiting and subsequently retaining individuals to become library school faculty. Underrepresented faculty assist in providing minority students an opportunity to experience learning in a multicultural environment.[11] Underrepresented faculty also provide minority students an opportunity to explore the variety of issues surrounding diversity.[12] In a profession where white library school students predominate, minority librarians need a powerful advocate in the organization to guarantee that they are provided equal access to opportunities.[13]

Library administrators and graduate library school programs must be proactive concerning the mentoring of minorities. Volunteers will not always come to the forefront offering their services as mentors because of peer pressure. This is especially true in institutions where racism exists or is an underlying factor in the hiring process. In addition, library personnel must make sure there is enough financial and human resource support available to promote the mentoring process. Without these resources, the mentoring process will continue to take a backseat to other less important initiatives.

The importance of reaching out to prospective students in order to attract them to the library profession has been documented for decades, but to a large degree, ignored by library administrators and graduate library science programs. The Library and Information Science Studentst Attitudes, Demographics and Aspirations (LISSADA) Survey in 1988 confirmed this fact. The LISSADA Survey was intended to identify attitudes and aspirations of students enrolled in accredited library and information science programs.[14] The Survey revealed clearly that individualized contact is the best mechanism for attracting new entrants to the library profession.[15] What better way to facilitate the mentoring process and attract minorities than through library faculty.

Finally, we must realize that many library faculty do not fully comprehend how important cultural diversity is to the library profession. There still remains a significant number of library faculty who have not worked in any library for years, individuals who fail to understand the changing complexion of the user population.[16] Part of this problem is the result of the insulated environment in which library schools function. Guided by the dictates of academe and not the parameters which libraries operate under, library faculty are more concerned with achieving their own personal goals and objectives.[17] They do not focus on the benefits which can be derived from the recruitment of minority students. In their estimation, research and teaching consume too much time for them to be involved in other duties. Thus, it is imperative that practicing librarians and administrators work together with library faculty and assist each other in the minority recruitment process so vital to the library profession.

Financial Aid

A number of programs exist which address the specific issue of minority recruitment to the library profession. The American Library Association's Spectrum Initiative is a good example. The program is attempting to improve service at the local level through the development of a diverse work force that mirrors the communities served by all libraries in the new millennium. Started in 1998, the Spectrum Initiative is designed to serve as a model which will bring attention to numerous other diversity issues during the next century. The program provides fifty $5,000 scholarships annually to students from the four largest underrepresented ethnic groups in the United States and Canada.

The LAMA Cultural Diversity Grant, although not funds which specifically go to a minority student, is yet another example of a program that focuses on the issue of diversity. Some of the key goals of the grant program include the following: fostering and sustaining diversity throughout institutions, increasing minority representation and advancement, and establishing various partnerships between LAMA and national organizations representing minority interests. Activities which potentially could get funded are educational activities such as workshops and seminars, research results, publications, mentoring and networking initiatives, resource lists, and studies on successful diversity-related initiatives in libraries or other organizations. Since only two awards can be given annually, it is not as attractive as it could be if more support and dollars were allocated to encourage additional applicants and promote continued research on the issue of diversity.

The prevalence of these programs and the monies made available for diversity initiatives are steps in the right direction, but financial aid at the university level in the form of scholarships, fellowships, assistantships, or other grants is still one of the most important factors in attracting minority students to the library profession. The literature is abundant with documentation that lists financial aid as a vital component in contributing to the recruitment and retention process. More financial aid sources need to be identified for prospective students so that this major obstacle can be eliminated prior to matriculation. Library school administrators should learn from programs such as the Spectrum Initiative that additional funding is available in the community and elsewhere if systematic plans are in place to acquire these monies. Likewise, state library organizations can be helpful in providing assistance. Many of these organizations are often willing to provide financial help, if they are encouraged to do so.

Recruitment from Other Disciplines

An amazing fact about the academic credentials required for getting into graduate library school is that you really don't need specific coursework. Unlike medicine where a foundation in the biological sciences is important, or business where some background in mathematics is essential, the library science curriculum is devoid of most prerequisites. Theoretically, the number of potential recruits is unlimited. Although most students who enter graduate library school programs have come from English, education, history, or the social sciences, this undergraduate training has never been required for pursuing an ALA-accredited master's degree. Even the Graduate Record Examination, if really required, has not been a factor regarding the admission of most library school students.

So why haven't library school administrators exploited this reservoir of undergraduate students, especially those minority candidates? Part of the reason is again attributable to the steady stream of traditional students who fill the enrollment ranks.

Unfortunately, the end result is that potential minority candidates get overlooked since it might require too much effort. A prime source of prospective librarians who might have changed the complexion of librarianship is bypassed.[18]

New approaches are rarely implemented regarding library school recruitment. Librarians and library school administrators believe that if it has worked in the past, don't fix it. This attitude may work well with some portions of the population, but some individuals need more encouragement and assistance with the decision making process. Those individuals who might require this added inspiration could end up being the best and brightest many library school administrators are looking for. As Wheeler and Hanson state, "Librarians from a traditional background, who are white and female, have not readily recognized that the tendency of some people to gravitate toward a library setting as their natural habitat is a characteristic that crosses all ethnic, cultural and national boundaries."[19]

Conclusion

The field of library and information science has changed dramatically in many ways during the past 30 to 40 years. Library school closings and openings, advances in technology, distance education, curriculum modifications, an influx of international students, and budget crunches have all affected the overall operation of both library schools and libraries in general.

Throughout these changes, two aspects of the profession have remained fairly much the same. First, there is still a dearth of minority librarians in the profession. Raw numbers may have increased, but these figures do not reflect proportionately the increase in the minority population in the United States. The other constant in librarianship is that it is still statistically a white female dominated profession. This fact has been confirmed for decades by ALISE statistical reports, the LISSADA Survey, innumerable research articles, ALA surveys, and miscellaneous reports.

What exactly does this mean for the library profession in the near future and beyond? What ramifications result because the library profession is composed and constructed the way it is? As Joan Howland states, "It is important to note that librarianship, a white female-dominated profession, has not become any more ethnically diverse than traditionally white male-dominated professions such as law, medicine, engineering, and architecture."[20] Her comment is straightforward and honest regarding the role the majority must play in making sure diversity exists in the library profession. For too long, diversity has been an issue and not a reality. Minority recruitment into the library profession must be more than a symbolic ritual.[21]

The field of librarianship is laden with the need to conform. Conformity is not unique to the library profession, but librarians have a much richer history regarding this attitude, According to various research studies, part of the reason for this practice may be the result of the insecurity felt by many librarians. Or it may simply be because many librarians see themselves undervalued both intellectually and materially. Whatever the reasons, these attitudes play a significant role in the recruitment and retention of minority librarians. "The bottom line is that it simply is neither logical nor good business practice to recruit and hire librarians from diverse backgrounds, only to expect them to assimilate and become mirrors of the generations of librarians which have preceded them."[22]

Another important part of this scenario concerns the climate that exists in the library profession. If minorities are going to be attracted to the library profession, the social environment will have to change. Libraries are too often seen by minorities as places with an indifferent climate.[23] Library administrators must develop work environments where everyone is valued for their own contributions. The caste system in place in most libraries needs to be eradicated.[24]

Finally, it must be emphasized that ALA must be more proactive in rectifying this situation regarding minority recruitment to the profession. ALA has been a strong advocate for diversity initiatives, but it is still an organization not in step with the nation's changing demographics. Although some very positive programs have occurred, and initiatives implemented, ALA must look beyond these individual events and assess its priorities on a regular basis. According to Joan Howland, "Members of diverse populations may find ALA, outside of the ethnic caucuses, if not threatening, at least very uncomfortable."[25]

Notes

1. Evelyn H. Daniel and Jerry D. Saye, *Library and Information Science Education Statistical Report 1998* (Arlington, Va.: ALISE, 1998), 59.
2. Evan St. Lifer and Corinne Nelson, "Unequal Opportunities: Race Does Matter," *Library Journal* 122 (November 1, 1997): 42–46.
3. St. Lifer and Nelson, "Unequal Opportunities," 43.
4. Maurice B. Wheeler and Jaqueline Hanson, "Improving Diversity: Recruiting Students to the Library Profession," *Journal of Library Administration* 21 3/4 (1995): 137–46.
5. Rosemary Ruhig Du Mont, "Recruiting Students Into Librarianship: Questions In Search of Answers," in *Librarians for the New Millennium* (Chicago: ALA/OLPR, 1988), 89–92.
6. Jonathan D. Lauer, "Recruiting for the Library Profession: 1970 to the Present," in *Encyclopedia of Library and Information Science* 44 (New York: Marcel Dekker, 1989), 277–83.
7. Ibid., 280.
8. Rosemary Ruhig Du Mont, Lois Buttlar and William Caynon, "Recruitment and Selection of a Diverse Staff," in *Multiculturalism in Libraries* (Westport, Conn.: Greenwood, 1994), 77–92.
9. Ibid., 78.
10. Joan Howland, "Beyond Recruitment: Retention and Promotion Strategies to Ensure Diversity and Success," *Library Administration & Management* 13 (winter 1999): 4–14.
11. Kriza A. Jennings, "Recruiting New Populations to the Library Profession," *Journal of Library Administration* 19 3/4 (1993): 175–91.
12. Jennings, "Recruiting New Populations," 181.
13. Howland, "Beyond Recruitment," 12.
14. Kathleen M. Heim and William E. Moen, *Occupational Entry: Library and Information Science Students' Attitudes, Demographics and Aspirations Survey* (Chicago: ALA/OLPR, 1989), 3.
15. Ibid., 186.
16. Virgil L.P. Blake, "The American Mosaic: Mapping Curriculum Reform: An Introduction and Overview," in *Mapping Curricular Reform in Library/Information Studies Education: The American Mosaic* (New York: Haworth, 1995), 1–13.
17. Jennings, "Recruiting New Populations," 182.
18. Wheeler & Hanson, "Improving Diversity," 139.
19. Ibid., 140.
20. Howland, "Beyond Recruitment," 6.
21. Wheeler and Hanson, "Improving Diversity," 137.
22. Howland, "Beyond Recruitment," 7.
23. Roberto G. Trujillo and David C. Weber, "Academic Library Responses to Cultural Diversity: A Position Paper for the 1990s," *Journal of Academic Librarianship* 17 (July 1991): 157–61.
24. Howland, "Beyond Recruitment," 8.
25. Ibid., 11.

Remote Control: Creating a Technology-Centered Library in Rural Alaska

Anne Duffy

Note: Paper unavailable at press time.

The Improvisational Nature of the Change Process

Felix T. Chu

To deal with change, the traditional view is to plan in order to rationally coordinate activities within an organization to meet the challenges of the future. One basic assumption is that any task may be decomposed to its various components, and each of these can be dealt with separately and sequentially. When adaptations are necessary, they are made from our understanding of the current environment. Then as soon as possible we try to get back "on track". In recent years, many people have challenged that view because of the need to interpret the environment from different points of view, craft strategies to deal with unpredicted external changes, and participate in teamwork characterized by shared values and shared responsibilities.

Traditional planning expects a long time horizon in a stable environment. A manager is supposed to deal with benchmarking and forecasting. The more information that one gathers about these variables, the better one can predict the future. However, the environment is not stable. The pace of change has increased and the amount of information that is available has increased and become easier to access. But because of the quantity, it is harder to digest and synthesize into a coherent whole. In my previous position as a data processing analyst at the Nebraska Department of Revenue, a colleague who worked with economic forecasting said that as soon as the forecasts become available, organizations will act on them to improve their positions within their industry. So the environment changes constantly and forecasts are never accurate in predicting the future. In a similar sense, as soon as trends are identified and the future forecasted in the information industry, we librarians act to mitigate the effects of potential changes. Thus, the environment becomes turbulent rather than stable. If we go back to Peter Vaill's metaphor, managing has become akin to paddling a canoe in "permanent white water.[1]" In order to move to a certain point in the river, one must know the paddle strokes, one's abilities and understand the canoe which in this case would be the available resources and organizational structure. One improvises according to current conditions of not only the environment but what one perceives as available resources. Improvisation is not possible unless one has mastered the basic traditional skills about handling a canoe.

In the real world, we do what is necessary at the moment to go where we want to go. What

---

Felix T. Chu is unit coordinator, Systems and Operations, Western Illinois University.

collection maintenance functions may move from the cataloging module under the old system to the circulation module in the new system because the menu choices are in that module and they can be done more appropriately there.

My library at Western Illinois University changed automation systems last summer. This is an instance of anticipated change. We, as a participant in a state-wide network of 45 libraries, moved from an old system based on the WLN software linked to a separate circulation system originally developed at Ohio State University to an integrated system from DRA. Of course, the process started a long time before last summer. In preparation for working with new software and hardware, our communication moved from dedicated lines to the Internet. We also acquired NT microcomputers to use as staff workstations according to earlier timetables because the newer software is being developed for the NT platform. Other parts in preparation for anticipated changes include barcoding the collection and attending training sessions for the new system and preparing for data conversion.

However, there were many changes we could not anticipate. We also could not adjust the implementation timetable to local conditions beyond our control nor modify internal workflow sufficiently based on descriptions for a product still under development. The result is to make-do with what we have at hand at the point of need. According to an earlier timetable, the public interface was to be Web-based. At that time, we intended to use some of our older machines running Netscape under Windows 3.1 as public workstations. Later on, when the timetable was revised with the provision that the primary public interface was to be based on the DRA Classic system accessible through telnet, a communications software was recommended by the vendor and the state systems organization that emulates a DEC VT-420 terminal. That software, however, runs under Windows 95 or Windows NT only. While we had fully intended to have microcomputers running Windows 95 in the public areas on Day One, funding through a grant was delayed. Initially, we tried loading Windows 95 onto those older 486 machines with limited RAM and were successful in running the communications software in testing. But those older machines

probably occurs more often than we care to admit is that we act and then try to make sense of what we did according to the structure we have in mind. We codify unplanned changes.[2] We "see what we believe" rather than "believe what we see" in trying to interpret an event.[3] Traditional ways rooted in Lewin's three-stage change model of unfreezing, change, and refreezing no longer seems to work.[4] There is no stability to regain in an environment of uncertainty, particularly in dealing with technology that is open-ended and customizable such as library automation systems. Thus the single sustainable competitive advantage has become how to learn faster and act faster since the raw information may be widely available.[5] The advantage is in re-casting the items of information into alternative frameworks to better understand the implications of impending changes. The view to planning being examined here is improvisational in nature. In improvisation, we are crafting strategy to build on one another's ideas within boundaries based on disciplined individual core skills that are understood by members of the team.[6] Those skills must constantly be sharpened, improved and updated. They form the basis from which to improvise, and the improvisation is local in nature.

Orlikowski and Hofman presented a model where they treat change as an on-going process, not as a scheduled event.[7] This model is particularly applicable in situations where the implemented change is open-ended and customizable such as a change in information systems. Therefore, it is not possible to craft a blueprint for the change process. In preparing for the future, there are three kinds of changes: (1) anticipated, (2) emergent, and (3) opportunity-based. An instance of anticipated change in many libraries is the move from one automated system to another with attendant timeline for preparation and implementation. The new system may be able to keep track and provide statistics on materials used but not charged out. Based on that knowledge and experience with the new system, an emergent change may be in the amount and nature of reference services provided during certain time periods. As we gain experience with the new system, an opportunity-based change that is purposeful and intentional may be a change in workflow. For example, some

were extremely slow and started to crash. Even though this plan looked good on paper, it did not work out. We had to develop an emergent plan based on running another communications software that will emulate at least a VT320 and run under Windows 3.1. Such a piece of software was locally available on every machine through an institutional site license. In this instance, the goal is to communicate with the mainframe at another location. The local boundaries are the abilities to communicate through a telnet session on Internet, emulate a high-end DEC terminal, and work with Windows 3.1. We also have the local expertise to make this work.

An instance of opportunity-based change came about in cleaning up error files created during data conversion in moving to the new system. One project involved writing macros on the preferred communication software on a Windows 95 machine to discharge more than 20,000 items. With the old system, materials placed in storage were charged to a special-use ID number. When the holdings records were converted to DRA, those items remained charged out. Initially, the Access Services Librarian thought of physically taking a scanner to the storage location to scan the barcode on every volume. A computer connection was not available in the storage location and the process would have been extremely time-consuming. Since a file of barcode numbers can be created, after a few tries, I succeeded in writing a macro to perform the job. This opportunity provided the beginning in the use of macros as a regular part of maintenance. Another macro was written and put to use in adding the word "storage" to all item records of material housed in storage. In case any of those items are requested, when it is returned and checked in, the workstation will beep and display the message on the screen to alert the student worker that the item should be returned to storage rather than for shelving in the stacks. More recently, macros have been written to change the permanent location of materials. Again, local resources are available to enable such an opportunity-based change. It is important to note that those circulation maintenance functions were performed by a cataloger for the benefit of reference and circulation so that reference librarians no longer have to explain to our users inaccurate or ambiguous messages on the computer screen. While the focus is for the benefit of the library, those tasks involve cooperation and trust among librarians from different departments.

Keys to such a change process are the alignment of internal support and dedication of resources. The support may involve cultural changes where library departments are focused on the function and performance of the total library within the institutional mission rather than performance of single departments relative to similar departments in other institutions. While changing the computer system affected the whole library, changing the communications software involved cooperation between Reference who must teach students how to use it, the Electronic Resources Unit who worked with the technical details, and the library representative to the state-wide organization who acts as the liaison between the local library and the organization. In using macros for maintenance, proposed solutions to perceived problems require cooperation among different departments and use of expertise that resides in different units in the library.

Thus, we look at the process in coping with change more as following recipes than blueprints where we must understand the assumptions behind the recipes, acquire intimate knowledge of available resources, and pay attention to the local environment.[8] Local perception is ultimately what determines success or failureCnot on how closely we follow the recipe but on the resulting dish that emanates from interactions between the cook and available ingredients within the environment provided by the local kitchen.

Notes

1. Peter B. Vaill, *Managing as a Performing Art: New Ideas for a World of Chaotic Change* (San Francisco: Jossey-Bass, 1991), 2.

2. Karl E. Weick, "Organizational Redesign as Improvisation," in *Organizational Change and Redesign*, ed. George P. Huber and William H. Glick (New York: Oxford Univ. Pr., 1993), 351.

3. Mary M. Crossan, "Improvise to Innovate," *Ivey Business Quarterly* 62 (autumn 1997): 39.

4. Wanda J. Orlikowski and J. Debra Hofman,

"An Improvisational Model for Change Management: The Case of Groupware Technologies," *Sloan Management Review* 38 (winter 1997):11–12.

    5. Crossan, "Improvise to Innovate," 38.

    6. Mary M. Crossan, Roderick E. White, Henry W. Lane and Leo Klus, "The Improvising Organization: Where Planning Meets Opportunity," *Organizational Dynamics* 24 (spring 1996): 20–35.

    7. Orlikowski and Hofman, 11–21.

    8. Weick, 350.

The Roles of Academic Librarians in Fostering a Pedagogy for Information Literacy

Gloria Leckie and Anne Fullerton

There is widespread agreement among academic librarians that they can make a crucial difference in ensuring that information literacy skills are integrated into university programs in some manner, and that they must make significant efforts to work with faculty to achieve this end (Warmkessel and McCade 1997; Baker 1995; Rader 1995; Lipow 1992). However, this is not an easy task, and numerous studies have shown that academic librarians and faculty do not understand each other's roles or expectations very well (Carpenter 1997; Crowley 1996; Hardesty 1995). The lack of understanding is further complicated by the existence of distinct pedagogical discourses for the two groups, which only serve to further distance faculty and librarians from each other. The purpose of this paper, therefore, is to examine the pedagogical discourses of faculty and librarians, and to put forward some ideas about how an understanding of discourse can aid academic librarians in developing pedagogical roles that will foster course/program-related integrated information literacy. The assumptions guiding the paper are that 1) academic librarians have an important role to play in higher education by helping students to become information literate, and 2) course/program-related integrated information literacy is a desirable way to accomplish this.

Pedagogical Discourse

What is meant by "pedagogical discourse"? Pedagogy is defined by most dictionaries as the science of teaching and so the phrase "pedagogical discourse" could be made a little more transparent by wording it as "a discourse of teaching". This wording is not entirely accurate, since pedagogy actually encompasses at least two aspects: teaching per se, and the study of teaching. Although it

---

Gloria Leckie is associate professor, Faculty of Information and Media Studies, University of Western Ontario, and Anne Fullerton is liaison librarian, Biology and Chemical Engineering, University of Waterloo.

is sometimes difficult to separate the two, this paper focuses a little more on teaching per se.

As for the word discourse, there are many meanings for the term, arising largely from the fact that a number of disciplines have developed the concept separately (McHoul 1993; Macdonnell 1986). The understanding of the term was revolutionized by Foucault (1970; 1972), who regarded discourses as bodies of knowledge with their associated practices (social control and social arrangements). Foucault also expressed the idea that knowledge and power are inseparable—one always occurs with the other (Barker 1998). Power does not arise as a phenomenon separate from knowledge, but is present in all of the social practices and relations of daily life. The Foucauldian notions of discourse and power, then, are intertwined:

> There are manifold relations of power which permeate, characterise and constitute the social body, and these relations of power cannot themselves be established, consolidated nor implemented without the production, accumulation, circulation and functioning of a discourse... We are subjected to the production of truth through power and we cannot exercise power except through the production of truth (Foucault 1980, 93).

In this paper, the sense of discourse used is from Vivien Burr (1995), who takes a socio-psychological approach to Foucauldian discourse. She describes a discourse as a "set of meanings, metaphors, representations, images, stories, statements and so on that together produce a particular version of events" or particular objects (p. 48). In other words, events or objects are socially-constructed and represented in particular ways by the discourses that surround them. Each discourse attempts to construct the event or object differently. Discourses are evident through the 'texts' of daily life (including speech acts of individuals, written documents, visual images, clothing, buildings etc.) and thus are available to be read. In other words, the texts of human activities or objects are the manifestations of the discourses which, in turn, inform and construct those activities and objects.

Pedagogy is one of those human activities that has a multitude of discourses surrounding it. What the discourse is depends upon who is doing the talking and the agenda being represented. For instance, 'standardized testing' is an object relating to the pedagogy of elementary and secondary education. Standardized testing is represented by several very different discourses. One is "testing as a means to ensure international competitiveness". Individuals (often from government agencies) who put forward this discourse argue that Jurisdiction X needs to know whether students are able to perform in mathematics and science as compared to students in other countries, and so standardized testing is needed to determine this. Another discourse is "testing as a control mechanism over teachers". Individuals who espouse this discourse are of the view that standardized testing is a sham, that it will do nothing to ensure competitiveness, and really represents a way to break the power of teacher's unions in meaningfully influencing the curriculum.

Each discourse has implications for a set of actions (or inactions) that flow from it, so the fact that one discourse prevails or becomes more powerful can have a very large impact on societal and institutional events. (Of course, even extremely entrenched and powerful discourses, such as communism, can be overturned and replaced by other discourses.)

Origins of Faculty Pedagogical Discourses

A discourse does not spring up from a vacuum. It arises from the context (objects, events) in which it is created, and in turn contributes further to the ongoing creation of that context by solidifying its representation. The pedagogical discourses of the faculty, then, cannot be understood outside of the dual processes of becoming a recognized scholar (through the attainment of a Ph.D.) and, for many, legitimizing that effort through becoming a tenured faculty member at an institution of higher education.

The essence of the Ph.D. process is that an individual must demonstrate that s/he can make an original contribution to knowledge within her/

his chosen discipline. How this is done depends somewhat upon the discipline. In the sciences, it is common to work on one's doctorate as part of a larger research project which is directed by established researchers. In the social sciences and humanities, it is quite often the case that the doctoral research is conceived and carried out by the student alone, with minimal guidance. Whether it takes place as part of a larger research project or not, the Ph.D. process is essentially a solitary endeavour in that it is a sink or swim situation. The wayside is littered with doctoral students who either could not start, or failed to complete, their thesis research. There is rarely a lifeboat in sight, and the old saying "Only the strong survive" is completely accurate.

To make an original contribution to any discipline is a daunting task. For the doctoral student, it may require years of studying the nuances of the discipline and its theoretical underpinnings, and passing a series of exams, before narrowing in on a particular area of study or research question. Within the area of study, it requires a thorough grounding in the literature related to the research question, an understanding of the theoretical and methodological limitations of previous research, and insights into alternate approaches to the problem or question at hand. Disciplinary expertise is respected and is not be taken lightly. Those who do not have the same level of expertise in a particular area will defer to those who do. Judgements about the value of one's scholarship and the quality of one's research are continually made, and are accepted as a fact of academic life. The discipline is paramount, permeating every aspect of the doctoral student's daily existence (Meadow 1998; Becher 1989, 19–35).

The process of acculturation to the discipline and to the academy continues even after the attainment of a faculty position. The new faculty member must develop a research program, must prove the value of his/her scholarship through faculty pedagogical discourses.

In the environment just described, teaching is often very much a second class citizen. In fact, as Hardesty (1995, 349) notes, university faculty often do not discuss teaching even with their colleagues. True, there are discipline-specific teaching journals, but are they widely read? For instance, when we asked the chair of a large social science department at the University of Western Ontario to find out whether any member of that department subscribed to the relevant pedagogical journal, he determined that no-one did. As well, the discipline-specific teaching journals are housed at the university's education library, which is removed from the main campus, making it highly unlikely that members of various departments will come there to read them. Nevertheless, whether discipline-specific journals are widely read or not, university faculty do teach, and there is a pedagogical discourse that surrounds their teaching. These discourses arise from, and further contribute to, the disciplinary focus and research-intensive nature of academia, and are bound up with the power relations bewteen the faculty and other groups on campus.

By using a variety of documentary evidence available at virtually any university (such as clauses in faculty union agreements, Senate minutes, campus newspapers), examining *The Chronicle of Higher Education* and comparable publications, or perusing discipline-specific pedagogical journals and the LIS literature, we suggest that it is possible to identify at least four dominant discourses, and two counter discourses. The following section provides an overview of each discourse, illustrating how they privilege certain types of teaching activities and inhibit others.

Dominant faculty discourses
Pedagogy as disciplinary integrity
This discourse represents the notion that each discipline has a sacrosanct core of concepts that students must assimilate before they can be allowed to possess an undergraduate degree in the discipline. Unfortunately, with new knowledge, most disciplines are expanding, so the amount of material that must be covered in a typical undergraduate degree is becoming increasingly unmanageable. This discourse, then, seeks to preserve the discipline by working against the addition of non-disciplinary and hence non-essential material (such as information literacy concepts) into courses. This discourse was quite evident in our interviews with faculty in science and engineering (Leckie and

Fullerton 1999), many of whom complained that there was just not enough time in the typical undergraduate course to cover the amount of material that needed to be covered to prepare students for more senior work.

Pedagogy as disciplinary expertise
This discourse reinforces the faculty member's right to present the discipline to students. As a scholar who has studied the discipline, the faculty member will decide what is important to teach and what is not, how concepts should be ordered, and will establish the rythym and flow for the course (De George 1997, 77). Strong adherence to this discourse may discourage the incorporation of other sources of expertise (such as librarians, and even colleagues) into the course. Ordering and timing of concepts may be a major issue, thus making it difficult to easily incorporate any information literacy activities into the course.

Pedagogy as academic freedom
A discourse closely related to the previous one, and arguably the most prevalent and powerful pedagogical discourse in evidence. In its pedagogical form (as opposed to its research form), the discourse of academic freedom upholds the classroom as the domain of the faculty member, who may teach any material that is deemed necessary, even if it is regarded as controversial (De George 1997, 76–81). Any interference with this right, particularly by those outside the discipline (such as administrators or librarians), is regarded as an attack on scholarship. Furthermore, the discourse of academic freedom includes the idea that faculty members, by virtue of their expertise, own the products of their pedagogy—they cannot be forced to give or sell their classroom materials to others.

Pedagogy as self-motivated learning, or bootstrap pedagogy
This discourse represents the idea that the university is a centre of individualistic, self-motivated learning. The discourse suggests that those who do not have the motivation will fall by the wayside, and rightly so, since there are too many students in university now who do not belong there. Numerous participants in the interview phase of our study (Leckie and Fullerton 1999) expressed variations of this discourse, noting that students who had not learned the basics of library research were "unmotivated" or "lazy". This idea has major implications for information literacy. It has been well documented in the LIS literature that faculty members often believe that students will learn library research skills on their own (as faculty members themselves did, by their boot-straps), either through exposure to the library or through contact with librarians (Thomas 1994; Hardesty 1991). Faculty members, therefore, feel little or no responsibility for students' lack of library research skills beyond giving assignments that require some library use.

Despite the fact that pedagogy is about teaching others, these four discourses appear to have less to do with teaching others than they do with the faculty themselves. This is because, traditionally, the faculty have been the most powerful group on campus, and still are, although on many campuses they view their power as increasingly under attack. As Burr notes (1995), discourses are about power relations - who has the authority to speak and to act, and thus maintain power. The dominant pedagogical discourses are part of maintaining faculty control over the classroom and its associated activities. Nevertheless, there are some faculty pedagogical discourses that run counter to the dominant discourses (hence the term counter discourses, borrowed from Henry Giroux's (1996) idea of counternarratives). Unlike the dominant discourses, these counter discourses tend to be more student-centred.

Counter faculty discourses
Pedagogy as the joy of discovery, of research
This discourse is voiced far less often but is still occasionally in evidence (for example, Weston 1993). Faculty who have bought into this discourse have a great deal of work ahead of them, because it requires a huge amount of effort to teach in a way that actually inspires the joy of discovery in perhaps hundreds of students. The traditional lecture course with an essay assignment does not necessarily fill very many students with joy. Faculty who are committed to this way of teaching may be more open to the idea of integrating li-

brary-based research skills into their courses and may welcome the input of librarians.

Pedagogy as integrated learning
There is also some evidence of this discourse, but it seems to be highly program dependent. The discourse represents the idea that there are areas of knowledge beyond the academic discipline that are very important for the future success of students. For instance, in the interview phase of our study (Leckie and Fullerton 1999), the nursing faculty were the strongest voice of this discourse. In the nursing program, critical thinking and research skills are heavily emphasized and are integrated into the health care curriculum, in the belief that nurses need to be able to understand medical research, respond accurately to patient inquiries, and think independently. Some medical science and engineering faculty in our study also voiced elements of this discourse. Obviously, this discourse holds the most promise for faculty-librarian collaboration, and for the incorporation of information literacy into the curriculum.

As a group, faculty have distinct ways of thinking and talking about pedagogy. For the most part, their pedagogical discourse does not involve notions of information literacy. As evidence of this, Julie Still (1998) determined that of over 13,000 citations that she found in the ERIC database from discipline-specific pedagogical journals, only 53 citations (less than one half of one percent) included some form of the word library. She concludes that "if the library and library instruction have been integrated into the academic curriculum, there is little evidence of it in the discipline specific teaching journals" (229). This fact alone would serve to distance faculty from librarians, who are very preoccupied with information literacy. A further complicating factor is that librarians have pedagogical discourses of their own, which differ from those of the faculty.

Origins of Librarians' Pedagogical Discourses
The pedagogical discourses of academic librarians are related to, and in turn reinforce, the values of the profession of librarianship. Librarians are acculturated not to the academy, but to a service profession. The values learned in library schools are concerned with responsibility to client needs, ethical behaviour, neutrality, and a commitment to making all kinds of information accessible in an equitable manner (Maack 1997). In addition, most library school curricula stress the development of rapid problem-solving and research skills, solid technology skills, team work, collaboration and professionalism (Buttlar and DuMont 1996).

At the risk of oversimplifying, it is likely fair to say that in many ways, the acculturation of librarians is quite opposite to that of the faculty. The values they adhere to have more to do with upholding the best interests of the group than they do with individual concerns. Librarians tend to place their clients' needs first and foremost and seek to work collaboratively, while faculty place their own research above all else and seek to work independently. Most academic librarians do not go through the individualistic process of attaining a doctorate, with its attendant acculturation, and so the tenets of academia that are so key to faculty do not have the same meaning for them. For instance, it is very rare to hear academic librarians speaking about academic freedom, yet this discourse is extremely prevalent in the context of faculty life.

Academic librarians are increasingly concerned with teaching information literacy skills and concepts, and so also have developed pedagogical discourses of their own. A few of these discourses overlap with those of the faculty, but most differ markedly. Through an informal scan of the literature relating to academic librarianship and bibliographic instruction (as represented in the *Journal of Academic Librarianship*, *College & Research Libraries*, and *Research Strategies*), we suggest that there are at least five dominant discourses, and one counter discourse.

Dominant Librarian Discourses

Pedagogy as disciplinary integrity
Like the faculty, librarians do have a strong pedagogical discourse that emphasizes the need to impart core concepts. For example, the ACRL Model Statement of Objectives for Academic Bibliographic Instruction (1987) is really part of the discourse of disciplinary integrity: these are the concepts that represent information literacy and thus should be

taught. As well, the LIS literature is full of examples of how difficult it is to adequately teach information literacy in limited time slots, because the information literacy curriculum is large and ever expanding. Adherence to the integrity discourse may make it difficult for librarians to think about new approaches to information literacy and may result in a high level of frustration that the integrity of the discipline cannot be maintained. It may also affect relations with faculty, who have their own version of disciplinary integrity and are not prepared to give time to ensure the integrity of another, less important discipline.

Pedagogy as meeting user needs
This is perhaps the most prevalent discourse underpinning information literacy pedagogy. It is slightly related to the faculty discourse about expertise, but has a different twist in that it is heavily influenced by the service and responsibility ethic (and, in turn, reinforces that ethic). Generally, faculty do not claim to be at all interested in their clients' needs—they assume that they already know what the needs are, based on the structure of the discipline they must present to their students. Librarians, on the other hand, want to know what their users' needs are so they can serve them better. With respect to information literacy, this usually entails figuring out what clients don't know, and then setting out to correct their lack of knowledge. For instance, the literature is full of examples of the mistakes that the average patron makes when attempting to search databases because they do not have the disciplinary expertise of librarians, who know how effective searching should be done. As the discourse goes, librarians have the responsibility to impart this knowledge to their patrons, who obviously have a need. Unfortunately, this discourse places all patrons (including faculty) in the position as the ignorant and uninformed. In some respects, then, it may work against true collaboration with faculty, who often are not regarded as having any real understanding of their own research processes and who cannot even identify their own informational needs.

Pedagogy as generic skills
This discourse represents the idea that librarians have a responsibility to teach generic skills (such as critical thinking and basic research skills) for lifelong learning. It is bolstered by government and institutional reports that suggest that the average citizen working in the knowledge society needs to have such skills to be able to continually learn and be productive (for example, Ontario. Premier's Council on Economic Renewal 1994). Some who voice this discourse also claim that academic librarians may be best positioned to do this work and should lead the way (Perkins, 1996; Editorial 1994; Hill 1991) Although the discourse seems to be gaining prominence, it is also highly contested, with other academic librarians suggesting that librarians are not equipped to teach generic skills and should stay within more familiar boundaries. The implications of this discourse are similar to those of the discourse on disciplinary integrity: increasing the range and scope of what ought to be taught, and thus possibly increasing frustration if not achieved.

Pedagogy as efficiency
It is frequently noted in the literature that academic reference librarians are faced daily with a barrage of similar questions regarding basic library skills. It is also pointed out that although one-on-one instruction is perhaps the best way to teach library skills, it is time-consuming, expensive and inefficient. The discourse that is related to these observations is one of pedagogy as a means to greater efficiency. If many students have similar questions, the most efficient approach is to gather them together and teach them all at once, thus making better use of the librarian's time and providing better service for more patrons. The efficiency discourse, however, leads to a dilemma in that it may promote stand-alone instruction, with no connection to the curricula of other disciplines, thus robbing it of much of its value. Interestingly, there is no comparable faculty discourse to this, since faculty have always primarily taught groups and not individuals, and are not known to be overly concerned with efficiency.

Pedagogy as peer status
Academic librarians have been involved in a well-documented struggle for decades about the nature

of their status vis-a-vis the teaching faculty. A large part of that struggle has to do with whether librarians do comparable work to the faculty and thus can be fitted into a similar model of career progression. Since most librarians cannot claim that they do the kinds of original research conducted by the faculty, it is even more imperative that they be able to demonstrate that they do contribute to pedagogy. This discourse, then, represents the idea that librarians are engaged in pedagogy and deserve to be considered as peers of the teaching faculty. Again, the discourse both arises out of and continually constructs the context—academic librarians actively seek ways to be more involved in teaching, thus reifying their claims, and lending weight to the discourse. There is no comparable faculty pedagogical discourse, since faculty do not have any doubts about their contributions to teaching. This discourse does not impress the faculty, who tend to regard anything less than full-time classroom teaching to be marginal.

Counter Librarian Discourses
Pedagogy as enhanced reference service
After more than two decades of teaching, and thinking and writing about it, the dominant pedagogical discourses of librarians are well established as part of the landscape of academic librarianship. Nevertheless, there is one persistent counter narrative that refuses to die, and that is the idea that librarians should stop trying to be teachers and should concentrate on doing what they do best, which is to offer good reference service. The most cited proponent of this counter discourse is Tom Eadie (1992; 1990) who stated that bibliographic instruction is a waste of time, ineffective, unproven and costly. He suggested that academic librarians would be far better off putting their energies and budgets into enhanced reference services. A more recent variant was put forward by Herrington (1998), who argued that bibliographic instruction is a cover-up for the fact the library systems are too difficult to use, and that librarians should be concentrating on making access easier, thus doing away with the need for instruction entirely.

If the BI literature can be taken as representative of the thinking of a wide spectrum of instructional librarians, many academic librarians involved in information literacy instruction do seem to espouse one or more of the dominant pedagogical discourses, despite the presence of counter discourses.

Discourse in Perspective
Faculty and librarians, who ostensibly are working to achieve the same goal of producing well-rounded, articulate and skilled graduates, do not seem to be on the same wave-length about how to do this, or what is important in doing this, particularly when it comes to information literacy. The dilemma continues despite evidence indicating that faculty across the arts, social sciences, sciences and engineering are favourably disposed to the idea that students should be information literate, yet many of them are doing nothing about it (Leckie and Fullerton 1999; Cannon 1994; Thomas 1994).

An understanding of the discourses that inform the work of the two groups can help us see why they have difficulty agreeing on the most appropriate courses of action, and seem to be at odds in accomplishing similar goals. Faculty are participating in discourses that serve to protect their disciplines, preserve their own disciplinary expertise and academic freedom, and uphold self-motivated, individualistic learning. Librarians are employing the pedagogical discourses related to meeting user needs, teaching important generic skills and providing efficient service. So, for instance, if instructional librarians on campus X employ the discourse of meeting students' needs, and the faculty in department X are using the discourse of disciplinary integrity, agreement on what to do about information literacy will be almost non-existent.

Of course, it is not quite so simple as that, either. Taken together, faculty pedagogical discourses work to actively maintain faculty control over the classroom. This frequently makes it difficult for academic librarians to insert themselves into classroom instruction in a meaningful way, or even to be considered seriously as a potential participant.

Roles of Academic Librarians in Information Literacy Pedagogy
As noted at the beginning, this paper takes the position that academic librarians have an impor-

tant role to play in the educating unversity students to be information literate, and that course/program-related integrated information literacy is a desirable way to accomplish this. But are the discourses so powerful and all-pervasive that there is no hope of a meeting of minds with the faculty? Does it mean that librarians have to diminish their commitment to information literacy? Not at all.

First, librarians should give some thought to their own discourses, and identify entrenched or established ways of thinking that actually impede their own efforts to understand and work with the faculty. As well, librarians should start to identify and listen to the faculty pedagogical discourses on their particular campus. For instance, the two counter faculty discourses that have been identified in this paper (and there may be others) are hospitable to ideas about information literacy and to potential collaboration between faculty and librarians. Librarians should concentrate early efforts on those faculty members or departments known to employ those counter discourses. As well, it may be that some of the counter discourses are more prevalent at institutions where the emphasis is placed on teaching more than research.

It is also important that librarians recognize that faculty are the more powerful group on campus and think of strategic ways to work for change within a system of essentially imbalanced power relations. It seems that librarians have not always clearly recognized this and have often dismissed faculty pedagogical discourses as somehow misguided or misinformed, preferring instead to employ their own librarian discourses as more appropriate. This approach is flawed: faculty pedagogical discourses arise out of, and reinforce, the faculty's view of the way in which academic life should be structured. It is foolish to assume that the faculty will be eager to embrace a librarian-centred pedagogical discourse that is essentially foreign to their experiences and ways of thinking. For instance, faculty will not abandon the discourse of disciplinary integrity in favour of one that stresses student needs.

Nevertheless, not all faculty adhere strongly to all of the dominant discourses noted previously, so there are opportunities within the pedagogical structures of campus to intitiate some blending of faculty and librarian discourses. Thus, even within the constraints of the dominant faculty discourses, it is possible, and important, for academic librarians to develop a number of different pedagogical roles in relation to information literacy. The roles that we have identified from our research and other studies include:

1) Librarians as Pedagogical Liaison

Perhaps the prime role for instructional librarians is one related to direct, interpersonal liaison with departments and programs. Numerous studies have shown that advertising the services of instructional librarians does not make much of an impact on faculty. This was confirmed yet again in our research where 31% of the faculty responding to our survey (Leckie and Fullerton 1999) and 40% in Cannon's 1994 study were not aware of the instructional services on their campus, despite advertising of such services. As well, numerous faculty whom we interviewed indicated that although they had seen advertisements for instructional services, they did not realize until the time of the interview that librarians were actually available to come into their courses. Although costly in terms of personnel resources, interpersonal liaison is the best way to inform faculty of the range of services available, and to suggest ways in which they might be able to utilize such services. Talking to faculty on their home turf is also a good way for librarians to get a glimpse into the pedagogical discourses espoused by various departments and programs.

2) Librarians as Pedagogical Collaborators

Our research has shown that a surprisingly high proportion (over 60%) of faculty, in science and engineering think information literacy is desirable for their students in the lower years, the upper years, or both (Leckie and Fullerton 1999, 14). Furthermore, about 46% of the faculty in the sciences and 50% in the arts/social sciences (Cannon 1994) would support some form of librarian collaboration to introduce more information literacy concepts into their courses. These findings would suggest that there is a role for academic librarians as collaborators in planning and delivering information literacy within specfic courses and programs. What form this collaboration would take, though, is very unclear, since the majority of faculty in our research also indicated they would not favour a team-teaching approach. It may be that a team approach is more appropriate at some institutions than others. Librarians should be aware that faculty may have varying definitions of what collaboration really means, and should be willing to work out several different models of collaboration in information literacy delivery.

3) Librarians as Pedagogical Leaders and Mentors

What about the 39% of faculty (Leckie and Fullerton 1999, 22) that do not favour a collaborative approach? Interviews with faculty in phase two of our study suggest that some faculty are willing to accept the discourse of librarians' own disciplinary expertise, and are quite happy to have librarians take the lead for information literacy delivery in their courses. Librarians ought to be prepared to take such a leadership role when it is warranted. This role has some drawbacks, however. First, in line with the discourse of respect for another's area of expertise, faculty frequently withdraw from the process entirely: 44% of our respondents did not attend the sessions delivered by a librarian in their courses (Leckie and Fullerton 1999, 23). Second, faculty then are subsequently unable to tell whether students have made any progress in developing their library research skills. Third, because they are unable to tell whether the information literacy components of the course have improved students' skills, faculty may be less inclined to continue incorporating information literacy in the future.

The leadership role, then, has some pitfalls. To be successful in this role, librarians should also develop a complementary mentoring role. Our interviews with faculty revealed that a large number of them did not have a very clear sense of what information literacy entailed, how to go about incorporating it into the course syllabus, or how to evaluate it. Librarians need to act as mentors to the faculty in this regard. They need to show faculty how information literacy concepts can be related to the course material, and it is especially important to help faculty determine effective ways to evaluate the information literacy skills that they expect their students to demonstrate.

4) Librarians as Pedagogical Supporters

Finally, librarians have an important role to play by supporting faculty in developing and broadening their own information literacy, and by assisting faculty who then feel comfortable incorporating information literacy into their teaching. In our research, 69% of survey respondents indicated that they wanted more hands-on workshops (76% in Cannon's study). Of all the instructional options presented, this was by far the most popular. There is no guarantee that assisting the faculty in developing their own information literacy skills will translate directly into the incorporation of information literacy in the classroom. Nevertheless, supporting faculty in this way does work to break down the discourse of "boot-strap pedagogy", as more faculty begin to realize that contemporary information retrieval is very complex and is not necessarily learned by osmosis.

Conclusion

This paper has attempted to illustrate how an understanding and consideration of the concepts of discourse and power relations can aid academic librarians as they attempt to foster a pedagogical environment that facilitates curriculum-integrated information literacy. Burr (1995) comments that "the discourses we employ often have political implications that we should investigate if we are interested in changing ourselves or the world we live in" (p. 57). Since universities are highly political places, this comment seems very appropriate when considering all the issues bound up with the teaching of information literacy on campus.

A dual process of self-reflection and informed listening may give librarians more insights into ways in which to approach faculty in different departments regarding information literacy. With respect to self-reflection, academic librarians would benefit from a thorough understanding of their own pedagogical discourses, and this entails some time spent in discussion with colleagues in the library system. Furthermore, as an object that is surrounded by discourses, information literacy cannot be viewed as separate from the power relations on campus. Librarians have tended not to see how information literacy activities construct and generate power, nor how their own pedagogical discourses may actually hamper their efforts to work with faculty.

With respect to informed listening, an understanding of faculty pedagogical discourses, and a better idea of how such discourses arise and function, will help librarians identify the particular discourses on their campuses. It must go further than understanding, however: face-face discussion with faculty is imperative. While this may seem like a time-consuming approach, it is the best way to gauge where information literacy fits in relation to how the faculty are thinking about, and representing, their own teaching activities. It is also the best way to determine what pedagogical role(s) should be taken in relation to the relative strength of each faculty member's disciplinary focus and his/her views on classroom autonomy, student needs, and collaborative approaches to teaching.

Bibliography

Association of College and Research Libraries. 1987. Model statement of objectives for academic bibliographic instruction. *College & Research Libraries News*, 48 (5): 256–61.

Baker, Robert K. 1995. Working with our teaching faculty. *College & Research Libraries*, 56 (Sept. 5): 377–79.

Barker, Philip. 1998. *Michel Foucault*. Edinburgh: Edinburgh University Pr.

Becher, Tony. 1989. *Academic Tribes and Territories: Intellectual Enquiry and the Culture of Disciplines*. Stony Stratford: Society for Research into Higher Education.

Burr, V. 1995. *An Introduction to Social Constructionism*. London: Routledge.

Buttlar, Lois and Rosemary DuMont. 1996. Library and information science competencies revisited. *Journal of Education for Library and Information Science*, 37:1 (winter): 44–62.

Cannon, Anita. 1994. Faculty survey on library research instruction. *RQ*, 33:4 (summer): 524–41.

Carpenter, Kenneth. 1997. The librarian-scholar. *Journal of Academic Librarianship* 23 (Sept. 5): 398–401.

Crowley, Bill. 1996. Redefining the status of the librarian in higher education. *College & Research Libraries* 57 (Mar. 2): 113–21.

De George, Richard T. 1997. *Academic freedom and tenure: Ethical issues*. Lanham: Rowman & Littlefield.

Eadie, Tom. 1992. Beyond immodesty: questioning the benefits of BI. *Research Strategies* 10 (summer): 105–10.

———. 1990. Immodest proposals: user instruction for students does not work. *Library Journal* 115 (Oct. 15), 42–45.

Editorial. 1994. A new order: BI librarians taking the lead. *Research Strategies* 12:4 (fall), 194–95.

Foucault, Michel. 1980. *Power/Knowledge: Selected Interviews and Other Writings 1972–1977*. London: Harvest Pr.

———. 1972. *The Archaeology of Knowledge*. London: Tavistock.

———. 1970. *The Order of Things: An Archaeology of the Human Sciences*. London: Tavistock.

Giroux, Henry et al. 1996. *Counternarratives: Cultural Studies and Critical Pedagogies in Postmodern Spaces*. New York: Routledge.

Hardesty, Larry. 1995. Faculty culture and bibliographic instruction: an exploratory analysis. *Library Trends* 44:2 (fall), 339–67.

———. 1991. *Faculty and the Library: the Undergraduate Experience*. Norwood, N.J.: Ablex.

Herrington, Verlene. 1998. Way beyond BI: a look to the future. *Journal of Academic Librarianship* 24 (Sept. 5): 381–86.

Hill, Patrick. 1991. Who will lead the reform of higher education? Librarians, of course! *Washington Center News* 5 (2): 3–8.

Leckie, Gloria J. and Anne Fullerton. 1999. Information literacy in science and engineering undergraduate education: faculty attitudes and pedagogical practices. *College & Research Libraries* 60:1 (Jan.): 9–30.

Lipow, Anne. 1992. Outreach to faculty: why and how. In Linda Shirato, ed. *Working with Faculty in the New Electronic Library*. Ann Arbor: Pieran Pr., 7–24

Maack, Mary Niles. 1997. Toward a new model of the information professions: embracing empowerment. *Journal of Education for Library and Information Science* 38:4 (fall): 283–302.

Macdonnell, D. 1986. *Theories of Discourse: An Introduction*. Oxford: Blackwell.

McHoul, A. 1993. 'Discourse', in *The Encyclopedia of Language and Linguistics*. London: Pergamon.

Meadow, A. J. 1998. *Communicating Research*. San Diego: Academic Pr.

Ontario. Premier's Council on Economic Renewal. 1994. *Lifelong Learning and the New Economy*. Toronto: Queen's Printer. Perkins, Michael. 1996. Bibliographic instruction? More than ever! *Journal of Academic Librarians*, 22 (May 3): 212–13.

Rader, Hannelore B. 1995. Information literacy and the undergraduate curriculum. *Library Trends*, 44:2 (fall): 270–78.

Still, Julie. 1998. The role and image of the library and librarians in discipline-specific pedagogical journals. *Journal of Academic Librarianship* 24 (May 3): 225–31.

Thomas, Joy. 1994. Faculty attitudes and habits concerning library instruction: how much has changed since 1982? *Research Strategies*, 12:4 (fall): 209–23.

Warmkessel, Marjorie M. and Joseph M. McCade. 1997. Integrating information literacy into the curriculum. *Research Strategies*, 15:2 (spring): 80–88.

Weston, Julian. 1993. Research made real. *University Affairs*, Nov., 6–9.

Unified Information Access for the 21ˢᵀ Century: A Project of the California State University

Gordon W. Smith and Marvin E. Pollard Jr.

Introduction
In 1994 the twenty-two libraries of the California State University produced a comprehensive strategic plan to prepare for the educational and information environments anticipated for the 21st Century. That plan, titled *Transforming CSU Libraries for the 21st Century*[1], identified as its first and foremost strategy a system of linking and integrating for easy access the full range of information resources available in all the CSU and other libraries as well as resources of the Internet. CSU libraries were facing frozen or declining budgets combined with prodigious increases in the rate of publication and in access methods to the expanding information cosmos. A new and innovative use of technology was seen as necessary to leverage the size of the CSU and its resources in order to continue to meet the information needs of students and faculty.

The Unified Information Access System (UIAS) initiative that arose from this strategic planning responds to a vision for the 21st Century that assumes that CSU students and faculty will interact with each other and with information using pervasive technology that enables every student and every faculty member to access, retrieve, display, and manipulate a vast array of recorded knowledge and information. The barriers of space—physical location of student, faculty member, or information—are expected to disappear, as well as the barrier of time.

Conceptualizing the UIAS
While our vision for UIAS was well developed in general terms, a great deal of work lay ahead in defining unified information access and determining its feasibility given the state of available technology in CSU libraries and the library automation industry. A consulting firm, RMG Consultants Inc., was retained in early 1995 with the charge to develop functional requirements of the UIAS, conduct an environmental scan of both CSU libraries

Gordon W. Smith is director, Library Resources, and Marvin E. Pollard Jr. is project manager, Unified Information Access System, California State University System.

and the industry, and develop recommended strategies for achieving unified information access. A particularly thorny concern was the use among CSU libraries of integrated library systems from several different vendors; a single system-wide vendor solution was not an option.

The consultants submitted their report[2] in October 1995. That report concluded, based on discussions with vendors and examination of CSU automated library systems, that UIAS was indeed feasible and attainable within CSU budgetary constraints. The report contained a proposed architecture for the UIAS and outlined a Request for Proposals process as an implementation strategy.

In developing their report the consultants also worked with CSU librarians to refine the desired outcomes of the UIAS project. That process yielded a vision of the UIAS as a dynamic and comprehensive tool for student access to information resources, for resource sharing among libraries, and for guidance and instruction in navigating the complexities of the expanding information environment. The UIAS is conceived as a single, easy to use, integrated, and coherent computer-based user interface which provides direct online access to or delivery of:

- print resources described in CSU Libraries' Online Public Access Catalogs and described in catalogs of libraries beyond CSU;
- print resources described in other bibliographic/abstract databases such as periodical indices;
- digital resources, including text, image, video, and multi-media;
- Internet-based resources including those on the World-Wide Web;
- guidance in the use and evaluation of information resources including access to self-paced information competence instruction.

The UIAS is dynamic both in its ability to respond to the rapidly changing information environment and in its ability to respond to the needs of the individual student. Students and faculty access the UIAS via a standard Web browser such as Netscape Navigator or Internet Explorer. The browser client software is linked by the UIAS gateway server on each campus to the library's patron data-file. This linkage not only provides authorization for users accessing licensed databases, but will also permit librarians to customize the interface for different categories of users. A faculty member, for example, can be presented a sequence of screens entirely different from one designed for a lower division undergraduate.

In summary, the desired outcome of the UIAS project is the creation of a powerful information access and educational tool that can meet the academic information needs of CSU students and faculty, a tool that is available anytime and any place.

Selecting the Development Partner

Our consultants had determined the feasibility of the UIAS and had developed an implementation strategy. Through a formal Request for Information (RFI) process conducted in the spring and summer of 1995, they had also discovered a high degree of interest in our project among library automation companies. Many of these companies had already identified Web-based access to integrated information resources as directions for development; our proposed project was seen as timely and felicitous.

The RFI determined that a number of vendor-proposed solutions met CSU's needs and had the ability to accommodate the diversity of CSU integrated library systems and to permit the incorporation of various systems and services. Interested vendors included Ameritech Library Services, OCLC, Innovative Interfaces, and several others. Many of the vendors regarded the UIAS project as the most advanced of its type, showing the way for other libraries. Some vendors suggested an ongoing partnership with CSU to develop their own solutions further to meet the needs of CSU even better than could be accomplished with their off-the-shelf systems and services.

It remained for CSU to identify a partner or partners with whom to contract to build the UIAS. Working with the consultants, we developed in early 1996 a Request for Proposals[3] for the UIAS. The RFP described the current CSU environment, detailed general system concept and the functional requirements of the UIAS, and set forth a process for proposal evaluation and vendor selection. It was written to serve as the basis for the ultimate contract for the system.

We were careful in the RFP not to prescribe a specific technical solution to providing unified access; rather, the document itemized a comprehensive set of requirements set within a broad technology framework conceived during the RFI process. We wanted to give the vendor community the opportunity to exercise its own creativity in proposing a design for the UIAS.

There were two significant areas of risk to the CSU in issuing the RFP. The first concerned the potential infeasibility of achieving the project's admittedly ambitious vision at all, either due to vendors' misunderstanding of the concept of UIAS or their ultimate conclusion that the system's objectives were unattainable. The second area of risk concerned cost. System-wide funds available for the project were limited; there was a distinct possibility that none of the vendors' proposals would be within budget. Both areas of risk were lessened somewhat by the groundwork laid during the RFI process, but they nevertheless remained sources of worry.

The RFP resulted in ten proposals; taken as a group, their quality was such that we concluded that at least our concern for the project's feasibility was unfounded. From the ten proposals, five were selected to proceed to a second phase of evaluation. Phase two of the evaluation involved confidential discussions with each vendor, pilot testing of features available in each vendor's system, and refinement of cost estimates based on the combination of hardware and software proposed. The last stage in the selection of a partner to work with the CSU in the development of the UIAS was the submission of a "Best and Final" offer by the five vendors included in the final round of the RFP process.

Selection of the winning vendor, Ameritech Library Services, was based on its submission of a "best value" solution to achieving the UIAS. Criteria included total system life cycle costing, maintenance and on-going support, technical excellence and state-of-the-art solution, vendor's performance, and system performance warranties. Following a period of contract negotiations, CSU and Ameritech signed a contract for development of the UIAS in June 1997. The name "Pharos" was selected as the new name for the system in its public manifestation.

The Architecture of Pharos

Pharos is created by the interoperation of the following systems:
- 23 Pharos Gateway Servers—one located at each of the twenty-two CSU libraries;
- the Union Catalog/Z39.50 server—located at the Chancellor's office;
- 4CNET—California State University's Wide Area Network;
- the twenty-two CSU libraries' local integrated library system (ILS) Z39.50 servers;
- other California academic and public library Z39.50 servers;
- the Internet;
- commercially operated Z39.50/HTTP servers providing access to indexing, abstracting, and full-text resources.

The Pharos Gateway Server is comprised of:
- IBM IntelliStation;
- MS NT 4.0 SP4;
- Apache Server 1.3.2 (HTTP);
- Ameritech WebPAC 1.35 with bibengine 1.35 (Multi-threaded version 3, Z39.50 Client);
- Ameritech RSS (ISO 10161 Protocol Server)
- MS SQL Server 6.5;
- Ameritech Remote Patron Authentication (RPA) Server.

The Pharos Union Catalog is comprised of:
- IBM RS6000—S70;
- AIX 4.3;
- Sybase System 11;
- Ameritech Horizon 5.x;
- InfoSphere—ProIndex.

Interoperation of Component Systems
Union Catalog

Because CSU libraries use integrated library systems from different vendors, the first step in developing Pharos was upgrading these local systems to include a Z39.50 V. 3 server. Building the union catalog was preceded by CSU's development of an algorithm that matches similar bibliographic records from the twenty-two library catalogs and then selects one of the matching records to be the *master record* retained in the union catalog. The program developed by Ameritech to implement this algorithm adds the local control number (LCN) to the master record from each of the matching CSU bibliographic records. The resulting MARC field in the Master Record is used to create a *Hook-to-Holdings,* which the Pharos Gateway Server resolves, using Z39.50, to dynamically retrieve the local call number and circulation status from each ILS. Holdings information is not stored in the Union Catalog. When fully operational, the union catalog will be updated on a daily basis with new, modified or deleted records from the 22 campus libraries.

The User's Perspective

To the user Pharos is a web site, or part of a web site, offered by the user's campus library. Pharos provides access to library information resources which can be obtained online, in the user's library, or requested from other libraries and/or document suppliers. The user is offered the opportunity to simultaneously search a number of catalogs and databases likely to contain the information desired by the user. Through the design of the screens generating the Pharos user interface, a novice user can begin with a general *Quick Search* that is intended to provide results that would lead the user to more specific information. Experienced users of the system can navigate quickly to topical screens that provide Quick Searches in subject domains. Expert users have access to more sophisticated searching options in specific databases or *native* interfaces offered by information providers that allow for more precise searching.

Authentication/Authorization

Integral to Pharos is an authentication/authorization system that provides a mechanism for controlling user access to impacted resources and services.

When using licensed resources or requesting materials not owned by the local library, the remote user is prompted to provide an I.D. number and last name by the Remote Patron Authentication (RPA) Server. The RPA submits this information to the library's ILS which then validates this user against its patron database. Assuming the user entered the correct information, the user is authorized to use licensed resources (in the library or anywhere else in the world).

Intercampus Circulation/Interlibrary Loan/Document Delivery

If a user has searched for information in Pharos and located a record or citation for an item that is not locally/currently available, he or she is prompted to request the item. The user generates a request for this item and is prompted by the RPA to enter his or her user I.D. and last name. Assuming the user entered the correct information, he or she is authorized to submit a request. The request will contain information about the user provided by RPA and the patron database, and bibliographic information provided by the database in which the user located the desired item.

Ameritech's Resource Sharing System (RSS) web service submits the request to the MS SQL server database. Based on profiling decisions made by the local library, requests can be automatically routed to: 1) a short list of CSU libraries owning this item; 2) other libraries, which the requesting library may have reciprocal borrowing agreements; 3) a document supply service contracted by CSU; and 4) national and international interlibrary loan services.

Users are able to check the status of their requests on the Pharos Website; doing so requires authentication by the RPA. The user is notified by an e-mail message when requested items are available. If the library chooses, the requested item can be delivered directly to the user.

Library Customization

Because each CSU library has its own gateway server, Pharos can be customized for each library in a number of ways. The library can select what combination of catalogs and commercial databases to offer in a broadcast search and can decide how to integrate Pharos with existing library web pages. The library can add a campus logo and other campus information sources and can create predefined searches and full-text hypertext links for faculty syllabi web pages, and web-based full-text course reserves. The Pharos Prototype Server can be reached at: http://pharos.calstate.edu:5080/

The Future of Pharos

Pharos is by design intended to be an expanding and evolving resource; as the educational, technological and information environments change, so will Pharos. The most significant area of refinement of Pharos that is planned for the immediate future is its customization for the user.

Pharos incorporates an important advance in library systems technology by linking the user interface to the patron database stored in each library's computer system. In addition to enabling authorization and authentication for resource sharing and access to licensed databases, this linkage permits the customization of Pharos to correspond to a variety of demographic characteristics of the user. The sequence of screens, branching options, help and guidance resources and search tools can be designed to accommodate the needs of faculty versus students, graduates versus undergraduates, residential versus distance learning students, and fine arts versus biology majors. Help screens, information competence tutorials, and pre-selected combinations of information resources can be packaged for lower division students, for example, while faculty can be presented with screens designed for more advanced searching. It is even possible to customize the Pharos interface to the level of the individual by creating and storing a user's own Pharos web page that contains profile and search history information.

As the CSU continues to refine and expand Pharos, it will build on two related ongoing system-wide initiatives: the Academic Information Services Cooperative (AISC) and the Information Competence Project. The AISC provides the content for Pharos. It combines the collective purchasing power of twenty-two libraries to acquire a core collection of electronic bibliographic and full text resources available across the system. It also encompasses a system-wide program of document delivery (books and articles) and agreements for expedited borrowing from University of California libraries. A new and innovative project within this initiative is the Journal Access Core Collection[4] consisting of a customized electronic full-text database of selected journal titles most often subscribed to by CSU libraries.

Information Competence Project[5] addresses the problem of making sense of the increasingly complex information environment; it is a critical element in the success of Pharos. Seventeen multi-campus projects have been completed or are presently underway and include both general education and major-specific instructional programs. Several are in the form of Web-based modules that will be incorporated into Pharos. An information competence fellowship program and faculty workshops are also being developed.

Conclusion

The scope and complexity of the UIAS project has entailed a daunting array of challenges, both in its conception and execution as Pharos. Through close collaboration with Ameritech Library Services, we have succeeded in creating a service to our students and faculty that has enormous potential for delivery of information and educational resources tailored the needs of the individual. Pharos in its present manifestation as a gateway to knowledge is far from perfect or complete, but it offers a framework we can build upon and adapt to the information and educational environments of the 21st Century.

References

1. The California State University, *Transforming CSU Libraries for the 21st Century: A Strategic Plan of the CSU Council of Library Directors* (Long Beach, Calif.: CSU Office of the Chancellor, September 1994). Available at http://www.calstate.edu/ITPA/itpd.html.

2. RMG Consultants, Inc., "Strategies and Plans for a Unified Information Access System (UIAS) for the California State University" (October 1995).

3. The California State University, " Request for Proposals for a Unified Information Access System" (Long Beach, Calif.: CSU Office of the Chancellor, June 1996). Available at the UIAS project home page http://uias.calstate.edu/UIAS.html.

4. Rogers, Michael, "Infotech," *Library Journal* 15 February 1999: 107–9.

5. See CSU Information Competence Project home page at http://www.lib.calpoly.edu/infocomp/.

Using the Scenario Approach for Achieving Sustainable Development in Academic Libraries

Steven J. Bell

Imagine in the not-too-distant future a hurried college student on the way to class. The student stops at the entrance to a classroom building and brings a miniature wrist computer up slightly and speaks to it saying, "Computer, make me an appointment with Professor Danzon for 4:00 p.m. next Tuesday, and remind me on Sunday night about that physics quiz I have on Monday—oh, and I have a paper to write on the development of the diesel engine during World War One for my History of Technology class—download some information that I can look at tonight." With impending advances in communications technology, computing miniaturization, voice recognition, artificial intelligence, and a host of other technical areas where new development occurs at ever increasing speed, this scenario may be less science fiction and more reality than we think possible. The implications of such change are significant for higher education institutions.

Under conditions of rapid, unpredictable change, library administrators will encounter increasing difficulty in achieving any semblance of rational planning. Consider the advent of Internet technology. What library administrator made technology acquisitions or planned for library service delivery based on the advent of the World Wide Web? None, because no one was able to determine the probability it would be created or the impact it would have as the primary conduit for electronic information.[1] Decision making can no longer depend on probability. Instead, we need, as Drucker suggested, to look at what has already happened that will create the future.[2] Environmental scanning and demographic, societal and technology trend analysis are all utilized to determine what an academic institution will need to survive and prosper.

Sustaining Our Values

W. Lee Hisle's theme for his year as ACRL President was "Facing the New Millennium: Values for the Electronic Information Age." Values are important to our profession. Hisle's concern was how will the profession maintain them in an environment of radical technology change, and he em-

---

Steven J. Bell is director of Gutman Library, Philadelphia College of Textiles & Science.

phasized that "stability can come from our values."[3] Therein lies the dualism that confronts our profession. How do we maintain our position as the primary change agents and early adapters of new technology within our institutions and still maintain the traditional values that are already being swept away by the floods of change? A known outcome of uncontrolled growth on a regional, planetary or professional scale is unsustainability. Unsustainability is a state characterized by the collapse of core values, progress, and prosperity. How do we preserve what is best about our present as we head into the future, and how can we, as library leaders, make wise administrative decisions to prevent unsustainability?

This dilemma is not unique to academic librarianship. Other disciplines are exploring a practice known as sustainable development in order to create a systems approach to preserving the core values of a profession or a service. This paper and associated presentation provide a discussion of sustainable development, and how academic librarians may use it as a guiding principle for progress. Environmental oriented professions, such as architecture or energy resource development, are able to more easily identify these principles and put them into practice. For academic librarians, the challenge is to identify a mechanism or process to provide an anchor to the positive values of the past and present as we head into an uncertain and unpredictable future? This paper suggests that such a process may be found in the scenario approach. Scenarios are stories about the future. The scenario approach offers promise to academic libraries for achieving sustainable development, and a model that explores the development of a scenario for achieving sustainable development is presented.

Sustainable Development and Organizational Change

Sustainable development is a difficult concept to illustrate. Good examples are nonexistant. Industrialized nations haven't figured out the sustainable part, and the rest of the world lags in development. There are many examples of where it hasn't occurred. In Carthage, the Roman Empire turned a successful agriculture system into a wasteland through over-cultivation and techniques that encouraged soil erosion. In the United States, we only have to think of whaling, the buffalo, and the Dust Bowl as historical examples of non-sustainable development.[4] Examples of unsustainability can be found throughout virtually every period of civilization and across all continents.

Contemporary thinking about sustainable development can be traced to the growth of the green movement that followed the first Earth Day in 1970. In 1987 the World Commission on Environment and Development put the idea of sustainable development in the form of an intergenerational golden rule: we must learn to meet the needs of the present without compromising the ability of future generations to meet their own needs.[5] The idea was formalized at the 1992 UN Earth Summit in Rio de Janeiro through Principle Number Three of Agenda 21. It stated "the right to development must be fulfilled so as to equitably meet developmental and environmental needs of present and future generations."[6]

Early developments in sustainability thought and policy applied mostly to environmental and ecological concerns. These are the arenas in which the failure to create sustainable development will profoundly harm our chances for survival. In time, organizational scientists began to explore the adaptation of the principles of sustainable development to the behavior of organizations. A number of different theories have emerged but two themes are consistent. First, organizational change causes instability that leads to an unsustainable environment. Second, organizations consist of people, and without a strong value system people fail to adapt to change. If people cannot change, organizations cannot change. Not unlike living organisms, organizations must also sustain or perish.

Organizational values provide a support system to enable people to survive times of instability. Harley, in a rare article on library sustainability, stated that because the pace of change in libraries is rapid and technological in nature, the possibilities for instability are high. To achieve sustained development in library automation, Harley recommended adopting a framework of ecological values. This framework consists of five instrumental values: (1) community; (2) wholeness; (3) posterity; (4) smallness; and (5) quality.[7] For library organizations, a key value within this framework is involvement in and support of both academic and regional library communities. Collaboration, internal and external, is a recurring theme in organizational sustainable development literature.

A Planning Approach for Rapid, Unpredictable Change

New technologies appear so rapidly that traditional strategic planning may now be too constrained to properly respond to crisis and opportunity. The new interest in scenario planning is in part a reaction to this weaknesses of strategic planning. Scenarios are stories about the future. This paper began with a scenario. Scenarios often appear outlandish. History provides repeated examples of the ridiculing of futuristic scenarios that later became reality (i.e., in the early 20th century Brigadier General Billy Mitchell was widely ridiculed when he proposed that airplanes would be able to sink battleships by dropping bombs on them). A scenario plan creates several stories. Each identifies how various elements might interact under certain conditions. Scenario planning does not create a single contingency plan, nor does it analyze how a change of a single variable can affect a process. It attempts to capture the richness and range of possibilities through narratives that are easier to grasp and use than great volumes of data.[8]

The steps for scenario planning are summarized here. Both Schoemaker and Giesecke provide greater detail on the process. First, determine the core issues or decisions for resolution, and the players affected. Second, planners identify, possibly through an environmental scan, the relevant issues of the immediate past, present trends and future possibilities. The planning horizon may be three to seven years. Third, critical uncertainties and driving forces are identified. For example, an uncertainty for an academic library is the degree to which constituents will seek out non-library resources over library resources; the force may be exponential growth in the ubiquitous access to global electronic data sources. Fourth, prioritize the uncertainties and forces according to their importance to the issues. Fifth, construct the initial scenario themes. The goal is to pull together ingredients for approximately four scenarios. A simple approach is to identify extreme worlds by grouping all positive and negative elements; a "winners and losers" scenario where conflict occurs is another suggested method. Sixth, develop the scenarios using a narrative sequence of events that shows possible and plausible happenings in each step. The final scenarios consist of plots that are easy to follow and remember. The final stage typically consists of evaluative or research methods aimed at testing the implications or potential outcome of the scenarios.[9]

Because it is difficult to conceive exactly what a sustainable library is or how the eco-framework would be implemented, the scenario approach offers a viable method for visualizing a sustainable library future. Using information about driving forces such as demographic change, changes in scholarly publishing, technological change, resource availability and change in higher education, a series of scenarios can be created to provide an image of what conditions would be necessary to allow for sustainable library development. Constructing scenarios can be an important part of the learning process, helping library leaders to clarify their vision of values to preserve for future generations of librarians and library users. The scenario approach can also enrich the process by identifying emerging risks and required actions for achieving sustainability.[10]

Scenarios for Sustainable Development

The scenario process begins with some thinking about the future. Three types of futures are typically envisioned: probable, possible and preferable. The probable future is based on trends that are fairly constant. For example, a private, four-year liberal arts college library could reasonably assume its future driving population force is an 18 to 22 year old demographic, while its economic force is tuition-driven revenue. The possible future attempts to consider "surprises." In the technology realm, a surprise force may be a new generation of light, handheld wireless computing devices that allows all students to connect to library resources from anywhere at anytime. The preferable future is the library's most desired image of itself. In a truly sustainable library, one that is guided by actions today that will create the stability needed for present and future generations, this image will grow from an organizational eco-framework.

When these driving future forces are identified and prioritized, main themes or assumptions can be developed for scenarios of sustainable library development. These themes emerge from the interaction between trends and driving forces. The themes suggested by this paper's matrix model are four different library futures: (1) failing library; (2) conventional library; (3) technocentrist library and (4) transformational library. They were derived using plot lines familiar to scenario developers, such as "winners and losers", "challenge and response", and "evolution". The matrix model itself is based on those driving forces with the greatest influence or priority. Two key forces are the eco-framework, which provides a set of principles for organizational sustainability, and values retention, which refers to the traditional set of organizational values that help libraries maintain stability. The initial matrix is presented in figure 1.

For each matrix quadrant a scenario results from intersecting driving forces. The initial matrix is further developed in figure 2. The scenario names suggest the outcome of intersecting forces in each quadrant. They also can provide a device to fuel participant discussions of the scenarios and their implications for a library organization. Participants, working together, create a narrative for each scenario that is tailored to the environment and driving forces particular to that organization. This model is designed for academic library organizations that want to initiate a scenario approach to imagine their own sustainable future.

Characteristics of the Scenarios

This paper does not allow for the unfolding of full scenario narratives. The intent of this discussion is to provide a model to engage others in thinking about sustainable development in academic libraries, and to provide a structure for developing a plan with the scenario approach. The short scenarios presented here briefly illustrate the context of each matrix quadrant and its characteristics:

Failing Library

This is a bleak scenario of a library organization that has faltered in sustaining its core values and neglected to develop an eco-framework to guide its development. This is the outcome of weak library leadership and decision making guided by short-term satisficing rather than sustainability. These decisions allowed the administration to gradually shift the library's resource base to other sectors of the institution. This situation was acerbated by the library's failure to keep pace with

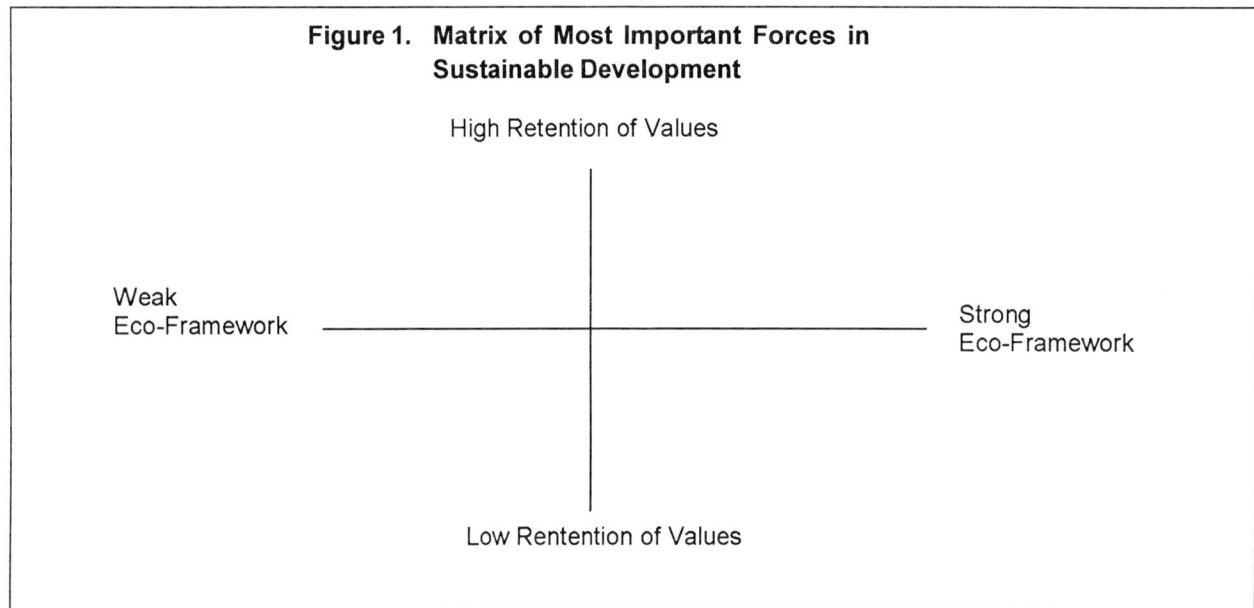

Figure 1. Matrix of Most Important Forces in Sustainable Development

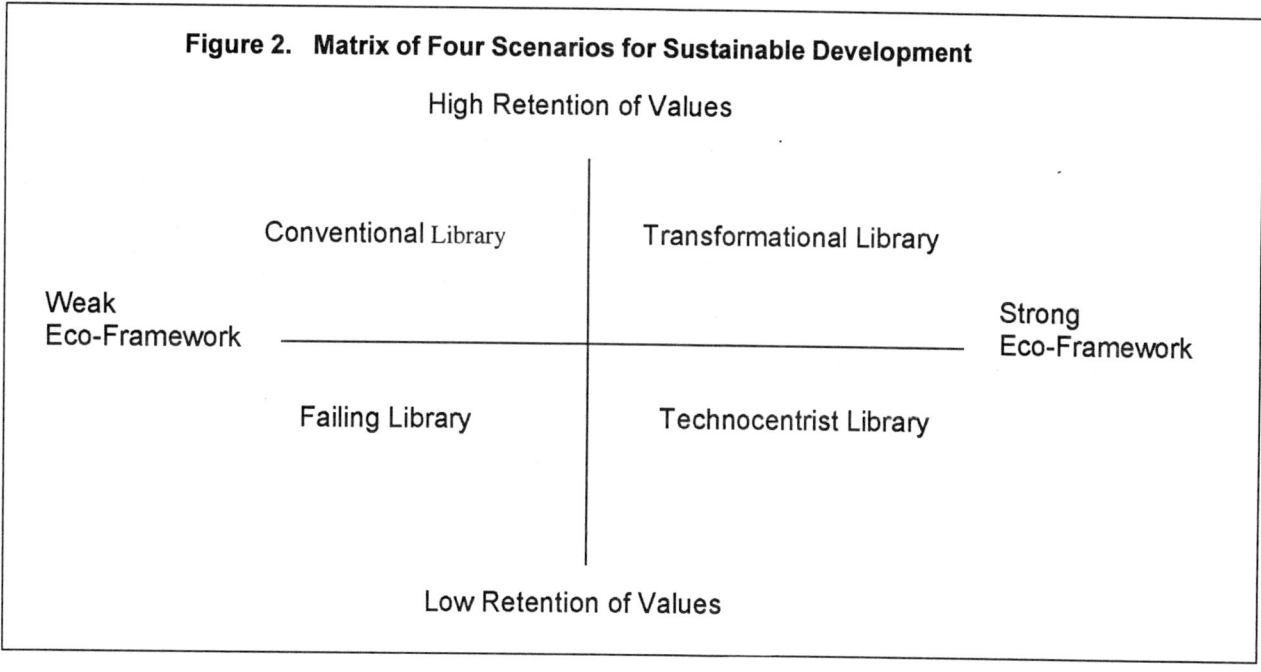

Figure 2. Matrix of Four Scenarios for Sustainable Development

information and educational technology, while other units embraced new technology for the delivery of educational programs, particularly Internet-based technology for reaching remote learners. Institutional administrators fell victim to the misconception that all information is available free on the Internet. Seeing the library's constant increases in periodicals as a weight dragging down the institution, decisions were made to cut library funding, and to encourage mass use of the World Wide Web as the primary vehicle for information retrieval. The library staff did little to counteract this movement. As the library drifted from its core mission and its ability to maintain its values, traditional user groups migrated to other avenues for obtaining services traditionally provided by the library. The library survives, but it's future is uncertain. Key characteristics of the Failing Library are:

- weak library leadership lacking vision and sustainability thinking;
- failure to innovate using latest information and computer technology;
- traditional functions are absorbed or acquired by other institutional units;
- control over library future has shifted to other administrators;
- collaboration with other libraries is virtually non-existent;
- fallen victim to "everything is on the Internet" syndrome.

Conventional Library

In this less pessimistic vision of library sustainability the Conventional Library sustains its commitment to traditional values, but an eco-framework does not guide planning for sustainability. The library is functional but stagnant. It stays afloat but drifts, rather than setting a course for growth and transformation. The library administration prefers to maintain the status quo. It maintains its value culture, and continues to be guided by the belief that library has a critical role to play in the educational process. However, there is a weak vision of a preferred future, and the library is slow to adopt new technology. The rest of the institution is moving ahead at a faster pace, especially on the technology frontier. The academic community perceives the library as an organization that is clinging to the past. In response, the library attempts to try to be what it thinks others want rather than being guided by a vision of achieving a sustainable, high-quality service organization. This results in a homogenized library organization that lacks excitement, diversity and community involvement. The library's progress is hampered by weak links with consortia. It

attempts to go it alone, ignoring the opportunities that might arise from cooperative activities with other library organizations. Key characteristics of the Conventional Library are:
- retains strong value culture;
- slow adaptation of technology;
- weak vision of future and direction library must take for sustainability;
- tries to be all things to all people; lacks service focus;
- aims for homogenization rather than diversity;
- weak consortia links.

Technocentrist Library

In some scenario matrixes this vision of a future library might be identified as "growth library". Progress is being made. The director has a strong vision of the organizational future, but the library's sustainability is still in doubt. The library's growth was fueled by shifting resources to technology development. New computers, networks, excess electronic resources, a shifting focus to remote over local users, and other new technologies were viewed as the path to organizational futurity. Technology, vision, and scale are important parts of the eco-framework, but in this scenario the library's technology centricism has blinded the leadership to other needs. Weak core values make sustainability an uncertainty in this scenario. More technology means less resources for staff training and development. Staff members are overwhelmed by the new technology, and grow unqualified to provide traditional library services. The loss of guiding beliefs leaves staff alienated and unfulfilled. Some leave for other opportunities. Those left behind are weaker in their ability to help constituents find their way through the maze of new technology. Key characteristics of the Technocentrist Library are:
- weak and disappearing value culture;
- technology perceived as solution to problems and link to future;
- human element critical to traditional services is de-emphasized;
- staff is alienated, overwhelmed and frustrated by fast technological change;
- strong vision of future.

Transformational Library

This scenario describes an evolving library. Improvement comes through a combination of strong commitment to values, and a leadership philosophy guided by the principles of the eco-framework. The Transformational Library is creating an environment of sustainability. Important decisions are examined through lenses that focus on sustainable development. Actions preserve the present library's traditional core values for future library leaders. Put simply, the Transformational Library's decision making is guided by its leaders concern for the library's future. The library director expends significant energy on creating a value climate and value culture. There is clear communication about organizational policies, practices and procedures to the library's staff and constituency. Organizational behavior is guided by a set of beliefs rooted in a tradition of service that extols the virtues of barrier-free access to information. The library views itself as a learning organization, and creates a setting for staff that encourages mastery, team development and learning through exploration and experience. Because individualistic organizations will be greatly challenged in the future, the Transformational Library builds bridges with partners both within the institution and beyond its walls. The key characteristics of this library are:
- guiding philosophy states present actions must sustain library futurity;
- emphasizes value climate and value culture internally and externally;
- embraces technology but allows staff to adapt to and master it;
- internal and external collaborative efforts are vital to organization;
- vision of future is library as evolving, permutable organization.

Conclusion

This paper is intended to challenge academic library leaders to think about, plan for, and develop sustainable organizations. They should be eager to take this challenge because the alternative is clearly unacceptable. A recent essay by Brian Hawkins, the President of EDUCAUSE, offers a vision of that alternative. In doing so he presents a similar challenge, but from a different perspective.

In the essay, Hawkins declares that traditional libraries are indeed unsustainable. Concentrating on just three issues, the costs of material, personnel and space, he explains that the traditional unit of analysis - the campus library - cannot exist in the current environment of higher education. Solutions to the dilemma of unsustainability, Hawkins suggests, lie in finding new models that focus on larger units of analysis (e.g., consortiums), finding greater efficiencies in the electronic distribution of information, changes in the scholarly publishing process, and sensible copyright policies for a digital environment.[11]

All of these suggestions make good sense, and will contribute to achieving sustainable development for academic libraries. This paper reinforces that effort by focusing attention on the importance of maintaining the traditional value climate and culture of academic libraries in tumultuous times. Sustainable development is a new concept for academic libraries. As library directors take their organizations into the new millennium and the specter of unsustainability looms larger, this is an opportune time to adopt sustainable development as a guiding philosophy in leading academic libraries. Our task is to better define what sustainable development requires and how it is achieved. The matrix model presented here is only the first attempt to accomplish that task, making use of scenarios to envision the characteristics and qualities of a sustainable library. The accuracy of these scenarios, like any prognostications, is open to debate, as is their ultimate utility for achieving sustainability. Robert Olsen put it best when he wrote, "The challenge is not to pick which scenario is best, but to create ever-better images of what a sustainable world could be like".[12] We can do the same for our libraries.

References

1. Foster, Clifton Dale and Steven J. Bell. "The Agile Technology Manager: Adapting New Technologies to Connect People With Information," in Haricombe, Lorraine J. and T.J. Lusher, eds. *Creating the Agile Library: A Management Guide for Librarians*. Westport, Conn.: Greenwood Press, 1998. 53.

2. Drucker, Peter F. *Managing in a Time of Great Change*. New York: Truman Talley, 1995. 40.

3. Hisle, W. Lee, "Facing the New Millennium," *College and Research Library News*, 58 (Dec. 1997): 764–65.

4. Muschett, F. Douglas, "An Integrated Approach to Sustainable Development," in Muschett, F. Douglas, ed. *Principles of Sustainable Development*. Delray Beach, Fla.: St. Lucie Press, 1997. 3.

5. Olson, Robert L., "Sustainability as a Social Vision," *Journal of Social Issues* 51 (winter 1995): 15–36.

6. Muschett, "Sustainable Development," 6.

7. Harley, Bruce, "Planning for Sustainable Automation," *Information Technology and Libraries* 14 (Sep. 1995): 176–79.

8. Schoemaker, Paul J. H., "Scenario Planning: a Tool for Strategic Thinking," *Sloan Management Review* 36 (winter 1995): 25–40.

9. King, James, "Scenario Planning: Power Tools for Thinking About Alternatives," in Giesecke, Joan, ed., *Scenario Planning for Libraries*. Chicago: American Library Association, 1998.

10. Gallopin, Gilberto C. and Paul Raskin, "Windows on the Future: Global Scenarios and Sustainability," *Environment* 40 (Apr. 1998): 7–19.

11. Hawkins, Brian L., "The Unsustainability of the Tradition Library and the Threat to Higher Education," in Hawkins, Brian L. and Patricia Battin (eds.), *The Mirage of Continuity: Reconfiguring Academic Information Resources for the 21st Century*. Washington, D.C.: Council on Library and Information Resources, 1998.

12. Olson, "Sustainability," 15–36.

"Why are you using the library?" or, The Real Goals of Library Research in the Academic Curriculum

Elizabeth D. Hammond

Good morning. I appreciate the opportunity to be on this panel and thank you for coming. As I begin my paper presentation, I presume the following story will probably date me but I'll just take that risk.

When I was an undergraduate student, there was one photocopier in the undergraduate library. It was a marvel to us, a big hulking machine that turned out smelly wet gray copies at 10 cents a page. The machine seemed to be broken as often as it worked but some people did use it. It seemed extravagant to pay so much for copies and so I, like a lot of students, kept to our habit of taking notes and writing laborious notes on note cards. It was inconceivable that I could or should photocopy a journal article or a page from a reference book. If I wanted a copy, I would do it the old fashioned way, by hand. Chances are, I would have located the sources I needed by using one of several print indexes or the card catalog. With any luck, I would have found some things related to my topic and I would have written down citations or call numbers for those as I progressed through the research process.

When I was an undergraduate student at the University of Illinois in the 1970s, library research was a labor intensive exercise. Many of you no doubt remember doing what I've described, It involved a lot of writing things down - call numbers, citations, quotations and other notes from sources. It involved choosing parts of the sources to use. It took a lot of time. I used lots of 3 x 5 cards. I had a system for keeping track of the bibliography cards and the related notes, of keeping it all in order. It was quite an effort. The process of putting a paper together involved shuffling lots of cards with cryptic notations and symbols, producing a draft paper and then a final paper, typed on my manual typewriter.

As I think back, I'm not sure what standards I was using to choose the material I used for my papers. My guess I was just glad to find anything

---

Elizabeth D. Hammond is interim director of university libraries, Mercer University.

and would have settled for what I could come up with. I have no recollection of a course instructor or teaching assistant providing any guidance about identifying, evaluating, or choosing sources. I was on my own. At that time academic librarians were just embracing the concept of the library as a teaching institution instead of as a self service book warehouse. I'm sure if I had asked for help, I would have received it but I don't think I did. If I had any notion of *why* I was conducting research, I would be surprised.

Looking back at that old photocopier, little did we know that smelly, messy machine was part of the first wave in the sea change for library technology and informational retrieval. For with that photocopier came the first shift from labor intensive information transcription to technology aided information gathering. Still to come were COM catalogs, integrated library systems, DIALOG, Infotrac, file servers, networks, scanners, floppy discs, ARIEL, sound cards, AMAZON.COM, and Java applets. So many new toys are now at our disposal if we want them and can afford them. While our work life has become one of troubleshooting PC's, un-jamming printers, and massaging HTML text, something else has happened and we all know it. The way students do research has changed. Students, and faculty, lead the charge for more and better information technology, for faster document delivery. As we can all attest, many students are averse to anything print and want the far more sexier and "easier" technology based material. We can all tell sad tales of wonderful print resources lying dormant while patrons pour over web sites of limited merit. Students also spend less and less time in the library building, using our networks and Internet providers to conduct research. We help that process through providing electronic reserves, full text or full image databases, and cataloged URL's on our webOPACS. And we will continue to try to keep up with patron demands while maintaining a workable balance of traditional and innovative library services and collections. In doing so, it may be said that some of us are on the cutting edge, some of us might argue we are on the bleeding edge, and some of us are on the trailing edge. Perhaps some of us are still looking for a foothold on the edge.

In thinking about technology and academic libraries, it is tempting to say that everything has changed, and indeed much has changed. But I would argue that one fundamental issue has not changed, an issue fundamental to how we conduct our business and how we interact with our constituents. And that is the question posed by my presentation title: Why are you using the library?

Just why *are* students given library based assignments? What is the purpose of a term paper, an annotated bibliography, or a book review? What does the course instructor expect the student to gain from the assignment? How does this project contribute to the learning goals and objectives for the course? And how is this communicated to the student? What kind of guidelines are presented for the completion of the assignment? What standards are put forward? Conversely, what does the student expect to get out of the experience? Does he or she *know* why this particular assignment has been given? For those of us involved in assessments and goal setting, using the vernacular of accrediting agencies: what is the desired student learning outcome? Unless we can answer these questions, our effectiveness as librarians, as libraries, and as partners in the education process will be hard to measure.

The common rationales for assigning students research assignments include (1) developing critical thinking skills, (2) gaining familiarity with the literature of the discipline, (3) reading, understanding and assimilating information, and (4) becoming an efficient and effective library user. I think we can all agree these are worthy goals and should be part of the academic experience. We certainly want to participate in helping students achieve those goals. The question is then, how can we arrive at a method that assures students learn what they are supposed to learn from the process?

If we briefly look at a research assignment, there are several components to the process. First, the instructor develops a course syllabus or outline for the entire term, listing textbooks, readings, topics to be covered, exams and due dates for papers or projects. Depending on the instructor, a document may be prepared that provides guidelines for the research project such as topic selection, scope, deadlines, etc. In some cases, guidance on information sources may be provided. Hopefully, a library instruction session helps students learn about the resources appropriate for the project. Thus prepared, students gather information, complete the project, and the instructor gives it a grade. With luck, the product fits the desired goals and the student is appropriately rewarded for his or her effort.

In considering that description, let's start with the information gathering component. We all know that technology has made finding information easier. Between online catalogs, full text databases, and web sites, students can generally find a plethora of sources to choose from. With technology, students and faculty are more inclined to do research. It seems easier; the electronic interface is attractive and eliminates much of the labor intensive transcribing of information. What used to seem tedious, difficult, obtuse, and time consuming is now more appealing, if not fun. In fact, it seems seductively easy. In the words of Tina Chrzastowksi "if you plug it in, they will come."[1] In short, the information gathering part of the process is generally no longer the issue. Our patrons can find plenty. The problem is finding, evaluating, and then selecting the most appropriate sources. It is now, and has always been, a matter of standards, of evaluation, of judgment. But whose judgment? The instructor's? The student's? The librarian's? Without guidance and standards, the student will indeed often take the first materials located and may not understand the consequences. Any five articles on capital punishment may fulfill the assignment requirements but what if there is no common thread to those five? What kind of final project will emerge? Is this knowledge? As one group of authors put it "all too often student forays into the library are papers that consist of information nuggets strung together by flimsy (but formal) transitions indicating that one source says X and another says Y."[2] Today, almost every day, we see students choosing the first five or six citations that come up on a screen, having satisfied what they believe the assignment requires. Observing this behavior, we worry about the other items not selected because they were on the next screen or in a different database. We are concerned that ease of access has replaced thoughtful judgment and care. As an aside,

I suggest that the dynamics of the selection process has certain similarities to a pre-electronic age. Take a volume of *Readers' Guide* from the early 1970s and open it to a subject such as gun control. Look at the citations. Note the little pen and pencil marks next to the first dozen or so citations, those at the beginning of the alphabet. Then look at the end of the citation list, those whose first words in the title start with R or S or W. Chances are there are few indications students got that far. They stopped at the first few, just as they now stop at the first screen display.

Without clearly articulated objectives for the assignment students will likely make poor choices for their sources as they do not know *why* they are doing the paper. If the purpose is to find a few supporting articles to support a simple thesis in a five-page opinion paper, the issue is not as complicated. If however, the point of the 15-page term paper assignment is to gather and assimilate material on a common theme, to employ critical thinking, to produce a product that exhibits true knowledge and understanding of the topic, then the research process will need to reflect the level of intellectual effort that will be demonstrated in the final paper.

How then do we approach the challenges of improving the quality of student research and the information literacy skills important for academic success? How can we as librarians participate in the measuring of our affect on student learning outcomes as demonstrated by library research? What role can we play at our institutions?

First, we can work with faculty to more clearly articulate the goals of a research assignment. The faculty member develops the course around certain objectives for learning. The relationship between the course objectives and the assignments can be strengthened and made more clear to students. It cannot be taken for granted that students inherently understand the relationship of a project to course content. Assignment design should also be considered; there is no "one size fits all" paper appropriate for every class or course objectives. The purpose of the assignment and the nature of the research intended should guide the project design and requirements.

In a 1995 article, Kathleen Garland discusses the purpose of research and how to make its purpose clear. She offers four elements that contribute to a meaningful research task,

> 1. students' understanding of the task, 2. their perceived connection between the task and other activities in the course, 3. whether they had any choices to make regarding the task, and 4. whether they felt they knew why their teacher wanted them to do this project."[3]

So, we need to encourage and work with faculty to clarify the point of the project in order to get things off to a good start.

We also need to articulate for ourselves and to others the difference between process and product. Too often students focus on the end result and shortchange the road that will get them there. As stated by Betty Dawn Hamilton,

> in research, the purpose of the assignment must be clear. If teachers want only content and perfection, then the product is what they are seeking. However, if teachers want students to learn how to find, assimilate, and synthesize information into a document to meet certain technological as well as intellectual requirements, then those outcomes must be made clear to the students and everyone who works with the students on the assignments".[4]

Second, we must find venues to provide instruction in the evaluation of sources. Faculty and students are bombarded with information choices. Making sense of these overwhelming choices should stem from the purpose of the assignment as articulated by the instructor and as understood by the student. Various criteria have been developed and suggested; the literature in this area is growing as educators face this dilemma. Many libraries provide web sites and handouts with suggestions for evaluating Internet resources and other unregulated materials. Teaching faculty and librarians need to work together to reach common understanding on what the instructor considers relevant information materials for a particular assignment so the librarian can be an informed partner in helping students in the classroom or at the reference desk. I'm sure you've had the same experience I've had of a student asking me if such and such a source is OK for a particular assignment. I am glad to give my opinion but always refer students to their instructors who can truly answer the question, and as I point out in language the student understands, I'm not giving the grade!

Third, the issue of resource evaluation leads to the arena of library research instruction. We already strive to present information skills training that is course related, and I would hope assignment related. A clear articulation of the assignment, standards, and goals ensures that our efforts match those expectations of students and faculty. Chappell et al, in discussing transforming research into inquiry, describe Evaluating Sources Workshops at the University of Washington and how students are instructed to put sources in context of the subject and to each other.[5] This is a good model for many librarians and faculty to consider, and provides the opportunity for true inquiry and information literacy skills that we desire for our students.

We need to also be mindful of not focusing too heavily on the technological side of research in our instruction while shortchanging guidance on the research process. Blandy and Libutti address this issue in an 1995 article saying "the addition of the technology layer to skills required for searching has narrowed the focus of library instruction almost exclusively to the use of technology."[6] Limited to an hour's presentation, we struggle to teach the tools but are often overlooking the process. True research does not progress in a nice straight line, even with the aid of computers and websites. There is a process of starting and stopping, making choices, changing one's mind, pursuing a certain point, that makes for a messy process. The computer is a tool; the intellectual process remains the same. In her 1994 article, Christy Gavin speaks to this issue, saying "treating research skills as a rote exercise negates its true nature, which demands a continual process of selection, elimination, and evaluation."[7]

Fourth, we can work closely with faculty to make sure they understand the world of research in the 1990's so they can best develop assignment guidelines and standards that fit the intended purpose of the assignment. Assigning "the Internet" as a source is not very helpful. Conversely, banning use of web based sources is not realistic for training life long learners. In articulating the research project, both students and faculty need to have the same basic understanding of the information world. Most students today, and many faculty, are fluent in computer use and demand more and better information technology. However, problems remain in sorting out what is useful and what is not for educational purposes. For many faculty research revolves around a small world of colleagues, listservs, journals, book editors, and scholars. This so called "invisible college"[8] is quite different from the broad, unfamiliar world of undergraduate research, and may mean that some faculty are not familiar with some basic information tools and how to use them. Faculty need to be fluent in the tools their students are using in order to help define which resources will best fit the assignment and the course goals. They need to understand what is available so they can help students make choices. Here, again, librarians play a role in educating and collaborating with faculty so that course objectives are met and these standards are articulated during library research instruction.

Fifth, we need to work towards identifying and teaching research core competencies in for students and then ways to measure students' grasp of those competencies. We should work with faculty and curriculum decision makers to make sure we are on the same page. My Mercer/ Atlanta colleagues are developing such a project that I hope we will adopt in Macon, too. Here is a perfect opportunity to directly measure the impact libraries have on student learning. If we can outline the goals and objectives for these competencies, then objective and subjective measures of those goals can follow. It must be more than technological fluency, however. Blandy and Libutti have identified four layers of learning in research in an electronic environment :

(1) the Inquiry layer, when the student becomes engaged in the forming of the questions, (2) the Library Layer, when the student interacts with library resources and personnel for information gathering, (3) the Technology layer, when s/he can manipulate information systems efficiently and effectively, and (4) the Scholarly layer, when the student can make judgments about information sources and content and assimilate information into knowledge and personal growth.[9]

The authors argue that the technology layer threatens to overshadow the other two, but it is the 1st and 4th, Inquiry and Scholarly, which provide the backbone for lifetime learning and intellectual growth.

Finally, I think it is obvious that the true goal of research is the same as that for the entire academic experience—the cultivation and assimilation of knowledge. Students engage in exploring the nature of an academic discipline during their course of study. They learn the way that discipline operates. They learn the structure, the language, the tools of the field. In large part, libraries provide the raw information for their inquiry. We enable students and faculty to locate the information sources that they need for their course work and intellectual development. Choosing the right sources is part of the intellectual exercise. Using various technological tools is only part of the process. The overall mission in which we all share, faculty, students and librarians, is making sense of the information arena. Maybe one of the reasons I look back at the ways I did research with some fondness is that I have a sense I may have learned more in writing down notes on note cards than in just highlighting pages. One can compress the time it takes to find information but one cannot compress the time needed for meaningful information processing, for thoughtful consideration of the text and the context of that text. These skills, the inquiry layer and the scholarly layer, are our goals. We must embrace the challenges and find the opportunities to ensure our students reach those layers for their academic success.

Notes
1. Tina E. Chzastowski, "Do Workstations Work Too Well? An Investigation into Library Work-

station Popularity and the 'Principle of Least Effort,'" *Journal of the American Society for Information Science* 46, no. 8 (1995): 638–41.

2. Virginia A. Chappell, Randall Hensley, and Elizabeth Simmons-O'Neill, "Beyond Information Retrieval: Transforming Research Assignments into Genuine Inquiry," *Journal of Teaching Writing* 13, no. 1–2 (1994): 209–24.

3. Kathleen Garland, "The Information Search Process: A Study of Elements Associated with Meaningful Research Tasks," *School Library Media Annual* 13 (1995): 171–83.

4. Betty Dawn Hamilton, "The Purpose of Information and Technology Assignments: Process or Product?," *Technology-Connection* 13, no. 10 (1997): 18–19.

5. Chappell et al., "Beyond Information Retrieval," 217.

6. Susan Griswold Blandy and Patricia O'Brien Libutti, "As the Cursor Blinks: Electronic Scholarship and Undergraduates in the Library," *Library Trends* 44, no. 2 (1995): 279–305.

7. Christy Gavin, "Guiding Students Along the Information Highway: Librarians Collaborating with Composition Instructors," *Journal of Teaching Writing* 13, no. 2 (1994): 225–35.

8. Ibid.

9. Blandy and Libutti, "As the Cursor Blinks," 293.

Contributed Papers

Acquiring New Knowledge Skills

Expansion of Electronic Resources: Superhighway to Campus Visibility

Francie C. Davis

Abstract

In an effort to provide easier access to databases, to expand resources to full-text, and to reduce the time-consuming process of updating loose-leaf paper subscriptions. Dowling College Library recently underwent a major transformation in its delivery of electronic information to its customers. The library went from DOS to Windows and online access, from CD-ROM to Internet delivery, from single stand-alone units to networked CD-ROMs, and from paper to a networked digital format. The disruptive transition required a total re-thinking of the delivery of information literacy to the library's customers, a serious look at library relationships, and a greater emphasis on communication, planning and training. In addition, the success of the project seriously improved the view of the role of librarians on campus by providing cutting-edge technology campus-wide.

For the success of Dowling's conversion project, teamwork was used to involve computer services, librarians, and administration in the planning and implementation of the project. Communication proved to be an essential component in fostering a cooperative environment maximizing the project's fruition. Faculty and administration reticence to attend classes attended by staff, was addressed by the librarians' using a well-known management technique and targeting specific interest groups to introduce them in the new information literacy program. The immense success of the entire project gave the librarians a new visibility that has proved quite positive and helped spur them into a leadership role on campus.

This paper will examine the lessons learned and provide some suggestions for the success of such programs. The audience will be asked to share their experience in bringing electronic resources to academic libraries. Discussion will focus on the diversity of techniques that can be used to accomplish this goal.

Francie C. Davis is reference librarian, Dowling College.

Introduction

What a wonderful opportunity we have as librarians. In one fell swoop, we can revitalize our image simply by doing our job, embracing the changes that are being thrust upon us, and demonstrating what we do best: evaluate, select, and disseminate information. At Dowling College, we have done just that. We recently converted to better access to our database subscriptions. We expanded from citation to full text access where available, upgraded from DOS to Windows 95, CD-ROM to online access, stand-alone to networked access, and paper to CD-ROM access. In so doing, we also converted the images of the library and the librarians to cutting edge and technologically astute. Formerly seen as stepchild members of the faculty, the librarians are now a respected segment of the faculty. How did all this happen?

Dowling College is a small liberal arts college located sixty miles east of Manhattan on the Connetquot River in an old Vanderbilt mansion on the south shore of Long Island, New York. Our student body is non-traditional and the main areas of specialization are Aviation and Transportation, Business and Education. Dowling, a relatively young institution, founded in 1955, relies heavily on its electronic resources to supplement its small collection.

When the librarians decided that access to full text databases would be beneficial to our customers, several key elements went into operation. All of them were essential to the project and comprise the *Critical Success Factors* necessary to the fulfillment of the operation. They are **planning**, **communicating**, and **training**. Do not undertake a project of this magnitude and breadth without considering those three elements. Let me repeat them. **Plan** for the conversion and consider the consequences. **Communicate** with *everyone* who will be affected by the conversion. And **train** everyone who will use the new system. All of this is simple, good common sense, you say? It is when you think about it. But when you are deeply involved in it, common sense can disappear.

Planning

You will need three plans to be prepared: a **Technology Plan**, a **Preparation Plan**, and a **Transition Plan**. The *Technology Plan* addresses how such a conversion will impact not only the immediate resources, but also the rest of the campus. For instance, we converted from Windows 3.1 to Windows 95 while the rest of our campus was still using Windows 3.1. The different Windows versions meant that access to our networked CD-ROMs was reduced from whole-campus access to library-access only. Thus, the improvement in resources resulted in a diminution of services instead of an expansion of access. Although we planned for multiple platforms, our technology support reneged on its commitment to our vision.

While formulating this plan, get your Computer Services Department involved. You will need their advice on hardware and the feasibility of the project. Because the success of the project will rely heavily on their technical expertise, it is vital to have their input and to get them to buy into the project. The plan will also need the administration's approval for funding. If you prepare a plan before approaching administration with your request, they will be more likely to support your project.

Your *Preparation Plan* addresses how you will proceed: What vendors will you consider? What databases will you purchase? What are your needs? How do you plan to access the information? What kind of authentication will you use? How will you distribute passwords? How will you deal with a change in password or URL? How will you keep everyone informed? What does everyone need to know? Who needs to know it? What is a fair price for the services?

Keep in mind the population you serve when you evaluate the various full text providers under consideration. Which databases will give you the best coverage for your curriculum? With our non-traditional student population, I sought a database that would support our curriculum and give the easiest, most intuitive access to our customers. One useful byproduct was that it would require the least amount of instruction. Be sure to be thorough in this evaluation because there undoubtedly will be challenges to your decision.

Preview the various resources and get feedback from as many users as possible. Then do a cost analysis to see which, if any, subscriptions can be cancelled to make this project affordable.

You may be fortunate with no budgetary constraints and, hence, cancellations. I was not.

Your Transition Plan is very important to the success of your project. You must anticipate all potential possibilities and disasters and be prepared for them. What will you do with the old version of the database when the new one is available? How will you deal with staff who much prefer the older version of *everything* that you are trying to upgrade? How will you inform everyone of the change? What do they need to know? I provided countless charts, lists, and timelines that served as security blankets to calm my staff's frustration during the "change."

Remember that the planning process helps you anticipate both the expected and the unexpected. Plan for the following:

- *Opposition to change*. How will you handle it?
- *Access to the databases*. What type of security will you use? Will you use IP authentication or passwords?
- *Web access to the databases*. Do you have control of your own web page? Is the web version as good as the CD-ROM?
- *Networked CD-ROMs*. Will access be possible from the entire campus? Off campus?
- *Transition from one system to the other*. What will you do?
- *Training* of staff, students, faculty, and administration. How will you approach it? Who will do it?
- *Reworking manuals* for your customers and staff. When will this be done? Who will be responsible?

It is vital to enlist the support of colleagues. Because change is not always welcomed, this is an important challenge. I found this step especially important. Budget cuts impacted this project and I needed to rely upon each of my colleagues to voluntarily offer a substantial portion of her budget to support my project's success. All of this takes time and patience so plan for it!

Communication

Because transition is really a four-letter word, one of the essential components to consider is communication. Communicate with *everyone*! Communicate more than you ever think is necessary. Let the administration know your plans and their benefit. Let Computer Services know what you are trying to achieve. Let the faculty know what is coming. This will help you to enlist their support. Tell the students what is happening. But above all, let your staff and colleagues know. Tell them what is coming, when to expect it and what the projected ramifications will be. Give them written lists of how the transition will unfold. Remember they will be on the front lines and they need to know what to expect. Do not assume they will understand the consequences of your announcements. Do not even assume they read or listen to your announcements. But if you put everything in writing, they will be able to refer to the written notices when they have the need. And they will.

Training

Training is essential to your project. If you want customers to be successful with your new, improved resources, you need to provide the best opportunity for them. You need to train them on the new features, the idiosyncrasies, and the databases' toots and whistles. Take advantage of every opportunity handed to you. We set up computer literacy classes for the entire campus, volunteered to address administrative councils, presented at faculty colloquia, revamped our Information Instruction classes, and gave interviews for the campus newspaper.

New Visibility

I have not told you of obstacles encountered during this project. You can read about those by going to our library web page at http://library.dowling.edu and reading my paper given at *Computers in Libraries '98*. Rather, I want you to benefit from the pearls of wisdom that I learned having successfully navigated a major conversion of access to electronic resources. More importantly, I want you to recognize the consequent benefits such a conversion can have for both the librarians and the library. To do so, I will use specific examples from our experience.

Let us now look at how the conversion of our electronic resources has changed the librarians' campus image. For some time, the librarians had been providing regional Internet classes and campus-wide computer literacy classes on Internet Searching, Database Searching, Microsoft Word, and PowerPoint. These classes had become quite popular, especially with the secretaries on campus. Although we tried many different approaches to getting the faculty to attend, we had limited success. When we converted our electronic resources, we provided ourselves with a golden opportunity. Everyone needed an introduction to the resources and each person could embrace the change, suffering no loss of face, an important consideration. A major effort to inform the campus of our new resources brought an excellent response. When we instituted catalog access to other colleges' library catalogs, the Associate Provost invited me to show off our gateway. Later, when we began to offer full text online, the Provost invited me to address the College administration. I gladly accepted. I volunteered to teach a faculty colloquium on the new resources available from faculty offices. The response was enthusiastic.

Perhaps the best response has come from two different programs that we now offer: off campus access to online databases and plagiarism detection on the Internet. Since our campus provides no dial-in-access, the faculty were frustrated that they could not research their topics from home. With Web Access Management, we now provide off-campus access to our online database subscriptions. The faculty are thrilled. From the number of students' calls I have had and my recent statistics reports, I know the service is well used.

In addition, I began to run a program to teach faculty how to identify papers that had been plagiarized from the Internet. It is a back-door way of teaching Internet searching techniques to faculty. And best of all, it works! It is a really satisfying to do a plagiarism search and find the dastardly source. It is especially gratifying when word-of-mouth publicity for this service increases its demands.

Your web page can become a major venue for accessing your databases. We were given control of our web page, redesigned it, converted to a web version of our catalog and provided off campus access to our online databases through Web Access Management, a module available through our library system. The seamless access to databases, catalog, and web page information are all customer friendly. In addition, our web page supports the curriculum with such sections as librarian-evaluated Subject Area Internet Resources and Course Support for our Information Instruction classes. These areas are all designed for ease of use and have been well received by our customers.

As I have mentioned, we now put individually tailored Course Support pages for each of the Information Instruction classes on our web page. Each librarian uses these as his/her basis for teaching each class. Students are able refer to this information from anywhere and we no longer need to print reams of paper and kill a forest to support our program. The teaching faculty is pleased with the customized job each class receives and impressed with the currency of the information.

Each of the librarians is responsible for maintaining the annotated Subject Area Internet Resources pages that are designed to supplement and support our curriculum. Faculty and students alike find these useful as starting points for their research. Among our criteria for inclusion are the following stipulations: each site must be the best on the subject and each site must be good enough to be included in and used as our own personal bookmarks. These criteria helped eliminate the tendency to list all sites on a subject and the pages are, in fact, replacing our bookmarks at the reference desk.

We have used the opportunity of having a library web page to bring visibility to the librarians and, in essence, to toot our own horn. We now put papers we have written and PowerPoint presentations we have given at meetings on our web page for others to see. While this allows meeting attendees access to the information, it also lets the rest of our faculty know that we are professionally active regionally, nationally, and internationally.

Our catalog provides immense customized service to our community. The catalog gateways to other library catalogs are very helpful when students are doing research. Customers can now do research, place interlibrary loan requests, renew their books, and request that items be held for them from home. All of this is great for public relations.

With the new union contract, the librarians are now represented on each of the campus standing committees. In addition, there are other key faculty posts filled by one or another of the librarians. While our new campus visibility is not the sole byproduct of the conversion of our electronic resources, I cannot help but believe that it has a great deal to do with the more positive way in which the other faculty interact with the library faculty today.

Conclusion

What have we learned from our experience? Go for it! Embrace the changes that are coming your way. Indeed, technology is making our job a lot more challenging. But by making our resources more accessible to our customers, by eliminating the tedium of the process of research, and by thrusting us into the forefront of the twenty-first century, libraries and librarians are benefiting from one of the unforeseen by-products of technology. Libraries and librarians are now viewed by many as leaders in this arena. Let's not lose that advantage.

Extinguishing Slow Fires: Cooperative Preservation Efforts

Brian J. Baird and Bradley L. Schaffner

For years filmmakers in Hollywood have relied on the image of a book burning to illustrate intolerance. In the movie *Indiana Jones and the Last Crusade* Steven Spielberg utilizes this image to make clear to the audience that Nazism was an evil ideology. It is safe to say that librarians would agree with Hollywood's view of book burning as the ultimate form of censorship and intolerance. Fortunately, book burning is a rare occurrence, at least in democratic nations. However, untold numbers of books are being destroyed, not by book burnings, but through the slow fires of deterioration. These flames of destruction are not being fanned by intolerance or censorship, but by a lack of funds or indifference to the problem. One promising solution is cooperative preservation programs that can provide a viable cost-effective way to preserve important and significant publications.

There is no question that the preservation of printed materials must be given a high priority if we are to save these resources for future generations of students and scholars. Large portions of most libraries' published holdings are printed on substandard acidic paper that will become embrittled. Paper is considered brittle when it breaks after less than two double folds. Recent condition surveys at the University of Kansas Libraries indicate that six percent of library holdings have embrittled paper. In addition, some holdings, such as Russian and Soviet publications, have a much higher percentage of brittle volumes with 17.43 percent currently evaluated as brittle. Complicating matters is the fact that over 65 percent of the general collections and 87 percent of all Russian and Soviet holdings at the University of Kansas Libraries are printed on acidic paper that will eventually become brittle. Although the percentage of brittle materials may vary by institution, most research libraries face similar challenges with significant percentages of brittle collections. If these

---

Brian J. Baird is preservation librarian, University of Kansas Libraries; E-mail: bbaird@ukans.edu. Bradley L. Schaffner is Russian studies librarian, University of Kansas Libraries; E-mail: bschaffn@ukans.edu.

items do not receive some type of preservation treatment, they will eventually deteriorate to the point where they will be unusable. There is no debating that preservation efforts must be made to save meaningful materials—the important question is how can this be accomplished?

Preservation specialists can employ a number of treatments to save publications. These treatments range from relatively simple repairs to rebinding materials to major conservation work to reformatting materials. Generally, brittle items are preserved by the latter. Reformatting involves the transfer of the information in the original publication to digital images, microforms, or preservation quality photocopy facsimiles. Unfortunately, the process can be expensive, and a single library could not afford to save all of its holdings that need this type of preservation treatment. In an effort to be cost-effective, libraries need to work together. This paper will briefly review reformatting options and then examine past and current cooperative programs which have successfully mobilized resources to preserve publications.

It is important to use the appropriate format when preserving materials. One should not fall into the trap of using one format for all preservation projects. For example, digitizing all items in a preservation project simply because it makes use of cutting-edge technology is not the best use of preservation funds. Many publications, such as individual volumes in the social science or humanities, are best preserved on microfilm or photocopy facsimiles.

There is no doubt that electronic formats are often more versatile than paper publications because full-text or key word indexing provides excellent searching capabilities. Many publications such as encyclopedias, indexes, bibliographies, and other reference works generally benefit from the enhanced access and storage capabilities of digitization. However, its limitations and drawbacks must be considered when working on preservation projects. First and foremost is the issue of cost. After an item is digitized, there are ongoing storage costs. A recent study shows that on-site storage of electronic information costs a library sixteen times more than housing books and serials. Moreover, there are many unanswered questions regarding the feasibility of archiving electronic information. Given the rapid development of computer technology and the lack of format and storage standards, one has to wonder if current electronic information will be accessible in five to ten years. As Marcia Watt and Lisa Biblo observed: "What use is a disc that can last 500 years, even 100 or 50 years, if there is no machine which provides access to the information on the disc?"

Furthermore, when choosing a reformatting treatment, one must also consider the patron's needs and preferences. In libraries we often see users printing off page upon page of electronic text. While electronic formats provide ease of access, users often prefer to print off the text into hard copy for their use. In a recent essay, Umberto Eco observed that rather than moving us towards a "paperless" society electronic texts have actually resulted in the increased production of printed material. Rather than dealing with published books and journals, we will have to cope with "tons and tons of unbound sheets of paper." Eco believes that new technologies will render only some types of publications, such as multivolume encyclopedias, obsolete. Most printed books which are durable, portable, and economical will continue to prosper.

Of course a similar argument can be made against the use of microfilm. Most patrons find it very difficult to read microfilm and use it as a last resort in their research, often printing articles that they need from the film. In addition, microfilm does not offer either enhanced or remote access to the resource like electronic formats. What microfilm does offer, however, is a relatively inexpensive way to preserve and store materials long term. This is a low-tech preservation solution that will remain easily accessible, regardless of technological innovations.

Another reformatting alternative, and one that addresses the user's preference for a hard copy, is the use of preservation-quality photocopy facsimiles to create reproductions of the original publication. When done professionally, photo reproduction technology enhances the text and illustrations so they are sharper than the deteriorated original. The reproductions are printed on acid-free paper and bound in book format for easy access and long term storage of several hundred years. Another advantage of preservation-quality photocopy is its cost. Orders for multiple copies of an individual title lowers the overall price making this ideal for cooperative programs.

Preservation-quality photocopy facsimile is the format currently used in two successful cooperative preservation ventures, *Brittle* and *SlavCopy*, which are operated at the University of Kansas. The goal of these programs is to preserve important individual works. While *Brittle* and *Slavcopy* currently use facsimile reproductions, both programs are exploring other options, such as digitization, that may optimize preservation resources.

Brittle and *SlavCopy*

Brittle is an international cooperative effort founded and administered at the University of Kansas. The purpose of *Brittle* is to facilitate the acquisition of preservation photocopies of embrittled volumes at reduced prices. The *modus operandi* for *Brittle* is an electronic listserver to which participating libraries post titles they wish to preserve. If other libraries wish to acquire preservation copies of a listed title, the price for that title is reduced. Currently there are over 60 active members of *Brittle* in the United States and Australia.

Building on the success of *Brittle*, a Slavic version of the cooperative program was established called *SlavCopy*. Brad Schaffner, the Slavic Librarian at the University of Kansas is primarily responsible for this effort and does most of the work. The focus of the list is the preservation of Slavic and other East Central European language publications. With over 20 members, *SlavCopy* is smaller than *Brittle*, but libraries actively participate resulting in the preservation of a number of important Slavic titles.

Brittle and *Slavcopy* essentially work the same way, but for ease, this paper will focus its discussion on *Brittle*. The preservation process begins when a participating library posts a title to the *Brittle* list. Full bibliographic information is given for each title along with the estimated reproduction price. Each citation also includes a list of libraries requesting a copy of the item. The *Brittle* list is distributed on the listserver weekly with updates that identify the libraries requesting a copy. Such information allows other librarians to make informed decisions regarding the need for their library to acquire a preservation copy of the work based on the number of other libraries planning to purchase the title. It is not necessary for each library to acquire a copy of every title posted, particularly if the monograph falls outside of the collection development parameters of the institution. Because *Brittle* identifies each library ordering a copy of the work other libraries know that the title will be available through interlibrary loan. Each citation appears on the list for one month so that libraries have time to examine their copy of the publication to determine if a preservation quality photocopy is needed to replace the original work.

After one month, the posting library sends the volume to the Preservation Department at the University of Kansas Libraries where it is processed as part of a *Brittle* shipment. Having all *Brittle* orders originating from the University of Kansas reduces the chance of error and helps the process run smoothly—ultimately reducing costs. In addition to the normal preparation procedures of erasing marks in the text, mending tears, and checking for missing text, the University of Kansas staff also prepare a special flag to notify the vendor which libraries have requested a copy of the title. Once prepared, the books are sent to National Bridgeport Bindery who is partnering with the University of Kansas to provide the *Brittle* photo reproduction service.

Generally, within six to eight weeks from the time a title is removed from *Brittle*, National Bridgeport Bindery will send a replacement copy and an invoice directly to each library that has requested a copy of the title. Bridgeport also returns the original volume, which was taken apart to facilitate the copy process, a replacement copy, and an invoice to the library which submitted the title for copying.

Benefits of Participating in *Brittle*

The primary benefit of participating in *Brittle* is substantial savings on the cost of preservation photo reproductions. The savings can be as much as 50 percent off the listed catalog price for photocopying services offered by some vendors. In addition to price reductions, libraries participating in

Brittle reduce the overhead costs involved with processing materials for preservation reformatting. These reductions are achieved through the distribution of processing activities amongst the members of the cooperative and represent a significant savings of time and money to participants.

Such activities include the elimination of the need to conduct bibliographic searches to determine if a reprint is available because this search has been conducted by the posting library. In addition, participating libraries are saved the hours of tedious work needed to prepare a book for photocopying. This includes reviewing the text page by page to mend tears, erase marks, and check for missing text. This process is further complicated when pages must be ordered through interlibrary loan to replace missing text.

Often, many of the titles posted on *Brittle* are heavily used and badly damaged. One of the advantages to this cooperative effort is that the *Brittle* citations indicate that the volume is badly damaged and request that other libraries consider supply their title for photocopying. On numerous occasions *Brittle* and *SlavCopy* have orchestrated the reproduction of a single title by using copies of the work held by two or more libraries. In some cases, these titles were only one use away from disappearing forever. Had it not been for the cooperative efforts of those participating in *Brittle* and *Slavcopy* it would have been impossible to create a complete preservation copy of the item.

It is clear that libraries can benefit through cooperative preservation efforts. When multiple libraries participate in cooperative programs such as *Brittle* and *Slavcopy*, significant amounts of time and money are saved. These savings can be applied towards the preservation of additional materials that are at risk. Given the current financial environment such cooperative efforts are extremely important.

Future Directions for Cooperative Efforts

Digitization and modern communication networks have opened many new possibilities for cooperative preservation efforts. *Brittle* and *Slavcopy* were made possible as a result of the creation of electronic mail which facilitates quick and easy communication with all of the participants. Thanks to digitization, it is currently possible to scan a book, store the information electronically, and print a paper copy with a high quality image; all done in less time than it takes to simply produce a preservation photocopy. Scanning and digitization allows for on-demand printing. Bridgeport Bindery is rapidly moving towards incorporating this technology into the *Brittle* and *Slavcopy* program. High resolution, high speed scanners make it possible to quickly capture, organize, and reproduce text and all types of images in a number of formats with very little degradation of text or image. A digitally captured original text can be reproduced as a near flawless book facsimile; as high resolution, high contrast microfilm; as image files on a web page; or it can be converted to a text file using OCR (optical character recognition) technology which is continually becoming more sophisticated. This technology, combined with the interactive capabilities of the Internet and World Wide Web, will allow cooperatives to maintain a catalog of digitized titles on a web site. Interested libraries, in return, may search the list at their convenience for desired titles to replace their embrittled volumes.

This on-demand capability to create copies of reformatted materials addresses a major concern that many funding agencies have had regarding the preservation of materials. In the past, government grant funds for the preservation of materials were limited to projects that used microfilm. Microfilm is a good preservation format because it has proscribed standards for the production and cataloging of three generations of film for each title including a preservation master, a print master, and a use copy to ensure the preservation of the title. It can be easily reproduced providing institutions or researchers around the world with access to the preserved material. Until recently, other formats did not offer such reproduction options, but thanks to technology there are several options available for capturing information, storing it long term, and reproducing it on demand. The success of microfilm projects have benefited national preservation efforts in demonstrating what can be accomplished with adequate leadership and funding. Funding agencies need to recognize that microfilm projects have limitations which can effectively be addressed with today's technology and, therefore, preservation initiatives should not restrict themselves exclusively to microfilm.

One limitation of past microfilm cooperative efforts was the focus on preserving information at a macro level. Materials were selected for filming based on their date of publication and general subject area. Like fishing with a net, collection level preservation projects captured many less important works and items that were not in need of immediate preservation attention along with core materials that were in dire need of preservation. This approach facilitated the preservation of important subject collections. However a collections based approach to preservation of embrittled materials is no longer necessary. Using current technological advances, institutions can work cooperatively to identify embrittled materials for preservation on a title by title basis allowing academic and research libraries to take advantage of their staffs' subject expertise to select materials for reformatting based on the scholarly or cultural value of the item.

Modern communications and digitization technologies enable libraries to be much more interactive in identifying texts to preserve. Moreover, these technologies allow a library to preserve a text in the format best suited to how the text will be used—be that film, preservation photocopy, or a permanent electronic format. The challenge is now for cooperative programs such as *Brittle* and *Slavcopy* and future ventures to utilize these resources to their fullest potential. Funding agencies and other institutions which support preservation activities also need to acknowledge that there are a variety of versatile preservation formats currently available. Therefore, preservation funds should not be restricted to a single format, such as microfilm or even digitization. All formats, from microfilm to digitization to codex form all have advantages and disadvantages. Funds are best spent when we choose the appropriate preservation format based on the needs of both the embrittled title and potential users of the title.

Conclusion

Cooperative programs are not without their challenges. It is difficult to maintain the level of energy needed to develop a program and make sure it continues to thrive. To have success requires a commitment from all involved. For cooperative programs to succeed they must be managed by an organization dedicated to the goals of the program, have secure funding, and operate under accepted standards which are flexible enough to accommodate the inclusion of new technologies.

We live in a world where the cost of acquiring library materials is growing faster than library budgets. For this reason, libraries must look to cooperative ventures to reduce preservation costs. We must utilize modern technologies to save important texts from around the world in the format best suited for the text, and use cooperative programs to preserve these texts in the most cost-effective manner possible.

Bibliography

Abbey Newsletter, September 1991, 83.

Baird, Brian J. "*Brittle*: Replacing Embrittled Titles Cooperatively," *College & Research Libraries News* 58:2 (February 1997): 83–84, 95.

Baird, Baird, Jana Krentz, and Bradley Schaffner, "Findings from the Condition Surveys Conducted at the University of Kansas Libraries," *College & Research Libraries* 58 (March 1997): 115–26.

Bond, Randall, et al., "Preservation Study at the Syracuse University Library," *College & Research Libraries* 48 (March 1987): 132–47.

Chrzastowski, Tina, et al., "Library Collection Deterioration: A Study at the University of Illinois at Urbana-Champaign," *College & Research Libraries* 50 (September 1989): 577–84.

Conway, Paul, *Preservation in the Digital World*, Washington, D.C.: Commission on Preservation and Access, 1996.

Eco, Umberto, "Gutenberg Galaxy Expands," *The Nation*, v. 264 no. 1 (January 6, 1997): 35.

Hazen, Dan, Jeffrey Horrell, and Jan Merrill-Oldham, "Selecting Research Collections for Digitization," Washington, D.C.: Council on Library and Information Resources, 1998.

Lowry, Charles B., and Denise A. Troll, "Carnegie Mellon University and University Microfilms International 'Virtual Library Project,'" *The Serials Librarian. v. 28, nos. 1/2 (1996): 143–69.

Schaffner, Bradley L. and Brian Baird, "Into the Dustbin of History? The Evaluation and Preservation of Slavic Materials," *College & Research Libraries* 60 (March 1999): 1–8.

Watt, Marcia, and Lisa Biblo. "CD-ROM Longevity: a Select Bibliography." *Conservation Administration News* (January 1995): 11–13.

Walker, Gay, et al., "The Yale Survey: A Large-Scale Study of the Book Deterioration in the Yale University Library," *College & Research Libraries* 46 (March 1985): 111-32.

Core Journal Titles in Full Text Databases

Jo Ann Carr and Amy Wolfe

Abstract

This paper describes a study initiated by the authors for a report to the Collection Development Committee of the Council of University of Wisconsin Libraries. The purpose of the study was to evaluate the content of four full text journal databases by identifying the coverage of core journals in specific disciplines. The databases studied were: *Academic Search Full Text* from Ebscohost; *Expanded Academic ASAP* from IAC; *Periodical Abstracts Research II Full Text* from ProQuest; and *Wilson Select Full Text..*

The Council of University of Wisconsin Libraries is comprised of the libraries of the University of Wisconsin-System. Beginning in 1997, the U.W. System allocated funds to libraries for cooperative collection development of full text electronic products. The U.W. System negotiated with full text vendors, selecting *Academic Search Full Text* from Ebscohost as a full text journal database for use by all libraries in the University of Wisconsin System. This allocation was intended to support a trial of a full text electronic journal product. As a part of this trial, the Collection Development Committee (CDC), comprised of collection development officers from the libraries of the U.W. system, wanted to supplement evaluations of the interface with an evaluation of the content of Ebscohost versus other full text journal databases.

Introduction

One of the legacies of the growth of the Internet and of the Web is that individuals are no longer content with computer services which only direct them to information. Rather they want computer services to provide indexing and abstracting of resources as well as the full content. This need was succinctly stated on the web site for the Electronic Library Network.

The continuing growth in the area of distributed learning requires libraries to revisit their current ability to serve students working from home,

---

Jo Ann Carr is library director, and Amy Wolfe is a student research assistant, University of Wisconsin, Madison.

faculty working from their office, etc. Also, library users want full text access. Increasingly, our professional literature reflects this trend. Users more often prefer electronic resources to print, and have become accustomed to information being accessible on demand, whether by E-mail, Internet or fax.

As databases have moved beyond indexing and abstracting resources based on print equivalents to include full text materials, librarians have been challenged to assess both interface issues, traditionally the domain of reference and information services librarians, and content issues which are the focus of those involved in collection development. This challenge has been exacerbated because of "the almost complete lack of empirical research proving or disproving vendor claims regarding content and capabilities". Because the cost of these full text products is often perceived as prohibitively expensive for a single institution (which still must sustain the costs of print equivalents because of unanswered questions regarding long term access and archiving issues) libraries are forming consortia which seek group pricing and access for full text database products. The development of these consortia means that collection development cannot simply be seen as the process of meeting a single library's current and future clientele needs, but must be based on a broad understanding of the basic information needs of specific disciplines. An example of this trend is demonstrated by the University of Wisconsin System. Beginning in the 1997–98 biennium the University of Wisconsin System provided funds to the Council of University of Wisconsin Libraries (CUWL) for System wide access to full text electronic products. CUWL is comprised of the libraries of the University of Wisconsin-System which includes doctoral campuses in Madison and Milwaukee; comprehensive universities at Eau Claire, Green Bay, LaCrosse, Menomonie (UW Stout), Oshkosh, Parkside, Platteville, River Falls, Stevens Point, Superior and Whitewater: and two year colleges at Baraboo/Sauk County, Barron, Fond du Lac, Fox Valley, Manitowoc County, Marathon County, Marinette County, Marshfield/Wood County, Richland County, Rock County, Sheboygan County, Washington County and Waukesha County.

The allocation of funds was intended to support a trial of full text journal databases. After negotiating with full text vendors, the University of Wisconsin System selected *Academic Search Full Text* from Ebscohost as the full text database for use by all the libraries in the System.

In the fall of 1997 Jo Ann Carr, co-author of this study, proposed that a content analysis of full text journal databases be conducted in order to assess the content of full text journal databases. The databases selected to be a part of this study include *Academic Search Full Text* from Ebscohost; *Expanded Academic ASAP* from IAC; *Periodical Abstracts Research II Full Text* from ProQuest; and *Wilson Select Full Text*. This content review as originally proposed had five objectives:

1) A review of current studies of full text databases.

2) Vendor definitions of full text coverage.

3) Comparison of journal titles in the discipline areas of the biological sciences, education,

social sciences, business, humanities and the physical sciences against the titles indexed and provided in full text by each vendor.

4) The number and percentage of peer-reviewed core titles covered by each database.

5) The number of regional titles in each database.

Due to a number of factors not all of these objectives were met. The mutability of the market provided challenges in obtaining and verifying definitions of full text as well as titles and years of coverage for the selected databases. Core journals were identified in only two of the identified fields- the biological sciences and education. Assistance in identifying core journals in the biological sciences was provided by Judy Wurtzler of the University of Wisconsin-Platteville library based on lists included in *Magazines for Libraries* (New York: Bowker, 1997) and *Using the Biological Literature: A Practical Guide* (New York: M Dekker, 1995). Three hundred thirty five titles are included on this list.

Core journals in education were identified by Jo Ann Carr using two widely acclaimed titles: Patricia Potter Wilson's *The Professional Collection for Elementary Educators* [New York: H.W. Wilson, 1996] and Nancy Patricia O'Brien and Emily

Fabiano's *Core List of Books and Journals in Education* [Phoenix: Oryx, 1991]. The combined list compiled from these two sources is 255 titles.

The study of the inclusion of core titles in the biological sciences and education included a literature review to determine if others were asking the same questions about full text database content. Database vendors descriptions of their databases and definitions of coverage, title changes and full text were also requested. *Ullrich's Plus 1998* was used to determine the number of core-reviewed journals in our core lists. Title lists for the four databases were acquired from the vendor's web sites or by contacting the vendors in March and early April of 1998. Excel spreadsheets were then constructed to compare between the core lists of journals in education and the biological sciences and the content of the four full text products.

Descriptions of the databases studied

In comparing the coverage of these four databases a review of how these databases are developed and described by their publisher is important.

Academic Search FullTEXT Elite provides "access to information from a wide range of academic areas including business, social sciences, humanities, general academic, general science, education and multi-cultural. This comprehensive database features full text for over 1,200 journals and abstracts and indexing for over 3,000 scholarly journals. It also includes coverage of over 1,700 peer-reviewed journals" Many titles are included back to 1990. Titles are identified as peer-reviewed titles by asking the publisher, checking serials directories or looking for information in the journal. Title changes are counted as separate journals with links to previous titles for ease in searching. Ceased titles and title changes are closely monitored with an indication of the stop date included in the journal authority file. Full text is defined as the complete text of articles including reviews and columns with indexing and abstracting. Selected illustrations are included as compound documents, and additional illustrations as PDF files. The indexing process includes the number of illustrations that are found in the article.

Expanded Academic ASAP from IAC (now part of the Gale Group) is described as offering "balanced, full text coverage of every academic concentration—from advertising and microbiology to history, political science, and art history. It also incorporates many interdisciplinary journals, national news magazines, and *The New York Times*. The IAC SearchBank includes 900+ full text titles as well as indexing for 1896 titles. The IAC SearchBank backfile provides coverage as far back as 1980. Articles selected for *Expanded Academic ASAP* must "contain substantive information on a field of study", be "one-half of a page or about 400 words in standard-sized journals, one-quarter of a page in tabloid journals, or one-half of a column in newsletters". Reviews from select journals are included as well as reviews from other publications which are one-quarter to one-half page. In addition to articles and reviews, the content criteria for *Expanded Academic ASAP* includes editorials, follow-up articles, letters to the editor from "authors who are prominent in their field", speeches, obituaries, product announcements, directories, bibliographies, and statistical compilations.

Periodicals Abstract Research II Full Text was the Proquest database used in this study. However, it should be noted that this product has been replaced by *Proquest Direct®*, "UMI's premier online information service...[which] provide[s] powerful, convenient search and retrieval, right from your desktop, to one of the world's largest collections of information, including summaries of articles from over 5,000 publications, with many in full text, full image format.

Wilson Select Full Text databases included in this study were *Education Abstracts Full Text* and *General Science Abstracts Full Text*. *Education Abstracts Full Text* contains the full text of more than 133 periodicals plus comprehensive indexing and abstracting for all of the periodicals covered in *Education Index*. These databases that cite every article of at least one column in length in 582 English-language periodicals and yearbooks published in the United States and elsewhere. English-language books related to education published in 1995 or later are also indexed. *General Science Abstracts Full-text* includes coverage of 40 periodicals back to January 1995 as well as indexing and abstracting for 167 popular and professional English-language science periodicals and the Science section of the *New York Times*.

Review of the literature

Our literature review indicated that "despite the recency of their development, a number of studies have been conducted which review...databases." Much of the research has focused on issues of access, design, user interface and cost, however there are also studies that looked at content issues.

Anna Grzeszkiewicz and A. Craig Hawbaker conducted a study at the University of the Pacific Library on 130 titles in Business Index ASAP from IAC. Although this database was not included in our study, this paper did consider issues relevant to the definitions of full text including problems with missing articles, missing issues, inconsistent availability of formats within titles and even issues, incorrect citations, and typographical errors. They also commented on the problem of editorial inconsistency in deciding what portions of journals should be included in the database.

Carol J. Richter and Thresa L. Wesley conducted a comparison study of UMI's *Periodical Abstracts Research II* (ProQuest CD-ROM stand alone stations) and IAC's *Expanded Academic Index* via Search Bank. This study was very useful in that it compared two of our four databases and produced some very good statistical information. They found that while UMI indexed approximately 11% more journal titles then IAC, IAC offered 15% more titles in the full text format. However, UMI offered more historical coverage of journals in the full text format than IAC (1988 average start date versus 1992 average start date). They also found UMI to have more journals the authors classified as recreational reading material than IAC. UMI had 112 recreational reading journals as compared to 22 for IAC.

Another useful aspect of this study was that the authors compared IAC and UMI in terms of subject emphasis (see tables 1 and 2). The study also focused on the number of titles included from ethnic and minority fields. IAC was found to contain significantly more full text titles (31) in these fields than UMI (14).

The information on subject emphasis provided by the authors was very helpful because it supplied us with an overview of the types of subjects covered in these two databases. The authors work in reviewing subject coverage differed from ours because they were not assessing the inclusion of specific core journals. Instead, the authors used Wilson subject indexes and *Ulrich's International Periodical Directory* (1995) to determine the subject classification of the titles covered.

A third study which focused on content rather than interface issues was conducted by Carol Franck and Holly Chambers of the State University of New York at Potsdam. Their study examined the inclusion of types of content (e.g. editorials, book reviews, articles), for completeness of text (e.g. author's affiliation, footnotes), the inclusion of graphics and of non standard text forms such as dialogue. This study concluded that none of the databases reproduced the paper issues in entirety with advertisements, classified ads and backcovers almost always excluded from coverage in the full-text databases. According to Franck and Chambers, UMI came closest to full content, followed by IAC, Ebsco and Wilson.

Another study which looked at the comparable content of print journals and their electronic full text equivalents was conducted by Laurie A. Preston and Corinne M. Ebbs looking at IAC's *Expanded Academic Index ASAP*. Two print issues from seventy titles from the James Madison Uni-

Table 1. Subject Distribution of Journal Indexed		
Subject	IAC	UMI
Social Sciences	543	539
Sciences	339	314
Humanities	428	477
Business	110	147
Education	79	105

Table 2. Subject Distribution of Full Text Journals		
Subject	IAC	UMI
Social Sciences	176	123
Sciences	82	51
Humanities	161	82
Business	50	41
Education	29	43

versity library collection, evenly divided among the sciences, social sciences and humanities, were compared for coverage with the electronic full text of those same journal issues. Only nine of the seventy five titles had an equal number of items covered in both the print and electronic versions of the journals, with the electronic versions lacking editorial policies, publisher's information, illustrations, reviews, editorials, sidebars etc. The authors noted "Whereas the editor decides what is included in the print version, the editor or publisher makes that decision for electronic full text access".

David Majka conducted a study comparing three database products: EBSCOHost, IAC InfoTrac SearchBank, and UMI ProQuest Direct. His study includes descriptions of the databases, and an enumeration of the challenges of a study of these products. His study provides an exploration of evaluation and implementation issues, user interface issues, and control issues as well as a comparison of the titles in these products against the holdings of the Robert Morris College Library.

Studies that are available on the Internet and which have been undertaken by specific colleges or consortia were also valuable to this project. Two studies (Electronic Library Network's *http://www.ola.bc.ca.eln/pands/descrip.htm* and St. Norbert and Edgewood Colleges Library's *http://222.snc.edu/~drewich/online.htm*) compared and provided descriptive information on the coverage provided by Ebsco *Academic Search*, IAC and ProQuest. According to the studies, *Academic Search* indexes 3,100 titles with 31% available in the full text format; IAC indexes 1,580 titles with 21% available in the full text format; and ProQuest indexes 1,800 titles with 25% available in full text. These studies also revealed that Ebscohost, IAC and ProQuest are updated on a daily basis. While these studies provided useful information they too lacked the aspect of evaluating the databases in terms of whether they included specific journal titles.

After conducting the literature review, it became apparent that our research methodology was unique. The use of core journal title comparisons as a method of content analysis had not been done before.

Preliminary Findings:

We have chosen to label the results of our study as preliminary finding in recognition of the fact that no single study can provide a complete picture of all aspects of full text journal databases. The lists used for our study are almost a year old and in a market where content changes on a monthly basis, these lists can only be regarded as a snapshot in time. In addition, the identification of core titles is only one way of determining what titles are most important to the each library or consortia. Given those caveats, we hope that our preliminary findings will serve to contribute to a growing picture of the comparative strengths of these four products.

Our results first provide information on the percentage of core journal titles indexed as well as an analysis of the percentage of peer reviewed core journal titles in each of the four databases in the fields of education and biology. Of the 255 core journal titles which we identified in the field of education the number of titles indexed ranged from 61 to 200 and the number of peer reviewed core journals titles ranged from 27 to 103 (see table 3).

The indexing of core titles in the biological sciences was much less extensive than in the field

Table 3				
Education	#Core journal indexed	%Core journals indexed	#Peer reviewed core journals indexed	%Peer reviewed core journals indexed
Ebscohost	126	49.4%	66	25.9%
IAC	62	24.3%	32	12.5%
Proquest	61	23.9%	27	10.6%
Wilson	200	78.4%	103	40.5%

Table 4				
Biological Sciences	#Core journal indexed	%Core journals indexed	#Peer reviewed core journals indexed	%Peer reviewed core journals indexed
Ebscohost	43	12.8%	36	10.7%
IAC	37	11.0%	31	9.25%
Proquest	30	8.9%	36	7.8%
Wilson	38	11.3%	30	8.9%

of education with less of a differential between the four vendors. Of the three hundred thirty five titles identified, the indexing of core titles ranged only from 30 to 43 and the indexing of peer reviewed core journals ranged from 30 to 36 (see table 4).

A second result of our study was an identification of the percentage of full text core journal titles as well as an analysis of the percentage of refereed core journal titles available in full text. The number of core titles available in full-text varied from 24 to 63 with peer reviewed core journals titles availability in full-text ranging from 13 to 34 (see table 5). There also appears to be differences in the effort to provide full-text for indexed titles with core journals that are both indexed and in full-text ranging from 31.5% to 77.0% and peer-reviewed core journals that are both indexed and in full-text ranging from 19.8% to 81.5%. This wide variance warrants further study to determine if some vendors regard their products primarily as indexes with full-text availability for selected titles while others regard their role as primarily full-text journal vendors.

Again the coverage is the biological sciences was much less than in education with only three to ten (1% to 2.98%) core journals being available in full-text and only three to nine (<1% to 2.7%) peer-reviewed titles being available in full text (see table 6).

The third item of information in our study was a determination (based on vendor's lists) of the average year of initial full text coverage of journals in these databases. For the field of education the initial year of full text coverage is shown in table 7. For the biological sciences the initial year of full-text coverage is shown in table 8.

Conclusions and Next Steps:

As noted above this study provides just a portion of the total picture needed for each library or consortia to make determinations regarding the best full text database product for their needs. The limited number of other studies conducted to date do provide other pieces of information needed to make this decision. If a fuller profile of the content of these databases is to be developed more frequent studies which attempt to keep pace with the changing title lists of these databases will need to be conducted. Jo Ann Carr, one of the authors of this study, is currently reviewing these same four databases coverage of the most frequently cited titles cited in *Journal Citation Reports*. In addition to studies reviewing core list in other disciplines or

Table 5						
Education	#Core jrls. in full-text	%Core jrls. in full-text	%Indexed titles in full-text	#Peer reviewed core jrls. in full-text	%Peer reviewed core jrls. in full text	%Indexed peer-rev. core jrls. in full text
Ebscohost	41	16.1%	32.5%	25	9.8%	19.8%
IAC	24	9.4%	38.7%	13	5.0%	40.6%
Proquest	47	18.4%	77.0%	22	8.6%	81.5%
Wilson	63	24.3%	31.5%	34	13.0%	33.3%

Table 6				
Biological Sciences	#Core jrls. in full-text	%Core jrls. in full-text	#Peer reviewed core jrls. in full-text	%Peer reviewed core jrls. in full text
Ebscohost	3	<1%	3	<1%
IAC	8	2.4%	6	1.8%
Proquest	10	2.9%	9	2.7%
Wilson	5	1.5%	4	1.2%

analyses comparing the holding of a specific library against the holdings of full text database, the products of other vendors which provide this full text journal titles must also be reviewed.

More complete analysis of the content of prepackaged full text journal databases is one avenue as we provide access to the best resources for our clients. A second approach is that which has been developed by California State University. The CSU system has submitted a request for proposals for the development of a customized database for the university's twenty three campuses. This request would require to the vendor to provide access to more than 1,250 journals selected by librarians in the CSU system. The similarity in the campuses and the fact that CSU was able to agree on the core list reflecting those titles held by at least twenty three campuses contributed to the development of this proposal by CSU. Their proposal also addresses archiving issues as its requires that the database include two print copies of each title, to be housed in the southern and northern halves of the state. Whether this proposal will allow CSU libraries to "break the mold" and find information providers who are capable of meeting [CSU's] requirements...rather than specify what they may want to sell.." remains to be seen. However, the fact that UMI's SiteBuilder, and the Gale Group's Infotrac Web now offers custom databases indicate that another option in providing full text access to journals is on the horizon.

Notes

1. Electronic Library Network. "Fulltext database initiative-project overview" Accessed at: http://www.ola/bc/ca/eln/pands/overview.htm on April 4, 1998.

2. Majak, David R. Remote host databases: issue and content" *Reference Services Review* 25 (3–4) fall/winter 1997. 23–35.

3. EbscoHost. "Academic Search Full Text Elite: About the Database" Accessed at http://gw5.epnet.com/ehost.asp?key=VKdt780&site=ehost, February 28, 1999.

4. Voltero, Kimberly. Personal Correspondence with Jo Ann Carr. February 17, 1999.

5. Information Access Company."*InfoTrac Products Expanded Academic ASAP*[TM]. Accessed at http://library.iacnet.com/html/eai.html on February 28, 1999.

6. Duval, Beverly and Linda Main. "Microcomputer

Table 7				
First Year FT available	Ebscohost	IAC	Proquest	Wilson
1989	0	3	0	0
1990	16	0	0	0
1991	0	1	0	0
1992	1	10	3	1
1993	0	5	0	0
1994	11	1	23	6
1995	0	1	9	1
1996	12	2	9	45
1997	1	1	3	4
1998	0	0	0	6

Table 8				
First Year FT available	Ebscohost	IAC	Proquest	Wilson
1989	0	2	0	0
1990	0	0	0	0
1991	0	0	0	0
1992	1	3	2	0
1993	0	2	0	0
1994	0	1	1	4
1995	0	0	2	0
1996	2	0	1	0
1997	0	0	3	1
1998	0	0	1	0

applications in the library" *Library Software Review* 17 (3) September 1998, 183–206.

7. University Microfilms International. "*Proquest Direct*". Accessed at http://www.umi.com/proquest/ on February 28, 1999.

8. H.W. Wilson Database Description. *Education Index, Education Abstracts, Education Abstracts Full Text.* Accessed at http://www.hwwilson.com/DDescriptions/EDI.HTM on March 1, 1999.

9. H.W. Wilson Database Description. *General Science Index, General Science and General Science Abstracts Full Text.* Accessed at http://www.hwwilson.com/DDescriptions/EDI.HTM on March 1, 1999.

10. Carr, Jo Ann. "Council of Wisconsin Libraries Collection Development Committee comparative study of full-text databases" (Paper presented at the Meeting of the Council of Wisconsin Libraries Collection Development Committee, Green Bay, Wisconsin, April 22 1998).

11. For example Duval, Beverly K. and Linda Main, "ProQuest Direct" and "EbscoHost's new face" *Library Software Review* 17 (2), June 1998 and Karp, Rashelle. "Comparing Three Full-Text Journal Services" *Booklist* 94 (18), May 15, 1998.

12. Grzeszkeiwics, Anna and A. Craig Hawbaker. "Investigating a full-text journal database: A case of detection" *Database Magazine* 19 (6) December 1996.

13. Richter, Carole J. and Threasa L. Wesley. "IAC and UMI go head-to head on full-text" *Database* 19 (4) Aug./Sept. 1996)

14. Franck, Carol and Holly Chambers. "How full is the full in full-text? A comparative study of paper periodicals with their web-based equivalents in the Ebsco, Information Access Company (IAC) UMI, and Wilson databases." A poster session presented at the ALA Annual Conference, Washington, D.C., June 27, 1998.

15. Preston, Laurie A. and Corinne M. Ebbs. "Full-text access evaluation: Are we getting the real thing?" *The Serials Librarian* 34 (4) 1998, 301–5.

16. Ibid., 303.

17. Majka. "Remote host databases, 23–35.

18. Guernsey, Lisa. "In a turnabout, California State U. calls for bids from data-base companies" *The Chronicle: information technology news*: 12/18/98. Accessed at http://chronicle.com/daily/98/12/9812801t.htm on December 29, 1998.

Getting It Right: Outcome-oriented Redesign of a Service Program in a Team-based Management Environment

Shirley W. Leung and Catherine Palmer

The University of California, Irvine (UCI) Libraries have emphasized and valued library instructional services for more than two decades. In the mid-1980's, an Education Services Coordinator position was established to coordinate and facilitate library instruction. Instruction activities were carried out in a distributed manner by public services librarians some of whom had subject bibliographer assignments. The Education Services Coordinator position was eliminated in Spring, 1994 when the UCI Libraries implemented a sweeping, new team-based management organizational structure subsequent to an Organizational Review and Design Project (OR&DP).

Impact of the Organizational Review and Design Project on Library Instruction Services
The new organizational structure created four divisions: Collections and Access Services, Research and Instructional Services, Technical Services, and Administrative Services. The Research and Instructional Services Division (R&I), was to be responsible for "reference, information, and research consultation services and instructional services". The R&I Division, made up of four departments, was further designated by the OR&DP (1) to establish department/site-based instruction teams to provide "site specific, general/lower division instruction"; and (2) to establish a cross-departmental team to facilitate coordination of instructional services for the Division as a whole. The OR&DP also stipulated that "upper division/graduate instruction" was to be delivered in a distributed manner given that subject specialists in the Collections and Access Services Division would also be involved with instructional services. It took five months to establish the sub-structure of thirteen teams for the R&I Division in accordance with the OR&DP recommendations.

Shirley W. Leung is university librarian, Hong Kong Baptist University, and Catherine Palmer is instructional services librarian, University of California, Irvine.

Although all members of the department teams and the cross-departmental team for instructional services made a concerted effort to carry out their functions in a team-based environment, it soon became that the design envisioned by the OR&DP was overly rigid in its desire to ensure consistency and uniformity across all the R&I departments. Therefore, soon after a formal assessment of the new structure by the University Librarian in Spring, 1995, a year after the OR&DP implementation, the R&I Division undertook a similar assessment effort of its divisional team-based management structure.

Comments from division personnel showed considerable consensus on what had worked well and what needed to be changed based on a year's experience. There was general consensus that there were more leadership opportunities for librarians and staff members and more opportunities to learn new and useful work skills such as problem-solving, conflict management, and meeting management; that meetings had become better organized and more productive; that the team-based environment was more inclusive; that project-based orientation to tasks had increased productivity; and that the process of team participation had allowed clearer appreciation of diverse workings styles and strengths. There were also concerns: too many meetings, teams did not work well for handling ongoing operations such as reference desk scheduling, supervising student assistants who support reference collection stack maintenance functions, or serving as liaison contacts with Technical Services units. More seriously, it was felt that the lockstep approach of identical teams across all four departments hampered more than facilitated their work when every department dealt with very different workload demands and constraints once they moved beyond a basic core of responsibilities.

As a result of the Libraries' overall assessment effort and the R&I Division's effort, the prescribed substructure of department teams was abandoned to allow more flexible and department-centered arrangements. Under the looser interpretation, each department could choose to set up its own project teams and appoint functional coordinators. The cross-departmental Instruction Services Team, however, was the only team retained out of the original thirteen teams. This may be attributed more to the recognition that the libraries needed an administrative structure to provide instructional services than to any acknowledgement that it had worked well. In fact, there were many concerns and questions regarding the purpose and function of the cross-department Instructional Services Team in terms of the mission, vision, and goals of library instruction at UCI.

A more fundamental concern was the bifurcation of general/lower division instruction from subject-based, upper division/graduate instruction. This bifurcation raised an array of management issues. The R&I Division was charged with responsibility for general and lower division instruction; the responsibility for subject-based instruction rested with individual subject specialist librarians. A large number of R&I Division Librarians are also subject specialists involved with graduate instructional functions while other subject specialists were members of the Collections and Access Services Division. How could the cross-department instructional services team be responsible for providing general and lower division instruction services when some of their colleagues choose to be exclusively involved with upper division/graduate instruction? Some of the librarians in the R&I Division were heavily involved with problem-based learning and course-integrated instruction for medical students and residents of UCI's teaching hospital. Lastly, some of the librarians in the Collections and Access Services Division continuously expressed the view that they wanted to be involved in instructional services planning and delivery efforts. Clearly, there was a need to have an open and meaningful dialogue between the R&I Division and the Collections and Access Division librarians. This need was made more significant since one of the outcomes of the formal assessment of the OR&DP was the pervasive concern regarding the structure for instructional services. The two divisional heads—the Assistant University Librarian for R&I (Shirley W. Leung) and the Assistant University Librarian for Collections and Access (Judith Paquette)—were assigned to address these issues.

The AUL's decided to put team-based management theory into practice by inviting all librarians involved with instructional services to attend two half-day working sessions with the Library's team management development resident consultant, George Soete. The goal was to take a grass-roots approach to identifying an administrative structure for instructional services by involving all the librarians who provided instructional services and collecting their ideas, aspirations, and suggestions for an effective instructional services program. The subsequent sequence of events went as follows:

February 29, 1996—Twenty-eight Librarians from the two divisions attended a half-day session held at the end of February, 1996. (This group were subsequently identified as "Friends of Instruction" or FOI for short.) Facilitator George Soete first provided the opportunity for all the participants to put their concerns and comments on the table. Then he held break-out sessions to brainstorm and prioritize lists of "What could/should we do more of" and "What could/should we do less of". This high-energy and high-participation session resulted in the spontaneous establishment of a fast-track inter-divisional team, made up of volunteers among the participants, to develop a draft conceptual framework and a draft instructional services proposal.

March 5, 1996—The two AULs constituted a four-member Fast-Track Team (with one member serving as facilitator) from the two divisions and established parameters for "Expected outcomes and objectives", "Focus of activity and charge", "Timelines" (one month) "Decision Points", and "Constraints".

March 28, 1996—Deadline for the Fast-Track Instruction Team to deliver its draft report to the FOI.

April 2, 1996—Mr. Soete facilitated a second forum for the FOI to gather feedback on the draft report by the Fast-Track Instruction Team.

May 10, 1996—The Fast-Track Instruction Team submitted its final report which contained five main components:

I. *Conceptual Framework*: This section discussed the Vision, Mission, Scope, and Goals of the program and included four objectives:
- Improve Library Instruction Across the Curriculum
- Improve Lower-Division Library Instruction
- Improve Upper-Division Library Instruction
- Support Graduate-Level and Faculty Instruction

II. *Instructional Services Program Proposal*: The Instructional Services Program Proposal discussed building blocks, campus partnership targets, and internal library partnerships such as the Library's Learning Team.

III. *Functional Description*: The function of the Instructional Services Program was to:
- provide Instruction;
- support Instruction;
- evaluate and improve instruction;
- create and maintain partnerships.

IV. *Elements for Success*: The Elements for Success section listed the resources and other environmental factors needed to make an instructional services program successful.

V. *Instruction Program models*: The Fast Track Instruction Team proposed four models for the administrative structure of the Instructional Services Program for consideration by the AULs.
- Model A: An instruction unit with assigned personnel including a unit head.
- Model B: An Instruction Officer/Coordinator who would work with a group or team of assigned personnel.
- Model C: An Instruction Team made up of an assigned instruction librarian within each R&I department and a subject librarian from the Collections and Access Division.
- Model D: Retain the current cross-departmental Instruction Team.

After extensive review of the Fast Track Instruction Team Report and the information generated in the two working sessions with George Soete, the two AULs presented a Model for the UCI Libraries Instruction Program in a report dated July 1, 1996. The report was the result of probing discussions on the pros and cons of each model, the overall resources needed for the implementation of each model and the perceived impact of implementation on the extant organizational structure in a team-based environment. The need for a strong evaluation/assessment component became clear as well as the need to implement a program that was resource-efficient and in consonance with the library's team-based management philosophy.

Administrative Model for Instruction Services at the UCI Libraries

The model selected and implemented was to provide an Instruction Services Librarian (IS Librarian) working with an instruction services team. The Instructional Services Team (IS Team) was specifically designated as a working team, not an advisory team with the IS Librarian serving as the team leader. The report went on to detail other aspects of the administrative structure of the program.

Duration and Focus of the Program

The program was implemented for a two-year pilot period which began upon the appointment of the Instruction Services Librarian in October, 1996. Based on analysis and assessment done and experience/data gathered during the two-year period, the program model and conceptual framework was to be reviewed and redesigned, if necessary.

Staffing Structure

The Instruction Services Program was staffed with an FTE librarian. In addition, the program was allocated 15 hours a week of clerical support to assist with operational functions such as room reservations, confirming instruction session schedules, and distribution of instructional materials.

Budget

Beyond the allocation of FTE, the program was given a budget allocation to support basic expenditures such as supplies and photocopying.

Reporting Line of the Instructional Services Librarian

The IS Librarian reported (and continues to report) directly to the AUL for the Research and Instructional Services Division.

Role of the Instructional Services Librarian

The AULs' report specified that the IS Librarian would work four hours per week on a general reference desk in order to stay in touch with user needs and information inquiry/use patterns. She was directed to consult, communicate and coordinate with the AUL for Collections and Access regarding subject-based instruction services. The IS Librarian position was designated as the key contact person for instructional services related matters with campus and off-campus units. In addition, the IS Librarian served as the Team Leader of the Instruction Services Team.

Membership and Function of the Instructional Services Team

With the IS Librarian as team leader, the IS Team was designated as the primary planning and working team for library instruction with membership composition as follows:

- a member from each of the four Research and Instructional Services Departments (Main Library, Government Information, Science Library and Medical Center Library).
- a Library Systems Department member appointed in an ex-officio capacity as the technology resources person for the team.
- at least one member of the team would also be a bibliographer, from the Collections and Access Division if possible (to ensure communication about subject-based instruction).

Identification and Appointment of the IS Librarian and the IS Team Members

The IS Librarian was appointed through an open internal recruitment process. The IS Team members were chosen by nomination or by volunteering to serve on the new Instructional Services Team.

Key Responsibilities of the Instructional Services Program

The Fast Track Instruction Team report identified areas of responsibility for the Instructional Services Program. The AUL report dated July 1, 1996, endorsed and prioritized key activities for the IS Program and the IS Team. (See appendix 1: Priority Ranking of ISP Activities) The key responsibilities were to provide, coordinate and support general instruction, library-based instruction and outreach instruction; to evaluate and improve instruction and to create and maintain partnerships with units within the library and on the campus, particularly in those areas which dealt with undergraduate education. In addition, the IS Program was charged with supporting subject-based instruction. One of the chief tasks given to the IS Program was the development of a strong assessment component to evaluate the effectiveness of the program offerings and the effectiveness of the program structure. (See appendix 2: ISP Activities Status Grid for a full listing of ISP activities)

The reconfigured Instructional Services Program structure was implemented in October, 1996 with a full-time Instructional Services Librarian acting as team leader for a seven member Instructional Services Team.

Assessment of the Two Year Pilot Period

The accomplishments of the Instructional Services Program were significant during the two-year pilot project. Activities fell into three categories: ongoing activities, new initiatives/partnerships, and evaluation activities.

Ongoing Activities

The Instructional Services Program (ISP) continued to coordinate general library and lower-division instruction and to provide library-wide and administrative support for the Libraries instruction efforts. The IS Librarian served as the campus contact for library instruction and acted as a resource for the improvement of teaching within the Libraries. With the assistance of the IS Team members, the curriculum of library-based classes was standardized and updated to reflect the changing complement of library resources.

New Initiatives/Partnerships

The IS Team designated the first year of the pilot period as a "Focus on Teaching Year". A variety of activities designed to improve and enhance the instruction provided by UCI librarians took place under this rubric. These activities included workshops, discussion forums and mini-seminars open to all librarians and library staff members who provided instruction.

During the two year pilot period, the Instruction program formed significant partnerships with campus units outside the library. The library was invited by the Division of Undergraduate Education to participate in a successful NSF grant application designed to improve undergraduate education in the areas of Science, Mathematics, Engineering, and Technology (SMET). In addition, the library also played a key role in a campus-wide initiative to develop an Electronic Educational Environment.

Evaluation Activities

The ISP was charged with three evaluation activities that were designated as critically important. The activities were to 1) conduct ongoing evaluation of the instruction program for continuous improvement and relevance to current needs, 2) conduct ongoing evaluation of instruction program participants (librarians), and 3) create statistical and narrative reports.

Assessment of the Administrative Structure of the ISP during the Two Year Pilot Period

The pilot period for the administrative structure of the Instructional Services Program covered October, 1996 through October, 1998. Many changes occurred in the upper administrative levels of the UCI Libraries during this time. One University Librarian retired, the former AUL for Research and Instructional Services acted as University Librarian for a year and then accepted a position in Hong Kong, a new University Librarian was hired and an acting AUL for Research and Instructional Services was appointed on an interim basis. Due to the numerous changes in library administration, the planned assessment of Instructional Services has not progressed as originally envisioned. A draft report is under review by the Acting AUL for R&I who will present it to the senior administrative team.

An Informal Summary of What Worked Well

From a practitioner's perspective, many aspects of the ISP worked well during the pilot program. Perhaps the biggest benefit was that the attention and focus on instruction created new enthusiasm and energy for the library teaching efforts. All instruction librarians had opportunities to reflect on their teaching experiences, to share their experiences with other interested and supportive colleagues and to learn and practice new instruction techniques. The make-up of the instruction team facilitated information sharing about instruction across all departments and units. Team members were able to report back to their units about instruction initiatives, needs and projects. In addition, team members were able to provide a variety of perspectives on instruction issues. Reporting to the AUL for the R&I Division, gave the Instruction Librarian a direct line of communication and facilitated information sharing about and resource allocation for instruction initiatives.

One area that improved significantly during the pilot project was the method for collecting statistical data about instruction. The data collection process was streamlined and standardized so that all librarians and unit heads had a clear understanding of what information was being collected and how to report it in a uniform fashion. For the first time, the library has reliable and meaningful data to help inform the allocation of resources to instruction. The ISP can generate detailed and accurate statistical reports on instruction activities by individual librarians, by schools and programs, and by academic discipline. The statistics gathered have helped identify underserved student populations and to target them for library instruction in the future.

The ISP made notable progress in the controversial area of evaluation of instruction. All Library-based classes routinely include an evaluation by participants and significant progress has been made toward designing an evaluation instrument for use in all classes taught by librarians. The issue of how to evaluate the performance of instruction librarians is still outstanding.

New partnerships and new initiatives gave campus-wide visibility to library instruction activities and the library's role in the academic and instruction mission of the University. In addition, the library was able to identify new avenues to ensure that all students had the opportunity to acquire both baseline information literacy skills and more advanced academic research skills in their disciplines.

An Informal Summary of What Could Have Worked Better

Although the ISP structure implemented was successful in many ways, there are some areas that need adjustment. The IS Team worked well as an advisory body, but did not function as a working team as originally envisioned. The intent was that IS Team members would serve as a core of instructors for the ISP classes. This did not happen. IS Team members continued to participate in instruction at the same levels and in the same areas as they had prior to their appointment to the team. There is not a library-wide standard for level of participation in the instructional service program classes. Although the library is able to meet current demands for instruction, it has proven difficult to expand instruction efforts because of personnel constraints.

Reporting directly to the AUL for R&I had benefits, but there were drawbacks as well. The structure did not enable close communication and coordination between the IS Librarian and other library managers and officers because the IS Librarian did not participate directly in management activities such as budget and goal setting meetings. Instead the AUL acted as the sole advocate for instructional services during management meetings.

These areas and others are currently being considered in the formal assessment of the Instructional Services Program at the UCI Libraries.

The IS Librarian's Assessment of the Process Used to Create the ISP Model

The process used to create the ISP model worked well in many ways. It was participative and inclusive. All interested parties had multiple opportunities and avenues to express their opinions and ideas. Because it was open-ended and value and judgement neutral, the process encouraged creative approaches to long-standing issues. The process itself focused attention on instruction and served to validate the importance of instruction as part of the UCI Libraries mission. In addition, resources were allocated to the creation of the model and to the program.

Some aspects of the process did not translate well when the senior administration underwent significant changes. The Fast Track Instruction Team Report identified issues, concerns and activities which fell under the auspices of Instructional Services. The AULs' report provided a context and endorsed ISP activities by assigning priorities to the issues, concerns and activities identified by the Fast Track Instruction Team. The IS Team was then free to set its own goals and objectives. It is safe to say that everyone who was involved in the process from the beginning had a shared understanding of desired outcomes for the ISP. However, personnel changes at the senior administrative level meant that those responsible for assessing the instruction pilot period had not been active participants in its design and implementation. The perceived lack of a formal charge or measurable goals presented challenges to measuring the performance of the IS Program.

The AUL's Assessment of the Process Used to Create the ISP Model

The process established to invite the full participation of all librarians involved with instructional services worked very well. It provided the opportunity for everyone to share their views on what was important, what should be given higher priority, and what should be given more attention. Through the facilitation of the consultant, the discussions stayed focused. Such accomplishments were not incidental. In fact, the two AULs had discussions with the consultant on the desired outcomes prior to the first FOI forum. However, the spontaneous formation of a small group to develop an instructional services program was not anticipated by the two AULs. They quickly supported this outcome given the participant's intense interest in forming such a group.

In order to ensure that the small group (later named the Fast Track Instruction Team) would accomplish desired objectives, the two AULs worked closely together to develop a very specific charge to the Team stating expected outcomes, focus of activity, membership, assigned facilitator, reporting relationship, timelines, decision points, and constraints. The detailed and careful attention given to the development of the charge for the Fast Track Instruction Team laid the foundation for the team's effectiveness.

A different approach was used with the Instructional Services Team formed later to be a working team in conjunction with the establishment of the Instructional Services Librarian position. The two AULs decided that it would be important to allow the team and the Instruction Services Librarian latitude to shape and determine their work within the established conceptual framework. In other words, a conscious effort was made not to give the same kind of specific directive to the (working) Team and the Instructional Services Librarian. Clearly, much has been accomplished in the ensuing two years. However, this may be more a result of the work by librarians with strong interests in instruction services than as a result of the team structure.

From an administrative perspective there was a major difference between the charges given to the Fast Track Instruction Team and the charges given to the IS Team. The Fast Track Instruction Team operated as team with a very specific charge whereas the Instruction Services Team was expected to function as a self-managed team.. They may appear to be very similar, but in fact they are vastly different.

Conclusion

This paper describes an academic library's effort to promote organizational agility by using a fast-track team-based management process to re-design an important library service program. The process used was inclusive, creative and facilitated by a professional library management consultant. Although there are still some areas which need clarification and adjustment, the overall assessment is that the process resulted in an effective administrative model for the delivery of the Libraries Instructional Services Program.

Appendix 1: Priority Ranking of Instructional Services Program Activities

The Administrative Team ranked these activities of the Instructional Services Team as **critically important**:

Goal/Activity	Status	Who	Activity
1) Evaluate and Improve Instruction			

a) Conduct ongoing evaluation of the instruction program for continuous improvement and relevance to current needs	Ongoing	IS Librarian, IS Team, Instruction librarians	1. Class Evaluations by students/participants
			   a. Intro to UCI Libs on the Internet
			   b. Pine Electronic Mail Classes
			   c. Writing 39C Library Orientations
			2. Ongoing consultation with program coordinators and instructors
			   a. Writing Program Coordinators
			   b. Teaching Assistants
			   c. Librarians
			3. Librarian evaluations of Writing 39C Library Orientation sessions (Spr, 98-)
			4. Writing 39C and Teaching Assistant evaluation of Writing 39C Handout (Spr, 96)

b) Conduct ongoing evaluation of instruction program participants (librarians)	In progress	IS Team, Administrative Team, Library Review Committee, Review Initiators, Instruction Librarians	1. Developed draft proposal for including evaluation of instruction in librarian reviews. 2. Develop criteria to determine when student evaluations of librarian instructors and instruction will be used. 3. Draft standardized form for evaluation by students of librarian instructors/instruction. 4. Direct observation of librarian instructors by IS Librarian and IS Team members. 5. Solicit feedback from faculty on librarian instruction.
c) Create statistical and narrative reports	In place	IS Librarian, IS Program Assistant, Acting AUL for R&I, R&I Recordkeepers	• Implemented standard procedures for reporting and tabulating instruction statistics.

The Administrative Team endorsed and ranked as a **high priority** the following tasks and responsibilities of the Instructional Services: The Instructional Services Program will:

Task/Activity	Status	Who	Activity
1) Provide Instruction			
a) Provide and coordinate the following types of instruction i. General, lower-division instruction (Writing 39B/C, Humanities Core) ii. Library-based instruction iii. Outreach instruction	Ongoing	IS Librarian → R&I Librarians → Outreach Services Librarian	Coordinates and provides Provide
b) Take on more instruction than other librarian-instructors	Level of activity varies by individual		See individual instruction profiles for a detailed report of instruction activities by librarian.
c) Evaluate Humanities 75	Evaluation complete	IS Librarian, IS Team	Recommendation: 1. Keep Humanities 75 as a credit course because it is extremely hard to get new courses approved. 2. Reconfigure course to make it more effective in reaching the target audience of lower-division students. 3. Develop a pool of instructors through who can teach the class on a rotating basis.
2) Coordinate administrative functions such as scheduling and maintaining statistics	In place/Ongoing	IS Program Assistant IS Librarian	Standardized and streamlined collection and reporting of statistics on library instruction activities at all levels and in all locations.
2) Support Instruction			
a) Provide orientation and training to end-users	Ongoing	IS Librarian all instruction librarians	See statistical reports for full range of activities.
b) Provide orientation and training for librarian-instructors teaching new and on-going classes	Ongoing	IS Librarian	
c) In collaboration with the Libraries' Learning Team, provide opportunities for in-service training to improve teaching.		IS Team, AUL for R&I (Learning Team did not participate)	Designated 96/97 as Focus on Instruction Year Betsy Wilson Workshops

Outcome-oriented Redesign of a Service Program

Task/Activity	Status	Who	Activity
d) Ensure that recognition of different modes of learning and cultural differences are incorporated into teaching program			
e) Create, develop handouts and other instructional materials such as overheads, PowerPoint presentations for use and/or adaptation by others		IS Librarian	Worksheets are available on IS web page.
f) Develop technology-based modes of delivering instruction	In progress	IS Librarian	Have grant to hire personnel to develop web-based interactive tutorial.
g) Schedule instruction (personnel, rooms, equipment)	Ongoing	IS Librarian	
h) Work cooperatively with the Libraries electronic classroom personnel	In place		
i) Engage in long-range planning	Unclear	IS Librarian, IS Team	IS Librarian is not a member of the Library Council. IS Program is over Sept. 30, 1998. Difficult to engage in long-range planning when opportunities for participation are not provided by the administrative structure.
3) Provide a forum for information and resource sharing among all participants in the Libraries Instruction Program			
4) Define levels of service and determine appropriate service providers for non-UCI patrons, especially high school students, community college students, CSU students	Provided	IS Librarian, IS Team, Friends of Instruction	Instruction Forums provided opportunities for sharing information. Brown Bag discussions provided opportunities for focused discussion on specific issues such as "Baseline Information Seeking Competencies for Writing 39C Students"

Appendix 2: ISP Activities Status Grid
UCI Libraries Instructional Services Program

CONCEPTUAL FRAMEWORK	Priority	Notes	Status
Vision: The UCI Libraries play an integral role in insuring that all members of the UCI community have the requisite information literacy skills to flourish in the 21st century		In general, endorse and support vision, mission, and scope. In particular, appreciate the clarity of the scope statement and endorse this definition of the program.	Instructional Services Program has adhered to the vision, mission and scope statement.
Mission: The mission of the UCI Libraries Instruction Program is to provide opportunities for the campus community to acquire information literacy skills based on a set of minimum competencies.			
Scope: The Instruction Program focuses on instructional services designed and provided for groups in classroom settings at assigned times. One-on-one and point-of-use instruction remains the responsibility of the units.			
INSTRUCTIONAL SERVICES GOALS			
1) Improve Library Instruction across the curriculum			
a) To recognize differences in library research methods and needs between disciplines and lower-div., upper-div., and grad. students, including medical students, and to design library instruction accordingly.		Agree/Endorse	Instructional Services offerings recognize these differences when designing instruction
b) To make library instruction an integral part of the UCI-wide critical thinking effort and information technology initiative by providing classes such as e-mail, Introduction to the World Wide Web, and database specific instruction.		Agree/Endorse	The Instructional Services program designs and delivers classes that meet this description.
c) To take a leadership role in incorporating technology in instruction by teaching technology, and promoting technology as a means of teaching.		Needs further development and clarificiation	The appointment of a Technology Training librarian has impacted this activity.
d) To serve as a resource for the improvement of teaching.	Low	Defer	The Instructional Services Team has provided opportunities for librarians to learn how to be better instructors.

ISP Goals, cont.	Priority	Notes	Status
e) To coordinate outreach services (e.g. library tours, special summer programs, general orientations) within established--or to-be-established guidelines		Needs clarification and definition of scope	ISP activities have been impacted by appointment of Outreach Services Librarian. Self-guided tour brochures for the Main and Science Libraries are available. ISP continues to provide opportunities for general orientation to library resources such as ANTPAC and MELVYL®
f) To define levels of service and determine appropriate service providers--esp. for high school students, CSU students, other non-UCI patrons	High	Agree/Endorse	ISP offers reasonable instruction opportunities for community college students who are UC-eligible. Other non-UCI patrons are not eligible for instruction services at this time. The ISP offers information about self-teaching tools available that can help non-UCI patrons understand how to use ANTPAC and MELVYL®
g) To improve information given about the Libraries during general campus tours conducted by undergraduates		Need clarification and scope definition.	The ISP has not pursued this directive.
h) To coordinate administrative functions such as schedule and maintaining statistics.	High	Agree/Endores	In place. ISP handles these activities.
i) To determine the feasibility of a for-fee instruction service [Low Priority]	Low	Defer	

ISP Goals, cont.	Priority	Notes	Status
2) Improve Lower-Division Library Instruction			
a) To ensure that every student fulfilling a lower-division writing requirement completes a library instruction assignment		Depends on external factors	In place. Library assignments are part of the curriculum in Writing 39B, 39C and Humanities Core Course.
b) To ensure that students in all lower division courses--across the disciplines--that require library-based research complete a library instruction component.		Depends on external factors	Many librarians provide library instruction to lower-division classes. See statistical report for details. ISP needs an science librarian who can design instruction to incorporate in lower-division science courses.
c) For BOTH of the above: Determine a set of COMPETENCIES that will serve as building blocks for upper-division and graduate [subject-specific] library instruction		Needs further exploration and development	ISP provides opportunities for librarians to develop a common understanding of core competencies.
3. Improve Upper-Division Library Instruction			
a) To ensure that students in upper-division course that fulfill the Writing Requirment and have library-based research requirements, complete a library instruction component.		Depends on external factors	Due to lack of manpower, ISP has not pursued this goal. Individual librarians provide subject-based instruction.
b) To ensure that all students, especially those in the Campuswide Honors Program and school-specific honors program complete a library instruction component as part of their Senior thesis course		Depends on external factors	Given the available manpower, the ISP understands that this goal is unrealistic.
c) To ensure that students participating in research-based mentorship programs successfully complete a library instruction component.		Depends on external factors	See previous comments.

Outcome-oriented Redesign of a Service Program

ISP Goals, cont.		Priority	Notes	Status
4. Support Graduate-level and Faculty Instruction				
a) To recognize the contributions of librarians outside the General Instruction program			Needs clarification	ISP offers opportunities for all librarians to participate in general instruction activities.
b) To provide a forum for information and resource sharing among all participants in the Libraries Instruction Program			Encourage development of forum	ISP sponsored a "Focus on Teaching" year.
INSTRUCTION PROGRAM PROPOSAL				
Building Blocks:				This section of the report describes the areas of instruction for which the ISP is responsible.
Instruction will have a rational, incremental flow starting with the following:			Good identification of major elements; expect further refinement of the organization of these major elements as group works on them and program evolves	There is a better understanding of the relationship between the levels of instruction after two years. See written report for more detailed explanation.
1. Curriculum-based Programs				
	a. Lower-division, course-based instruction such as Humanities Core, Writing 39B/C			
	b. Upper-division, subject-based instruction			
	c. Graduate level, subject-based instruction			
2. Library-based Instruction				ISP designs and delivers instruction in these areas.
	a. ANTPAC/MELVYL® Training			
	b. Internet Training			
	c. Research resources and methods			
	e. E-mail			
Instruction will build partnerships with			Agree/Endorse; depends on some extent on external factors; needs further development	ISP has strong relationships with units such as OAC, DUE, Writing Program
	a. Academic Programs			
	b. Office of Academic Computing			
	c. Academic Support units and Student Support Units			
	d. Campus Computer Labs			

	Priority	Notes	Status
Instruction Program Proposal, cont.			
When appropriate, the Instruction Program will collaborate with:			ISP collaborates as appropriate depending on activity.
a. The Libraries Learning Team			
b. All library units			
FUNCTIONAL DESCRIPTION			
1. Provide Instruction			
a. Provide and coordinate instruction: general instruction, library-based instruction, outreach instruction	High	Agree/Endorse	Ongoing ISP activity
b. Take on more general instruction than other librarian-instructors	High	Agree/Endorse	This is not the reality.
c. Design and facilitate provision of library-based instruction	High	Agree/Endorse	Ongoing ISP/IS librarian activity
d. Teach Humanities 75		Needs evaluation and assessment	Recommend keeping Humanities 75.
e. Develop equivalent course to Humanities 75 (e.g. Soc. Sci.)		Needs assessment	Not a realistic goal.
2. Support Instruction			
a. Provide orientation and training		Agree/Endorse	Orientation and training is provided
b. Provide orientation and training for librarian-instructors teaching new and on-going course.		Needs assessment and more specific program development	The ISP provide orientation and training in areas b, c, and d.
c. Provide orientation for TA's and instructors who teach library assignments			
d. Provide orientation and training for student assistants who teach E-mail and other basic skills			
e. Provide consultation for design/production of point-of-us and electronic instruction resources			The ISP has not provided consultation in these areas.
f. Ensure that different modes of learning and recognition of cultural differences are incorporated into teaching programs		Agree/Endorse	
g. Create, develop handouts and other instructional materials such as overheads, PowerPoint presentations for use and/or adaptation by others		Support group development of new skill; expect will evolve	IS has web page which makes handouts and worksheets available.

Instruction Program Proposal, cont.	Priority	Notes	Status
i. Develop technology-based modes of delivering instruction		Agree/endorse	IS librarian has grant money available to develop web-based tutorial.
j. Provide consultative assistance for the design and production of point-of-use and electronic instruction resources			Happens on an informal basis.
k. Provide consulting services for those who teach upper-div. and grad. students			
l. Schedule instruction (personnel, rooms, equipment)		Agree/Endorse	In place and ongoing.
m. Work cooperatively with the Libraries electronic classroom personnel		Yes	We do.
n. Engage in long-range planning		Evaluation=key component; within the framework, need to focus on evaluation and high priority activities	Difficult to engage in long-range planning when program is in state of flux.
3. Evaluate and Improve Instruction			
a. Conduct ongoing evaluation of the instruction program for continuous improvement and relevance to current needs	High	Critically Important	Evaluation activities are enumerated in report.
b. Conduct ongoing evaluation of instruction program participants	High	Critically Important	Proposal developed.
c. Create statistical and narrative reports	High	Critically Important	Procedures and policies are implemented.
4. Create and Maintain Partnerships			
a. Create and maintain partnerships with		Depends on external factors	
• Academic Units			ISP has partnerships with units.
• with library units such as R&I, C&A, Publications, Learning Team			
• other units such as the Writing Program, Humanities Core, academic departments with large enrollments & library assign. summer programs, Welcome Week organizers			ISP works with all units
b. Work with high school, public library, and community college librarians			ISP has met with these groups.

Instruction Program Proposal, cont.	Priority	Notes	Status
c. Consider the feasibility of a for-fee instructional service/program	Low		Not addressed by ISP.
d. make appropriate referrals for requests which fall outside the scope of the Libraries Instruction Program			
ELEMENTS FOR SUCCESS			
In order to be successful, the ISP must have:			
Defined scope of responsibility and authority (vision, mission, goals)		Yes	
Administrative Team recognition of instruction as an essential function within the Library		Yes	
A two year commitment to new structure		Yes	
Autonomy to pursue goals		Yes, within framework	
Decision-making authority		Yes, within framework	
Effective evaluation mechanism	High	Critical responsibility to develop	
Recognition of instruction as an essential function in the Library		Yes	
Recognized place in Libraries' organizational chart		Yes	
Clearly defined relationships with other Library units		Not yet developed	
A match between existing resources and the program		Yes	
A commitment of resources by Administration to the program		Yes	
Affiliate practitioners with instruction as part of position profile		Yes	
Assigned personnel both professional and administrative		Yes, within two year period	
Stable membership to form and maintain partnerships and undertake long-range plan		Provides opportunity	
Representation of both (current) R&I librarians and bibliographers		Yes, through team and coordination	
Centralization of library-based and lower-division instruction activities			IS librarian, not team, provides coordination
Clerical support		Yes	
Office space		Yes	
Equipment		Yes	
Budget (line item)		Yes	

In Search of Services: Analyzing the Findability of Links on CIC University Libraries' Web Pages

Barbara I. Dewey

Abstract

This paper examines Web-based services from the 13 member libraries of the CIC (Committee on Institutional Cooperation). Information was gathered from a survey of member libraries and from an analysis of each Web site. Particular attention was given to the placement and "findability" of service links on the sites. Successes and problems are summarized with suggestions for further individual and CIC-wide Web development focusing on services.

CIC Libraries—A Unique Consortia
The exploding development of Web-based services is a critical activity for college and university libraries. This is especially true for the 13 member libraries of the Committee on Institutional Cooperation (CIC) consortia. This paper analyzes access, reference, information and user education services reflected on the CIC pages related to where these services are located or their "findability" by users. By using the CIC libraries as the target population for this study it is hoped that the findings might provide a possible model for next generation developments of the CIC Virtual Electronic Library (VEL) as this consortia of research libraries seeks to advance collaboration and cooperation, not only in collection provision, but also in innovative service delivery.

The CIC Libraries vision is as follows:

By the beginning of the 21st Century, the CIC libraries will have a cohesive consortial organization guided by a vision of the information resources in the CIC as a seamless whole, whether those resources are developed or owned individually or collectively. Through shared planning and

---

Barbara I. Dewey is director, Information and Research Services, University of Iowa Libraries.

action, the libraries and their patrons will have equal access to the total information resources of the CIC. In addition, the libraries will provide the students, faculties, and staffs of the CIC universities with access to comprehensive resources throughout the world. **Through collective leadership and cooperative action, each CIC library will realize extensive value-added services for its clienteles.** The CIC libraries will be in the forefront of efforts to preserve, expand, and access both electronic information resources and traditional collections.

Its mission:

Through cooperation and collaboration, to advance the missions of the individual CIC libraries in their support of teaching, research, and service by:
- *creating*—individually and collectively— new ways to fulfill the information needs of the faculties, students and staffs of the CIC universities;
- *extending* and *enhancing* the information resources and services available on each campus by providing equal access to complementary resources throughout the CIC; and thereby, improving the collections, information resources, and services of the individual CIC libraries.

While collection cooperation is paramount in the CIC mission an interest in cooperative services is coming to the fore, particularly with the emergence of the CIC Virtual Electronic Library (VEL), a Web-based catalog of the CIC holdings, and patron-initiated interlibrary loan services. The experience of cooperative development related to the VEL and to creating the CIC Libraries Strategic Plan has provided CIC librarians with incentive to move forward with many other cooperative projects and ideas. Collaboration is particularly critical as each individual library is challenged with limited resources and staff to create similar platforms and Web-based services.

Web Design and Evaluation

The literature is exploding with articles related to Web design and usability though research libraries are just beginning to conduct specific needs assessment and evaluation related to their Web site. More libraries have included questions about their Web presence in general user needs assessment surveys but these focus most often on whether the respondent uses all or specific parts of the Web site. Few are involving users at the front end of the Web design. Abels, White, and Hahn developed and implemented user-based criteria for designing a Web page for the academic business community. They note that in the past usability testing is most often conducted after the Web sites are developed, usually in the evaluation stage. They propose determining the criteria that influences the community's use of the Web, integrate these in the design and involve users in the evaluation phase. Wan and Chung examine Web page design in terms of network analysis, and classify Web sites according to the complexity of their designs, a factor strongly related to effectiveness and efficiency for users. After mapping the structure of Web sites they concluded that it is desirable to keep Web pages within a close distance to the homepage. McMurdo agrees with the concept of a shallow structure for Web sites. Roy Tennant summarizes that "determining a logical structure that supports multiple uses" is the key to developing information for different people who seek and use the information in a wide variety of ways.

Specific analysis of research library Web sites is beginning to emerge in the literature. For example the University of Arizona Library conducted user-based testing to develop and evaluate their Website. In a descriptive article, King examined the home pages of the 120 libraries in the Association of Research Libraries with a goal of comparing design similarities and differences. Allen and Prabha are in the process of analyzing data from a study of user perceptions of the CIC Virtual Electronic Library (VEL) using the critical incidence methodology where a recent experience by a user is studied.

Emergence of Web-Based Services: An Initial Survey of CIC Libraries

CIC libraries all have Websites containing a wide variety of information about collections, digital resources, and services. This paper will focus only on a preliminary analysis of the inclusion and placement of services in these Web sites. A questionnaire was completed by 12 of the 13 member libraries concerning their Web sites. Service areas of each site were also examined individually for placement and "findability." Linkage of these services from the libraries' homepages was also reviewed. Table 1 summarizes the number of library Web sites where a particular service is found, the number found on the libraries' homepage and the number of "clicks" to get to the particular service from the homepage.

Specific services

Electronic reference, library instruction, interlibrary loan, and circulation policy information sites were the most frequently noted service sites. However, they were not located, in most cases, on the libraries' homepages. Electronic reference was most frequently on the homepage (5 of 12). Interlibrary loan (3 of 12) and circulation policies (only 2 of 12) appeared on very few homepages. Circulation recalls was the next common site (11 of 12) with circulation renewals, electronic suggestion box, campus document delivery, and acquisitions suggestions following in frequency. Other common sites include interactive library instruction, circulation renewals, reserves, disability services, frequently asked questions, electronic tours, and technical support. Less frequent were sites for research consultations, distance education or subject-specific interactive library instruction.

CIC VEL

As members of the CIC consortia, all 13 libraries provide access to the CIC Virtual Electronic Library or VEL. However, only four have this service located on their homepage. Allen and Prabha found that in libraries where the VEL is embedded it takes users an average of three clicks to locate it. Also none of the libraries link to the CIC Website, itself (although currently it does not contain many specific services for library users). It takes four clicks to get to the "Links to CIC Libraries" page from the CIC consortia homepage. Another possible barrier is that users cannot go to a CIC library catalog within the VEL and then move to that library's Website.

"Findability" Issues in CIC Libraries

Locating service sites can either be easy or almost impossible on the various CIC library sites. Two major barriers exist for users. First, the service must be found and, in some cases, important service points are imbedded in the Website site requiring two or more "clicks." For example, electronic reference, one of the most prolific service sites, can be found on the homepage of only five of 12 libraries. Circulation is only found on two homepages. Interlibrary loan is found on three.

The second major barrier to locating services is terminology. Although the service might be on the homepage its label may be obscure to users. Examples of this linguistic obscurity include words like lending services for circulation (which is also an obscure word to some), library outreach ser-

Table 1. Services on CIC Libraries Web Sites

Services	Libraries	On Homepage
Circ. - policies	12	2
Electronic reference	12	5
ILL	12	3
User education	12	3
Circ. - recalls	11	1
Acquisitions suggestions	10	0
Campus document delivery	10	0
Circ - renewals	10	3
Electronic reserves	10	3
Electronic suggestion box	10	4
Reserves (directory)	10	3
Disability services	9	3
Interactive library instr (gen)	9	5
FAQ	8	2
Electronic tour	7	3
Distance education	6	1
Technical support	6	1
Reference consultation	3	1
Interactive library instr (subj)	2	0

vices for distance education, virtual reference for electronic reference services and 7-Fast for document delivery. Librarians are becoming keenly aware of this problem and are applying new, hopefully more understandable names to the services. For example, five CIC libraries use "Ask a Librarian" as the title for their electronic reference site. Another library uses the phrase "a.k.a. assigned reading, after reserves and another puts "borrowing books" in parentheses after "circulation." Interactive tutorials also suffer from the naming problem. Everything from *Library Explorer to netTutor* is used to identify these very useful interactive tutorials.

Web searching and subject gateways

Seven of 12 libraries offer users the ability to search their entire Website and eight of 12 libraries have some kind of subject-based gateway to the Internet. One library removed the Web searching capability because users were confusing it with the online catalog. Another library solved this problem by including a phrase under the search link "excluding the library catalog." The increased blurring of online catalogs with Web-based resources is quite confusing and will not diminish until the catalogs and Web resources are more effectively integrated into a single, easily searchable gateway. Although this paper does not address staffing issues, construction of individual subject-based gateways can be quite demanding and most libraries have a difficult time keeping these sites current as well as applying effective search capabilities to them.

University homepages

Findability of libraries' Web sites is also related to whether or not the universities' homepages feature the library as a direct link. Five of 12 CIC institutions have a clickable link to their respective library. At other CIC institutions it is difficult to find the library because it is not always located where it might fit logically. For example, searching under "research" did not lead to the library Web site in several of the CIC institutions while searching under faculty and staff did. King found similar results in the ARL Web pages study where only 44% of library homepages could be found in one step from the institutions' homepage.

Web Site Assessment and Evaluation

All of the CIC libraries are strongly interested in user-based needs assessment, particularly now that the first wave of more comprehensive Web sites has been created and used for a period of time. Three CIC libraries report conducting some a specific assessment of their Web site using surveys, focus groups, individual interviews, and desk interaction data. One library has hired consultants to conduct an in-depth study of their Web presence. Others are in the process of conducting general library user needs assessment projects which have selected questions related to Web use.

All of the libraries are reviewing their Web sites and some are doing major overhauls with an eye to improving design features, adding more services, improving the organization of information, improving access to specific sites such as electronic journals, improving ease of use, and relocating buried sites. One library reported that their Web redesign was part of a larger intellectual effort to aid in resource discovery and selection through reconceptualize of information zones or spaces. It is likely that many of the libraries' Web pages will continue to change as the assessments are completed and new information about usability applied to design and placement of services.

Web Site Successes

CIC libraries reported a number of successes with their Web sites. These included elevating services to a level equal to that of information resources, the ability to use electronic request forms for various services, self service features for reference and instruction, delivery of full-text content, and the ability to develop a one library view for library users entering the Web space. Many libraries also reported positive experiences with Web versions of their OPAC integrated into their Web presence.

Web Site Problems

A number of common problems exist with the CIC libraries' Web sites. Users cannot understand categories where services are placed. Current designs are often heavily based on the individual library's organization structure which is not intuitive to the user or does not have a bearing on their particular information need. Service features are buried. The Web sites contain too much information poorly placed. One library indicated the need for "a demolition and rebuilding project" to address this problem. Several libraries indicated the need to improve design to take advantage of virtual information delivery rather than to rely on conventional models of delivery in the virtual environment (rather like using the card catalog as a model for the online catalog environment).

Next Steps

CIC libraries are committed to advancing Web-based information services and new developments will continue to appear on individual Web sites as more is learned about user needs and interface design. This analysis reveals a growing priority for the member libraries to bring Web-based services to the forefront of their Web presence through a variety of methods including better placement and improved user-friendly design. Though not part of this study the importance of marketing the sites is becoming obvious to CIC librarians based on results of user surveys and anecdotal evidence.

CIC libraries are also interested in advancing projects that promote the rich resources contained on their individual Websites. Developing effective searching capabilities across CIC library Websites is one such effort underway. Other projects of interest include a searchable database to electronic reference sites and improved links to digital initiatives. CIC libraries are developing strategies to advance their collective virtual presence to the next level. A major challenge for CIC libraries will be how to develop selected cooperative Web-based services in a user-friendly and seamless way. Services could include cooperative reference consultation services and joint user education program development. A more multidimensional CIC library Website could be developed containing not only the resources found in the VEL and the electronic Web-based resources located on member library Websites, but also services and expertise. Place these elements in a searchable and responsive site and the search for services will be fulfilled.

The Changing Nature of Work in Academic Libraries

Kimberley Robles Smith and Beverly P. Lynch

This paper reports the first stage of an investigation of the changing nature of academic library work. Through a content analysis of job advertisements appearing in *College & Research Libraries*, the paper reports on an analysis of the stated requirements for academic library jobs in terms of knowledge of computing and desirable behavioral characteristics. It also addresses changes occurring in some jobs.

Previous Investigations
Most of the studies based on job advertisements in library and information science have had as their purpose an analysis of the job market and the predictions of employment trends. In 1980 Block analyzed job announcements in a file maintained by the Graduate School of Library and Information Science at the University of Texas at Austin. Cataloging and reference positions comprised nearly half of the total jobs listed there.

Reser and Schuneman carried out a content analysis of 1,133 technical service positions and public services positions advertised in *American Libraries, College & Research Libraries News*, and *Library Journal* in 1988. They found that technical services jobs required more computer skills, greater foreign-language requirements, and previous work experience. Public services jobs required more advanced degrees.

Hong Xu conducted a content analysis of job ads appearing in *American Libraries* from 1971–1990 in order to identify similarities and differences in the jobs of catalog librarians and reference libraries working in academic libraries. Xu was particularly interested in identifying jobs brought about by developments in library automation. He analyzed 574 jobs stratified into four periods representing technological change in libraries: 1971–75; 1976–80; 1981–85; 1986–90. Xu found increasing needs for computer skills in both groups. Differences remained, however, in the major job responsibilities and in the knowledge and skills needed.

Robinson, seeking to identify skills and experiences required for collection development jobs, analyzed 433 ads in *College & Research Libraries News* from 1980–1991. Fifty-eight percent of the ads (251) combined collection development jobs with another function; about 80% of these were combined with reference jobs. Seventy-nine percent of the positions required degrees from ALA accredited programs; only 23% of the ads mentioned faculty status. Robinson also includes a good

---

Kimberley Robles Smith is reference librarian, California State University, Fresno, and Beverly P. Lynch is professor, Graduate School of Library and Information Science, UCLA.

review of the literature on the use of job ads to assess the nature of library work.

Zhou analyzed trends in requirements for computer skills in academic library jobs. He found that jobs in technical and public services now require specific computer skills. Further, in the 1994 data, the last year of his analysis, nearly 88% of administration positions listed computer related qualifications. Zhou concludes that knowledge of computing now is integral to all jobs in academic libraries.

Using a different methodology, Buttlar and Garcha carried out a survey of 271 catalogers in order to determine through questionnaires the change catalogers identified in their work activities and roles during the period 1987–1997. More than 90% of the respondents reported that the core activities of their jobs remained the same: descriptive cataloging and the assignment of call numbers and subject headings, activities long associated with their careers. The catalogers did report that their roles had expanded to include managerial tasks, the training of others, and the inclusion of electronic materials. Buttlar and Garcha also found that some catalogers were becoming involved in the activities relating to database development and maintenance. A small but growing number of catalogers reported being engaged in reference desk work, collection development and bibliographic instruction, with job sharing on the rise.

Questions Guiding This Study

Our interest is in the changing nature of library work. We expect that change in work will lead to change in organizational structure and design. Several questions thus guided this investigation.

• Do the jobs being advertised in the 1990s show significant changes in content over the jobs being advertised in the 1980s?

• How wide spread are job requirements relating to technology? That is, do more jobs include specific technologies in their requirements?

• Are behavior skills such as "ability to work in a team environment" appearing more frequently? Were such behavioral requirements found in 1980s ads?

• Does job content, as reflected in advertisements, show significant differences depending upon the type of institution the job is in?

• What change can be observed in the administrative patterns in academic libraries and in the functional departments in those libraries? We expected this change to be observed in that fewer assistant director and assistant department head jobs would appear in the 1990s.

Methodology

A content analysis of job advertisements was selected as the methodology for this study. The assumption is that the advertisement will indicate the ideal job as defined by the employer at a particular point in time and the library will include in the ad those knowledge, skills, and abilities it believes to be important at the time. The ad defines the job without making the necessary adjustments to the job when a person already is in the job. Since we were looking for indicators of changes in library work, the ideal design is what we sought.

Job advertisements appearing in *College & Research Libraries News* for the month of March in 1983, 1988, 1993, and 1998 were used, a total of 211 ads. *College & Research Libraries News* was selected because jobs advertised here reach a national audience of about 12,000 subscribers, not a regional or local audience. It was assumed that these jobs would reflect change occurring in academic libraries and thus would display a variation over time. We assumed that 1983 would be a baseline year and that technological imperatives would grow over the next fifteen years. March was selected arbitrarily.

The job categories used in this study were based upon those used in the placement center at conferences on the American Library Association. Twelve categories were used:

A. Administration (deans, directors, AULS, etc.)

A1. Other Administrative Positions (Personnel Officer, etc.)

A2. Head of a subject library (Chemistry, Art, etc.)

A3. Head of a Library Dept. (function: Reference, Cataloging, etc.)

D. General and Subject Reference.

E1. Instruction Librarian. (coordinator of instruction)

E2. Extension/Distance Learning Librarian.

F. Technical Services (acquisitions, cataloger, serials).

H. Collection development.

I. Special materials (any position) government documents, maps, rare books, archives, audio-visual, etc.

J. Information systems (automation, bibliographic utilities, networks, systems, etc.

K. Non-library settings.

Table 1 lists number of positions advertised by job title by date. The title of the job was used, although if the title was not descriptive enough, assignment of the title was taken out of the content of the ad.

The *Classification of Institutions of Higher Education*, published in 1994 by the Carnegie Foundation for the Advancement of Teaching, was used to classify the libraries advertising. The classifications used were: Research Universities, Doctoral Universities, Master's (Comprehensive) Colleges and Universities, Baccalaureate (Liberal Arts) colleges, and Associate of Arts Colleges. While the Carnegie Classifications includes two groupings in most classes, the groups I and II in each category were collapsed into a single class in this study. Table 2 shows the distribution of the ads. 48% of the ads were for jobs in libraries serving research universities. Of the 3,595 institutions included in the 1994 Carnegie classification, 125 or 3% were research universities. We assumed that these large libraries were more able to design new jobs reflecting new demands in technology than smaller libraries were and we further assumed that the large libraries have more freedom to experiment with new job designs than small libraries do. Historically the large libraries have pioneered in most change in academic libraries.

The authors did a small pilot study of twelve jobs advertised in a February 1998 issue of the *Chronicle of Higher Education* in order to assess coding and determine the presence of some of the variables. Of these, seven jobs had traditional titles, e.g., Social Science Reference Librarian, Assistant/Associate Director of Technical Services. One job displayed a title which extended the reference librarian's job, Information Ser-

Table 1. Positions Advertised by Job Title

Job title	1983	1988	1993	1998	Total
A	8	16	6	13	43
A1	0	2	0	0	2
A2	2	6	0	0	8
A3	3	10	5	6	24
subtotal in A:					77
D	1	11	7	9	28
E1	0	0	0	0	0
E2	0	1	0	0	1
F	6	8	3	6	23
H	0	1	1	3	5
I	3	6	2	2	13
J	1	3	0	2	6
K	0	1	0	0	1
subtotal in D–K:					77
A2/D	2	3	2	0	7
A3/D	1	1	1	1	4
D/H	2	11	4	5	22
A3/F	0	1	0	0	1
D/F	0	2	0	1	3
E1/D/H	0	2	0	0	2
A2/D/H	0	1	0	1	2
H/J/D	0	1	0	4	5
A2/H	0	0	2	0	2
E1/D	0	0	1	2	3
H/J	0	0	1	0	1
A3/J	0	0	0	1	1
D/F/H	0	0	0	1	1
D/H/A3	0	0	0	1	1
D/E1/A3	0	0	0	1	1
I/J	0	0	0	1	1
Subtotal in Combination:					57
Total	29	87	35	60	211

Table 2. Job Ads by Institutional Class and Date						
Class	1983	1988	1993	1998	Total	%
Research Universities	17	42	19	23	101	48%
Doctoral Universities	3	17	2	6	28	13%
Master's	3	17	9	16	45	21%
Baccalaureate (Liberal arts)	5	9	3	11	28	13%
Associate Arts	1	1	2	4	8	4%
Total	29	86	35	60	210	*

* 99% due to rounding

vices Librarian. Two jobs had what we called emerging titles, e.g., Access Services Manager. One job, advertised by a Research I university, was an innovative or new title, Information Consultant.

To assess the job content relating to computing the authors used the checklist of computer-related codes developed and used by Zhou. The computer codes used were

1. bibliographic utilities, such as OCLC or RLIN;
2. automated library systems, including general knowledge of library automation;
3. online database searching, such as DIALOG or BRS;
4. microcomputer applications;
5. mainframe computer applications;
6. CD-ROM products;
7. computer languages or programming;
8. computer hardware;
9. possession of a degree in computer science.
10. networks, such as LAN or WAN;
11. Internet searching.
12. resources in electronic formats;
13. image technology or multimedia.

To assess job requirements relating to behavioral descriptions, the authors developed a set of codes from an examination of the pilot data and a review of the literature on organizational change in libraries. The paper by Roy Tennant was particularly helpful. The behavioral codes used were:

1. communication skills (includes oral and/or written);
2. interpersonal skills;
3. service orientation/public service;
4. work effectively with faculty, students, staff;
5. collegial environment;
6. creative/creativity;
7. energetic/enthusiastic/outgoing;
8. flexibility;
9. team member/team environment;
10. work in a changing, dynamic, expanding environment.

The authors analyzed a sample set of ads to assess the level of agreement in coding. One author did the job title coding and both authors reviewed the coding and, in the event of disagreement, arrived at a consensus.

For the purposes of this paper we analyzed three groups of jobs. The first group, Group A, Administration (Deans, Directors, AULs, etc.), was analyzed because of our interest in change in organizational structures in academic libraries. We expected to see a significant difference in the duties and responsibilities of the AUL position. We expected to find job ads that stated a description of organizational change from a hierarchical structure to a team-based, flattened structure.

The second groups of job was the general and subject reference jobs, Group D. We were interested in how electronic resources were incorporated into the job. We also sought some indication of the role of instruction in the reference jobs.

The third group of jobs comprised those which displayed a combination of jobs, those showing a combination (A2/D,etc.) in table 1. Our purpose is to study the changing nature of work in academic libraries, so this latter group is of particular interest to us. These fifty seven positions combine many of the tasks that have defined the work of the academic librarian: collection development, reference, cataloging. Buttlar and Garcha had reported that a growing number of catalogers were engaged in reference desk work, collection development, and bibliographic instruction. These participants reported "job sharing" on the rise. Robinson also reported a wide spread sharing of collection development work with other jobs. We interpret this as reflecting a change in professional work in academic libraries and we wanted to assess such changes.

Results

Over 80% of all jobs being advertised required a degree from an ALA accredited program. This replicates the finding of Robinson who reported that 79% of the ads he studied required a degree from an ALA accredited program. The largest libraries, those in Research I and II universities, are more likely not to mention the ALA degree, but in general the policy adopted by ACRL in the 1970s has been accepted by the field:

> The master's degree from a program accredited by the American Library Association is the appropriate professional degree for librarians. (Source: Policy 54.2. *ALA Handbook of Organization 1998–99*, p.45.)

A second policy adopted by ACRL in the 1970s, Faculty Status of College and University Librarians, was less widely accepted. ACRL has, as policy:

> The intellectual contributions made by academic librarians to the teaching, research, and service mission of their colleges and universities merit the granting of faculty status. Faculty status for librarians should entail the same rights and responsibilities granted to and required of other members of the faculty. (Source: Policy 54.5. *ALA Handbook of Organization 1998–99*, p. 45.)

Forty-three percent of the ads in this study included faculty status in the ad.

Administrative Jobs

Fifty percent of all administrative positions in this study required some knowledge of or experience with automated library systems, this most often being a general knowledge of library automation (50% of ads in 1983; 50% in 1988; 40% in 1993; 62% in 1998). More specific aspects of automation, such as knowledge of particular bibliographic utilities or online data base searching, were not included in the administrative job ads.

In terms of behavioral requirements, strong communication skills, both oral and written, emerged as the most frequently mentioned skill (25% in 1983; 50% in 1988; 80% in 1993; 45% in 1998). Communication skills were followed by interpersonal skills and the ability to work effectively with faculty, students, and staff.

From the data on administrative jobs we could not identify much interest in "ability to work in a team environment" nor was change identified in the administrative patterns in libraries. Only one job ad, for an AUL position in a Research I library, stated explicitly that "The library system, as it evolves into a functional team rather than a traditional line management approach, is seeking someone to initiate change".

The job content for the administrative jobs reflected the historical approach to library management. The interest in strong communication and interpersonal skills and a general knowledge of library automation have been added to the general management knowledge and skills of planning, organizing, budgeting. Generally speaking, the knowledge, skills, and abilities required for director and associate/assistant director jobs are well known and the job easily defined.

Leadership was not a variable that was included in this study. It emerged, however, as a important consideration in the administrative job category. Forty-two percent of all jobs required some evidence of leadership (25% in 1983; 38% in 1988; 67% in 1993; 46% in 1998).

Reference Jobs

The duties of the reference librarian included instruction and online searching in the 1980s. The one job ad in 1983 mentioned "orientation," which we interpret as the earlier form of the library's instruction program. Eight of the 10 ads in 1988 included instruction, seven included online searching, and six had collection development responsibilities. Two of the ads titled the jobs differently, one being "Information Services Librarian" and other being "Automated Information Access/Reference Librarian".

In the 1980s behavioral characteristics began to appear in the reference ads. Oral and written communication skills emerged most often.

In the 1990s oral and written communication skills were common in the reference jobs ads. Instruction duties were included in all job ads. Online searching and collection development were mentioned in four.

In 1998 the variable, leadership, appeared in three of the nine ads.

The title, "reference librarian" continued to be the most common title until 1998. In 1998 the reference jobs were called:
- Electronic Services Reference Librarian
- Information Literacy Librarian
- Library faculty/Reference Librarian
- Reference/Agricultural Librarian
- Reference/Business Librarian
- Reference/Science Librarian
- Reference/Social Science Librarian
- Social Science Reference Librarian

One continued to use "Reference Librarian." All reference jobs required the degree from an ALA accredited program.

Combination Jobs

The emergence of the combination positions may be the results of budget concerns, "we must do more with less." We suspect, though, that the current jobs in academic librarianship are shifting from the traditional, functional specialist positions, to more expansive and complex jobs. It is clear that these types of positions are on the rise. In the data set from 1983, combination jobs represented 14% of the total positions advertised. The percentage increased to 25% in 1988, 31% in 1993, and 32% in 1998.

While it might have been expected that computer related skills would increase dramatically in the 1990s, the combination jobs are not laden with such requirements. In positions requiring reference services, online database searching was often mentioned and the cataloging positions referred to knowledge of the bibliographic utilities. There was no tendency, however, to list numerous computer skills across the board. The most consistent computer related skills were broad and general, eg., "working with resources in electronic formats" or "knowledge of computerized systems."

The requirement of behavioral traits also increased with time in these jobs. The earliest data emphasize skills, not behaviors, in the ads; communication skills are listed in two jobs and only one mention is made of public service. In the 1998 set, however, communications skills occur in 12 of the 19 positions. Terms such as "creativity," "enthusiasm," "flexibility" begin to show up in the 1988 data and increase into the 1990s sets. Only in the 1990s do the concepts of "team environment" or "changing environment" appear. Tennant suggests that it may be more productive to look at personality traits instead of specific skills when hiring for the future. These new combined positions show a growing interest in behavioral characteristics.

Discussion

The results of the first stage of our investigation do enable us to conclude that most academic library jobs require a degree from an ALA accredited program. Over 80% of the jobs require the degree. The master's degree from an ALA accredited program, adopted as policy by the Association of College and Research Libraries in the 1970s, has been adopted by the field as the appropriate professional degree for academic librarians.

The field has incorporated the computing technologies into all jobs. The computer requirements in the 1990s ads were stated in broad terms, not in specific skill requirements. Since the ALA accredited degree is a requirement, the assumption of employers is that knowledge of all aspects of computer technologies as they relate to library and information science will be an integral part of a graduate's knowledge base. Therefore, computer skills, a solid knowledge of technological design and application, and knowledge of information resources in all formats must be integral components of all LIS educational programs, and the educational programs must keep pace with change in technology as must the academic libraries.

Instruction has become an integral part of every reference job and some responsibility for collection development is emerging as an important component of these jobs. Job titles are displaying these content changes. How LIS programs deal with these changes in jobs and the requirements for the knowledge base is an important question. Avery and Ketchner report that library instruction is not taught formally in many LIS programs. Programs, however, must look carefully at what kinds of teaching skills and learning theories should be included in the curriculum in order to meet the instructional responsibilities now found in jobs.

The titles of reference jobs and the emergence of more combination jobs do suggest the changing nature of library work. The administrative job ads, however, did not reflect change in organizational structures. The data simply do not describe what we are searching for in terms of organizational structure. Organizational changes, however, have begun to appear in the more entry level jobs where departmental and unit team environments were mentioned. These results are tantalizing and require further investigation using different methods.

The growing requirement for behavior skills, especially oral and written communication skills, in entry level and well as administrative level positions, also suggest changes in the nature of the work librarians do. Technical skills continue to be important, but jobs now require the ability to communicate well with people inside and outside the library. Requirements for "flexibility", "creativity", and "leadership" also suggest that jobs are changing and that libraries are too.

These findings require more detailed and careful study of the jobs themselves, not just of the advertisements for these jobs.

Notes

1. David Block, "Emerging Personnel Requirements in Academic Libraries as Reflected in Recent Positions Announcements." ERIC (ED 215 703) 1980.

2. David W. Reser and Anita P. Schuneman, "The Academic Library Job Market: a Content Analysis Comparing Public and Technical Services," *College & Research Libraries*, 53 (January 1992): 49–59.

3. Hong Xu, "The Impact of Automation on Job Requirements and Qualifications for Catalogers and Reference Librarians in Academic Libraries," *Library Resources & Technical Services* 40 (January 1996): 9–59.

4. William C. Robinson, "Academic Library Collection Development and Management Positions: Announcements in *College & Research Libraries News* from 1980 through 1991," *Library Resources & Technical Services* 37 (April 1993): 134–46.

5. Zhou Yuan, "Analysis of Trends in Demand for Computer-Related Skills for Academic Librarians from 1974 to 1994," *College & Research Libraries*, 57 (May 1996): 259–72.

6. Lois Buttlar and Rajinder Garcha, "Catalogers in Academic Libraries: Their Evolving and Expanding Roles," *College & Research Libraries* 59 (July 1998): 311–21.

7. Zhou, 260.

8. Roy Tennant, "The Most Important Management Decision: Hiring Staff for the New Millennium," *Library Journal* (February 15, 1998): 102.

9. Tennant, 102.

10. Chris Avery and Kevin Ketchner, "Do Instruction Skills Impress Employers?' *College & Research Libraries* 57 (May 1996): 249–58.

Thinking Style Preferences Among Academic Librarians: Practical Tips for Effective Work Relationships

Linda Marie Golian

Introduction

Thinking is like breathing—we take it for granted (Parlette, & Rae, 1993). But how we think is just as vital to our success as leaders in the library profession as breathing is to life. A person's thinking style is an interactive mix of inherited tendencies and conditioned responses to early behavioral experiences. As a result, each person favors a particular method of thinking (Harrison & Bramson, 1984).

This paper, and subsequent ACRL conference presentation, is an executive summary of a doctoral research study that investigated the popular assumption that public service librarians and technical service librarians think differently. The information presented in this paper is organized into four sections: (a) description of the research study; (b) theoretical, descriptive, and background information concerning thinking styles; (c) conclusions of the study; and (d) practical applications.

Part I: The Research Study

This first section introduces the research problem, provides a brief explanation of the research methodology, describes the data analysis techniques, and concludes with highlights from the findings of the study. This completed research study was conducted in partial fulfillment of an education doctorate from the Florida Atlantic University, College of Education, Department of Educational Leadership.

The purpose of this study was to scientifically investigate whether differences in thinking styles exist between senior level library administrators working in public and technical service areas in libraries with an institutional membership in the Association of Research Libraries (ARL). Sample size was determined by a power analysis, which calculated that a mean score of 66 dyads (132 participants) was required in order to avoid a Type II error (failing to reject a false null hypothesis).

Linda Marie Golian is associate university librarian, Florida Gulf Coast University.

Once sample size was determined, 66 ARL institutions were randomly selected. Of the randomly selected libraries, the Assistant Director for Public Services and the Assistant Director for Technical Services were then mailed a packet of survey materials. If the Assistant Director for Public Services was not available, the packet was sent to the Head of Reference. If the Assistant Director for Technical Services was not available, the packet was sent to the Head of Cataloging.

The packets included a brief explanation of the study, a consent form, a demographic data form, and a copy of the Inquiry Mode Questionnaire (InQ). Because of the nature of the study, confidentiality, but not anonymity, could be guaranteed to participants. Despite this concern, an 80.3% (106) return rate was achieved. Due to incomplete demographic data forms or improperly completed InQ instruments, a total of 97 surveys were used for the data analysis.

Data analyses included five analyses of variance (ANOVAs) to determine relationships, differences, and interactions based upon the subject's administrative role (public or technical), gender (female or male), and thinking style preference (synthesist, idealist, pragmatist, analyst, or realist). The dependent variable associated with this study was thinking style preference (synthesist, idealist, pragmatist, analyst, and realist). The two independent variables associated with this study were administrative role (public or technical service) and gender (female or male). As part of the ANOVA process, the interaction between gender and administrative role was analyzed. Data analysis also included descriptive information analysis, a cross tabulation computation, and a dyad comparison.

Using a .05 alpha level, none of the 15 null hypotheses could be rejected based upon the ANOVA statistical computation. However, the cross-tabulation and dyad analysis did reveal several noteworthy findings. These findings included: (a) an indication for a strong naturally occurring ability for developing the flat thinking style existed among librarians participating in the study; (b) the relationship between gender and thinking style needed further investigation; (c) the relationship between area of administrative responsibility and thinking style needed further investigation; and (d) a significant difference (84.4%) in preferred thinking styles existed among administrative peers working in the same institution.

Part II: Theoretical, Definitional, and Background Information Concerning Thinking Styles

The second section of this paper provides additional theoretical, definitional, and background information concerning thinking style research. This section focuses upon the InQ instrument developed by Harrison and Bramson in 1977, and revised in 1980. Definitions for six specific thinking styles are provided, with detailed information concerning the strengths and weaknesses of these styles highlighted in three informational tables.

Believing that differences exist among cognition, learning, personality, and thinking, Harrison and Bramson (1982) began investigating inquiring systems in the 1970s. As part of their research investigation, Harrison and Bramson conducted a series of seminars. From these seminars they inferred that the incongruities between learning and thinking were attributed to individual differences in ways of thinking rather than to attributes of personality (Bruvold, Parlette, Bramson, & Bramson, 1983). Interested in the disparity they noticed between cognition and behaviors exhibited during in the decision-making process, Harrison and Bramson (1982) reasoned that thinking styles were integrated collections of perceptual and conceptual strategies.

Based upon these conclusions, Harrison and Bramson then used Buchler's (1961) and Churchman's (1968, 1971) works for identifying five specific approaches in the way an individual perceives, makes meaning, and communicates. This research resulted in the five dimensions of thinking. The five dimensions of thinking identified by Harrison and Bramson's InQ are: (a) synthesist, (b) idealist, (c) pragmatist, (d) analyst, and (e) realist. The following brief explanation of these thinking style dimensions is included for additional definitional clarification:

Synthesist Thinking: A dimension of thinking associated with concentrating on underlying assumptions and abstract ideas. The orientation of synthesist thinkers is focused on integration while their behavior is often viewed as challenging.

Idealist Thinking: A dimension of thinking associated with focusing on process, aspirations, and values. The orientation of idealist thinkers is focused on assimilation while their behavior is often viewed as receptive.

Pragmatist Thinking: A dimension of thinking associated with examining problems within their situational context. The orientation of pragmatist thinkers is focused on payoff while their behavior is often viewed as adaptive and incremental.

Analyst Thinking: A dimension of thinking associated with abstracting facts into theories and problem-solving approaches. The orientation is

Table 1: Summary of Thinking Style Orientations					
Orientations	Synthesist	Idealist	Pragmatist	Analyst	Realist
Characteristics	Integrative view.	Holistic view.	Eclectic view.	Deductive view.	Empirical view.
	Seeks conflict and synthesis.	Seeks ideal solutions.	Seeks shortest route to payoff.	Seeks "one" best way.	Seeks solutions that meet current needs.
	Interested in change.	Interested in values.	Interested in innovation.	Interested in scientific solutions	Interested in concrete results.
	Speculative.	Receptive	Adaptive	Prescriptive	Corrective
Strengths	Focuses on underlying assumptions.	Focuses on process and relationships.	Focuses on payoffs.	Focuses on method and plan.	Focuses on facts and results.
	Points out abstract conceptual aspects.	Points out values and aspirations.	Points out tactics and strategies.	Points out data and details.	Points out realities and resources.
	Good at preventing over-agreement.	Good at articulating goals.	Good at identifying impacts.	Good at model building and planning.	Good at simplifying, "cutting-through"
	Best in controversial situations.	Best in value-laden situations.	Best in complex situations.	Best in structured situations.	Best in well-defined situations.
	Provides debate and creativity.	Provides broad view, goals, and standards.	Provides experimentation and innovation.	Provides stability and structure.	Provides drive and momentum.
Liabilities	May screen out agreement.	May screen out "hard data."	May screen out long-range aspects.	May screen out values.	May screen out disagreement.
	May seek conflict unnecessarily.	May delay from too many choices.	May rush too quickly to payoff.	May over-plan, over-analyze.	May rush to over-simplified solutions.
	May try too hard for change, newness.	May try too hard for "perfect" solutions.	May try too hard for expediency	May try too hard for predictability.	May try too hard for consensus.
	May theorize excessively.	May overlook details.	May rely too much on what "sells."	May be inflexible, overly cautious.	May over-emphasize perceived "facts".
	Can appear uncommitted.	Can appear overly sentimental.	Can appear over-compromising.	Can appear "tunnel visioned."	Can appear too results-oriented.

Source: Harrison, A.F. and Bramson, R. M. 1988. *InQ inquiry mode questionnaire: A measure of how you think and make decisions.* Berkeley, Calif.: Bramson, Parlette, Harrison & Associates.

focused on method while behavior is often viewed as prescriptive and logical.

Realist Thinking: A dimension of thinking associated with emphasizing available resources and apprehendable facts. The orientation of realist thinkers is focused on the task at hand while their behavior is often viewed as empirical and objective.

Flat Thinking: A dimension of thinking associated with a natural predisposition towards using all five of the thinking styles with equal effectiveness depending upon the situation. The orientation of flat thinkers is focused on using the most effective thinking style for the situation while their behavior is often viewed as inconsistent.

Building upon the basic concepts of the five dimensions of thinking, Table 1, table 2, and table 3 provide additional information concerning the characteristics of each style. These tables also provide information concerning the strengths and liabilities for each of the five primary thinking styles.

Part III: Conclusions of the Study

The third section of this paper addresses the conclusions of the study. Seven conclusions were highlighted in the full study, with three having special merit for this paper and presentation. These three conclusions are: (a) the tremendous potential for librarians participating in this study to develop the flexible, and highly effective, flat thinking style; (b) the effect of highly structured, or differentiated organizations, upon individual thinking styles; and (c) the lack of previous research connecting thinking style with the library science profession.

The first conclusion, the natural potential for librarians to develop a flat thinking style, is based upon a thorough analysis of the actual scores for each participant concerning the scores for each of the five thinking style dimensions. To understand

Table 2: Quick Behavioral Clues to Help Recognize Thinking Styles	
Thinking Style	Behavioral Clues
Synthesist	bounces from topic to topic in a conversation asks "what if" questions argues theoretical points and talks a lot speculates about new ideas and concepts
Idealist	is a good and interested listener talks about long range goals, values and ideals wants to please you so you won't be upset often sounds disappointed in others
Pragmatist	Interested in a quick payoff quick-witted and quick on their feet playful and cheerful interested in a short time frame
Analyst	insists on technical data generally appears neat and orderly asks detailed and concrete questions is reluctant to change from the tried-and-true
Realist	is direct and frank seems impatient and restless and interrupts a lot says ... If you look at the facts ... Do we really need it? states opinions as if they were facts is quick to provide solutions to issues

Source: InQ Educational Materials, Inc. (1994). *Workbook for recognizing and influencing others' thinking styles*. Berkeley: Holland Parlette Associates.

Behavioral Clues	Synthesist	Idealist	Pragmatist	Analyst	Realist
Apt to appear	Challenging, skeptical, amused.	Attentive, receptive, supportive.	Open, sociable, humorous.	Cool, studious, hard to read.	Direct, forceful, quick, non-verbal expression.
Apt to say	On the other hand... No, not necessarily...	It seems to me... Don't you think...	I'll buy that... That's one sure way...	Logically... It stands to reason...	It's obvious to me... Everybody knows that...
Apt to express	Concepts, opposite points of view.	Feelings, Ideas about values. What's good.	Non-complex ideas, Personal anecdotes.	General rules, supporting data.	Opinions, factual anecdotes.
Tone	May sound argumentative, sardonic.	May sound tentative, hopeful, and resentful.	May sound insincere, enthusiastic.	May sound stubborn, careful, dry.	May sound dogmatic, forthright, and positive.
Enjoys	Intellectual, philosophical arguments.	Feeling-level, discussions.	Brainstorming, Lively give-and-take.	Rational examination of issues.	Short, direct, factual discussions.
Apt to use	Parenthetical expressions, qualifying phrases, adjectives.	Indirect questions, Aids to agreement.	Case examples, illustrations, and popular opinions.	Long, discursive, well-formulated sentences.	Direct, pithy, descriptive statements.
Dislikes	Talk that seems too simplistic, superficial, mundane.	Talk that seems too factual, conflictive, dehumanizing.	Talk that seems too dry, dull, humorless, "nit-picking."	Talk that seems too irrational, aimless, "far-out."	Talk that seems too sentimental, impractical.
Under stess	Pokes fun.	Looks hurt.	Looks bored.	Withdraws.	Becomes agitated.

Source: InQ Educational Materials, Inc. 1994. *Workbook for modifying your thinking profile*. Berkeley, Calif.: Holland Parlette Associates.

this conclusion, a brief explanation concerning InQ scoring is provided.

Table 4 provides an illustrated summary of the strength of thinking style preferences based upon InQ scoring. Scores between 90 and 72 in any one style of thinking indicate a very strong preference for that style, with scores between 71 and 66 interpreted as a strong preference, and scores between 65 and 60 revealing a moderate preference for a specific thinking style. A score of 48 or less in any one style of thinking is considered a disregard for a thinking style, with scores between 48 and 43 considered moderate disregard, and scores between 42 and 35 considered strong disregard for a specific thinking style. Scores of 34 or below are considered a virtual neglect of a specific thinking style. A score between 59 and 49 notes a neutral preference for a specific thinking style. Differences between any two scores that are less than four points apart are considered too small to indicate a preferred thinking style (Harrison and Bramson, 1982).

A relatively low preference or disregard for any specific thinking style, coupled by an overall evenness among the scores for the five specific thinking styles, indicates a natural tendency toward the flat thinking style. The inclination towards a flat thinking style is viewed as an asset since these thinkers are considered more flexible, creative, and

Table 4: Summary of InQ Thinking Style Preferences						
90–72	71–66	65–60	59–49	48–43	42–35	34–18
Very strong preference	Strong preference	Moderate preference	Neutral preference	Moderate disregard	Strong disregard	Virtual neglect

Source: Harrison, A. F., and R. M. Bramson. 1977. *InQ administration and interpretation manual.* Berkeley, Calif.: Bramson, Parlette, Harrison and Associates.

better adapted to use the best thinking style to resolve problems based upon the situation (Svendsen & Svendsen, 1995).

Prior to the ANOVA calculations, the raw scores from the InQ instruments indicated that 57.6% of the sample had a moderate to neutral preference for the most preferred thinking style. After calculating the 20 mean scores necessary for the ANOVA analysis, a neutral preference for 16 thinking styles (80%) was noted. These scores reveal a natural tendency towards a flat thinking style.

The second conclusion highlighted for this paper involves the influence of organizational differentiation upon an individual's thinking style preference. According to the theory of differentiation, when organizations grow in size their environments become more complex. In an attempt to manage the organization, sub-units, such as library public service and technical service departments, are created. In time, these organizational sub-units become more differentiated from other sub-units in order to address specific work routines. Conformity in these sub-units becomes the desired norm, with individual members quickly realizing the need to behave, and think, like the rest of their unit, or like their immediate supervisor, in order to be considered effective, successful, and part of the group.

According to research conducted by Frankie (1980) and Lowry (1988), libraries are highly differentiated organizations. Data analysis for this study revealed that 84.4% of the organizational dyads (administrative peers working in the same library organization) had significant differences in thinking style preferences. In accordance with differentiation theory, it can be reasoned that in some library organizations, differences in thinking style preferences among administrative peers can affect the preferred thinking style among sub-unit members due to the desire to adopt the preferred thinking style of the immediate supervisor. Additional research is needed to verify and substantiate this conclusion.

The final conclusion highlighted for this paper involves the lack of previous research concerning thinking style research and the library science profession. Although librarianship is a profession that requires specialized cognitive and higher level mental organizational skills, very little research has been conducted concerning thinking styles and librarianship, with no previous studies found using the InQ instrument with library science professionals (Golian, 1998). However, the literature review conducted for the dissertation study revealed numerous research studies analyzing library professionals using other self-discovery instruments such as the Myers-Briggs Type Indicator or Kolb's Learning Style Instrument.

This lack of research concerning thinking styles and the library science profession severely limits the practical application and incorporation of thinking style research within the library science profession. Librarians must first become aware of thinking style research before they can attempt to understand, and finally, incorporate these concepts into every day library administration situations. As additional research is conducted and shared in the professional library science literature, more librarians and library administrators should begin to employ thinking style research for both personal and organizational growth.

Part IV: Practical Applications

The final section of this paper presents suggestions and advice on how librarians can become more creative and flexible thinkers. The literature review, findings, and conclusions of this research study indicate that incorporating thinking style research can help facilitate understanding among coworkers and can help improve organizational communication. This is possible since thinking style research can be linked with opportunities for personal growth and with opportunities for organizational growth.

For personal growth, research shows that thinking styles can be modified when change and growth are considered important for professional growth (Harrison & Bramson, 1982). Research shows that individuals who strive to utilize the thinking style most appropriate for the situation (flat thinkers) have greater flexibility and creativity and are more effective problem-solvers (Harrison and Bramson, 1977; Svendsen and Svendsen, 1995).

Benfari (1991, 1995) created a four-step plan to modify skills for effective professional growth. In his plan, Benfari recommends taking the time to understand yourself, your co-workers, and your organization's culture. Only when understanding is achieved can modification begin. Using the information available in table 1, table 2, and table 3, Benfari's four steps, modified to include thinking styles, include:

Reflect: Take the time to understand yourself and others in terms of strengths and weaknesses concerning thinking style preferences.

Identify: Find work situations in which you have been effective and those in which you have been ineffective.

Determine: Recognize what aspects of your thinking styles play a role in both the positive and negative outcomes in these situations.

Modify: Work to achieve positive outcomes at all times by using the thinking style most appropriate for the situation, and try to align these outcomes with the mission of the organization.

For organizational growth, research shows that when thinking style awareness is used with daily work routines, improved work effectiveness for individuals and the organization can occur (Robinson, 1995; Sheldon, 1991). By encouraging workers to learn and reflect upon how thinking styles are viewed by others in the organization, library administrators help support team-based management and total quality management in their organizations. Table 5 provides additional information concerning how organizations can utilize thinking style research to enhance organizational growth.

Summary and Comments

Inter (1993) indicated that the relationship between library public service and technical service departments is strained by many variables including diversities in management orientations, differences in public service philosophies, and varying approaches towards descriptive cataloging. In 1966, Xu concluded that the administrative area of responsibility (public or technical service) and the level of responsibility had a direct relationship to communication behaviors of individuals within a library. The conclusions of this study indicate that thinking style research can help lessen these

---

Table 5. Applications For Using Thinking Style Research in Organizations

1. To broaden and deepen individual competencies in thinking, problem solving, and influencing others.
2. To support team building since the process has been proven to be a non-threating way of indentifying collaborative resources.
3. To coach others by helping them to strengthen under-used strategies and modify styles that are over used.
4. As an aid in the selection of key personnel, especially for providing strengths that are needed for enabling teams and the organization to work more effectively.
5. In integrating new employees into the organization by using the selection-process data to plan how best to orient and supervise new staff.
6. In matching persons to projects so that thinking styles and experiences can be applied to tasks appropriately.

Sources: InQ Educational Materials, Inc. 1994. *Workbook for modifying your thinking profile.* Berkeley: Holland Parlette Associates.

strained relationships by encouraging a more effective means of understanding and communication.

The literature review associated with this study reveals that librarians and library organizations have been using self-discovery tools as an effective means for developing effective library organizations (Golian, 1998; Scherdin, 1994). For example Kolb's Learning Styles Inventory and the MBTI personality style indicator are two very popular self-discovery tools that have been used in numerous library research studies. Although these instruments provide critical information to the success of building effective library organizations, in recent years they have provided very little new information and knowledge for the library science profession. It is therefore suggested that library leaders and library administrators consider alternative methods and self-discovery tools for developing more effective communication patterns and staff development. One tool that can help in acquiring this new perspective and knowledge is the InQ.

The contributed paper that will be presented at the ACRL 9th National Conference will incorporate a PowerPoint display of the most significant facts from this paper. To help increase awareness of this powerful self-discovery tool, the first 90 people attending the presentation will be given a free copy of a simplified version of the InQ for their own self-discovery.

References

Benfari, R. C. (1995). *Changing your management style: How to evaluate and improve your own performance.* New York: Lexington Books.

———. (1991). *Understanding your management style.* New York: Lexington Books.

*Bramson, R. M., and S. Bramson. (December 1987). What kind of thinker are you? *Reader's Digest,* 131 (788), 149–51.

Bruvold, W. H., N. Parlett, R. M. Bramson, and S. J. Bramson. (1983). "An investigation of the item characteristics, reliability, and validity of the inquiry mode questionnaire." *Education and Psychological Measurement* 43, 483–93.

Butcher, J. (1961). *Concept of method.* New York: Columbia University.

Churchman, C. W. (1968). *Challenge to reason.* New York: McGraw-Hill.

———. (1971). *The design of inquiring systems: Basic concepts of systems and organization.* New York: Basic Books.

Frankie, S. O. (1980). "The behavioral styles, work preferences and values of an occupational group: A study of university catalog and reference librarians." (Doctoral dissertation, George Washington University, 1980). *Dissertation Abstracts International* 41, 3307A.

Golian, L. M. (1998). "Thinking style differences among academic librarians." (Doctoral dissertation, Florida Atlantic University, 1998). *Dissertation Abstracts International* 59, 07A.

**Harrison, A. F., and R. M. Bramson. (1984) *The art of thinking.* New York: Doubleday.

———. (1977). *InQ administration and interpretation manual.* Berkeley, Calif.: Bramson, Parlette, Harrison and Associates.

———. (1988). *InQ inquiry mode questionnaire: A measure of how you think and make decisions.* Berkeley, Calif.: Bramson, Parlette, Harrison and Associates.

———. (1982). *Styles of thinking: Strategies for asking questions, making decisions, and solving problems.* Garden City: Anchor Pr.

InQ Educational Materials, Inc. (1994). *Workbook for modifying your thinking profile.* Berkeley, Calif.: Holland Parlette Associates.

———. (1994). *Workbook for recognizing and influencing others' thinking styles.* Berkeley, Calif.: Holland Parlette Associates.

Intner, S. S. (1993). *Interfaces: Relationships between library technical and public services.* Englewood, Colo.: Libraries Unlimited.

Lowry, H. M. (1988). "An investigation of cognitive style and preferred conflict handling mode of cataloging and reference librarians in academic libraries." (Doctoral dissertation, University of New York at Buffalo, 1988). *Dissertation Abstracts International* 49, 1073A.

**Parlette, N., and R. Rae. (1993). "Thinking about thinking." *Leadership,* 70–74.

Robinson, R. D. (1995). *An introduction to dynamics of group leadership and organizational change.* West Bend, Wisc.: Omnibook.

** Scherdin, M. J., ed. (1994) *Discovering librarians: Profiles of a profession.* Chicago: Association of College and Research Libraries.

Sheldon, B. E. (1991). *Leaders in libraries: Styles and strategies for success.* Chicago: American Library Association.

** Svendsen, E., and V. Svendsen. (1995). *Building bridges: Using thinking styles to facilitate communication.* Colorado Springs, Colo.: Help Desk Institute.

Xu, H. (1996). "Type and level of position in academic libraries related to communication behavior." *Journal of Academic Librarianship* 22 (4), 257–66.

In addition to these resources, the copyright holders of the InQ instrument and cited workbooks can be contacted at the following address and phone number:

Holland Parlette Associates, Inc.
P O Box 10213, North Berkeley Station
Berkeley, California 94709-5213
1-800-338-2462

* This article includes a simplified version of the InQ copyrighted instrument.

** These items are highly recommended readings.

That's My Bailiwick

Carol Ann Hughes and Paul Soderdahl

The University of Iowa Libraries provides a unique new scholarly publishing outlet for its faculty and graduate students. With the prevalence of personal faculty home pages and course web sites in just about every department on campus, it's not very hard for faculty to find a web server somewhere for storing an HTML file. And, with some work, faculty can often find some "techie" to help convert a document to HTML or to save a list of links.

What is rare, however, is a space on the web where faculty from all disciplines can find a home for their scholarly research interests, coupled with a computing environment and a knowledgeable staff to help them "follow their bliss" in digital form. The Information Arcade's new Bailiwick project does just that.

The Need for Something New

For a number of years, academic departments in the humanities and social sciences have been able to mount departmental information on the University of Iowa's central web server maintained by academic computing. More recently, two centrally administered course web servers have been made available to any faculty member or teaching assistant offering a credit course. Based on feedback from faculty and graduate students, however, the University Libraries learned that there was no place for a research idea or other academically oriented "pet project" to be published on the web. Instead, faculty and students needed to bury these somewhere on a personal home page, often with a commercial Internet Service Provider at their own expense. Rising to address this need, the University Libraries sought to provide a well-respected, institutionally supported web server for just this sort of electronic publishing endeavor. What originally started as simply a "projects" directory on the library's general web server has now grown into the Bailiwick project.

Officially launched in March of 1998, Bailiwick provide a space on the web where academic passions can be realized as highly specialized and creative web sites. It is not simply a place for personal home pages, nor is it intended for course

---

Carol Ann Hughes is head, Information, Research, and Instructional Services, and Paul Soderdahl is team leader, Libraries-Wide Info System and Multimedia, University of Iowa.

web sites or academic departmental information. It is not meant to serve as the new model for scholarly publishing in peer-reviewed journals. Rather, Bailiwick is designed to provide faculty, staff, and graduate students with web space where they can focus on a particular area of scholarly interest.

Most electronic publishing initiatives arise from an attempt to transfer existing models of print publishing to the digital environment. A small number of electronic scholarly journals are currently published on the University of Iowa campus. The University Libraries already provides a number of ways to support this medium, from archiving to cataloging to hosting journal sites, all as one element of the University Libraries' new Scholarly Digital Resources Center.

Bailiwick, instead, provides a web space that allows authors to harness and exploit this new electronic medium, permitting new models of publishing with multimedia, hypertext, and the ability to incorporate anything in digital form. It is not intended to substitute or even compete with traditional scholarly publishing or electronic journal publishing. Rather, it provides an opportunity to engage in an entirely new medium for scholarly communication.

A History of Innovation

The heart of the Bailiwick Project within the library environment is the Information Arcade, an award-winning facility located in the University of Iowa's Main Library. Opened in 1992, the Information Arcade is a place that provides access to published electronic information resources coupled with state-of-the-art multimedia development workstations that allow faculty and students to digitize and manipulate source materials that are not already in electronic form. The facility also houses a fully networked electronic classroom, with 24 student workstations, where classes from throughout the University are held—some for the whole term and others for one or two class sessions.

In support of its unique service mission "to facilitate the integration of new technologies into teaching, learning, and research," the Information Arcade is well regarded as a place for innovation and risk-taking on the University of Iowa campus. It is a place where ideas can be fleshed out, a place that can respond to the real technology needs that faculty and students present. When the Information Arcade first opened, it was the only fully wired electronic classroom on campus, with a workstation at every student's desk. It was the only publicly accessible facility on campus where any faculty member or student could create digital video on a drop-in basis. It was the only computer facility on campus where anyone could anonymously access the Internet for free. All of these innovations are now mainstays on campus.

In 1998, the Information Arcade expanded its offerings with three new innovative web-based services:

• ***The MOO Project.*** This text-based virtual reality campus for the University of Iowa community is made possible through the magic of MOO, a piece of software that creates a networked environment on the Internet that is part e-mail, part chat-room, and part programming interface. Known collectively as "The Mediatrix," this educational MOO currently houses two distinct academic projects. The Scholar's Web Project, devoted to the possibilities of digital communication in graduate education, makes its MOO home in "The Cave." The MOOniversity Project, which strives to provide a virtual learning environment that encourages collaboration across campuses and disciplines, is located in "The MOOniversity." Co-administered by D. Diane Davis, assistant professor of rhetoric in the Rhetoric Department and Michael Calvin McGee, a professor of rhetoric in the Communications Studies Department, The Mediatrix is available to any faculty member wishing to make use of it for teaching and research.

• ***The Streaming Video Project.*** With text-based virtual reality at one end of the spectrum, the Information Arcade simultaneously launched a new streaming video server, to meet the high-end multimedia needs for delivering real-time motion video and audio over the Internet. With a 50-user license to Real Networks' Real Server, the Information Arcade now provides students and faculty with the ability to serve digital movie files to several locations simultaneously. Because of the streaming quality of the video files, users do not need to wait for an entire file to download before playing it. Already used by Bob Boynton, Professor of Political Science, for his Multimedia Politics class, the streaming video server provides a delivery mechanism for the digital videos created by students and faculty at the Information Arcade's multimedia development stations.

- **The Bailiwick Project.** Linking these two new modes of communication, and providing an outlet for any number of other scholarly publishing projects, the Bailiwick server becomes a publishing medium for research projects that complements the University Libraries' TWIST (Teaching With Innovative Style and Technology) course web server. Space is available on this research web server to any University of Iowa faculty, staff, or graduate student publishing a scholarly academic web site that might be experimental in nature, or consist of a comprehensive examination of scholarly resources in some subject area, or perhaps explore a narrow, highly specialized topic.

Open by simple proposal, Bailiwick runs on a dedicated web server within the library and is supported by the University Libraries' web server infrastructure. Content providers retain editorial control and freedom, and have the ability to define their topic of interest, identify the target audience, and design a customized web site. Each bailiwick is initially limited to 5MB of space, with the ability to petition for more based on specific needs for a given project. In addition to disk space, authors can turn to library staff at the Information Arcade for consultation on site design, graphics and layout, technical support, and training.

An individual bailiwick might:
- serve as a home page for artistic expression and collaboration between artists working in Iowa and other countries;
- be a showcase for digitally produced art that incorporates interactivity meant to be viewed on a computer screen;
- provide a natural home for hypertext experiments that explore new forms of multilinear argument or open-system documents that welcome, even depend on, links to other web sites to expand or counter those arguments;
- host a site not full of bells and whistles but simply a collection of narrowly focused pages of links to resources on a given topic;
- offer an electronic publishing medium for delivery of specialized bibliographies or digital reproductions of rare documents

There are currently 11 bailiwicks in production, with another eight more being developed. The authors of bailiwicks represent 13 different academic departments, including Communication Studies, Political Science, Athletics Administration, and Theatre Arts, and they range from teaching and research assistants to full professors.

Sample Bailiwicks

In general, the bailiwicks developed to date fall into one of four categories: (1) a collection of Internet links on a specialized topic of study, which could range from a small set of links on a particular page to an annotated Internet bibliography of thousands of links; (2) a hypertextual or multimedia essay or thesis that necessitates publishing in this medium; (3) a scholarly research project that is dynamic or updated with such frequency that print publishing would be ineffective, including, for example, ongoing findings from a research study; or (4) a collaborative project that makes use of a shared electronically accessible work space.

The Internet Bibliography

Karla Tonella, a graduate student in Mass Communication, has authored three different bailiwick sites that loosely fall into the category of Internet bibliography. As a former graduate assistant on the Information Arcade staff, Tonella was the one who first identified the need for this sort of publishing medium on campus and articulated the concept of the Bailiwick project. She was very much instrumental in bringing the server to fruition and quickly adopted it as a home for two comprehensive and award-winning sites of Internet resources in her areas of expertise: Women's Studies Online and Journalism and Mass Media. Both of these sites have been given widespread praise in those subject areas and have helped bring attention to the Bailiwick project, both on campus and around the country.

Her Border Crossings site also relies on Internet links as its core content, but it is experimental in its design and published in a way that is intended to "encourage the browsing reader to consider the areas of their postmodern world where traditional boundaries are being renegotiated and blurred." The site explores the notion of "border crossings" from a number of different perspectives and has received numerous citations in the mainstream press, including a sidebar in the *Chronicle of Higher Education*, inclusion in *Britannica Online*'s catalog of recommended sites, and a feature article in *Search*, a monthly newsletter for advanced graduate students published out of Northeastern University in Boston.

The Multimedia Essay

The most popular use for Bailiwick thus far has been for publishing multimedia essays. The Information Arcade itself has been a proponent of the multimedia essay since it first opened in 1992, and most semester-long courses now held in the Information Arcade's electronic classroom incorporate some sort of multimedia term paper as part of the course requirements. The Information Arcade is one of the leaders on campus in the adoption of electronic theses and dissertations, working closely with the Graduate College and academic computing on a pilot project this semester. It is not surprising, then, that faculty and graduate students are turning to Bailiwick as a medium for publishing these sorts of materials.

Michael Calvin McGee, Professor of Communication Studies, has published his essay, "Suffix it to Say that Reality is at Issue," as a bailiwick. Jennifer Lawrence-Gentry, a Ph.D. candidate also in Communication Studies, created a comprehensive site on the work of Mikhail Bakhtin which is now seen as one of the most complete online resources on Bakhtin. Patrick Muller, a teaching assistant in Preventive and Community Dentistry, developed a bailiwick essay entitled, "Complexity Studies: The Fluid Multifaceted Nature of Knowledge." The sites are all very different in design, target audience, and perhaps even scholarly value. Nonetheless, Bailiwick provides an ideal way for the University of Iowa to support this sort of experimental multimedia publishing outside the rubric of a class assignment for a multimedia term paper or a more traditional electronic scholarly publishing environment.

The Scholarly Research Project

Aside from the hypertextual and multimedia aspects of publishing on the web, the most unique advantage to the web for publishing scholarly research is the ability to maintain currency on a published project. The most well developed example of this is a bailiwick on Gender Equity in Sports, sponsored by the Women's Intercollegiate Athletics department. The site monitors the current state of affairs of gender equity in intercollegiate and interscholastic sport, and tracks Title IX compliance and pending Title IX litigation at colleges and universities. This resource has received significant national attention and acts as a research tool in and of itself that is published out of the University of Iowa Libraries and now available for students and scholars across the country.

Another example is the Dogon bailiwick, published by Chris Culy, Associate Professor of Linguistics. This dictionary of the Dogon language was compiled by Marcel Kervran, a member of the Pères Blancs, who lived in the town of Bandiagara, Mali for about 30 years. The dictionary has over 7,000 head words. A second expanded edition was published in 1993. Partially representing the varieties of Donno SO spoken in and around Bandiagara, the dictionary is being expanded from its earlier HyperCard format, and it may soon be ported into an SGML environment. It is an excellent example of an academic tool that would be difficult to create and deliver in paper form.

The Collaborative Work Space

Finally, the Bailiwick server provides a way for researchers at the University of Iowa to work collaboratively and in a public forum with colleagues at other institutions. This collaborative space can be used as a way to gather research data, or to allow others to comment on or contribute to the development of a site. Barbara Bianchi, a graduate student in Counselor Education and an art therapist, has established a bailiwick for Global Connections, a set of online art and notes from travel journals. One component of the Global Connections site, called "Russia Revisited," includes materials from a number of contributing artists and students in Russia, who are jointly working together to create a collaborative artistic travel journal.

Policies Regarding Bailiwick Sites

Bailiwick sites run the gamut in subject area, nature, and scope. No attempt is made to centrally control the content of someone's site. After all, it is their bailiwick and they have complete editorial freedom. On the other hand, there are certain guidelines in place for establishing a bailiwick in order to maintain the focus as an innovative research web server.

First, the site is not intended to be a space for student class assignments. Short-term projects intended to meet course requirements can already be accommodated on one of the University's centrally administered course web servers. In addition, the site is not meant to be a place for a personal home page, or even a student's portfolio. This type of activity can be better accommodated on a student's personal account through academic computing or through a commercial Internet Service Provider. Sites that are commercial in nature are refused, as are sites that are completely divorced from the University's mission.

Content providers need to abide by the University's Acceptable Use Policy which identifies inappropriate uses of information technology resources on campus, such as hacking, forgery, inserting viruses, violating intellectual property rights and software licenses, interfering with others' access to information technology resources, or personal campaigning, lobbying, or commercial activities.

These modest restrictions notwithstanding, most proposals for bailiwicks have been approved. Inappropriate use of existing bailiwick web space has not yet been an issue.

Library Resources to Support the Project

The hallmark of the Information Arcade is its dual strength of providing a facility with state-of-the-art high-end computing equipment for electronic publishing and multimedia development combined with a large and diverse public services staff that can work closely with faculty and students, often one-on-one, to help them harness the technology and integrate it effectively into their teaching, learning, and research. The facility is staffed with six half-time graduate assistants selected from a variety of academic programs in an attempt to achieve a balance of technologists, information specialists, graphics artists, and instructional designers. The primary benefit of this unique staffing arrangement is that the Information Arcade is much more than just another computer or library lab. It is a place where faculty and students can find qualified consultants trained in a subject specialty with expertise in almost any area related to technology.

With this high-tech high-touch model, the Information Arcade is uniquely suited to host a project like Bailiwick. Within the walls of this one facility, the library provides support for every piece of a bailiwick development from inception to creation to delivery. With expert consultation, access to equipment, technical support, and web server space, the library becomes a one-stop place for this model of publishing scholarly research.

With respect to staffing, support includes consultation in any aspect of the Bailiwick project, including design issues, interface development, and training in software. Staff do not provide programming nor do they do any of the work in researching or assembling sites. At the point where a faculty member submits an application for a bailiwick, that faculty member is assigned an Information Arcade Consultant as a primary contact person for technical support, troubleshooting, basic interface design guidance, and referrals to other staff both within and without the Information Arcade. At present, the current level of staffing has been sufficient to accommodate this sort of assistance, which is not unlike the assistance provided to any patron who walks in the door.

As a computing facility, the Information Arcade provides public access to a host of multimedia development workstations for scanning images, slides, and text, and for digitizing video and audio. At these multimedia stations, a large suite of multimedia integration software and web publishing software is made available for public use. Staff at the public services desk have a strong background in multimedia development and web design and can provide some one-on-one training on a walk-in basis beyond technical support and troubleshooting. All of these hardware and software resources are available to Bailiwick content providers, who can choose to do their development work in the Information Arcade or at their home or office.

Finally, since there is a close relationship between the Information Arcade and the University Libraries web, system administration and web server support is all handled in house as well. Thus, there are few artificial barriers imposed by the technology permitting content providers to focus on their creative expression and scholarly communication.

Therefore, with only minimal reallocation of existing resources, the University of Iowa Libraries has been able to launch the Bailiwick project and continue to grow it at a modest pace. One of the components most essential for its continued success, however, is the ability to scale up to meet the expected demand over the next several years. Technical infrastructure challenges are not overwhelming as yet. An analysis still needs to be made to determine how quickly creators are developing their sites, what are the implications for network delivery of these resources, what are reasonable projections for disk space, and who is using the resources.

Perhaps more importantly, though, adequate staffing will always remain a concern. Some faculty are desirous of working more closely with library staff consultants than they can now manage, and the consultants would certainly find it enriching to be more intimately involved with the development of each bailiwick site than time now permits. Marketing of the Bailiwick project has been discrete to say the least because of the limited staffing available. However, embedded in the collaboration inherent in bailiwicks is the potential for stronger involvement with faculty on obtaining grant funding to support the development of specific bailiwick sites.

This path is being tested in a project with two scholars – one from the University of Iowa and one from a university in Germany. With grant funding, these scholars would work with the library to create a new academic resource consisting of a searchable critical edition of an author's corpus coupled with thematic web sites containing bibliographies, a hypertext archive, and searchable commentaries. This bailiwick would then result in an unprecedented resource for scholars from many disciplines and present a model for the development of academic web sites that not only reflect serious study but actually nurture the creation of new, international scholarship. Other site proposals are also candidates for outside funding and can follow this lead.

A Model for Research Libraries

Bailiwick has been a way for the University of Iowa Libraries, and specifically the Information Arcade, to focus on the integration of technology, multimedia, and hypertext, in the context of scholarship and research publishing. To date, most of the bailiwick sites represent disciplines in the arts, humanities, and social sciences, which not only matches the overall clientele of the Information Arcade (given its location in the University of Iowa's Main Library), but also reflects the fact that these disciplines have been traditionally underfunded with respect to technology. Nevertheless, faculty in these disciplines have integrated some of the most creative applications of the technology in their everyday teaching and research, in part because of the existence of the Information Arcade and the groundwork laid by the Libraries for the past several years.

With the Information Arcade's visibility on campus, and with similar resources and support in the Information Commons—a sister facility in the health sciences library—the University of Iowa Libraries is well regarded on campus as a leader in information technology, electronic publishing, and new media. Thus, faculty and students alike are accustomed to turning to the library for innovation in technology, and the Bailiwick project is a natural fit. As part of a palette of new technology services and resources provided by the library, Bailiwick is now integrated as one of the scholarly digital resources included in the Libraries' support of the teaching, learning, and research mission of the University of Iowa.

Contributed Papers

Emerging Roles for Librarians

Building a Campus Presence One Page at a Time: Web Strategies for the Small College Library

Nancy H. Dewald

Small college libraries do not have the large numbers of staff and professionals of universities to create and maintain a significant Web site which may include extensive library and Web information, online tutorials, and guides to print, database, and Web resources in a variety of disciplines. Yet those of us at small college or campus libraries wish to be seen as up to date on the campus, and we also wish to reach out to faculty and students and stretch our reference and instruction capabilities. This combination of needs and limitations can be frustrating, yet there are strategies for achieving a greater online presence and furthering the library's campus presence.

An opportunity the online environment offers is collaboration with faculty in combining class syllabi with library reference and resource information. Many faculty are placing their syllabi, including details of term paper assignments, on the Web. By the same token, many librarians provide class handouts of library and Web resources appropriate to particular assignments. On the Web, these two can be combined, and students can read about their assignment and have information available at the same place on how to start their research. An e-mail connection to the reference librarian and a connection to the online catalog add to the value, and all of this is available anytime, anywhere, at the convenience of the student.

Large universities have the capabilities to create major projects involving faculty/librarian collaboration on the Web. For example, the TWIST project at the University of Iowa[1] is a "project to create a model training program for librarians and faculty on networked information resources." This site includes collaborative pages of many faculty and librarians, and it offers not only resource help for particular assignments but also tutorials in a variety of library and Web research skills.

Collaboration with faculty need not be limited to major projects of a university, however. Even a librarian at a small campus can create a collaborative page with one interested faculty member at a time. The library portion of the Web page may include links to the online catalog and/or helpful

---

Nancy H. Dewald is reference library at Penn State Berks.

online databases (or referral to specific CD-ROM databases), guidelines for Web evaluation, a few significant reference sources and Web sites, information on making bibliographies, and an e-mail connection to the librarian for personal help.

The Berks Campus of Penn State University, located in Reading, PA., has 1,750 full-time equivalent (FTE) students and 97 FTE faculty, and courses are primarily lower division. The library has three full time librarians, two full time staff, four part time staff, and several student assistants, including two during the summer sessions. Inspired by the University of Iowa's TWIST Project, as Reference Librarian I thought a collaborative Web page could be developed with one faculty member in political science whose students needed help with term paper research.

There are four political science courses offered each year at the Berks Campus, and there were several problems in these classes. The students were using the World Wide Web indiscriminately for their research. The students were also ignoring print resources and/or were not seeking help from a librarian. The professor could not devote a full class period to library instruction, and in any case the classes were large and unwieldy in the library. In an effort to guide students, I had created a general handout in the past, but this needed to be updated and did not include Web information.

From the professor's point of view, he did not have a Web page and had neither the time nor the desire to learn a Web editor. Yet he felt frustrated by subtle pressure on the campus to have a Web site for his courses. In this environment, it seemed that both the professor and I could benefit from a Web collaboration, and when I approached him in January of 1998 with this proposal, he readily agreed. This was to be a summer project in preparation for classes the following fall.

Although I knew both basic HTML and how to use a Web editor, I also recruited help from a summer student assistant who knew a Web editor and had some experience creating Web pages. The student assistant, the political science professor and I met and planned the layout for the site, using content provided by the professor and me. The student could do the manual work, including finding and adding copyright-free graphics and backgrounds for the site. Making Web pages can be time consuming, partly because creative activity is seductive, but with this arrangement my time was only spent on content, layout, and troubleshooting, rather than on the manual labor.

The resulting Web site includes the professor's professional and course information, and a research paper help page, which contains links to:
- his guidelines for term papers;
- the university's plagiarism information for students;
- the university library's online catalog and database system;
- a help link to my e-mail;
- political science Web sites collected by the professor and by me, some of which have brief annotations;
- a short information sheet on evaluating Web pages;
- a section on citing print and Web sources in a bibliography using MLA, APA or Turabian formats; and
- for each of the four political science courses, a page listing appropriate reference books and databases, with annotations, including a link to the library system from each database name.

These last four items were written by me. The site can be viewed at http://www.bk.psu.edu/faculty/newnham/RNHOME2.htm.

During the semester, I spent fifteen minutes in each political science class showing the Web site, explaining its features for the students as they began work on their papers, and encouraging them to e-mail or come to me for assistance at any time.

In order to accommodate students who are not comfortable with computers or the Internet, or who have limited access to computers, the professor had handed out his syllabus and assignment information in class. However, at the end of the semester over half (57%) of the class members reported having accessed the course Web site. Of those that used the Web site, 80% found it helpful and informative for information about the course, and 86% found it helpful and informative for working on the term paper. Comments indicated that students appreciated having access from off campus at any time, having information on creating bibliographies, having a link to the online catalog, and having access to the professor's pages, even though those had been given to them in class. Even those students that chose not to use the Web were introduced to the reference librarian in class and were made aware of the availability of help for their research.

Strategies for Success

The elements for success in a project such as this are: building relationships with faculty, being prepared to author Web pages, and planning the collaborative Web page.

Building Relationships with Faculty

- It is important to be building relationships with faculty from the time you begin work at a college library. If possible, volunteer for committees with faculty, eat where they eat, visit their offices, or otherwise spend time with them. Offer new faculty an orientation to the library and its services, including library instruction. Use any new library development as an excuse to invite faculty to come to the library, such as a presentation on new databases or CD-ROMs in their field.

- Be assertive with any faculty who assign term papers, and offer your help with library instruction, handouts, or any way you can help them and their students.

- When planning a Web collaboration, try to meet a faculty need as well as your own, which will be more likely to lead to agreement. For example, the political science professor needed a faculty Web page. As another example, a science professor for whom I have done library instruction had mentioned that his class Web page needed to be updated and reorganized, so I have offered to help him if I can also add library content, and he has agreed.

Preparing to Author Web Pages

Before approaching a faculty member, it is a good idea to prepare for the work involved in this project.

- Look for student or staff assistance. The librarian's time need not be spent on the mundane aspects of Web page creation except for design, planning, and troubleshooting. Some students, especially upperclassmen, have some experience in Web page creation. Ask professors of computer science to suggest students who might want a job with the library, or even ask current library student workers if they have Web page experience. Sometimes staff members in a library develop an interest in Web authoring, as well. Check with the Head Librarian for permission to use staff members for these projects, which could actually make their jobs more interesting.

- Even with help, the librarian needs to know how to create Web pages as well, in order to be able to make quick changes or corrections in the future, and also in order that the librarian, not the assistant, is the final designer. There are many good Web editors that produce pages in a What-You-See-Is-What-You-Get (WYSIWYG) manner. However, one should also know the basics of Hypertext Markup Language (HTML), as even good Web editors do not always perform as expected. In those instances, the page must be brought into a simple word processing program such as Notepad or WordPad for manual correction to the source code.

- *Smart Computing* published a primer called "Build a Web Site" in two parts[2] which explains very basic HTML and recommends learning it before progressing to WYSIWYG authoring of Web pages. There are also a number of Web sources for learning HTML. An excellent place to start is the National Center for Supercomputing Applications, which has published the *NCSA Beginner's Guide to HTML*[3]. Another excellent resource is the *HyperText Markup Language Home Page* at the World Wide Web Consortium (W3C)[4].

Steps in Planning the Web Pages

- Get all the faculty member's information, such as syllabus and assignment handouts, in electronic format. These are probably on a disk already. If there is a problem such as MAC/IBM incompatibility, having the professor save documents in plain text (ASCII) format to send to you as an attachment to e-mail will work, or you can simply have him/her copy the documents into the body of e-mail messages to send to you. If the materials are only in paper format, a program called Omni Page Pro Version 8.0 allows scanning text into a word processing program. In this form, a student assistant can clean up the text to make it look like the original.

- Plan the library portions of the Web pages. Type into word processing the library information, such as annotated lists of helpful reference sources, descriptions of appropriate databases, a cheat sheet on creating a bibliography, and a brief Web evaluation page. Plan to use fonts, colors, and white space judiciously to make the pages appealing, and try to keep each page relatively brief, as students usually do not want to read a wall of text.
- Decide on the layout for the site as a whole, in conjunction with the professor and the assistant. The site should not be confusing to students, and consistent links at the bottom and/or top of each page will facilitate movement around the site.
- Decide on links, such as an e-mail connection to the librarian and/or the professor, links to the online catalog and databases, and appropriate Web links for the subject. In the case of database links, be sure not to bypass security systems, as Web users from outside your college or university will also be able to read these pages.
- Decide with the professor whether to edit his/her information. The professor may or may not wish to do this, and there may be only a few instances where it is necessary. For example, it is best to be non-specific with dates on the syllabus, so that online changes need not be made every semester. It is simpler to list classes as week one, week two, etc.
- Be willing to create a basic faculty home page also, as this is part of the incentive for faculty. The professor's curriculum vita can be used, as well as a list of his/her publications. However, do not include any personal addresses or phone numbers, only the office address and phone.

Conclusion

As a result of this project, the political science professor and I have an even more comfortable relationship than previously, and more political science students are aware of the availability of library assistance for their research. More information is available online than I would have had time to present in one library instruction session, and each semester a number of the students approach me in the days and weeks following the brief in-class presentation of the Web page. Students report the course Web site is helpful and informative about the course itself, the expectations for the term paper, and the resources available for writing the term paper. Many students like the user-friendly interface of the Web, and they appreciate being able to access the course information and research assistance when they need it.

As reference librarians try to reach more students on and off campus and offer more research information, the World Wide Web is a logical venue. A Web page created in collaboration with a faculty member offers increased visibility of the librarian and of research assistance. Students can be guided to good quality, relevant Web sites for the discipline, appropriate databases and reference sources, and help with their bibliographies. As the Web becomes increasingly prominent as a campus resource, reference information can be combined with course information to attract students to see the library and the librarian as up-to-date resources for their research. With development of faculty relationships, careful planning, and wise use of student or staff assistance, even a librarian at a small campus or college library can build a Web presence on the campus, one page at a time.

References

1. *TWIST, Teaching With Innovative Style and Technology* [online]. TWIST, University Libraries, The University of Iowa. September 2 1998 [cited 10 December 1997]. Available from: http://twist.lib.uiowa.edu/

2. "Build a Web Site, Part 1," *Smart Computing,* July 1998, 46–50. "Build a Web Site, Part 2," *Smart Computing,* August 1998, 50–53.

3. *NCSA Beginner's Guide to HTML* [online]. NCSA [National Center for Supercomputing Applications]. February 16, 1999 [cited February 17, 1999]. Available from: http://www.ncsa.uiuc.edu/General/Internet/WWW/HTMLPrimer.html

4. *HyperText Markup Language Home Page* [online]. W3C [World Wide Web Consortium]. User Interface Domain. December 16 1998 [cited February 10, 1999]. Available from: http://www.w3.org/MarkUp/MarkUp.html.

First-Year Learning Communities: Redefining the Educational Roles of Academic Librarians

Tony Stamatoplos and Terry Taylor

First-Year Classes & Learning Communities

Colleges and universities increasingly find themselves in the position of competing for enrollment, and the average student body is a mixture of traditional residential, commuter, and adult returning students. As a result, new issues have emerged concerning the assessment of learning and retention of students after their first year. Studies indicating the success of collaborative learning environments have given new weight to the concept of learning communities and the impact they have upon learning outcomes. Faith Gabelnick, et al., describe key advantages of today's learning communities:

> Learning communities [...] purposefully restructure the curriculum to link together courses or course work so that students find greater coherence in what they are learning as well as increased intellectual interaction with faculty and fellow students. Advocates contend that learning communities can address some of the structural features of the modern university that undermine effective teaching and learning. Built on what is known about effective educational practice, learning communities are also usually associated with collaborative and active approaches to learning, some form of team teaching, and interdisciplinary themes.

The Coalition of Networked Information (CNI) initiated a New Learning Communities program that highlighted "increased student involvement in learning [...] and the realization that students can create knowledge and meaning out of their learning experience." Learning communities foster both social and academic involvement, the integration of which appears to be central to the students' perceived success in their transition to university life. As Vincent Tinto explains: "Often, social and academic concerns compete, causing students to feel torn between two worlds so that students have to choose one over the other. Learning communities [help] students draw these two worlds together."

Tony Stamatoplos is assistant librarian/instruction team, Indiana University Purdue University Indianapolis, and Terry Taylor is corrdinator of library instruction, DePaul University.

Recognizing the significance of the first year in creating a baseline for the students' entire college experience, many institutions have revisited their general studies programs and have created opportunities for the development of new learning communities. According to Tinto:

> Membership in the community of the classroom provides important linkages to membership in communities external to the classroom. For new students in particular, engagement in the community of the classroom becomes a gateway for subsequent student involvement in the academic and social communities of the college generally.

Information Literacy in the Curriculum

For many years academic librarians have advocated the integration of library instruction or information literacy into the curriculum of colleges and universities. Librarians assert that students must learn information skills in the context of their courses in order for those skills to be meaningful. True integration implies that information skills are accepted as a natural and essential part of the curriculum. Attempts at integration have had varying degrees of success. Successful integration appears to be related to a few key factors. Administrative or institutional support and commitment are vital to success, as is a clear connection to the educational mission of the institution. Specific, well-defined goals are important. Hannelore Rader points out that where there has been successful integration at an institution, the institution "had a strong commitment to excellent educational outcomes for the students in the areas of critical thinking, problem-solving, and information skills."

Perhaps most important to success are collaborative and collegial relationships between teaching faculty and librarians. Such relationships often take the form of a true partnership between faculty and librarians. D.W. Farmer goes even farther and calls for faculty, librarians, and students to step out of their traditional roles and form an "active partnership in a genuine learning community." Marian Winner emphasizes that librarians "must demonstrate to faculty that they have the background and knowledge to be useful partners for faculty in curriculum planning, so that information literacy becomes an integral part of the course structure and so that skills the students develop are assessed."

At the same time, and paralleling higher education curriculum reforms, many instruction librarians and programs have shifted focus to better empower students and foster independence and life-long learning. This has become particularly important as more information is readily available, and our students try to meet their information needs through the use of the Internet and the World Wide Web. There probably has never been a better opportunity to demonstrate both the need to integrate information literacy into the curriculum and the significance of the librarian's role as information educator. According to Rader: "It is up to librarians to maximize their potential and to be in position to assume their role in the teaching and learning process as reforms take place."

The role of teacher is not really a new one for academic librarians. We have provided instruction as part of our reference service and have taught sessions and entire courses of bibliographic instruction. Several years ago, instruction programs began to move away from library orientation and instruction in the use of specific research tools. More recently, library instruction has emphasized the teaching of process, problem-solving, and critical thinking. As this trend continues, we open up opportunities for a more direct impact on the curriculum and clearly respond to the educational goals of our institutions. As Evelyn Haynes asserts: "Librarians must be granted the authority, responsibility, and time to develop the programs that will accommodate institution-wide curriculum needs, rather than merely responding to individual requests from those faculty who already recognize the importance of information research to their teaching." This sometimes means re-defining our roles or taking on new roles in the educational mission of our institution. According to Abigail Loomis we "must recognize and accept that our contribution to that educational mission involves much more than making information resources available on demand. It also involves teaching—

teaching students how to find, select, evaluate, and use that information effectively and efficiently."

Two First-Year Programs

New program initiatives at DePaul and IUPUI have expanded the possibilities for integrating library instruction into the university curriculum. The learning communities developed as a result of these programs present unique opportunities to integrate information and library skills into the first-year curriculum.

DePaul

As part of a larger initiative to restructure the Liberal Studies curriculum, DePaul University revised and expanded its First-Year Program. The First-Year Program has two overarching goals: 1) introducing students to the process of intellectual inquiry in a university, and 2) community building. Most students take a required sequence of English composition courses in the first year, and it is in those courses that the Library has provided a basic level of library instruction. Two new components in the First-Year Program are taught by a faculty/staff team: *Discover Chicago*, an experiential course with Chicago-related field experiences, and *Focal Point Seminar*, a small interdisciplinary seminar. The instruction team for the Discover Chicago classes also includes a student mentor. The staff professional teaches the *Common Hour* portion of the course, a seminar focusing on transition skills in four areas: student success skills (e.g., note taking and time management); university resources (e.g., student services and the library); academic and career planning; and diversity/community issues.

At its inception, the Common Hour was viewed as an extension of the services offered by Student Affairs, but as the program grew, the opportunity to work with these new first-year learning communities was extended to staff professionals throughout the university. In the first year of the program, a librarian served as a consultant to the faculty planning committee. In the second year, one librarian taught a section of the Focal Point seminar. This past year, six librarians taught eight sections of the Focal Point seminar. For the first time, inclusion of a library experience, activity, or assignment was required in all sections of the Common Hour. Two librarians currently serve on the steering committee charged with designing the curriculum for next year's Common Hour component and the job descriptions for those who will teach it.

IUPUI

First-year classes have become a primary focus of library instruction activity at IUPUI. First-year seminars are now a part of the Learning Communities Program. All learning communities include a first-year experience class, and many link two or more classes. IUPUI learning communities address the general goals of learning communities, and many also serve to introduce students to their prospective majors. As an integral component of the Learning Communities Program, instruction librarians have worked primarily with the first-year experience classes.

IUPUI learning communities use an instructional team approach in the first-year component. An IUPUI instructional team is a collaborative venture that brings together a teaching faculty member, a librarian, an academic adviser, and a student mentor. The faculty member leads the team, which collaboratively develops and implements the curriculum for a particular class. Each team member plays an active role in designing and delivering the course, depending upon his or her particular expertise. Librarians are assigned to several learning communities each semester and their roles vary from team to team, always centering on the library- and information- based learning objectives.

Common Elements of DePaul and IUPUI Programs

• A history of "traditional library instruction" placed in writing courses;
• A focus on first-year programs that introduce students to the university, build a learning community, and promote academic success;
• Administrative support, both from library administration and from the university;
• Well-defined outcomes that relate to the educational mission of the university;
• A team approach in which librarians collaborate with faculty and others, expanding our role as educators.

Benefits

The advantages of first-year learning communities such as those at DePaul and IUPUI are numerous. The impact of these programs is most evident in the following areas:

- Integration of library instruction into the curriculum from the beginning of the student's college experience;
- Development of collegial relationships with others outside the library (both faculty and staff);
- Increased visibility of librarians within the university community, which expands the perception of what are considered the "traditional" responsibilities of library professionals;
- New opportunities for librarians to participate in students' socialization into the university;
- Extension of the librarians' teaching experience in areas that can benefit from a generalist's approach.

Challenges

Innovative programs and new course models present challenges and opportunities to examine various aspects of the endeavor. One needs to ask questions, such as:

- What skills are required, and what are the existing skills, of the librarians?
- How much preparation will the librarian need, and how will the additional responsibilities balance with his/her workload?
- How are these new responsibilities relevant to the overall goals of the library?
- What impact can the librarians' participation in the new programs have on their identity and role within the university, and how does that involvement complement other public service activities?
- How might librarians pursue or maintain administrative commitment and financial support?

Conclusion

At DePaul and IUPUI, the information component, including librarians' active participation, is an integral part of students' first-year experience. Early in their academic careers, students see the value of information and connect with information professionals. This demonstrates the importance of information literacy and presents the librarian as expert in this arena. Not only are students able to see librarians as knowledgeable and skilled with information and library research but also as teachers, guides, and coaches. Most students, as well as teaching faculty, are unaccustomed to librarians fulfilling these roles. Whether working one-on-one with a student or leading a library instruction session for a group, librarians have a lot of teaching experience. First-year learning communities can demonstrate this experience to the larger university community. It is not only our opportunity; it is our professional responsibility to become involved in programs that foster these new learning environments.

Harvesting Hyperspace: Developing Technological Solutions to Internet Resource Discovery and Description

Gregory A. McClellan and Thomas P. Turner

Abstract

Many students and faculty make use of Internet search engines to locate information on the World Wide Web. The increasing interest in these resources challenges collection development specialists to find more resources, technical services librarians to describe them, and public services librarians to support them. This paper addresses experiments underway in the Technical Services unit of the Albert R. Mann Library at Cornell University to make use of the underlying World Wide Web indexing technologies in a local setting, to develop new ways for catalogers to approach Internet resources, and to discover cost effective methods for approaching the wealth of resources available on the Internet. We have worked to link this new, more detailed information into the Cornell University Library Gateway, a local database of network-accessible resources. The authors discuss technological solutions for indexing large aggregations of Web resources, electronic serials, Web sites containing multiple file formats and Web sites that make use of frames.

Introduction

Many students and faculty make use of Internet search engines to locate information on the World Wide Web. However, these general resources do not serve our scholars and students well because they lack the care and attention that our local bibliographers and catalogers give to choosing and describing individually selected resources. This paper will address experiments underway at the Albert R. Mann Library at Cornell University to make

---

Gregory A. McClellan is cataloging librarian for networked information resources, and Thomas P. Turner is metadata librarian, Cornell Unviersity.

use of the underlying World Wide Web indexing technologies in a local setting, to develop new ways for catalogers to approach Internet resources, and to discover cost effective methods for approaching the wealth of resources available on the Internet.

Providing access to locally selected Internet resources involves decisions that impact collection development, public services, and technical services units in very different ways. Bibliographers face the difficulty of discovering relevant materials for our users and gathering enough information about resources to make appropriate choices. Public services staff need to identify which parts of a complex Internet site are appropriate for a user's needs. When Internet sites are added to our on-line catalogs, technical services staff are challenged to find ways to describe these resources, which are often large, complex sites, so that the wealth of materials available will be apparent to our users.

In this environment, librarians must develop new methods for discovering, collecting, and describing. We will discuss current efforts at Mann Library to make use of a locally mounted World Wide Web indexer, based on the Harvest gatherer, to explore large, complex sites. The information is used to create a "metadata tank" because automated indexing provides a finer level of granularity than is available through traditional cataloging. Making use of this technology may help the library take a new approach to dealing with Internet resources. Although we will focus on the technical services perspective, we will also address collection development and public services concerns related to the inclusion of Internet resources in local collections. We will propose a model for the automated generation of metadata for Internet resource description.

In January, 1998, the Cornell University Library administration made money available for a variety of projects through an internal grant program. This program enabled Mann Library Technical Services staff to experiment with the local use of Internet indexing technology to grapple with the difficulties that Internet resources present. By seeking technologically enhanced, rather than strictly human, approaches to these resources, we hope to improve access to these materials as well as the speed with which we are able to process them. Without the additional funding of the Cornell University Library administration, this experiment would not have been possible.

Finding and Describing Resources on the Web

Finding the right resource on the Internet can be difficult. Library patrons can turn either to large-scale Internet search engine services or to local on-line catalogs which provide access to locally selected and cataloged materials. Internet search engine companies create databases of Internet citations by making use of indexing technology to find and organize materials, such as AltaVista and HotBot, (Kimmel 1996) or by having employees select, annotate and/or assign subject captions to Web sites, such as Yahoo! (Lester 1995, Steinberg 1996). These services often result in the creation of large databases without a clearly defined audience.

Libraries are struggling to find ways to approach the Internet and its resources for local, specific audiences. Some libraries have chosen to limit the selection and cataloging of Internet resources. Many libraries have also started to select and catalog Internet resources using the MARC record. However, this task has presented several challenges to libraries in terms of establishing selection criteria for a variety of complex documents, determining cataloging processes, maintaining cataloging records over time, and supporting public use of a vast assortment of materials. Many libraries have approached the selection of Internet-based resources in the same manner as other resources. They have developed selection policies and procedures that analyze the quality, consistency and applicability of each site for the library's collection (Demas, McDonald and Lawrence 1995). Internet-based services are presenting new challenges as well. Walters et al. (1998) describe the complex issues surrounding the selection of aggregations of resources available over the Internet. In addition, although Internet-based and other electronic resources are being added to library collections, print materials will continue to require the attention of technical services and collection development staff. This hybrid collection will require a sharper focus on methods for adding value to the entirety of the library collection (Atkinson 1998).

Defining the Control Zone

The addition of Internet-based resources in the library collection has had an enormous impact on the work of technical services units. New methods for electronic resource description have emerged for cataloging units dealing with electronic resources (Younger 1997, Dillon and Jul 1996). New sets of standards have emerged for working effectively with electronic resources. Most of these new standards require catalogers to broaden their sense of resource description beyond the MARC record and to look at other forms of metadata. Clifford Lynch (1998) describes metadata in the following ways:

> Metadata is literally "data about data," information that qualifies other information. Bibliographic description is a form of metadata, so also is information about intellectual property rights and terms of use, formats of electronic information, reviews, errata, abstracts and summaries, provenance information, and a host of other data. Some metadata can be derived mechanically from objects; other metadata has independent standing as intellectual creation in its own right (p.5).

This wide scope of resource description possibilities involves an assortment of new metadata schemes. Options include MARC, the Dublin Core, PICS, among others, and involve related developments like the Resource Description Framework (Gill 1998, Chepesiak 1999). With the rise in the number of metadata and descriptive options, finding a way to manage those possibilities becomes more important. Libraries need to find methods for building on the strengths of all resource description possibilities rather than trying to impose one method on all resources (Vellucci 1997).

In this complex metadata environment, making use of technological solutions to resource discovery and description should be considered as much of an option as making use of human-dependent methods (such as traditional selecting and cataloging of materials). Looking at the scope of the digital library, Atkinson (1996) calls for the establishment of a "control zone" in which libraries determine which resources are essential for scholarly endeavors. He contrasts this collection with the "open zone," or the network at large. One way to develop this control zone would be to perform traditional selection and cataloging on sets of materials that are defined as essential to scholarly pursuit, such as high-priced items or digital materials created by the library. For materials that may be of interest outside this core set, making use of cheaper, less-perfect methods of automated indexing may be appropriate. Martin Dillon, director of the OCLC Institute, defines four possible methods of description based on the importance of materials: traditional MARC-based cataloging, the use of the Dublin Core, the use of Internet indexing software with some editing and the use of Internet indexing software with no editing. Michael Gorman suggests a similar four-tier scheme: traditional MARC-based cataloging, "enriched" Dublin Core records, basic Dublin Core records and simple full-text searching (Oder 1998). Several initiatives are attempting to develop methods for using traditional as well as new technological solutions, including OCLC's Cooperative On-line Resource Catalog (OCLC 1998) and INFOMINE (Oder 1998).

Project Overview

Cornell University's Mann Library has been selecting and cataloging electronic resources for over a decade. Selection criteria, which have evolved over time, are based on standards set by print materials in terms of quality, reliability, and appropriateness for the collection (Demas, McDonald and Lawrence 1995). Current efforts include, among others, selecting free and for-fee electronic serials (Weintraub 1998) and aggregations of resources (Walters et al. 1998). Subject bibliographers identify networked materials within the library's scope. They usually select specific titles for cataloging (such as Ecological Monographs) rather than entire sites (like JSTOR). Once they have determined that selection criteria have been met, acquisitions staff create preliminary records in the on-line catalog and record contact information and price and contract limitations as applicable. Cataloging staff complete the work of describing the items using full-level cataloging.

As part of the cataloging process, a Cornell University Library Gateway record is created. The CUL Gateway (http://campusgw.library.cornell.edu) is a Web-based system which provides a single point of entry to all networked electronic resources selected by the library. This system consists of a searchable database of electronic resource surrogates and is able to dynamically generate a list of resources appropriate to user queries. The records provide a hypertext link to the resource, the title, a description, the genre of the material, summary holdings, general subject categories and similar information. The CUL Gateway also handles many authentication issues related to for-fee networked electronic resources (Garrison and McClellan 1997). In addition, the CUL Gateway contains links to library home pages, library services, and other resources available to library users. For a more detailed discussion of the CUL Gateway and its users, please see the article by Karen Calhoun and Zsuzsa Koltay in this volume (Calhoun and Koltay 1999).

The main technical focus of this project was to integrate an Internet indexer into the already existing architecture of the CUL Gateway. The Har-

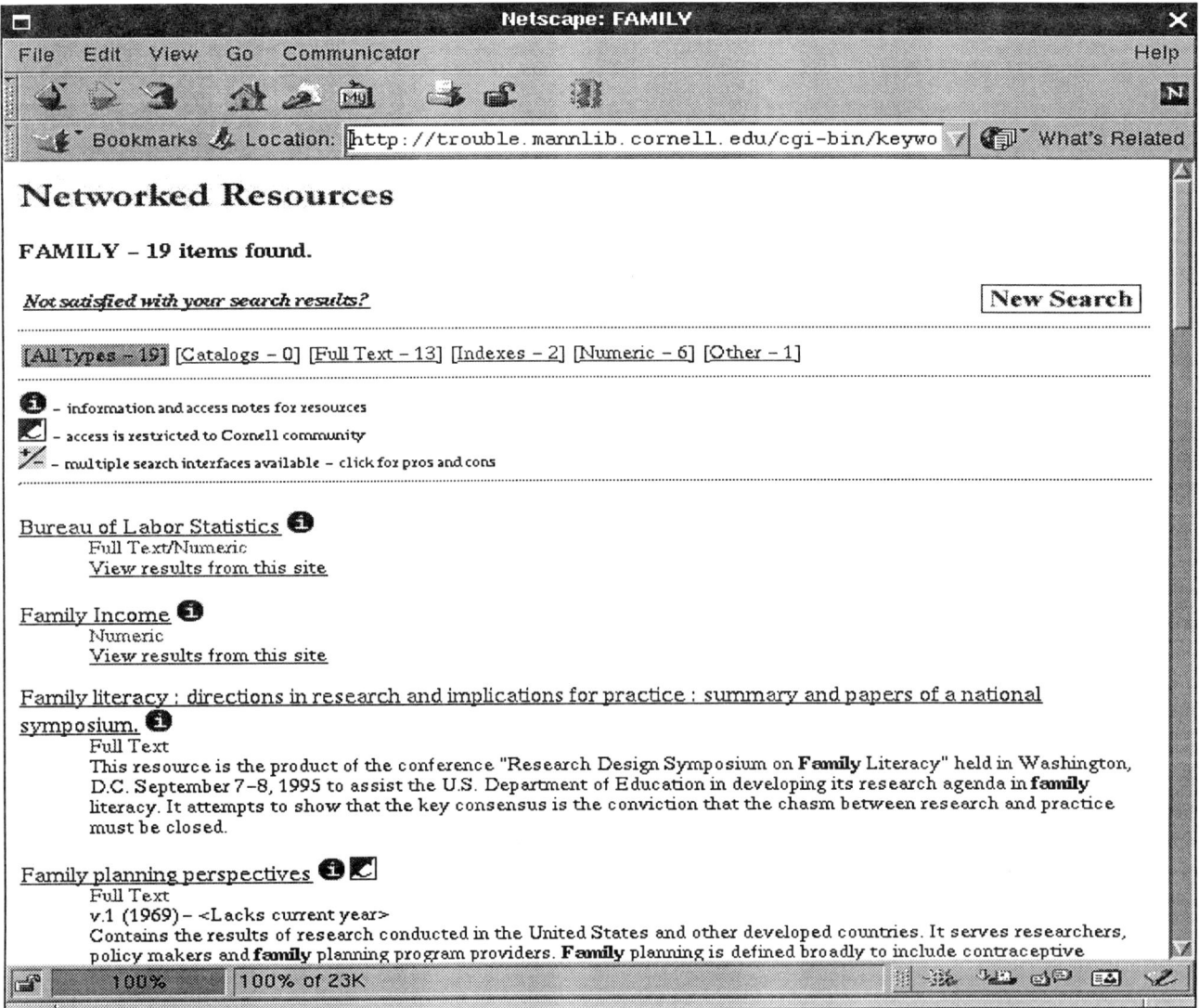

Figure 1. A sample top-level results page from the experimental version of the Cornell University Library Gateway.

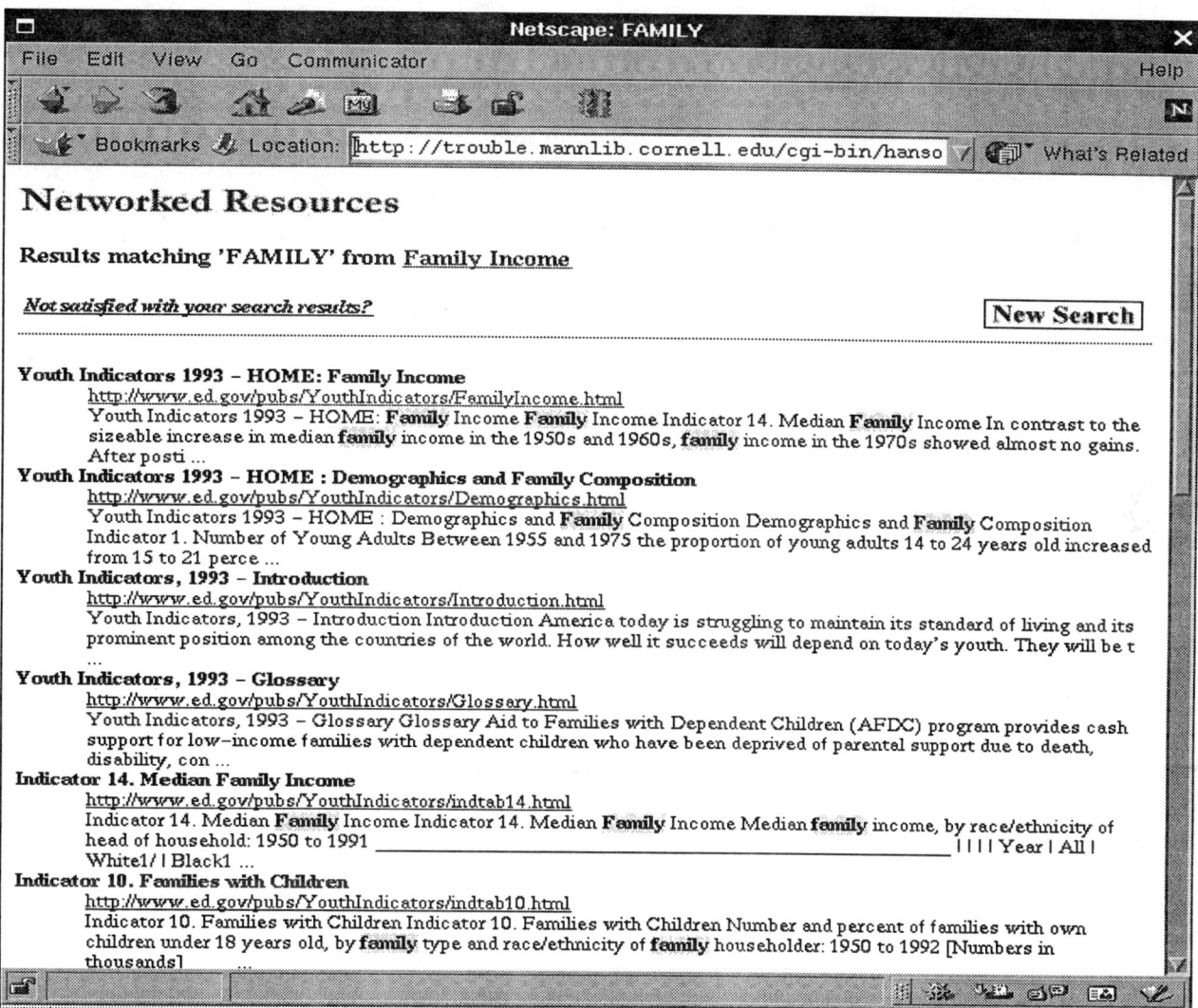

Figure 2. A sample of the pages indexed using Harvest-NG.

vest-NG indexer (http://www.tardis.ed.ac.uk/harvest/ng/) was chosen, mainly due to its flexibility and extensibility. The task of integrating Harvest-NG into the CUL Gateway was made easier by the fact that both were written using the Perl programming language. After Harvest-NG indexes the requested documents, the system imports the automatically generated metadata into its MySQL database (http://www.mysql.com/). The metadata is then available to be searched via the Gateway's keyword search function.

Each keyword search actually performs two searches: one of the Gateway's human-generated metadata and one of the automatically generated metadata. The results are merged into a single HTML document (figure 1). In this example, you see four results: the first two are the result of the Harvest-NG indexing and the second two are the results from a "traditional" CUL Gateway search. Notice that the traditional results have a cataloger-generated description, whereas the other results have no description. The Harvest-NG indexed titles also have an additional link to the "deeper" results available through the indexing (figure 2). These results present each document's title, URL, and an automatically generated description. The description is taken from the HTML description META tag if available, otherwise it is generated from the beginning of the document. This page will give the user quicker and easier access to the relevant information on that site.

Eleven Internet resources were indexed to test the ability of the indexing software to cope with both simple and complex Web sites. Most of the resources indexed were selected by staff of Cornell University's Catherwood Library, but were not yet on the CUL Gateway. The Web sites fell into three categories: four serials, four aggregations, and three sites including non-HTML-based document formats such as GIF and PDF. This small test was planned as the first step in the process of determining the effectiveness of automatic metadata generation from Web documents identified by library staff. Not all of the sites had been fully cataloged and, as a result, information about each site varied in detail and human effort. Four of the Web resources had received full cataloging and had a detailed description written of it by cataloging staff. This variation provided an opportunity for staff to determine the optimal amount of information needed about each site. However, all resources chosen for this test were freely available over the Internet. Resources available for a fee will require a somewhat different approach. For a list of the resources indexed see table 1. A twelfth site, an aggregation, was identified for indexing. However, the site, GPO Access: Keeping America Informed (http://www.access.gpo.gov/), does not allow robot-indexing software to analyze its components. As a result, GPO Access could not be included in this test.

Evaluation

This limited-scale project provided an opportunity to test the adequacy of indexing large, complex sites as well as sites containing multiple file formats. The indexing was analyzed for technologi-

Table 1. List of Titles Indexed Using Harvest-NG	
Title	URL
Serials	
Family Income	http://www.ed.gov/pubs/YouthIndicators/FamilyIncome.html
Journal of Extension*	http://www.joe.org/
Poultry Slaughter*	http://usda.mannlib.cornell.edu/reports/nassr/poultry/ppy-bb/
Rice Yearbook*	http://usda.mannlib.cornell.edu/data-sets/crops/89001/
Aggregations	
Bureau of Labor Statistics	http://stats.bls.gov/blshome.html
Demographic Data Viewer	http://plue.sedac.ciesin.org/plue/ddviewer/
Office of Technology Assessment Publications	http://www.wws.princeton.edu/~ota/ns20/pubs_f.html
World Wide HR	http://www.WorldWideHR.hq.dla.mil/
Multiple Document Formats	
U.S. Census Bureau PDF Publications	http://www.census.gov/prod/www/titles.html
United States Labor and Industrial History Audio Archive	http://www.albany.edu/history/LaborAudio/index.html
Wisconsin Herpetological Atlas Project*	http://www.mpm.edu/collect/vertzo/herp/atlas/atlas.html
* Indicates title was fully cataloged as well as indexed using Harvest-NG.	

cal success as well as for usefulness by technical services, collection development and public services staff.

Technologically, automated indexing of these sites showed potential for dealing with complex resources. Due to file "summarisers" available through Harvest, Web sites containing WK1 (Lotus spreadsheet) and PDF (Adobe Acrobat) file formats were indexed well. Other formats, such as audio files, were also indexed adequately because links to these files used descriptive text phrases In addition, the automatic indexing found and referenced aspects of the site that catalogers would not have. This detailed analysis could lead to reduced time and effort by selectors and catalogers.

However, several technological difficulties were discovered. Sites that exclude the use of robots to capture information, like GPO Access and many for-fee sites, were inaccessible via this process. This could result in discrepancies in the database in terms of expected levels of granularity or detail. In addition, the use of frames caused significant problems for this automated indexing method. Determining the proper context and document to return was made more difficult by the use of frames because sites using frames were broken into their sub-parts. It is possible, however, to develop automated methods to deal with the difficult structures that frames present to automated indexing software.

In addition to testing technological feasibility, preliminary feedback was gathered from public services, technical services and collection development staff. As a means of concept testing, staff were asked to evaluate the results from two searches based on: expected results generated by searches, relevance of results to the search conducted, adequacy of information presented about sites and documents, and satisfaction with the extent of the indexing of each site. These questions were asked to determine whether or not we should pursue indexing only sites already cataloged as well as the amount of a site that would be indexed.

Staff members tended to view this project in relation to their experiences using, and helping patrons to use, Internet search engines. Not surprisingly, they preferred summaries produced by catalogers rather than text summaries produced from recording the text at the beginning of a page. Internet search engines usually generate descriptions of resources from the words at the beginning of a page, however, this text often does not provide adequate information to determine whether or not a document is relevant to a search. The summary of the site as a whole was more important to staff than human-generated summaries for each sub-part. Most staff preferred having at least the site-level summary because it allowed them to make a quick determination of relevance. They did want better quality results and more information to determine relevance than they usually receive from Internet search engines. Staff were not bothered by similarities to Internet search engines since they provide a well-known paradigm for information discovery on the Web.

Staff saw the results as a possible improvement over traditional Internet search engines. Staff members were enthusiastic about the possibilities of merging this level of detail with traditional cataloging. However, several staff pointed to indexed pages that were not particularly relevant to their searches suggesting that some clean-up of indexed items would be required. For instance, a search for the word "family" resulted in one site with only a passing use of this word, hence not a particularly useful result. In addition, staff were concerned about providing a context in which different levels of results could be understood by users; most felt this could be done through interface adjustments. Staff were less interested in the results generated from the indexing of serials than they were in the results from the indexing of aggregations and Web sites with multiple documents formats. One public services staff member was concerned that having some, but by no means comprehensive, results for very detailed search terms might lead patrons away from using more appropriate resources like bibliographic databases which would not be automatically indexed in this way. However, this is a problem for the traditional on-line catalog as well as databases of Internet resources.

Conclusion

This project was designed to test of possibility of using automated indexing software to enhance a library's database of Internet resources. This small-scale project is not a production system but could be used as the basis for a much larger initiative. Automated indexing software successfully improved the amount of information that was retrievable about complex Web resources, such as aggregations and electronic serials. Similar initiatives, like OCLC's CORC project (1998), will expand the set of tools that libraries can use to approach the Internet and enhance its usefulness for library users. In addition, more robust embedded metadata, such as the HTML META tag (Turner and Brackbill 1998) and XML (Flynn 1998 Light 1997) will continue to improve automated means of selecting and describing electronic resources available over the Internet.

The authors have identified several issues that require further development and consideration as libraries develop technological approaches to the Web. All of the resources that were tested in this project were available to any user of the Web. Resources requiring passwords, containing firewalls or limiting access in other ways will require very different technological solutions. Most for-fee resource producers will not permit robot-indexing software to scan their sites. In addition, we must provide better ways for users to understand the context of their search results. Interface improvements as well as selective editing of indexer output can help to provide such a context. Lastly, it is necessary to determine the number of levels of a site that should be indexed. At what level do most sites become too disorganized to be useful? Deciding the extent of indexing for each site is at the heart of determining the ultimate usefulness of automated indexing.

References

Atkinson, Ross. 1996. Library functions, scholarly communication, and the foundation of the digital library: laying claim to the control zone. *Library Quarterly* 66, no. 3: 239–65.

———. 1998. Managing traditional materials in an on-line environment: some definitions and distinctions for a future collection management. *Library resources and technical services* 42, no. 1: 7–20.

Calhoun, Karen and Zsuzsa Koltay. 1999. Designing for WOW!: The optimal information gateway. In *Racing toward tomorrow: Proceedings of the Ninth National Conference of the Association of College and Research Libraries*. Chicago: ACRL.

Chepesiuk, Ron. 1999. Organizing the Internet: the "core" of the challenge. *American libraries* 30, no. 1: 60–63.

Demas, Samuel, Peter McDonald, and Gregory Lawrence. 1995. The Internet and collection development: mainstreaming selection of Internet resources. *Library resources and technical services* 39, no. 3: 275–90.

Dillon, Martin and Erik Jul. 1996. Cataloging Internet resources: the convergence of libraries and Internet resources. *Cataloging & classification quarterly* 22, nos. 3/4: 197–238.

Flynn, Peter. 1998. Frequently asked questions about the Extensible Markup Language. Version 1.3. On-line. Available: http://www.ucc.ie/xml.

Garrison, William V. and Gregory A. McClellan. 1997. Tao of gateway: providing Internet access to licensed databases. *Library hi tech* 15, nos. 1/2: 39–54.

Gill, Tony. 1998. Metadata and the World Wide Web. In Baca, Murtha (ed.). *Introduction to metadata: pathways to digital information*, Los Angeles, Calif.: Getty Information Institute. 9–18.

Kimmel, Stacey. 1996. Robot-generated databases on the World Wide Web. *Database* 19, no. 1: 40–43+.

Lester, Dan. 1995. Yahoo!: Profile of a Web database. *Database* 18, no.6: 46–50.

Light, Richard. 1997. *Presenting XML*. Indianapolis, Ind.: Sams Publishing.

Lynch, Clifford. 1998. The Dublin Core Descriptive Metadata Program: strategic implications for libraries and networked information access. *ARL: a bimonthly newsletter of research library issues and actions* no. 196: 5–10. Available: http://www.arl.org/newsltr/196/dublin.html.

Oder, Norman. October 1, 1998. Cataloging the Net: can we do it? *Library journal* 123, no. 16: 47–51.

OCLC. 1998. CORC—Cooperative Online Resource Catalog. Online. Available: http://www.oclc.org/oclc/research/projects/corc/index.htm.

Steinberg, Steve G. 1996. Seek and ye shall find (maybe). *Wired* 4, no.5: 108–114+.

Turner, Thomas P. and Lise Brackbill. 1998. Rising to the top: evaluating the use of the HTML META tag to improve retrieval of World Wide Web documents through Internet search engines. *Library resources and technical services* 42, no. 4: 258–71.

Vellucci, Sherry L. 1997. Options for organizing electronic resources: the coexistence of metadata. *Bulletin of the American Society for Information Science* 24, no. 1: 14–17.

Walters, William H., Samuel G. Demas, Linda Stewart, and Jennifer Weintraub. 1998. Guidelines for collecting aggregations of Web resources. *Information technology and libraries* 17, no. 3: 157–160.

Weintraub, Jennifer. 1998. The development and use of a genre statement for electronic journals in the sciences. *Issues in science and technology librarianship* no. 17. Online. Available: http://www.library.ucsb.edu/istl/98-winter/article5.html.

Younger, Jennifer A. 1997. Resources description in the digital age. *Library trends* 45, no.3: 462–81.

Reorganization: The Next Generation

Rhoda Channing

Library reorganizations are difficult, time consuming, and evoke in staff a fear of change exacerbated by the knowledge that the change will not be an abstraction, but something that will directly affect their lives and jobs. Existing job classifications and descriptions, and perhaps even salaries, are in question when the library embarks on a reorganization, and there are, inevitably, winners and losers. After a library goes through a major reorganization, however thoughtful the process, however participatory it was, and however well staff understood it, once it has been implemented there is often the feeling of "Well, that's over and now we don't have to think about it any more". There is relief and a return to the emphasis on activities in the immediate work unit or team. If we think seriously about the reasons we reorganize in the first place: rapid change, the impact of technology on our operations and collections, budget imperatives, or other motivators, we will recognize the need to put in place a mechanism for regular assessment, reality checks and review. Implementation does not mean the end of a reorganization effort, merely round one.

I'd like to share with you a brief history of our reorganization effort at Wake Forest's Reynolds Library, setting it in the context of the university, and then describe our process of reassessment and continued change. Let me provide a thumbnail sketch of the university and the library.

Wake Forest University is a private liberal arts university in the Piedmont area of North Carolina. It is small in size, but large in other ways, and with only 3800 undergraduates, boasts inclusion in *US News & World Report*'s list of the top national universities, a peculiar categorization for our little institution. In 1995, Wake Forest University developed and implemented a major plan for the class of 2000. It had several elements, including adding 40 new faculty positions and requiring first year seminars, but the element that attracted national attention was the technology plan. In partnership with IBM, we began to give all freshmen IBM laptops, later adding color printers. Another element of the very complex plan included replacing the laptops and the software for students after two years. Faculty were also to receive new machines on a 2 year cycle, and the library was given the huge new responsibility for computer orientation and training.

The Z. Smith Reynolds Library is one of three Wake Forest libraries, each with separate governance, the other two being the Carpenter Library, serving the medical campus, and the Professional

---

Rhoda Channing is library director, Wake Forest University.

Reorganization: The Next Generation

Center Library, serving the graduate law and management schools. Reynolds serves the College of Arts and Sciences, the Calloway (undergraduate) School of Business and Accountancy and the Graduate School of Arts and Sciences, which offers several masters' programs and Ph.D. programs in the Sciences. With a budget of $5 million plus, over 1 million volumes in print and large microfilm and electronic research collections, the Reynolds Library offers much more support than the average library serving such a small population. The staff has had little growth, numbering 54 positions although some were added as a result of the new responsibilities. Like many academic libraries we rely heavily on student workers and have about 150 students on the payroll as well.

I undertook the reorganization of the Reynolds Library after several years of waiting for the opportunity and the right moment. They converged when one of my assistant directors left to become a director, and when the library was given the new charge to train the first year students in the use of their computers. Figure 1 shows the organization chart I inherited as of September 1989.

It was a bit odd, as Technical Services included Automation, Cataloging and Circulation, and the Reader Services Division included Reference, Collection Development, and Acquisitions. The two Special Collections departments, and the Information Technology Center, created in 1992 following our building addition project, reported directly to me.

There were many reasons to consider reorganizing. From a purely selfish standpoint, I needed someone to monitor budget information very closely, handle administrative paperwork, keep up with facilities issues, and initiate systematic staff development. My own responsibilities on campus but outside the library were taking much of my time, and my own efforts in day to day administration were not enough to accomplish my goals for the library. I also wanted to see more synergy, the development of processes that were unhindered by departmental boundaries, and the strengthening of leadership skills among our librarians and other managers. Our library had undergone many changes, an addition and renovation project, automation, introduction of approval plans and many other new activities since my arrival. I had done some tinkering with the original chart, combining some units, but basically we were the same organization.

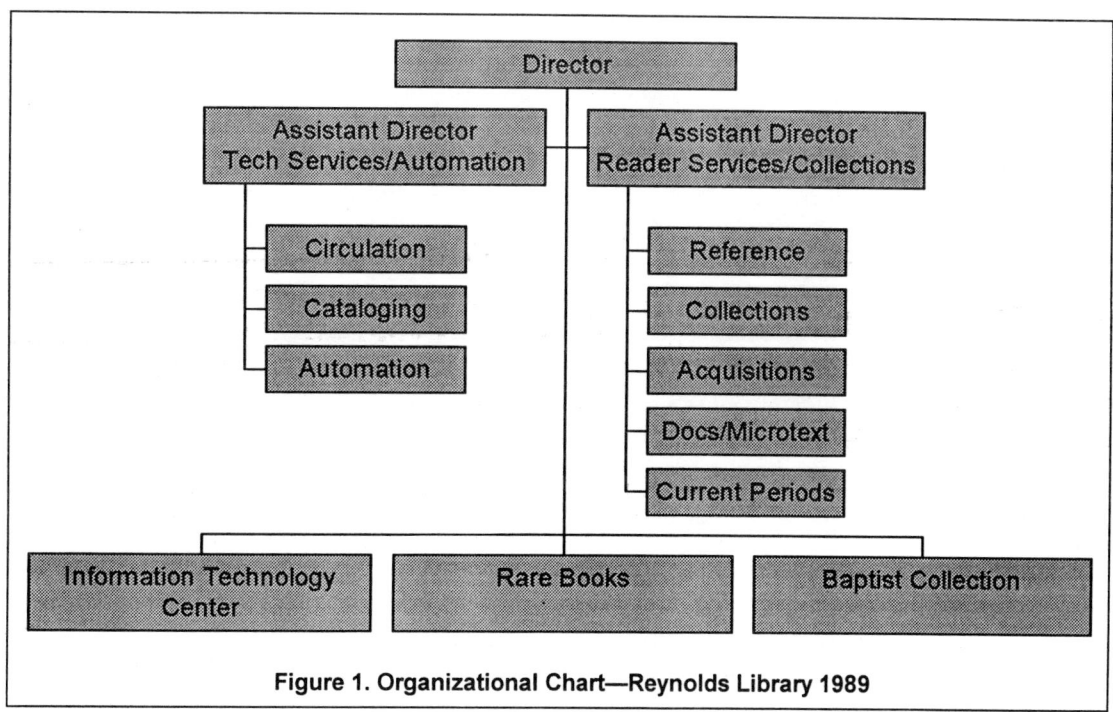

Figure 1. Organizational Chart—Reynolds Library 1989

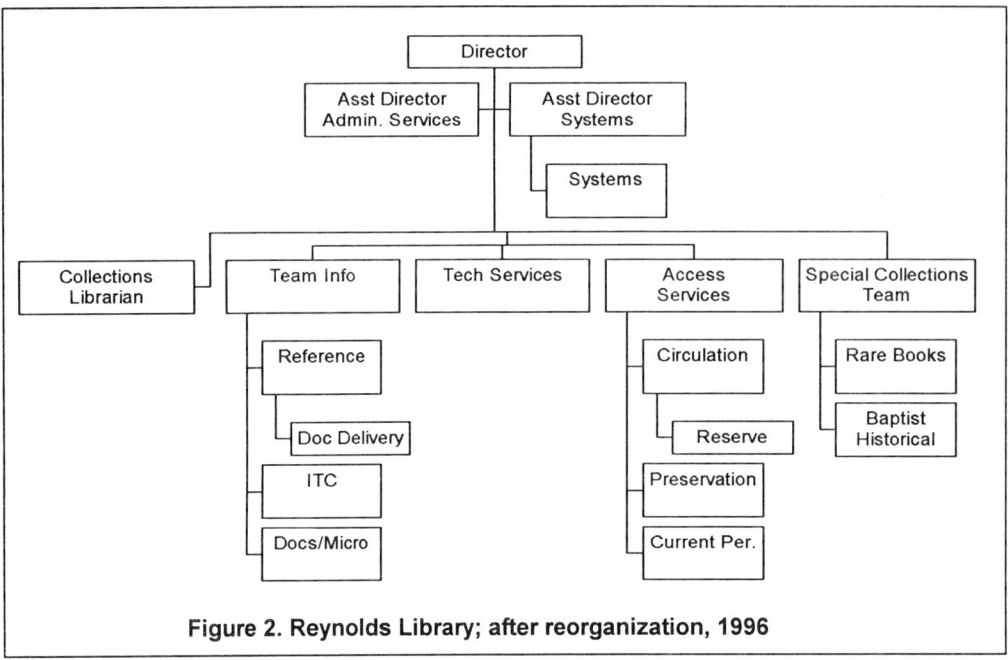

Figure 2. Reynolds Library; after reorganization, 1996

In the fall of 1995 we began a thorough yearlong reorganization process. With a Steering Committee, representing all areas of the library with professional and support staff, a Technology Task Force, a Work Processes Task Force and a Communications Team, we revised our mission statement, developed alternative future scenarios, identified gaps in our processes, and kept the entire staff informed. We had a daylong retreat with a facilitator to do scenario building, based on Marvin Weisbord's work *Future Search*, read much of the literature about other library reorganization processes, and met with focus groups of faculty and students. We set up an anonymous communication system for staff so that we could deal with their concerns. Many staff members came to talk to me individually to voice their opinions. At general staff meetings we made sure to update our staff on what was happening behind closed doors. We debated all kinds of changes from peer review and upward evaluation to rotating Team Leaders, to eliminating departments altogether. We reached consensus, and put the organization chart shown in figure 2 into effect in July of 1996.

The new organization eliminated the two line assistant directors, substituting an Assistant Director for Administrative Services, and Assistant Director for Systems. Both were to be essentially staff positions, although the A.D. for Systems would supervise the Automation librarian and a technician. There would also be a Collections Librarian, another staff position. The rest of the staff would be divided into four teams: Technical Services, eliminating separate acquisitions and catalog departments, Access Services, which includes Circulation, Reserve, Current Periodicals and Preservation, Information Services which promptly rechristened itself TeamInfo, including Reference, Document Delivery, the Information Technology Center and Government Documents and Microtexts. The fourth team was Special Collections, consisting of Rare Books and Manuscripts, Archives and the Baptist Historical Collection. The major training function involved staff from all teams in the library, over 20 people, coordinated by a Task Force chaired by the Director. Collection development was organized using the department liaison model and also included people on all the teams, coordinated by the Collections Librarian. Our reorganization plan called for three of the team leaders to be appointed by the director and to rotate every three years. The Technical Services Team leader was made a permanent position, in part because the Technical Services Department and the team were identical. Team leaders received an extra stipend of $2,000 per year. In addition to the teams, there were to be a number of library wide committees, such as publications, policies and procedures, statistics, staff development, etc. All the teams were to be coordinated at the Administrative Council level. The Administrative Council included the Director, Assistant Directors, Collections Librarian, Team Leaders and an elected representative of the support staff. This group would meet monthly, with the teams meeting more frequently. To reflect the changes in our expectations and in the work, we conducted a thorough review and rewrite of all staff position descriptions and secured salary and classification adjustments totaling $120,000 to the payroll. Not all staff were affected by the adjustment processes, but more than half were.

In addition to my selfish goals for the reorganization, we had identified increased customer satisfaction, for both internal and external customers, as the measure of effectiveness. Although that is hard to measure, we had senior surveys and a web-based faculty survey administered in the 1997–98 academic year which indicated we were doing well. From 1996 to 1998 we worked within our new organizational structure, formed some of the new committees and generally put structural issues and structural change at the back of our minds as we became involved in the ongoing progress of our work. We had workshops on teamwork and related topics for staff to aid in their transition to the new behaviors we wanted to encourage. I had some feedback from our staff, especially the Team Leaders, but nothing that was systematic or comprehensive. Then in the beginning of calendar 1998 we began a formal review of our reorganization.

We formed a Reorganization Review Committee, made up of some of the original steering committee members, again including support and professional staff from the different parts of the library. We went over the original report. We had discussions as a committee and met with each team, with some departments and with individuals in a series of scheduled "hearings." Before meetings we sent out a questionnaire asking the following:

- How has reorganization changed your work processes?
- How has reorganization changed your communication within the library?
- How is a Team Leader different from a Department Head?
- In what ways has the reorganization met, or not met, your expectations?
- What do you see as next steps or objectives to be addressed by the library?

We found that it is difficult for some people to identify cause and effect, and there were many vague replies to the first question. Much depended on the team. For example, Technical Services had made great changes in the work processes and physical layout of the workplace, but some of the other teams didn't see much change or change attributable to the reorganization. Most staff agreed that there was more and better communication within teams, but felt that more needed to be done to improve communication across team boundaries. There was lots of confusion about the role of the Team Leader vis a vis the Department Heads. Some of the confusion was from the Team Leaders themselves! Although by eliminating line assistant directors, I thought we had flattened our organization, several individuals experienced the change as adding hierarchy. The individuals who were parts of teams, but not Team Leaders, no longer reporting directly to me expressed that perception. Few staff members were able to articulate their expectations for the reorganization, but did believe that they were working more collegially and making the decisions related to their work. They pointed out some of the areas in which clarity was lacking, and others in which we had yet to implement the committees or structures. The rotation of team leaders was and continues to be a sensitive subject. The first team leaders were all department heads, but the position is not restricted to department heads, and, jumping ahead of myself a bit, in the next rotation, beginning July of 1999, two of the Team Leaders will not be department heads. In Access services, there was another issue. As there is only one professional, the new team leader would come from outside the department. I am not yet proposing to have a support staff member coordinate the work of a professional librarian. After the one professional retires, in about three years, we may have no professionals in Access Services, and that will require another look. We will make a decision then.

Budgeting	Hardware	Liaison to IS	Data Migration	Networks
Software	Printing	Website	Training	Multimedia
Digitizing	OCLC	User interfaces	Library systems	Y2K
Electronic Resources	Office Processes	Programming	Administrative applications	CD and other technologies

Figure 3. Technology roles.

Other issues that arose in our review included the reluctance of the Reorganization Review Steering Committee, the Team Leaders and Department Heads to move toward peer review or upward review. Every academic library exists in a broader context, that of the parent institution. Wake Forest is an anomaly in a number of ways: librarians are classed as administrative staff, and administrative staff are not evaluated! Only support staff are evaluated annually. One could ask if it is reasonable to expect anyone who does not have to be reviewed to submit to having his or her work evaluated. In general people dislike being judged, and the value of performance appraisal in improvement of performance is dubious. Yet I felt, and still do, that for teams to be effective, there must be a level of trust that permits both peer review and upward review as well as the traditional review by supervisors. I started the ball rolling when I asked the members of the Administrative Council to evaluate me anonymously, and then met with the whole staff to discuss the outcome. I would like to pursue this as part of regular pulse-taking.

Life happens, while we are making plans, and in November of 1997, the Assistant Director for Systems left, prompting a long look at the way we organize, or manage, our technology functions. We had identified many different technology roles that needed someone to coordinate efforts by individuals in each team (see figure 3).

Although there is a large IS operation on campus, there are still many things that the library chooses to do, or is expected to do for itself. Library Staff are also heavily involved in software testing and documentation for the university in relation to our training responsibilities. It was easy to identify a core of employees whose jobs were primarily concerned with technology, well beyond the boundaries of the two people in the systems office. The Information Technology Center staff, the technician in the Reference Department, and the systems staff spent most of their time on the tasks outlined above, but the Director, the Assistant Director for Administrative Services and people in several departments also were heavily involved in the technology challenges. Our solution was to form a technology team, put systems, the ITC, and the technician from reference in it and have others representing administration and all the other teams participating at varying levels. Pending the hiring of a new team leader, we have the head of the ITC acting in that capacity. Thus our latest chart (see figure 4).

We are finding that our relationships and work extend beyond our boundaries. Collections projects involve the state and sometimes the region. Our systems projects involve IS and the other university libraries, as well as registrars, controllers and vendors, and so many of our efforts require teamwork at all levels of the organization that we must

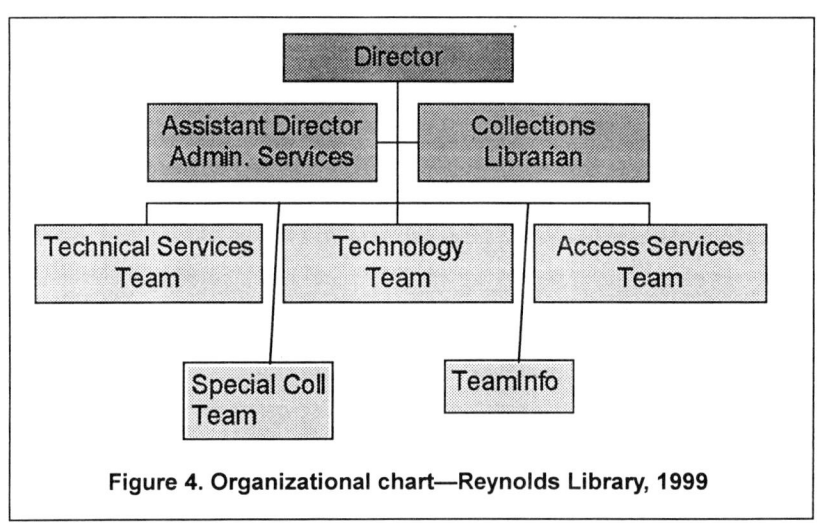

Figure 4. Organizational chart—Reynolds Library, 1999

remain flexible as organizations. This means that several people, not just one or two, must be empowered to speak for the library, and must be knowledgeable beyond a specific task. Our structures must support and encourage this, and if they don't, must be altered. Our experience, at Wake Forest, indicates that some staff seek to be directed, others seek self determination, and still others, movers and shakers, seek to influence others. No structure or organization chart perfectly slots staff according to their abilities and desires, but if we can be flexible, use freer structures, whether teams or something else, we may allow more people to contribute at their highest level. We need to have a process in place to take our organizational pulse at regular intervals, and to make course corrections.

As our October 19, 1998 Reorganization Update suggests:

- *Communication and coordination still seem to be goals for continuous*
- improvement, and continuing staff development will inevitably lead to
- increased staff involvement in decision making at each appropriate
- level. This is already happening and must be encouraged and supported
- by supervisors and team leaders.

In July of 1999, three or four new team leaders will replace existing ones, bringing their fresh perspectives to the coordination of library activities, and getting opportunities to develop greater skills in facilitation and management. Stay tuned!

Role Call—What are Library Students Training For and What Will They Be Doing?

Elvira Embser and Philip Coen-Pesch

Note: Paper unavailable at press time.

Snowbird Leadership Institute: A Survey Of The Implications For Leadership In The Profession

Teresa Y. Neely and Mark D. Winston

Introduction
This research reflects the results of a study of the individuals who have participated in the Snowbird Leadership Institute (Institute) from its inception in 1990 to 1998. The Institute participants were asked about their career backgrounds and career progression since they participated in the Institute, the level and type of involvement in leadership and professional activities, and about their perceptions regarding the impact of the Snowbird experience on their career paths and progression. They were also asked about their perceptions regarding the importance of the other participants and the program mentors on the value of the experience, and a number of demographic factors.

Background and Review of the Literature
The review of the literature reflects the increased emphasis on leadership in library and information science. In an environmental scan of leadership development programs, the Association of Research Libraries Office of Leadership and Management Services (ARL/OLMS) identified a number of such programs that met a number of guidelines for inclusion, such as the following:

[T]he leadership program is a continuing offering, held regularly.
[T]he focus of the program is on leadership development, not technical skills or policy analysis.[1]

The results of the environmental scan indicate the following:

In addition to ARL/OLMS programs, a wide variety of learning events are being offered by diverse organizations. Three North American residential programs, the Senior Fellows Program at the Long Island University's Palmer School of Library and Information Science [although the future location of the program appears to be in question], the Snowbird Leadership Institute, and Northern Exposure to Leadership, offer comprehensive opportunities for growth and development at different stages of librarians' professional careers. These events effectively combine experiential and theoretical learning in order to engage participants

---

Teresa Y. Neely is interim personnel librarian/staff development and training coordinator, Colorado State University and Mark D. Winston is assistant professor, Department of the Library and Information Studies, Rutgers University.

in discussion/dialogue of current leadership issues.[2]

It is important to note that a number of other organizations sponsor leadership development programs, as well.

The American Library Association (ALA), through the Association of College and Research Libraries (ACRL) and Library Administration and Management Association (LAMA), offer a number of programs geared to provide participants with an overview of leadership and the skills required to foster individual development. These events are shorter in duration than residential programs and offer varying levels of expert advice, theoretical learning, and practical application.

Library consortia, state library associations, library schools, and individual universities also offer varying levels of leadership development programs. While there are similarities in program content, the defining factors seem related to instructional approach, duration of learning experience and depth of exploration.[3]

As has been suggested, leadership programs may focus on individuals in different stages of their careers. For example, the Senior Fellows program, "a biennial leadership and executive development experience,"[4] and the new ACRL/Harvard Leadership Institute, which has been "Developed for directors of libraries and those who report directly to them,"[5] represent offerings for those who are currently in senior administrative positions.

In contrast, programs for those who are relatively new to the profession include the Snowbird Leadership Institute and the Northern Exposure to Leadership program. Donna Brockmeyer-Klebaum, Coordinator of the Northern Exposure to Leadership Institute, and a 1993 participant in the Snowbird Leadership Institute has noted that

> Junior professionals often look to senior colleagues for leadership, for guidance, and for role models. While we may have energy, creativity, enthusiasm and good intentions, we may lack vision and confidence based on experience. We lack not in our ability to contribute, not in our ability to do things right, but sometimes in our instinct to do the right thing.[6]

Certainly, the changes that are being encountered with regard to the advent and proliferation of information technology and changing organizational structures that allow new professionals to take on leadership responsibilities early on in their careers create the need for, as Brockmeyer-Klebaum suggests "a skill set never before required. We need to be quick, nimble, flexible and able to deal with constant ambiguity in an ever-changing environment."[7]

The Snowbird Leadership Institute provides a leadership development opportunity for individuals who are relatively new to their careers. Snowbird "is a five-day residential, primarily experiential, program of leadership training for people who are at a relatively early point in their library careers. This event takes place in August at a ski resort called Snowbird in the Wasatch Mountains rising above Salt Lake City."[8]

The Canadian equivalent of Snowbird, the Northern Exposure to Leadership, is a "five-day experiential and theoretical learning institute held at spectacular Emerald Lake Lodge in Yoho National Park, B.C."[9]

According to F. William Summers and Lorraine Summers, who have been involved actively with the Institute since its inception in 1990,

> It is the brainchild of J. Dennis Day, [then] director of the Salt Lake City Public Library. Day was a strong supporter of 1987–88 American Library Association President Margaret Chisholm's call for special training for young leaders, and when ALA's proposal for a much broader project to carry this out was not funded, he decided to do something on his own.[10]

Since its inception, the Institute has been funded in large measure by Ameritech (formerly, Dynix), under the leadership of President, and now CEO, Paul Sybrowsky.

In an article regarding the first of the Institutes, Nancy Tessman, then Institute Coordinator, described the program as "a series of experiences that encouraged self-exploration and discovery."[11] The program is structured around a number of learning activities, group activities, and interaction with mentors.

The mentors have included "library school deans and faculty, directors of major public and academic libraries, and state librarians. The role of the mentors is to share their wisdom and experience with participants. They work and interact with learning groups and in one-on-one situations throughout the [I]nstitute."[12]

According to the Summers, "If there is a key identifying concept of the Snowbird Leadership Institute it is probably the belief that being a leader depends as much as anything else upon knowing and being comfortable with who you are and having confidence in yourself."[13]

With thirty or so participants, normally with less than five years of experience since completion of the MLS degree, there is also the provision of "plenty of time for personal reflection and evaluation."[14]

According to Marilyn Miller, who has served as one of the program mentors,

> The profession is empowered by Snowbird, because year after year a small group of emerging leaders joins a developing cadre of librarians who have had a vital leadership experience at a crucial time in their career and who are committed to professional growth. Snowbird also empowers the profession because it brings together librarians across all types of libraries and types of library functions and responsibilities to explore common interests, concerns, and opportunities.[15]

In their December 1991 article, F. William Summers and Lorraine Summers posed a significant question about Snowbird. "Will the annual output of thirty to thirty-five early to mid-career young people with special training make a difference in the quality and quantity of leadership in the field over time?"[16] They suggest that with only two institutes having been completed, "it is too early to tell in any real sense."[17]

The data and analysis presented here are intended to begin to answer that question.

General Methodology

This paper presents the findings of a research study of individuals who have participated in the Snowbird Leadership Institute. The primary focus of this original research is analyze the impact of the knowledge and insight gained on the career progression and professional activities of the participants, as well as specific knowledge and skills gained as a result of participation. Survey methodology was used and data collection was completed by direct mailing the questionnaire to each known Snowbird participant.

Instrumentation

The survey instrument used in this study is designed to address issues related to demographics, educational background, work experience prior to entering librarianship, and professional experience prior and subsequent to participating in the Institute. This instrument was adapted from an instrument used in a 1997 research study, and one used in a 1997 dissertation. In the November 1997 issue of *College and Research Libraries*, Julie Brewer reported on a study designed by the American Library Association Office for Library Personnel Resources (OLPR)[18] on post-master's residency programs. The instrument used was designed to "gather information about residency experiences from the perspective of former program participants."[19] The second instrument used was from Mark Winston's 1997 dissertation which investigated the role of recruitment in the education and careers of academic business librarians.[20] The resulting survey instrument was expanded to make allowances for the leadership activities of both academic and public librarians, and for the Snowbird population.

The Winston instrument provided the basic structure of the Snowbird Leadership Institute instrument (See Appendix A). Basic demographic queries and items on educational background were taken directly from this instrument or adapted (See Appendix A, items 5–7a, 9–16, 17, 19–25 and 33–36).

The Snowbird survey adapted a number of relevant areas from the Brewer/OLPR instrument such as queries requesting the year of participation, and the individual who nominated the respondent for participation (See Appendix A, items 1 and 2). The Professional and Career Development section of the Brewer/OLPR instrument provided the basis for a similar section in the Snowbird instrument relating to the participants' perception of Snowbird's overall impact on their careers and professional development (See items 27–31). Snowbird items 29–30e were constructed to gather information on specific aspects of the Snowbird experience which continued after the Institute itself. Items in the summary section of the Brewer/OLPR instrument were adapted to construct queries about the participants status before and after the Institute (See items 11–16).

Both researchers are from academic librarianship and therefore, defined and interpreted leadership activities as publications and participation in committees and professional/scholarly associations. Item 26 asked for other leadership activities; however, many respondents from public librarianship were critical of the academic slant of the survey and implied that the inclusion of item 26 and other items as the sole mechanism for collecting additional qualitative data were not adequate.

Prior to survey distribution, the instrument was reviewed by Institute administrators and consultants for their approval and comments. In October 1998, surveys were mailed to the entire population of individuals (n=213) on the most current list of Snowbird Leadership Institute participants (1990–1998) as obtained from the Salt Lake City headquarters.[21] In mid-November, a follow up mailing was done. In total, 150 useable surveys were returned, reflecting a response rate of nearly 71 percent. Thirteen surveys were returned by the postal service as a result of non current addresses; and, one survey was returned with a note from the respondent, but was not completed. The latter survey and those returned but incomplete were included in the response rate; and the data on incomplete surveys (those where the participant inadvertently skipped items or pages of items) were included in the data analysis. Surveys were accompanied by a letter and a self-addressed envelope. Postage was not included, although at least one participant indicated that this would have been a welcome addition and may contribute to a higher response rate. Prior to the mailing of the surveys, an email message was sent to the Snowbird listserv[22] announcing the intended research, that the surveys would be arriving shortly and to encourage the return of completed surveys.

Although a large amount of data was collected, this paper will present only relevant selected findings related to the demographic profile of the population and leadership activities, career progression and development. A more complete discussion is forthcoming.

Selected Findings and Discussion

The researchers intent to collect relevant data from all participants from the beginning of the Institute (1990) until 1998 took into consideration that the 1997 class was a reunion and did not include new participants; however, the instrument did not make allowances for 1998 participants who had recently completed the Institute and therefore could not adequately answer many of the queries. Therefore, the 1998 participants will be discussed where relevant. All statistical analysis was done on a n=150 scale and throughout much of the analysis, null and N/A responses will be reported where appropriate.

Demographics

Of the 150 useable surveys, 1994 and 1998 classes showed the highest return rate, as shown in Table 1.

The population is somewhat homogenous in that it is predominantly White (85.33 percent) and female (76 percent), and in the 40+ age range (55 percent). However, nearly 24 percent reported their age in the 31–35 range. One hundred and forty-eight of the total respondents reported their gender and ethnicity, and 145 reported their age range, as shown in table 2. The Ethnic Background section of table 2 shows the *Other* category with three respondents. Of those three, one respondent reported her ethnic background as White Australian, and a second identified as a U.S. citizen, Jamaican heritage; the third *Other* was not identified.

Table 1. Breakdown of useable returned surveys by year of attendance.

Year	# of useable surveys received	%
1990	11	7.3
1991	14	9.3
1992	22	14.6
1993	11	7.3
1994	25	16.66
1995	21	14
1996	17	11.3
1998	25	16.66
	4	2.66
Total	150	

Academics

Undergraduate Careers

The academic backgrounds were of interest to the researchers because it helps in providing a complete profile of the Snowbird participant. All but 4 of the respondents reported having attained an undergraduate degree and the major subject area. Nearly 23 percent (34) reported English as their undergraduate major. Other subject areas worth noting include history (8 percent), social sciences[23] and other (7.3 percent each). Fine arts and business tied with 6.6 percent (10). More than fifty percent (92) of respondents reported not having an undergraduate minor. Three persons reported library science as an undergraduate minor.

Nominations

An important aspect of the Snowbird Leadership Institute which determines the pool for selection is the person who is doing the nominating. Participants are selected from a pool of nominees; therefore, one can not be selected if he or she is not nominated. It should be noted that responses include respondents who reported more than one person nominating them. Thirty-five percent (or 53 respondents) of the participants were nominated by their library school dean or department head. State librarians were instrumental in nominating 25 percent (or 38 respondents); nineteen percent (or 29 respondents) of the participants selected the *Other* category; library directors nominated 18.6 percent (or 28 respondents); and 2 percent (or 3 respondents) of the respondents did not know or could not recall who nominated them.

MLS/MLIS and Other Graduate Degrees

The terminal degree for the library and information science profession is considered by the American Library Association and the majority of the profession to be the master's degree. Findings in this area, 96.66 percent, overwhelmingly confirm this assumption; however, of the respondents, 2 percent (3) reported not having acquired the degree; and, an additional 1.3 percent (2) did not answer the question. Although more than a third of the participants were nominated by their library school deans, there was no concentration of participants from specific graduate schools. The University of Arizona ranked first with 11 participants; the University of Pittsburgh and Emporia State University each had 9 participants; and Brigham Young University and the University of Wisconsin-Madison each had 8 participants.[24]

One hundred and fifteen respondents, nearly 77 percent, reported not having earned an additional graduate degree at the time of the survey. Thirty of the Snowbirders have earned master's degrees; 3 have earned doctorates; and 1 reported earning the equivalent of a master's degree in education. Almost 27 percent (40) of the respondents reported that they had

Table 2. Gender, ethnic background and age range of Snowbird population.

Gender		Ethnic Background		Age Range	
Female	114	White	128	21–25	0
Male	34	Black/African American	11	26–30	9
Null	2	Hispanic/Latino	3	31–35	35
		Other	3	36–39	17
		Asian/Asian American	2	40–45	38
		American Indian-Native American	1	46 +	46

completed additional graduate credits, which had not been applied toward a degree, in a variety of disciplines.

Career Background and Progression

An important component of the profile of the Snowbird Leadership Institute participants is a discussion of career backgrounds and career progression since participation in the Institute, and the level and type of involvement in leadership and professional activities. It is important to indicate that the concept of leadership is, and probably should be, defined broadly, with respect to the types of organizations in which individuals are employed and personal and professional goals.

Career Progression

Certainly, a significant part of this discussion is the respondents' perceptions regarding the impact of the Snowbird experience on their career paths and progression. The discussion of the career backgrounds and career progression of those who have participated in the Institute includes information regarding years of professional library experience, years of prior experience in other professions and as paraprofessionals in libraries. It also includes the types of libraries in which they worked at the time of their attendance and at present, the types of positions they have held and are in currently, and career progression since participation in the Institute.

In terms of professional experience, the participants have been librarians for an average of 8 years (See table 3). More than half of the respondents have been professional librarians for between 6 and 10 years, and slightly more than one-quarter have 5 years or fewer of professional experience. In contrast, with regard to when they participated in Snowbird, the respondents indicated that they had an average of just under 4 years of professional library experience, reflecting the program focus on individuals who are relatively new to the profession. In fact, 85 percent had five or fewer years of professional experience at the time of participation.

With regard to the types of libraries in which they have been employed, nearly all of the Snowbird participants worked in public libraries (44 percent) or academic libraries (34.66 percent) at the time they attended the Institute (See table 4). Of those who did indicate the type of library in which they are working now, the majority are still working in public (29.33 percent) or academic (16.66 percent) libraries. However, providing a comparison between the types of libraries in which the respondents were working at the time of their participation and the types of institutions in which they are working now is difficult based upon the fact that exactly one-third did not indicate the type of library in which they are working now. The fact that such a large percentage of the respondents did not provide an answer for this survey item may be based on the fact that an earlier question addresses their current job situation in reference to their Snowbird participation. (See Appendix A, item 15). In fact, 38.66 percent indicated that they are in the same position (and same institution) now, as was the case at the time they attended the Institute. Another 25.33 percent are in the same insti-

Table 3. Professional Experience currently and during Snowbird.

	Currently		During Snowbird	
0 to 5 years	39	26%	128	85.33%
6 to 10 years	83	53.33%	10	6.66%
11 to 15 years	14	9.33%	4	2.66%
16 to 20 years	8	5.33%	4	2.66%
More than 20 years	3	2%	0	
No response	3	2%	4	2.66%

Table 4. Employing Institution currently and during Snowbird.

	Currently	During Snowbird
Academic	25	52
Public	44	66
Special	5	8
Government	7	12
School	0	1
Other	7	10
Not working in a library	12	3
No response	50	

tution but in a different position. It should be noted that some respondents selected more than one category in response to this item.

In fact, of the 58 respondents who indicated that they are in the same position that they were in at the time of the Institute, half (51.72 percent) are working in public libraries now. Nearly one-third are in academic libraries, with 10.34 percent in government libraries, and approximately 5 percent in special libraries. In contrast, a slightly larger percentage (55.26 percent) of those who are working in the same institution but in a different position are in public libraries, with fewer (23.68 percent) in academic libraries. It should be noted that almost half of those who are working in different institutions than was the case at the time of their participation in the Institute are in academic libraries, with approximately one-quarter in public libraries.

It is interesting to note the changes in the types of positions held by the respondents now as compared to the time of participation. More than a third (38.66 percent) of the respondents were working in public services at the time of their participation in the Institute (See table 5). With regard to administrative positions, 22.66 percent were department heads or heads of branches, 12 percent were directors or deans, and 3.33 percent were assistant or associate deans or directors at the time of their participation. Only 10 percent were working in technical services; and, 14 percent worked in other areas of library and information services. In contrast, only 20 percent are working in public services now. And, slightly fewer (8.6 percent) reported working in technical services now, as compared to their positions at the time of participation in the Institute. As would be expected on the basis of the fact that they have been in the profession for a greater period of time, more are in administrative positions now. At present, 30.6 percent are heads of branches of departments; 6.66 percent are assistant or associate deans or directors; and, 14.6 percent are deans or directors. Certainly, it is not possible to indicate a direct correlation between the respondents' participation in the leadership institute and their career and upward mobility. However, discussion of the respondents' perceptions of the impact of their participation with regard to their obtaining subsequent positions and their perceptions regarding whether their careers (discussed below) would have been different had they not had the Snowbird experience provides additional information regarding the role of the Institute.

While it is important to consider the promotions and what appears to be the upward mobility of those who have participated in the Institute, it should be noted that not all progression is vertical. Thus, being promoted or obtaining a higher level position elsewhere is not the only measure of career progression. Also, the size and availability of promotion opportunities in the employing institution and the relative mobility of the respondents are factors, as well. However, factors such as these are outside of the scope of this study. In addition, some of the respondents were already in administrative or managerial positions at the time of participation. Certainly, the comparison of the level of leadership activity prior to and since participation in the Institute is an important consideration in considering the role of the Institute in the careers of the respondents.

With regard to their career backgrounds prior to entering librarianship, more than 60 percent have held paraprofessional positions in library and information science prior to becoming librarians. Of those who have held such positions, the average number of years of such experience that the respondents reported was 6.4 years, reflecting the fact that 34 percent of those with such experience had five or fewer years of paraprofessional experience in library and information science; and, 19.33

Table 5. Type of Position held currently and during Snowbird.

	Currently	During Snowbird
Public Services	30	58
Technical Services	13	15
Department or Branch Head	46	34
Asst. or Assoc. Dean/Director	10	5
Dean/Director	22	18
Other	26	21
No response	3	2

Table 6. Paraprofessional experience.		
	LIS	Other Fields
0 to 5 years	52	128
6 to 10 years	29	10
11 to 15 years	12	4
16 to 20 years	3	4
More than 20 years	3	0
No response	51	4

percent had 6 to 10 years paraprofessional experience in library and information science (See table 6). In contrast, slightly fewer than one-quarter (22 percent) reported having held positions in some other field prior to becoming librarians. And, of those who worked in other fields prior to entering librarianship, did so for relatively short periods of time. In fact 85 percent of those who did work in other fields had five or fewer years of such experience, with the average being 3.84 years.

Leadership Activities

One limitation of the study relates to the discussion of leadership activities. As the two researchers are working or have worked in academic library settings, the leadership activities about which the respondents were queried reflect an emphasis on activities that are often required of academic librarians, and which may, thus, reflect a greater degree of participation by participants in these types of settings than may be the case for others in public, school, or special libraries. The respondents were asked to indicate other leadership activities in which they have been involved. It is important to indicate that a full discussion of the leadership role taken by individuals in such a broad array of settings is not possible if the focus is on only scholarship, professional association activities, and other committee activities.

The leadership activities considered include scholarly activities, such as research, publication, and presentations. For the purposes of this discussion, the discussion of participation will be limited to research and scholarly activities. In order to consider the impact of the Institute on their level of professional activity, the participants were asked to indicate their level of scholarly activity and professional participation prior and subsequent to attending the Institute. Certainly, any discussion of these factors must include the indication that the fact the individuals have simply been in the profession for longer period of time is likely to have some impact on the level of scholarly and professional activity. In addition, the fact that the Institute focuses on leadership development for those who are at relatively early stages in their career suggests that at the time of participation, the level of activity reported is not likely to be directly comparable to that reported later. It should be noted that only 15 percent of the respondents indicated that they are required to write, publish, and/or engage in research in order to obtain promotion and/or tenure or a tenure equivalent. Fewer (12 percent) have held other positions with these requirements since participating in Snowbird.

The data gathered reflects the respondents' publication activity in terms of journal articles, books, book chapters, book reviews, and publications in conference proceedings.

Of the 150 respondents, only 36 had authored or co-authored articles that had been published prior to participating in Snowbird (See table 7). Since their participation in the Institute, there has been a 15.29 percent increase in the number of respondents who have published articles. Greater increases are also reflected for all other types of publications as well. Not surprisingly, the largest increase (43.75 percent) appeared with regard to the number of respondents who have written book reviews. However, it should be noted that a larger number of individuals wrote journal articles than did book reviews.

A more consistent level of increases was noted with regard to presentations reported. The partici-

Table 7. Leadership Activities: Respondents reporting publication activity.		
	# of respondents before Snowbird	# of respondents since Snowbird
Journal articles	36	49
Books	12	17
Book chapters	18	33
Book reviews	18	46
Conference papers	20	25

pants were asked about presentations that they have made at professional library conferences at the national and international levels, the state level, and other library conferences, as well as conferences in other disciplines. The increases ranged from 14 percent to 25 percent, with the greater increase being reflected in relation to presentations at national and international library conferences, although the largest number of presentations reported were as a part of state library association conferences as shown in table 8.

Attitudes about the Institute and Perceived Impact

In order to gather data on the participants' attitudes about the Institute, the researchers included survey queries which asked about the participants' perceptions of the impact of the Institute on their career progression, as well as learnings and interaction with other Snowbird participants, and benefit and learnings from the Institute itself. Forty percent of the respondents reported that the Institute contributed somewhat to their obtaining subsequent positions, 19 percent reported that it contributed to a great extent. However, 31.33 percent (47) reported that it did not contribute at all to their obtaining subsequent positions. The latter statistic is in line with the 38.66 percent (58) who reported that at the time of the survey, they were in the same position as when they attended the Institute.

In a question related to career progression, nearly half of the respondents (48.66 percent or 73) selected yes when asked if they believed their career paths would have been different without the Snowbird experience. Forty-two percent answered that it would not have been different and 14 respondents declined to answer the question.

Individuals who have participated in the Institute are selected from a larger pool, and are ostensibly, the cream that rose to the top during the selection process. With this in mind, the researchers included queries which were intended to gather data about learnings and interactions with other Snowbird participants. One hundred and fourteen (76 percent) of those surveyed noted that interaction with other participants contributed a great deal to the overall quality and experience of the Institute. Twenty-two percent noted that it contributed to some extent and one person reported that interactions with other participants did not contribute at all to the overall quality and experience.

Recognizing the proprietary nature of the content and curriculum of the Institute itself, the researchers generalized the overall Snowbird experience, including all learning techniques, literature, and structured group and individual occurrences, by asking respondents about the perceived benefits and learnings from activities which occurred after the Institute. The survey instrument included a number of opportunities for gathering qualitative data about the Institute and this data will be analyzed and disseminated at a later date. Four categories of post-Institute activity were identified and participants were surveyed using multiple choice format queries, modeled on a Likert scale.

Listserv

The Snowbird listserv is an electronic discussion list, open only to Snowbird participants. Selection and participation in the Institute does not guarantee automatic signup and many respondents expressed a lack of knowledge about the existence of the listserv and some included requests in their comments to be subscribed. Several offered comments about the traffic on the listserv including its perceived primary existence as being a method for announcing job and address changes, as opposed to being a tool for discussion of leadership and related issues. As primarily a lurker on this listserv, one of the researchers observes that there

Table 8. Leadership Activities: Respondents reporting presentation activity.

	# of respondents before Snowbird	# of respondents since Snowbird
National or International Library Conferences	30	50
State/Regional Library Conferences	63	84
Other Library Conferences	40	63
Other Conferences	54	81

have been attempts to introduce and sustain stimulating and intellectual discussions; however, it is difficult for one or two persons to provide the continuing dialogue for an entire list. Table 9 shows the responses regarding the listserv as well as the other categories: informal reunions at professional conferences, collegial relationships developed with other participants, and mentoring relationships.

Informal Reunions

The Snowbird Leadership office in Salt Lake City hosts an annual reception for participants and mentors at the American Library Association's annual conference each summer. Depending upon the location of ALA's Midwinter conference, and/or division conferences (e.g., Public Library Association, Association of College and Research Libraries, etc.), local participants sometimes organize dinner, lunch, or other informal meetings for Snowbirder's attending those conferences. Table 9, column 3 shows that 41 percent of the respondents reported that these informal reunions contribute to a great extent or to some extent to the overall quality of their post-Institute interaction. Nearly 60 percent (89 respondents) did not answer or reported that these reunions did not contribute to the quality of the experience. An analysis of the years of participation of the 89 respondents did not reveal any statistically significant relationship between year of participation and attitude about informal reunions.

Collegial Relationships

Collegial relationships were identified as an area for further analysis because the researchers recognize the importance of collegiality in the profession of librarianship. Collegial relationships are developed and maintained via listservs, at annual and biannual conferences, and via other professional development opportunities. Networking professionally and socially has long been associated with advancement in the corporate, private, public and higher education sectors. Table 9 reveals that collegial relationships have contributed greatly or to some extent to the quality of the experience for 114 (76 percent) participants.

Mentoring Relationships

Mentoring is an important component of the Snowbird experience. In fact, in the majority of the leadership institutes previously discussed, mentoring is an aspect that is given much consideration. The mentoring aspect of the Institute was more informal in that for the duration of the Institute, small groups of individuals were assigned to 2 mentors. These relationships have the potential to continue after the Institute, but this post-Institute activity is not directly structured. Mentors have ranged from lawyers to directors of large public library systems, to library administrators from universities, both public and private. Table 9 shows that more than 50 percent (87 respondents) of those responding to the survey rated mentoring relationships as contributing to a great extent or to some extent to the quality of their Snowbird experience. Thirty-eight percent of those surveyed reported that the mentoring relationships did not contribute to the quality of their experience and 4 percent declined to answer the question. The fact that a significant portion of the population did not rate the value of the mentoring relationships highly may be based on the lack of individual mentoring relationships and/or as factor of the population demographics and the difficulty of building such relationships.

Table 9. Responses for categories identified as post-Institute relevant activities.

Contributions to individual benefits and learning	Listserv	Informal	Collegial reunions	Mentoring relationships
To a great extent	15 (10%)	14 (9.33%)	35 (23.33%)	26 (17.33%)
To some extent	57 (38%)	47 (31.33%)	79 (52.66%)	61 (40.60%)
Not at all	69 (46%)	62 (41.33%)	31 (20.66%)	57 (38%)
No response	9 (6%)	27 (18%)	5 (3.33%)	6 (4%)

Other Library Leadership Programs

Based on the authors' interest in the effects of library leadership programs, item 31 inquired about participation in other library leadership programs. Twenty-two individuals responded about participation in *Other* Institutes, citing state or regional leadership programs. Seventy-eight percent reported that they had not participated in any other programs; eight percent reported they attended the ALA Emerging Leaders Institute, and 6 percent reported they had recently participated in the Association of Research Libraries Leadership and Career Development Program.[25] Although the former Institute appears to have been a one-time opportunity, plans are underway for the second ARL program; and, as participants in the latter, the researchers look forward to examining that population for trends and evidence of acquired outcomes.

Summary and Recommendations for Future Research

It is difficult to identify a direct relationship between participation in the Snowbird Leadership Institute and career progression and greater participation in leadership activities. However, it is clear that the respondents report an increased level of activity in a number of different categories of leadership activity. In addition, their perceptions regarding the value of the Institute with regard to their career progression are largely positive and reflect that many of their career paths would have been different had they not had the Snowbird experience.

In terms of the respondents attitudes about the Institute and perceived impact, it is difficult to determine the relationship between the impact of the Institute on the obtaining of subsequent positions. The fact that nearly 40 percent reported that they are currently in the same position as when they attended the Institute does not allow a clear analysis of this particular occurrence. Other activities engaged in, however, while remaining in the same position may begin to shed some light on this aspect of the study; and, as mentioned previously, the number of individuals increased in every category in the presentation and publication categories.

Interactions with other Snowbird participants, categorized as Collegial relationships, and mentoring are rated highly among most participants. However, the nearly 40 percent answered that mentoring did not contribute to the quality of their overall experience. As previously mentioned, mentoring is critical and the informal, unstructured approach may not have been the best method for introducing the mentoring component.

The listserv and informal reunions were not highly rated, as well. This could be contributed to the informal nature of both.

The researchers recommend further analysis of the data collected, with a special emphasis on the qualitative responses to the queries on leadership, career progression and impact of the Institute on individual careers. It would also be beneficial to track the participants of the Spectrum Initiative, for more in depth qualitative data on the mentoring component and the proposed Spectrum institute[26]; as well as the participants of the Senior Fellows program, the Emerging Leaders Institute, and the ARL Leadership and Career Development Program.

Notes

1. "Leadership Development Programs: An Environmental Scan." Washington, D.C.: Association of Research Libraries Office of Leadership and Management Services. Unpublished document, 1.

2. Ibid.

3. Ibid.

4. Ibid. 1–2.

5. "ACRL/Harvard Leadership Institute." *College and Research Libraries News* 60 (February 1999): 71.

6. Donna Brockmeyer-Klebaum, "Leadership Institutes: The Living Legacy They Can and Can't Leave," *Feliciter* (October 1995): 18

7. Ibid.

8. F. William Summers and Lorraine Summers, "Library Leadership 2000 and Beyond: Snowbird Leadership Institute," *Wilson Library Bulletin* (1991): 38.

9. Ibid.

10. Ibid.

11. Nancy Tessman, "Learning to Be Library Leaders," *Wilson Library Bulletin* (October 1990): 16.

12. Ibid.

13. F. William Summers and Lorraine Summers, 39.

14. F. William Summers and Lorraine Summers, 40.

15. Marilyn L. Miller, "Snowbird: An Experiment in Leadership," *American Libraries* (October 1992): 812.

16. F. William Summers and Lorraine Summers, 41.

17. Ibid.

18. Julie A. Brewer, "Post-Master's Residency Programs: Enhancing the Development of New Professionals and Minority Recruitment in Academic and Research Libraries," *College and Research Libraries* 58 (Nov. 1997): 528–37.

19. Ibid., 531.

20. Mark D. Winston. "The Recruitment, Education and Careers of Academic Business Librarians." Unpublished doctoral dissertation, University of Pittsburgh.(1997).

21. For information on the Snowbird Leadership Institute, contact Bobbi Bohman, Salt Lake City Public Library, Salt Lake City, Utah. In 1997, a "reunion" Institute was held for participants from earlier years, instead of the usual Institute. Thus, respondents were asked to complete the instrument on the basis of their first participation in the Institute.

22. The Snowbird Leadership Institute listserv is openly only to Snowbird participants, mentors, and administrators. To be added to the list, contact Mike Silvia at msilvia@etal.uri.edu.

23. Includes double majors, international affairs and American studies.

24. Other schools attended include: State University of New York-Albany, University of Alberta, University of British Columbia, Clarion University of Pennsylvania, Emory University, University of Michigan, University of North Carolina at Chapel Hill, University of North Carolina at Greensboro, San Jose State University, St. John's University, University of Texas at Austin, Wayne State University, University of Wisconsin-Milwaukee, Columbia University, and the University of Southern California—1 participant each; University of California-Los Angeles, Catholic University of America, Kent State University, University of Kentucky, North Carolina Central University, University of South Carolina, University of Tennessee, and University of Washington—2 participants; Drexel University, University of Hawaii, University of Iowa, University of Oklahoma, Rutgers University, Simmons College, and University of California, Berkeley—3 participants; University of Illinois, Indiana University, University of North Texas, and Texas Women's University—4 participants; Louisiana State University and University of Missouri-Columbia—5 participants; University of South Florida and Florida State University—6 participants; and University of Maryland—7 participants.

25. For additional information on the ARL LCDP, contact DeEtta Jones, ARL Program Officer for Diversity at <deetta@arl.org> or at 202-296-2296; and for information on the Emerging Leaders institute, contact Emily Melton <emelton@ala.org>; or see Teresa Y. Neely, "Diversity Initiatives and Programs: The National Approach," *Journal of Library Administration* (forthcoming 1999).

26. See the Spectrum Initiative Mission at <http://www.ala.org/spectrum/mission.html> and also, Spectrum Initiative: Scholarship Requirements and Expectations at http://www.ala.org/spectrum/mission.html.

Training ITAs: A Program for Student Information Technology Assistants

Angela Myatt Quick and Eugene Engeldinger

Note: Paper unavailable at press time.

Contributed Papers

21st-Century Learners

Faculty Use of Electronic Journals at Research Institutions

Deborah Lenares

Introduction

The meteoric rise in the number of electronic journals published during the 1990s (see Figure 1) is documented in the *ARL Directory of Electronic Journals, Newsletters and Academic Discussion Lists*, published annually since 1991. The number of electronic journals listed in the 1991 directory was 27. The first significant increase in the number listed was a jump from 45 in 1993, to 181 in 1994. In 1995 the number rose to 306, in 1996 the number listed surged to 1093, and it surged again in 1997 to 2459 (ARL, 1997). Although the exact numbers of new journals published since 1997 cannot be reported until the release of the 8th edition of the *ARL Directory*, an extrapolation of the growth curve shows the expected increase (see figure 1).

The popularity of the World Wide Web helped to stimulate the growth of electronic journal publishing in the mid 1990s, but much of the growth since 1996 can be attributed to the electronic debut of many commercial publishers. The growth in parallel publishing, which may be defined as the publication of an electronic version of a traditionally print journal, has greatly increased the number of scholarly journals available electronically and may possibly have affected the attitudes of acceptance toward journals in this format. Together, these changes could have a dramatic af-

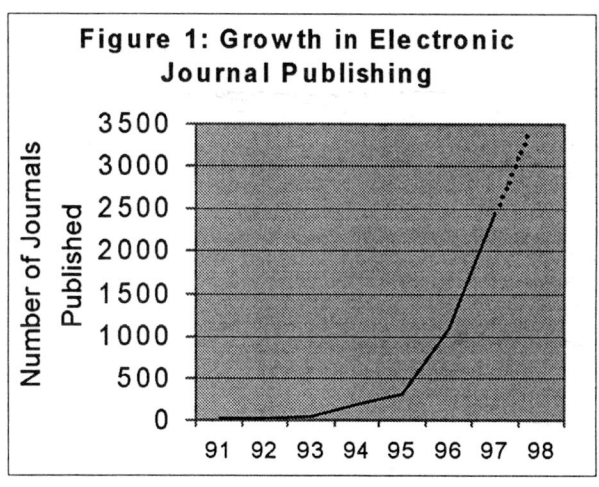

Figure 1: Growth in Electronic Journal Publishing

Deborah Lenares is Electronic Resources reference librarian, University of New Orleans.

fect on the use of electronic journals within the scholarly community.

If the introduction of parallel published journals greatly increases the acceptance of journals in electronic format, the transition to an electronic only environment that many predict could be hastened.

Robert Bovenschulte, Director of the American Chemical Society Publications Division, predicts that electronic journals will dominate the serials marketplace within ten years (Wilkinson, 13). Peter Boyce of the American Astronomical Society, predicted in 1998 that within three years electronic access to journals would replace print (Wilkinson, 13). Others, while not specifying a timeline, assume the complete transition to electronic (Varian, 1, Barnes, 404). If a complete transition to electronic does occur, there will be broad implications for the future of journal publishing.

Although many articles have been written in the past fifteen years examining the state of electronic publishing, there has been little empirical research published which examines the levels of use and acceptance of this new format within the scholarly community. One study of note is a 1995 project by Lisa Covi and Robert Kling. One hundred and twenty four faculty members at eight universities were interviewed to determine their use of "digital library services in the course of their routine work" (Kling, 1.0). The research focussed on "the social practices and organizational arrangements" of digital library use, and not on "static behaviors" such as the percent of faculty using electronic journals (Kling, 2.1). Conclusions drawn from these interviews were that, few informants had much knowledge of electronic journals, and few read them (Kling, 7.0), but that this low rate of acceptance was caused largely by the marginalization of electronic journals (Kling, 7.6).

With the phenomenal growth of electronic journal publishing since 1995, this research is necessary to examine the changes in attitude and acceptance that have occurred in these pivotal years. This study will provide librarians, and others interested in scholarly communication, with information about the current use of electronic journals. Using the 1995 Kling and Covi study as a baseline, changes in the acceptance of electronic journals within the scholarly community will be examined. Understanding the changes in acceptance and the current amount of use of electronic journals will help librarians to determine what resources are necessary to meet present and future patron needs.

Methodology

A survey was distributed in January of 1998 and, after slight revision, distributed again in January of 1999. The research design was a descriptive, fact finding survey, using multi-stage sampling of a stratified two-stage sample with systematic sampling at each stage. Descriptive surveys are useful for "collecting data around as well as directly on the subject of study, so that the problem is brought into focus and the points worth pursuing are suggested" (Moser, 4). Because there has been little research estimating faculty use of electronic journals since Since Covi and Kling's 1995 study, this type of survey was chosen to collect basic data that can be used in the future for more complex research.

Instrumentation

A survey was designed to collect basic information about the level of use of electronic journals as well as other factors contributing to and associated with their use. The survey was self-administered and was delivered using electronic mail. The instrument collected nominal and likert scale data, as well as qualitative data through comments and lists of titles read.

Sample Population

The population sampled from was faculty at institutions whose libraries were members of the Association of Research Libraries. The primary sampling unit from this population was the list of member universities provided on the ARL website. The second stage sampling unit was departments within these universities or a directory list of faculty. A sample population was then chosen from this second stage. A total sample of 500 faculty members were chosen from 20 research universities, departments were chosen to equally represent the disciplines.

Distribution

Systematic random sampling of institutions from the list of ARL members was performed. Every third university on the list was selected. Non-university institutions were not included in the sample. From the university's homepage, faculty email addresses were located using one of two methods. The preferred method was to use the university's faculty directory to randomly select addresses. Searches were entered into directories in a number of different ways depending on the requirements of the directory. First priority was to include the word professor if a title field was available. If further fields were required, the letters "ca," "al" or "jo" were entered into the name field. From the list provided by the directory search every third faculty member was chosen until twenty-five were selected. If a directory search was not possible, academic department homepages were selected, and addresses were selected from departmental faculty lists. Five departments were selected from each university. Every third faculty member was chosen from the departmental list until five were chosen from each department, for a total of twenty-five from each university.

Distribution by email has limited the sample to faculty exhibiting some involvement in electronic services. This may create a bias in results, but a great majority of faculty members did have email links available, and I have sampled from this group. A survey has been distributed to faculty members by mail to study this bias. Results from this survey are not yet available.

Initial Results
Return Rate
Of the 500 surveys distributed in 1999 41 were returned as undeliverable, and a total of 120 responses were received, for a response rate of 26%. The response rate for the 1998 survey, with the same number of surveys distributed, was 22% with a total of 112 respondents. All results will be presented as comparisons of data collected in 1998 and 1999.

Percentage of Use
The 1999 survey revealed that 61% of faculty surveyed do use electronic journals (see figure 2). This is an increase from the 46% of respondents reporting electronic journal use in 1998. Examination of this use by discipline (see figure 3) shows that the number of faculty using electronic journals has increased in all disciplines. The physical sciences and arts and humanities exhibit the greatest growth. Ninety percent of respondents in the physical sciences reported that they use electronic journals. Across the disciplines a majority of faculty members report that they do use electronic journals.

Frequency of Use
Questions about frequency of use for both print and electronic journals help to further define this large percentage of electronic journal readers. Figure 4 displays the frequency of usage for those that do read electronic journals. Half of the respondents that read electronic journals report that they read journals in this format infrequently. The frequency of electronic journal usage has remained steady over the one year period. The frequency of use of print journals was also examined. Figure 5 charts the percentage of respondents reporting frequent use of electronic and print journals. Sixty five percent of respondents reported frequent use of print journals in 1999 a substantial decrease from 1998. It should be noted however, that when the percentage of respondents who reported frequent use of print journals are added to the percentage of respondents who reported fairly frequent use, there is only a 2% decrease from last year.

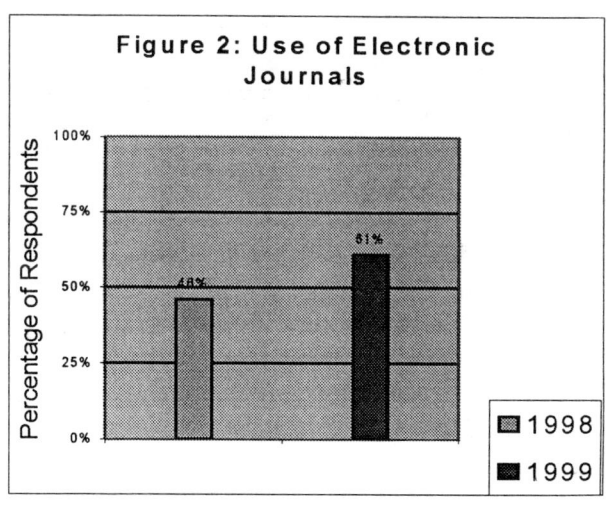

Figure 2: Use of Electronic Journals

Choice of Format

Respondents were asked to rate a number of characteristics of electronic journals that would affect their choice of the electronic format over print. Respondents in both 1998 and 1999 reported that the characteristics of convenience, timeliness and the ability to search text were the most important factors in their choice of electronic over print. The least important characteristics in this choice were interactivity, the ability to compute and the animation of graphics. It is possible that these characteristics are considered unimportant because they are not yet available in most electronic journals. When asked to rate characteristics that would affect their choice of the print format over electronic the most important characteristics were the ability to browse, portability, physical comfort and convenience. The least important characteristics were familiarity with format and the ability to underline.

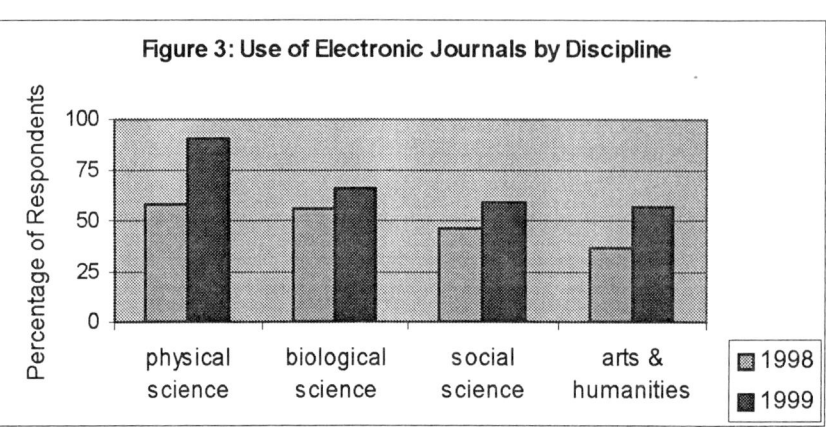

Non Users

Respondents that reported that they do not use electronic journals were questioned to further to explain why they do not. Figure 6 shows that a majority of those that do not use electronic journals do not do so because they do not know of any well-respected electronic journals in their field. A comparison of results from 1999 and 1998 show a large increase in the percentage of respondents answering that the quality of electronic journals is not equal to the quality of print. There was also a slight decrease in the number of respondents that answered that they were not resistant to using electronic journals.

Initial Conclusions

The initial results of this research provide evidence of the rapidly growing acceptance of electronic journals within the scholarly community. Results from the mailed survey will be important to determine whether the distribution by e-mail has skewed these results. It is important to remember that these results report only faculty use of electronic journals at research level institutions, levels of use may be very different at others institutions with fewer resources. When compared to the Kling and Covi study, which showed that few faculty members knew of or used electronic journals in 1995, the rapid acceptance of this new format is remarkable. The increase in electronic journal usage is accompanied by a decrease in the frequent use of print journals. Print journal usage, however, continues to dominate electronic journal usage, with only 14% of respondents using electronic journals frequently as compared to the 65% using print journals frequently. It will be interesting to track changes in the use of print in the coming years.

When these results are viewed using the Diffusion of Innovation Theory (Rogers, 1971) interesting conclusions can be drawn about where we currently are in the adoption of the innovation of electronic journals, and conjectures can be made about when complete adoption may be attained. Rogers states that adoption of innovation has generally been found to follow a bell shaped curve

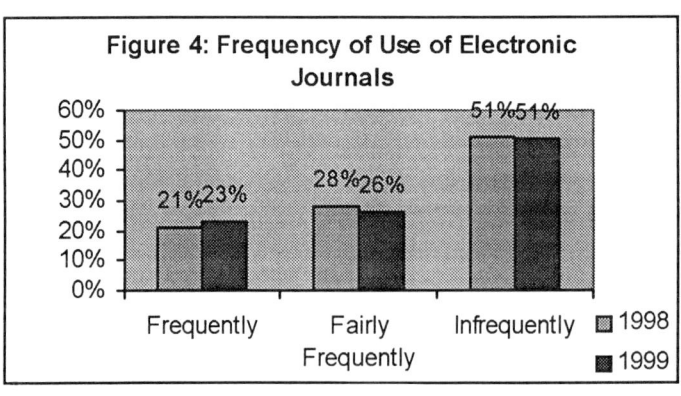

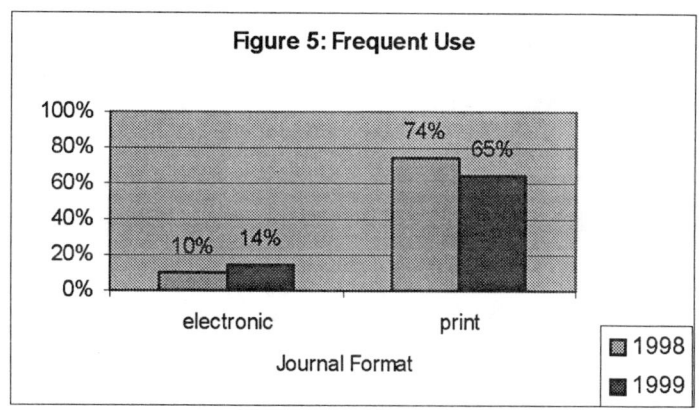

Figure 5: Frequent Use

over time, that adoption of innovation follows a normal distribution (Rogers, 179). Within this normal distribution, adopter categories, describing an individual's ability to adopt change, can be defined. Figure 7 shows the normal distribution for the rate of adoption and the adopter categories. The dotted line in Figure 7 represents the percentage of respondents that in January 1999 reported using electronic journals. When this is plotted on the normal curve, it is clear that we are in the late majority adopters stage.

It is important when examining the current placement of the adoption of the electronic journal innovation on the normal distribution curve, to remember that those who do use electronic journals must be considered incomplete adopters at this point (Rogers, 182). The high level of infrequent use shows that complete adoption has not occurred in most electronic journal users. Incomplete adoption does effect the accuracy of this model, but for general representation of the adoption of innovation the model is useful.

The reasons given by faculty who are not using electronic journals as to why they do not, show in-creasing resistance to change. The percentage of responses to negative statements: "physically uncomfortable," and "quality not equal," have increased. The percentages of responses to neutral statements: "inadequate network resources," "the library does not subscribe," and "no knowledge of respected journals in their field," have all decreased since 1998. The percentage who responded to the only positive statement: "not resistant," has also decreased. The normal distribution shows that of the 39% of faculty surveyed that do not currently use electronic journals, a large percentage are of the most resistant adopter category, the Laggards. Individuals in this category are described by Rogers as traditionalists who are suspicious of innovation and who are "alienated from a too fast moving world" (Rogers, 185).

Another factor, which affects the rate of adoption, is the diffusion effect. This is the effect of the cumulative pressure to adopt an innovation within a system, caused by the incorporation of the innovation into the culture of the system (Rogers, 161). Or, as described by one of the survey respondents, "Electronic articles of scholarship simply don't fit into the manner of colleagueship and discussion I have with fellow faculty members and graduate students. When it does, then I will read journals electronically." Each innovation and each system has a unique threshold for the diffusion effect, and it seems clear that electronic journals have not yet reached the threshold of assimilation that would

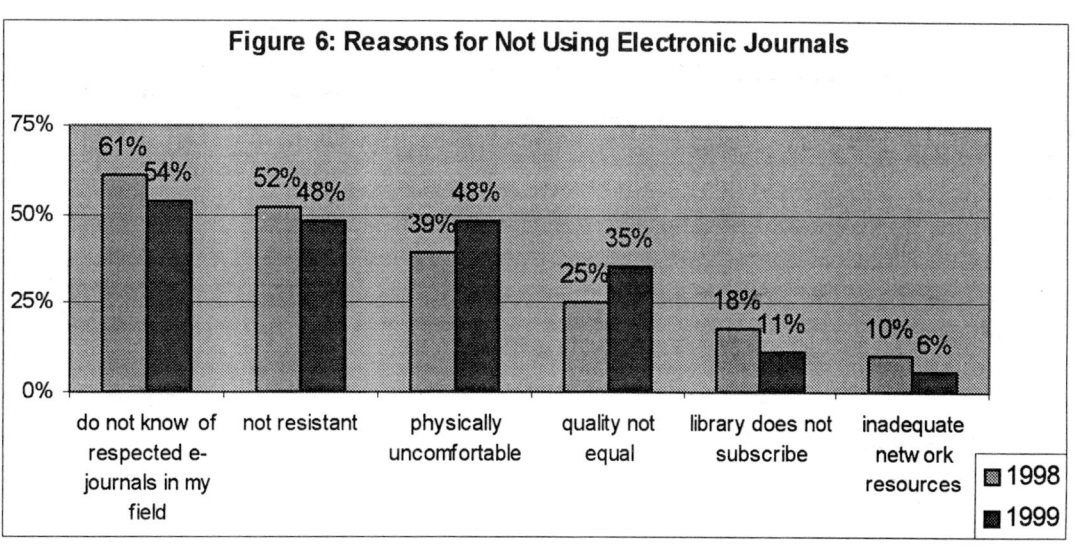

Figure 6: Reasons for Not Using Electronic Journals

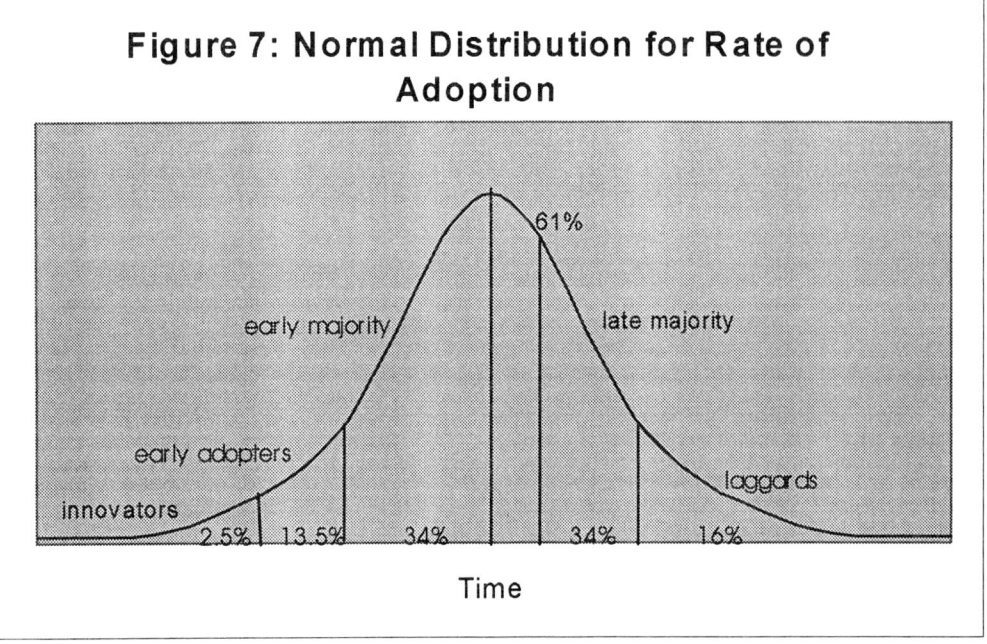

Figure 7: Normal Distribution for Rate of Adoption

lead to their more rapid adoption throughout the academic community.

It would appear that electronic journals are clearly on their way to more complete adoption. The rate of adoption may still be undetermined, as the integration of electronic journals into the culture of the scholarly community is not yet complete. Once electronic journals become integrated into the scholarly community the diffusion effect is likely to stimulate the rate of adoption, and we will begin to see complete adoption of the innovation. Librarians and others involved in scholarly publishing must be prepared for this complete adoption and continue to track its progress.

References

Association of Research Libraries. 1997. *Directory of Electronic Journals, Newsletters and Academic Discussion Lists*. Washington D.C.: Association of Research Libraries.

Barnes, John H. 1997. One giant leap, one small step: Continuing migration to electronic journals. *Library Trends*. 45 (3), 404–15.

Kling, Rob and Lisa Covi. 1997. *Digital libraries and the practices of scholarly communication*. Available at: http://www.slis.lib.indiana.edu/~kling/scit/SCIT97.html

Moser, C. A. and G. Kalton. 1972. *Survey Methods in Social Investigation*. 2nd edition. New York: Basic Books

Rogers, Everett M. 1971. *Communication of Innovations: A cross-cultural approach*. 2nd edition. New York: Free Press

Wilkinson, Sophie L. 1998. Electronic Publishing takes journals into a new realm. *Chemical and Engineering News*. 76 (20), May 18, 10–18.

Varian, Hal R. 1998. The future of electronic journals. *The Journal of Electronic Publishing*. 4 (1). Available at: http://www.press.umich.edu/jep/04-01/varian.html

How Students Use Web-Based Tutorials and Library Assignments: Case Studies from The Ohio State University Libraries

Nancy O'Hanlon and Fred Roecker

Abstract

Use of the World Wide Web to teach information retrieval skills to college students is a rather new phenomenon. Understanding how students react to and interact with this new media is essential for building successful instructional programs. This paper presents and analyzes data from several studies of user behavior and perceptions of Web-based instruction at The Ohio State University Libraries.

The *net.TUTOR* program of self-paced Web tutorials on using the Internet for research was introduced in Fall 1997. Ten interactive lessons focus on basic skills (Web browsing, e-mail), tools (mailing lists, newsgroups, browser plug-ins and customization), searching (cross-resource skills as well as Web search tools), and research skills (evaluation of sources, research strategies, citing sources). Several large enrollment classes at The Ohio State University as well as a number of smaller classes have incorporated the *net.TUTOR* program into their syllabi. Numbers of independent *net.TUTOR* users not connected with courses continues to grow on campus, nationally and internationally. User log data collected by the course management software provides a unique and detailed picture of how students interact with lesson components. Additional data collected from user surveys offer insights into student perceptions of this new instructional program.

Additionally, the existing library instruction program for new students at Ohio State, which enrolls approximately 10,000 students each year, has migrated to Web-based library assignments and now teaches skills that are essential to success using today's online information resources. Hands-on lessons focus on the evaluation of Web resources and on practicing search skills needed to efficiently use online encyclopedias such as

---

Nancy O'Hanlon is user education librarian for Internet instruction and Fred Roecker is acting head, library user education, The Ohio State University.

Britannica Online, full text periodical indexes, or the Libraries' catalog. *net.TUTOR* lessons are offered as supporting resources for those students requiring additional instruction in searching and evaluation techniques. Data collected from surveys of students completing these new library assignments sheds light on comfort levels and perceptions of success as well as the impact on library personnel and resources.

Introduction

For the past 20 years, the User Education program at The Ohio State University Libraries has reached over 23,000 users annually with some form of bibliographic instruction (BI). Most of this instruction employed traditional methods of general workshops, in-class presentations, and tours.

In the past few years, however, with the availability of networked and Web resources, there has been an increased need to help users sort through the information readily available from any computer connected to the Internet. The OSU Libraries' Web page alone offers access to over 170 networked databases, as well as online catalogs and e-journals.

Even selecting an online resource had grown to be an arduous task. Conducting a search, evaluating results, and then printing, downloading, or otherwise manipulating the data were skills most users did not possess.

Established methods of BI proved impractical to address these needs. Decreasing attendance figures showed that users no longer desired "specific time/specific place workshops" to learn skills, even if the Libraries could recruit enough staff to teach these additional classes. Printed instructional guides could be expanded, but were useless to the many users who connected to the Libraries from remote computers.

By 1997, the User Education Office was convinced that to expand instruction to a larger audience, online instruction must be developed. Networked instruction would not require staff to teach new classes, could be accessed remotely at any time, and could help large numbers of users learn a wide variety of research skills.

Since then, two major online instructional projects were developed, tested, and implemented in the OSU Libraries. The first, *net.TUTOR*, provides interactive, Web-based tutorials for learning to use the Internet for research. The second project delivers a Web-based library assignment to 10,000 freshmen yearly.

Web-Based Tutorials

Web-based learning is increasingly popular with college students. They like the convenience and flexibility in scheduling their time, but poor Internet skills inhibit their ability to fully participate in these course offerings. Administrators and faculty at The Ohio State University wanted a program that could be used across the curriculum to insure development of baseline skills and provide a platform to build distance education courses upon.

The Ohio State University Libraries received an Academic Enrichment Grant from the University in summer 1996 to develop a program to enhance the Internet skills of students. *net.TUTOR* <http://gateway.lib.ohio-state.edu/tutor>, first deployed in Fall quarter 1997, provides instruction on various aspects of using the Internet for research.

The program consists of self-paced tutorials on using Web browsers, electronic mail, mailing lists and newsgroups, searching concepts and techniques, Web search tools and strategies, general research strategies, evaluation of Web sites, intellectual property issues and methods for citing Internet sources. Content was determined through a needs assessment of library staff and input from an advisory panel of university faculty, computing center and library staff.

Each tutorial includes a "classroom" portion, where content is presented succinctly. Practice opportunities are provided throughout, but are not mandatory. Classroom lessons are followed by optional multiple-choice quizzes. Additional content includes a list of links to sites that offer further information and in many cases a "Quick Guide" which presents lesson information in a concise fashion, optimized for printing.

net.TUTOR utilizes Docent (formerly IBTauthor) course management software and runs on a Windows NT server. The Docent software handles user registration and authorization, serves content pages, manages quizzing, records quiz and other user history data, and provides reports on usage.

The *net.TUTOR* program began with the "interactive" version running under Docent software, but it expanded in Winter 1998 to include a second "basic" version, available to users without prior registration. This basic version mirrors the lesson content exactly, but does not include interactive quizzes or track usage.

Usage Data

From Fall 1997 through Fall 1998, 4,301 individuals registered to use the "interactive" version of *net.TUTOR*. Of these, 72% were undergraduates, 11% were graduate students and 17% were faculty or other types of users. Overall, 86% of registered users were affiliated with The Ohio State University and 94% listed their place of residence within the U.S.

A growing number of Ohio State faculty now use *net.TUTOR* in their courses. Twenty-six courses, ranging from the large enrollment freshmen survey course, UVC 100, to graduate level courses in education, law, music and business, have incorporated *net.TUTOR* assignments into their syllabi. Eighty-six percent of registered users are students completing a course requirement.

More than 8,800 individual lessons have been completed by users of the interactive version of *net.TUTOR*. The most popular lessons are those related to using Internet tools (Web browser and e-mail), with the lesson on evaluation of Web sites ranking third. Lesson choice, to some extent, is determined by the nature of the course assignment. The evaluation lesson, quite popular with faculty, is frequently required.

The survey forms appended to each lesson provide other data. From Fall 1997 through Fall 1998, 6,651 surveys were returned. Twenty-eight percent of these respondents indicated that they were new to the Internet, 59% had moderate prior experience and 13% reported extensive experience.

A question about user location was added to the survey forms in Spring 1998. In 3,335 surveys submitted from Spring 1998 through Fall 1998, 46% of respondents were working from home or dorm room, 35% were in a campus computer lab, 12% used a computer in the library and 7% were in other locations, such as an office.

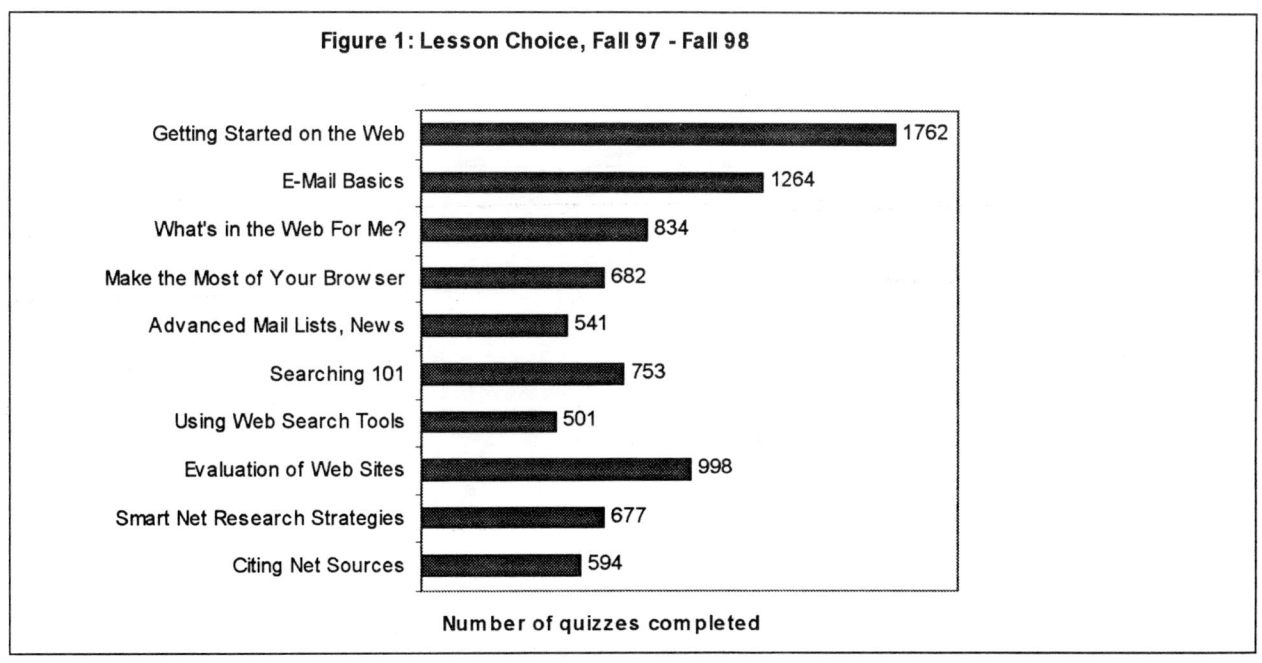
Figure 1: Lesson Choice, Fall 97 - Fall 98

User Attitudes

Responses to survey forms also provide a view of user satisfaction and help to identify problems and lessons requiring revisions. Overall satisfaction (for all lessons combined) was high. On a Likert rating scale of 1 (lowest) to 5 (highest) satisfaction, 50% of respondents chose 4 or 5. 31% of these users chose 3, while 19% disliked the lessons, choosing a 1 or 2 rating. Some of this dissatisfaction may be attributed to software failures during periods of intense demand. These are being addressed by implementation of new hardware and more robust web server and database software to manage these peak loads.

Considering mean satisfaction ratings for specific lessons, respondents were most satisfied with the lesson introducing the Web browser (3.6) and least satisfied with lessons on searching (3.3) and evaluation (3.2). The searching lessons have also consistently received a higher difficulty rating, despite several revisions to the content. User quiz scores for these lessons are also lower.

Those who classify themselves as new to the Internet have the highest overall mean satisfaction level (3.6), but there are no significant variations by user experience level. Those with extensive experience (often faculty evaluating the program for use in their course) have an overall satisfaction rating of 3.5, while those with moderate experience, the great bulk of the user population, have an overall rating of 3.4.

User motivation reveals more interesting differences. Those users who are required to complete lessons have consistently been less satisfied. Using Fall 1998 as a representative quarter, the mean satisfaction level of those completing a course requirement was 3.2, while the mean rating of those choosing the program independently was 4.0. To some extent, this may reflect residual resentment toward inappropriate assignments by their instructors. Attempts to educate instructors about how to use the program have helped, but some faculty still require students to complete all lessons rather than letting them choose those matching their needs.

User Behavior

Four studies of usr's history log files were completed. A total of 465 detailed user histories were examined. Time spent and tutorial components used were tracked for each lesson viewed by the user. Two studies utilized random samples of all registered users during Fall 1997 and Winter 1998. Two other studies focused exclusively on Communication 140 students during Winter and Spring quarters in 1998. Each data group represents between nine and twenty percent of all registered users during that quarter and offers a somewhat different slice of user activity.

As Figure 2 shows, those viewing all parts of a tutorial ranged from 10-14% in these studies. During Fall 1997 and Winter 1998, more than one-third viewed both lesson and quiz components and approximately the same number skipped directly to the quiz.

In an attempt to encourage more users to view the instructional portion of the tutorials before taking quizzes, changes were made to quiz grading protocols in Spring 1998. Prior to that time, users

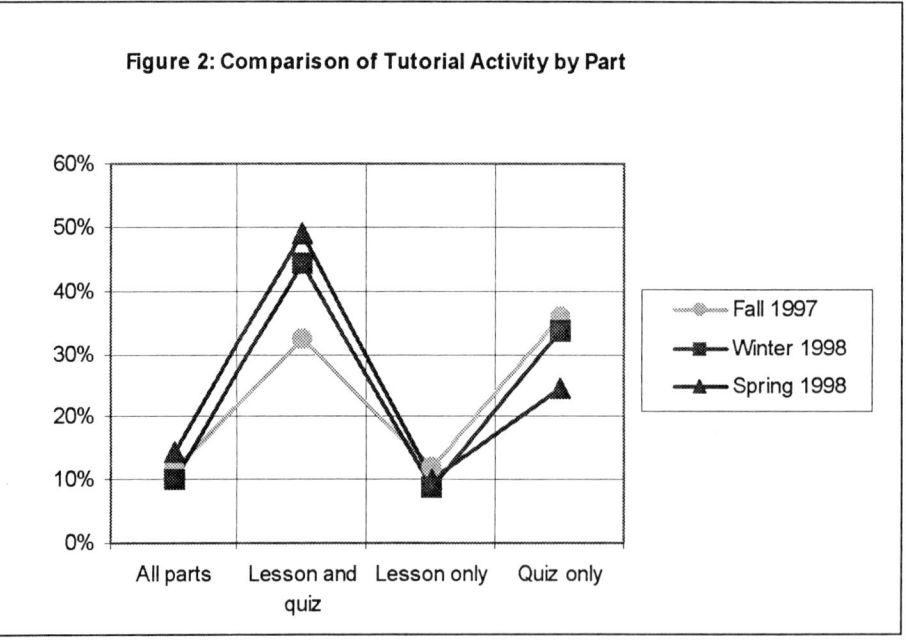

Figure 2: Comparison of Tutorial Activity by Part

were allowed unlimited attempts to answer quiz questions correctly and once a correct answer was selected, received full points for it. Now users are limited to one attempt at each multiple choice quiz question and points are deducted for incorrect answers selected prior to choosing the correct one. As the Spring 1998 study data indicate, this tactic was successful. Those skipping the lesson content dropped to 25%, while almost 50% viewed lessons before taking quizzes.

Course-affiliated users spent on average twelve minutes per tutorial. Those in upper division or graduate courses (300+) spent about two to three minutes longer on searching and research skills related tutorials than students in lower level courses. General users spent almost twice as much time (twenty-three minutes) viewing content in the tutorials. Some of this difference may be attributed to users connecting via modem versus those using campus computer labs or other speedier Internet connections. General users may also be somewhat more likely to try suggested activities in the tutorials, thus lengthening time spent viewing pages.

The Online Library Assignment
The Ohio State University Libraries have enjoyed a 20-year instructional relationship with OSU's University College. All 10,000 incoming freshmen and transfer sophomores receive a Libraries' orientation session and two research assignments as part of their one-credit University College general survey class (UVC100). Scores from these assignments comprise 25% of the student's final grade.

When the OSU Undergraduate Library closed in 1997, however, UVC students lost their primary facility for completing their assignments. While students could use any OSU library for their project, the Undergraduate Library's general collection and friendly staff were geared to novice researchers. Other OSU libraries lacked the staff and collection resources to absorb additional UVC users.

Designing and Implementing the Online Library Assignment
In Winter 1998, based on discussions with public services librarians and demographic information about UVC students, a team of three librarians re-designed the second library assignment to be completely Web-based. University College studies showed that 80% of all incoming OSU freshmen brought a computer to campus. Coupled with the recent wiring of all OSU dorms for direct Internet access, the team felt many students would be able to complete an online assignment from their dorm room.

Rather than emphasizing print resources housed in a specific buildings, the new assignment now focused on networked materials available remotely without reliance on library facilities or staff. This addressed OSU librarians' concerns about the old UVC assignment regarding damaged print materials and overcrowded facilities. The online assignment would tap into students' enthusiasm for computers and Web searching, teach them needed skills, and help create an image of the Libraries as managers of high-tech information resources, not just buildings with books.

The new assignment was pilot-tested on 300 UVC students during Spring and summer quarters in 1998. Librarians gave in-class presentations to each UVC class and distributed instruction sheets with information on how to access the assignment Web site <http://www.lib.ohio-state.edu/uvc/assignment.html>.

From this site, students selected one online resources for exploration (*Britannica Online, Social Issues Researcher, Britannica eBLAST* or *OSCAR*, the OSU online catalog) and connected to a corresponding worksheet. This HTML worksheet provided the assignment instructions and embedded links to online databases and other "helper" resources. Students had to print a copy of this worksheet to complete and turn in, or they could pick up a paper copy in several libraries.

In three assignments, students followed step-by-step instructions through keyword searches on their topic using Boolean operators, noting variations in number of hits for each search. They recorded related subject headings and sub-topics, then selected a relevant article or book and created an citation. In the fourth assignment option, students identified relevant Web sites from *Britannica's eBLAST*, evaluated the quality of information and created a citation.

The assignment was distributed during Fall quarter 1998 to all 7,000 UVC students. Students had one week to complete the assignment, which then were graded by University College. Attached evaluation forms were returned to the Office of Library User Education for analysis.

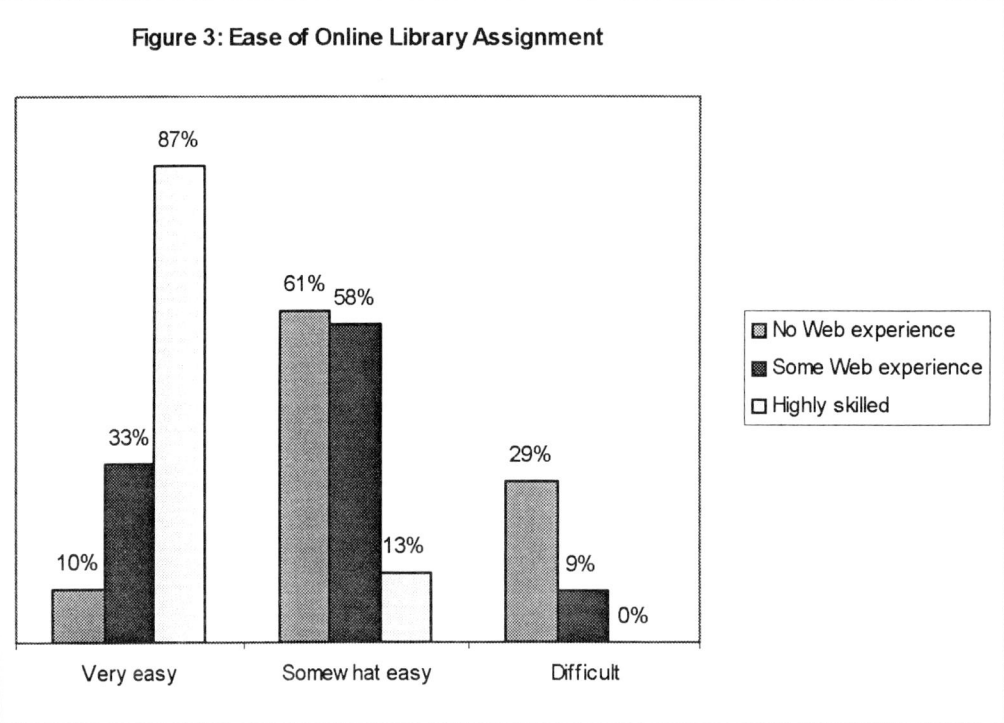

Figure 3: Ease of Online Library Assignment

Data from Evaluations

Data from a sample of 303 student comment forms during Fall quarter showed that this online assignment provided a quality learning experience for students and addressed many concerns of the Libraries.

Students rated their Web experience prior to this assignment as "Highly Skilled" (16%), "Somewhat Skilled" (65%), and "No Web Experience" (16%). Yet 86% indicated the assignment was "Very Easy" or "Somewhat Easy," including 67% of those with no previous Web experience.

Overall, students indicated they felt "Very Confident (39%) and "Somewhat Confident" (51%) using the online resources. In connecting to the Libraries Web site, 51% overall felt "Very Confident, and 39% were "Somewhat Confident." Even 75% of those with no Web experience indicated confidence in these areas.

Comments on the evaluation forms indicated students were genuinely grateful for this hands-on experience with Libraries' resources. While some felt the assignment was "too easy," the vast majority indicated an appreciation of the research concepts presented.

Problems Anticipated

The design team anticipated there might be problems with printing the assignment, increases in support needed from staff, and technology breakdowns. The data, however, showed these were not major problems.

Only 20% of the students needed staff help to complete the assignment. Seventy-nine percent of students did not even come into the Libraries, opting to complete their UVC assignment in computer labs or from their home or dorm. Seventy-five percent of those with no Web experience completed the assignment remotely.

Although some students mentioned problems in printing the Web worksheet, their comments indicated most eventually either figured it out or opted to pick up a worksheet in the libraries. A poll of library staff noted that the 15% who choose to pick up worksheets were able to get their assignments from folders at the reference desks without staff assistance.

Happily, there were almost no technology glitches noted. Although OSCAR was down for about five hours one day, no other network-wide problems were noted. Assignments were distributed throughout the quarter to prevent overload of the resources, with about 1,500 students receiving the assignment each week.

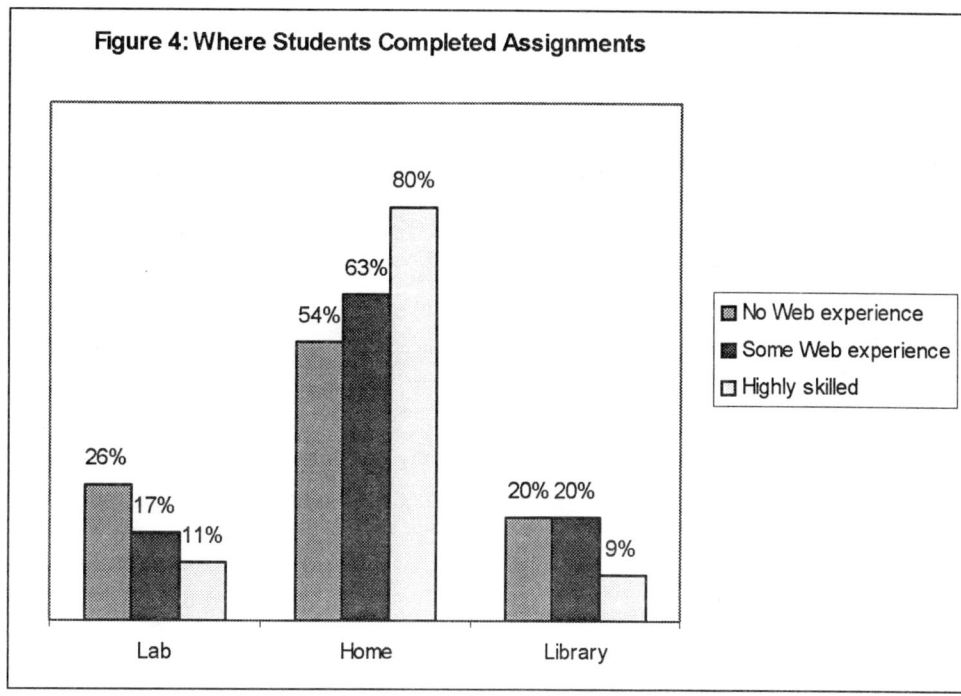

Figure 4: Where Students Completed Assignments

Prospects for Web-Based Instruction at Ohio State University Libraries

Based on evaluations from users, both the online library assignment and the tutorial program are successful. Both will undergo some changes over the next year. New online resources will be evaluated for inclusion in the library assignment. Designers will continue to monitor whether the major instructional emphasis for the assignment is appropriate. New *net.TUTOR* tutorials will be developed.

Other *net.TUTOR* enhancements are planned. In order to optimize access to tutorial content while minimizing duplication of effort and user confusion about which version to use, only one version of the lessons will be available. This version will not require prior registration. "Quick quizzes" will be available within lessons for user self-assessment purposes. Courseware will continue to be used to manage scored tests and other assignments for OSU students in a secure environment.

The library assignment design team will also consider feasibility of a worksheet that could be submitted and graded online. Making the answers multiple choice rather than open-ended would facilitate electronic grading, a tempting thought when faced with 7,000 assignments to mark.

Both the online assignment and the interactive tutorial program are extensible models for library instruction in a large university environment. Each will be modified and expanded as the Libraries' technology and student baseline skills change. The biggest challenge in implementing these programs has been uncertainty over whether the campus network could handle the extreme load during Fall quarter. Close collaboration with computing center staff to find new ways to address infrastructure issues will be important to the future development of both programs.

Related Web Sites:

net.TUTOR
<http://gateway.lib.ohio-state.edu/tutor>

net.TUTOR Annual Report
<http://gateway.lib.ohio-state.edu/tutor/about.html>

net.TUTOR Survey Form
<http://gateway.lib.ohio-state.edu/tutor/open/les2/survey.html>

net.TUTOR Survey Data
<http://gateway.lib.ohio-state.edu/tutor/stats>

UVC 100 Assignment Instructions and Survey
<http://www.lib.ohio-state.edu/guides/uvcinstruct.pdf>

UVC 100 Second Library Assignment
<http://www.lib.ohio-state.edu/uvc/assignment.html>

E-Reserves: Home Grown vs. Turnkey

Shane Nackerud

Abstract

Obvious reasons for implementing e-reserves abound, the most compelling of which is better access to reserve readings for students on campus and off. The question then is not whether your library is going to begin making e-reserves available, but how are you going to do it? One decision which must be made before any work can begin is will your library use a home grown system to deliver and maintain e-reserves, or will your library use a turnkey system such as Eres, Contec, or Nousoft? This paper will focus on the decisions and pilot projects at Southern Illinois University, Carbondale, and the University of Minnesota concerning this question and e-reserves implementation.

Introduction

Chances are if your library has not yet decided to implement an electronic reserves project, it soon will. A wide variety of decisions must be made before a project can take off, including what scanning hardware and software to use, how much staffing to hire, and, of course, how to handle the copyright issue. However, possibly the most important decision a library will make regarding e-reserve implementation is whether to create a management and maintenance system from scratch, a homegrown system, or purchase a turnkey solution such as ERes, Contec, or Nousoft. On the one hand, a homegrown solution gives your library complete control over the entire program and is relatively inexpensive, but your library may not have the technical expertise or the manpower to create a homegrown product. A turnkey solution gets your library up and running quickly and comes complete with usage instructions and support, but a turnkey solution may not be in your library's budget.

Shane Nackerud is Web Services Coordinator at the University of Minnesota Libraries.

Implementing E-reserves: Home-grown vs. Turnkey

The libraries at Southern Illinois University, Carbondale (SIUC) and the University of Minnesota have both recently grappled with this decision. While SIUC decided to build a homegrown product, the University of Minnesota went with a turnkey solution, specifically ERes from Docutek. What follows is a discussion of the reasoning that went behind these decisions, as well as reviews of both SIUC's homegrown product and Docutek's ERes version 3.1 in terms of ease of use, customizability, labor, and cost.

SIU: The Setting

Morris Library of Southern Illinois University, Carbondale serves the needs of over 22,000 undergraduate and graduate students with a collection of over 2.4 million physical volumes and a wide range of user services. Divisions within the library include Instructional Support Services, Humanities, Social Studies, Education and Psychology, Science, and the Undergraduate Library. The Undergraduate Library contains a reference collection, a small circulating book collection, a busy reference desk, and the reserve collection, among other responsibilities. The reserve collection averages about 400 courses and approximately 3,000 unique readings per semester. During the fall semester of 1997, it was decided that the Undergraduate Library would begin an electronic reserves pilot project to be rolled out the spring semester 1998.

A team of three librarians was created to look at other e-reserve implementations and recommend hardware and software purchases as well as suggest staff requirements. After reviewing various e-reserve home pages and touring Northwestern University's E-Reserve department, it became obvious Adobe Acrobat products were the dominant software tools to create reserve readings. Adobe Acrobat Capture 2.0 and Adobe Acrobat 3.0 were purchased as well as an HP ScanJet 4c. Two student workers were hired for approximately 20 hours a week a piece. Thirty-five classes signed up for the pilot project.

A scanning schedule was developed using professor supplied course syllabi. Reserve readings were scanned as they were needed with an attempt to scan them two weeks in advance of the assigned reading date. A large desk calendar was used to schedule readings, and as they were finished they were crossed out. A reserve reading flow chart was also created which included fields for file name, scanned, processed, reviewed, cropped, copyright attached, uploaded, and erased from the PC. The flow chart was important in case a student worker left in the middle of a job; the next student worker could pick up where the other left off. Approximately 450 articles were scanned that semester with about 7 to 10 being scanned per day.

Although scanning reserve readings is time consuming, there is little that can be done to avoid this process other than requiring that instructors do it themselves. What quickly became the most frustrating aspect of the project was the time it took creating the HTML pages to access the readings. Flat HTML pages were created including an instructor list, a course list, and all the individual course reserve home pages. Early in the project the supervisor found little time for anything else besides coding HTML for the e-reserves web pages. Authenticating users also became problematic. Straight IP address authentication was out of the question due to the large number of distance learners using off-campus ISPs. Using Netscape's FastTrack server to password protect directories, each individual course page received a unique username and password which then had to be passed back to the instructor and finally on to the students. And to top it all off, a separate Microsoft Access database was created to maintain information about the courses and readings. This too needed daily maintenance. Due to all these time consuming duties the project quickly became too overwhelming.

A Better Way

The above narrative may sound familiar to many librarians attempting to implement e-reserves. It was quickly decided that the project at SIUC needed a software program to aid in the management of electronic reserves. SIUC considered a turnkey product to alleviate the situation, but because of cost and time constraints this option was not feasible. The library simply did not have money for electronic reserves software in its budget. A homegrown solution was the only option, but it had to be easy use for both administrators of the system and student workers. A series of benchmarks were produced:

1. The program must be web based, utilizing forms for the entry of course and bibliographic data.

2. The program must be database driven, and create the e-reserves web site dynamically based on thisdata.

3. The program should require that bibliographic information be entered only once, have the ability to use that data in multiple ways, and have the ability to retrieve that data in subsequent semesters.

4. The program must be able to remove a reserve reading at the end of the semester that reading is intended for without intervention, as well as allow administrators to place a reading on reserve for as little as a day and remove it without intervention.

5. The program must authenticate user access to readings through an easy to use password, preferably one they are already familiar with such as SSN or student ID number.

6. The program must have both a browse and a keyword search feature that allows users to search for courses and instructors, but not specific readings.

7. The program must include a log file to evaluate usage patterns and detect problem areas.

8. The program must be able to handle a variety of file types such as PDF, DOC, XLS, PPT, ZIP, etc, as well as links to web based material such as course syllabi and external sites.

Other necessities were conceived as the project went along including the ability to allow student workers to upload reserve readings into the server, but not overwrite or have the ability to erase any existing readings, and to somehow have the program maintain copyright information for each individual reading. There was also a concern that once a user had authenticated, there was nothing to stop this user from book marking a reading or even placing a link to that reading on a personal web page. Luckily, Morris Library employs two extremely capable web applications programmers. Work began in the spring of 1998 by one of these programmers to tackle the above criteria.

Technical Information

Development began using the Perl programming language. Using the above benchmarks as a guide, the programmer spent approximately 50 hours total creating the program which includes 12 individual scripts and three directories. The scripts include:

input—the input program for e-reserves processing

input.courses—creates or modifies information for a particular course (page one of e-reserve processing)

input.readings—to create or modify reserve readings (page two of e-reserve processing)

input.help—help regarding filling in the two pages of processing

list—the patron processing form for displaying e-reserves

list.courses—displays courses or instructors based on user selection

list.readings—displays course page and readings after user clicks on course link

maint.pl—a maintenance routine which removes deleted records from the data files

fileUpload.pl—uploads new files to the server

proc.pl—performs common procedures throughout the e-reserves program

ssn—text file holding all the valid IDs

wrong.id—displays error screen if user leaves ID field blank or if the ID isn't listed in the ssn file

Three directories named temp, data, and readings are also essential parts of the program. Temp holds temporary files created by search functions used in list.courses and list.readings. The data directory contains four flat text files data.courses, data.readings, data.dates, and data.logs. The data in these files are retrieved by the scripts listed above for display to the adminstrators and patrons using the program. The readings directory obviously holds the reserve readings uploaded to the server. After completion, the program was unveiled on schedule during the 1998 summer session for use by the library staff and patrons of SIUC's Morris Library.

User Interface

The user interface begins with an opening screen

which requires that the user authenticate with a student ID number (See figure 1).

Upon entering the student id, the user then has a choice to either browse for courses or instructors, or to search for instructors or courses. The search mechanism automatically right truncates and uses Boolean AND for multiple term entries. It does not search for any information about reserve readings such as titles or authors. A small bit of JavaScript is used on the opening page to focus the cursor into the student ID entry box when the page finishes loading. Finally, the user may click "submit." If the user enters an invalid student ID or leaves the field blank, an error screen appears giving the user another chance to enter a valid student ID.

After clicking "submit" the user is presented with the results from his or her search, a list of available courses or instructors (see figure 2).

Upon choosing a course the user is sent the actual course reserve page with links to all the various readings the instructor has assigned (see figure 3). Readings are categorized by date to be read, group number, or alphabetical order if no date or group number is available. A complete citation for the reading is included as well as a bolded note to the user that is an optional field input during the e-reserve processing phase. This bolded note may warn the user that the reading is large or poor quality, among other possibilities. This is followed by the link to the reading which denotes the format of the reading as well as the overall size of the reading in bytes.

What's in the URL?
Copyright compliance was a major concern for everyone involved with the project. By placing readings on the WWW, libraries with e-reserve projects run the risk of the readings being made available to anyone with a browser and access to the Internet. It became apparent in the early stages of SIUC's project development that once a user had authenticated there was no way to stop the user from either book marking the reading or making it available on a private web page. The chances of the latter actually happening may seem remote to most reserve librarians (getting students to actually read the material is hard enough), but something had to be done to fix the problem. One option was to dedicate a server session to each authenticated user and have it time out after a period of inactivity much like database vendors such as ProQuest or FirstSearch. However, it was decided that individual sessions would be too much of a burden on the server. Everything can slow down when a server gets low on process space and memory.

Instead, the programmer built into the URL a time-out feature which times out course and reading links after six hours. In other words, each course page and individual reading has a dynamically created URL with a time-out limit of six hours. The time-out feature begins as soon as the user selects a course or a reading. A user may still bookmark or place a link to the reading or course page on a private web page, but it won't last long.

The URL also calls other functions such as verifying that the user has properly authenticated. It also pushes the reading to the patron using a byte serving script for PDFs from Adobe (http://www.adobe.com/prodindex/acrobat/byteserve.html). Byte serving, or page-at-a-time downloading, serves up PDFs to the user one page at a time rather than downloading the entire file before displaying. This is especially useful for users with slow modem connections since downloading the complete reading is not required to view the beginning of the document. In order for byte serving to work, the user must have the Adobe Acrobat Reader installed as a plugin on their browser of choice, as opposed to a stand alone application.

Processing Interface
Courses and readings are entered into the system using the two page Electronic Reserves Processing Form. However, before a person can begin, the program must recognize that person as a "super user" or a person with administrative privileges. Rather than require a unique password like the patron interface, the processing form recognizes the remote host name of the workstation trying to access the program. If the program doesn't recognize the remote host name the user is sent to the patron interface home page and a log entry is created stating someone tried to gain access to the processing form. The remote host name and the

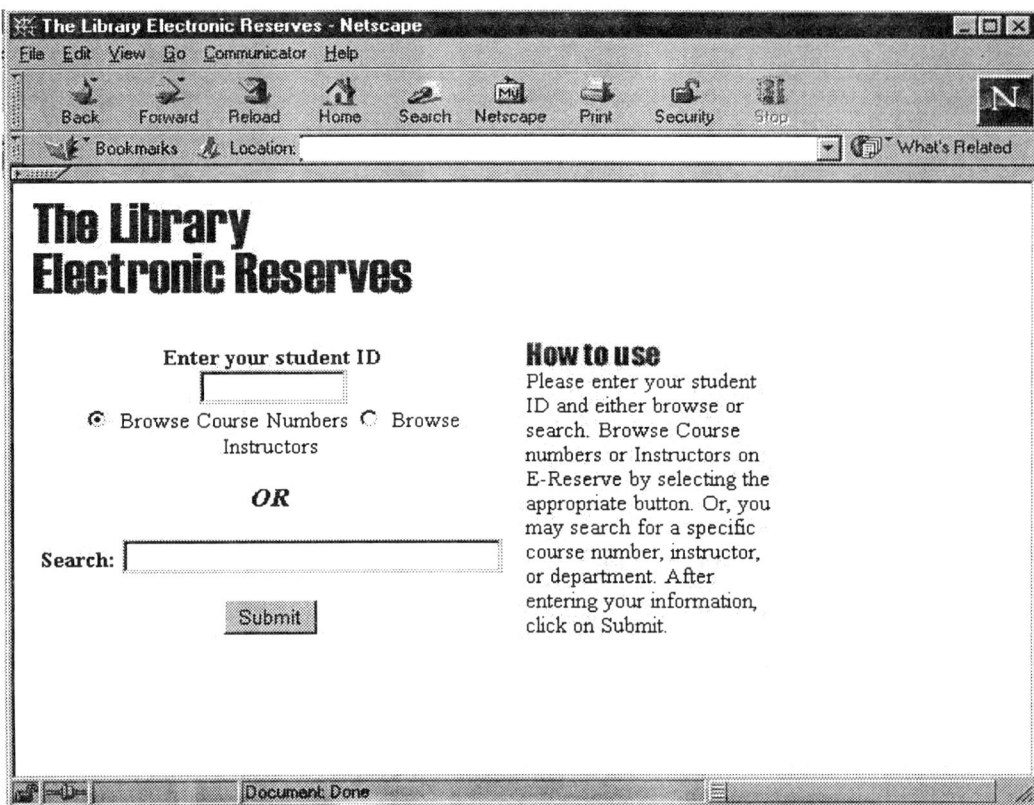

Figure 1: Patron Interface

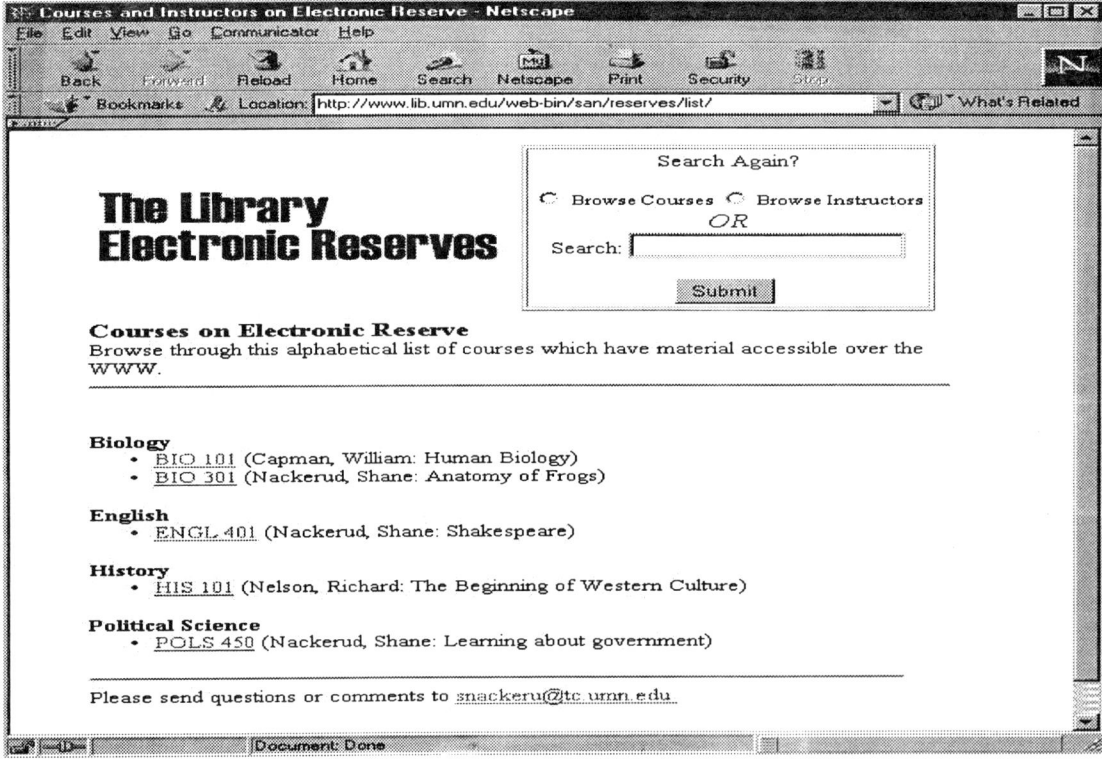

Figure 2: Course Selection

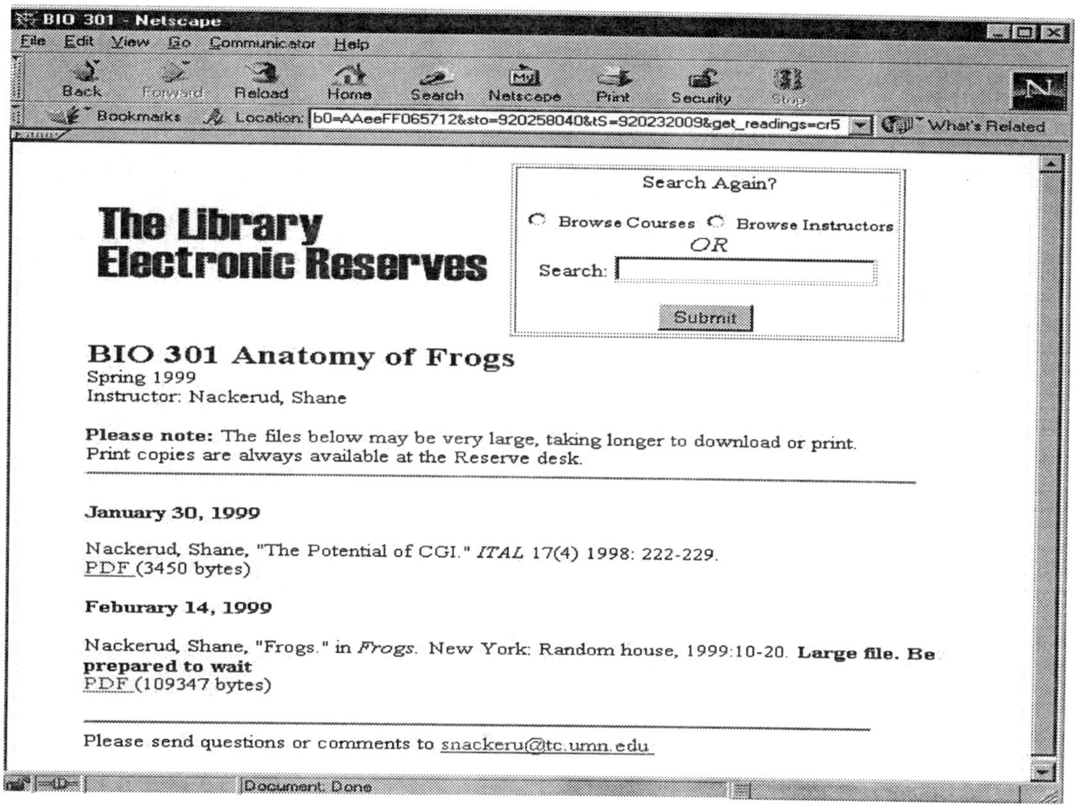

Implementing E-reserves: Home-grown vs. Turnkey

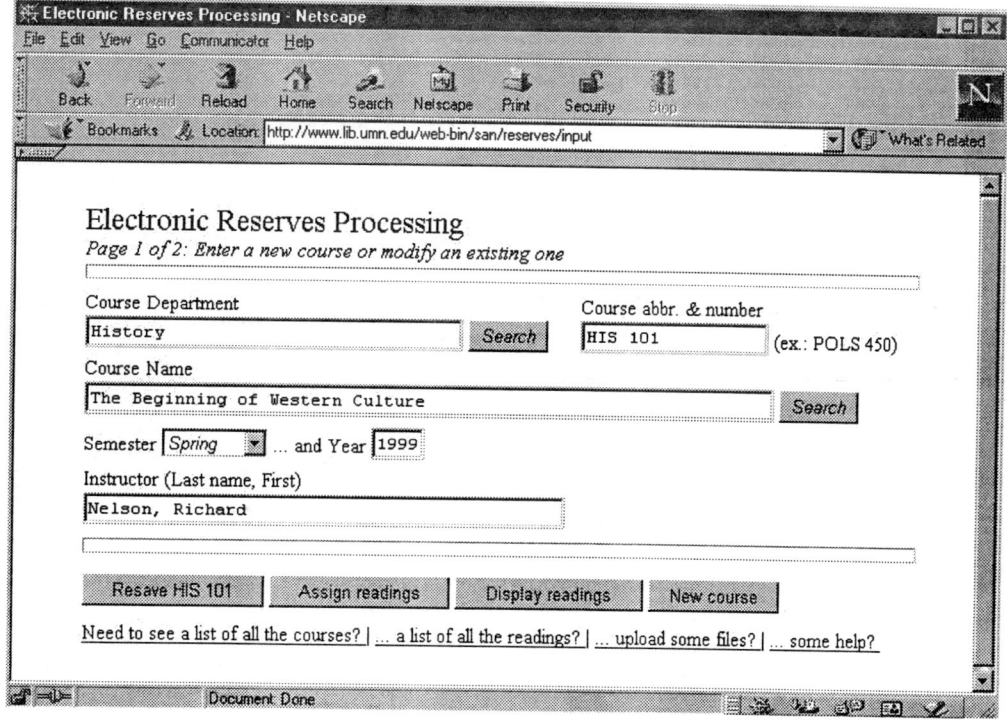

Figure 3. Course page

Figure 4: Electronic Reserves Processing First Page.

date of the attempt is also noted in the log (more about the log file later).

Figure 4 illustrates the first page of the Electronic Reserves Processing Form, the course entry form. Everything about the course is entered onto this page including the department, the course number, the course title, the semester and year of use, and the course instructor. Users may also search the course data file for an existing entry to avoid redundancy. After clicking "submit," the user is then presented with a verification screen allowing for modification of the course information, assignment of readings, display of current readings assigned to the course, or the option of creating a new course. Clicking on "Assign Readings" will open the second page of the processing form and allow users to assign readings to that course.

Page two of the Electronic Reserves Processing Form assigns reserve readings to a specific course. (see figure 5) On this page, the user enters bibliographic information such as author of the selection, title, source, publisher, date, and the pages scanned or used by e-reserves. Again, the user may search for the author or the title of the work being processed to make sure that the data hasn't already been entered or to verify that the reading doesn't already exist on the server. After entering the bibliographic information for the reserve reading a note may be attached to the reading. (see figure 6) This note will be visible to patrons accessing the corresponding course page and may include information on the quality of the scanned reading, size of the document, or a note from the instructor. This is followed by the name of the file to be uploaded to the server or the URL for an external link to the selection. The file extension is not required because the script will recognize the extension on the file after it is uploaded to the readings directory.

Copyright information is maintained for the reading by making a selection, fair use or copyright, from the copyright drop down box. If copyright is granted for a fee, that information may also be entered. With this data, administrators may reliably track whether or not the reading is being used as fair use, or with copyright permission. If this reading is accessed again in subsequent semesters, this information will appear again as well as a note telling the user the last semester the reading was used. Next, corresponding dates must be entered. The first field "Date to be Read or Group" allows the user to specify the assigned reading date or reading group supplied by the instructor. This date is then shown to the student on the patron accessible course page (see figure 3).

Finally, the dates on reserve must be entered for the reading including a beginning date and an ending date. Users may leave the reading on for the entire semester or a shorter period of time depending on copyright restrictions. The field was initially created to take advantage of the "guideline of spontaneity" which is a guideline stating that material may be reproduced and made public for a short period of time without copyright.[1] When a reserve reading falls in between the two dates entered, the reading is displayed to the student, and after the ending date the link to the reading is removed from access. This all happens without user intervention. Upon completion of the form the user has the option of showing the link (to verify accuracy), saving and assigning the reading, resetting the form, or entering a new course. Once the reading has been assigned to a specific course and the actual file (pdf, doc, ppt, etc.) is uploaded to the server, the reading is ready for patron access.

Other Features

Two other features available to "super users" worth mentioning include the fileUpload.pl script and the log file. The upload script allows student workers or others without access to the server the ability to upload readings into the readings directory. Again, this is a function that is only available to workstations with recognized remote host names. Another characteristic of the upload script is that users can only upload files, files cannot be deleted or overwritten.

Super users also have access to the log file. The log file can be viewed by typing "log" into the search box of the patron interface home page from a super user workstation. The log file counts access to course pages as well as hits on the readings themselves. The remote host name of the computer accessing the files is also noted as well as the date and time. The log file also tracks illegal

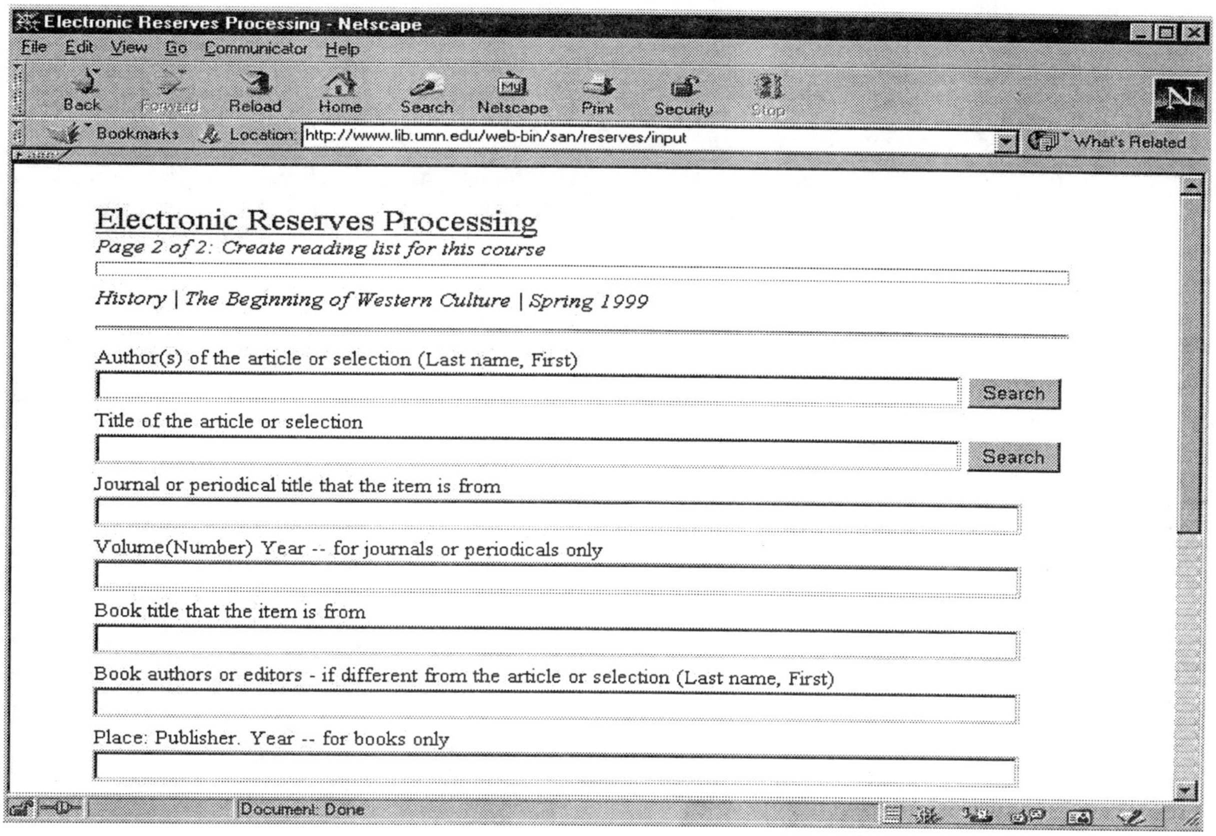

Figure 5: Electronic Rerserves Processing Page 2

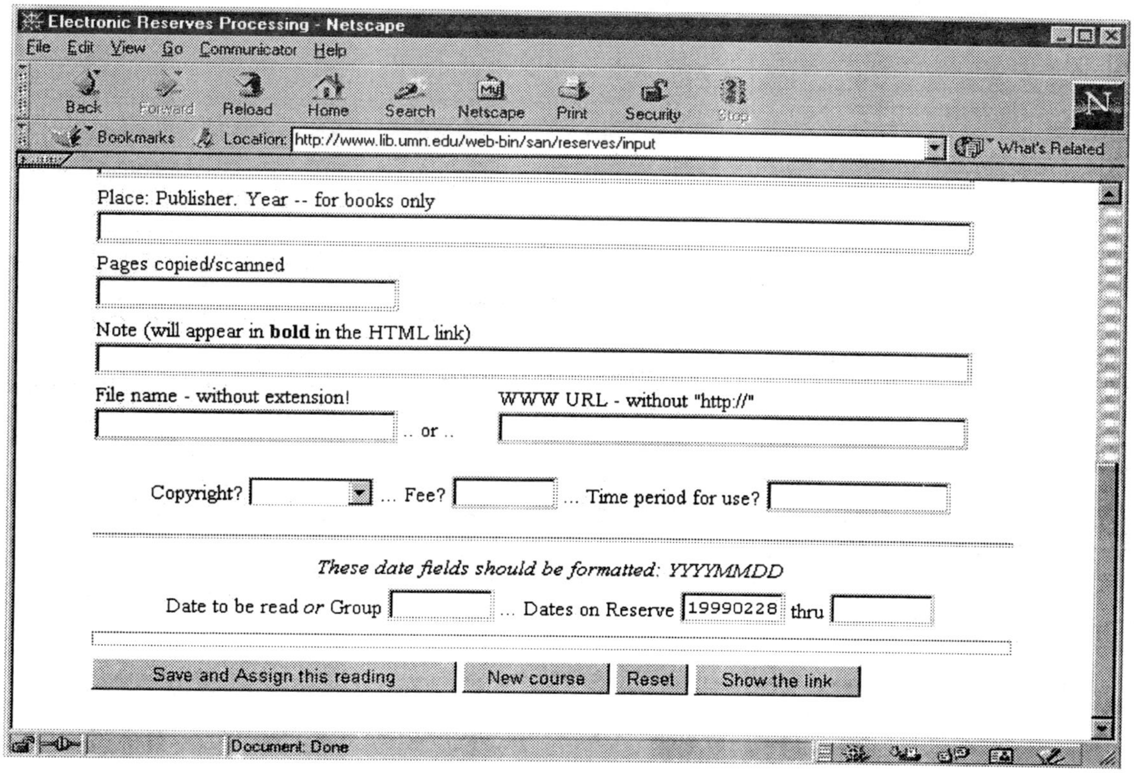

Figure 6: Electronic Rerserves Processing Page 2 (Cont.)

attempts to access the processing form and attempts to use links that have timed out.

Limitations

The program has been in place for two semesters now and in that time some limitations have become apparent. For one, not everything is automatic. The current semester must be manually input into the script "list" in order for the correct semester's readings to display. This is a minor irritation that will be worked out in future versions. Secondly, although only providing "super user" access to workstations with recognized remote host names provides good security, it makes it difficult to work on the system from home. Unless you can figure out what remote host name the campus, library, or ISP modem pool has given your connection the system won't let you in. While it is possible to find this information out and enter it into the scripts, it is still an annoyance.

Another limitation is the fact that everything in the system is protected by a password including non-copyrighted material. This means that non-copyrighted material such as course syllabi or final exams are also behind a wall of security. And just as users are unable to link or book mark specific readings or course pages, this also means that instructors can't link to assigned readings from their own course web pages. If an instructor has built a course web page and has material on electronic reserve, the link to this material must go to the e-reserve home page where the user can first authenticate and receive authorization. If authenticated and authorized, the user may then proceed to the assigned readings.

Future Plan: Introducing FreeReserves

Library staff and patron response to the product has been very favorable. Due to this success and the portability of the Perl programming language, the developers of the program intend to make the source code available to anyone who wants to use it under the GNU General Public License agreement (http://www.fsf.org/copyleft/gpl.html) and under the name FreeReserves. By making the code open source and free to the library community, the developers hope that the program can continue to grow and improve. All that we ask in return is that if you make an improvement to the program that you pass it back to the developers so that it can be built into future versions of FreeReserves. System requirements for the program include a Unix based web server running at least Perl 5.003. Currently, FreeReserves is not available for Windows NT servers. Hopefully, a compatible program for NT servers will be worked out in future versions.

Most importantly, in order to correctly install FreeReserves at your institution, there must be someone there that has at the very least a basic understanding of Perl. This is not a program that can simply be "double-clicked" to install. The beauty of FreeReserves is that it is open source. This means that everything from the data structure to the interface can be modified to comply with your institutions' desires or standards. However, whoever modifies the program must be knowledgeable in Perl. For more on FreeReserves including a demonstration, and downloading and implementation information, please visit http://www.lib.umn.edu/san/freereserves/.

The University of Minnesota

Rather than take the time to develop, test, and implement a homegrown solution to maintaining electronic reserves like SIUC, the University of Minnesota instead went with a turnkey product, specifically ERes from Docutek. What follows is a discussion of the ideas and reasoning behind this decision as well as a review of the ERes software. Although it was the original intention of this paper to give a detailed discussion of the U of M's electronic reserves implementation, as of the writing of this paper, the pilot project has not started.

The Setting

The University of Minnesota—Twin Cities campus has an enrollment of over 37,000 students, graduate and undergraduate. The University Libraries are housed in five main facilities and eleven branch sites, and contain over 5 million print volumes, as well as numerous serial, microform, and government document collections. Because of its vast holdings the University of Minnesota Libraries is the 17th largest research library in the nation. In terms of reserves, the collection is spread out across

16 individual sites. The three largest reserve collections are contained in Wilson and Walter Libraries in Minneapolis, and Magrath Library in St. Paul. To give the reader an idea of the volume of the operation, Wilson Library reports an average of 61,000 reserve items circulated per year and between 100-120 courses on reserve per quarter. Walter Library reports a circulation of 36,000 items per year with an average of 100-120 courses on reserve per quarter. St. Paul's Magrath Library reports a circulation of 35,000 items per year and around 100 courses per quarter. Obviously, these statistics do not include the 13 other reserve collections on campus.

Because of the overwhelming size and spread out nature of print reserves for faculty and students of the University, as well as staff of the Libraries, electronic reserves was seen as a way to consolidate the operation. Talk began in March of 1998 and an ad hoc committee of four reserve staff members was created to discuss electronic reserves. The group was given a small budget and began inspecting e-reserves sites on the web and visiting local area college implementations. Based on this field research the group quickly formulated a series of criteria for an e-reserve system at the University of Minnesota. First of all, the system must be able to handle usage by multiple reserve sites, 16 to be exact. Secondly, in order to comply with copyright guidelines, the system must include password protection capabilities. The University of Minnesota currently uses a campus wide authentication system known as x.500 which requires a username and password for authentication and authorization to licensed resources. It was the group's hope that x.500 could be incorporated into any e-reserve system developed to minimize university student and staff confusion. There was also a concern about the compatibility of the system with future automated system upgrades (new OPAC, etc.). It was decided that the system should be stand-alone.

Essentially, however, the two main criteria for the system were ease of use and support. The system would be used primarily by student workers and staff members with little or no technical knowledge, and little time to learn. The potential number of documents, and the potential number of courses desiring to have digitized material also meant that the system had to be learned quickly. Support was also a major concern. Would the already overworked automated systems staff at the libraries be able to effectively develop and support the system? These criteria and others moved the group into the next phase of discussion: home-grown or turnkey?

The Players

Based on research, discussion, and field trips, the group decided that a turnkey system was the way to go. It was decided that a homegrown system required too much technical expertise and would require more support than the group thought the automated systems department could handle. So, four major players emerged for the right to provide electronic reserves to the students of the University of Minnesota: Docutek (ERes), Nousoft, OCLC SiteSearch, and DRA. DRA was considered as an option due to the University Libraries' commitment to use the DRA OPAC. With implementation of the DRA OPAC so far in the future, and the e-reserve committee's resolution to use a stand alone product, DRA quickly fell out of the running. Nousoft was considered due to its complete package including copyright maintenance features, password protection capabilities, and archiving features. However, cost was an issue as well as San Diego State University's decision to no longer use the product (SDSU was the first library to use Nousoft). Excitement for OCLC's SiteSearch was also minimal due to the fact that only one other institution was using it at the time. Eventually, it was decided that ERes from Docutek would be the electronic reserves system for the University of Minnesota.

ERes

ERes version 3.1 from Docutek is a series of CGI scripts which use the Perl programming language and a unique backend flat file database system. Library staff or instructors with little of no knowledge of HTML may enter course and document information into ERes using a web based interface. This information is then automatically organized into specific course web pages much like FreeReserves. ERes may currently run on any web server platform including UNIX and Windows NT, and can handle a wide variety of document types including MS Office products, gif, jpeg, WordPerfect, HTML, text, postscript, and PDF, among others. Other unique features of ERes include optional password protection at the course level, and an automatic interactive bulletin board and live Java chat room for each course page. This makes discussion of course related material outside the classroom easier and has obvious uses for courses catering to distance learners.

Unlike FreeReserves, ERes uses a user name and password system to allow access to the administration functions of the program. This user name and password system also has four levels of access privileges from the Manager, who has complete control of the system, to the general account level which has the power to create course pages and work with page entries. The beauty of this system is that it allows for access to the system by library staff and course instructors from any location with a connection to the web. If a library so desires, it can allow the instructors themselves to maintain their own course pages with a lower level account. This account could include the ability to not only maintain the course readings, but also administer the bulletin board and chat room for the course as well as include pertinent announcements for students accessing the course page. In essence, these capabilities allow instructors with no technical expertise to maintain their very own course home pages complete with course readings, course syllabi, reading schedules, announcements, and a bulletin board and chat room, among other possibilities.

The University of Minnesota was impressed with what they saw, especially of the fact that over 60 colleges and universities currently use the product. Docutek also offers a product called ERes Pro that includes not only the program, but also a Pentium computer running Linux and the Apache web server with the software pre-installed. According to the ERes web site "unpack the boxes and plug it in...your ERes Electronic Reserve System is running!"[2] The University of Minnesota went with ERes Pro and purchased a Pentium II 400 MHz Widows NT server with a 9.1 GB hardrive and monitor for approximately $4,500. The size and speed of the server were based in part on the overall student population of the University of Minnesota as well as the potential number of reserves to be put on the system. The software license cost approximately $6,000 with a yearly fee of $900 for maintenance and support.

Patron Interface

The University of Minnesota ERes home page at http://scooter.lib.umn.edu looks much like other ERes implementations (See Figure 7). Users may find their desired course page, or look at a manual, software requirements, or links outside of the system. The home page also includes links to the administration functions of the system. Upon entering the second level of the system users may search for course pages or browse for course pages by instructor name or department name. The interface is very intuitive and leads users to the appropriate courses with minimal difficulty.

Eventually a user finds the appropriate course page (see Figure 8). Before entering the course page the user is presented with either a copyright notice page or a copyright notice and password page depending on whether or not the course page is password protected. This password is assigned by either the professor or library staff member who originally created the course page and is one word (alpha-numeric). The course page includes the name and number of the course, instructor name and email, links to the course chat room and bulletin board, an announcement from the instructor (if the instructor has decided to post one), and information about the course readings or documents. The document information includes the title of the reading, the format, and the size of the document in pages.

Administration Interface

Again, administration privileges are determined by the administrator's account level. There are four account levels. The General account level allows for the creation of course pages and page entries. Anyone with the general account level may only work with the course pages he or she has created. This would be an obvious choice for an instructor who has been given access to maintain his or her own course page. The second account level is the

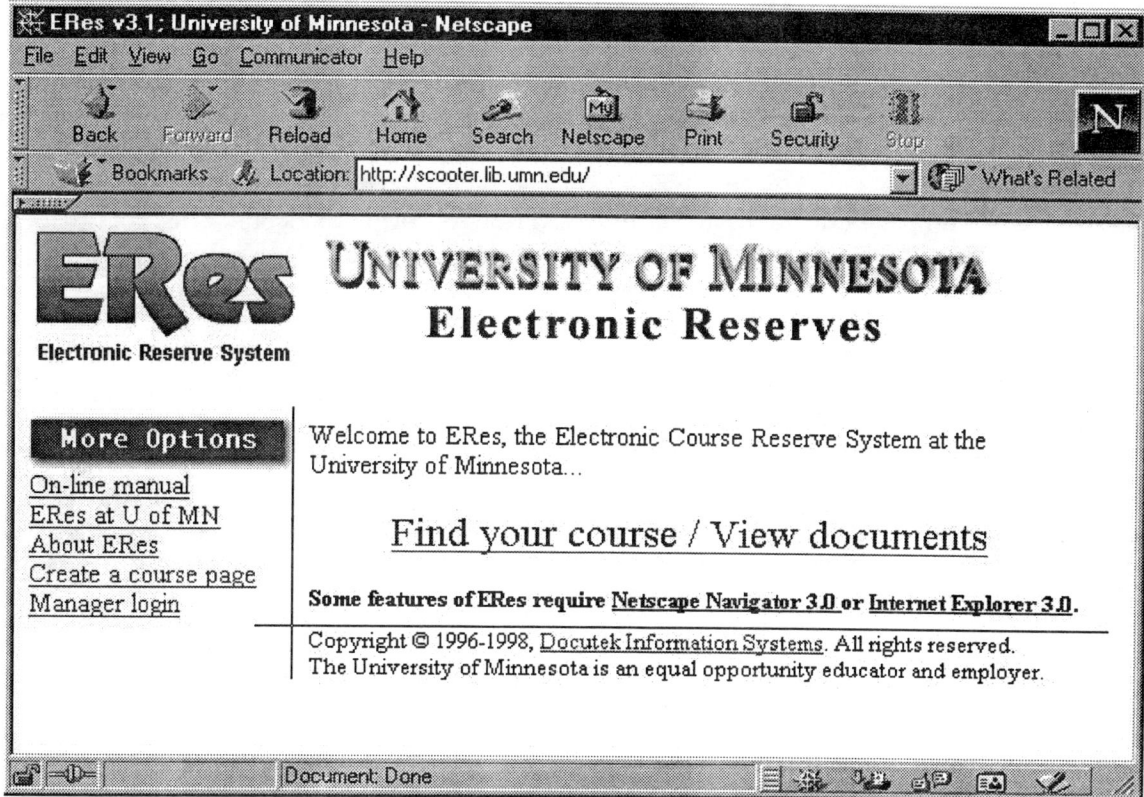

Figure 7: ERES Home Page at the University of Minnesota

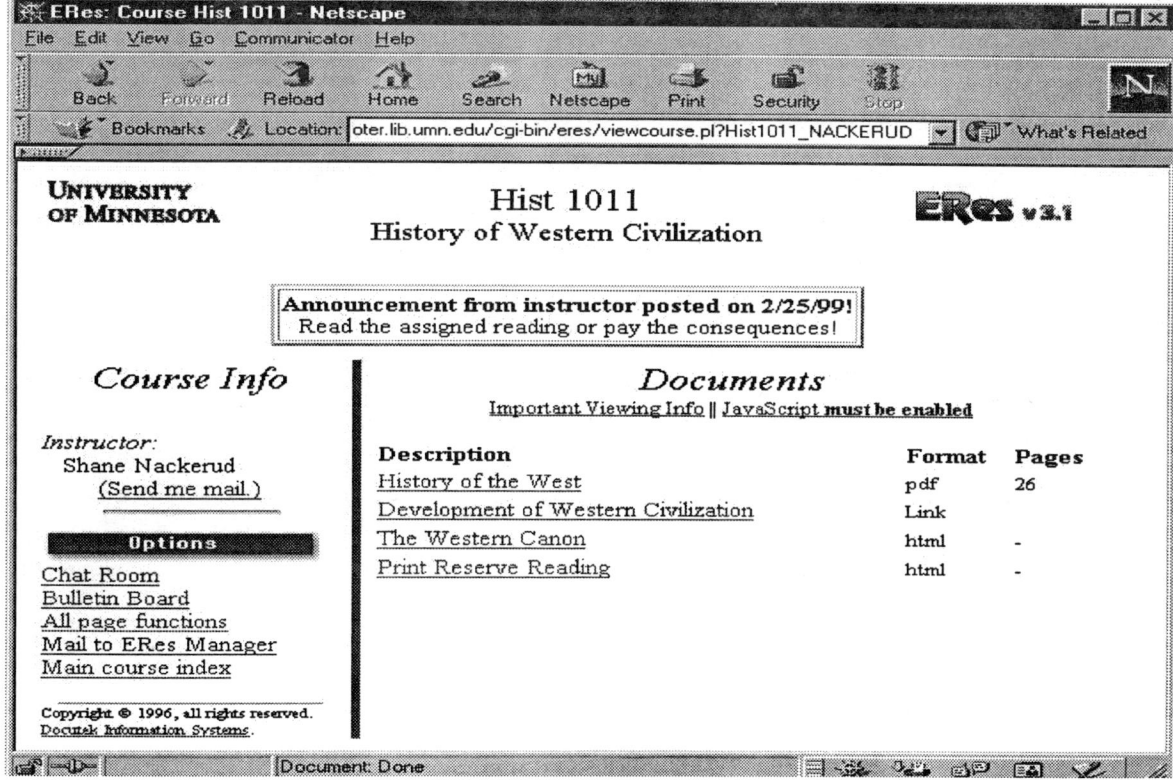

Figure 8: ERES Course Page

Helper who has the same privileges as the General user, but may also add readings to any course page. A Helper may delete readings only from course pages he or she has created. The third account level, Assistant, may create course pages and work with page entries for any course page.

Finally, the ERes Manager account level is authorized to not only create course pages and modify page entries, but also create and maintain user accounts, as well as perform other administrative functions (see figure 9). These include the ability to add or remove departments, gather usage statistics, create departmental internet resources web pages, delete course pages, link to course pages created outside of ERes, and send email messages to all account holders. According to Phil Kesten, Docutek's Information Systems Representative, only one Manager account exists in the ERes system, and this is usually given to one person. Again, there is no need for this person to have any technical knowledge or expertise outside of knowing how to use a web browser.[3]

At the heart of the ERes system, however, is the ability of any account holder to create course pages and add or delete documents from it, among other possibilities. Any account holder may create a course page by clicking on "Create a course page" from the ERes home page. This will then prompt them for their user name and password to gain access to the first screen of course page creation. (see Figure 10) After the course page is created, the account holder may begin to attach documents to it. In order to gain access to a course page account holders besides the Manager must first find the course page in the user interface system and then click on "All page functions." This will again prompt the account holder for user name and password information and finally forward the account holder to the Course Page Functions screen. The account holder may then add, modify, delete, or change the order of documents, post announcements, manage the course bulletin board, gather access statistics, or even delete or archive the course page (see Figure 11). Again, the privileges an account holder has are determined by the account level his or her user name and password is given.

Limitations

The most obvious limitation concerning the ERes product is the ability to customize the interface or the overall system. The ERes license agreement prohibits any modification of the code without the prior approval of Docutek. This is in part because of support issues. Docutek obviously can't support code it doesn't recognize. In terms of navigation issues and screen text and layout, Docutek prefers to keep the same look and feel of the program from site to site as each installation is a potential advertisement to the world. However, Docutek does promise that it will develop an ERes system that meets the wants and needs of the school. This may require extra software engineer hours, and possibly an extra fee attached to the overall price. For example, the University of Minnesota would prefer to use its own x.500 authentication system for student access to the program. This may require that Docutek modify the original code. Obviously, developing a homegrown system allows for as much customization as you want without the hassle of dealing with any license restrictions or programmers outside of your library. To their benefit, it is remarkable that Docutek allows for any customization and it certainly shows their commitment to customer satisfaction.

Secondly, unlike electronic reserves systems like Contec or Nousoft, and even to a lesser extent FreeReserves, ERes version 3.1 currently does not contain any copyright management applications. The ability to password protect course pages is as far as the software goes concerning this sticky issue. Granted, systems like Contec and Nousoft are far more expensive, and most libraries already have copyright management guidelines in place. ERes will, however, be developing a copyright management piece into future versions of its product.

Finally, although course pages may be password protected, there is no password protection at the document level. All documents have world access rights in the ERes system. If a person knows the URL to a reading, the course page and password protection can be bypassed. This, of course, means that a student may not only bookmark a reading, but also link to it from a personal web page. Again, the chances of this happening are rather slim, but who can guess the mind of a ma-

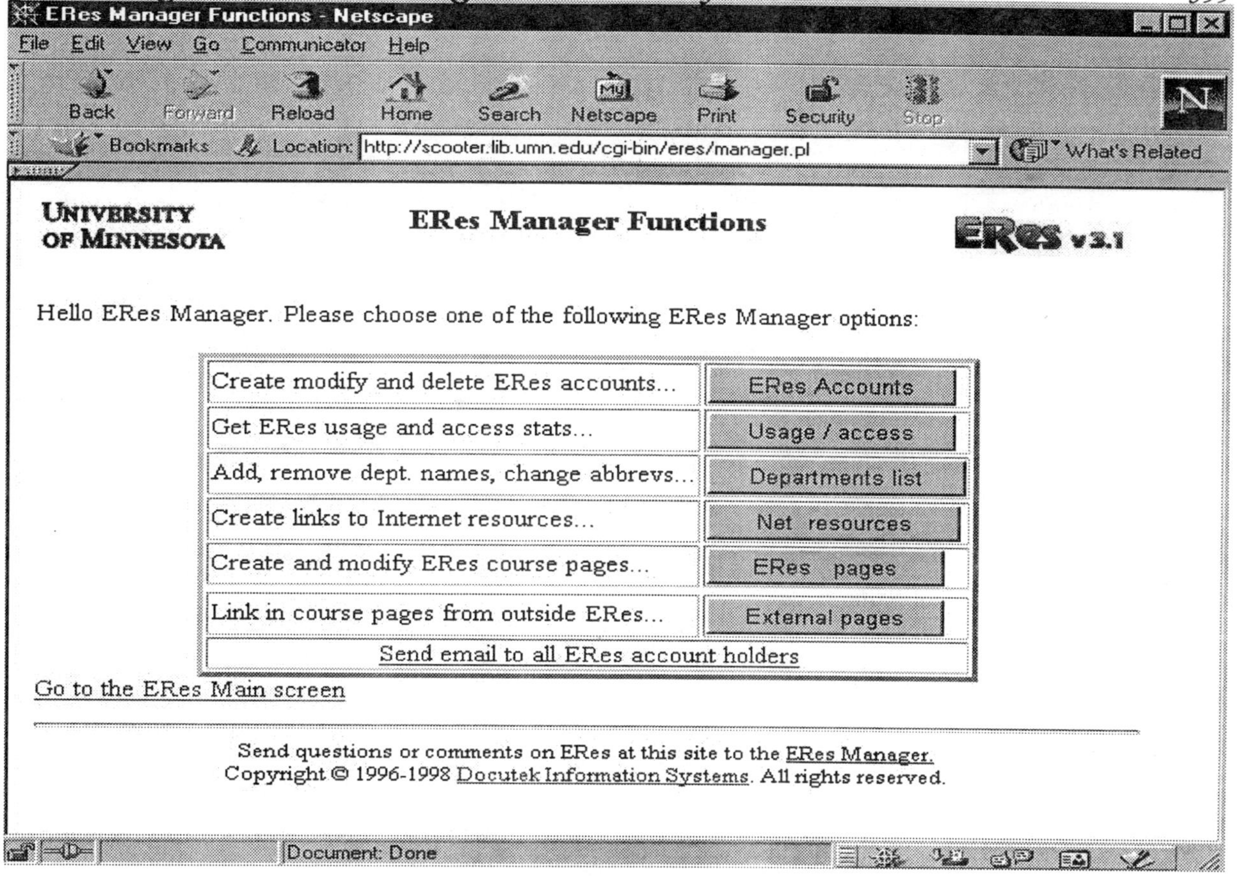

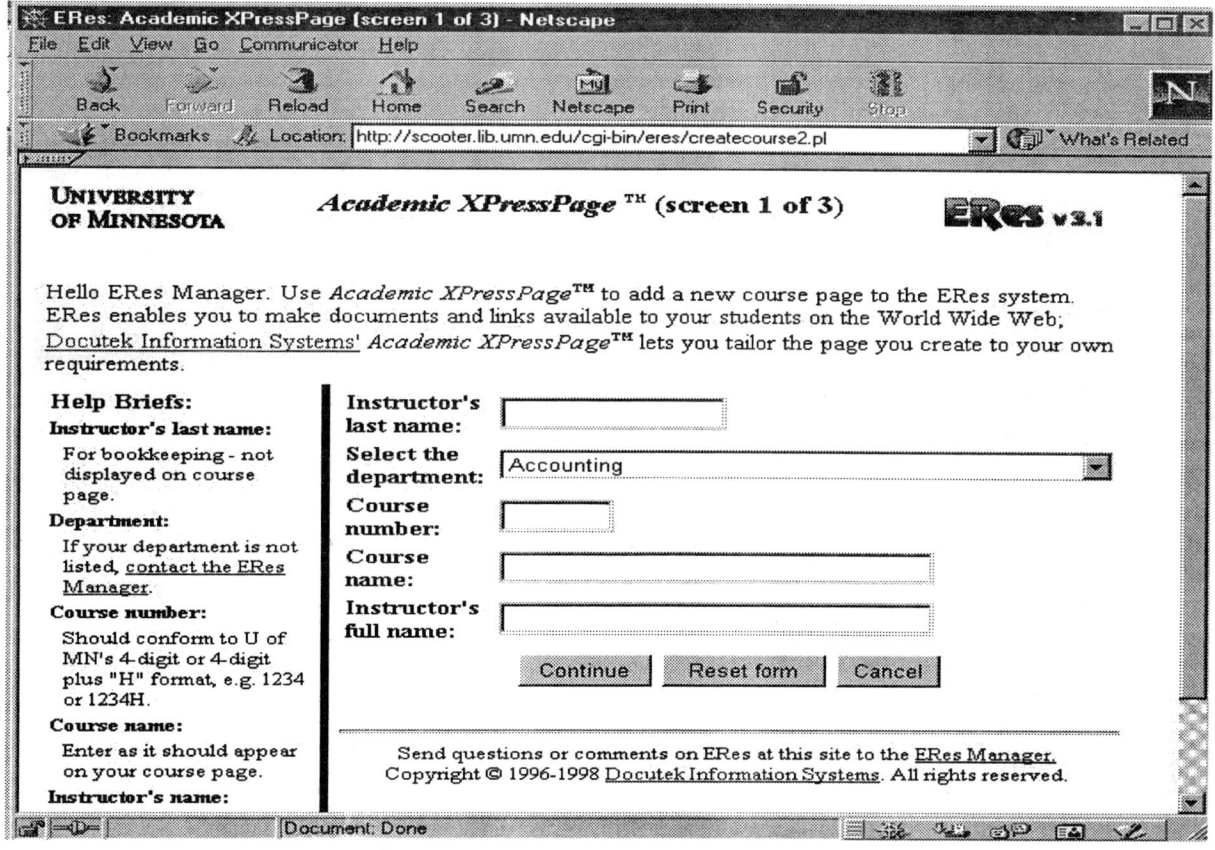

Figure 9: ERES Manager Functions

Figure 10: Course Page Creation Page 1

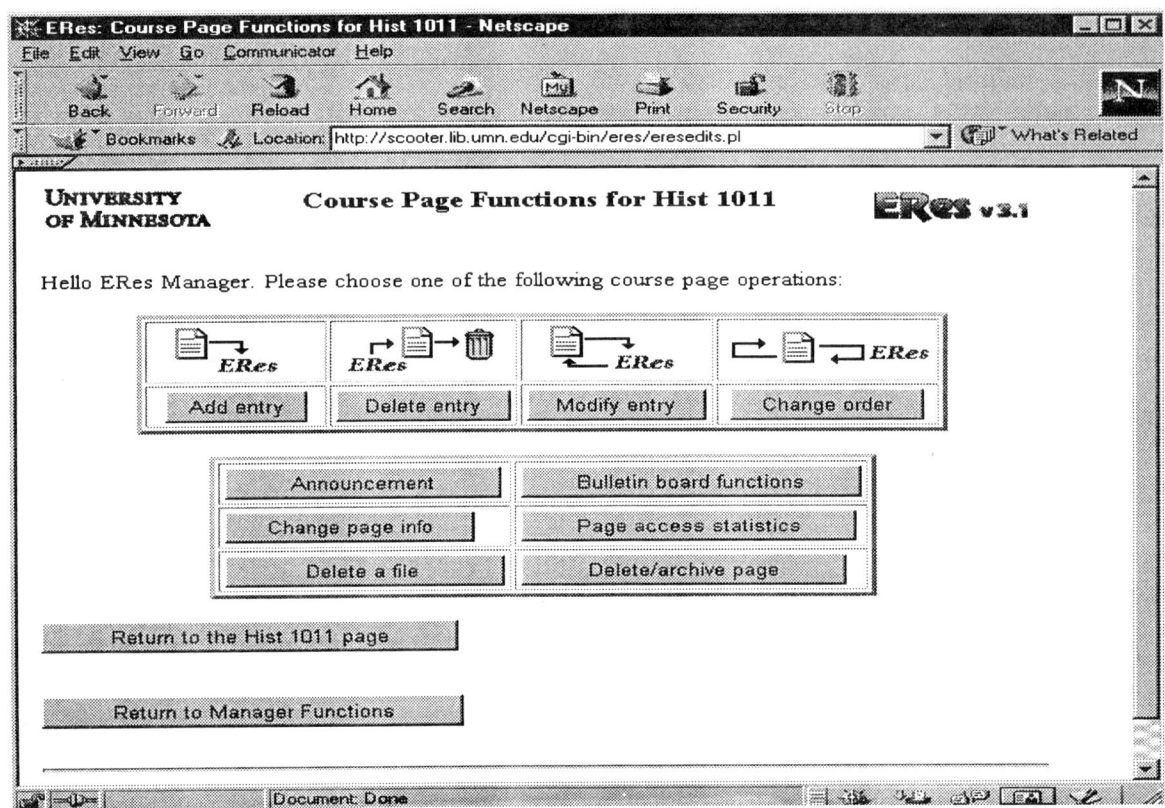

Figure 11: Course Page Functions

licious user? According to Phil Kesten, the new version of ERes will offer greater security at the document level by making the URL impossible to determine.[4] Nonetheless, the URL will still be world accessible.

Future Versions

Currently, ERes version 3.1 uses a flat file database as its backend. ERes 4.0 will use an SQL database and VBScript/ASP technology to drive the program. This will offer the database a great deal more flexibility. By using Active Server Pages this of course means that ERes 4.0 will require a Windows NT server running Microsoft's Internet Information Server (IIS). Although ChiliSoft (http://www.chilisoft.com) has developed software that allows ASP programming on UNIX based servers, Docutek reports that the software is still "buggy" and has not yet reached the level of relationship between ASP and Microsoft's IIS.[5]

The database behind ERes 4.0 will also include a number of new fields concerning copyright and the flexibility to add new fields for copyright management at the request of individual schools. This will include the ability to flag documents based on copyright compliance causing affected documents to be viewed only as permissions warrant. Each document will be tagged as either "Copyright Registered" or "Copyright Not Registered" with additional fields for "Claim Fair Use," "Request Copyright Permission," "Reveal to Public Pending Permission" or "Do Not Reveal to Public until Permission is Granted," and "Permission Granted."[6] This additional functionality will almost certainly allow ERes to keep its dominance of the electronic reserves market.

The U of M: What's Next

Using ERes version 3.1, the University of Minnesota Libraries hopes to conduct its pilot electronic reserves project during the Spring Quarter beginning March 15, 1999. Until then, various decisions still need to be made concerning courses to take part in the project, equipment, staffing, and workflow. For now, no more than 10 courses will take part in the pilot project giving the University

Libraries time to learn the new software, determine how much each reserve collection can handle, and decide what each reserve unit needs in terms of staffing and equipment.

The reserve unit of Wilson Library (Minneapolis campus) will direct the pilot project. One HP 6100C scanner has been purchased, as well as Adobe Acrobat 3.0 and Adobe Acrobat Capture 2.0. The University Libraries' Copy Service has agreed to scan, process, and upload reserve readings, while the actual reserve unit will handle data entry, advertising, and correspondence with instructors. Some of the responsibilities between the Copy Service and the reserve unit may begin to blur as the pilot project goes on, but it is important that these workflow issues be resolved before the word gets out and the reserve units are inundated with courses desiring the service. It is hoped that after a successful pilot project the lessons learned will enable the three Copy Service centers at Wilson Library, Walter Library and Magrath Library to not only take care of the electronic reserve scanning needs for their corresponding libraries, but also all the branch libraries on the Twin Cities campus.

Conclusion

Based on the experiences of SIUC and the University of Minnesota, the main differences between homegrown and turnkey e-reserve systems can be found in a discussion of labor, cost, and customizability. Homegrown systems can be quite labor intensive to develop and support. Developing the homegrown system at SIUC took over 50 hours of programming time and countless hours taking care of minor adjustments and "tweaking" the product. Developing a homegrown system also requires staff members with technical knowledge and web development expertise. This obviously includes knowledge of HTML, not to mention advanced programming languages such as Perl. Although creating a homegrown system using only HTML is possible, this type of endeavor can quickly become overwhelming for institutions with large reserve collections.

Turnkey systems like ERes offer a distinct advantage over homegrown systems in terms of the time and effort it takes to get a product up and running. For the University of Minnesota, the lack of programming skills and the desire for on-going, reliable support prompted them to purchase ERes from Docutek. Docutek in particular has made it easier for libraries to begin offering e-reserves through its ERes Pro product line. With ERes Pro, Docutek will build and configure a server for you, complete with the software already installed and ready to go. Of course, this comes with a price.

Developing a homegrown system obviously saves money, especially when compared with turnkey systems like Contec or Nousoft. This is not to say homegrown systems are without costs. There is, of course, the staff time required to develop the program, as well as software and hardware costs. SIUC spent an estimated $3,000 on hardware and software, and an indeterminable amount in programming hours. This is far less than the University of Minnesota, however, which will spend approximately $11,000 on the ERes software and server, not to mention possible customization costs and yearly license fees. Of course, the total cost for the University of Minnesota is based in part on the overall size of the university. Some smaller libraries using a turnkey system may have lower costs.

Finally, the biggest difference between homegrown and turnkey systems lies in the customizability of the end product. Libraries developing homegrown systems can conduct usability testing to determine the most appropriate web interface, or use existing graphics and web site appearance to create a satisfactory e-reserves site. Anything from graphics, to screen layout, to navigation can all be customized to meet library web page standards or the desires of your library's webmaster or web committee. By creating a homegrown site, SIUC was not only able to customize the patron interface, but also the backend database in order to create a system which totally catered to the needs of their reserve unit. With a turnkey system, a library is somewhat hampered in the choices it has concerning customization. Although Docutek does claim to allow for some modification of the product, extensive modifications may require an added fee. Some modifications may be completed by the purchasing library, but the license agreement prohibits any modifications without the approval of Docutek in advance.

In defense of Docutek, their willingness to modify their product at all is commendable. ERes is also already extremely easy to use and requires very little in the way of modifications for most colleges and universities.

The decision to go with either a turnkey system or a homegrown system to deliver electronic reserves is based on the unique situation at your library. For libraries without the technical expertise or manpower to create and support a homegrown system, products like ERes are

the clear choice. ERes in particular is used by over 60 libraries worldwide both large and small, and does not require any knowledge of HTML or advanced programming languages. A homegrown system, however, gives a library significant cost savings as well as the power to customize the product at will. Obviously, there are advantages and disadvantages to both types of systems that must be considered before determining the most suitable method for electronic reserves maintenance and delivery at your institution.

Notes

1. Janis H. Bruwelheide, *The Copyright Primer for Librarians and Educators* (Chicago: ALA, 1995): 32.

2. *"Docutek Information Systems, ERes Technical Overview"* Online. Available http://www.docutek.com/products/eres/techno.htm. 28 February 1999.

3. Philip R. Kesten and Slaven M. Zivkovic, "ERes—Electronic Reserves on the World Wide Web." *Journal of Interlibrary Loan, Document Delivery & Information Supply* 7, no. 4 (1997): 43.

4. Philip R. Kesten <kesten@docutek.com>. "ERes questions" Private e-mail message to Shane Nackerud. 25 February 1999.

5. ———.<kesten@docutek.com>. "ERes questions" Private e-mail message to Shane Nackerud. 24 February 1999.

6. ———.<kesten@docutek.com>. "Copyright questions" Private e-mail message to Shane Nackerud. 26 February 1999.

Learning Communities, Adult Learners, and Instructional Teams at IUPUI

May Jafari

Introduction

Adult independent learners are becoming an increasingly important and sizable segment of the college student population. It has been projected that within the next ten years the majority of students will not be the eighteen-to twenty-four-year-olds who come to higher education directly from high schools. Instead, the largest group will be students who are older and attend school on a part-time rather than full-time basis. Recent studies show that not only is there a shrinking pool of the traditional "younger" students and a rapid expansion of the older population but also that part-time students are the fastest growing population in higher education (Hussar, 1993).

Access to library resources and developing skills are important elements of the academic experience for all students. Yet, adult learners experience barriers in the use of the library and its many resources. In the meantime, the advent of electronic information retrieval in university libraries has caused resources available to our users to grow exponentially. Technology has sensitized us to potential differences in skill levels and "learning styles." Institutions of higher education and their academic units and libraries have been asked to re-examine their roles and to come up with innovative methods or alternative services to accommodate the needs of adult learners as well as the needs of their traditional students. Through establishing learning communities, several universities have begun to address and accommodate the learning and teaching needs of their students. As a result of this new environment, libraries and other academic and computing units on campus have become partners in the new learning environment.

This paper describes Learning Communities Program in development at Indiana University Purdue University Indianapolis (IUPUI). It draws upon the experience of one of the Learning Community which utilizes an "instructional team" approach to teach various information literacy and technology skills to adult learners over 25 years of age. It examines the unique needs and learning

May Jafari is instructional librarian at IUPUI University Library.

objectives of an adult learner. The paper investigates the issues and challenges of collaborating with faculty, other team members and adult learners operating in a team environment.

Learning/Teaching Paradigm and Academic Libraries

Increasingly, institutions of higher education are being asked to provide students with critical thinking and problem solving skills. Equally important has been a paradigm shift within colleges and universities to move toward "learning paradigm" rather than "teaching paradigm". As a result of this new learning environment, some of the universities and academic units responsible for teaching and learning efforts on their campuses have been forced to come up with innovative ways to educate their students to prepare them to participate in the "lifelong" learning process. This new shift on learning has resulted in new research, new methods, and new considerations, creating a new learning environment for faculty, librarians, and learners as well. As a result, various academic and computing service units have joined efforts to expand and enhance the teaching and learning mission of their institutions.

In most universities and colleges, academic libraries are part of the academic units of the campus and are expected to contribute to the institution's educational mission. Support for the role of libraries in educational reform through the integration of information literacy skills into the curriculum can be found in works such as the article written by Patricia B. Knapp over 40 years ago which states" if we wish the library to function more effectively in the college… we must direct our efforts toward the curriculum, working through faculty" (Knapp, 1958: 831). In 1989, the American Library Association Presidential Committee on Information Literacy issued its Final Report, in which they noted "ultimately, information literate people are those who have learned how to learn…they are people prepared for lifelong learning because they can always find the information needed for any task or decision at hand" (American Library Association, 1989).

In more recent years, other writers such as Patricia S. Breivik and E. Gordon Gee (Breivik and Gee, 1989), Hannelore B. Rader (Rader, 1997), Brendan A. Rapple (Rapple, 1997), and Gabriela Sonntag and Donna M. Ohr (Sonntag and Ohr, 1996) have emphasized the need for forming partnerships between the library, faculty, classroom, and university administration to integrate electronic information and information literacy instruction into the curriculum. Kimberley M. Donnelly lists four distinct approaches that librarians have used to develop and integrate information literacy into the curriculum of their respective institutions (Donnelly, 1998). The four approaches are:

• The Required, core-curriculum, for credit model;
• The Required, discipline-specific, for credit-course model;
• The Elective, for-credit course model;
• The Course-integrated model.

Faculty and librarians' collaboration has been a major factor in developing the above successful information literacy programs. Another recent development has begun in some colleges and universities to better understand "how their students learn," "in what kinds of environment or setting," and "what educational reform" are needed to enhance their learning experience. As a result of this renewed interest in "students' learning," some universities have created innovative approaches that attempt to create rich, challenging and nurturing academic communities for their students. One such approach has been the creation of "Learning Communities." Once again, academic librarians have emerged as active partners in the educational arena through their involvement in the learning communities program of their respective institutions.

Learning Communities

How do we define "learning communities?" One major proponent of the learning communities movement, Barbara Leigh Smith, states that the, "learning community approach fundamentally restructures the curriculum, and the time and space of students…link together courses or coursework to provide more opportunities for active learning, and interaction between students and faculty" (Smith, 1993). In another recent article, Philip Tompkins, Susan Perry and Joan K. Lippincott discuss the " new learning communities" movement in several universities such the University of Washington (UW-UWired Program), and the Southern California (USC, Jump Start Program). These educators note that "New Learning Communities Program was developed to support pioneers in education who use networking and networked information to support student-centered teaching and learning" (Tompkins, Perry and Lippincott, 1998). They also state that "important models existed that demonstrated the convergence of the increasingly important role of collaboration and collaborative learning, the availability of Internet and networking... and the importance of including information literacy in the higher education curriculum" (Tompkins, Perry and Lippincott, 1998).

IUPUI Learning Communities Initiative

IUPUI is a public, four-year urban university of some 27,000 students. About 98 percent of the students are Indiana residents and 48 percent are part-time students who work and have family obligations. There are 1,400 full-time and approximately 800 part-time faculty employed at IUPUI. IUPUI was formed in 1969 when Indiana University and Purdue University merged their Indianapolis operations. IUPUI is recognized as a leader in urban higher education, ranked as Indiana's third largest and most comprehensive university.

Since 1996, IUPUI has been the home institution of one of Coalition for Networked Information's (CNI) New Learning Communities (NLC) project leaders. IUPUI offers students a variety of educational and career opportunities. The size and complexity of IUPUI, however, may create problems for all students, especially the adult learners, who have not been in school for a number of years. Some may find it difficult to make connections with other students, faculty members, and campus resources. The Learning Community Program provides an environment where students are supported in making those connections to better ensure a successful transition to college. Learning Communities are facilitated by an Instructional Team which is a collaborative effort of a faculty member working with a librarian, and supported by a student mentor, an academic advisor, and a technologist.

Since Fall 1996, the IUPUI University Library has been involved in collaborating with faculty and other academic units in providing support to the Learning Community program. The IUPUI Librarians were able to devote more attention to understand and accommodate the needs of our First-Year students as well as our adult learners with respect to information literacy and technology skills. All Learning Communities include a first-year experience class. Some learning communities link two or more classes, and some are specifically designed to introduce students to their majors. All students entering IUPUI for the first semester in college are eligible for a Learning Community.

Instructional Teams and Adult Learners at IUPUI

Instructional Teams are an integral component of the learning communities program. In fall 1996, there were 23 instructional teams on campus. Called together by the faculty member to prepare and/or revise a course, the instructional team moves through four phases in the development of a successful learning experience for students enrolled. The four phases of development within instructional teams are:

1. Team Formation
2. Development Design
3. Implementation
4. Evaluation

In each of these stages, team members have particular roles to play. For further information about Instructional Teams at IUPUI see our Web page: (http://www-lib.iupui.edu/itt/itt.html).

The library assigned a team of librarians to support instructional teams. The author was one of the librarians assigned to work with two non-discipline specific courses whose linkages were based on generally connecting students to the university and to the scholarly community. The objectives of each course were intended to reflect the student population they targeted. The description printed in the Schedule of Courses reads: First Year Success Seminar: "Designed to help returning students ages 25 and over, or any student who is a parent, develop habits and skills that will enable them to be successful in the intellectual and cultural environment of IUPUI."

The Instructional Team members met to discuss their roles and to develop an understanding of "learning styles" of adult learners. They decided to study Malcolm Knowles' works. In his writings which date back to the 1960s, Knowles discusses the concept of "andragogy, or the art of teaching adults" (Knowles, 1968). In the andragological perspective the librarian or any other team member becomes a 'facilitator" rather than the "giver" of all knowledge. Students learn by methods such as collaborative strategies and link what they already know to newly acquired skills. As Knowles and Brookfield noted in their separate works on andragogy, the adult learner is self-directed, more motivated to acquire information and skills relevant to real life situations. The adult learner is also well experienced professionally and personally and expects an immediate payoff or practical application (Knowles, 1990; Brookfield, 1986).

After studying the above works, the instructional team met several times to develop and provide learning opportunities to enhance educational experiences for adult learners. The team members worked together to develop roles, to achieve goals of planning, developing, implementing, and evaluating each course. By collaborating on curriculum development and design, the team members were able to teach various information technology skills and other critical skills. The unique needs of adult learners were incorporated into the assignments and projects. Listed are some of the unique ways the team members were able to contribute and enhance the learning experiences of adult learners enrolled in Learning Communities Program.

Faculty
Introduce students to the culture and society of the university; provide academic status for the program; course planning; maintain an academic course orientation; model success strategies; assessment of students products and projects

Librarian
Expand the range of teaching and learning materials; participate in course planning, and learning objectives; incorporate information skills into the curriculum; facilitate discussions, contribute to critical thinking and evaluation of information sources; employ active learning; assessment of student products.

Student Mentor
Role model; mediator between students and the faculty; students' advocate, expert on campus resources; course planning; email & technology assistant

Academic Advisor
Expert on campus resources; academic policies; university regulations; facilitator on the use of a variety of learning styles

Technologist
Technology expert on e-mail & basic Internet searching

Issues and Challenges
As with any new initiative, the Instructional Team members faced issues and challenges in teaching information literacy and technology skills to the students. Some issues included:

For students:
- Various age groups, 25 to 60 years old, different needs, learning styles and motivations;
- Low-self esteem among some students, a high level of confidence (not realizing how to ask for assistance);
- Computer & technology apprehensions;
- Family and job obligations, not enough time to establish contact with the instructional team members and campus community.

For the instructional team:
- Technologist's lack of knowledge about the adult learners learning styles;
- Faculty & academic advisor lack of knowledge about the library and its online resources;
- Insufficient infrastuctue (networking, personnel, equipment, facilities, etc);
- Difficulty scaling projects (adding more courses and more students);
- The significant time commitment required to develop such projects has taxed the ability of faculty and librarians to carry out other "traditional" responsibilities, and limits involvement;
- Problems with off-campus access;
- Copyright of materials that might be incorporated in the network resources.

Conclusion
As academic libraries engage in widespread re-

definition of goals and reallocation of resources, the above pilot project should be evaluated from the perspective of value to academic faculty, its students and the positive roles that library faculty have taken to represent the institutional role of the library. Instructional Teams have provided many learning opportunities for its members and the student body. Having a voice in the course planning, integrating information literacy into the curriculum, and being involved in student learning at a more fundamental level has been beneficial to team members, and especially the instructional librarians. Having closer connection with the institution's teaching & learning mission and playing another role central to meeting the changing information needs of the academic community has contributed to higher visibility for librarians involved in the Learning Communities Program.

References

American Library Association. *Presidential Committee on Information Literacy, Final Report* (Chicago, Ill.: American Library Association, 1989): 1.

Patricia S. Breivik and E. Gordon Gee. *Information Literacy: Revolution in the Library* (New York: Macmillian, 1989).

Stephen Brookfield. *Understanding and Facilitating Adult Learning* (San Francisco, Jossey-Bass, 1986).

Kimberley M. Donnelly. "Learning from the Teaching Libraries," *American Libraries* 29, no. 11 (December 1998): 47.

William J. Hussar. *Projections of Education Statistics to 2003*. U.S. Department of Education, National Center for Education Statistics (Washington, D.C.: GPO, 1993).

Patricia B. Knapp. "College Teaching and the Library," *Illinois Librarian* 40 (December 1958): 831.

Malcolm S, Knowles. "Andragogy, Not Pedagogy!" *Adult Leadership* 16 (April 1968): 351.

Malcolm S. Knowles. *The Adult Learner, a Neglected Species*, 5th edition (Houston: Gulf Publishing, 1990).

Hannelore B. Rader. "Library Instruction and Information Literacy 1996," *Reference Services Review* (fall/winter 1997): 103–18.

Brendan A. Rapple. "The Electronic Library, New Roles for Librarians," *CAUSE/EFFECT* 20, no. 1 (spring 1997): 45–51.

Barbara Leigh Smith. "Creating Learning Communities," *Liberal Education* 79, no. 4 (fall 1993): 32–39.

Gabriela Sonntag and Donna M. Ohr. "The Development of a Lower-Division, General Education, Course-Integrated Information Literacy Program," *College & Research Libraries* 57 (July 1996): 331–38.

Philip Tompkins, Susan Perry, and Joan K. Lippincott. "New Learning Communities: Collaboration, Networking, and Information Literacy," *Information Technology and Libraries* 17, no. 2 (June 1998): 101–6.

Revelry, Revelation, or Research: What Are College Students Really Doing on the Internet

Rebecca A. Wilson

Introduction

What are college students really doing on the Internet? To what extent, if any, are they seeking information for course-related assignments? To provide a context for this paper, think back a few years to 1994 and 1995. Lynx and other gophers were on the way out; the Mosaic browser was still in use; and Netscape had recently made its debut on the Internet scene. You may recall that 1995 was touted as "the Year of the Internet". Nationwide, costly networks were being implemented on college campuses, many with Internet connectivity from computer labs, libraries, and even residence halls. Little could be known about how these networks would be used once students were connected to the vast, limitless, indiscriminate, and unedited ocean of data known as the Internet.

Brief summary of the research study

What impact would such access have on students, libraries and the research process? Would students flock to the keyboard, surf the Web, and crank out papers based on data plucked from amorphous, unauthenticated web sites? Would they fritter away valuable time in aimless wandering? These questions and others prompted the study. This paper is based on research conducted in 1996 which investigated whether and how students were using the Internet to access information for course-related research, and what accounted for such use or non-use. For purposes of this paper, *course-related research* refers to research undertaken by students to fulfill specific class assignments, including term papers, for credit courses. Although Internet technology is evolving at the speed of light and some of the terms may already appear dated, data is presented here as reported by students. Partial responses to three of the research questions are discussed:

1) purposes for which students are using the Internet;
2) factors that influence use or non-use of the Internet for research;
3) how Internet research compares to traditional library research.

The qualitative study was conducted at five small, independent, residential, undergraduate colleges in central Pennsylvania. The campuses had varying degrees of connectivity, but all had some access to the Internet. Although the sample population was small, students were randomly selected from all four academic levels from the aggregate

Rebecca Wilson is associate library director, Susquehanna University.

college population. Ultimately, seventy-three students participated and were divided into two groups: those who had used the Internet for course-related research (users), and those who had not (non-users). Methodology used was that of small, scheduled, focus-group sessions, in which students as users (36, or 49%) were asked a series of eleven questions about Internet use; non-users (37, or 51%) were asked a series of four questions regarding non-use.

Purposes of Internet use
- Email use
- Course-related research
- Recreational purposes
- Academic purposes
- Practical purposes

When asked the question, "For what purposes do you use the Internet?," the answer came as no surprise. The reason cited most often for using the Internet, reported by 46 students (63%) in the study, was for e-mail purposes. Students reported e-mailing to friends, peers at other colleges, and to family members, largely as a social function and a way to stay in touch. Intensity of use varied, with some students checking e-mail a few times per week and others logging on twenty times a day. Of interest was the fact that twice as many students in the non-users groups used the Internet for email than in the users groups.

The second most often cited reason for Internet use was for course-related research. This was somewhat surprising because, in 1996 when the Internet was not widely promoted and was still incredibly difficult to navigate, almost half of all participants in the study (36, or 49%) were already using it on their own to find course-related information simply because it was there.

Three additional reasons for accessing the Internet, cited less frequently by students in both groups, were for recreational purposes, for academic purposes and for practical purposes. Recreational use varied widely and included chat lines, news groups, music-related activities, sports, games and humor, dating, and sending postcards. Academic use could include seeking information about other colleges, scholarships and online applications, and creating web pages and JAVA script. On a practical level, students accessed course-related software on the campus LAN, used FTP to locate archived files, sought background information on companies for job interviews, and investigated other career-oriented applications.

On average, all students used the Internet for all purposes 2.6 hours per week. Students (as users) spent an average of 3.7 hours a week on the Internet, while non-users averaged 1.6 hours a week.

Factors affecting Internet use for course research
Students as Users
What factors encouraged or hindered Internet use for course research among college students? Why did some students choose to search the Internet, while others did not? When asked these questions, the three primary reasons (in rank order) most often cited by users for using the Internet for course-related research were:
- convenience—faster, easier than searching books and periodicals for information;
- information type and content—breadth, variety and currency of data;
- as a library alternative—ability to access from residence halls, computer labs, etc.

In their own words:

I think it's faster; instead of walking to the library and looking it up in the catalog, then going to find the book or magazine . . . just type in the subject you're looking for and it's right there.—*freshman, female*

For the kind of information I can't find in the library—up-to-date, up-to-the-minute statistics, or a subject that's not very common and you can't find books or magazine articles on it.—*junior, male*

Less often, students also reported using the Internet:
- upon recommendation of a faculty member;
- for the advantages of hypertext links.

Among users then, while several factors influenced Internet use for research purposes, it is note-

worthy that peer influence was rarely cited as a reason. When users were asked to describe *what* they were seeking when they searched the Internet for course-related research, they most often said they wanted to:
- find various kinds/types of information;
- find information about a specific topic;
- find information for a specific course.

Examples of information types included: articles or entries on a topic (web-based, not journal articles); government documents; teacher pages/lesson plans; pictures and home pages of people, especially politicians; current news and events (same day news—too recent for books); journal articles; recent scientific data; research studies; primary documents; statistical data; papers written by faculty; and term papers written by students at other colleges which they could download and use.

Examples of specific topics included: company information; wetlands/everglades; animal testing; campaigns, elections, and presidents; Star Wars movie; Women's Conference in China; euthanasia; DNA fingerprinting; genetics; and forensics. To quote one student when asked why he had used the Internet:

> . . . For U.S. campaigns and elections. We had to do a candidate profile on the Republican candidates for president. I went on the WWW and to each candidate's home page . . . then I would go to the Democratic National Committee page to look for information against the candidate.—*junior, male*

Information sought for specific courses ran the gamut from political science and urban economics to business policy and biology. Not all students were equally clear about their objectives when searching the Internet, but they had few preconceived ideas regarding what they would find. About 10 students in this group (28%) were "unsure of what they were seeking" but reported that they would know it when they found it.

Students as Non-Users

Among non-users surveyed (51% of the sample population), students provided several responses when asked why they chose not to use the Internet for course-related research. In rank order, non-users reported that they:
- had no reason or need to use it; had never used it; had never been told to use it;
- were unable to access the Internet or to conduct a search and locate useful information;
- preferred other more traditional methods of research with which they were more familiar.

Many students in this group regarded the Internet as a tool for social or recreational purposes, and had not considered its use for academic or research purposes. Often, these students reported being able to satisfy all their research needs in the library.

> I never thought about using it. I think . . . a lot of professors ask you if they want to you try and get something up-to-date, but none . . . have asked me, so it never occurred to me to use it; but I don't think I even know how to get on it without help.—freshman, female

> Teachers . . . didn't really stress the Internet or show us how to use the Internet; they stressed looking up catalogs and . . . the Humanities Index, e.g., or Psychological Abstracts and . . . I was able to find all the information I needed through those sources.—sophomore, female

Other reasons for non-use, ranked but cited less often, included:
- the need for instruction or documentation;
- a general dislike of computers;
- difficulty with locating computers and gaining access to the Internet;
- lack of knowledge about what the Internet was;
- confusion as to what kind of information could be found.

Recall that in 1996, search engines were far less efficient than they are today. Yahoo and WebCrawler were most familiar to the student sample at that time, and a search would result in tens of thousands of hits, many completely irrelevant to the query. Most students were still using modems which in their view took forever! The

Internet experience was often frustrating and overwhelming to a number of students.

Internet research vs traditional library research

How did the experience of students who used the Internet for research compare to those who did not, when using more traditional Library resources? Did Internet users rely heavily on the Internet for their research—to the exclusion of other sources? Surprisingly, they did not. In fact, students who used the Internet for course research made greater overall use of all types, sources, and formats of library materials. To quote one senior:

> For me, I use besides the Internet, encyclopedias, books, periodicals - periodicals are probably the biggest thing I use, because it's the thing that I can get here at the school and it's up-to-date and it's pretty recent and that seems to be my most-used source for research.—senior, male

When asked which resources they used, however, the responses of both groups were more comparable, with users citing by name 33 specific resources and 69 uses, and non-users citing 21 resources with 71 uses. The following sources were cited by both groups:

InfoTrac
Psychological Abstracts
Social Science & Humanities Index
Humanities Index
Reference Books
Social Sciences Index
FirstSearch
ERIC
New York Times
CD-CAT
PsycLit
Readers' Guide to Periodical Literature

In addition, users could recall by name:

Chemical Abstracts
Am. Occupational Therapy Database
Oxford Compendium of English Literature
Wall Street Journal
Historical Abstracts
Biology Abstracts
Moody's Manuals
NewsBank
MLA Database
GeoBase
Times Literary Supplement
WilsonDisk
Biography Index
Value Line
Encyclopedia Britannica Online
Congressional Quarterly
America: History & Life
Art Index
Washington Post
Book Review Digest
Business Periodicals Index

Non-users mentioned as well:

Cinahl
Social Sciences Citation Index
LIAS (PSU Online Catalog)
Contemporary Literary Criticism
Sport Discus
LA Times
Purdon's Law
Religion Index One
SocioFile

One non-user, a senior, described her research process:

> I have used Psychological Abstracts, Readers' Guide, Social Sciences Index, Humanities Index and the New York Times... The InfoTrac I've used more often because most of the time I need more current information. The books here in the library are not up-to-date really... and there's no point even looking for a book itself. Interlibrary loan, I use heavily, heavily, especially in psychology we're lacking a lot of journals in the psychology area so these have to be interlibrary loaned.—senior, female

Neither group was averse to using electronic databases, either online or in CD-ROM format. Among users, 27 of the 36 students (75%) had used electronic databases, and 28 out of 37 Non-Users had (76%). This would imply that for research purposes, both groups made comparable use of online databases but clearly, non-users made a distinction between online resources and use of the Internet. Taken as a whole, the data indicates that users overall conducted more active research than non-users, and simply regarded the Internet as one more tool in the research process. Concerns that the Internet would become a substitute for scholarly library resources were not substantiated by the study.

Some distinctions can be made among campuses. An interesting observation was that students from the campus with the highest number of non-users were able to recall by name the greatest number of different reference sources; and conversely, students from the campus with the highest number of users recalled the fewest number of sources by name. Another finding of the study, which came as no surprise, was that physical access to the Internet also affected students' willingness and ability to use or not use this tool. The study revealed that the numbers of students using the Internet for course research correlated positively with the degree of network connectivity on each of the five campuses. In other words, the "most-wired" campuses had the highest number of users. This suggests that Internet use for research could increase as more students gain easier access to networked computers, and as incoming students find a fully-networked campus at the outset.

Differences were also noted among academic levels. Freshmen and sophomores preferred electronic and/or Internet access for conducting research, having received early exposure to the technology. Juniors and seniors in both groups (users and non-users) preferred to conduct research using traditional library resources and were less apt to embrace unfamiliar, computer-based methods. Seniors were most able to articulate a logical and comprehensive library-based research strategy, often revealing a number of higher level cognitive skills utilizing printed sources.

No distinctions were noted between male and female students regarding their comfort levels with, willingness, or reluctance to use computers. They also exhibited similar search patterns on the Internet, using comparable techniques to conduct a search strategy, and using topic or menu searching in the default search engine. Gender did not appear to be a factor in the study.

In summary, then, we know that students are using the Internet for a variety of purposes which includes email, course-related research, recreational, academic and practical purposes. Convenience, speed of access, and breadth of data are factors that encourage their use for research. Students as non-users cited lack of need, lack of knowledge, and inability to conduct successful searches as reasons for non-use. Both groups made comparable use of traditional library resources; the Internet was simply one more tool for students as users to consult.

No recent studies could be found to update this data and it is entirely possible that students' research patterns regarding the Internet have changed in the last two years. Until further research is available, I will conclude the paper with this question: Do you know what *your* students are doing on the Internet?

APPENDIX

The study was based on the following set of research questions, posed to two groups.

A. Questions for students who HAD used the Internet for course-related research:

    1. In what ways do you use the Internet for course-related research?

    2. WHY do you use the Internet for research?

    3. How did you learn to use the Internet for course-related research?

    4. In conducting course research, what other sources, if any, do you use?

    5. What is the search process you typically use in accessing the Internet for course research?

    6. What kinds of information are you seeking?

    7. How do you evaluate the information you retrieve?

    8. How successful are you when using Internet searches for course research?

    9. What do you like best about using the Internet for course research?

    10. How could your use of the Internet for research be made more effective?

    11. What else do you do on the Internet?

B. Questions for students who had NOT used the Internet for research:

    1. Since you have NOT used the Internet to do research for a course, explain why not?

    2. Describe which resources you use for research instead? Which resources and where?

    3. For what purposes have you used the Internet?

    4. What would encourage you to use it for research?

Wilson, Rebecca A. *Students' Use of the Internet for Course-Related Research: Factors Which Account for Use or Non-Use.* University Park, Penn.: Pennsylvania State University, 1997.

Strategic Positioning and the Building Project: Penn State Harrisburg's "Library of the Future"

Harold Shill

The academic library has historically been viewed as an institution's repository of knowledge and gateway to recorded human knowledge. This perception, which placed the library at the center of the academic enterprise, was a valuable positioning asset during the print era. Although studies of scholarly communication have demonstrated the presence of parallel, informal communication systems within academic disciplines,[1] the library has remained the preeminent point of access to accepted knowledge for students, faculty and many community users. However, in a period of decentralized, networked access to electronic databases, expanding use of the World Wide Web, and distance education, some administrators and commercial information providers have questioned the future importance of print collections and the need for additional physical space for libraries.

Early challenges to the library's primacy emerged in the mid-1980s, as online database vendors began targeting the end-user as a customer.[2]

A much more serious challenge has been provided by the exponential growth of the Internet, particularly the World Wide Web, during the 1990s. With a growing body of information readily available from classrooms, faculty offices, dormitories and off-campus locations, a widely used, parallel system of information access has developed in less than five years.

Academic libraries have responded to this trend by adopting Web-based automated library systems, offering a proliferating array of subscription databases through their online public access catalogs (OPACs), and incorporating both Web and online database search training into their bibliographic instruction programs. They have also scanned unique resources, particularly materials usually kept in special collections, to provide remote access from their Web pages. The terms "library without walls," "virtual library," and "digital library" have been used to convey the library's growth from a site-based resource provider into a networked access point to a fast-growing body of information

Harold Shill is director, Capital College Libraries, Pennsylvania State University, Harrisburg.

available, without regard to physical location, in electronic formats.[3]

While these initiatives have expanded the range of resources available to the academic community and demonstrated the library's ability to use technology creatively, they have not assured its continued primacy as an information and knowledge provider in the academic community. Indeed, spurred on by Internet "hype" and their own positive experiences, administrators, faculty and students have increasingly embraced the Web as a primary source of information.

This growing acceptance of the Web has already had important implications for the future of the physical library. Brian Hawkins has demonstrated the libraries are acquiring an increasingly smaller proportion of the world's information in their print collections.[4] A California State University-Monterey Bay administrator announced in early 1995 that his new campus would open without a physical library, relying instead on document delivery; although a library has indeed been built at CSU-MB, the idea of reliance on a virtual library was introduced into the higher education dialogue.[5] Database vendors have approached university administrators, bypassing library directors, with the idea that full-text journal subscriptions could eliminate the need for future expansion of library facilities by containing the physical growth of library collections. The University of Phoenix has developed an extensive collection of databases to provide remote access to research materials for students in its far-flung programs. In some cases, academic departments and computer centers are initiating their own subscriptions to electronic resources without consulting the library.

While administrators have discussed the need for expansion of library facilities in the Information Age, students have increasingly incorporated Web materials into their research strategies. John Lubans has found that middle and high school students in a summer program are more likely than current Duke University freshmen to rely heavily on Web sources for their research and feel more confident in performing Web searches without librarian assistance.[6] As new generations of students reach college age with growing experience and skill in using Internet resources, print resources may seem increasingly staid and uninteresting, their intellectual value notwithstanding.

The library facility has been generally perceived by the academic community as a place for research, study and the storage of collections. While automated systems, databases and bibliographic instruction have been seen as welcome enhancements, they have largely been viewed as initiatives requiring, at most, rewiring of facilities. In an information environment characterized by increasing use of electronic databases and the World Wide Web, the case for expansion of library facilities can be difficult to make. In many instances, administrators may see investment in technology-enhanced classrooms and wired dormitories as a better investment for bringing electronic resources closer to the student end-user.

It is the position of this paper that library facilities, as well as electronic resources, new services and expert staff, are crucial to the future of academic libraries. Indeed, if technology-enhanced library facilities are not developed through new building projects, additions, and renovations of existing buildings, the library's historic function of providing systematic access to validated knowledge will slowly be undermined. In addition, the library will become increasingly marginalized as information users access Web resources from other locations through Internet service providers. At the same time, librarians must not overlook the importance of the traditional library to many of our stakeholders. Although humanities and social sciences faculty are becoming increasingly comfortable with electronic resources, they are the core constituency supporting the intellectual function of the library in the college or university. In short, it is important to provide the platform necessary for future information services without alienating the library's traditional constituency.

Librarians face three challenges in making the case for new, expanded or renovated buildings. First, they must demonstrate the need for improved facilities in terms of larger institutional objectives, such as expanded enrollment. In this context, they must demonstrate that emerging librarian roles and competencies are essential for institutional and academic success. Second, they must demonstrate the "value-added" contribution of improved library facilities to institutional objectives. Third, they must develop a new model for the academic library building in the 21st century, one, which redefines "the library as place," rather than arguing for a larger and newer facility doing the same things.

This position paper describes the experience of a medium-sized academic library in advancing the "Library of the Future" concept as a strategy for creating a state-of-the-art, transformational library. It identifies the library's efforts to align the building project with broader institutional objectives, such as economic development and expanded enrollment. It addresses the political issues encountered in persuading administration, faculty, physical plant and technical experts to "buy into" the library's vision. It will analyze both successes and failures encountered in the use of that strategy.

Penn State Harrisburg Case Study

Efforts to secure funding for a new library building at Penn State Harrisburg were initiated in 1978, when a metal "Butler building" annex was connected to the existing facility to accommodate collection expansion for an anticipated five years. Following prolonged efforts to secure State funding, design of a new library was begun in early 1996, with construction starting August 31, 1998. Occupancy is anticipated in January 2000. The evolution of this project from a simple expansion of library space into a "Library of the Future" offers an informative case study, one in which a new building model has been utilized to mobilize institutional support and to align the library with broader institutional objectives while providing a technology-enhanced environment for 21st century students.

Founded in 1966, Penn State Harrisburg is an upper-division and graduate college located on the site of a decommissioned Air Force base site in Middletown, PA, nine miles from the State Capitol in downtown Harrisburg. It offers 25 baccalaureate, 17 master's degree, and 2 doctoral programs to its 3600 students, 55 percent of whom hold full-time jobs and 24 percent of whom work part-time. Its undergraduate students are primarily graduates of Harrisburg Area Community College and various two-year Penn State campuses. Its programs are focused in five schools: Behavioral Sciences and Education; Business Administration; Humanities; Public Affairs; and Science, Engineering and Technology.

The college has a strong commitment to community outreach and economic development as important components of its mission and as one college in a land-grant institution. It is actively engaged in a number of economic development organizations, and its faculty members have developed a strong network of relationships with state government, school districts, corporations and businesses, and non-profit organizations.

Although its enrollment has increased steadily in the 1990s, the College faces significant local competition for students from a number of distant institutions offering center-based programs in high-demand areas, such as business administration, information systems and education. The College also faces a challenge from the long-time mayor of Harrisburg, who has repeatedly campaigned for a four-year institution within the city limits of Harrisburg.

The Penn State Harrisburg library holds the third largest collection among Penn State's 27 libraries. Its 251,000 volumes, 1557 periodical subscriptions and 1.1 million microforms are surpassed only by the Paterno/Pattee Library at the University Park campus and the Dickinson School of Law Library. In addition, the library offers its students access to more than 160 databases, most of them funded centrally by University Libraries. As a member of the Associated College Libraries of Central Pennsylvania (ACLCP), the library is able to offer PSH students reciprocal borrowing privileges at 21 other academic libraries in the region. Ironically, the current Heindel Library receives significant use by students from Penn State Harrisburg's distant, non-ACLCP competitors, many of whom have launched academic programs in the Harrisburg area without providing significant library collections or services.

A draft program statement for a library/classroom building was completed in 1986, the first year that a library for Penn State Harrisburg was included in Penn State's request for capital funding from state government. This document envisioned the new library as the centerpiece of a campus mall. In addition to library facilities, the building would include classrooms and might include an auditorium or an art gallery, depending on size. However, the project suffered successive line-item vetoes from the governor in 1986, 1988 and 1990, while moving gradually upward on Penn State's capital projects priority list. It was clear that both political support and a more compelling vision were needed to secure funding.

The initial step toward development of that vision was a concept paper, entitled "Toward a Library of the Future," drafted in early 1992 by the library director. Recognizing the building project as an opportunity for transformational enhancement of collections and services in a medium-sized library, the concept paper argued that the new library should anticipate and accommodate new technologies and formats as paralleling print collection growth in importance. In short, it took the position that the academic "clout" of the new library could be increased profoundly through creative use of technology, rather than incremental improvement and enhancement of space.

This paper was shared with the Task Force on the New Library, an ad hoc committee appointed by the Provost to generate support for passage of funding for the new building. The committee endorsed this document, which recognized that development of a more extensive, in-depth print collection was unlikely within the library's acquisitions budget, while viewing sharply increased use of the Internet and electronic databases as an appropriate strategy for expanded access to information . Copies of the paper were sent to all state legislators that year as part of an informational packet encouraging funding for the new library.

The "Library of the Future" vision was given a significant boost in Summer 1992, when a capital campaign feasibility study recommended that the College establish a "unique niche" in order to raise funds. The report noted that there were numerous academic libraries in Central Pennsylvania and that major donors had already given to many of them. In order to raise the funds needed for an expected "match" of state construction money, a different focus would be needed. The Library viewed this assessment as legitimizing the technology-focused vision developed earlier that year, and the "Library of the Future" concept was used consistently thereafter as a focal construct.

Following a shift in party control of the state Senate in November 1992, a capital budget bill including the new library was passed, with a funding level set at $17.33 million. The library project survived the Governor's line-item veto and received funding authorization in late December 1992. That action placed the project in a queue of approved projects awaiting the release of funding. Design and construction funds were finally released on January 13, 1995, Democratic Governor Robert P. Casey's last full day in office.

While the College awaited the release of project funds, the library director was asked in February 1993 to prepare a program statement in two weeks. With substantial input from library faculty and staff, a 44-page program statement had been completed by late 1993. This program statement retained the campus enhancement focus of the 1986 document, but expanded upon it to propose a facility in which print and electronic resources would have parallel importance. The document included several new features, such as: data access from all seats in the building; a state-of-the-art library instruction lab; a document delivery/ copying center; and a 24-hour reading room.

In addition, the new program statement included the Pennsylvania State Data Center (PSDC) Operations Unit as the only non-library unit to be housed in the facility. The State Data Center is the major unit providing analysis of demographic and economic Census data for businesses, state government agencies and non-profit organizations in Pennsylvania, responding to 12,000+ data requests annually. The Library sought the inclusion of the State Data Center, rather than the Computer Center, Audio-Visual Services or an auditorium, in the building to provide a unique partnership which would advance the College's economic development mission. So far as the College is aware, this is the only collocation of an academic library and state data center under the same roof in the United States. The addition of the State Data Center should promote a unique, symbiotic partnership between two major information utilities. It also underscores the Library's commitment to the College's economic development mission.

The appropriateness of the "Library of the Future" vision was further reinforced in September 1994, when the library director visited the new Indiana University-Purdue University at Indianapolis (IUPUI) Library. Opened in fall 1993, the IUPUI library was the first large academic library in the United States to offer data access (CAT-3 and fiber optic cable) at every seat to students. The IUPUI director, Barbara Fischler, described the development of the vision for that library and offered ongoing encouragement over the next few years for implementation of the PSH vision. Photos taken during the IUPUI visit were used to demonstrate the possibilities for ubiquitous access to electronic databases and the Internet at PSH.

A formal Program Committee, appointed by the University Provost and including Penn State Physical Plant and Telecommunications officials, was appointed to develop and refine the existing program statement. This committee, chaired by a retired colonel serving as Special Assistant to the Penn State Harrisburg Provost, completed its work between January and June 1995. The Library Director, the Head of Public Services and the Associate Dean of University Libraries for Planning and Administration represented the library on a twelve-person team. Most of the facilities included in the library draft were retained, but an Art Gallery/Reception Hall was added to address the College's need for art displays and an elegant setting for receptions. The 24-hour reading room was eliminated due to low projected demand from commuter students, while the document delivery/copying center was eliminated for staffing and copyright reasons. Ubiquitous access to power and data from all seats was retained, as was the State Data Center. Telecommunication officials, who maintained that unshielded twisted pair category 5 (UTP CAT-5) wiring was the industry standard, were persuaded to allow the inclusion of fiber optic wiring to the desktop as a bid alternate.

Selection of an architect could not proceed until the newly elected administration of Governor Thomas P. Ridge, a Republican, had appointed an Architectural Selection Board in July 1995. The Board announced the project in the *Pennsylvania Bulletin* in October, and 80 bids from architectural firms were submitted. The unusually large interest in the project was significantly attributable to the Library of the Future focus, providing an early indication that the project would receive substantial visibility in the library community. Following interviews with the top five bidders, the joint venture team of Shepley Bulfinch Richardson Abbott (SBRA) of Boston and Hayes Large (HL) of Altoona and Harrisburg received the design award. The design process was completed between February 1996 and April 1997.

The architectural team successfully delivered the facility design anticipated in the Library of the Future vision. One creative enhancement during the design phase was the upgrading of the snack bar to an "Internet Café" or CyberCafe. Data and power access were provided at 92% of all general user seats, a raised floor was planned to permit easy rearrangement of the library instruction lab and two technology-enhanced classrooms, and video ports were added for the Art Gallery/Reception Hall, two seminar rooms, the library instruction lab and two technology-enhanced classrooms. A 115,000 square foot building with more than 700 seats, extensive seating in natural light areas, and an aesthetically pleasing curve was created.

Consensus Building

The advancement of the Library of the Future vision over a multi-year period required attention to political issues, as well as technological advances occurring while the funding campaign, program statement development, and building design were taking place. Three distinctive political phases in the mobilization of academic community support for this vision can be distinguished during 1992-97 period.

First, it was important to build as much community consensus as possible during the early, pre-Web years of this period. The academic community did not universally accept the Library of the Future concept during this period. Humanities faculty, among the strongest supporters of the existing library and the need for a new facility, were not initially enthusiastic about a project giving substantial focus to Internet and electronic resources. Numerous articles articulating the vision were published in the library's newsletter during this period to increase understanding and build support for a different type of library.

Nevertheless, some faculty continued to express concern about the direction in which the project was proceeding. As a result, the Penn State Harrisburg Provost appointed an ad hoc committee, excluding the library director and chaired by a European History professor, in spring 1994 to review the library draft of the program statement. After receiving consulting input from the University Libraries' Associate Dean for Planning and Administration, the committee concluded that the focus was generally appropriate. This endorsement substantially legitimized the Library of the Future concept. However, faculty input in the library director's fifth-year review, in fall 1995, still indicated that the vision did not enjoy universal support.

Ironically, the 1995-96 flowering of the World Wide Web, a technological advance that threatens libraries in some ways, served to quietly vindicate the library's vision. Although one faculty complaint about the need to focus on "the library of the present" appeared in the student newspaper, criticism of the futuristic vision largely evaporated as students and faculty made increasing use of the Web and new electronic databases, such as Lexis-Nexis and ProQuest, offered by the library. The library also recognized the need to make the facility welcoming to users at all levels of comfort with technology. Library Faculty offered approximately 250 Electronic Resources workshops in the 1995–96 year.

The library also began referring to the new building as a "hybrid print/electronic facility," reassuring traditional supporters that the printed book and journal would not be relegated to marginal status. Regional visibility was secured for the first time in August 1996, when a three-page article on "The Library of the Future" was included as one of four projects impacting the area's future in a "Harrisburg—A City on the Move" section of a widely read public television magazine.[7] The Library continued to use its own newsletter as a vehicle for communicating the concept within the academic environment and to interested community members, such as the College's Board of Advisers.

Finally, as the April 1998 groundbreaking and the August 31, 1998 construction start approached, a few faculty and students began questioning the need for a new library since "everything's on the Internet." At this point, it became essential for library personnel to draw distinctions between the higher-quality subscription material offered in library databases and the unfiltered information available on the Internet. Although the library's bibliographic instruction program was already emphasizing critical thinking about electronic resources, the quality distinctions needed to be explained often to Internet enthusiasts inside and outside the library. The library director also tailored his groundbreaking ceremony remarks to clarify and reinforce the vision of a hybrid print/electronic library.

The phrase "visible signs of progress" has been used to emphasize the positive visual impact made upon individuals by physical change. The importance of the facility for the College's future became dramatically evident in December 1998, when the erection of the building's structural steel framework began. Project supporters and doubters alike were amazed by the building's massive scale, which makes it slightly taller than the old, three-story Air Force classroom building in which the majority of College classes are held. A unique uplifting of morale College-wide was observable, as administrators, faculty, students and staff recognized that the building would both provide a first-rate research environment and make an impressive statement to potential students, the community and the Mayor of Harrisburg. Plans were initiated to level a low hill partially obscuring views of the library from the main entrance road, thereby making it visible from all parts of the campus as a landmark building. Central University funding for five new positions was made the College's top budgetary priority in its 1998–99 strategic plan update.

In The Meantrime...Advancing Library Services
A bold vision cannot be implemented readily if the library is not already showing itself to be an innovative organization. The Penn State Harrisburg library undertook a number of initiatives in the 1990s to permit the delivery of strong, technology-enhanced services even as plans for the new library were being developed.

Four innovative librarians comfortable with technology were recruited between 1992 and 1995. Two of these librarians assumed positions, Electronic Services Reference Librarian and Public Affairs/Government Information Librarian, restructured when existing reference positions became vacant. The Electronic Services Reference Librarian: 1) upgraded equipment, replacing dumb terminals with PCs with printers; 2) Implemented a Novell LAN providing access from one menu to the OPAC, online databases, CD-ROM databases, and the Internet; and 3) created a Web page focused around subject linkages to high-quality Web sites. The Public Affairs/Government Information Librarian developed a strategy for systematic access to government information in a non-depository library in 1995 and 1996.[8]

A new Head of Public Services was appointed chair of the Electronic Services Task Force, which embarked upon a major print index cancellation project in Fall 1994 and replaced those indexes with online databases. This project was so successful that the cancellation of 24 print indexes was accomplished without a recorded complaint. The Head of Public Services also launched a broad, continually-evolving series of Electronic Resources workshops to familiarize users with new databases and the Internet, while also increasing their comfort levels with these resources. A new Business Reference Librarian assumed leadership for the library portion of the American Association of Collegiate Schools of Business Administration (AACSB) accreditation effort, resulting in full accreditation of the College's master's and baccalaureate programs in Spring 1998.

The library's strategy of complementing print resources with access to relevant Web sites and electronic databases drew favorable review from the accreditation team.

The contributions of these four librarians helped to create a climate conducive to the implementation of the Library of the Future vision. Had the implementation of innovative programs been deferred, it is likely that fewer positions would have been requested from the University budget and other units would have placed claims on vacant spaces in the new facility, such as group study rooms.

Advancing Institutional Objectives

Penn State Harrisburg's Library of the Future was planned to address a broad array of institutional needs. As library personnel repeatedly advanced the vision, the College leadership gradually came to view the new facility as an academic enhancement, a recruiting tool, an economic development resource and a political asset in the regional higher education context.

The academic benefits of the new library will become evident shortly after it is opened in early 2000. Students will have ample, comfortable spaces for individual and collaborative study, and the facility will seat 20% of the student body at any one time. Faculty and graduate carrels will be available for the first time. A state-of-the-art instruction lab on raised flooring will provide workstations for 35 students and flexibility for easy room reconfiguration. Laptop users will have access to data and power at 92% of all seats.

Despite the rapid increase in Web use among prospective students, recruitment officials still report that students expect a strong library. While collections and services remain important, a state-of-the-art facility makes a bold statement about the institution's commitment to embrace new technologies and to support technologically sophisticated students with rising expectations. Meetings with recruitment personnel are being planned to familiarize them with the new library and to alert library staff to the recruitment opportunities provided by the new building. Librarian selectors will continue to give brief candidate tours as part of the faculty recruitment process. Both printed brochures and visitor tours are being developed. The Library will be featured on the cover of the 1999-2000 catalog and on the College's Web page. Increasingly, the library facility is being recognized as a major asset for both student and faculty recruitment, and College officials are giving it prominent attention in their presentations.

Regional visibility is a third College need. As an upper-division and graduate college that has discontinued intercollegiate sports, Penn State Harrisburg is at an inherent disadvantage in contacting high school seniors and gaining attention in the local media. However, the library project has received periodic attention from the Harrisburg *Patriot-News* newspaper, and relevant articles have been scanned onto the Library's Web page. A January 1994 ice-damming incident, which caused moisture damage to 400 bound periodicals, was covered by two area television stations. The *Central Pennsylvania APPRISE* article provided welcome publicity in 1996. Extensive television coverage was received for the April 30, 1998 groundbreaking.

The building opening and dedication ceremonies will provide excellent opportunities for media coverage in spring 2000. A major symposium celebrating the Library's opening is tentatively planned for that year. Since the library will be open to the community, it is expected to receive significant use from high school students and adult learners. These students, in turn, may boost the College's enrollment by transferring to Penn State Harrisburg for upper-division or graduate programs or share favorable word-of-mouth reactions with their friends.

The Pennsylvania State Data Center (PSDC) was the only non-library unit actively sought by the Library as a building occupant. Its presence was considered desirable to support the College's economic development and academic missions. Substantial referrals between the Data Center and the Library already occur even though they are in separate buildings. Their physical presence in the same building is expected to promote a unique symbiosis, which will increase business, government, nonprofit and general public use of both facilities. This use, in turn, should promote greater outside funding support for both organizations.

By introducing a wired Art Gallery and Reception Hall, the Library sought to address a variety of cultural, educational and social needs. The Gallery will present a much-needed, elegant location for receptions and art exhibits. With data and video ports installed, the Gallery can also be converted into site for videoconferences or on-site programs. By making it multifunctional, the Library has both aligned itself with College needs and made itself the delivery site for them.

The only facility "imposed" on the Library is the art slide library, now housed in the School of Humanities. The College Provost asked that it be relocated into the new library to provide longer hours of service and College-wide access. The slide library will be housed in a room originally designated for seminars, while the seminar room will displace a planned general reading area.

Finally, as the second largest (behind the State Library) and most technologically advanced library within a 20-mile radius of the State Capitol, the new facility will be a major political asset for College's initiatives to discourage creation of a University of Harrisburg. The presence of a substantial, state-of-the-art library can demonstrate that the College is much more than a "commuter college" which cannot address broad educational needs in the Capital Region. If it is successful in enhancing the College's visibility and reputation, the Library will help confirm that, in combination, Harrisburg Area Community College and Penn State Harrisburg really do constitute a four-year institution serving regional needs.

Building Features

When completed, the Library of the Future will seat more than 20 percent of the College's 3600 students and provide 26.6 years of growth space for print collections. It will provide data and power at 92 percent of its 700+ seats, enabling students to access both print and electronic information at nearly every seat. Raised flooring in the library instruction lab and technology-enhanced classroom permits flexible reconfiguration of seating arrangements, thereby facilitating both formal and collaborative learning.

The building also offers a CyberCafe where students can relax with a snack while continuing their research. Twelve video ports will permit the delivery of videoconference programs in six different locations. In addition, the building walls are modular, allowing for redesign of many areas to address future use requirements. This facility will be 3-1/2 times the size of the current library and will have approximately five times as much seating, most of it wired for data and power.

The only real disappointment in the experience has been the State's rejection of a request that unactivated fiber optic cabling be run to all data ports alongside CAT-5 wiring. However, the State did agree to run parallel pathways for a later installation of fiber optic cable, and that is being done in construction. While it would have made a later fiber installation unnecessary, this partial setback is not devastating, since the campus backbone currently supports transmission of only 4.5 mbps of data, with an expected increase to 30 mbps in several years. Since the necessary pathways are being installed, a later fiber installation can be accomplished without excessive inconvenience.

While the facility will be a major academic asset for the College, its larger significance for the library community is twofold. First, its unique combination of multifunctional and technology-enhanced spaces should permit it to be a center of excellence supporting academic programs well into the 21st century. Second, its careful inclusion of facilities which address broader College goals is an instance of strategic positioning to enable the library to be a central player in future college planning. This combination of technological enhancement and strategic alignment can both demonstrate the library's continued relevance in the Information Age and enable it to remain a vital center of the academic community, even as information access becomes increasingly decentralized.

The "library as place" in the 21st century can continue to be a physical place for access to selected print materials. It can provide a safe, nonthreatening environment for individual and collaborative learning, user training, reference assistance, and preservation. It can be a gateway to the Web and electronic databases, providing a place where print and electronic research can be conducted side-by-side. It can retain its symbolic value as the centerpiece of learning on a campus while evolving to accommodate new technologies, new formats, Web-savvy students and new learning strategies. By strategically positioning itself to utilize technology and to creatively address broad institutional needs, the library can remain a robust academic entity while also establishing its importance as an asset for the pursuit of institutional goals. The building project offers an important opportunity to create a hybrid print/electronic learning environment serving future instructional and research needs. It is also an opportunity to make the library an essential resource for the attainment of institutional goals.

The "Library of the Future" focus has served Penn State Harrisburg well by defining a new, relevant model for 21st century library service and by enhancing the institution's stature in the region. Other libraries may be able to attain similar prominence in their institutions' planning through the infusion of information technology into their buildings and by careful alignment with institutional strategies. This approach will preserve the best of past library experience while alerting administrators to new, supportive institutional roles.

Notes

1. See, for example, Derek J. de Solla Price, *Little Science, Big Science* (New York: Columbia Univ. Pr., 1963); Diana Crane, *Invisible Colleges: Diffusion of Knowledge in Scientific Communities* (Chicago: Univ. of Chicago Pr., 1972); and William D. Garvey, *Communication, the Essence of Science: Facilitating Information Exchange among Librarians, Scientists, Engineers, and Students* (New York: Pergamon Pr., 1979).

2. For an early assessment of the challenge from alternative media, see Judith Axler Turner, "Campus Libraries Seen Threatened by Other Sources of Information," *The Chronicle of Higher Education*, vol. 31 (December 4, 1985), 30.

3. See John R. Sack, "Open Systems for Open Minds: Building the Library Without Walls," *College & Research Libraries*, vol. 47, no. 6 (November 1986), 535–44; see also Laverna M. Saunders, "The Virtual Library Today," *Library Administration & Management*, vol. 6, no. 2 (spring 1992), 66–70.

4. Brian Hawkins, "The Unsustainability of Traditional Libraries," *Executive Strategies*, vol. 2, no. 3 (1996), 1–15.

5. David L. Wilson. "New California State Campus Has Ambitious Plans for Technology," *The Chronicle of Higher Education*, vol. 43 (October 18, 1996), A23–24.

6. John Lubans Jr., "Key Findings on Internet Use among Students" (1998) [online]. Available: http://www.lib.duke.edu/staff/orgnztn/lubans/key.html. Accessed: February 26, 1999.

7. Philip K. Eberly, "Library of the Future," *Central Pennsylvania's APPRISE*, vol. 16, no. 2 (August 1996), 53–55.

8. Harold B. Shill and Lisa R. Stimatz, "Government Information in Academic Libraries: New Options for the Electronic Age," *Journal of Academic Librarianship*, vol. 25, no. 2 (1999), forthcoming.

Students Versus the Research Paper: What Can We Learn?

Barbara Valentine

Abstract

If we are to develop library services that meet the expectations of our patrons in this changing technological environment, we must first understand how they currently interact with our information services and systems. This paper presents preliminary results from a qualitative study that elicits perspectives of undergraduates engaged in writing research papers. Because this study has been in progress since the early nineties, results also reflect ways in which technological advances such as the Internet may have altered strategies. Findings highlight some commonly used information gathering strategies, issues which impact motivation and use of time, and sources of help students consult most often in the process. Implications and recommendations for librarians conclude the paper.

I came here with the attitude, oh god, if I don't get an A, I'm hosed. But I sorta like looked at people and thought, "listen, it's too much stress on my body to worry about something that's going to be difficult to get." Learn what you can and put out enough effort that you need to get by. I want to do good work, but if I'm not interested, it's like I don't want to be here. Problem is you have to do it to get out of here. Have to do it to get that rubber stamp that says,

"I'm educated. Next! Next!" You're educated and you walk out into the world. It's a big assembly line. They don't even give you a real diploma. They give you some blank piece of paper. I'm not gonna kill myself over 4 years of school or 5 or 6. I just want to have fun while I'm here and learn a lot. (TD)

Introduction

This is the voice of a junior describing his overall

Barbara Valentine is reference and systems librarian, Linfield College.

university experience. He raises issues that were echoed over and over again in the present study. Students come into the institution with anxiety about grades. They note a disparity between what they want to learn and what is required to graduate. Over time, they learn what they have to do to satisfy both the institution and themselves. They make decisions about how much effort they will invest in various parts along the way to meet both their academic and personal expectations for the undergraduate experience.

When it comes to research, there is a similar disparity between what librarians provide in services and what students seem to want.[1] Rapid changes in technology demand that librarians rethink the usefulness of current services and modify or completely change them to work in the new electronic research dynamic. The more academic librarians know about how undergraduates relate to the information gathering process, the better able they will be to design effective services.

Relevant Research

In 1989[2], when the author first started conducting focus groups, there was little research in the library literature on student perspectives with the important exception of Mellon's[3] study on library anxiety and Kuhlthau's work[4] on the information search process. Fortunately, a decade later, research on the user perspective is more commonplace. Most of these studies focus on library-centered activities such as database searching,[5] reference,[6,7,8] bibliographic instruction,[9] attitudes toward librarians and services,[10,11] and, more recently, on use of digital libraries,[12,13] and the Internet.[14,15] Few studies[16] consider what impact the larger academic environment has specifically on undergraduate research behaviors. The current study is an attempt to add to that research. By looking at how students complete a research assignment from the perspective of the classroom experience, we may gain new insights about motivations and strategies.

Methodology

In 1993,[17] the author interviewed 28 undergraduates, either in focus groups or individually, about how they accomplished the task of completing a substantial research paper during the course of a particular class. The study was repeated with 31 students in 1998. The 59 participants represented at least a third of the students enrolled in each of 9 different classes in academic institutions in the Pacific Northwest—4 classes from a large state university and 5 from two different small private colleges. Course professors from each class also answered questions about expectations and what, in their view, students delivered. A preliminary questionnaire gathered information on other factors such as major, class standing, and GPA. By gender, there were 25 males and 34 females. By class there were 34 seniors, 16 juniors, and 9 sophomores. The average GPA of volunteers was 3.25 with college students averaging slightly higher than the university students. Five students interviewed were non-traditional age. Except for one Asian American and two Hispanic Americans, all participants were Caucasian, which is fairly representative of the ethnic breakdown in the classes as a whole (see tables 1 and 2).

The author avoided asking students any direct questions about the library, preferring to let those responses come from the context of the experience. Using Kuhlthau's Information Search Process as a framework for the interview questions, she probed instead the thoughts, feelings and actions of the students at the beginning, middle and ending stages of the research process. She also asked students whom they consulted and, if the issue was not raised naturally elsewhere, whether or not there had been library instruction. Focus group interviews worked well at eliciting fresh perspectives, while the individual interviews added support to those perspectives and provided more context.

This research is very much a work in progress. Transcriptions of interviews were coded using qualitative software called Atlas.ti and are being analyzed according to standard grounded theory procedures.[18] This paper will present some preliminary observations of the most commonly used strategies for gathering resources, specific institutional and classroom issues that seem to impact motivation and use of time, and a discussion about whom students consult most often in the process. Implications for the library field in general and reference librarians in particular will follow.

Table 1. Undergraduate Profile					
University students					
4 classes	Subjects	Class	Major	Gender	GPA
1993 (2 classes)	14 (1 adult)*	11 Senior 3 Junior	14 History	5 F 9 M	2.91
1998 (2 classes)	11 (1 adult) *	8 Senior 3 Junior	5 Music 6 Human Dev/ Family Services	8 F 3 M	3.34
total	25 (2 adult) *	19 Senior, 6 Junior		13 F 12 M	3.13
College students					
5 classes	Subjects	Class	Major	Gender	GPA
1993 (2 classes)	14 (1 adult)*	10 Senior 3 Junior 1 Sophomore	11 History, 2 Education 1 Commun.	8 F 7 M	3.37
1998 (3 classes)	20 (2 adult)*	5 Senior 7 Junior 8 Sophomore	4 Art, 4 Psychology, 7 Political Sci, 1 Classics, 1 Religion, 1 Music, 1 Exercise Sci, 1 Business	13 F 7 M	3.38
total	34 (3 adult)*	15 Senior 10 Junior 9 Sophomore		21 F 14 M	3.375
*nontraditional age					

Gathering Sources

Although students demonstrated individual styles and attitudes toward the project at hand when gathering resources for the paper, some aspects of the process were quite common. Most described

Table 2. Professors			
	University	College	Dept
1993	2 Male	2 Male	History
1998	1 Male 1 Female	1 Male 2 Female	Art Music Sociology Education Political Science

the information gathering stage of the process as they might describe a trip to the store. They expected to be able to find what they needed within a particular framework of time and were frustrated when this was difficult or the results unsatisfactory. It is true that a certain number enjoyed browsing through books and journals, especially in pursuit of a topic, but even these students noted this activity was at the cost of other pending commitments. So from the beginning most students were pressed for time.

As might have been predicted using Kuhlthau's[19] research model, the information gathering and focus phases were the most traumatic in the process, eliciting the strongest negative feelings. It is no wonder then that students, in order to alleviate uncertainty and confusion, leaned toward strategies that were most familiar to them. They might try scanning relevant textbooks or papers and books from previous courses. Some tried to locate specific items suggested by professors or librarians in classes. Others browsed the online catalog or another database they had used in the past. Some hopped onto a familiar search engine such as Yahoo. Having something in hand gave students the most immediate relief. In fact, a few in one focus group mentioned that they would modify the topic to match what they found in the home library because getting things from other libraries was too uncertain and time intensive.

Though most did use the home library, many said they went to other libraries, often a public library, because it was smaller, more familiar, closer to home or because a friend knew that library and helped them do the research. Students also used other libraries to avoid competition for books with classmates working in the same subject area.

When these familiar paths did not pan out adequately, most moved into the unfamiliar realms in a disorderly fashion, best described as chaotic. Things were found "in random places," by "luck," "stumbling around," "by accident," or "by trial and error." One sophomore admitted:

> "Basically I stumbled into everything I found and maybe I wasn't really looking for it, but I stumbled into it." (LH)

Most students did not distinguish among the databases they used to find articles and books, simply referring to "the computer" as the place they went for everything. When pressed, they mentioned the online catalog, but few could be certain of the periodical databases used. Of those who could talk about a specific database experience, many used them in ways librarians might find less than effective. For instance, one student used MLA to find articles on Hitler. Another preferred to search ERIC for ED rather than EJ records and spent $20 in photocopies because she discovered the microfiche was all located in the same place, obviating the hassle of going up and downstairs in the quest for journals. Similarly students relished finding full text articles wherever possible since they not only saved time locating journals, but also money on photocopying costs. Frustration doing research was echoed constantly:

> "I hate [the library]. It is the most overwhelming place on campus. I have no idea where anything is or how to use anything. And everything changes all the time, especially here with everything under construction. It's like I think it's useless. I can't find anything so I just don't want to come in here and was really relieved when I got it done." (SB)

In sum, research energies are focussed on the familiar and convenient perhaps at the expense of the most relevant.

Enter the web

Although all the students interviewed in 1998 mentioned searching the Internet at some point in the project, most of them did not use research retrieved from search engines such as Yahoo or Alta Vista. Many complained that their surfing experiences for reliable information in the past had not been cost effective in terms of time and results. This was a typical response:

> "But I didn't use Lycos or any of the search engines on the web because I knew I wouldn't find anything. I never find the right things when I search on the web like that. It takes hours…so the web isn't really an option for me." (KW)

More often students tried specific web links mentioned by professors or presented by librarians in instruction sessions. Even with the expected relevance of these pages, students had varied success. They complained about the quality and depth of materials they found or that they had trouble narrowing the search.

The advent of one stop web shopping may have increased the likelihood of students hitting pay dirt. But it has also added to the confusion about the kinds of sources students are retrieving. Typical library web sites now feature the online catalog, library-purchased databases, electronic journals, and other web sites that are equally selectable from a single list. One student was totally confused by the journal situation in the library due to this integration.

> "I went into the library's web site and they have resources there. With the search engines for journals that are available on that web site, there is also a listing of electronic journals. I just perused the titles of these journals and it didn't look like there was a single thing that matched my topic. I was also kind of confused. Was this everything that was available to me [on the Internet] or is that just what the library knows about?" (AD)

Motivations

Students in this study appeared to put forth varying degrees of effort for an assignment depending on several institutional and class specific factors which had little to do with the library itself, but impacted their activities there.

Grades

Grades are a fact of academic life and had a large impact on the research process in this study. Howard Becker and others, who conducted a two-year qualitative study of student activity at the University of Kansas, discovered that grades are the "currency of campus," "the main institutionally recognized commodity in the academic community."[20] Although most professors in this study intended that the research papers give students the opportunity to explore intellectual spheres outside the range of class discussion, the bottom line for most students was the grade.

There were a handful of students who de-emphasized the grade as the most important factor in the process. They pointed to the value of the assignment outside of school or their interest in learning. But even students with the highest GPA's still saw the bottom line as the grade.

> "I like to do well on everything I write, so the grade really had a lot of influence. If I had more time, I would have liked to do more...Actually the grade does have a good effect on me cause it gets me going. I know that deadline for the grade is when the axe drops." (AE)

Students agreed that the best way to get a good grade was to focus on what the professor wanted and most students spent considerable emotional capital and time trying to solve this sometimes enigmatic puzzle. For some, the key to getting good grades was the relationship one developed with the course professor. Those who did not know the professor from a previous class felt the pressure to make a good impression for the future.

> "I'm not going to get what [grade] I feel I deserve...I have not [had him before] so I think I have to win his trust and have to go through that initiation with him." (NE)

Many students tried to guess what the professor wanted by paying attention to clues dropped in class, what was written in the syllabus, or by consulting the collective wisdom of classmates. These students focussed on assignment specific features such as how many pages constituted a "legitimate effort."

Surprisingly, most students did not ask the professor direct questions about the assignment. One professor, who had set time aside in class for just this purpose, remarked on how few students consulted her. Even students who talked with professors were careful to note that these relationships were built around other conversations having little to do with a particular assignment.

Class standing

There was a noticeable difference in the attitudes and strategies of the 9 sophomores in this study compared to the juniors and seniors. Although freshmen were not interviewed, comments by seniors who reminisced about their freshmen year indicate that sophomores and freshmen do share more in common than the upper division students.

> "I really feel if we were doing research when I was a freshman it would be completely different because now I am confident writing research papers. I know what I'm doing and I know what [the professor] wants. That's something that I've learned and acquired over the 4 years here. I know when I was a freshman I was scared to death." (MB)

Lower division students are all in the process of trying to figure out how to succeed in college. The sophomores tended to be more anxious about the paper assignment throughout the process than the upper division students in their classes. Many of them had never written a paper of any consequence before and had trouble finding and narrowing topics. They would obsess more about the weight of the paper on the course grade and how the professor would view the product. They were just developing their GPA's and establishing their strategies for accomplishing academic work. One student explained:

> "I'm a sophomore and this is judgement year!" (DS)

In contrast, juniors and especially seniors were more confident. Upper division students often had smaller classes, more focus in one discipline area, and some relationship with the course professor. They had well-established strategies for accomplishing academic work and had figured out what they could let slide and where they had to concentrate time. Seniors especially seemed to put more effort into those assignments that had relevance to their future employment, were good preparation for graduate school or would weigh heavily on their GPA's. In fact, when an assignment had little weight or was otherwise uninteresting, they might blow it off with little effort. "Senioritis" was mentioned over and over again across classes as a very real disease, especially in the Spring weather.

While the lower division students were becoming entrenched in academic life, then, the upper division students were looking toward leaving.

Other institutional factors
Several other institutional factors surfaced which need further development.

First, students engaged in many activities outside academic work. Employment, both on and off campus, sports, campus organizations, and musical and theatre performance can take lots of time. It would be interesting to see what proportion of time students on average allot to academic work.

The quarter system limits the time students can spend on a substantial research paper. This especially constrains the time available for research exploration, false starts, and Interlibrary loan requests. On the other hand, the semester system, while affording more time for Interlibrary loan, did not seem to change significantly the effort put into papers in this study. In fact, in one class, a professor required a bibliography early on urging students to spend the rest of the semester preparing the paper. Most of the students in that class said they submitted the bibliography and then put the paper on the back burner until the end of the term.

For this study, it was difficult finding classes which required a substantial research paper, especially at the university, despite the fact that the general curriculum in all institutions emphasizes more writing intensive classes now than it did in 1993. Larger class size seems to be partly to blame. A study is needed to determine if fewer research papers are being assigned and what, if any, impact this might have on undergraduate research.

Students have gained increased timely access to books from other libraries as a result of patron-initiated consortial borrowing through union catalogs such as OhioLink. Those undergraduates interviewed in 1998, who came from schools with small library collections, used the union catalog as much or more than the local catalog to do research. Undeniably a boon to research, this access also increased information overload, overdue fines, and possibly under-utilization of local collections.

Course specific issues
Issues relating to the presentation and support of a specific assignment also influenced the time and effort research received.

The clarity of guidelines and expectations for assignments and grading varied widely among professors. Student stress levels and time spent trying to guess at expectations increased when written guidelines were non-existent or vague.

Stress levels decreased in those classes where the professor provided a graded library assignment that introduced them to the range of resources they would use for the final paper. In these classes students seemed to take more ownership of the process and at the end appreciated the research experience more.

Topic choice was important to most students. Personal commitment to the assignment seemed to decrease as choice was denied, steered, or made very narrow by the professor. There were exceptions to this among sophomores who appreciated as much direction as possible.

Bibliographic instruction classes conducted by librarians were more meaningful when tied to the course assignment than provided as part of freshmen orientation. When successful, they provided an effective start to the research process, with both a list of resources and a friendly contact in the library. More students visited the librarians when they were promoted as experts by professors. When BI classes did not work for students it was because the sessions came too late in the research process and/or provided too much new information, adding stress rather than reducing it. Students, who had several sessions for different classes in a term or year, sometimes found them redundant, indistinguishable one from the other, and tuned them out.

Whom do they ask for help?
The literature on help-seeking is well-explored in the area of psychology and suggests that students have trouble asking experts for help.[21,22,23] This was true in this study as well. As noted earlier, although students spent a great deal of time trying to figure out what the professor wanted, very few asked direct questions about the assignment itself. When they did get help, it was usually as a result of a required meeting to approve a topic or hand in an outline.

Students indicated there was a certain amount of risk attached to contacting a course professor. Some students said they did not want the professor to see a draft, a messy version, of their paper or even really know what was on their minds until the work was complete. Others had heard "war" stories about unpleasant encounters with this professor and were simply too intimidated to initiate contact. Many mentioned that required meetings with professors often left them more confused than before the contact, with the added burden of having to find more information. Perhaps because grades were so much attached to the relationship with the professor, many wanted that relationship to be as positive as possible and exposing doubts was not the thing to do. Whatever the reason, for many, the professor was not an optimal choice to pursue help.

Apparently they did not like to ask librarians for help either. Only one third of the students mentioned asking a librarian or other library staff person for help in the library. Three of those students actually consulted friends who worked as student assistants in the library.

Expectations of library personnel seemed rather low. Students would ask for help in locating a specific book, journal, or Internet site, but more than that was considered "handholding." It was also acceptable to get help with a particular database such as Lexis/Nexis or the Internet at the suggestion of a professor or as a result of a BI session. They also expected to consult some experts, such as the government documents librarian, if one wanted anything in that area.

But students were generally reluctant to ask for general help, such as getting started with a topic or finding an appropriate database. Only four students admitted that consulting a librarian was the most efficient way for them to begin research. One noted:

> "I didn't even attempt to research [my topic]. I just went to the library assistant and said this is my topic can you help me find it and she...just put it in the computer. [I asked] just because I knew if I would have sat down at the computer it would have taken me hours to [find stuff]...I knew that she knew what she was doing..." (SB)

Some of those who did ask for help met with less success and did not get what they needed from library staff. Sometimes librarians were simply unable to meet specific requests, help out with a technical problem, or find the right articles. A few students had unhelpful experiences consulting non-librarians. In any case, these failures required time and indicated an inherent cost to asking for help in the library.

Many students in this study, however, were inclined to ask for assistance from more informal sources, such as friends, relatives, roommates, and classmates. They asked acquaintances for a whole range of help including ideas for selecting and even narrowing a topic, developing themes, locating relevant sources, providing keywords, and proofreading and editing, sometimes even typing, papers.

Classmates were the most popular source of help. They shared the same assignment and understood many things about what the professor wanted. They might be experienced at navigating the same computer systems and topics. Many classmates knew each other already, especially if they shared a major, and were a source of moral support. And in classes which had a mixture of upper and lower division students, those who knew the ropes could offer help to the novices.

It may not be surprising that students asked peers for help instead of experts, such as librarians and professors, at critical times in the process. Peers are more available since they travel the same institutional circles. It may be less emotionally risky to appear uninformed before a friend or classmate and, in fact, may even be a source of bonding.

It appears, then, that when students considered sources of help for research in this study, they selected the most familiar and cost effective first, moving to the more formal sources of help only in desperation. Yet this is perhaps too simplistic a view. Further exploration of current research on help-seeking and learning[24] may provide increased understanding of an undoubtedly complex issue.

Discussion

This research suggests that undergraduates generally set priorities for how much time and effort they can or will allot to a particular assignment. They start with familiar strategies that have worked for them before, which may or may not be effective for this project. Many do eschew popular Internet search engines for serious research, but that does not mean they hit the best library-purchased databases for their topics.

In general, they avoid asking for help, but in a bind they find it more comfortable and convenient to ask friends than professors and librarians. If one ever makes it to asking a librarian for help, that student, in most cases, has already tried a variety of approaches that have failed or provided little progress.

Implications and recommendations

A growing number of students have begun to do research outside the library, in their dorms or the computer lab, only making an appearance in the library to retrieve books or articles researched electronically. Although only a few students in this study from the 1998 group fall into that category, it is clear this is a trend that will continue. How can librarians help make the information gathering stage more productive for undergraduates who already shy away from spending time in the library?

For one thing, we can provide library systems that are readily available, familiar, and easier to use. But simply improving the interface that connects the plethora of electronic resources is not enough. The databases themselves are so varied and complex that even librarians struggle with them. Students find that stumbling into something is easier than actually learning how to use the system effectively. In fact, studies on faculty researchers suggest that people expect to use the systems with little or no help[25] and do not want to invest time in learning new systems.[26] It is doubtful more can be expected of undergraduates. Additional work has to be done to standardize the searching interfaces and minimize the effort it takes to select among hundreds of choices.

Research suggests that helping patrons to select sources is a key role for reference librarians. But making connections with students on their terms and at their level of need is essential. When recommending sources, reference librarians can be more aware of both the anxiety level and time constraints under which students operate. Lower division students may have more anxiety, less experience, and fewer strategies that work for them. Reference librarians can be more proactive in the library in locating students who are having trouble by roving around the areas containing research computers. Unobtrusive inquiries, such as "are you finding what you want?" may go further than directly asking if students want help.

Librarians must find better ways to connect with students both in and outside the library. This research indicates that perhaps the greatest value of bibliographic instruction for undergraduates is not in the teaching, but in providing a link for students with the library and those who can help them outside of the classroom. If this is true, it might be worth working with the course professor to meet briefly with students informally in the classroom, on their own turf, and to provide brief information and more importantly librarian contact information.

As a complement to this first contact, librarians can do a better job collaborating with professors on providing instruction that is timely and more meaningfully connected to a course assignment. All the professors interviewed in this study noted that, with the exception of a few papers, their expectations of the students' papers were generally not met. Working with faculty on course specific goals will not only improve these results, but provide clearer guidance for students. Whitmire's[27] study also suggests that greater librarian-faculty collaboration is key for fostering critical thinking. It is time to evaluate seriously the strengths and weaknesses of bibliographic instruction and reshape it to work more effectively.

In addition, there is increasing potential to connect with students through email. One of the professors in this study communicated heavily by email. Similarly, the author's experience is that students increasingly ask questions via email as a direct result of a library instruction class. Maybe email communication connected with instruction can become one answer to low-risk library contact and an opportunity to invite students in for research appointments.

Finally, since peers are a key source of information to students, librarians need to use student library assistants more wisely. Sensitize them to the importance of their roles in the library and train them better to refer patrons to librarians, especially for selecting databases.

In the end, the effort must be spent thinking of ways to connect appropriate resources to people. The information field is in some ways in great disarray during this transition to electronic research. Undergraduates are increasingly disconnected from expert help both physically and psychologically. Librarians can certainly become more creative in finding effective ways to be lifelines in the changing research climate.

Notes

1. Ward, Maribeth. "A "Disconnect" Between Academic Librarians and Students." *Computers in Libraries* (1996): 22–23.

2. Valentine, Barbara. "Undergraduate Research Behavior: Using Focus Groups to Generate Theory." *Journal of Academic Librarianship* 19, no. 5 (1993): 300–4.

3. Mellon, Constance A. "Library Anxiety: A Grounded Theory and Its Development." *College and Research Libraries* 47 (1986): 160–65.

4. Kuhlthau, Carol C. "Longitudinal Case Studies of the Information Search Process of Users in Libraries." *Library and Information Science Research* 10 (1988): 257–304.

5. Yang, Shu Ching. "Information Seeking As Problem-Solving Using a Qualitative Approach to Uncover the Novice Learners' Information-Seeking Processes in a Perseus Hypertext System." *Library and Information Science Research* 19, no. 1 (1997): 71–92.

6. Alafiatayo, Benjamin O., and John C. P. Blunden-Ellis. "Reference Transactions and the Nature of the Process for General Reference Assistance." *Library and Information Science Research* 18 (1996): 357–84.

7. Kuhlthau, Carol C. "Impact of the Information Search Process Model on Library Services." *RQ* 34, no. 1 (1994): 21–26.

8. Julien, Heidi. "A Content Analysis of the Recent Information Needs and Uses Literature." *Library and Information Science Research* 18 (1996): 53–65.

9. Morrison, Heather. "Information Literacy Skills: An Exploratory Focus Group Study of Student Perceptions." *Research Strategies* 15, no. 1 (1997): 4–17.

10. Bailey, Edgar C. Jr. "Help-Seeking Behavior in the Research Process of College Students." *Choosing Our Futures: Proceedings of the Eighth National Conference of the Association of College and Research Libraries* Nashville Tenn.: Association of College & Research Libraries, 1997. Available online: http://www.ala.org/acrl/paperhtm/d35.html

11. Massey-Burzio, Virginia. "From the Other Side of the Reference Desk: A Focus Group Study." *Journal of Academic Librarianship* (1998): 208–15.

12. Jacobson, Frances F., and Emily N. Ignacio. "Teaching Reflection: Information Seeking and Evaluation in a Digital Library Environment." *Library Trends* 45, no. 4 (1997): 771–802.

13. Seiden, Peggy, Kris Szymborski, and Barbara Norelli. "Undergraduate Students and the Digital Library: Information-Seeking Behavior in a Heterogeneous Environment." *Choosing Our Futures: Proceedings of the Eighth National Conference of the Association of College and Research Libraries* Nashville, Tenn.: Association of College and Research Libraries, 1997. Available online: http://www.ala.org/acrl/paperhtm/c26.html

14. Lubans, John Jr., Deputy University Librarian. "How First-year university students use and regard internet resources." Web page, April 1998 [accessed 12 February 1999]. Available at http://www.lib.duke.edu/staff/orgnztn/lubans/firstyear.html.

15. Nahl, Diane. "Ethnography of Novices' First Use of Web Search Engines: Affective Control in Cognitive Processing." *Internet Reference Services Quarterly* 3, no. 2 (1998): 51-72.

16. Whitmire, Ethelene. "The Campus Environment for African-American and White Students: Impact on Academic Library Experiences." *Choosing Our Futures: Proceedings of the Eighth National Conference of the Association of College and Research Libraries* Nashville, Tenn.: Association of College and Research Libraries, 1997. Available online: http://www.ala.org/acrl/paperhtm/e42.html

17. Valentine, Barbara. "The GPA Perspective Revisited: Agents Vs. Recruits." (M.A. Thesis. University of Georgia, Department of Sociology, 1994).

18. Strauss, Anselm L. *Qualitative Analysis for Social Scientists*. Cambridge: Cambridge University Press, 1987.

19. Kuhlthau, Carol Collier. *Seeking Meaning: A Process Approach to Library and Information Services*. Norwood N.J.: Ablex, 1993: 43.

20. Becker, Howard S., Blanche Geer, and Everett C. Hughes. *Making the Grade: The Academic Side of College Life*. New York: Wiley, 1968: 55.

21. DePaulo, Bella M., Arie Nadler, and Jeffrey D. Fisher. *New Direction in Helping: Volume 2: Help-Seeking*. New York: Academic Press, 1983.

22. Knapp, John R., and Stuart A. Karabenick. "Incidence of Formal and Informal Academic Help-Seeking in Higher Education." *Journal of College Student Development* 29 (1988): 223–27.

23. Bell, Jennifer, Jana Grekul, Navjot Lamba, Christine Minas, and W. Andrew Harrell. "The Impact of Cost on Student Helping Behavior." *Journal of Social Psychology* 135, no. 1 (1995): 49–56.

24. *Strategic Help Seeking: Implications for Learning and Teaching*. Edited by Stuart A. Karabenick. Mahwah, N.J.: L. Erlbaum Associates, 1998.

25. Barry, Christine A. "Critical Issues in Evaluating the Impact of IT on Information Activity in Academic Research: Developing a Qualitative Research Solution." *Library and Information Science Research* 17 (1995): 127.

26. Barry, Christine A, and David Squires. "Why the Move From Traditional Information-Seeking to the Electronic Library Is Not Straightforward for Academic Users: Some Surprising Findings." *Online Information 95: 19th International Online Information Meeting*. Eds. David I. Raitt, and Ben Jeapes. Oxford: Learned Information Europe Ltd, 1995: 181.

27. Whitmire, Ethelene. "Development of Critical Thinking Skills: An Analysis of Academic Library Experiences and Other Measures." *College and Research Libraries* 59 (1998): 266–73.

The Classroom vs. the Web: Comparing Two Ways to Teach Web-based Resources

Elizabeth Burns

Abstract

The Classroom vs. the Web is a presentation of research-in-progress of two methods to teach competency with web-based resources. The study was carried out at the Mansfield Campus of the Ohio State University during the Autumn, 1998, and Winter, 1999, quarters. The Ohio State University and OhioLINK recently converted access to their resources from VT100 terminal emulation to web-based interfaces. A one credit hour, bibliographic instruction course was created to teach the required skills in the new web environment. Students divided themselves into two groups. One group attended the weekly one-hour lab class with the instructors; the other used a web-based instructional program. Each population was given identical content and projects. At the beginning of the quarter, a pre-test was administered. At the end of the quarter, a post-test was administered and the results compared. Comments from the students on each method were also studied. The study was continued with a second set of students during the Winter Quarter.

Introduction

The Ohio State University and OhioLINK recently converted access to their resources from VT100 terminal emulation to web-based interfaces. To teach the required skills in the new web environment, a one credit hour bibliographic instruction course was approved to be taught beginning the Autumn, 1998, quarter. The students divided themselves into two groups: one group attended the weekly one-hour lab class with the instructors; and the other group used a web-based instructional program with email and personal contact with the

Elizabeth Burns is reference librarian, Ohio State University Mansfield.

instructors occurring only as needed by the student. Each population was given identical content and projects. The study was continued with a second set of students during the Winter Quarter. The purpose of this paper is to describe the research-in-progress of a study comparing two methods of bibliographic instruction for students at a branch campus of a large university: classroom/lab-based and web-based.

Methodology
The Autumn, 1998, course was team-taught in the classroom/lab, using individual computers, a Proxima projector/computer, the blackboard, handouts, in-class activities, and out-of-class assignments. Web-based students received their instructions via email and the web. Both groups of students were required to attend a final library session on reference books.

The Winter, 1999, course was taught by a single instructor, in the classroom/lab, using individual computers, a Proxima projector/computer, the blackboard, handouts, and in-class activities and out-of-class assignments. Web-based students received all of their instructions via email; the web only provided the resources they were using for their assignments. Both groups of students were required to attend a final library session on reference books. Students again chose which class version they wanted to attend: via the web or via the classroom/lab.

At the beginning of the each quarter, a pre-test was administered. At the end of the quarter, a post-test was administered and the results compared. Comments from the students on each method are studied and evaluated.

The pass/no pass, one credit-hour course does not have any quizzes, midterms or finals. Assignments are turned in, corrected with suitable notations, and returned to the students. Attendance is taken in the classroom/lab version of the course.

Results
Sixteen students enrolled in the Autumn, 1998, class; nine students participated in the classroom/lab version and seven students worked via the web. Enrollments included ten freshmen, three sophomores, and two juniors. Two students failed the course by not turning in enough completed assignments. Student comments and student evaluation forms were positive. Twenty-seven students enrolled in the Winter, 1999, class; 14 students participated in the classroom/lab version, and 13 students worked via the web. Enrollments included 23 freshmen, three sophomores, and one junior.

Since the method of teaching the class changed from the Autumn quarter to the Winter quarter, the two groups tested were not instructed in identical fashion, nor with identical content and projects. This project will be continued for two more quarters as a pilot study. Then during the Autumn, 1999, and Winter, 2000, quarters, the students will be surveyed for the purposes of research.

Discussion and Conclusion
Bromfield Library is a shared facility on the campus of The Ohio State University at Mansfield and the North Central Technical College. Our students' knowledge and expertise in library skills and research strategies range from expert to non-existent. We had to revise all the bibliographic instruction materials before the Autumn, 1998, quarter since we installed web-based OPACS during the summer.

Our library's professional staff is composed of the reference librarian/bibliographic instructor and the director. During an average Autumn quarter, the reference librarian teaches an average of 50 instruction classes to approximately 1000-1200 students from both institutions on campus. The reference librarian teaches everything from basic library skills in English classes to specialized research skills in graduate level education and social work classes.

While teaching in the classroom, the reference librarian is leaving the reference desk unattended too many hours a week. I am researching whether I can design a web-based course that can effectively reach an unlimited number of students, with a limited amount of out-of-the-library time for the instructor. My past experiences taught me that most students do not volunteer to attend workshops; therefore, I felt that a "for credit" course was the solution.

As with any pilot research project, a number of things have changed. In the eleven months since the conception of this course, our library building was renovated, with the staff moving the collection out of the building in late June and returning the collection to the library in September, as school was starting. In mid-September, the director took over the teaching of two courses in computer science at North Central Technical College, in addition to team teaching our class and directing the library. In December, he resigned his director's position to teach computer science full time.

During the Winter, 1999, quarter, I was acting director/reference librarian/bibliographic instructor and teacher for this class.

When we devised our plan for the course, I was to write up the lessons, send them to him, and he placed them on the library's home page. In the classroom, we both took part in the teaching. With his resignation, I lost my "web page" person. The web-based students during the Winter quarter got their instructions entirely from email. It would have been more proper to call them email-based students, not web-based students.

The winter quarter was also bombarded with snow. It was the third week of classes (out of a ten week quarter) before I saw all of my classroom/lab students. In fact, during the third week of school, the campus closed down halfway through our class. Weather was not the only problem; we ran into equipment shortages (no Proxima/project) and computer systems failures.

In spite of this, student feedback has been positive. After talking to the student advisors, I am offering the course two different times this quarter (Spring, 1999, quarter) and again in the Autumn, 1999, quarter. The course will be offered on Wednesday, 11:20 a.m.–12:20 p.m. and again 5:45–6:45 p.m. During the Summer, 1999, quarter, the course will be offered on Wednesday, at 9:00 a.m. and again at 8:00 p.m. This will allow evening and part-time students to take the course, via the classroom, if they need the additional help of an instructor.

I came to a number of conclusions about the way that I taught this class. At the beginning of the Spring, 1999, quarter, I made the following changes.

Freshmen often don't get their email accounts activated until the third or fourth week into their first quarter in school. That is too late if they are planning to take the course via the web. Starting the Spring quarter, students were given three choices: 1) to activate their email accounts before the end of the second week of classes, or 2) to take the classroom version of the class, or 3) to wait until their second quarter of college before signing up for the course. Financial aid problems often keep students from activating their accounts on time; they cannot activate their email accounts if their fees aren't paid.

Students must take six credit hours to qualify as a part-time student for their financial aid or they have to take 12 credit hours to qualify for full-time student status. Most of our academic courses are five credit hour courses. A student may take my course and one regular course; e.g., American History, or English, to be considered a part-time student. If that student is taking two 5 credit hour courses as a part-time student, drops one of them, the student must grab a one-hour course to remain part-time. My course is a perfect solution for the students and their academic advisors. However, I no longer allow a student to enter the classroom version of the class later than the beginning of the third week. If the student is an experienced user of computers and the Internet, I will allow them to join the web-based version of the course through the fourth week of class.

The Ohio State University Libraries' *net.TUTOR* tutorial, via the web, formed the backbone of my *Research Strategies* course the first two quarters. I lectured as we worked our way through the tutorial, adding more steps, and going into more details wherever I thought something wasn't clear or I overheard students' having problems.

During the Winter quarter, several students attended class whenever they could, completing their work via email when they couldn't attend class. As our enrollment increases, students will have to choose a method of instruction and stick with it. At this time, it isn't a problem. We have room for twice the number of students in our computer lab as I have enrolled in the class.

However it does compound the problems of instructional materials and methods of delivery. The number of students working in a lab is in direct ratio to the amount of time it takes for everyone to complete the exercise. Internet response time can change the amount of time that it takes to teach a class. A class that may have taken an hour the first quarter only took half an hour the second. The day that the computer system went down, I hadn't prepared enough lecture to speak for an hour and let them out of class early, forcing us to play catch-up the next class.

This quarter, I made several changes. PowerPoint to the rescue! I no longer depend on the computer system being up the day of the class. Everything is prepared ahead of time; I have a much better idea of the amount of time that each demonstration is going to take. Downed computer systems may keep the students from following my demonstration on their own computers but it won't keep us from covering the material planned for that class.

Students in the classroom had few written instructions. If they couldn't remember or hadn't taken notes, and few of them did, they had nothing to fall back on when they wanted to do it on their own in the library or at home. The web-based students had the email instructions to follow, if they had printed them out. After discussing this problem over with the students, I decided to create a workbook/manual that follows along with their assignments. I am printing up a week's lesson at a time this quarter, will have a completed draft for students this summer, and hopefully, a finished work by this fall. I am not using *net.TUTOR* as my text this quarter; however, I am using the ideas expressed in each lesson of *net.TUTOR* as the basis of my own lessons.

Since all the course work will be contained in this workbook, if a student misses a class, they can do the work on their own, turn in the assignment and be ready for the next class period. If web-based students want to complete the entire course during the first several weeks of school, that will also be possible, as long as they turn their assignments in on time, as required. That is another change that has evolved since last fall. The wording of the syllabus has changed from "assignments must be turned in to me in a timely manner" to "assignments must be turned in by the Monday following the previous class on Wednesday." Morning classes are offered four or five times a week but afternoon and evening classes are scheduled on a Monday/Wednesday or Tuesday/Thursday pattern. Our campus is a commuter campus; I didn't want students to make a special trip out to the campus just to hand in assignments.

Since instigating this policy, three missed assignments equal a "no-pass." Attendance was taken the first two quarters as part of the grade; now attendance is taken only for my benefit. I want to have a gauge of the number of students that are attending every class for the purposes of statistics. At the beginning of each class period, after taking attendance and conducting any other necessary housekeeping, we go over the assignments turned in two days earlier, thereby reviewing and reinforcing the material taught the week before. The web-based students are sent an email the same day, going over their assignments in the same detail.

The first two quarters, the final day of class was held in the library for all students. I had to hold this class several times to fit everybody's time schedules. I felt that the students needed to "meet" these reference resources earlier in the quarter. This quarter, I am experimenting by giving them several reference books to locate and review, in between class periods, with several questions on their assignments pertaining to each book. I feel that integrating the paper library materials with the electronic and Internet sources will give them a better feel of actual research. It is also the only way that I can see to introduce paper library resources via web-based classes.

In the pre-test/post-test, I ask the students to briefly define a number of terms that they need to know and understand for the class to be meaningful. The first time we taught the class, we discussed each term during the second class period and handed out a glossary for the students. The second quarter, I just handed out the glossary. The results of the post-test taken last quarter revealed that the students needed more participatory reinforcement than that. This quarter, in addition to the glossary list, I am introducing and discussing several of these terms each class period.

At this time, I don't have any conclusions to report about my original research. I don't know whether students will prefer one method of instruction to another method because they want more personal instruction or if they just need the credit and can't fit it in any other way. However, I do know that even though changes in format have prevented me from concluding my research as per my original timetable, the information gained during the last three quarters of research has yielded some interesting statistics. After finishing this research project, I am sure that I will have several more projects ready to go.

The Librarian as Mediator: A Significant Change in the Educational Role of Librarians

Donna Roe and David Moody

The face of academic librarianship is changing. While much attention has been focused on the impact of new technologies, new sources of information, and new ways of management, perhaps the most significant change is in the faces across the desk.

Students in higher education are becoming more multicultural, their needs and demands shifting, their personal backgrounds and values diversifying. Today multiculturalism includes such factors as race, national origin, religion, gender, age, sexual orientation, physical and mental enablement, and socioeconomic status. No longer is the typical college student male, fresh out of high school, and of Anglo/European American heritage.

The numbers of students from diverse ethnic and cultural heritages are steadily growing. In this paper the term "minorities" will be used to describe those people not of "white" (Anglo/European American) background. However, a phrase such as "diverse cultures" better represents the broad spectrum of individuals described: Arabic/Eastern Mediterranean/Semitic American, African American, Asian American, First Nation/Indigenous/Native American, Hispanic, Latino, Mexican, Puerto Rican and a full complement of other international students.

The Changing Minority Student Population

From 1990–1995, total enrollment in institutions of higher education increased by 3.21%. However, in this time period, the actual number of Anglo/European American enrollees decreased by almost four percent, while enrollment from diverse groups rose nearly 30%. Overall, the percentage of those diverse groups rose steadily by about 1% a year, from 23% to 28%.[1]

Should this trend continue through the year 2020, the percentage of academic students from diverse groups would stand at 53%, outnumber-

---

Donna Roe is head of cataloging/database management, and David Moody is cataloging librarian, University of Detroit Mercy.

ing those from Anglo/European American backgrounds. Examination of population projections from the United States Census Bureau show a persistent decrease for whites is indeed likely to continue. In 1995, 75.26% of the population of this country was of Anglo/European American background; by 2020, this is expected to shrink to 67%. In 2020, it is projected that the increase in the minority population will be almost 18% greater than the increase in the Anglo/European American population. To look at this another way, in the period 2015-2020 the Anglo/European American population is expected to rise about 3.1%; the population of diverse ethnic groups is expected to rise almost 10%, or more than three times as much.[2]

Do these changes have implications for instruction of the academic library user? Tucker points out several areas where non-traditional students have different expectations than their younger counterparts. One of the most important is that they prefer to learn "horizontally", that is, in an environment that recognizes and builds on the expertise and skills they bring to the classroom. Rather than simply accepting information uncritically, they want it to be relevant to their life, to have meaning that relates to their experiences.[3]

Such an approach would seem to be vital when instructing users of diverse cultural and ethnic backgrounds. Language barriers are the most obvious hurdle to effective communication, but by no means the only one. Different groups interact with people and process information in different ways, leading to a need for flexibility without which even basic communication can become difficult.

These changes offer new opportunities and challenges for librarians as educators. To best instruct the increasing numbers of multicultural library users, librarians need to communicate and teach in a manner that is relevant for the individuals, that has meaning which they can relate to their own experiences. In addition, as librarians examine the ways of working with diverse groups, there is an opportunity to explore methods which take into account the individual learning style of each user.

No longer can one generic instruction session be expected to serve the vast majority of users. Students approach the search for information from different angles, with different viewpoints, with various backgrounds and abilities. They want to know how to find and evaluate information on their own, without being restricted to only the physical resources of the library. The time has arrived when the emphasis is less on the information itself and more on the strategy of the search which may be different for each person; the same old answers will not fit all.

The Unchanging Minority Academic Librarian Population

One possible way to meet the challenge of providing effective education to an increasing number of multicultural users would be a similarly dramatic increase in the numbers of multicultural librarians. Their presence would make the library a more welcoming place for users and help to improve library instruction by providing a diversity of viewpoints, ideas, and teaching styles.

Recognizing the value of this, ALA and academic library institutions and programs have set up incentives designed to recruit from diverse cultures into the library profession. Initiatives introduced to improve these circumstances include such plans as: ALA's Spectrum Initiative which is targeted to recruit minority librarians with annual $5000 scholarships to minority students of ALA accredited library schools,[4] the scholarship incentives offered by many library schools to increase the number of minority librarians (some reach $10,000 annually),[5] higher starting salaries or contract bonuses offered to potential minority employees, academic libraries with diversity policies to recruit and retain minority librarians, and the addition of collection development funds for Diversity, African American Studies and other specialty areas.

Despite these efforts, results have been disappointing. While research describing the racial/ethnic makeup of academic librarians is limited, the number of librarians from minorities lags far behind the increase in minority student population.

Mary Jo Lynch states in the November issue of *American Libraries* that the *ALA Survey of Librarian Salaries 1998* includes statistics on the racial and ethnic makeup of librarians actively working in academic libraries. The 1998 figures show that 13.22% of academic librarians are other than Anglo/European Americans. In the article Lynch goes on to ask and respond, "Can we compare this data to any older data in order to determine if the field is changing? The short answer is 'no'." The 1985 and 1991 ALA samples cannot be legitimately compared because they included both full-time and part-time employees, some of whom did not have master's degrees from ALA accredited library schools.[6]

In the fall of 1992, *The Chronicle of Higher Education* published an article which listed the racial/ethnic characteristics of full-time faculty, including librarians.[7] This study showed that in 1992, 11.3% of academic librarians were other than Anglo/European Americans.[8] This may be a little like comparing raisins and grapes but in six years there was only a 1.82% increase in minority librarians working in academic libraries. Minority academic librarians actively working in the field are increasing by a rate of three-tenths of a percent each year. The minority student population is increasing at three times the rate of minority librarians. Even though these numbers cannot be *legitimately* compared they give an overall picture on which to build a premise. If these figures are extrapolated into the next century, it becomes apparent that there is not going to be a significant increase in minority librarians. At a maximum, only 19.92 % of academic librarians will represent other than Anglo/European Americans by the year 2020.

Presently, minority academic librarians, 13% of all academic librarians, serve a multicultural student population of which 32% is minority. Obviously in academe there is a discrepancy between the number of minority librarians and the number of minority students. And it is going to get worse. By the year 2020, a maximum of 19% minority academic librarians will serve a multicultural student population of which 53% is minority.

Even though measures must be taken to attract, educate, get, and keep minority librarians in the field, it is the position of these writers that the number of minority librarians will not dramatically increase. Part of the reason for this is that minorities seem to be choosing fields other than library science, often fields more related to information technology than traditional library science career fields. Another reason is that tuition scholarships and other incentives may not be enough to attract and keep minority librarians. The demands of minority students are frequently different than those of non-minority students. Scholarships may need to include housing (possibly for entire families) and subsistence allowances as well. The third barrier to increasing the number of minority enrollees in library schools and hirees at American colleges and universities is reverse discrimination lawsuits, where Anglo/European Americans are suing because they do not have the same opportunities as minorities.

Clearly the minority librarian pool is not changing as much as the minority student population. Under these circumstances, can academic librarians effectively teach and communicate with a multicultural student population?

Reuven Feuerstein

Promisingly, there has been a movement going on in education for the last fifty years that provides a bridge. The movement is designed to provide educators with the ability to teach all cultures in a way that is meaningful, relevant, and effective. The movement is based on two theories called Mediated Learning Experience (MLE) and Structural Cognitive Modifiability. The founder is Reuven Feuerstein, an Israeli psychology professor and a protégé of Piaget. Feuerstein worked from Piaget's educational theory in which it is postulated that when a learner is stimulated by a learning experience, the result is a change *to* the learner. This concept can be represented as <S - O - R> [stimulus/learning situation—organism/learner—response/change to learner], a model which suggests an association between Piaget and his contemporary Pavlov.

Feuerstein developed the theory in another direction, stating that the learning experience is effective when it produces a change *in* the learner and this can only be accomplished through a humanitarian interchange. Feuerstein's redesign of the theory can be expressed as <S - h - O - h - R>. [stimulus/learning experience—human connection—organism/learner—human connection—response/change in learner]. In other words Feuerstein was stating that the learning situation could neither have meaning nor be effective without mediation to guide and convey the educational message (stimulus). The "h" is a small letter because the mediator guides rather than controls the learning situation.

Feuerstein was given the opportunity to use his theories in the 1940s when he worked with a group of children who had been diagnosed intellectually and developmentally retarded. These children were survivors of the Holocaust who had lost family and all connection to their cultural heritage. Feuerstein believed these "at risk"children were not only capable of learning but were also capable of excelling. He gave new meaning to the term culturally deprived, which he defined as people who are deprived of their birthright culture. These theories were confirmed when every one of the children mediated by Feuerstein went on to college and a professional career.[9]

Mediated Learning

During the years that Feuerstein worked with these children, he developed his theory of Mediated Learning to include essential criteria for learning. They are: 1. Intentionality and Reciprocity; 2. Meaning; 3. Transcendence; 4. Mediation of Competence; 5. Self Regulation and Control of Behavior; 6. Sharing and Individuation Behavior; 7. Challenge and Goal Planning; and 8. Self-Change. The first four of these criteria are fundamental for a Mediated Learning Experience to take place. To briefly define these four concepts: Intentionality occurs when the mediator purposely guides the interaction in a certain direction. Reciprocity occurs when the mediatee indicates involvement in the learning process. Meaning occurs when the learning experience has value and significance for the mediatee. Transcendence occurs when a learning interaction transcends or goes beyond the immediate situation. Mediation of Competence occurs when the mediator conveys to the mediatee a sense of confidence to engage successfully in the learning experience. The goal of MLE is to make students autonomous and independent learners.[10]

Multiple Intelligences; Modalities of Learning

Feuerstein worked with children who were members of his culture. Another educator, Howard Gardner, who studied Feuerstein's work recognized certain modalities of learning, any one or more of which could be used to teach to the cultural values of any nation or group of people. Gardner defined these learning modalities as: Verbal/Linguistic, Logical/Mathematical, Visual/Spatial, Body/Kinesthetic, Musical/Rhythmical, Interpersonal, and Intrapersonal. Recently the modality of Nature/Natural World has been added to reach the learning styles of indigenous peoples.[11]

Mediating in the Library

What does this have to do with diverse academic student library users who by the very nature of being in college make a statement about being not only highly intelligent but also possibly gifted?

While Mediated Learning was initially used with culturally deprived children the principles involved apply universally because they deal with the common processes of thought rather than information that is subject specific. Mediated Learning is not primarily concerned with differences in cultural backgrounds or learning styles. It is designed to teach educators how to mediate learners to become aware of their thought processes so that they can effectively utilize their own particular backgrounds and learning styles to become autonomous, independent learners.

The nature of the Mediated Learning Experience in the library will vary according to the situation. A user in a quick reference interview cannot be mediated in exactly the same manner as a staff member who will be mediated over a long period of time. One common factor must be kept in mind for any type of Mediated Learning Experience: the human connection. Within the human connection, the mediator must focus on the thinking/thought processes/mind of the learner in such a way that the learner, not the librarian, answers the question. Learning occurs when change takes place in the mind of the learner.

Within the focus of this paper it is not possible to help librarians to understand all cultures or all the concepts of Mediated Learning. What is intended instead is to instill a sensitivity to the fact that cultural and learning differences exist. What is intended is to foster a willingness on the part of librarians to accept students as they are and not expect them to subscribe to the librarian's way of thinking/reasoning. Imagine for instance, librarians who initiate interpersonal contact with students, much as good teachers roam the classroom. The librarian who physically goes to the student, at a place where the student has chosen to learn, is more likely to reach the student cognitively. In this way, the librarian invites the student to show how that student learns best.

The remainder of this paper will focus on some ideas for using Mediated Learning in library situations. These ideas are intended to provide librarians with some strategies they might adapt to their own particular circumstances and libraries.

The Public Services Mediator

The demands on public services librarians often leave little time for them to actually instruct users. Instruction is seen as a process that is handled during bibliographic instruction sessions. While BI sessions would be the ideal place to practice Mediated Learning because there is sufficient preparation time to create the session, librarians spend more time at the reference desk than in the BI classroom. It is more difficult to use Mediated Learning in the spontaneous interview that takes place at the reference desk. The spontaneous reference question seems to negate the possibility of using the MLE motto, "Just a moment let me think." Unless there are few students who need assistance, the librarian is not able to give users time to think about forming research strategies. Instructing one student is not a problem; but when several students need instruction at the same time, an MLE strategy that could work is to ask the group of students in front of the desk, "Who has questions about operating the system?" and "Who has questions about forming specific research strategies?" If another librarian is available, it may be expedient for each librarian to take a group. Mediating a small group can facilitate the librarian's responsibility because after some basic instruction, at the invitation of the librarian, the students can interact with and help each other. In giving an overview of an MLE instruction, it is important to remember that it is never only a matter of finding the answer but instead how best to guide students to find it.

A few quick questions will assist the librarian in knowing how to mediate—input from and interaction with the students provide cues on how to best mediate. The librarian can also readily identify some potential pairing of students, those with experience paired with those who have no experience, by asking such questions as, "Have you used our catalog before?" "Have you ever used an automated system?" Other questions can help form the intentionality of the instruction: "Do you want information from materials that you can borrow from this library?" The librarian should be direct, friendly, and interactive. The librarian mediator should stand beside or smile naturally at those who seem most uncomfortable. Any student who has a question about using the library is "at risk". If these students are not mediated in humanitarian ways, they will avoid using libraries, particularly YOUR library.

The librarian must always consider that some of the students may be from cultures and/or have learning styles different than the librarian. Daily preparation, before attending the reference desk, should include search strategies for current places, events, and people from different cultures, especially cultures that may be represented by the students to be mediated that day.

Having the students, not the librarian, operate the workstations will help the librarian connect with those students who learn best in verbal/linguistic, logical, visual/spatial, kinesthetic, and possibly rhythmical modalities. Verbal and non-verbal interactions between the librarian and students will promote understanding in those students who learn interpersonally (personal share) or intrapersonally (awareness about self) as well.

It is important to remember that in order for MLE to take place, there must be Intentionality and Reciprocity, Meaning, Transcendence, and mediation of a feeling of Competence. After the librarian ascertains student interest, Intentionality or purposeful direction might look like this: "To teach students how to use the catalog by having them complete a search." Intentionality and reciprocity are highly interactive. The librarian can recognize reciprocity when the students' facial expressions and questions show interest.

As the librarian seamlessly guides students to the Meaning phase, the instruction is given importance and energy. It is a matter of engaging students in the "why" of the process. Simply asking a question like, "Why does this step seem important?" will involve students in the mental process of learning. This act helps them move toward independence and autonomy.

To push the learning experience further and to give it value in terms of the students' individual cultures, the librarian must get the students to transcend or bridge the prevailing experience. In the Transcendence phase, the students must relate generalizations from the learning experience to a similar principle in their own lives. For example, the librarian might make a generalization, such as "There is no set amount of time that is right for completing a search task." Ideally the librarian could follow up with a question like, "Where else does that apply in your life?" And ideally students would have time to reply. More likely, however, is the situation in which the librarian will have to set the stage for the transcendence to happen in the students' minds, with a statement like, "Is that also true when you eat dinner at home or prepare for a holiday?" The *association* provided allows students to immediately transcend to their own cultures and values.

The next and final phase that is needed for an effective MLE is, in actuality, an ongoing phase and one that should be peppered throughout the instruction. Mediation of a feeling of competence is accomplished when the librarian communicates positive feedback to the learner. The librarian mediates a feeling of competence by verbally rewarding individual learning achievements, by acknowledging explicit strategies used by a student, by focusing on the successful completion of parts of the learning activity. As the librarian observes a student implementing a successful search, he or she might say to the student, "That was an exceptional search strategy." A rule of thumb is to emphasize the positive strengths to remediate the weakness.

The Technical Services Mediator

Mediation in the technical services environment offers opportunities not always available in public services. The audience is better known to the instructing librarian, which makes it easier to devise a plan that will accommodate diverse cultures and backgrounds.

Assume that five members of the Cataloging Department require instruction in use of a new automated system. All are experienced users of the old system. English is a second language for two of the members.

For this session, the instructing librarian could set up three workstations. One would be connected to a liquid crystal display unit, while a fluent and non-fluent department member could be paired at the other workstations. A set of handouts would be prepared for each cataloging function to be covered, consisting of two parts: a step-by-step outline of each function as performed in the two systems, arranged in parallel columns, and practice examples.

The instructing librarian should demonstrate a function, comparing its operation in the two systems. As department members work on the examples, the librarian should meditate by moving around to answer questions and discuss the work.

When everyone seems comfortable with performing the function, there should be general discussion. The mediating librarian can ask members to comment on the differences in the way the function was performed in the new system, whether these differences make the work easier or harder, and how workflow and procedures might change to accommodate the new system.

In designing this session, the librarian knows that some department members could have language barriers. Therefore, a decision is made to avoid reliance on the verbal-linguistic learning modality. Also, the suggestion that members be paired during the practice phase is made so that the fluent English speakers can help to bridge communication gaps which might occur during the demonstration phase.

The greatest emphasis is placed on discerning relationships and patterns (logical/mathematical thinking), taking advantage of the members' knowledge of the old system. Other learning modalities employed are physical performance of the new task (kinesthetic learning), interaction between members (interpersonal learning), and reflection on the lesson just learned (intrapersonal thinking).

In terms of the Mediated Learning process, the intention of the mediating librarian is to select functions of the new system which are most familiar and provide a good basis for comparison. Reciprocity is apparent when department members show interest in learning the new system, overcoming a resistance to change.

Meaning becomes reality when learners provide an answer from their own experience to the question, "Why is this important?" Transcendence occurs when learners can bridge the process to something familiar in their own lives.

A sense of competence is also a necessary part of the session. This can be mediated by an enthusiastic, "can-do" attitude on the part of the instructor, encouraging a similarly positive response from the learner. This attitude also helps the learner to perceive the process of change as a challenge rather than a problem. Department members can think of the new system as a chance to improve their skills and knowledge, and have confidence in their ability to solve future problems that may arise.

Finally, the general discussion after the practice session is an important element of the process. This human connection gives the mediating librarian a sense of how well the lesson has been learned, and gives learners material to build more bridges of their own. Mediated Learning is a two-way street, on which the mediator and mediatee are constantly learning from each other.

Notes

1. *Digest of Educational Statistics 1997* (Washington, D.C.: U.S. Department of Education, Office of Educational Research and Improvement, 1997, 214.

2. *Population Projections of the United States, by Age, Sex, Race, and Hispanic Origin, 1995–2050* (Washington, D.C.: U.S. Department of Commerce), Economics and Statistics Administration, Bureau of The Census, 1992), 32–37.

3. Robert W. Tucker, "The New American College Student and Workforce Competence: Seven Generalizations that Challenge Traditional Accreditation and Licensure," in *The Challenge and Practice of Academic Accreditation*, ed. Edward D. Garten (Westport, Conn.: Greenwood Pr., 1994), 101–12.

4. *ALA Spectrum Initiative: Information and Application.* c1999 [Online]. Available: http@www.ala.org/spectrum/index.html (25 Feb. 1999).

5. *The Big Book of Minority Opportunities: the Directory of Special Programs for Minority Group Members* 7th ed., ed. Elizabeth Oakes Chicago, Ill.: Ferguson Publishing, 1997).

6. Mary Jo Lynch, "Librarians' Salaries: Smaller Increases This Year," *American Libraries* (Nov. 1998): 66–70.

7. "Characteristics of Full-Time Faculty Members with Teaching Duties, Fall 1992," *Chronicle of Higher Education*, 43 (Sept. 2, 1992): 24.

8. "College Enrollment by Racial and Ethnic Group, Selected Years", *Chronicle of Higher Education*, 43 (Sept. 2, 1992): 24.

9. Howard Sharron, *Changing Children's Minds: Feuerstein's Revolution in the "Teaching of Intelligence* (London: Souvenir Press (Education & Academic), Ltd., 1987).

10. Cognitive Research Program Division of Specialized Education, University of the Witwatersrand, South Africa, *Mediated Learning; In and Out of the Classroom* (Arlington Heights, Ill.: IRI Skylight, 1996).

11. David Lazear, *Seven Ways of Teaching: the Artistry of Teaching with Multiple Intelligences* (Arlington Heights, Ill.: IRI Skylight, 1991).

Web-Based OPACs: A Leap of Faith?

Norm Medeiros, James Beattie, and Carol Wu

Abstract

A three-month study explored and evaluated user satisfaction with the Web version versus the character-based telnet version of Ehrman Medical Library's online catalog, MEDCat. Methodologies included analyzing responses from a questionnaire, monitoring system statistics, and recording observations by Circulation and Information Services staff working one-on-one with users. The results will be utilized to gain insight into user needs, expectations, and satisfaction with the Web-based OPAC.

Introduction

The World Wide Web has permeated many aspects of academic reference services. The Web's presumed ease of use and computer platform independence are supplanting telnet- and CD-ROM-based resources. Consequently, academic libraries and system vendors are scrambling to provide Web-based OPACs (WEBPACs) to a browser-oriented clientele. In our haste, traditional character-based OPAC features are often sacrificed in order to provide the point-and-click interface users have come to expect. Although WEBPACs offer features distinct from their character-based counterparts, the assumption that they will be embraced with the same enthusiasm as other Web-based products needs to be investigated.

In January 1998, the Ehrman Medical Library (EML) of New York University School of Medicine released the Web version of its online catalog, MEDCat. In the following month, a "digital

---

Norm Medeiros is technical services librarian, James Beattie is educational services librarian, and Carol Wu is information services/electronic resource librarian, New York University School of Medicine.

premiere" showcased new electronic products and services available through EML. MEDCat via the Web was officially unveiled at the premiere and established as the default OPAC interface in the Main Reading Room. In mid-March, a "Lunch-n-Learn" session was held for the NYU Medical Center community to demonstrate features of the Web version of MEDCat. By the end of April, based on informal feedback and staff observations, the need to evaluate the visibility and performance of this interface was apparent.

Review of Literature

In the literature there are no similar projects aimed at determining user search habits and satisfaction with telnet versus Web-based online catalogs. However, a number of articles explore overall design of WEBPACs.

Green and Head[1] examine the Web catalogs of Stanford University and the University of California at Berkeley. Their research promotes the Web catalog as making "one-stop shopping possible." Although their work studies the difference in search patterns between command-line searching and the use of pull-down menus, it does not pair the telnet and Web-based catalogs in a way that provides for direct comparison. Instead, the emphasis rests with WEBPAC design principles.

Cherry[2] discusses the bibliographic display differences between telnet and Web-based catalogs. Issues such as telnet's "screen" versus a Web "page" are addressed. However, this paper does not give a comparison of user satisfaction between the competing interfaces for a specific OPAC.

Dennis, Carter, and Bordeianu[3] address immediate concerns of migration from a character- to Web-based online catalog. This work highlights advantages of WEBPAC such as the common gateway to electronic resources and the graphical user interface. The authors extend beyond a mere checklist of tangible WEBPAC benefits, and refer to the "fundamental change" resulting from such a migration. Additionally, one-to-one comparisons between the different access methods highlight features sacrificed in the WEBPAC in order to achieve the "holistic computing environment" users demand. However, a qualitative analysis of user satisfaction is not examined.

Environment and Methods

NYU School of Medicine is the academic component of NYU Medical Center, a large urban health care facility. EML serves the School of Medicine, the Medical Center, the larger NYU community, and a number of affiliated hospitals.

This paper reports a three-prong approach to data collection that took place from September to November 1998. The first method employed a questionnaire (Appendix I) aimed at gaining a perspective on the MEDCat search interface used and preferred by EML users. The questionnaire was made available within EML for one week in each of the three months. Additionally, 837 full-time compensated faculty received a direct mailing of the questionnaire in October 1998, and 634 MD and MD/Ph.D. students received a similar mailing in November 1998.

The second approach to this study gathered search statistics generated by MEDCat. These statistics were examined on a weekly basis. Principally targeted were the telnet and Web searches performed on the catalog by those outside EML. These data supplied concrete evidence of interface access.

The third and final approach to the study analyzed anecdotal evidence gathered from both informal interactions by EML staff with users using MEDCat within the library, as well as feedback which was requested on the questionnaire.

Results

Section A: Questionnaire.

Table 1 represents distribution and rate of return. Table 2 represents the responses to completed questionnaires distributed within EML, and those mailed directly to faculty and students. The questionnaire consists of five questions. The authors considered a completed questionnaire to include answers to the first two questions (1. Status; 2. Where do you use MEDCat) and part one of the third question (3. Which version of MEDCat do you use). Table 2 also includes responses that are not necessary criteria for a completed questionnaire, but that provide useful information regarding user preference.

Section B: Search Statistics

Graph 1 demonstrates the percent of searches per-

Table 1

	September	October	November	Faculty Direct Mailing	Student Direct Mailing
Total # Distributed	150	130	75	837	634
# of Surveys Returned	63	66	8	72	13
Rate of Return	42.00%	50.77%	10.67%	8.60%	2.05%
# of Completes	58	60	7	61	13
# of Incompletes	4	6	1	11	0

Table 2

Status	Faculty	Student	Staff	Resident	Fellow	Nursing	Admin	Other	Totals
	80	66	22	15	10	2	1	3	199
Where do you use MEDCat?									
Office/Lab	64	8	6	3	6	0	1	1	89
Home	31	21	2	3	4	0	0	0	61
Ehrman Medical Library	47	57	18	13	7	2	1	2	147
Other Libraries	2	4	0	0	1	0	0	0	7
Other	1	2	0	1	0	0	0	0	4
Which version do you use?									
Telnet access	13	6	5	4	0	0	0	0	28
Web access	37	39	11	6	7	2	1	3	106
Both	30	21	6	5	3	0	0	0	65
If Web access, how did you find out about it?									
Digital Library Premiere	4	1	0	2	0	0	0	0	7
Lunch-n-Learns	2	0	0	0	0	0	0	0	0
Library staff	22	18	12	5	2	1	0	0	60
Library Web site	29	18	6	0	3	0	0	3	59
Using it in the library	12	31	6	3	5	1	1	0	59
Other	5	2	0	1	0	0	0	0	8
Preference									
Telnet	15	9	3	5	1	1	0	0	34
Web	40	35	10	5	8	1	0	2	102
Both/Neither	2	2	2	0	0	0	0	0	6

formed on MEDCat from September through November 1998. Public searches performed via telnet steadily declined each month (Sept.=36.77%; Oct.=33.83%; Nov.=29.23%). Searches performed via the Web interface steadily grew during the same period (Sept.=33.11%; Oct.=34.59%; Nov.=37.20%). Web usage exceeded telnet usage for the first time in October 1998.

Section C: Anecdotal Evidence

Staff observations and comments from returned questionnaires indicate that there is a wide spectrum in the use and knowledge of MEDCat. A number of users did not know or were not familiar with the purpose or capabilities of MEDCat. Another group of users could not distinguish the difference between telnet and Web, while some more experienced Web/computer users requested more integration between MEDCat and other online databases. Additional comments included suggestions for additions to EML print and electronic collections.

Discussion

When this study began in September 1998, the Web version of MEDCat was already established as the default interface within EML. This in effect created a "force feed" situation. Except for two dumb terminals, users were forced to use the Web version of MEDCat that was available from the various PC and Macintosh stations located throughout EML.

Section A: Questionnaire

The MEDCat questionnaire was used to collect data about who was searching the online catalog, where they were doing their searching from, and which interface they employed. Data collected from the 199 complete surveys provided useful demographic information about MEDCat usage and a framework within which to increase awareness of Web MEDCat.

Of interest is the percent of all respondents (14%) who said that they used telnet access to MEDCat (Figure 1). While this is considerably less than the actual percent of telnet sessions logged by the system (Section B), it is higher than expected given the WEBPAC "force feed" situation within EML. This indicates that a dedicated segment of our user population has not fully embraced the Web as a means of accessing MEDCat.

A reliance on telnet is further supported by 33% of all respondents who claim to use both telnet and Web interfaces. Unfortunately, it is impossible to know if "both" means that a respondent used one or the other of the interfaces once, or if they employed both on a regular basis. The response of "both" may point to several other factors influencing how our users access MEDCat. The NYU Medical Center community may be used to the character-based interface, senior faculty and research staff may lack the computing and techno-

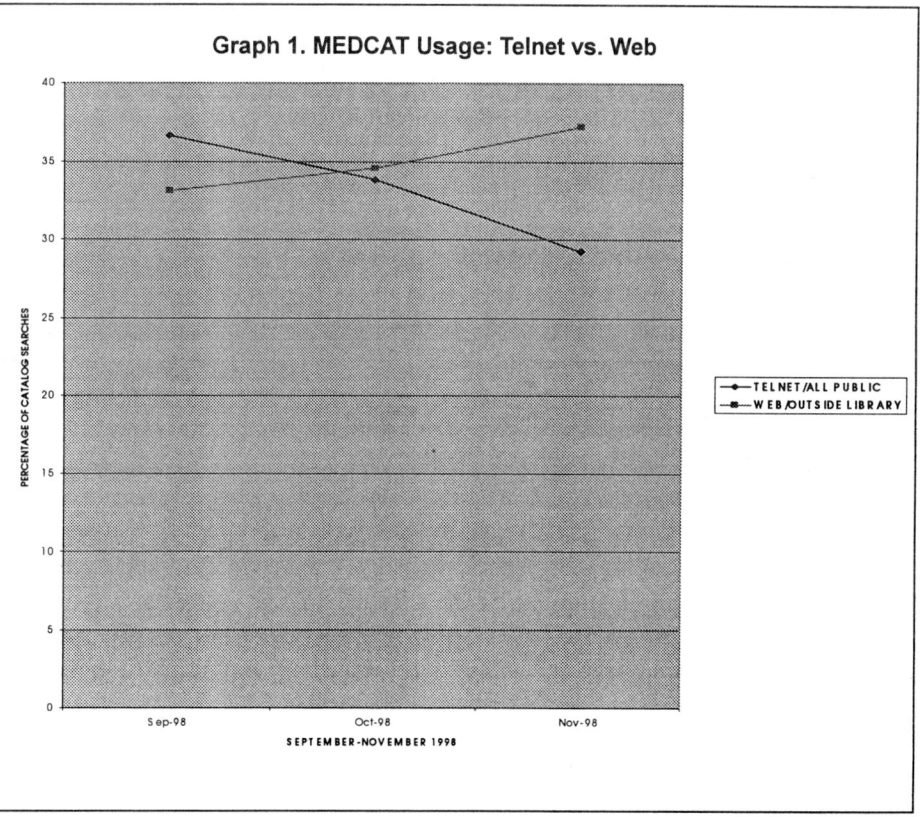

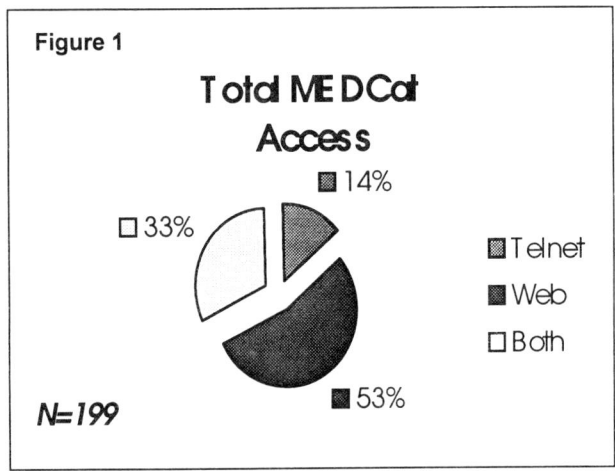

Figure 1

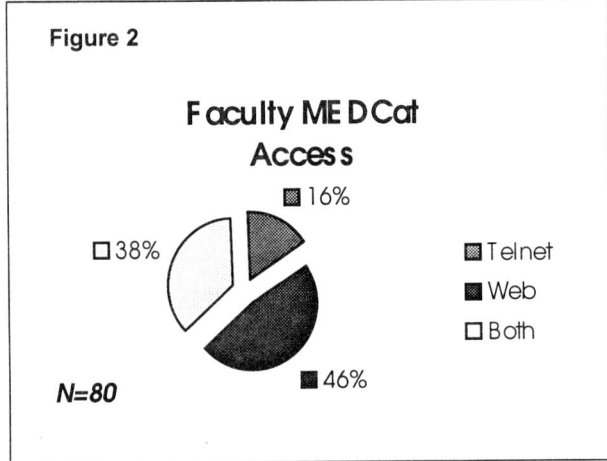

Figure 2

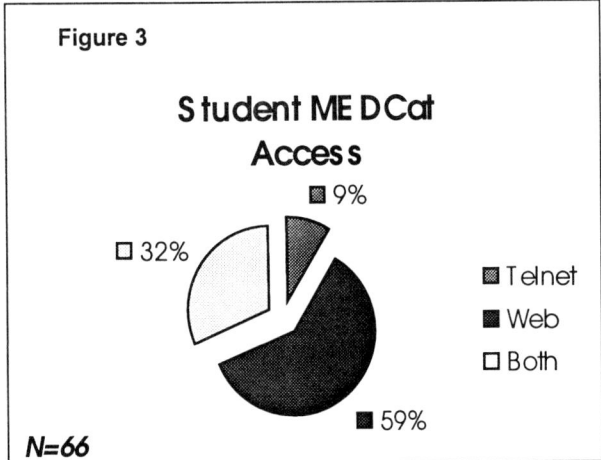

Figure 3

A comparison of faculty and student reported usage of telnet versus WEBPAC (Figures 2 and 3) is interesting for several reasons. The comparison indicates that faculty may rely more upon the telnet interface because it is what they are used to, or they are unaware of the Web interface given their library use habits. A significant number of respondents (Table 2) to the questionnaire noted that they learned of the WEBPAC in the library or from library staff. The fact that students spend considerably more time in the library than faculty may explain a higher percent of them using and being aware of the WEBPAC. This difference may also be explained by a greater sophistication in computing and technological skills that many students possess when compared to faculty.

Section B: Search Statistics

The Web interface to MEDCat is an Innovative Interfaces Incorporated product. In addition to creating on-the-fly conversion of MARC bibliographic data to HTML pages, the server software allows libraries to examine particular groups of users based on IP ranges. This method of examination allowed the authors to monitor certain areas of WEBPAC usage and compare it to the telnet searches being performed on the catalog. It was decided that the most pertinent statistics in regard to tracking preference would be to compare Web connections from outside EML to all telnet searches.

Statistics were gathered weekly during the study. The percent of searches performed on MEDCat via telnet versus Web was noted. As demonstrated in Graph 1, telnet access steadily declined as Web usage increased. In October 1998, Web connections exceeded telnet connections. The numbers for November 1998 showed an even greater percent of Web connections.

Of interest are the questionnaire results from those who noted a preference for a particular interface. By a three to one ratio, respondents preferred the WEBPAC (Figure 5). The relatively high number of searches still being performed on the catalog via telnet (29%) surprised the authors. Clearly the expectation was that the Web-to-telnet ratio would mirror the three to one found on the questionnaire. Furthermore, the prominent marketing of the Web version of MEDCat within EML

logical skills necessary to navigate in a Web environment, and remote users may still use telnet sessions to access MEDCat for increased speed. Alternatively, users unfamiliar with MEDCat may have checked both to avoid appearing ignorant.

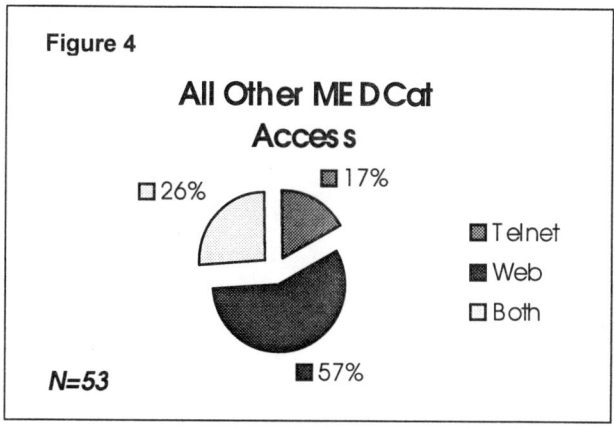

Figure 4. All Other MEDCat Access. Telnet 17%, Web 57%, Both 26%. N=53

may not have made as much difference to users as was previously considered. A large number of faculty and staff accustomed to accessing the character-based catalog for the past eight years no doubt contributed to telnet's strong numbers. Yet the combination of prominence within EML, marketing, and the continued integration of services into the framework of the Web medium, should help enlarge WEBPAC usage in the years ahead.

Section C: Anecdotal Evidence

It was a learning experience to gather anecdotal information on the use of MEDCat. Interestingly, most comments did not correlate much to the original intent of the survey.

Several conclusions may be drawn:

• An overwhelming number of users preferred Web access. They found the Web to be easier to use, faster, and more user friendly. In several cases, Web is the only way users know how to access MEDCat. This could also be an indication that Web dominates how users seek information, as the Web provides a more graphical and visual interface.

• Those who still prefer telnet cited the same reasons as those preferring Web. These users believed telnet provides faster and "easier" access.

• A number of users did not have an interface preference. These users may be more flexible and responsive to different computing systems.

• Several respondents indicated that they did not know what MEDCat was or what it could be used for. Those who did not know about MEDCat suggested that EML should provide more marketing and publicity. This led us to wonder what purpose the online catalog serves these users.

• MEDCat displays information on e-journals EML subscribes to, and in the Web version offers direct links to them. However, some users clearly did not understand how to interpret the information displayed. More user education is certainly required.

• Some users have confused MEDCat with databases such as Medline and asked that articles be placed in MEDCat. Users also did not understand that different databases may utilize different types of subject headings, and are created by different vendors. Perhaps an uniform search engine for online catalog and bibliographic databases could be useful in the future.

• Many users did not understand the type of restrictions (e.g. IP addresses) or licensing agreements libraries enter with publishers. Several requested integration with the NYU main campus library (which uses a different online catalog) or abandoning password protection when accessing from outside the library or remotely from home. The issue here would be how to educate general library users about licensing.

• It was also evident that a number of users disregarded print sources and would prefer to obtain electronic versions. One user even suggested an improvement to MEDCat would be "if it included all complete texts!" Is it a library's mission to replace all print with electronic materials?

• Many respondents used this survey to lobby for additions to the library's print and journal collection. Requests ranged from specific titles to entire subject areas.

• MEDCat is open to the public to browse on the Web. However, there are users who do not

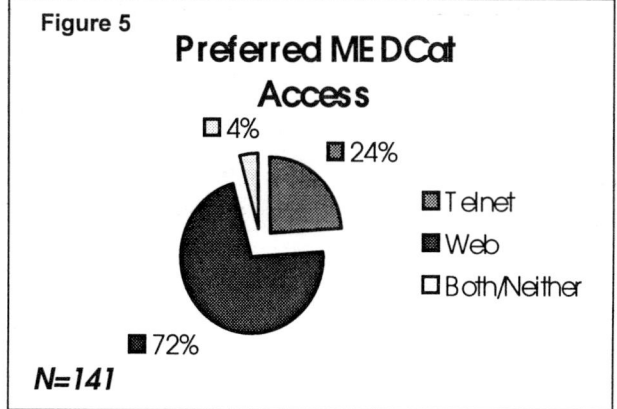

Figure 5. Preferred MEDCat Access. Telnet 24%, Web 72%, Both/Neither 4%. N=141

have complete grasp on how the Internet functions and have requested that the library open access to MEDCat via commercial Internet Service Providers or provide modem pools. Is it the responsibility of libraries, commercial ISPs, or users' parent institutions to educate about general Web access?

• Finally, several comments indicated a need for better tutorials and online help. We will need to explore different venues to educate our users.

Conclusion

As expected, the majority of searches performed on MEDCat were via the Web interface. However, system statistics and questionnaire responses demonstrate greater than expected telnet usage by certain segments of the NYU community. Given the defined samples, these data have significant implications for marketing, bibliographic instruction, and overall display and design issues. This study has raised unanticipated questions that are in need of further examination. Nevertheless, WEBPAC has been accepted, is the preferred interface, and has become the gateway to the EML digital library.

Works Cited

Green, Elisabeth and Alison J. Head. "Web-Based Catalogs: Is Their Design Language Anything to Talk About?" *Online*, 22:4 (July/Aug. 1998).

Cherry, Joan M. "Bibliographic Displays in OPACs and Web Catalogs: How Well Do They Comply with Display Guidelines?" *Information Technology & Libraries*, 17:3 (Sept. 1998)

Dennis, Nancy K., Christina E. Carter and Sever Bordeianu. "Vision vs. Reality: Planning for the Implementation of a Web-Based Online Catalog in an Academic Library" *Library Hi Tech*, 15:3–4 (1997)

Appendix I
Ehrman Medical Library
New York University School of Medicine
MEDCat Questionnaire

Objective

In an effort to improve MEDCat, *the library's online catalog,* please complete the following questionnaire and return it to the library. Your comments will help us in our ongoing effort to deliver the best possible library services to the New York University community.

1. Are you:
    - ☐ Faculty
    - ☐ Student
    - ☐ NursingResident
    - ☐ Staff
    - ☐ Administration
    - ☐ Fellow
    - ☐ Other (specify) _____

2. Where do you use MEDCat? (Check all that apply)
    - ☐ Office / Lab
    - ☐ Home
    - ☐ Ehrman Medical Library
    - ☐ Other Libraries
    - ☐ Other (specify) _____

3. Which version of MEDCat do you use to locate library materials?
    - ☐ Telnet access
    - ☐ Web access
    - ☐ Both

If Web access, how did you find out about it?
    - ☐ Lunch-n-Learns
    - ☐ Library staff
    - ☐ Library Web site
    - ☐ Using it in the library
    - ☐ Other (specify) _____

4. If you have used both versions of MEDCat, which do you prefer?
    - ☐ Telnet access
    - ☐ Web access
        Why?

5. How do you feel MEDCat could be improved?

_____
_____
_____

On the Threshold of Discontinuity: The New Genres of Scholarly Communication and the Role of the Research Library

Clifford Lynch

Introduction

Research libraries have historically shaped much of their role through a relationship to a canon of scholarly publication and the system that produces it. The boundaries of this canon have always been indistinct and problematic, and implicitly captured in the well-established notion (and problem) of "gray literature". The largest portion of the acquisitions budget traditionally has supported the purchase of the canonical print scholarly literature—in recent years, predominantly journals—and the construction of the supporting apparatus of catalogs and abstracting and indexing databases.

Innovative scholarly use of the networked information environment is creating complex and rapidly evolving new genres that raise both tactical and strategic issues for research libraries. The products of scholars' engagement with new technologies increasingly fall well outside of the traditional canon, yet encompass some of the most important and vital new scholarly communication.

And many of us still attempt to understand these new genres through analogies to print, just as their creators mimicked both print layout and formatting and social practices of print early in the development of the new genres. Print conventions conferred legitimacy as well as a familiar point of departure.

Electronic journals are a case in point. Traditional print journal publishers are going electronic; through the 1990s de novo electronic journals sprang up in huge numbers. Both types of network delivered journals are very tied to conventions, organization, and practices of print journals, no matter how strongly they emphasize and celebrate the ways in which they differ from, enhance, or supplant print journals.

The implications of these developments have been, and continue to be, discussed at great length. The developments impact both scholarly communications generally and libraries specifically, as a key component in the overall system of scholarly

---

Clifford Lynch is executive director of the Coalition for Networked Information.

communications. The discussions simultaneously fascinate, engage, threaten, and energize scholarly publishers, authors, editors, readers, and librarians. Yet we may, in the heat of rhetoric and analysis, fail to recognize that our discussions have chosen to focus on developments that really continue the evolution of traditional scholarly publishing. We've chosen to emphasize extrapolation rather than to identify and understand emerging discontinuity. The prism of the print tradition is a comfortable and comforting one. We are bringing electronic journals into the shelter of the traditional canon, and we are finding that this really isn't so difficult.

In this paper, I will argue that a new wave of materials is emerging that have much less connection to the recent history of print-dominated scholarly publishing and that cannot be understood or managed from a print-based perspective. In some ways, these new materials combine pre-Gutenberg (perhaps Medieval) traditions of communication with 21st century capabilities (instantaneous worldwide dissemination, electronically enabled and hosted communities, and the ability to capture, record, and archive events as they occur, building upon the capabilities of photography and sound recording, and later the capability to capture moving images that have had such profound effects over the past century). With these new genres, the scholarly canon will expand massively, and its boundary regions will become much broader, more diffuse, and more uncertain than those inhabited by the historic print gray literature. The inherent uncertainties of these materials (new questions of ownership, archivability, and content stability which are well settled for printed materials) will compound the difficulties libraries face in defining their roles in the management of the new scholarly communications.

Let me be clear: I am not predicting the demise of print, but rather the emergence of a new and important body of materials that fall within a very different intellectual regime; libraries will have to come to terms with the new while continuing to manage the old.

The paper begins with a look at some of the emerging genres and the technology trends in which they are incubating. It then considers the major historic functions of research libraries—selection and acquisition; organization; access; and archiving and preservation—in the context of these new forms.

New Genres, New Literatures, New Technical Enablers

The change to the canon of scholarly literature began with informal electronic-mail-enabled communication, soon supplemented by more structured listservers and electronic-mail-based journals. At first, these tools were largely, and sometimes slavishly, modeled on print predecessors; but they made scholarly communication more rapid, more global, and also more ephemeral and informal. Scientific research in many areas (most particularly and prominently, perhaps, molecular biology and the earth and space sciences) was fundamentally changed by the creation of shared, network-accessible data and knowledge bases. The Worldwide web is actually changing the conduct and dissemination of scholarship as it is used both for the distribution of papers prior to their publication in the print literature, and for the creation of major academic instructional and research resources completely outside of the traditional authoring and publication framework. The results are visible everywhere: in preprint archives, in scientific databases that complement the journal literature, and in the development of monographic and encyclopedic web sites in the humanities and sciences.

Similarly extensive changes are rippling through mass-market products such as newspapers, magazines, newsletters, music, sensor data and telemetry, and, perhaps soon, films. Because these mass market products represent the raw materials of future scholarship, the changes are of importance to research libraries. While we will not consider these shifts in any detail here, it is worth noting that they are taking place; the transformation of scholarly communication is part of a larger change, and is not occurring in isolation. Because scholarly communication innovation occurs in a limited environment that is characterized by the availability of advanced, precommercial technology, the developments there are likely to provide insight into the broader shifts. Scholarly communication may well prove to be a bellwether for the mass market.

Scientific databases—with molecular biology and genomics being perhaps the most prominent example—represent a much greater discontinuity, in some senses, that the other developments such as journals delivered over the network. They represent a new literature that is evolving alongside the traditional journals and books, closely linked to the traditional literature but standing independently. They encapsulate new social structures and new usage patterns that borrow heavily from the print tradition. They both point towards the future and hark back towards the past. Space does not permit a full consideration of these databases as new genres that are detached from publishing as we have understood it, but they should be recognized as one of the first key points of departure, and as content that has very high impact on the research community.

What we see today is just the beginning. Even more extensive shifts are on the horizon. They will be enabled and fueled by technologies such as the new high-performance networks such as those developed under the Internet 2 and Next Generation Internet programs to link our major universities and research centers, and by a whole range of dramatic price-performance improvements in storage, computation, and input/output devices.

It's helpful to consider concrete examples of what's rapidly becoming feasible on a reasonably large scale and the ways in which they are radically different from the print-inspired networked information developments. Network-based seminars provide a good place to start, in part because much of its technology base is shared with the other examples I'll discuss later.

Network-Based Distributed Seminars

With enough network bandwidth, it is now fairly easy and inexpensive to conduct a lecture, seminar, or other discussion across multiple sites (including individuals sitting at workstations as well as classroom settings). To be sure, there are real limitations on the group of technologies that make this possible. High quality is still expensive and is best accomplished through specially designed and instrumented rooms, rather than with cheap consumer-grade digital cameras. It takes a fast network connection and a fast workstation to provide high-quality, full-screen video playback. But these constraints are easing with each new generation of technology.

More fundamental, and more deeply problematic, are the limitations on effective interaction. As Michael Schrage has observed, a true interactive discussion, there's an inexact but real limit on the number of participating sites. Above that limit, videoconference essentially becomes a broadcast (possibly moving from one source site to another over the course of the conference in a rather structured way), perhaps augmented with a few rather formal questions and responses. While we can broadcast easily to a very large number of sites, and even allow people at these sites to queue to submit questions, we do not know how to scale really interactive discussions to large numbers of sites. (It is worth noting that this is not purely a technology problem; in meetings involving a large number of people organizers typically resort to the mechanism of breakout discussion groups that report back in plenary in order to inject some sense of interactivity and participation, even though this organizational approach is very limited. Collaboration and interaction in large groups is a hard and poorly explored problem.)

The critical point to understand about the digital capture and dissemination of a lecture is that it need not be a strictly real-time event. It costs very little more to capture the lecture, store it, and make it available for replay on demand if it's being digitally transmitted in the first place. It is even feasible to provide random access to specific clips within the lecture, though not necessarily in terms that are helpful to a viewer—it's easy to respond to a request to view a lecture starting at a given minute, as opposed to a request for the segment when the lecturer discusses a specific topic. But the key point is that the event takes on a dual existence as an artifact that can be preserved and delivered on demand.

Much discussion has focused recently on the implications of distance education in the networked world and, in particular, on two controversial and emotionally laden scenarios. In the first situation, universities worldwide engage in a competitive battle to service distance learners as individuals who attend courses through the net. In the second scenario, a few major universities (or for-profit commercial concerns) become the suppliers of many of the large enrollment lecture courses that are part of the core undergraduate curriculum for hundreds of other institutions. These recipient institutions would no longer need faculty to teach locally (or at least a lot fewer of them), but could just purchase material that's delivered over the net.

While these are undoubtedly going to be serious long-term issues, we may find that the mixture of available technology and academic needs creates a rather different opportunity in the near term. On a technology basis, high performance networks don't currently or in the very near future reach enough of the players in the scenarios described above. The political, economic, business, credentialling, labor relations and similar factors involved are extremely complex and controversial. And the strongly ingrained conservatism of higher education means that change from within the academy will be slow and incremental.

But consider: At research universities, there are always courses at the advanced graduate level that departments would like to offer but don't have the faculty expertise or critical mass of students to support. The ability to make a broad range of specialized offerings available is a very important component of the quality of advanced graduate education. The best universities, when two or more are geographically close, often offer their graduate students cross-registration and collaborate to develop and coordinate the richest possible collective range of educational offerings. These formal course offerings are further supplemented by opportunistic, ad hoc seminars in which visiting researchers present and discuss the latest research results.

These advanced courses are not commodities in the sense that one might argue that, say, most Calculus I course lectures (except perhaps in the hands of a magnificently gifted teacher) are commodities, covering nearly identical material in nearly identical ways; each advanced seminar or course covers relatively unique content and has some lasting value. Indeed, it is not uncommon historically for lecture notes from such courses to be written up, informally distributed, and even placed in departmental libraries or published is series titled "lecture notes in...." These courses and seminars often also ultimately give rise to formal papers or books that eventually become part of the traditional print literature. And they are generally not part of a competitive economic battleground between universities. The spirit is really one of collaboration among colleagues in a scholarly discipline.

Internet 2 is interconnecting the major research universities in the United States with capabilities that will be extremely hospitable to digital delivery of these kinds of distributed seminars, lectures, and advanced courses. They have always been an important part of scholarly communication and advanced education, but the new networked environment will make them much more accessible. Recordings will preserve what have historically been events as permanent content that can be managed and delivered on demand. Even further, digital recordings can readily be annotated and linked to documents, computer programs, or other recordings.

Collaborative Research Environments
Videoconferencing technology and network-based interaction is also evolving in another important direction. About a decade ago, the concept of a "co-laboratory" was first articulated as a place on the network that would provide a forum for scientific collaboration and research; this was a very powerful vision that captured the imagination of many scientists, scholars and educators. We are now finally witnessing the actual development of operational collaboratories that serve communities of researchers. (An excellent example of this technology is the Upper Atmosphere Research Collaboratory, UARC.) These environments variously combine videoconferencing, synchronous and asynchronous text-based messaging, shared control of scientific instrumentation, access to data (from observational sensors, simulations, or data archives), analysis and visualization tools, shared whiteboards, literature databases, and authoring tools. Their scale is sufficiently limited that the interaction problems that characterize very-large-scale seminars don't seem to be a major factor.

The technical requirements for using these collaboratories vary widely, from access to routine workstations (perhaps augmented with inexpensive digital cameras and microphones) at the low end, all the way through use of very costly, experimental, immersive, virtual reality "caves" at the research frontiers. At the high end, participation assumes not only very sophisticated input/output equipment (the caves), but an accompanying very-high-bandwidth, low-latency, quality of service managed communications infrastructure.

The focus of such collaboratories, naturally, is science, or more generally research—the vast majority of the systems built to date are in the physical sciences, and it still remains somewhat unclear how to translate these working environments to host and serve the practice of scholarship in some other, more individualistic and less data intensive disciplines, particularly in the humanities and some of the social sciences. But to the extent that we have learned how to create collaboratories, these systems also document the research and knowledge creation process. Actually recording the process of science research is something of an afterthought, a byproduct of the development of collaboratories, but it's important to note that events and activities that take place in these collaboratories can be stored, reviewed, replayed, and annotated.

It is worth also recognizing the generalization of this effort. In academia, we honor the processes of science, the work of scholarship, the processes of collaboration and analysis and authoring, as having a special importance, so it seems natural to build systems to facilitate these processes. But technologies very similar to those at work in the collaboratory can be used to provide electronic "places" to host routine meetings for organizational problem-solving, and to also record and make available the record of these activities. It may well be the case, in the not too distant future, that in information technology intensive organizations every meeting has an indefinitely long afterlife as a recorded artifact which can be reviewed, annotated, and referenced, and shared as an intrinsic byproduct of the meeting itself, rather than through surrogates such as meeting minutes that may sometimes be specially prepared to document the event.

Instructional Media Systems
Under the auspices of the Educause (formerly Educom, prior to the CAUSE-Educom merger) National Learning Infrastructure Initiative (NLII), there has been a great deal of work on the development of standards for an Instructional Management System (IMS). The IMS can be viewed as a special-purpose digital library that houses digital instructional media objects. The scope of the standard transcends a simple repository to explore links to evaluation and course delivery management as well as to links between instructional objects and the scholarly literature. Many specifics remain unresolved, but the broad scope of the initiative is clear. In terms of the new genres of scholarly communication, the IMS represents a confluence and formalization of traditional classroom activities (involving not only teaching tools and materials but also the evaluation of student learning results) with an archivable record of the processes of classroom teaching and learning. And, of course, materials within the IMS can be linked in very complex ways to other IMS materials, to the more traditional published scholarly literature, or to other new genres such as records of network-based seminars or collaboratory participation.

The implications of the IMS are far-reaching. They raise the possibility that instructional materials will be acquired and managed on an institutional basis, rather than individually by students directly purchasing textbooks or their electronic successors. Each faculty member can continually customize the instructional media objects if he or she wishes. The IMS environment creates a much more detailed record of the use and impact of these materials; this record can be managed, owned, accessed, shared and annotated.

Classroom practice itself, or more generally the construction and use of a distributed, network-based learning environment, and even potentially the interpersonal interactions and collaborations that occur when groups of students learn together, becomes an artifact that is subject to collection in the digital world.

Web Sites as Monographs and Encyclopedias
We are seeing both individual scholars and groups of faculty and students (not necessarily at a single

institution) developing subject-specific web sites that represent a new genre in scholarly communication, somewhat akin both to monographs and to highly focused encyclopedia. I've discussed these developments elsewhere (see my paper and others in the proceedings of the conference *The Specialized Scholarly Monograph in Crisis, or How can I get Tenure If You Won't Publish My Book*, at www.arl.org) and will not repeat these details here. However, some of the key characteristics of these works are that they are often collaboratively developed; they evolve continuously; and they are rich in image, sound, and moving images in a way that published print works cannot afford. Because of the ability of the web to make links among independently managed information, they also have the have the property that their boundaries are unclear; they exist in and define a continuously evolving relationship between the scholarship of multiple individuals or groups, and in this sense represent collaboration as a dynamic process rather than a static series of citations among fixed, published works.

These sites are becoming very important, particularly in the humanities and some social sciences, but also in niche areas of the sciences where they are replacing or supplementing monographs and specialized textbooks. In some cases, they are folding together extensive primary source materials with commentaries and analysis, thus confusing boundaries that have been well-established in print literature through the publication of authoritative editions of primary source materials on one hand, and of critical and analytical works that make reference to these primary source materials on the other. The growing availability of a new range of digitized source materials from cultural heritage organizations such as museums and archives is also providing exciting new opportunities to integrate materials which can enrich these sites, particularly again in the humanites and social sciences.

Coping with the New Genres: What are the Roles for Research Libraries?

As organizations, research libraries have a set of specific functions with respect to scholarly communication: they select and acquire; they organize and describe; they provide access; and they archive and preserve the record of communication. For the traditional print canon of scholarship, the practice of these functions is well understood and well established. For the new genres described above, it will be necessary for libraries to reconceptualize their activities virtually from first principles. This section of the paper does not provide comprehensive answers; rather, it makes a series of observations and comments that may help to structure the discussion of how the research library will ultimately respond to the challenges offered by the new, discontinuous, technology-enabled forms of scholarly communication.

A caveat is appropriate here. Libraries do not define an era's practice of scholarly communication; rather, libraries must respond to the construction of these practices by communities of scholars. This is a time of enormous change, and of exciting new possibilities: it remains to be seen which of the possibilities offered by technology will prove to be fruitful in improving the practice and documentation of scholarship. These determinations will not be made by libraries, but rather by scholars, teachers, and students, and the criteria for acceptability will not be driven by the convenience of libraries. It is crucial that libraries maintain a posture that is both skeptical about the importance of emerging genres and at the same time accommodating and responsive to new genres as they do emerge into broad use and acceptance by the community of scholars. This is going to be a very difficult balancing act, particularly given the attraction of innovation, the lure of the new, which will tempt libraries to engage new genres early in their development. At the same time, I believe that libraries do have a legitimate role in the dialog and debate about which emerging genres should find acceptance, because the ability to organize, provide access, and preserve these genres is an important factor in establishing their viability; it's essential that libraries make their voices and perspectives heard in the discussions.

Selection and Acquisition

It is clear that the new genres are not yet controlled or marketed by traditional publishers; no commercial marketplace exists for most of these new works. Libraries will need to take a much broader view of how they define the potential universe of materials that are candidates for acquisition and incorporation in their collections. There will be no catalogs to shop from, no approval plans. For the new genres, price will be a very poor indicator of quality; some of the best may be free, subject only to the effort of working out appropriate agreements with the creators. Identifying materials for potential acquisition will require a close, continuing and open-minded dialog and collaboration with working scholars.

Historically, publishers have served an important role in clearing and clarifying rights to works that they offer for sale. Libraries have not had to worry about who owns materials—when they purchased works from publishers, these publishers would provide implicit answers to questions about ownership, and would in effect indemnify libraries with regard to intellectual property liabilities. As libraries consider "acquisitions" (whatever this ultimately turns out to mean; see below) from the new, broader array of genres of scholarly communication, it is not clear who, if anyone, they are acquiring the materials *from*; ownership of these new information objects is debatable and often diffuse. Some of the material is free for use worldwide via the web, but it's unclear whether this extends to copying. Other complicating factors include the involvement of students as well as faculty in the creation of materials, and the multimedia character of many of the new genres, which invoke intellectual property questions not only about authorship but about participation and depiction of individuals in the events that the works document (Think about model releases for people who are part of a video record, for example: will seminar participants be asked to fill out a form, or will policies be established that say that enrolling as a student or entering a particular classroom implies consent to be imaged?). Intellectual property issues, particularly as they relate to libraries, are much better understood for textual materials than for images, sound, performances, records of events and activities.

Further: libraries used to purchase published material, and their subsequent use of this material was defined within the framework of copyright law, the doctrine of first sale, and fair use. More recently they negotiated licenses for materials, extrapolating from this framework. The new genres are different. Consider the network-based seminar for example. Agreements about what rights the library may have and the duration of those rights is unexplored territory that will have to be mapped through negotiation, institutional policy development, and the emergence of social norms; perhaps occasionally even by law or litigation.

There is a problem of content stability with some of the new digital genres. Unlike print publications, many of these works are continuously evolving. It's not clear what the library would acquire, or how to draw boundaries around the acquisitions.

For some of the new digital genres acquisition costs are not established by publishers, but rather are determined by the costs of the deployment of the technology necessary to record and to store the record of events. Thus, acquisitions costs are related to technology costs in a much more direct, volatile and local way. For example, libraries may in essence be offered the opportunity to selectively fund the creation of content by deciding when they will fund audio or video recording.

Finally, there is an enormous problem with quality control and ranking, and the setting of priorities. Assessing these materials and prioritizing them for potential acquisition will involve a much closer collaboration with faculty and researchers and a much greater exercise of judgement by libraries. A lack of bias towards traditional, well-understood and well established scholarly publishing will be essential for libraries that successfully recognize and exploit the emerging opportunities. Indeed, more than a lack of bias will be required—there is tremendous inertia in the commitment to the print canon: the traditional forms are supported, and promoted through salespeople and marketing campaigns, and also by all of the assumptions of legitimacy implicit in printed literature which manifest themselves in settings such as tenure and promotion practices. They are endorsed and validated by citation indexing, library statistics, journal impact ratings, editorial board members, faculty authors and reviewers—journals in particular are wide-reaching social activities that mobilize large numbers of people in the academic community as advocates.

Organization and Description

Content stability, or fixity is a problem for description and organization. It is not clear what needs to be described. So much of the theory and practice of description is predicated on static, fixed representations as a basis.

The content of these new genres involves multimedia, especially sound records and video. The technologies of capture will provide an enormously large corpus of information at relatively low cost. There will be a need to apply automatic indexing tools, to the extent that this is feasible, just because of the sheer volume of material. Most of the content is unique, and shared cataloging or indexing models historically used to control and distribute the costs of description and indexing thus offer little economic relief. The pragmatics of indexing video and audio in useful ways will be critical; as speech to text technology comes along, for example, even if it is imperfect, it will be important because it will allow us to leverage text indexing technology against multimedia content.

There is no longer—at least at any practical level—a single, cost-independent "right" way to describe and organize materials that are characteristic of the new genres. For the foreseeable future, the "gold standard" of description will be detailed, human-expert-supplied description (which is very expensive) both of the work itself and, in many cases, supplementing the content of the work with navigational aids; increasingly we will see various computational services that provide indexing and other organizational services competing with human description, offering admittedly inferior quality but at much lower cost and with much greater timeliness. Library managers will need to learn to make what are ultimately engineering decisions about how to execute these cost-performance tradeoffs. To make these decisions we will have to understand technology's capabilities and costs, but also what users of the materials really need.

Further, the materials involved are not only dynamic but also represent complex, interlinked and autonomously evolving works, which present major conceptual challenges to traditional descriptive practices. Addressing the new genres will require not only near term pragmatic approaches, but, in the longer term, new foundational research and deep intellectual consideration. This, in turn, has major implications for how we train new professionals and for the research agenda in library and information sciences.

Access

Provision of access is intimately related to control and rights, which in turn will be negotiated as part of the acquisitions process. Given the ambiguities of ownership and library rights surrounding the new genres, it is unclear that research libraries have, or can acquire, a clear, unlimited and permanent mandate to offer access. It seems likely that research libraries will find themselves engaged in increasingly complex and delicate negotiations about who can have access to these materials, for how long, and under what conditions. It will be very important for libraries to learn to link access capabilities and selection, to decide when materials are *not* worth acquiring because access is too constrained and they can't afford to keep the materials for close to a century until they enter the public domain.

We are also going to have to sort out what levels of access are responsive to the user community, and this is closely tied to the ability to organize and describe the new genres. It is clear that we can provide superficial description of large scale records of events, for example, and provide access to them. It is much less clear that it will be practical to offer descriptions and provide access at a finer level of granularity, within an object, at least in the near future. We'll have to identify situations when it's not worth acquiring content because the library cannot afford to invest in organizing it in a way that's useful to the user community.

Preservation and Archiving

How long should materials that are part of the emerging genres be archived? Who decides? This, of course, is closely related to who owns them and who controls them—who has the ability and authority to make preservation and archiving decisions? The economic and legal models that surround printed scholarly communication place these decisions in the hands of libraries; licensing of electronic information from traditional publishers has changed this balance, and has made the ability to choose to archive part of a license negotiation. (It is worth noting that as libraries have recognized that archiving decision-making and capability has to be part of a licensing discussion, they have been relatively successful in getting scholarly publishers to address the issues.) For the new forms of scholarly communication, preservation decision making is likely to be a very delicate discussion, and one that will in part be driven by the conversion of content to traditional scholarly communication channels: once a technical report, or a lecture, or a collaboratory session is represented in the traditional scholarly literature, the justification of maintaining the "raw materials" for this publication becomes much weaker, and is often likely to be justified more on grounds of capturing history than an active, vital record of scholarship that will be revisited and reused by disciplinary scholars and students rather than historians. The "author" rather than the publisher will be much more prominent for the new genres. Authors will want to assert "moral rights" over their works – they will want to be able to withdraw inaccurate or out-of-date lectures, or even performances that just did not go well, in a way that they never could with published journal articles, for example.

Stability is a problem for archiving as well: It is not clear what is being archived, or in how many versions, or for what purpose. There are some very complex technical issues here. These have been explored elsewhere and I won't belabor them here.

It is unclear how to finance archiving and preservation of these materials. Their volume is no longer driven by acquisitions budgets or by the scholarly publishing system, but by activities that may talke place largely beyond the control of the library. And, of course, costs are open ended and unpredictable for digital preservation, unlike the costs associated with preserving modern printed materials (on acid-free paper).

Conclusions

It is clear there are some common and problematic themes: Content stability and ownership or usage rights are particularly prominent. Libraries will need to consider downstream use of materials as part of the acquisitions process—lifecycle costs and benefits, not just pure acquisitions costs, will be key in determining selection. Archivability, rights to archive and preserve, as well as access restrictions and a realistic assessment of the ability to organize material should and will factor into acquisitions and selection decisions. These are not totally new considerations, but they will take on vastly greater importance.

One fundamental challenge will be to balance resource allocation (not just in acquisitions dollars, but resource commitments at a financial, operational and intellectual level, over the full spectrum of acquisitions, organization, access and preservation activites) to traditional published literature—supported by well-understood economic models, an intensive social advocacy, and an aggressive sales force—with the commitment to new forms of scholarly communication.

This is a time for independent thinking, for intellectual courage, for leadership, innovation and pioneering. It is a time to recognize that we must move to a view that is broader than the print tradition and the published canon. Libraries can embrace or delay the emergence of the new genres; to the extent that they move to engage them, they have the opportunity to shape the landscape of scholarly communication for the next century, and their roles in managing it.

Index of Authors and Titles

A

A Successful Partnership Library 43
Academic Publishing: Networks and Prices 13
Anderson, Scott 98
Assessment Outside of the Box: The Need for a Focused Study of Information Seekers in a Changing Environment 127
Automated Storage and Retrieval—The Next Generation 49

B

Baird, Brian J. 228
Beattie, James 402
Bell, Steven J. 207
Blome, Patricia M. 43
Bringing LOGIC to Local Government Information: A Multi-type Partnership to Organize Local Government Information 87
Building a Campus Presence One Page at a Time: Web Strategies for the Small College Library 289
Burke, John 127
Burns, Elizabeth 390

C

Calhoun, Karen 154
Carr, Jo Ann 234
Changing Collaborations to Deliver Information in New Ways: Lessons Learned in the Illinois Digital Library Initiative Project 53
The Changing Nature of Higher Education 37
The Changing Nature of Work in Academic Libraries 264
Channing, Rhoda 306
Chu, Felix T. 187
Classroom vs. the Web: Comparing Two Ways to Teach Web-based Resources 390
Coen-Pesch, Philip 312
Cole, Timothy 53

Common Cause: Creating a Unified Environmental Information System Through Stakeholder Partnership 134
Core Journal Titles in Full Text Databases 234
Creating Our Roles as Reference Librarians of the Future: Choice or Fate? 140
Cry Me a River: Searching for Revenue Streams in Academic Libraries 60

D

Davis, Francie C. 223
Designing for WOW!: The Optimal Information Gateway 154
Developing and Maintaining Instructional Web Sites: The Library Starter Kit 94
Dewald, Nancy H. 289
Dewey, Barbara I. 259
Digital Libraries Support Distributed Education 29
Directly to the Source: Will Academic Libraries Become Wholesalers of Information? 98
Dobb, Linda 60
Duffy, Anne 186

E

E-Reserves: Home Grown vs. Turnkey 342
EDI—Slow Walk to Fast Forward 63
Embser, Elvira 312
Engeldinger, Eugene 325
Estabrook, Leigh S. 8
Expansion of Electronic Resources: Superhighway to Campus Visibility 223
Extinguishing Slow Fires: Cooperative Preservation Efforts 228

F

Factors That Influence Online Database Use 68
Faculty Use of Electronic Journals at Research Institutions 329

First-Year Learning Communities: Redefining the Educational Roles of Academic Librarians 293
Fullerton, Anne 191

G

Getz, Malcolm 13
Golian, Linda Marie 271

H

Hammond, Elizabeth D. 214
Harmony, Stephena 127
Harvesting Hyperspace: Developing Technological Solutions to Internet Resource Discovery and Description 297
Horn, Judy K. 87
How Students Use Web-Based Tutorials and Library Assignments: Case Studies from Ohio State University Libraries 335
Hubble, Ann 80
Hughes, Carol Ann 280

I

The Improvisational Nature of the Change Process 187
In Search of Services: Analyzing the Findability of Links on CIC University Libraries' Web Page 259
Intercepting Departmental Fumbles and Running with the Ball 104

J

Jafari, May 359
Jones, John 76

K

Kirk Jr., Thomas G. 161
Kirsch, Sarah Elizabeth 49
Kochan, Carol A. 115
Koltay, Zsuzsa 154

L

Langschied, Linda 134
Learning Communities, Adult Learners, and Instructional Teams at IUPUI 359
Leckie, Gloria 191
Lee, Daniel R. 115
Lenares, Deborah 329
Leung, Shirley W. 87
Librarian as Mediator: A Significant Change in the Educational Role of Librarians 395
Library Program Assessment 161
Lund, Nick 43
Lynch, Beverly P. 264
Lynch, Clifford 410

M

Markley, Susan B. 166
McClellan, Gregory A. 297
McMillan, Gail 29
Medeiros, Norm 402
Mischo, William 53
Moody, David 395
Murdoch, Robert G. 115
Murphy, Deborah A. 80, 94

N

Nackerud, Shane 342
Neely, Teresa Y. 313
New Forms of Distance Education: Opportunities for Students, Threats to Institutions 8

O

Ochs, Mary Anderson 120
Odom, Dennis 104
O'Hanlon, Nancy 335
On the Threshold of Discontinuity: The New Genres of Scholarly Communication and the Role of the Research Library 410

P

Pacheco, Manuel 37
Palmer, Susan Szasz 140
Partnering for the Future: Integrating Traditional Interlibrary Lending and Commercial Document Delivery Into a Seamless Service 115
Pay for Print: Implementing Fee for Service Programs 76
Pollard Jr., Marvin E. 202
Presley, Roger 63

Q

Quality Undergraduate Education in a Research

Index of Authors and Titles

University—The Role of Information Literacy 109
QUEST: A Collaborative Approach to Information Literacy 166
Quick, Angela Myatt 325

R

Racing to Keep Up With An Electronic FDLP: Its Effect on Professional Relationships of Academic Government Document Librarians 171
Remote Control: Creating a Technology-Centered Library in Rural Alaska 186
Reorganization: The Next Generation 306
Revelry, Revelation, or Research: What Are College Students Really Doing on the Internet? 364
Roe, Donna 395
Roecker, Fred 335
Role Call—What are Library Students Training For and What Will They Be Doing? 312
The Roles of Academic Librarians in Fostering a Pedagogy for Information Literacy 191
Roselle, Ann 171

S

Schaffner, Ann C. 109
Schaffner, Bradley L. 228
Shifting Gears: A University President's View 3
Shill, Harold 370
Smith, Gordon W. 202
Smith, Kimberley Robles 264
Snowbird Leadership Institute: A Survey Of The Implications for Leadership in the Profession 313
Soderdahl, Paul 280
Stamatoplos, Tony 293
Stebbins, Leslie 109
Stein, Merrill D. 166
Stephens, Joan 63
Strategic Positioning and the Building Project: Penn State Harrisburg's Library of the Future 370

Strout-Dapaz, Alexia 104
Students Versus the Research Paper: What Can We Learn? 380

T

Taylor, Terry 293
TEEAL: The Essential Electronic Agricultural Library—Getting the Literature of Agriculture to Developing Countries 120
Tenopir, Carol 68
That's My Bailiwick 280
Thinking Style Preferences Among Academic Librarians 271
Thiss, Mona 76
Training ITAs: A Program for Student Information Technology Assistants 325
Turner, Thomas P. 297

U

UCSC NetTrail: Web-based Instruction for Online Literacy 80
Unified Information Access for the 21st Century: A Project of the California State University 202
Using the Scenario Approach for Achieving Sustainable Development in Academic Libraries 207

V

Valentine, Barbara 380

W

Walker, Michael 76
Web-Based OPACs: A Leap of Faith? 402
"Why are you using the library?" or, The Real Goals of Library Research in the Academic Curriculum 214
Wilson, Blenda J. 3
Wilson, Rebecca A. 364
Winston, Mark D. 313
Wolfe, Amy 234
Wu, Carol 402
Wyman, Sally 109